The Scroll of Kurzeniac (Kurenets, Belarus)

Translation of
Megilat Kurenits; ayara be-hayeha u-ve-mota

Original book edited by: Aharon Meirovitch

Written by Aharon and other former residents of Kurzeniec in Israel and in the USA
Originally published in Tel Aviv 1956

A Publication of JewishGen, Inc.
Edmond J. Safra Plaza, 36 Battery Place, New York, NY 10280
646.494.5972 | info@JewishGen.org | www.jewishgen.org

©JewishGen, Inc. 2023. All Rights Reserved
An affiliate of New York's Museum of Jewish Heritage – A Living Memorial to the Holocaust

The Scroll of Kurzeniac (Kurenets, Belarus)
Translation of *Megilat Kurenits; ayara be-hayeha u-ve-mota*

Copyright © 2023 by JewishGen, Inc. All rights reserved.
First Printing: September 2023, Tishrei 5784

Editor of Original Yizkor Book: Aharon Meirovitch
Written by Aharon and other former residents of Kurzeniec in Israel and in the USA
Project Coordinator: Eilat Gordin-Levitan
Cover Design: Irv Osterer
Layout: Jonathan Wind
Name Indexing: Stefanie Holzman

This book may not be reproduced, in whole or in part, including illustrations in any form (beyond that copying permitted by Sections 107 and 108 of the U.S. Copyright Law and except by reviewers for public press), without written permission from the publisher.

JewishGen Inc. is not responsible for inaccuracies or omissions in the original work and makes no representations regarding the accuracy of this translation. Digital images of the original book's contents can be seen online at the New York Public Library website or the Yiddish Book Center website.

Library of Congress Control Number (LCCN): 2022946110

ISBN: 978-1-954176-59-1 (hard cover: 512 pages, alk. paper)

About JewishGen.org

JewishGen, an affiliate of the Museum of Jewish Heritage - A Living Memorial to the Holocaust, serves as the global home for Jewish genealogy.

Featuring unparalleled access to 30+ million records, it offers unique search tools, along with opportunities for researchers to connect with others who share similar interests. Award winning resources such as the Family Finder, Discussion Groups, and ViewMate, are relied upon by thousands each day.

In addition, JewishGen's extensive informational, educational and historical offerings, such as the Jewish Communities Database, Yizkor Book translations, InfoFiles, Family Tree of the Jewish People, and KehilaLinks, provide critical insights, first-hand accounts, and context about Jewish communal and familial life throughout the world.

Offered as a free resource, JewishGen.org has facilitated thousands of family connections and success stories, and is currently engaged in an intensive expansion effort that will bring many more records, tools, and resources to its collections.

Please visit https://www.jewishgen.org/ to learn more.

Executive Director: Avraham Groll

About the JewishGen Yizkor Book Project

Yizkor Books (Memorial Books) were traditionally written to memorialize the names of departed family and martyrs during holiday services in the synagogue (a practice that still exists in many synagogues today).

Over the centuries, as a result of countless persecutions and horrific atrocities committed against the Jews, Yizkor Books (Sefer Zikaron in Hebrew) were expanded to include more historical information, such as biographical sketches of famous personalities and descriptions of daily town life.

Following the Holocaust, the idea of remembrance and learning took on an urgent and crucial importance. Survivors of the Holocaust sought out other surviving residents of their former towns to memorialize and document the names and way of life of those who were ruthlessly murdered by the Nazis. These remembrances were documented in Yizkor Books, hundreds of which were published in the first decades after the Holocaust.

Most of these books were published privately, or through landsmanshaftn (social organizations comprised of members originating from the same European town or region) that still existed, and were often distributed free of charge. Sadly, the languages used to document these crucial histories and links to our past, Yiddish and Hebrew, are no longer commonly understood by a significant percentage of Jews today. As a result, JewishGen has undertaken the sacred responsibility of translating these books into English so that the culture and way of life of these communities will be preserved and transmitted to future generations.

In 1986, a group of farsighted JewishGenners started a project to pool their efforts together in groups based upon their ancestors from each town and donate money to get the Yizkor books of their ancestral towns translated into English. As the translated material became available, it was made accessible for free at www.JewishGen.org/Yizkor. Hardcover copies can be purchased by visiting https://www.jewishgen.org/Yizkor/ybip.html (see below).

It is our hope that the translation of these books into English (and other languages) will assist the countless Jewish family researchers who are so desperately seeking to forge a connection with their heritage.

Director of JewishGen Yizkor Book Project: Lance Ackerfeld

About JewishGen Press

JewishGen Press (formerly the Yizkor Books-in-Print Project) is the publishing division of JewishGen.org, and provides a venue for the publication of non-fiction books pertaining to Jewish genealogy, history, culture, and heritage.

In addition to the Yizkor Book category, publications in the Other Non-Fiction category include Shoah memoirs and research, genealogical research, collections of genealogical and historical materials, biographies, diaries and letters, studies of Jewish experience and cultural life in the past, academic theses, and other books of interest to the Jewish community.

Please visit https://www.jewishgen.org/Yizkor/ybip.html to learn more.

Director of JewishGen Press: Joel Alpert
Managing Editor - Jessica Feinstein
Publications Manager - Susan Rosin

Notes to the Reader

The images in the original book were reproduced from photographs from the time of the first edition. These reproductions were already of poor quality, being pre-war and at least 30 or more years old. As a result, the images in the book are the best achievable.

A reader can view the original scans of the book on the websites listed below.

The original book can be seen online at the Yiddish Book Center website:

https://www.yiddishbookcenter.org/collections/yizkor-books/yzk-nybc313842/meirovitch-aaron-megilat-kurenits-ayarah-be-hayeha-uve-motah

OR

at the New York Public Library Digital Collections website:

https://digitalcollections.nypl.org/items/87e7bb00-6c7e-0133-efad-00505686d14e

To obtain a list of Shoah victims from **Kurzeniac (Kurenets, Belarus),** the reader should access the Yad Vashem web site listed below; one can also search for specific family names using family name option. These lists are continually updated by Yad Vashem, so it is worthwhile to periodically search these lists.

There is more valuable information (including the Pages of Testimony, etc.) available on this website: https://yvng.yadvashem.org/

For additional information about Kurzeniac, please visit:

http://www.eilatgordinlevitan.com/kurenets/kurenets.html
and
https://kehilalinks.jewishgen.org/kurenets/kurenets.html

A list of all books available from JewishGen Press along with prices is available at: https://www.jewishgen.org/Yizkor/ybip.html

Photo Credits

Cover photos:

Courtesy of Eilat Gordin-Levitan

Cover Design: Irv Osterer

Project Coordinator Introduction

Kurenets (English, Hebrew), also known as *Kurzeniec* (Belarussian, Russian and Polish) and *Kuznitse* (Yiddish)

Introduction by Eilat Gordin Levitan, a granddaughter of two Kurenetzers. Project coordinator and translator of the Yizkor book, with help from her siblings, children, cousins and a few others - all descendants of Kurenetzers.

Brief Timeline of the Kurenets region
- 1323 - 1790s: Part of the Polish-Lithuanian Kingdom. According to local testimony, the Jewish community in Kurenets formed in the late 17th century
- 1790s - 1915: Vileika uyezd, Vilna Gubernia. Part of the Russian Empire
- 1915- 1920: War years. During the First World War most of the region was under German occupation. Later, the region alternated between the Soviets, the Polish and the Lithuanians, who were at war with each other.
- 1921 - 1939: Vileika district, Vilna region, part of Poland (split from Eastern Belarus, which became part of the Soviet Union)
- 1939 - 1941: Annexed by the Soviets
- 1941 - 1944: Under Nazi Occupation
- 1944 - 1991: Part of Soviet Union
- Today: a small town *(shtetl)* in the Minsk district, the capital of Belarus. Not far from the border with Lithuania.

Kurenets and nearby Vileika are situated at a road junction and a railway that leads deep into Russia. Because of this significant location on a noteworthy geographic artery, the area has suffered from many foreign army invasions. According to local testimony, the Jewish community in Kurenets started in the late 17th century. The founders were Jews who fled the Spanish Inquisition and escaped to western Europe. After the Spanish Inquisition, which required Jews to convert to Catholicism or die, survivors fled to neighboring countries such as France and Holland and discovered that they were physically safer but still could not live authentically as Jews. Many Jewish people subsequently moved to the Polish-Lithuanian kingdom, as the rulers invited them to immigrate there. The rulers sought an educated middle class to be between the noblemen, who owned most of the land but lived far away in major cities, and the local serfs who worked the land for them. It was appealing for Jewish people that they could be the majority of the population of newly established small towns in the Polish-Lithuanian kingdom. They were able to live an autonomous life there, leading their own communities and openly practicing Judaism. In addition to Kurenets, there were many other small towns (*shtetls*) with large Jewish populations in the area between Minsk and Vilnius (*Vilna*). Vileika, which is located 7 kilometers from Kurenets, was founded by Catherine the Great's regime in the 1790s, about a century after the founding of Kurenets. The rumor according to Jewish locals was that Catherine the Great personally chose the name Vileika.

At the Jewish cemetery in Kurenets we find tombstones without last names that date before 1800. In the Kurenets of 1800 most Jews did not have a last name. They were identified by adding a parent name, adding their profession or adding a unique quality they possessed.[1] However, in 1815

Russian authorities ordered the Jews to take a last name so they could be easier identified for tax purposes and for the dreaded czar army service for their sons. Military service was for an arduous period of 25 years! It excluded sons who had no male siblings.

When Jews were ordered to take a last name in the Russian Empire, some Jewish families in the area chose the surname "Norman" to commemorate a French relative that came to the area with Napoleon's army circa 1812.[2] About one third of the Jews of Kurenets took the surname Alperovich/Alperowitz, which originated in 1815 in Kurenets. This last name became very popular in Kurenets, as Jewish families tried to spare their sons from 25 year military service by tricking the authorities into registering their second sons with Alperoviches who only had daughters[3]. The Alperovich name was so popular that it became synonymous with Kurenets. Anyone with that last name, historically or even today, has ancestry in Kurenets. This is common with Jewish surnames in general, as there are some others that are closely associated with different regions. Until around 1920, all Jewish marriages in Kurenets were arranged by matchmakers (*shidduch*). Alperoviches widely varied in terms of wealth, education level, class and worshiping styles. There were therefore Alperoviches that were not considered a suitable match for marriage, according to relatives I interviewed who grew up in Kurenets. However, Alperoviches married their cousins to ensure they were from the same class. Kurenetzers and their descendants with the last name Alperovich (and its variations) are not all related on the male line. Y DNA (paternal line) tests of many Alperovich males today show that they are not a match to most other Alperoviches but all of them know of ancestry from the Kurenets region. For example, in our family, Dr. Zeev Alperovich, whose father was my grandfather's first cousin, matched only two other Alperoviches (who had changed to Alperts in the United States). He matched many others' YDNA with different last names. Many DNA tests by Kurenetzers' descendants are found on FTDNA, MyHeritage, 23andMe, Ancestry DNA and GEDmatch. We find many more matches with each other (from Kurenets ancestry) that are not on the male Alperovich line.

According to the census taken in 1867, the population of Kurenets was more than two thirds Jewish: 1325 Jews among a total population of 1955 inhabitants of Kurenets.[4] During those years, circa 1860, Kurenets became the spiritual center for the neighboring Jewish communities. Kurenets was renowned for its Jewish scholars, in particular the *gaon*, Rabbi Ziska.[5] The religious focus in Kurenets was Lubavitch Chasidim, yet the region of Vilna was known as the center of Mitnagdim who fought bitterly to eradicate Chasidut about sixty years earlier during the time of Hagaon from Vilna. Still, most of the Jews of Kurenets were by the end of the 1800s Chabad's Chasids on good terms with the Mitnagdim minority in town. Reb Dan, who was born in Kurenets, married the granddaughter of the famed Rabbi Menachem Mendel of Lubavitch (1789-1866), known as the "Tzemach Tzedek." He was the third Rebbe of Chabad. According to the chapter that came from the Memorial Book to Moshe Eliezer Kramer who was born

---

[1] Recommended reading on naming conventions: the chapter in *Megilat Kurenets* by Morris Cohen of New Haven.
[2] As told by by descendants of the Norman family.
[3] As told to me by a relative of mine from Kurenets.
[4] Additional census records available online at the JewishGen Belarus Database, which you can search by name or by town: https://www.jewishgen.org/databases/belarus/
[5] You can read about him and about other rabbis of Kurenets in the chapter written by the Av Beit Din of Bnei Brak, Rabbi Yaakov Landau, who was born in Kurenets.

in Kurenets in 1867, the first person who introduced Kurenets to the ways of Chasidut was the well-known Gvir, the Righteous Rabbi Zalman Kurenetzer: *"Still, this day, all the town natives are very proud of him. Adding to his glory were well known scholars as well as other respected men from those days like Rev Yehuda Lev Ephron, Rev Yehuda Zusman, Rev Josef Halevi, and others."* Note the other well-known Rabbi Zalman Kornitzer - born in Kurenets c1900 to the Alperovitz family - perished in the

Holocaust and was named after him. From a story[6] about him, *"There were two students in Tomchei Tmimim in Lubavitch who went by the last name of Kurnitzer: Berel Kurnitzer and Zalman Kurnitzer. The two were not related. Berel's real last name was Garfinkel and Zalman's was Alperowitz. But in those days, everyone went by the name of the town he came from, and both boys had come from Kurenets. "*

There were four synagogues in town, which were filled to capacity on Shabbat and holidays. Among the rabbis officiating in the community were the illustrious Rabbi Yaakov Landau, who later became Av Beit Din and chief rabbi of Bnei Brak, where he served the community for 40 years. As previously mentioned, he wrote a chapter in the Yizkor book. Rabbi Aharon Feldman was the last rabbi of Kurenets. He perished in the Holocaust. The Feldman family of Kurenets is related to author Herman Wouk's mother. She had many relatives in Kurenets.

Kurenets had a lasting imprint on Judaism. Immigrants from Kurenets were the first people to introduce Chabad to the United States. Many Kurenetzers settled in New Haven, Connecticut at the end of the 1800s and the early 1900s. From "the Kurnitzer Shule in New Haven's archives, *"In 1889, a group of Chassidic followers of Rabbi Menachem Mendel of Lubavitch, who was a descendant of the celebrated R. Schneaur Zalman of Liadi, founded the Congregation Sheveth Achim Anshei Lubavitch in New Haven. shortly after arriving here in 1894, and in 1898 erected its Synagogue."*

Among the charitable organizations in Kurenets, there was *gmiluth chasadim* (interest-free loans to small businesses to buy merchandise to be repaid when the merchandise is sold), *Hchnasat Kalah* (gifts to brides), *maot chitim* (food for the needy) and *matan baseter* (anonymous givings). The camaraderie and kindness continued when Kurenetserst immigrated. They were kind to other immigrants as well as to the people they left behind in Kurenets. From the Memorial Book to Moshe Ellezer Kramer,

"After many years in America, where he became very well off and renowned, Moshe Lazar traveled to his hometown Kurenets in the year 1920. He was 56 years old and during those days there was war between Poland and the Bolsheviks for control of the area. Truly it was many years that his soul yearned to see his hometown and to meet with his relatives, and to go pay his respects to the graves of his forefathers. But this trip, more than it was for himself, was for the sake of other people. He was a messenger of Mitzvah or charity. He had with him more than $25,000 that he planned to divide amongst hundreds of families in Kurenets and the surrounding towns that were devastated and impoverished during the days of the war. Many, many came to see him off at the ship, and he received many blessings from his friends, other Kurenets natives in America. One old man, Shmaryahu Fingerhut, couldn't contain his excitement for the moment, and he immediately made a vow to roll twice if Moshe Lazar would return peacefully from his trip. The old man did complete his vow. "

While the Jewish residents of Kurenets spanned the income spectrum, most were middle class in 1900. Middle class Jews in Kurenets earned their living in the central market, which was the heart of the town. The homes all around the market were Jewish owned and had workshops and other small shops operating in the front of the buildings. The clients were mostly low-income Belorussian peasants (non-Jews) who lived in the surrounding villages. My grandmother told me that as a young child she was very proud of being a Jew. The majority of the people around her were Yiddish speaking Jews. The only non-

---

[6] http://www.eilatgordinlevitan.com/kurenets/k_pages/stories_2kurenetsers.html

Jewish children she ever saw in public were from peasant families. By contrast, her family had a home in the center of the town in the *best* location, and her father was a tanner who made a good living. Some of the poorer Jews were peddlers who sold their wares in the surrounding villages. There were a few wealthy Jews in Kurenets. However, most lived week by week, taking interest-free loans to buy merchandise and paying them back after selling their merchandise.

At the turn of the 20th century many young Jews became more secular. They sought general education and better opportunities in bigger cities. Some left for cities in western Europe and others went to the United States. Many of the young people of Kurenets at that time were influenced by the revolutionary socialist and anarchist Jewish youth of Smorgon, a bigger town in the area. Some took part in the socialist revolution in 1905. After the revolution failed, many who were active escaped to North and South America.

During World War I the area was under German occupation for several years. Some Jewish youth escaped to Russian controlled districts, while others stayed in Kurenets and had German teachers. After the Germans lost the war there were difficult years of war between Poland and the newly formed Soviet Union for control of the area.

Jewish youth looked for new solutions and in 1918 and 1919, Zionist activities started in town. Many concluded that the solution for Jews is having their own country. In preparation for a new country the Hebrew school *Tarbuth* was founded and functioned till the outbreak of World War II in 1939. Most classes were conducted in Hebrew. The school was very highly regarded within the greater region and was known for its literary program. Zion, Herut and Techiya, a branch of *Hehalutz* (socialist zionist movement) was opened in 1922, at a time when such branches were opened all over the district. The *Hehalutz* members went to an agricultural training camp, *hachshara*, at a farm called *Trumpeldoria* near Vilna. This was in preparation for making *aliyah* to Eretz Israel to work the land. After the training, many of the Zionist socialist Jewish youth in town immigrated to Eretz Israel and joined newly formed *Kibutzim and Moshavim*. Among the immigrants to Eretz Israel were my grandmother (Bela nee Shulman) and her sister (Rivkah Yaakobi). My grandfather (Meir Gurevich), his sisters (Batia Bender, Sima Herbert and Luba Bardan) and their parents (Frida nee Alperovich and Moderchai Gurevich) followed them as well.

There was a very active branch of *Hashomer Hatzair*, a leftist socialist Zionist movement, in the 1930s. Members of Hashomer Hatzair later formed a resistance cell in Kurenets during the Holocaust. In 1939 there were 1,500 Jews in Kurenets.

The Holocaust Period:

Following the Ribbentrop-Molotov Accord, which was signed by Germany and the U.S.S.R. in August 1939, the Red Army entered the district containing Kurenets in September of that year. The Red Army installed a soviet government there. After the German attack on Russia on June 22, 1941 and the retreat of the Red Army, panic spread among the Jews of Kurenets and they tried to escape into Russia. A few of them succeeded. Jews who did not manage to escape Kurenets endured severe limitations imposed upon them as soon as the Germans entered town. Their conditions progressively worsened as days passed. Rumors spread among the shtetl that killings were taking place in the greater region.

During the first days of the Nazi occupation, an underground cell was formed in town. Its purpose was to sabotage the German army in any possible way. Amongst the core members of this resistance group were Shimon Zirolnik, Yitzhak Einbender, Motik and Elik Alperovich and several of my relatives: Neyomka Shulman (my grandmother's brother), Zalman Gurevich (my grandfather's nephew) and Nachoom Alperovich (my grandfather's first cousin). They were later joined by Yankele Alperovich, Shimon Zimmerman, Noah Dinerstein, Berta Dimenstein, Shalom Yoran and others. They fled into the forests and formed fighting partisan groups with the Russians. After the war they gained public recognition and were honorably mentioned and decorated by the Soviets. This book contains the stories of a few partisans who survived.

The Jewish population of Kurenets was gradually liquidated during World War II. From time to time the Nazis executed individual Jews in town. On Simchat Torah in autumn 1941, the Nazis killed 54 Jews. A short time later, an additional 33 people and then another 13 Jewish community members were killed. On September 9, 1942, three days before Rosh Hashana, a horrific massacre took place. The local German garrison carried out an *aktion,* an act of total liquidation. Early in the morning the day of the liquidation, the town was surrounded by Nazis. Some of the Jews realized it and knew what was coming.

About 200 Jewish community members managed to escape the gunfire because it happened to be a very foggy morning. 1040 Jews of Kurenets were killed on this day - young and old, women and children.

The Kurenets area is surrounded by lakes, rivers and forests. The 200 Jewish people who escaped Kurenets on the day of liquidation in September 1942 fled deep into the forest and built underground shelters. The young single men of the group joined the Soviet resistance. The rest of the group spent the next two years in the forest and lived in the man-made underground shelters that they had built. After enduring starvation, Nazi raids and being in two harsh cold winters in the forest, half of the group - about 100 people - survived until the end of the war. Of these 100 or so survivors, some stayed in Russia after the war, some made *aliyah* to Eretz Israel and some immigrated to the United States and South America. The kind spirit of Kurenetzers who came before them was seen in all these destinations. For example, the Holocaust survivors from Kurenets who came to New Haven, Connecticut, were helped by the Jewish families who had immigrated there from Kurenets about fifty years before them. The same is true for the survivors who came to Eretz Israel after the Holocaust. They received much help from those who came there 20 years earlier. Kurenetzers across the globe supported each other through this difficult post-war period.

According to Soviet archives[7]:

The organized Jewish pogroms have begun from autumn of 1941, on October 14th a group of Jews have been accused of sympathy to the Soviet authority. Among 54 people in this group, 20 were children in the age of from 4 till 12 years old. According to witness Simon Rayhel (born 1892), "these people were from a poor class" and had received welfare from the Soviet government. Jews were given out to the Germans by local residents Roman Savievich, Ivan Sorokvosh, Grigory Bolvak, Vladyha and some other, who were in police service. Arrested people have been shot on Kasutskaya st. Witness Joseph Bekach (born 1917) has added, that the SS command and policemen selected well educated and better qualified people among Jews along with their families, who " stood close to communists ". In February of 1942 a special command under the direction of the chief of prison Yasinsky arrived at Kurenets. Together with assistant Sharangovich and others (surnames in the document are not named) they have shot 33 Jews. After some time at the same month Kazimir Sokolovsky, Peter Drozdovsky, Peter Glitoft, Nikolay Bliznjuk, Nikolay Yaroshesky under direction of Vileyka's SD chief Egof had arrived from Vileyka. Jews were demanded to hand over valuable things, gold, watches, etc. Not having received anything, this command killed 120 Jews, including children in the age of 1 till 10 years old. At the end of March of 1942 Egof had unexpectedly appeared in Kurenets again and " without any reasons " had shot 6 more Jews who had no time to hide. Basya Zaltsman (born 1889) had added that at the end of February or at the beginning of March 1942 Germans together with local police from the Belarus nationalists had shot 17 Jews, 5 from whom were

---

[7] information from the Soviet archives, translated to English by Tikhon Bykov, my 3rd cousin from our Alperovich of Kurenets side. His great grandmother was from the Beker family from Kurenetsl (the Original of this document is stored in GARF, f. 7021, op. 89, d. 8, ll. 3-76; copies are in Yad Vashem Archive, M-33/1141).

children. They burned 11 houses together with their attachments and also had stolen 408 heads of cattle. The final action had been carried out on September 9th 1942. Large forces of police (up to 400 people) arrived at three o'clock in the morning under the command of SD officer ober-lieutenant Grave from Vileyka. Jews had been gathered on the square under the pretense that they would be sent for work. More than half of them were old people and children. Covered motor vehicles transported people to Mjadelskaya st. There all the people were put in a shed and burned, those who tried to run were shot from automatic guns. Together with SD chief Grave, chief of regional police Schiller and chief

of a military police ober-lieutenant Voltman an active participation in this action was taken by local policemen. The shed was set on fire by members of the local fire-fighting crew of Kurenets led by Vladimir Birjuk. At the same time the firemen were watching the fire not to spread on other houses. 1052 people died in this fire. The total number of people killed during occupation in Kurenets and surrounding area is 1201. Among them 107 women, 59 children and Soviet war prisoners of all nationalities The author's note: Kurenets, a village in Vileysky region of the Minsk area, is located on the river Sang, 7 km from Vileyka. For the first time it is mentioned in 1519, as a place in the Great Princedom Lithuanian. In 1665 it became town. In the beginning of 20th century, it is the center of Vileysky (Vileyka) region of province. In 1847 - 844 Jews, in 1897 - 1613 Jews (at the same time the total population is 1.774 inhabitants). In 1921-1939 it was part of Poland. Since 1939 in BSSR, in prewar years there have been 1131 Jews. The German army occupied the Kurenets area from June 25th, 1941 till July 2d 1944. There is a tomb of victims of fascism, a communal grave of the Soviet soldiers and the guerrillas, a monument to participants of a patriotic underground. Any information on Jews as victims of nazi genocide is absent.

After the unspeakable tragedy of the Holocaust, surviving Kurenetsers remained a close-knit community. On a personal note, Rivka Gvint told me that attending my parents' wedding in Eretz Israel in November 1947 was very special for her, her mother and other survivors from Kurenets who had arrived to Israel shortly after the Holocaust. My mother's parents, who immigrated from Kurenets circa 1925, invited every surviving Kurenetzer in Israel to the wedding. It was a beautiful wedding with 500 people. It was the first happy celebration for many of the survivors in their new country.

In 1958 it became feasible for former Polish citizens to leave the Soviet Union for Poland. As a result, more Holocaust survivors arrived in Israel via Poland. They were greatly helped by the Kurenetzers who came before them. In later years when more survivors arrived from the Kurenets area, Shimon Zimmerman, the head of the Kurenets society in Israel, arranged a new community in Kfar Harif. He gave land and homes to the newcomers from Kurenets and they worked the fields together. This was another example of the supportive community spirit of Kurenets that carried on well after the war.

One may wonder why I have devoted so much of my life's work to Kurenets: through research, translations, collecting photos, creating websites for Kurenets and other Eastern European shtetls, and uniting many Israeli descendants with their long-lost cousins in Argentina, Brazil, Mexico, the US, Canada, South Africa Australia and more. Some people have contacted me about their ancestors from Kurenets and nearby locations after Googling and finding my website. I was able to unite cousins who for fifty years were assumed to perish in the Holocaust. I even traveled to Kurenets and about 20 other shtetls and cities on my quest to learn as much as I can about its history and people. I was not born in Kurenets and in fact, my more recent roots are in Israel. I was born in Israel to a mother who was also born in Eretz Israel. My father came to Eretz Israel as a young child. All my grandparents were secular and socialist Zionists who left Eastern Europe by age 20. Even four of my great grandparents made *aliyah* during the 1920s and 1930s following their children.

Two events in 1995 precipitated my interest in Kurenets. First, my son Ron asked me to tell my story as an immigrant for a high school school project. I feel there is an oversimplified immigrant narrative that society perpetuates: a refugee escapes war and their good life begins as soon as they enter the United States. I didn't feel that my personal immigration story neatly fit that narrative. I am from a happy upper middle class Israeli family and like many immigrants in the 1970s, I came to the United States on a student visa. Entering the U.S. on a student or work visa is very common but frankly, I thought that story might come across as less compelling. I therefore dug deeper and began teaching my son about my ancestors from Kurenets and other places in Eastern Europe, who were immigrants too. One of my great grandparents from Kurenets was a victim of the Nazis and I shared his story with my son. I decided to expand my own research about our family history in Kurenets, for the purposes of my son's high school project. My mother sent me the book from Kurenets and also my grandmother's photo

album, which was filled with pictures of friends and family members in Kurenets before the Holocaust. Those photos had been sent from Kurenets to Eretz Israel before the war.

The second event that contributed to my devotion to Kurenets took place about a month after my son's high school project I reached out to all of my mother's first and second cousins who were Holocaust survivors from Kurenets and I recorded their stories. The first on my list was her first cousin Zalman Gurevich, who wrote about his time in Kurenets and in the resistance in Megilat Kurenets and in other books. While talking to Zalman, I said something about a picture I have of him, his parents and his siblings from the 1930s in Kurenets. In shock he said "You have a picture of my mother? The last time I have seen her was in 1941, the year she perished. We lost our albums during the Holocaustt and I have no pictures of her." A few relatives who left Kurenets had the pictures but for fifty years not one shared it with Zalman or his siblings. They were under the impression that it is best not to remind them anything about the tragic past. At that moment I knew that beside sending copies of the pictures to my mother's cousins, I must put Jewish Kurenets online immediately. Now, when people Google Kurenets they find old pictures, translated chapters from the Kurenets book and everything else I can find. It is meaningful to connect descendants of Kurenets of Kurenets to their heritage and to help revive these lost treasures of the past.

After the war there was a code of silence about Holocaust victims. My grandmother mentioned many times to us that her brother Nyomka (Benjamin Shulman) was a hero of the resistance and was killed in action. She spoke about him with pride but never mentioned her father Aharon Shulman and her sister Chanale who perished at age 14. In fact, I asked my mother and she told me that she was never told that her grandfather and her aunt perished in the Holocaust. I feel it is important to bring these stories to light - not just the stories of resistance fighters but also the heroism of everyday people who survived unspeakable atrocities and protected their families as long as they could. There is a tendency to stereotype Holocaust victims as lambs to the slaughter. However, much like many of us today, they were smart and resilient but the circumstances were beyond their control. For example, my great grandfather Aharon Shulman hosted his son's resistance meetings in his house despite knowing the dangers involved. Heroic family members like this were not technically members of the resistance but were equally heroic in supporting resistance efforts.

How can we preach "never again" while disassociating from Holocaust victims and never teaching our children in the Jewish tradition of thinking of themselves as if they were there? How would they ever learn that populist racist slogans and hate speeches against people of color or immigrants or refugees calling for division are never okay? My ancestors from Kurenets told me to spread love and tolerance. The only way I know of doing it is by educating the public so they will recognize evil, racist, soulless leaders with no redeeming values who spread chaos and hate. Whether it be Trump, who admires Hitler or Putin, who most likely admires Stalin, we must never elect dangerous leaders to office again. We must realize that "never again" applies to all marginalized peoples around the world and we must not become complacent. We should not take comfort in a false image of pre-war Europe as being far removed from modern society. People thought then that such a tragedy could never happen to them. They kept saying to each other that Germany is a very cultured country and Hitler is just saying racist staff to be popular with the masses. We must never take for granted that hate speech is only speech.

One of my passions is to help connect members of the Jewish diaspora to their long-lost relatives and to keep alive the stories of our ancestors. I would also like to challenge the stereotypical image of shtetls as old-fashioned, quaint villages, as depicted in Fiddler on the Roof. I hope the story of Kurenets is an example of the forward thinking, progressive, vibrant and courageous communities that flourished. I also hope to challenge oversimplified immigration narratives of upward mobility and to expand people's associations of pre-war Jewry. We must never forget the Holocaust but also we should not forget the full lives that were led before the Holocaust either, which were not as far removed from

today's society as one might imagine. Whether it be bringing the Chabad movement to the United States, supporting secular socialist Jewish movements, founding Kibbutzim and moshavim in Israel or joining activist and partisan movements, the people of Kurenets were clearly not afraid to think outside the box and pave the way for a brighter future.

While it can be challenging to discuss Kurenets due to the collective trauma of the Holocaust, we should honor our ancestors by sharing their stories and photos and by remembering their full vibrancy. I feel that Kurenets is a powerful microcosm of diverse Jewish thought, activism, heroism, resilience, kindness and community. Every Kurenetzer I interviewed through the years was very proud of their hometown and its legacy. My hope is that this book captures the unique spirit of Kurenets and honors its history and people.

For additional information about Kurenets, visit:
http://www.eilatgordinlevitan.com/kurenets/kurenets.html
https://kehilalinks.jewishgen.org/kurenets/kurenets.html

Geopolitical Information

Kurenets, Belarus is located at 54°33' N 26°57' E and 51 miles NNW of Minsk

	Town	District	Province	Country
Before WWI (c. 1900):	Kurenets	Vilejka	Vilna	Russian Empire
Between the wars (c. 1930):	Kurzeniec	Wilejka	Wilno	Poland
After WWII (c. 1950):	Kurenets			Soviet Union
Today (c. 2000):	Kuraniec			Belarus

Alternate Names for the Town:

Kurenets [Rus], Kurzeniec [Pol], Kornitz [Yid], Kuraniec [Bel], Korenetz, Kuzhenets, Kuranec

Nearby Jewish Communities:

Vilyeyka 4 miles SSW
Nivki 10 miles NE
Vyazyn 13 miles SE
Maladzyechna 17 miles SSW
Ilya 17 miles ESE
Zaskevichi 17 miles SW
Kryvichy 18 miles NE
Liebiedzieva 19 miles SSW
Myadzyel 22 miles N
Kraysk 22 miles E
Daŭhinava 22 miles ENE
Krasnae 23 miles SSE
Smarhon 23 miles WSW
Budslav 26 miles NE
Haradok 28 miles S
Narach 29 miles NNW
Radashkovichy 30 miles SSE
Svir 30 miles NW

Jewish Population: 1,613 (in 1897)

Map of Belarus showing the location of **Kurenets**

Table of Contents

Title	Author	Page
Introduction to Megilat Kurenitz	Aharon Meirovitch	2
Our withered town, Kurenitz, Villeyka County, Vilnus District	Baruch Zukerman	12
Should You Wish to Know		15
A Place of the Torah	Ysrael Isar Katzervitz	16
My Hometown	Rabbi Yakov Landau, Av Beit Din, B'nei Brak, a former Rabbi of Kurenets	20
Grandma Marisha	Max Alberts	36
During those Days	From a Memorial Book to Moshe Eliezer Kremer who died in the US	38
Images	David Krivitzky	46
The Big Boulder	Yosef Weiss	49
Matia, son of Pesach (Zavodnik)	Maris Cohen	50
Kurenitz (Poem)	David Krivitsky	52
Old Images	Yaakov Alpert son of Eliyau Alperovich	53
Impressions	Alter Zimmerman	67
A Little Bit From A Lot	Rabbi Itzhak Dov Oshpal	72
Self Defense	Levik son of Mendel Alperovich	74
From There to Now	David son of Leib Motosov	78
Beloved and Unforgettable Kurenets	Dov Benes	83
Lost Tunes	Yehoshua Alperovich	91
Beloved Person	Avraham Alperovich	98
A Few Lines	Tzvia née Cohen Even-Shoshan	104
The Tarbut School	Israel Gvint	106
Memories, Memories	Pesia née Taubes Norman	115
Illustrations	Avraham Dimmenstein	118
Dolhinov Street	Chaia Altman	121
From the Notebook of a Teenager	Itzhak Arieli son of Moshe Alperovich	122
A Miracle of Spring	Chana Alperovich	126
A Journey in Your Vistas	Aharon Meirovitch	129

Part Two: In Your Shining Face

Your Youth and the Loveliness of Your Wedding Will Always be Remembered ...From the Siege I saw you Soaked in Blood

Title	Author	Page
My Hometown	Aharon Meirovitch	136
My Ravished Home	Fayga Alperovich	136

Amongst the Fifty-Four	Yente née Dinerstein Rudnitsky Baranovitch	141
The Struggle to Survive	Wolf Zev Rabunksi	146
One Month	Yosef Zuckerman	171
Three Years	Itzhak son of Nethka Zimmerman	175
A Little Drop	Yosef Friedman	195
In the Luben Farm	Nathan Alperovich	200
By the Nail of the Eradicator	Rivka Dudik daughter of Sima and Zalman Gvint	211
The Day of the Massacre	Tuvya Sosensky	221
In the market on the day of the slaughter	Avraham Bergstein	224
In the Vostok Territory	Abraham Aharon son of Naftali Alperovich	227
Resistance	Zalman Uri Gurevich	238

Part Three: On Hills of Dust

A Small Remnant	David Motosov	260
The Broken Limb	Sima Gvint	265
After the Liberation	Zev Rabunski	267
Bakatz	Aharon Meirovitch	269

Part Four: A List of the Martyrs

List of the Martyrs	274

Part Five: Supplement

The Day the War Started in Grodno	Shimon Zimmerman	316
The Escape from the Ghetto	Jehoash Alperovich	326
Memories of Solomon	Shlomo Alperovich	337
Thus It Began	Nachum Alperovich	349
Memoir of infancy in the Vileyka camp	Jay (Yosef) Rabunski	395

Name Index	402
Supplements	409

The Scroll of Kurzeniac
(Kurenets, Belarus)

54°33' / 26°57'

Translation of:
Megilat Kurenits; ayara be-hayeha u-ve-mota

Original book edited by: Aharon Meirovitch

Written by Aharon and other former residents of Kurzeniec in Israel and in the USA

Published in Tel Aviv, 1956

Acknowledgments

Project Coordinator:

Eilat Gordin Levitan

Our sincere appreciation to Shimon Zimmerman, of the Kurenets Landsmanshaften, for permission to put this material on the JewishGen web site

This is a translation from: *Megilat Kurenits; ayara be-hayeha u-ve-mota*; The scroll of Kurzeniac, Editor: A. Meirovitch, Tel Aviv, 1956, Former Residents of Kurzeniec in Israel and in the USA.

This material is made available by JewishGen, Inc. and the Yizkor Book Project for the purpose of fulfilling our mission of disseminating information about the Holocaust and destroyed Jewish communities. This material may not be copied, sold or bartered without JewishGen, Inc.'s permission. Rights may be reserved by the copyright holder.

JewishGen, Inc. makes no representations regarding the accuracy of the translation. The reader may wish to refer to the original material for verification.
JewishGen is not responsible for inaccuracies or omissions in the original work and cannot rewrite or edit the text to correct inaccuracies and/or omissions.
Our mission is to produce a translation of the original work and we cannot verify the accuracy of statements or alter facts cited.

[Page 4-7]

Introduction to Megilat Kurenitz

Aharon Meirovitch – editor/writer, 1956

Translated by thirteen year old, Talia Bela Levitan

*"In honor of my great-grandmother Bela Shulman Gurevitz,
my namesake from whom I am told I inherited my beautiful voice
and for her beloved family who perished in Kurenitz."*

Memoir of our town: the quest of our mourning soul became a reality. It's been three years since we began our difficult journey. We had times of worries: Did we have the strength for this heavy mission? Would we find sufficient numbers of reporters and writers? Did we have the financial means to carry out the task? Mostly could we find the right balance to put forward the shining face of our town of days gone and her successive annihilation?

   Rooted in the essence of this manuscript is the upcoming tragedy. We must observe rules pertaining to style, pace, and editing. The future horrors control the expressions even in the periods prior to the time of annihilation, even as she flourished during the good old days of youth. The voice has to be controlled. The shades even when light and bright must express a melancholy essence. The typical criticism we assign to literary works must be replaced and our hearts should be filled only with sorrow and pity.

As you can see, the editor's job is difficult. He must embroider the stitches carefully. He must observe and analyze the sentiments, yet keep carefully to the true facts. To chronicle the days of the Holocaust is to acquire a unique set of problems. One must report carefully. Many tend to eulogize, but eulogizing will tell only of the pain. Rather than just the bigger picture, we want to know the little picture, that tells of those days with the little things. The expressions of our brothers, their tears and their shouts. Not in the general but in the particular.

In many letters, meetings, and phone calls, I try to express these concepts. "Do you see these bushes?" says Chaim Itzee while we were taken to Luben, "do you see these bushes?" "Our bones will lie there and there will be no one to bring them to Jewish Burial… we must run, we must escape, but I have no idea where to…" This incident was reported as an unimportant statement. The person reporting it questioned whether it should be reproduced, never thinking that this phrase contains the entire experience of the Holocaust.

In many letters and pleas, we demanded that the residents of our former towns chronicle their memories. We explained that the book is a collective work of art, and the more voice that would be heard, the greater the value of the book. Many of them could have contributed greatly with helpful testaments, but they didn't. Others gave it to us only at the last moments when the book was already being printed, and we did our best to include their stories in this collection.

The most worrisome part was the list of our beloved martyrs. We were extremely concerned with including the name of every martyr. In some cases, their entire families had perished. We knew that some names would be omitted, so we sent letters to all of the former residents in Israel and later to all of the former residents in the USA we could find. There were few replies, and so we gathered all the people we could in Haifa. Most of the people who came were people who left our town after the Holocaust. If we omitted some names we will make an addendum.

We decided to arrange the list according to streets so that the townspeople could recognize their beloved neighbors, the homes, and the streets all as one complete entity. I have to specially thank Yitzhak Zimmerman, who made the list, checked the corrections, and even corrected the list that had been corrected by others.

Every letter and a sign of concern were of real encouragement for me, and many did care! But I must specify the names of some of our town natives whose involvement was crucial to our project. First and foremost I must mention our dear respected town native Mr. Baruch Zukerman, who kept in constant touch with me by mail the entire time. His help and support were immense. Not to be forgotten is our shtetl's former resident the honorable Mr. Chaim Peykin and Mr. Ben Glazer of the USA; their more practical concerns made this book a reality. I must mention Shmuel Spektor of the USA who kept a mail connection with me. And last my dear friend, like a brother to me, Israel Gvint. His hand never left my hand and his limitless commitment made this mission much easier to accomplish.

All that I recognized and others that I did not will be blessed.

Aharon Meirovitz, 1956.

Israel, 1950, the house of Emma née Alperovitz Zivoni
[top row] in Tel Aviv
A meeting of Kurenitz natives in regards to publishing a
Kurenitz Yizkor book.

Top right; Moshe [son of Rashka and Zalman Alperovitz]
Middle row right to left; Bela Gurevitz [daughter of Rachel and Aharon Shulman]
Batia Bender [daughter of Frada nee Alperovitz and Mordechai Gurevitz] Rivka
[daughter of Rachel and Aharon Shulman] Zalman Zivoni [Emmas' husband], David
[son of Leib Motosov], Zionist leader; Baruch Zukerman [original last name was Chait]
, Mr. Pintov [related to the Shulman family, father of Badana Dori], Alter Zimerman. In
the bottom row left; Doba [daughter of Pesia née Kastrol and Michael Alperovitz], next
to her is the author; Aharon Meirovitz [son of Perla née Shafer and Ben Zion Meirovitz]

Leib Yakov Torov, his wife Chaya Frumka and their daughter Sara – perished on the day of slaughter, 9-9-1942. Their son Moshe-Eliezer perished while hiding in the woods.

Ytzhak Rabonski and his wife Lea – perished on the day of slaughter, 9-9-1942 their son Shmuel and their daughter Chaya perished in Velyka.

Mina Fidler daughter of Ytzhak Fidler – perished in Velyka, her brother – perished in unknown.

Chyena (nee Torov) Alperovich, her daughters: Dvushel, Taybel, and Elka. Her son, Yakov – the day of slaughter, 9-9-1942

Ark Alperovich son of Reuven – perished with the fifty-four (Simchat Torah, 1941) he attacked the policemen that were taking him and was killed while running away. His wife, Nehama and daughter, Zelda – perished on the day of slaughter, 9-9-1942.

Sheina-Lyba (nee Torov) Charas – perished while hiding in the woods.

Avraham Roytstein, his wife and three children – perished on the day of slaughter, 9-9-1942.

Eliezer – Shlomo Shulman, his wife, two sons, one daughter – the day of slaughter, 9-9-1942.

Feybush Shulman, his wife, Henya. Her mother, their son, Chanan, their daughter, Rivka – perished while hid in in the wood.

Aydale Zimerman – perished on the day of slaughter, 9-9-1942. Yosef Zimerman – perished with the thirty-two, the Jewish month of Adar, 1942.

Eeta Gilberstein – joined the fighters, was renowned for her bravery, was killed while fighting in the woods.

Zev Gilberstein – killed in battle.

Chaim Jokovski, his mother, Pesya – Yente, – perished with the fifty-four, Simchat Torah, 1941. His wife, Shifra, their daughter, – the day of slaughter, 9-9-1942.

Dvushel Jokovsky (Chaim's sister), Kurenitz beloved teacher, her husband and daughter – the day of slaughter, 9-9-1942.

Neta Zimerman, his wife, Elka, their granddaughter – perished on the day of slaughter, 9-9-1942.

Yermiyau son of Neta Zimerman, his wife, Chasya – the day of slaughter, 9-9-1942. Their son, Shimon – perished while giving back his rifle, the first days the Germans arrived. Their daughters, Chayka and Ettel –perished in Velyka. Elka – perished while hiding in the woods.

Hilel son of Neta Zimerman, his wife, Fraydel – perished while hiding in the woods.

Nechma – Racha Shmukler – perished on the day of slaughter-1942.

Yishayau Shmukler, his wife, their son and daughter – perished on the day of slaughter, 9-9-1942

Chaya-Sara Shmukler, her husband Berel and two daughters – perished on the day of slaughter 9-9-1942.

Yosef Zimerman, his daughter, Lea – perished on the day of slaughter, 9-9-1942 his son Shimon – the first day the Germans arrived, while giving back a rifle.

Chaim, son of Hevos Alperovich, Shapira, his wife, Marishka nee Zimerman, their son Yakov – perished on the day of slaughter, 9-9-1942

Menucha Peykon – perished while hiding in the woods.

Barka Chadash – perished while hiding in the woods; Sara Chadash – perished on the day of slaughter, 9-9-1942, Eetka Chadash – perished in Vilyka

Ytzhak Feyglson, his wife, and their grandson, Nisan Rayz – the day of slaughter, 9-9-1942

Moshe – Chaim (Feema) Feyglson – perished unknown, his wife Duba, nee Motosov, their daughters; Miriyam and Sara – perished on the day of slaughter, 9-9-1942.

Moshe Alperovich, his daughters, Rashka and Dishka – perished on the day of slaughter, 9-9-1942. His son, Ytzhak – perished while hiding in the woods. His daughter, Batya – perished unknown.

Lipa Zemushzik, his wife Elka, and four children – perished on the day of slaughter, 9-9-1942.

Shlomo Zaif – perished in Shrekovishtzina. His wife Duba and their four children – perished in Vilyka, while hiding another Jewish family.

Menachem – Mendel Kramer – perished with the thirty-two, the Jewish month of Adar, 1942. His wife, Chana and their son Yishayu – perished while hiding in the woods. Their daughter Henya and their sons, Moshke, and Gershon – perished the day of the slaughter, 9-9-1942.

Baruch Kramer – perished with the thirteen, the Jewish month of Shvat, 1942. His wife – perished in Molodechno.

Meir – Shmuel Makler, his wife, Pesya, and their daughter – perished the day of the slaughter, 9-9-1942. Their son, Hilel – perished unknown.

David Ziskand, and two daughters – perished the day of slaughter, 9-9-1942. His wife, Nechama and another daughter – perished with the thirty two, the Jewish month of Adar, 1942

Reuven – Zishka Alperovich, his wife, Marke, their son, Avraham – perished while hiding in the woods, their sons Elihu (Elik) and Mordechai (Motik) joined the resistance and perished during a battle.

Meir Shkolnik – perished while hiding in the woods.

Eliezer Roytstein, his wife, their two sons, their one daughter – perished the day of the slaughter, 9-9-1942.

Rivka Zimerman, her son, Chaim – Ytzhak – perished on the day of slaughter, 9-9-1942.

Sheyna-Chaya Zimerman, her son – perished with the thirty-two, the Jewish month of Adar, 1942. Her husband – perished unknown.

Nechamka Zimerman, her husband, their child – perished with the thirty-two, the Jewish month of Adar, 1942.

Sara Shulman – perished the day of slaughter, 9-9-1942. Her daughter – perished in Vilyka.

Pesach Alperovich, his wife, Rivka, their daughter – perished the day of slaughter, 9-9-1942.

Chana Fridman (nee Torov) – perished while hiding in the woods.

Yoel and his wife – perished on the day of slaughter, 9-9-1942. Their son – perished unknown.

Avraham-Shimon Torov, his daughter, Sara-Shifra, his grandson – perished the day of slaughter 9-9-1942.

Chaim Ben-Zion Torov, his wife – perished unknown.

    Yakov Kramer and his family – perished in the shtetl Svyer.

Yehuda – Leib Dinnerstein, his wife, Sara – perished on the day of slaughter, Yehuda jumped to the fire wearing his talit, before the murderer could kill him. Their son Moshe – perished in Lublin, their son, Yakov, missing.

Avraham Blinder, his wife, Bluma, their daughter – perished on the day of slaughter, 9-9-1942.

Moshe Taubes – perished in Velyka.

Yakov Taubes and six of his children – perished on the day of slaughter, 9-9-1942. One son – perished unknown.

Tzvi Alperovich, his sons, Zev, Moshe, and Israel – perished the day of slaughter, 9-9-1942. His daughter, Chana, her husband, Mordechai, their daughter, Shifra – perished after the day of slaughter, when there hiding place was found.

Chalvina Torov – perished while hiding in the woods. His wife Rivka-Hinda and their two children – perished on the day of slaughter, 9-9-1042.

Chaim Sotzkover, his wife, Sara Eshka, her mother, Shashe-Reyse, their son – perished on the day of slaughter, Chaim fought the policeman that came to get them, he started choking him, and the other policemen shot him.

Chaim Zirolnik – perished on the day of slaughter, 9-9-1942. His wife Chaya – Eetka, their daughter, – while hiding in the woods.

Moshe –Benjamin Alperovich, his wife, Malka – perished on the day of slaughter, 9-9-1942.

Zalman, son of Moshe –Benjamin Alperovich, his wife, Chana-Tzipa, their son, Reuven – perished in Vilyka.

Tanchum Zimerman, his daughter, Sara – perished the day of the slaughter, 9-9-1942.

Neta Rodinski, his wife, Riva-Zlata, and their two children – perished on the day of slaughter, 9-9-1942.

Shalom Catzovitz, his wife, their two children, his sister – perished in Vileyka.

Ben-Zion, his wife, Sara-Gitel, their two children – perished on the day of slaughter, 9-9-1942.

Yecheskel Fridman, his wife, Hinda, three of their children – perished on the day of the slaughter, 9-9-1942.

Beela, wife of Moshe Alperovich, – perished on the day of slaughter. Her daughter, Chaya-Shtirl – perished in Shtzotzin.

Fruma Sosanski, her granddaughter, Chayale – perished on the day of slaughter, the teen-ager, Chayale scratched the faces of her killers, and cursed them, she was tortured.

Mordechai Kuzniatz, his wife, Lea, two sons and a daughter, – perished on the day of slaughter ,9-9-1942. One son perished while hiding in the woods.

Yadz'ze Kuzniatz – perished while hiding in the woods. His wife – perished in Dolhinov.

Eliezer Racha – Rasha's– perished on the day of slaughter, his wife and child – perished in Dolhinov.

Ytzhak Zimerman – perished with the thirteen, the Jewish month of Shvat, 1942. His son, Shimshon – perished unknown, Fayga – perished in Vilyka.

Yosef Zimerman, his wife, Lea, two children – perished on the day of slaughter, 9-9-1942.

Mirka nee Zimerman, her husband and their child – perished in Globoki.

Shmuel Gordon, his wife Chasya, his son, Yakov – perished on the day of slaughter, 9-9-1942.

Avraham-Moshe Forman, his wife, Chana, his son, Levi-Ytzhakhis daughters, Lyba and Tzipa – perished on the day of slaughter, 9-9-1942.

Chana (nee Gurevitz) wife of Elchanan Alperovich, the (ha katzav) – perished on the day of slaughter, 9-9-1942.

Chaim Alperovich, the son of Elchanan and Chana, Marishka, his wife, their baby girl – perished in the woods, when their hide out was found.

Hirshel son of Elchanan Alperovich, his wife Marishka, – perished when they tried to leave their hideout. 9-9-1942

Zusia Benes, his wife –Lea – perished by committing suicide and burning down their home on the day of slaughter, 9-9-1942.

Mordechai Ziskind – perished while hiding in the woods his sister , Eetka – perished in Velyka.

Chaim Israel Gurevitz, his wife – perished on the day of slaughter, 9-9-1942. Her daughter, Sonia, her husband and three children – perished in Dolhinov.

The wife of Faybush, the "shochet", their son and daughter – perished on the day of slaughter, 9-9-1942. One son – perished while hiding in the woods.

Ysrael Alpervich, his wife, Chaya, their sons Zundel and Yosel, their daughters; Chana and Eetka – perished while hiding in the woods.

Shmaryau, son of Ysrael Alperovich – perished on the day of slaughter, 9/9/1942. His wife and two children – while hiding in the woods.

Yosef Dubin, his wife, Malka, their daughter – perished on the day of slaughter, 9/9/1942.

Gdalyau Kopelovich, his wife, Frayda, their son, Yosef – v perished on the day of slaughter, 9/9/1942. Their son, Tebel perished while hiding in the woods,. Their daughter, Dvosha-perished in Velyka.

Baruch Kopelovich, Frumka, his wife, their two children – perished in Velyka.

Tzipa Ashknazi, her son Avraham – perished on the day of slaughter, 9/9/1942.

Lyba, daughter of Noach her husband, their son-perished while hiding in the woods,. Their daughter, Shifra – perished in Vilna.

Nechama, wife of Ytza – Michael Alperovich, her daughter, Tzirel – perished on the day of slaughter, 9/9/1942. Her daughter, Lyba – perished in Velyka.

Herzl Alperovich, his two sons – perished while escaping the Velyka camp.

Shmuel – Ytzak Eesak, his wife, Shosha, their daughter, Freydel with her two children, their daughter, Chaya-Racha, her husband, Nachum their two children – perished on the day of slaughter, 9/9/1942.

Eliyhu Eesak, his wife, two girls – perished on the day of slaughter, 9/9/1942.

Feyga Berger [de Lyubiker], her daughter, Chaya, and Chaya's husband – perished on the day of slaughter, 9/9/1942.

Isar Berger, his wife and children perished Dockshitz.

Zev Berger, his wife and children – perished in Smorogon.

Aharon Dinnerstein, – perished while hiding in the woods,. His wife, Ester, their son, Yosef, their daughter, Yenta – perished on the day of slaughter, 9/9/1942.

Mina Berez, daughter of Neta Zimerman and her baby girl – were tortured to death in Velyka.

Nachum Zimerman, his wife Sheya [Neta Zimmerman's' daughter] and their daughter – perished when they tried to run away in Velyka.

Chaim Gvellman, his wife, Gita, their three girls – perished on the day of slaughter, 9/9/1942.

Zisha, daughter of Aba Alperovich – perished with the thirteen, Shvat 1942. Her sister Malka – perished in Troki.

Neta Alperovich [son of Ytzhak-Elchanan], his wife Hayka, their daughter Sima perished on the day of slaughter 9/9/1942, their son Israel and their daughter Yohevet perished in the woods. Their daughter Rivkah perished in Vileyka; Yonah Chayim – her husband, David Yonah perished in Ponar.

Mendel Alperovitz son of Shimon – perished on the day of slaughter, 9/9/1942. His son Shimon and the son's wife Golda perished in Voloshin.

Ziskint Alperovitz, son of Shimon – his wife Batia Chana, their children Shimon and Yachiel perished while hiding in the woods.

Vellvell Rodinisky – perished with the 54. His son baby Zalman perished on the day of slaughter, 9/9/1942.

Shmoel Cherney – his wife Chana, daughter of Asher Rodinidky and 3 children perished while hiding in the woods.

Shmoel Alperovitz, son of Taybe – his wife Hinda, their son and their daughter perished with the 54 on Simcha Torah, 1941.

Shlomo Mizel – his wife Chana Kaya perished on the day of slaughter, 9/9/1942.

Israel Soliminsky – his wife Esther nee Mizel and 2 children perished with the 32. Their two other children perished on the day of slaughter, 9/9/1942.

Shmuel Mizel – his wife perished in an unknown place.

Henia Gvellman – wife of Zelig and their daughter Faygale perished on the day of slaughter, 9/9/1942.

Meir Gordon – his wife, and 4 daughters perished on the day of slaughter, 9/9/1942.

Yitzhak Tsinstung-his wife Rachel perished in Vileyka. Rachel's sisters Hinda and Chana (with her 2 daughters) perished on the day of slaughter, 9/9/1942.

Leib Charnas – perished in Kribitz. His wife Asna perished on the day of slaughter, 9/9/1942.

Avraham Charnas – his wife Racha Batya perished in Kribitz.

Eliezer Charnas – his family perished in Rochee.

Menachem Charnas – his wife Rachel, their daughter Chaya and their son Moshe perished on the day of slaughter, 9/9/1942.

Daniel Alperovitz, son of Chaim Avraham – caught in the woods and died a painful death. His sister Sertyl perished in Vileyka. His sister Chaya and her family perished in an unknown place.

Menachem Mendel son of Yecheskel Alperovitz – his wife Gittel and their son Aaron perished on the day of slaughter, 9/9/1942.

Arye Leibchik Fistonovitz – perished in Vileyka. His wife Nacha, daughter of Mendel Alperovitz perished on the day of slaughter, 9/9/1942. Their daughter Nina perished in Vileyka. Their daughter Pesya and sons Yeheskal and Zalman perished on the day of slaughter, 9/9/1942.

Yosef Alperovitz, son of Menachem Mendel – perished in the woods. His wife Leah nee Mizel and their son Shimon Motel perished on 9-11-1941.

Rashka Alperovitz nee Gurevich, wife of Zalman, son of Yaheskel – perished in the woods. Her son, Meir perished in Vileyka. Her grandchildren Zalman and Moshe perished on the day of slaughter, 9/9/1942. Her daughter Piya and the daughter's husband Shimshon Rubin and her grandchildren Zalman and Yakov perished in Dolhinov.

Pesia Alperovitz, wife of Moshe, son of Yaheskel – her son Benjamin perished with the 54. Her daughter Rachel with her child perished on the day of slaughter, 9/9/1942. Eliezer, husband of Rachel perished in an unknown place.

Aaron, son of Tzvi Shulman, his wife Frada, and their daughter Chana perished on the day of slaughter, 9/9/1942.

Benjamin "Nyomka" Shulman son of Aaron and Rachel – perished as a partisan while blowing up a German train. Nyomka's grandmother Batia Raizeh perished on the day of slaughter, 9/9/1942.

Yosef Zeev Sandler – his wife Rachel and their daughter Osnat perished the day after the slaughter. They hid in the attic of the synagogue. They were caught and they tied them to a horse and buggy and they pulled them to the graveyard.

Zalman-Mendel , son of Chaykel-Velvel Alperovich, – perished in unknown, his wife, Lea-Malka, their sons, Chanoch and Chaykel, their daughter, Rachel, – perished in Poken 9-10-1942.

Mendel Levine – perished with the thirteen, Shvat, 1942. His son, Elimelech, – perished on the day of slaughter, 9-9-1942. His son Chaim, – perished in Velyka.

Yehoshua Limon – perished with the thirteen, the month of Shvat, 1942, his wife, their daughter- – perished on the day of slaughter, 9-9-1942. His son – perished while hiding in the woods.

Asna Lemon – perished in Kobilanik.

Asher Limon, Chaya-Eshka, his wife, their son, Shlomo, their daughter, Batya, – perished in unknown.

Chana-Rivka, daughter of Asna Limon, – perished on the day of slaughter, 9-9-1942.

Mordechai – Leib Kopershtuch, his wife, Chana-Ester, – perished on the day of slaughter, 9-9-1942.

Yosef Kopershtuch, his wife, Rachel, their son, Avrahmel, their daughter, Reyzel – perished on the day of slaughter, 9-9-1942.

Zev Kopershtuch – was tortured to death in Velyka. His wife, Shayna, – perished on the day of slaughter, 9-9-1942.

Shabtai Gordon, his wife, Sonya, their children; Aaron, Zalman, Chaim, Golda – perished on the day of slaughter, 9-9-1942.

Rivka, sister of Shabtai Gordon, her husband, Mordechai. Two children, – perished on the day of slaughter, 9-9-1942.

Nathan, son of Meir Shalom Shulman, his wife, Sara, their daughters, – perished on the day of slaughter, 9-9-1942. Their son Zalman – perished on the way to Velyka.

Tzipa Tzipilevitz, sister of Zalman-Mendel Tzipilevitz – perished on the day of slaughter, 9-9-1942.

Pesya Brunstein, wife of Zalman – Asher, – perished on the day of slaughter, 9-9-1942.

Zalman Shulman, his wife, Rivka – perished on the day of slaughter, 9-9-1942.

Yakov Shulman – perished in /unknown his wife and son, – perished on the day of slaughter, 9-9-1942.

Tzvi Shulman and his wife, – perished on the day of slaughter, 9-9-1942.

Shneorson (the pharmacist) his wife, their son Liyona, his wife, Riva nee Anzelevich and their daughter, – were murdered ten months after the day of slaughter.

Shmuel Zipelovitz – perished with the thirteen, the Jewish month of Shvat, 1942.

Duba Zipelevitz, wife of Moshe. Her son, Chaim, – perished on the day of slaughter, 9-9-1942.

Rachel Lea Meltzer, – perished on the day of slaughter, 9-9-1942.

Yakov Sotzkover. His wife, Sara [daughter of Rachel – Lea] their sons, Benjamin and Avraham, – perished on the day of slaughter, 9-9-1942.

Yakov-Mendel Fladsher – perished in Leeda.

Shmuel Gurevitz – perished in unknown, his wife, Henya nee Motosov, their children, Avraham, Ytzhak, Meir, Sara, , – perished on the day of slaughter, 9-9-1942.

Chaya [nee Motosov] Einbinder, her son, Zev. Her daughter, Rachel, – perished on the day of slaughter, 9-9-1942. Their son Mendel – killed while walking to Velyka.

Sara Alperovich [Zukerman], – perished on the day of slaughter, 9-9-1942.

Bluma Alperovich, wife of Ysrael Munis, her grandchildren, Shifra, Yente, Eesar, – perished on the day of slaughter, 9-9-1942.

Rivka Alperovich, wife of Reuven Natan Zalman – perished on the day of slaughter, 9-9-1942.

Tzvi Kopilovitz – perished in Kurenitz, his wife, Feygel, their son, Yakov, their daughter, Lea. – perished while hiding in the woods, Feygel Lea Serls was found alive, she was badly tortured but would not tell that the farmers gave them food.

Zalman Shulman, his wife, Rivka, – perished on the day of slaughter, 9-9-1942.

This is only a partial list. There are six pages that have not yet been translated.

[Page 8-11]

Our withered town, Kurenitz, Villeyka County, Vilnus District.

by Baruch Zukerman

Translated by Carmel Levitan

In honor of her grandfather, Sali Gordin, who had the good sense to marry her grandmother, Rachel, a daughter of Kurenitzers.

Her destruction was a drop in the days of annihilation of the European Jewry, reflecting in miniscule the currents of the sea in its enormity, so would the destruction of the little shtetl reflect the desolation of the whole Diaspora.

The force of the sea is the combined force of its many rivers and streams as is the creative force of the Jews, the intermingling of shtetls and cities, that in their midst flows the Jewish spirituality, generation after generation.

The book we are writing is a memorial to the life and death of a little unknown shtetl, one eternal flame in the enormous cemetery of shtetls and towns. These eternal flames will enlighten future generations and spark the thousand-year-old Jewish entity of Europe: the thousand year-old Jewish creativeness, original and constant. In the presence of the memorial, our sons and the sons of our sons will stand enlightened. It will let them comprehend "Where did you come from" and "Where are you going" and there they would realize from the glittering lights to the shadowy annihilation that the history notebook is ajar. There is an observing eye and a hand recording. The king of all kings in his divinity is listening, whether a metaphysical god or our eternal universal conscience. We couldn't collect a thousand years of our shtetl's history in these pages. We don't know the days of her life, and what was her origin.

When did they lay the foundation? And who put in her doors? By contrast, we know the continuance and it's clear to a tear her terrible annihilation. So we did the best that we could to make a megillah-like book of everything that we could collect and gather. We were helped mainly by the memories of living natives, but we also melded chapters from writings about her from former generations. So we believe that we were able to embroider on her life-quilt the way she was in her last hundred years.

Her financial picture was not complicated. The shopkeeper and tradesmen comprised a majority. Some shopkeepers had large shops, and some had miniscule shops. Some tradesmen had one or two workers, and some did all the work themselves. The city had tailors, shoemakers, hatters, woodworkers, butchers, and metalworkers. There was a large number of very poor peddlers that went from village to village trying to sell housewares, tools, and for that they would either get money or food from the farmers, and that they would sell to the storekeepers, and they would sell it to the bigger towns. Most of the exchange of merchandise was with the city of Smorgone that had real industry in those days. But this financial basis was falling apart, and the natives of the town, especially the young ones, didn't stay and started going into the outside world, first to Smorgone and then farther, to Vilnus and Minsk. Some of them found their way to Dvinsk, and in their travels they arrived to cities outside of the Pale of Settlement, like Riga and Libo. Later on, when poverty spread, the wandering spring found a new path: immigration to America.

Towards the end of the 19th century, many families in Kurenitz prevailed because of the infusion of American dollars. The dollar became a very important element in the economy of the town and America became the land (harbor) of opportunity for hundreds of families. In the final 20 years of the town, Eretz Yisrael became the harbor and the haven.

The general picture of the shtetl was similar to other shtetls in Eastern Europe and in the pale of settlement. Her spiritual life was very special and original. And I hope that the collections here will show us the uniqueness of her profile.

Unlike most shtetls in Lithuania and Belarus, Kurenitz was mainly Hasidic. It had three synagogues and two minyans. And from this, only one synagogue belonged to the "mitnagdim". Spiritually, the town was very blessed. The leaders were noble of spirit and spread their noble spirit on her image. Rabbi Yaakov Landau gives true image to the influence of this unique people. He tells us about the deep effect that the beloved renowned famed genius Rabbi Zishka, and the influence of the articulate and intuitive Rabbi Moshe Leib Landau. From his childhood memoirs of home, we picture essence of modesty, excitement of Torah studies and love of humanity.

Jacob Alpert vividly describes his family and long list of beloved neighbors, and with all their individual differences the commonality through the stories is the deeply committed social and spiritual essence of the town.

The town was blessed with a large number of unique teachers. They were not credential, (except for the beloved and respected Moreh , Ben-Zion Meirovitz) . What they lacked in pedagogical methods, they compensated for with the deep desire to awaken their pupils' spirits with love for God, Jews, Zion, and the high ideals of our prophets. The teachers and rabbis spread their deeply spiritual essence on their flock and opened their hearts to experience a spiritual treasure that enabled them to withstand the extreme poverty and the severity of life in the Diaspora and unable them to continue to live as complete Jews. The ones that left for America will be witnessed that despite the enormous new influences of a new country, they could not erase the strong childhood impressions and values that they brought from their homeland. We witness this in their stories, especially in the spiritual journey of Rabbi Moshe Laser Kramer.

Then came the days that the flame of enlightenment spread around the town. Stronger yet, were the effects of the unstoppable radical socialist movement. The firebrands that tried to evoke hate to the tsarist regime did not need to use much persuasion. Their job was done by the evil deeply anti-Semitic authority. But neither the spirit of enlightenment nor the revolution would affect the town's spirit. Externally, things changed, but the deeper essence stayed the same till the arrival of Zionism that let yet unique new expression and longing surface. New tunes and ideals were heard in the hills and the valleys- Hebrew schools, beloved teachers that only spoke Hebrew, Zionist organizations, like Histadrut, youth movements, like hachaloot, and Hashomer Hatza'ir. But in some ways it was a new tune for an old song. Old wine in a new bottle…

The size of the population hardly changed. Many immigrated, but new births replenished the departures. Hundred of families were left prey to the Nazi murderers. Our town collapsed in the bloody battle where the terrorists annihilated left and right millions. Millions of morally and spiritually committed and religiously obedient Jews.

The Jews of Kurenitz were also among the contributors and heroes of the resistance during the dark days of the Holocaust. Their sacrifice and braves had many faces. Can we forget the teenage girl, Chayaleh Sesonsky, while taken to be murdered on the day of the slaughter 9/9/42, she scratched the faces of her killers with her tender fingers, and on her grave she cursed them, prophesying that the sounds of bleeding souls would scream from the earth and the day of revenge would come… Can we forget the courageous actions of the teenage sons of Kurenitz, organizing underground fighting, and connecting with the Russian army? Motik and Ellik Alperovich, Yunkle Alperovich, Yitzhak Einbinder, Nachum Alperovich, Zalman Uri Gurevich, Benjamin Shulman, and Zalman Alperovich, amongst others… Will we forget old Leib Motisov, passionately calling Jews to action, warning and prophesizing the bitter end, and on the day of slaughter, jumping into the fire, wearing his talleet, before the killer's bullet would get him? Is it possible to forget the series of tortures of Yisrael Alperovich, the meat vendor that escaped the slaughter to the woods with a few hundred other Kurnitzers? Yisrael, a god fearing Jew, ate only potatoes, refusing to compromise the kosher rules until starvation and died. And what about the torture and killing of Sarl's Faiga Leah. It reminds us of the torture of Hannah. She was caught alive by the enemy while hiding in the woods. She suffered every physical torture but would not give the names of the gentiles that fed them, even denying the words of ones that had already confessed.

All these testaments that tell about the life and the death of the Jews of our town will be printed in this memorial for eternity. But the most shaking testament is the list of the holy martyr, man and woman, old and babies slaughtered in the hands of the evil. The voice of their blood rises from the book. Their shouts combine with the shouts of the millions that perished that demand from us: remember what the pharaohs from Ashkenaz did to us.

Books of testament and memoirs are the answer to all those that want to deny our enormous destruction, the mark of shame on the forehead of humanity. By denying it they want to erase the enormous crime as if the number of our slaughtered is only 2 million and not 6, it makes less the crime of humanity that stood there and didn't intervene to save or help. As If the weight of the blood and the number of the victims are the only measures of the collective human order, "do not stand on the blood of your friend".

It's our duty and holy mission to register in all books like this the vastness of our destruction and the huge measure of our slaughtered . It's our responsibility to each victim that didn't get to be brought to Jewish burial and for the whole Jewish nation.

For eternity our nation remembered our martyrs and this helped to us to endure. The memory of this mother of all annihilations that has no brother in our recorded history should be the weapon in our war for the future survival of the nation. And this will support us in the future as it supported us in the past: that our biggest enemy that wanted to annihilate us all did not succeed. The nation of Israel lives and will continue to live. And the high ideals of Isaiah and Micha will endure and their prophecies will come on the judgement day. The enemy wanted to kill our spirit, but they failed and will always fail.

Our little shtetl was killed only physically, she was erased from the maps of the Diaspora but her spiritual contribution will float to the horizon to mix with the rest of Judaism. These pages will bear witness that the spirit of our town did not die, and from the ashes will come life and faith.

[Page 12]

Should You Wish to Know [1]

Translated by Jerrold Landau

Should you wish to know the wellspring
From which your murdered brethren drew
During the days of strong evil, the strength of the soul
When they went out joyously to greet death, to extend their necks
To every burnished knife, to every extended axe,
To ascend the stake, to jump into the fire
And to die the death of a martyr with "*echad*"[2]

Should you wish to know the wellspring
From which your oppressed brethren drew
Between the straits of the netherworld and the tribulations of destruction, amongst the scorpions –
With the consolations of G-d, faith, courage, steadfastness of spirit
And the iron power to bear every burden, the shoulder
Extended to suffer a life of filth and degradation, to suffer
Without end, without bounds, without an end – – –

Should you wish to know the bravery
On their heads, through which your fathers fortified their souls,
Their Torah, their holy of holies – and it would save them;
If you wish to know the hiding place in which it was guarded –
And the essence of purity – the mighty spirit of your nation,
Which even though it was sated with a life of shame, spit, and degradation
Its hoary age did not shame the pleasantness of its youth –

Should you wish to know the merciful mother,
The elderly mother, loving and faithful,
In whose great mercy she is suffused with tears for her lost son
And in her great compassion is bound all her affirmations,
And when he returns, humiliated, tired, and weary
To the shelter of her roofs, she will wipe his tears
Cover them with the shadow of her wings, lull him to sleep upon her lap –

[Page 13]

O, just answer, if you do not know all these –
Go to the House of Study, the old, the ancient,
On the long, desolate nights of Tevet
On the burning, fiery nights of Tammuz,
In the heat of the day, in the morning, or in the darkness of night,
If G-d still leaves a small remnant of survivors –
Then perhaps even to this day your eyes will see
Under the influence of the shade of its roof, in the cloud,
In one of its corners, or next to its oven
Lone sheathes, as a shadow of what was lost,
Wizened Jews, with wrinkled, pitted faces,
Jews of the exile, who bear the weight of its yoke,
Who relieve their toil with a page of Gemara,
They forget their poverty through the study of ancient discussions
And calm their worries with hymns of Psalms –
(Aha! How strange and gloomy does this appear
To the eyes of a stranger who does not understand!) But your heart tells you,
That your feet should tread upon the threshold of our house of life
And your eyes should see the treasury of our souls. – – –

Translator's Footnotes:

1. An online translation of this poem exists at https://www.poemhunter.com/poem/should-you-wish-to-know-the-source/ However, this appears to be more of a summary style adaptation than a literal translation.
2. A reference to the first verse of Shema, which ends with *Echad* (One), declaring the unity of G-d.

[Page 15-18]

A place of the Torah

Written in the 1880s' by Yisrael Yisar Katzovitz

Translated by Alon Meir Levitan

*"In honor of my great grandfather, who is also my namesake.
He loved books and was the librarian of Moshav Bitzaron"*

…It's already the end of summer. I feel refreshed, energetic and content. I sleep deeply and soundly, I devour my food, I like my job and I am never idle. My uncle is very happy with me, so you might ask, "What's the problem?" Out of nowhere these negative thoughts started penetrating my peaceful existence - "You are bound to stay an idiot and a simpleton!" What does it mean to be an idiot, you might ask? The entire summer I did not touch a book, and in no time the little knowledge I have gained will be erased. I find myself being pulled back to my days of Torah studies, but every time I remember Minsk and its yeshivas' I get a bad taste in my mouth and my skin shivers. I want to go to Kurenitz where I could study the torah on my own.

In my childhood I spent some time there studying in the cheder. Kurenitz is a very short distance from my fathers' home in Kribitzi and I can see my folks as often as I like. In Kurenitz I can study as I wish and I'll be rid of the arrogant, rooster-like heads of the Yeshivas and their police-men type aids, and all the Ta Ra Ram!

My father and my uncle like the idea. My uncle paid me twenty rubles that he owed me and I gave some of the money to my father. I had the tailor make me some clothes with the rest, and immediately after "Sukkot" I walked to Kurenitz.

Amongst Chasidim

If you want to know the essence of the Hassidim you must live with them, mingle with, and observe them. The Hassidic movement has had a profound impact on the Jewish experience. It revolutionized the old, tired Jewish class system with a sense of equality and love and respect for the common man. It suited the aching Jewish heart to assuage it of the hardship of the Diaspora. Kurenitz is a shtetl of Hasidim and I must say in my childhood it was like a splendid oasis for me. As I enter Kurenitz I immediately feel that I entered a new world, a different kind of people.

Here you won't meet Jews who are full of themselves, who assume self-importance, and will constantly let you know that they are Jews of "Aliah." Here you won't find the rabbis who prance around like proud turkeys and look with distaste at the common person. Everyone is equal here - poor, rich, son of the Torah and the handyman. On holidays and days of celebration everyone mingles and you feel like you are part of one big, happy family. In addition to the beauty of friendship and sense of equality, I particularly enjoy the fact that you won't see here the spineless Jews with solemn faces, as you do in other towns. The Hassid says sadness is a curse. Work God in happiness. For the Hassidim, it is a mitzvah to be happy, a commandment. The Baal Shem Tov would say that a man who lives with joy fulfills the wish of his God. There are shtetls where after the three meals at the ending of Shabbat the Jews retain a sense of bitterness on their faces. Extreme despair comes over them and they start saying Tehilim with a whiny tune as if a dead person is in front of them and they are eulogizing him. Here they say Hassidut. They tell wonderful tales and sing wonderful, melodic, sweet tunes. It does not seem like a big deal, songs and tales, but I feel like my soul rises to heaven and my heart fills with good feelings and aspirations more than when I read the Mussar (moralizing) books.

The prayers are done here with special excitement. They give their heart and soul in their prayer. It is never done in haste. Every word is pronounced slowly with perfect enunciation and tune. Hassidut is discussed here often. One gives drasha and explanation and the rest listen. I started going to hear drashot. At the beginning it was a foreign thing to me, but slowly I started understanding. The Hassidut teaches us to see man as a partner of God, helping God in the creation of the world. Without the deed of the human beings here on earth, God could hardly do much in heaven. The essence of man and his aim and desire is to be God-like, to improve his personality and his deeds. The first Mitzvah, or commandment, is to get rid of the "have," to stop putting such importance to small physical bodily urges and to selfish desires. Man must remember that he is the sparkle in the eyes of the creation, and that without him, the world means nothing.

The Hassidut will also teach us that the mitzvoth and bible studies must be done out of love, and not out of fear. A man should not do the commandments for his reward in heaven or the other world, but only for the sake of the commandment and its goodness. The prayer to God is not only the words written in a book, or the fasts and physical sacrifices, but it must heighten the spirits with excitement and should be done with extreme concentration. If its done properly it will transport the soul and enable it to reach higher levels of spirituality. With the help of such prayers man would ascend from a physical being to one that is one with God , one that has an unending splendor....

During the long winter nights, sometimes I find myself all alone in the shtetl, and I study until midnight, sometimes even later. I wake up when I wish, sometimes just before dawn. The short of it is that I am free and independent and I do whatever I desire. I don't have anyone watching over me and I study what I wish. In summer nights I stay awake all night and study, especially when there is a full moon. I open all the windows, a light wind blows around me and I dive with sweet tune into the passages of our scholars. Now I understand them and I admire them. If I meet a very difficult passage and I cannot understand the complicated ideas of our scholars, I have a solution. I stand with my face to the wall and I say with deep reverence, "Ahavat Olam." And when I reach the passage "Vten b'libanu bina l'haveen" I start begging, "God, open my heart and light it so I can understand and comprehend the saying of your Torahs."

After saying that, my eyes open wide and my thinking becomes clear. I read the passage again, slowly with no haste, and with deep concentration. God helps me. After a short time the difficult passage is absolutely clear. "Yagata Umatzata Taamim"

- "The one that tries and studies hard at the end will comprehend." That is what our sages said. Sometimes I feel drawn to something new, and not to the Gammara, so I study the Midrash. Among the books I found in the synagogue was a book *Bchinat Olam*. It is an extremely difficult book, but that does not scare me…

Yuda son of Zushas – A land owner and a Hassid

I study in the shteble of Yuda Zushas'. To a house of study they call here shteble. Yuda Zushas is a handsome Jew. Tall, with a round black beard, his eyes are black and he has a very deep, penetrating stare. He is a serious person, but usually a relaxed aura surrounds him. He is always dressed in a clean, and elegant manner. Everyone says that he is a brilliant man, and has a thorough knowledge of the Bible and the laws. His Hassidic lessons are very lively. He also speaks Polish and Russian well. Even among the gentiles he is known as a very smart and decent man. He has two children: a son and a daughter. He also adopted an orphan girl. He rents a land parcel from the wealthiest landlord in the area, the Paritz. He has a *pundak* (a wine making and tasting establishment). He owns a boarding house. In addition, he has claims in numerous businesses in the wood processing and clothing manufacturing industries. Many of the town Jews work for him. He supplies for all of his relatives, and no one complains. In spite of the fact that he has so many businesses, he finds time for the Torah and every morning when morning prayers end, he reads from the Olam, a chapter from the Mishnah. Between Mincha and Maariv he reads from "Ain Ya'akov".

I love to listen to his prayer when he is left all alone in the shteble. I especially enjoy the Shabat prayer. On Shabat I eat at his house. After everyone else has left the shteble, his son and I stay and wait for him. He faces the wall and prays with excitement and his beautiful voice fills the room with pleasant sounds and words of God. His prayers make you forget the rest of the world.

How beautiful is this house when we return from the synagogue! There are six silver candle sticks with long candles standing on a very long table that is covered with a white table-cloth. His wife, with her gentle, modest, yet proud face, sits on the "tzena vereyena". The orphan girl and the daughter listen intently to every word she reads.

Yuda Zoshas starts signing "Shalom Alechem" in a sweet voice. Holy quietness surrounds the home. The son, and I softly join the singing in hushed voices. Now its time for him to bless the wine. We stand slightly bowing our heads. He holds the big silver wine glass that is filled to the top. For a moment he'll shut his eyes and fall into deep thought. And then, his voice lifts in song. Each word vibrates the air. The holiness of the Shabat becomes a reality. I breathe deeply and the experience fills me. We sit around the table, late into the night when the fish is all eaten, and we sing "ezamer - beshvacheen". After we are done with the noodles, the son will recite a Mishniot chapter that is commonly told on Shabat.

Herschel the Tzadik (Righteous)

Another person who receives a lot of respect here is Herschel the Tzadic. In Kurenitz it's not common to be honored with the title "tzadik." Herschel, a short, skinny Jew, is always in a hurry and at all times, busy with some chore or another. He is Yuda Zushas' assistant. The entire alcohol business is his responsibility – he makes the wine, he measures and mixes it, he sells it and he registers the sales. His other important job is to observe the sun. He watches for the sunrises and sunsets. When he sees the first rays of the sun, he runs to all the houses of prayer, and sets the clocks. His job is to ensure that all the town's clocks are set in accordance with the sun, and with each other. In this way, the Jews will not set, God forbid!, the schedule for the daily prayers at the wrong times, or even worse, misjudge the time of the 'blessing of the candles' ceremony on Shabat evenings.

One night, on the month of Shvat, everyone had tired of scanning the sky for the moon. Not a single sighting of the moon had been reported. It was already the last night, and still the ceremony of moon renewal had not ended. The Jews sat late through the night, waiting and waiting, but all in vain. Eventually, all departed and returned to their homes to sleep. I had already fallen into a deep sleep, when all of a sudden, I was awakened by a loud knock on the window. I approached the window and heard a voice scolding me, "Get up quickly!", and announcing, "It's time to renew the moon." I washed my hands, got dressed, and ran hastily outside. Outdoors, I saw many Jews who also were hurrying from their beds, and were gathering from all corners.

As I later realized, Herschel the Tzadik hadn't slept the whole night. Instead, he had sat awake, and waited. He had hoped, 'Maybe God would have pity after all, and reveal the moon.' And as it turned out, Herschel the Tzadik hadn't waited in vain. The moon appeared and immediately he woke up all of the neighbors, and these neighbors woke up their other neighbors, until everyone was outside. We stood in the shivering cold, but the moon was shining and the beautiful sounds of the Jewish voices spread through the night air, and Herschel the Righteous, beamed with happiness…

Chaim Zalman – My Friend

I have a friend in the shtetl. His name is Chaim Zalman. He's the one and only son of Yuda Zushas'. He's only a few years older than I, but he is much taller than I am, and skinny, like a *lulav*. His face is elongated and pale, with a long nose, and long *curly cues payas'*. He is slightly sickly, and the doctors from Vilna have ordered him to drink plenty of milk and eats raw eggs. The doctors also recommended that he take walks in the fresh air. For this reason, his father, Yuda Zusha, asked me to take a daily journey with Chaim. Every evening, even during the winter time, we would stroll around the shtetl.

During the summer, and especially on weekends, we would take walks in the forest, in addition to our evening stroll. There, we would lie under a tree and discuss what a 'good Jew' is, the study of Hassidut, and everything that happens in Heaven and Hell. Both of us were confident that he, respectively, knew everything that happened in Heaven. On the other hand, we knew very little about what was happening on Earth. Newspapers never reached our area, and strangers would never visit.

One day, I learned about the world outside Kurenitz. Here is a tale that concerns a stranger who came to stay. One Shabat evening, Chaim Zalman approached me in haste and asked me to come to his house at once. He said "I want to show you something". I entered his home, and he pointed to a *Paritz* that was sitting in the next room, eating *gefilta* fish. "The person you see here, is a Jew," said Chaim Zalman. "He's a lawyer from Vilna, and he's visiting our *Paritz*." I stood there and observed the stranger carefully, from top to bottom. He had no side burns! His beard was completely shaved, he ate without a kippa on his head, and his whole face was un-Jewish- like. I couldn't believe what Chaim Zalman had said to me. I went to his mother and asked if he had indeed told me the truth. She answered me, sighing deeply, "Yes, yes, my dear, this one is also a Jew."

At dusk, Yuda asked me to sleep in the same room with the guest. He explained that the guest would get lonely, sitting alone at nightfall, and falling asleep by himself. When I went to the guest's room, he welcomed me warmly. He was very friendly and he spoke Yiddish eloquently, and with great depth of expression. He asked what chapter I had studied in my Talmud studies and mentioned many passages from different Talmudic chapters. He told me that just like me, he had been a poor *yeshiva* boy, but that was many years ago now. Some good people, he explained, had helped to put him on the right track, aiding him in becoming educated and learning the ways of the world until he succeeded in becoming a lawyer. While he was talking, I thought, "God forbid that this man truly exemplifies what it means to have found the 'right track'!". Later he urged me, "Come with me to Vilna, my dear, and there we'll make a man out of you." I thought, "Your concept of what is a fine man is really foreign to me." As he spoke, he began preparing for bed. Suddenly, I felt something was very wrong. This "cool" man had taken his clothes off and he hadn't even bothered to put a *talit*. I began to shiver, I felt anxious and uncomfortable at the idea of sleeping in the same room as him. I left the room quickly, and didn't return… …That was, and still is, the way the days in Kurenitz pass. Life is good here, when I feel lonely I walk to my fathers' home, visit my family, and then I go back to Kurenitz to study the Torah…

בית הכנסת   Kurenitz Синагогука

[Pages 20-34]

My Hometown

Rabbi Yakov Landau, Av Beit Din[1] of B'nei B'rak Israel. Former Rabbi of Kurenets

Translated by Danny Koor and Eilat Gordin Levitan

In her image and her essence, Kurenets stood apart from her neighboring shtetls. A holy spirit engulfed her in all her events and its spiritual essence was embedded with the stems of the giants of spirit who guided her through many generations. A splendor of holiness spread on her Sabbaths, her holy days, and her festivals. How pleasant it was to experience the sounds of the approaching Shabbat at dusk on Friday. When Rabbi Shmuel der Viner, the father of Shlomo Asna's, would leave my father's house (the Rabbi) to go to the central market, he would pass through all the stores in the center of town and announce in a special singing tone, "Ein shul ariyan (Into the synagogue)." And the Shabbat would spread its wings around the town and fill it with sacredness.

How I was filled with joy when I as a young boy stood by the gate of our house to see the scene. My father would say, "Reb Shmuel, it is time to announce Ein shul." And I would closely follow Reb Shmuel to see how that as soon as he would announce it, all the merchants would close their shops, as a small storm would start. The shutters would be closed and the locks would be turned. Immediately this would be followed by a holy tranquility and peacefulness, and the town would robe itself in its most majestic Shabbat clothes.

And here we see coming from Myadel Street, Shimon from the brothers [Zimmerman]. He is going to the Beit Midrash, wearing a velvet hat and soon, from all corners of town, Jews dressed in Sabbath clothes rushed to the synagogue. Here comes Reb Yehuda Meir Freda's (Alperovich). He was a very learned Jew. And here comes Avraham the Tailor, who we called Avramtzik der Schneider, a very respectable looking person. And from another direction comes Reb Eli Muniz, with a Midrash Rabba under his arm. He would teach midrash before the assembled members of the central synagogue, De Nyer Shtiebel. - The new Shtiebel. And here comes Moshe Nehemsik's, wearing a velvet yarmulke most of which can be seen from under his hat. And there makes an appearance, Cheikel Welwel, with him his youngest son Yakov Yoseleh, a devoted Lubavitch Hasid. His expression gleams from the splendor of Sabbath. And here is Mordechai Gurevich, husband of Freda, with his curly peyas, and his face is radiant, illuminated from the delight of Sabbath. Could anyone tell that this is the same Reb Mordechai that just a short time earlier was busy with selling iron goods to the gentiles? And here comes Mendel Zalman Roshka's. His hair is neatly combed and his essence is brimming with the refinement of the Sabbath.

In our minyan, my father would walk slowly from one side to the other and with a tune that was laden with piety and holiness, he would say, "Hodu and Patach Eliahu" before the minha prayer. In the minyan synagogue[2] simple oil lamps spread their lights, but still every corner shone splendidly in the reflection of Shabbat. And while the congregation starts saying their prayer, "Lehu neranena Lahshem, nariya letzur yishano" Come let us sing to God let us call out to the rock of our salvation, the heart would beam with elevated sentiments that would come to an apex at the passage "Mizmor Le David havu lashem bnei eilim." A psalm of David, render unto heaven you sons of the powerful" Kol hashem bakoach kol hashem chotzev lehavot eish. The voice of God is in power the voice of God is in splendor." This psalm is said one sentence at a time, with a pause in between each verse, and the hearts would get more and more ecstatic when they reached the tune of "Leha Dodi." It would not be sung with as regular tune, rather with a Hasidic melody and the prayers would go on, and the people would be filled with a thirst for more as they neared the height of joyfulness. In my early youth I would leave the minyan synagogue and go to the central market between the prayer of the Inauguration of the Sabbath and the evening prayer. At that point Reb Shlomo Asna's would read before the congregation from the book Beir Mayim Hayyim or Siddoro Shel Shabbat, but I wanted to become part of the holy silence that spread in the streets. To tell the truth, we didn't have to wait for Shabbat to feel the holiness around us. Early on Friday morning you could already feel the new holy face of the town. Smoke would rise high above the chimneys of the town, you could hear the sound of the Hakmasa while the women prepared the fish, and the wonderful smells of the Sabbath food would foretell the advent of the impending Sabbath.

On Fridays, as soon as the melamdim(teachers) would finish teaching the youth in the chadarim they would quickly go in town to collect from everyone the weekly tithes (donations) for the different charity organizations. One would be for the institution of Bikur Holim (which took care of the sick); here the Gabbai was Reb Abba Lubka's. Others would be collecting for the Gm'ch, which was a sort of savings and loan organization, it would be used for loans and in every big synagogue there would be a collection box for it.

Once a year, after Shabbat Parashat Mishpatim, there would be a big celebration where all the pledges that were not paid would be sold.

There were a few teachers that before Sabbath would collect money for different Hasidic dynasties. For example, for Lubavitch, for Lyadi… Each one would come with his own notebook and on each page there would be a table, and each square would represent one week for all the people who gave donations. They would write in detail the exact amount; usually it would be one or two kopecks. So the teachers of the town would be busily running around town, amongst them Reb Yitzhak Moshe, Reb Avraham Yitzhak, Reb Yosef Leib, and Reb Moshe Baruch the Shamash. This would also add to the special spirit of Friday.

The Festivals

A saying that was repeated many times by Reb Mendel son of Reb Yosef Zaev, the baker who lived in the shtetl Lebedove, was, "If you wanted to feel the true essence of Rosh Hashanah during the shofar blowing, you must always compare it with the shofar blowing of the Rabbi's minyan in Kurenets."

I must agree with his assessment because what was experienced during the days before Yom Kippur in Kurenets is almost impossible to describe. I would like to point out that in Kurenets, people would not smoke on Rosh Hashanah although there was no clear rule against it. During Sabbath Shuva (The Shabbat between Rosh Hashana and Yom Kippur), they would never carry outdoors despite the fact that there was eiruv in the shtetl. I also liked to write about a very splendid custom that took place during the ten days of Penitence. In all the synagogues they would light huge candles made of wax that we would prepare specially in our house. When the time of "Shuvalicht" repentance lights would arrive, a certain woman would go from house to house and would announce to all the women in town that now it was time to prepare for "Shuvalicht". On a set day, all the women in town would get up early and come to our house and throughout the entire day they were busy preparing candles. They would come and go through the entire day, taking turns, and each one of them took part in this important mitzvah. Heading the women was Bilka, the wife of Benny the Baker. The wax was always bought by my mother from Sarah Rachel, the wife of Avraham Mendel the Melamed, who had a small wax factory in their home. Once in a while Bilka would repeat, "Have you prepared (banged) wax?" Then she would say, "Have you prepared a wick?" each woman would do these two things. During the time of adding the wick, each woman would recite prayers for the souls of their relatives, and naming all the ones who had died, and also" the souls of the holy people who have fallen in the field and the forest." Each woman would then put a donation for the enterprise on a plate that was specially put on the table for this purpose. Before leaving each woman would go to a special room to pour out her heart in prayer, and plead with tears before God. At dusk only Bilka would be left there and she would start preparing the actual candles. The melted wax was put in a huge pail with hot water until it became even softer and then she would make it into candles that were one and a half meters tall, and five centimeters thick, five candles for each one of the synagogues in town.

Before Shabbat Shuva, each Shamash came to our house to get the candle for his synagogue. The candle would be burn halfway during Shabbat Shuva, and the rest during Yom Kippur. I would also like to relate about another beautiful, special custom that our town would experience during Shmini Atzeret and Simhat Torah. It would start with the special enterprise Lehem Evyonim. In our town we would give real loaves of bread to the needy. The Gabbai of this enterprise was Reb Yosi Velvul, the baker, he would distribute the bread. During the day of Simhat Torah, a few volunteers would go around all the homes, blessing everyone with a passage, "Mi Sheberach", and each family would promise to take care of distributing a certain amount of bread for the next year. Each week someone would go and collect the loaves of bread from each home. Sometimes people would give money instead of bread and the baker would then bake the bread on their account. When the volunteers for Lehem Evyonimn finished their rounds in town, they would come to our house to take part in the celebration of the festival. They would sit by the table for a meal that would last until after dark. Birkat Hamazon (Grace after meals) would always be said in the evening[3].

Obviously there was also the enterprise of Kimcha d'Pischa[4] every year. My father, the Rabbi of blessed memory, would head this enterprise. He would go with one of the most prominent town members and together they would go to the houses of the well to do people and the generous people of the town, and then they would give to the needy, matzos, wine, and mead. The amount of matzos for each needy person was four kilograms. Prior to that on Purim, all around town there would be Purim spielers. They would ride horses dressed up as policemen and rode happily through town. Once they finished their parade, they would stop at our house for the Purim feast.

The spiritual leaders of the town, formulators of the spiritual character

In all the different aspects of life, you can see the distinct influence of the town's leaders. First and foremost, the pious brilliant, filled with knowledge and intelligence, Rav Avraham Meshulam; Zalman Landau from the lineage of the most prominent Rabbi of Israel, the Gaon Yehezkel Landau (author of the Noda Beyudah), and from the lineage of the "Hacham Zvi" who originally came from Brody. Long ago, there lived in Kurenets a wealthy man by the name of Itzha Raha's. Rav Zalman married his daughter when he was very young. Already at that point he was well known as a most amazing genius and even the most well-known, learned men would make testament that he was able to dispute and debate with the best scientists even in their own fields of expertise. When he heard of the well-known Hassidic Rebbe, author of the Tanya and Shulhan Arukh Harav[5] he was very drawn to him, so secretly he left together with his brother-in-law Leib, the father of Zalman Roshka's, to visit this Rebbe, and in spite of the fact that his mother-in-law chased after them to bring them back, they succeeded in reaching their destination.

On their return, Reb Zalman established the "minyan synagogue" that was named the Rabbi's Minyan, the same place that was destroyed by the Nazis, may their names be erased from memory. The first building that was put up in this location was destroyed by fire and my father rebuilt it. When that building caught fire again in 1925, my deceased brother Rabbi Shmuel Hillel of blessed memory rebuilt it. Zalman was amongst the main Hasidim of the "Admor Hazaken" and for that reason, his sons and grandsons had tremendous influence on the image of Jewish Kurenets which eventually became an overwhelmingly Chabad (Lubavitch) shtetl. Of the five synagogues in Kurenets, in four they prayed in the style of Ha'ari and only in the Beit Midrash did they continue in the Ashkenazi style. The pious Gaon, Reb Zalman Landau had two sons and one daughter. One was Reb Tzvi Hirsch, who was nicknamed Reb Hirscheleh Reb Zalman's. He was a merchant and had business connections with Konigsberg and would travel there often . He was splendid in piety and purity. In Kurenets they often repeated a passage first spoken by him, "A Jew can swap a calf for a young horse and live off the profit a whole week.." He once said to my father, of blessed memory, that in his opinion, one must donate ten percent to charity of money that one loses as well as from money that one earns. His sons were the pious Rabbi, Reb Avraham Landau, who was the father of Leah Sherl. When he lived in Kurenets he worked as a businessman, but later on he became Rabbi in the town of Zabin, and he was related to the Tzemach Tzedek[6]. His son in law, Reb Yakov, who was nicknamed Yakov Leah Sherl's, was a pious and learned Jew. The second son of Reb Hirsheleh was Rabbi Dan, who was the husband of the granddaughter of Tzemach Tzedek. The second son of Rabbi Zalman Landau was the adored Rabbi of our town, the genius, pious and renowned all over, Reb Mordechai Ziskind Zal, known by everyone as Reb Zishka. All the people of the town and surrounding area saw him as a most amazing man, and his name and his memory are held in deep respect. He was extremely pious towards God and very respectful to all people. Reb Zishka was a Hasid in the court of the Tzemach Tzedek, and was greatly loved by him, both on account of his father, the genius pious Zalman, but also for his own personality. As a Rabbi in our town, Reb Zishka was active until the year 1884. He didn't have any sons, only two daughters. One was Leah Margalit, the other was Cherna. He married his daughter Leah Margalit to my father, the Gaon Rabbi Moshe Leib Zal. He took his place as a Rabbi in Kurenets after he died. His daughter Cherna lived in Vilna. Rabbi Zishka passed away on Shabbat, the fourteenth of Sivan, 1884. They tell that before he passed away he got up and walked to the window and looked outside and said, "Ah sheina walt. Ah sheina walt A wonderful world." Although he sat in his chair and didn't lie down, at certain points he felt that he was on the verge of death and a few times asked if the doctor Yehoshua Kremer was still present, since he was very worried that his soul would depart while there was still a Cohen in the house (Cohanim-Priests are not allowed to be in the presence of dead people). During the day when people asked him questions he said, "You must ask my son-in-law those questions because on the day of my death I cannot give answers anymore." The manifest of the rabbinical transfer that was given to my father after he passed away started in those words…

The holy, who was light to our eyes, a crown to our head, went to Heaven[7]. We gathered here…

This Rabbinical transfer was written by the famous Hasid, Reb Yehoshua Castrol[8] the uncle of the shohet in our town, Nahum Castrol.

Rabbi Zishka loved my father and was very close to him, and as my father would say, he withheld nothing from him. For fourteen years, my father lived with him and he would converse with him about passages of the Torah and Hasidic tales everyday from the evening meal until 3 in the morning. He would also tell him the most intimate details of his life. He opened his soul to him. His love for my father was unending, While he was still alive he ordered my father to sign all the papers replacing him as Rabbi of Kurenets. The transfer to my father as a Rabbi of Kurenets is from Tuesday the 17th of Sivan in the year 5684 (1884). It seems that during the first days of mourning the Rabbinate was already transferred. When all the townspeople returned from the cemetery, they gathered and the heads of the community took my father as the Rabbi of the town.

My father the genius and pious Rabbi was born in the town Haluvakah. From his father's side he was from the dynasty of Shlah[9] and from his mother's side from the dynasty of Mahar'sha[10]. My paternal grand father was the pious Rabbi, Reb Schneur Zalman. He was an exemplary genius, and he was one of the important Hasidim in the court of Tzemach Tzedek. He was the son in law of the genius, important Rabbi Reb Leib Ha-Cohen, Av Beit Din of Haluvkah, who was nicknamed Reb Leibeleh Tsertele's. In his youth, my father was famous as a genius prodigy and all the Rabbis of the time wanted to take him as a son-in-law, but he chose the daughter of the well-known Hasid when he was 23. He got a letter of endorsement from some of the great Rabbis of this generation, amongst them the genius from Dinabourg (or Dvinsk) who wrote, "Although I usually avoid giving these kinds of endorsements, I felt obligated to give this endorsement to such a worthy person." When he reached the age of 25 the genius Yeruham Leib from Minsk who was known as the Minsker Hagadol (the great Rabbi from Minsk), said about him, "When a smart man asks something, he gives half an answer in his question. when he asks something he gives a full answer in his question." He was fluent in all the Talmud and commentaries and he had a detailed knowledge of all the different parts of Shulhan Aruch and Shelot and Teshuvot[11]. Already in the days when he lived with his father-in-law, he was well known as a wonderful teacher. His mouth was filled with pearls of wisdom and whoever heard him instructing in the Hasidic and the Chabad traditions would be drawn towards him by his tremendous charisma. He would travel to all the sons of Tzemach Tzedek and at the end of his days he traveled a few times to the Rashab[12], who deeply respected him and took note of his instructions. And if the way the community in Kurenets treated his father-in-law Reb Zishka Zal with respect and admiration, they treated my father as if he was father to all. The way he treated them back was as if all the townspeople were his children. Mordechai Gurevich (son of Zalman Uri and Sara nee Zimmerman Gurevich) told me that once he came to study with my father for his daily lessons and he was very depressed that day. My father, who was very close to him, could see from his face all that was bothering him, even down to the tiniest of details.

During the fire of 1910, three synagogues were burnt down, these three synagogues were situated in the shulhaif circle and my father spared no trouble in trying to rebuild them. Finally he was able to rebuild them with more modern buildings and he also was able to collect money for people who could not afford to rebuild their homes after the fire. From his first wife, the daughter of Reb Zishka, my father had two sons: Reb Avraham Schneur Zalman and Reb Yosef Zvi. He also had five daughters. When he was still young, his wife passed away and he then married my mother, Gita Fega nee Loria, also from a Hasidic family. Her father was first a Strashali Hasid and later a Hasid of the Tzemach Tzedek. They had two sons, my brother who passed away, Rabbi Shmuel Hillel Zal, and myself[13] (may I be spared for life).

From the customs of my father's house

Every festival people would come to our home, the home of the Rabbi, they would come on the last day of Passover, on the second day of Shavuot, and on Simhat Torah. During the day of Simhat Torah, people would come to visit from morning until late at night. Everyone wanted to join in the rejoicing. People would sing, "The Gemara asks a difficult question ay ay ay ay, the answer is ay ay ay ay ay." And then someone else would start singing, "A dudla", holding the edges of his coat in his hand. Mushka Hashia Riva's was especially adept at that song. He would sit on the floor, surrounded by a crowd of people standing around him, and he would start, in a very quiet voice, "Doo doo doo doo…" Slowly his voice would become louder and louder until he would get up and start dancing with all the people who surrounded him, and he would continue dancing and singing like this throughout the night. My father would intersperse passages from the Torah and clever Hasidic tales between the dancing.. On other festivals the visits from the townspeople would only last until noon. Every festival my house would be busy with preparations for the visits. The women would bake all kinds of cookies and sweets to give to the visitors. For Passover, they would bake goods made from potato flour because we didn't use gebrochts[14]. The potato flour would be made from scratch in our house. Already during the winter months they would make certain rooms of the house Kosher for Passover, especially my father's room, where they would prepare the potato flour. Beetroots were also prepared for Passover, as well as the Passover wine. Mainly Reb Shmuel der Viner and Hirshel der Vaser Trager (water carrier) handled the preparation of the wine. A few days before Passover the house would be sparkling clean and all ready for the holiness of the festival. And if Passover happened to fall on Tuesday, then on Shabbat hagadol[15] we wouldn't eat at home, but in the shed that we had in the yard, a place where we stored the Hametz.

During regular weekdays we had visitors from the town everyday. There were certain designated hours to drink tea from the samovar, in the morning and in the afternoon. We would always have friends of the family coming to drink with us. Some of them would be invited specially; among them would be Daniel Yakov der Muler (the miller), a perfect example of a Lubavitch Hasid. Also Reb Yoel Nahum the Painter, who would sit studying in our minyan until someone would let him know it was time for tea. From my earliest days (2-3 years old) I can remember the image of Shmuel der Malach (the angel) coming to drink tea in the morning. I loved to sit on his lap. I would always ask him, "Why do they call you the Angel?" but he never answered my question. He was a very dear person. He was the court's envoy and he wrote all the contracts in those days. I saw many papers that my father had that he had signed. His sons were Efraim der Malach, Israel der Malach, who made an extremely impressive image when he would pray as chazzan for the congregation, and his third son Aaron who was nicknamed Arad der Eiser . He first lived in a community called Eisa, but later his family moved to Kurenets to a house near that of Nehama Risha Alperovich.

Another person who would come to our house was Avraham David the butcher who I will tell you about later. Also Aron Yosef, the Scribe who was a Koidanov Hasid. He was the brother-in-law of Avraham Itza Shohel's. Mezuzot and tefillin written by him were very desired by everyone, but he didn't write too many of them despite the fact that he was very poor. He used to say that he surely would not be punished for mezuzot he refused to write. He was also a shamash in our minyan and he would write the divorce contracts for the community members.

In the summer of the year 1912, my father became sick and this was his last illness. He traveled to see doctors in Konigsberg, but they lost hope. When he returned he said, "Just look at my diagnosis and you will understand my situation." The word spread in the town and everyone panicked. Everyone came to the house and I welcomed them saying, "In my opinion, all that is left for us to do is to pray." There was nothing the doctors could do anymore so I told them to go to the synagogue and say passages from tehillim and continuously recite psalms. I was very young but since the community was so respectful of my father, they accepted what I said and the next day all the stores and businesses were shut down, and everyone gathered in the synagogues and with deep sadness as they prayed for mercy for the beloved Rabbi. When they finished reciting psalms, they went to the cemetery to ask mercy from the deceased souls. Also, many in the neighboring town of Vilejka were upset and came to Kurenets to ask for God's pity. Letters were sent to the Admor of Lubavitch in the name of the communities of Kurenets and Vilejka, asking him to ask pity from the Kingdom of Heaven. My father was very tormented with his sickness. This was at the end of the month of Av, but by the time Elul came, all of a sudden he was much better and a day later he rose from his bed, and on Rosh Hashanah that year he prayed in the synagogue and he also fasted on Yom Kippur. During that winter his situation greatly improved and he was like a new, healthy man. But on Passover the next year the situation was grave. And in Elul of 1913 he passed away.

When he was sick he kept expressing sorrow that he couldn't go to the Synagogue to arrive before the congregation, so they wouldn't have to stand up when he arrived. All his life he took care to reach the synagogue before the congregation. At 3 in the afternoon on his last day, he still instructed me in Torah. His passing away was almost like a Torah scroll being burned. Until his very last minute he remembered every passage of the Torah. He was laid to rest next to his father-in-law. I was pressed by friends of my father and theAdmor from Lubavitch to replace my father, in spite of my young age. The Admor of Lubavitch received members of the community like Shalom Yitzhak Baker, Mordechai Gurevich, and Leib Motosov in Lubavitch. I also went there and explained to the Admor how difficult it would be to accept the position but I couldn't change his mind, and with reluctance I took the job.

During that winter, Nahum Castrol the shohet became blind, and when I again went to Lubavitch to ask the Rebbe to let me leave Kurenets, I again received a refusal. The Admor expressed to me that Reb Nahum Castrol must not continue his job as a shohet. Reb Nahum Castrol who was also a Lubavitch Hasid had already visited the Rebbe some time earlier. So as soon as I returned I let everyone know about the Admor's orders and now there was a question of who should be the new shohet. As is usual in such cases, there was a dispute on the subject of who should be the shohet.. I brought R.Schraga to see if he could handle the job. R. Schraga later became the shohet of our town. Mendel Dinestein who was nicknamed Mendel Shmuel Naha's, greatly helped me. According to the rules, the person who was the karaka[16] was supposed to decide about the shohet and somehow Mendel by some kind of trickery was able to become the karaka during the bidding process for the job. So now he was responsible for giving the old shohet the money owed to him for his pension. The community sent a letter to the Admor asking his opinion if Reb Schraga should be the shohet, and once he sent his approval, Reb Schraga became the shohet.

In the month of Tishrei 1915, the Germans conquered our town. I was away at that point from Kurenets, and the war prevented me from returning until the Germans were pushed out of the area. At the point when I returned, I found out that all the cheder studies were cancelled during the war, and the youths were running freely in the streets. So I gathered a group of youths and started lessons with them in Talmud and bible. Later on, I sent a few of them to the Lubavitch yeshiva in Karachi, amongst them was Zalman, the son of Yitzhak Mikhail Alperovitch, and Berl, son of Binyamin Hirshel Gorfinkel. Both of them were very good students and became well known among the Chabad Hasidim. We also organized an assistance committee, Zemstava that distributed food to people in the area. I became the head of the local committee. I was very busy with this until I had to leave the town and go to Rostov, where the Chabad Rebbe lived in those days. From that time on I didn't go back to Kurenets until the year 1934.

In the winter of 1926, I was in Moscow, and I received a letter from the townspeople inviting me to return to Kurenets and to become the Rabbi there. The letter said:

Second of Shvat, 1926 (Taf Reish Pei Vav), Kurenets. To the honorable, splendid friend who is dear to our hearts and filled with goodness and honesty, Rabbi Yakov Landau. We would like our friend to come to you with a suggestion, since not too long ago Rabbi Noah left our town after he received a Rabbinical position in another town. All the townspeople came to an agreement to try to talk to the heart of our friend that maybe he will agree to return to our town and accept the Rabbinical position in our town, in spite of the fact that many good Rabbis inquire about the job every day, and all with excellent Rabbinical credentials, we would like to return the crown of old to our town, since you are from the pedigree of a family of Tzadikim, Rabbis who are part of the town's past. If you will return, maybe it will save our town's respect. Signed by Israel son of Zalman Pinhas Alperovich, Mordechai son of Zalman Uri Gurevich, Mendel son of Zalman Alperovich, Zalman Mendel son of Pinhas Tsipilevich, Shimon-Michal son of Shaul Hurwitz-Gurevich, Shimon Leib Zimmerman, Yakutiel Meir Hakoen Kremer, Menachem Mendel son of Shmuel N. Dinestein. We ask you to send us a telegram if you will be able to fulfill our request. Written by Mendel son of Shimon Alperovich, Zelig son of Meir-Michal Gvalman, and Dov-Bar Himmelfarb.

My heart at that point was far from accepting such an offer and I suggested they take my brother, Shmuel Hillel as a Rabbi, but this was not accomplished. In the month of Elul in 1934, on my way to Eretz Israel, I visited Kurenets and I met some of my old friends, the shohet Reb Schraga, Leib Motosov, Reb Yekutiel Meir Hakoen Kremer, Reb Mendel son of Shimon Alperovich, and others. Who could ever imagine in his worst nightmare what their fate would be in the future?

Respected Characters

Rabbi Yehuda son of Zusha Alperovich

I was about six or seven at the time when Yehuda Zusha's passed away. In spite of that I can clearly see his image in front of my eyes. He was an elevated person in all his actions, both physically and spiritually. I remember him from my father's house, the Rabbi Z-L. I remember that at that time the Chabad Rebbe from Lyadi came to us as the town invited him in the winter of 1889 or so. I still remember the excitement he had on his face during that visit! On the other hand I remember the darkness that spread in town on the day that Yehuda Zusha's passed away. The red eyes of my father, who was crying, I can remember until today. Reb Yehuda Zusha's was a very learned man, and a paragon of piety in his very essence. He made a very good living from a winery and an inn, Privana Lakava. I remember that once, on a market day, the house was filled with Christians and all of a sudden no one could find Reb Yehuda. Everyone started looking for him, and finally he was found sitting in the minyan synagogue that was in his backyard and was named after him "Yehuda's Minyan" (destroyed by fire in 1906).

He was sitting in the minyan and writing Hasidic works. He didn't care at all that this was a market day and he should be busy with his merchandise. He was at that time in a totally different world, busying himself with the Holy Scripture.

On the last Simhat Torah of his life, he was extremely happy. I still remember him dancing on the table with excitement of the mitzvah, the happiness of the holiday was one of the last events that he took part in. At the beginning of the winter his soul passed away, to the deep mourning of every citizen of the town, from the young to the old, and his pure soul returned to its source.

Moshe Alperovitz,
grandson of Yehuda Alperovich

Other than the very well known Reb Yehuda Zusha's, Reb Leib Ephron was well known among the Koidanov Hasidim and Reb David Shihanover was a well known Lubavitch Hasid who was very clever and learned, there were other special people who were modest in their ways but were extremely special. Amongst the Melamedim (teachers) of the town, I must emphasize the special character of Reb Reuven Malisker. Not everyone was privileged to be accepted as a student at the cheder of Reuven. He had a very limited number of students, usually no more than 8, and normally more mature boys. For the sake of my respected father, I was accepted into this cheder when I was only six years old. Reb Reuven was very knowledgeable, and very well versed in the Halacha and grammar. He also had secular knowledge in medicine. Since his wife Frieda was sick, he would visit Professor Bora, who invented Borov Liquid. The professor became a close friend of his and taught him a lot about medicine. He had an extensive knowledge about common pharmaceuticals of the time so in Kurenets he was treated like a doctor.

There was another teacher named Yossi the Melamed. He was a very knowledgeable in Mishna and in general was very learned, pure in deed and honest in his ways. In Kurenets there was a Jew nicknamed Itzha Meir der Koymen Karer. He was the father-in-law of Mikhail the forester from Myadel Street. Even when he was very, very old, he would still clean all the chimneys in town. Every time he would come to our minyan synagogue, he loved playing with me since I was a young child, and he would tell me about his life. When he was very young, he was a secretary of Reb Hirsheleh son of Reb Zalman. One time, when the family of Hirsheleh went to Lubavitch for the marriage of Reb Hirshel's son Dan to the granddaughter of Tzemach Tzedek, Reb Itzha Meir went with them. It was a very cold winter and his feet froze, and when he took off his boots and showed his legs to a doctor, the doctor said that he was going to die in a few days. When the Tzemach Tzedek came to visit him, Reb Itzhak Meir started crying. When the Rebbe asked, "Why are you crying?" he told him that the doctor said he had no more than a month to live. The Rabbi started admonishing him, saying, "Patak, patak. You will live for [so-and-so] years." At the time Itzhak Meir told me this, his eyes filled with tears. He was already very old and he commented that according to the years the Rebbe gave him, he only had a short time to live. He said that when he left Lubavitch to go to Kurenets the Tzemach Tzedek blessed him, "Go in health." By the time he entered Kurenets in the central market he was a healthy man. When his wife met him there, he asked her that she should go and help the family of Hirsheleh with their belongings and he would go home to rest. He dragged his legs along until he got home. He immediately lay by the oven and for a few months was bed ridden. He had surgery on his toes at one point, but in spite of all the problems, as soon as he became well he went on top of the houses' roofs to clean the chimneys until he reached old age. Every night between the hours of 2 and 3 am, he would run to the Beit Midrash and recite Psalms.

Reb Meir Shmuel

I knew him when he was very old and could hardly see. He was practically blind. During the daytime he would try to read a book, and had some difficulties, but at night he had regular lessons in Talmud with Yoel Nahum, the painter who prayed in our minyan. Despite the fact that he listened to whatever Nahum read, it was clear that he knew much more than Yoel Nahum. Every passage in the book was memorized by him. He was a Jew with special spiritual gifts, very religious. When he was younger he used to teach Talmud to the children. His living was made from a store that his wife ran. The store was in the middle of the central market, in a building that contained other stores. His wife would sell simple medicines and some kind of oil, but his main occupation was Torah studies.

Reb Meir-Bar der Einbender   (Bookbinder)

The truth is he was not a professional bookbinder. The professional bookbinder was Reb Menachem, son of Zusia. It must be that he chose this profession since he was a deep thinker and he didn't want his work to disturb him in his deep thoughts. My brother Shmuel Hillel Z-l was right when he would comment every time we passed his house on Kosita, how can we not stop near this house where such a deep thinker lived? A person that in his very essence was a Chabad thinker. Every year he would make a pilgrimage to the Rebbe in Lubavitch, and that was the main event in his life. Once he was on a train to Lubavitch when he met a German Jew. The German Jew asked him, "Why are you wearing two hats?" He was referring to the kipa that Meir-Bar wore under his hat. The answer of Reb Meir-Bar was, "Since there are some Jews who don't even wear one hat, I feel that it's my duty to wear two."

Reb Meir Tziras

During that time, the letters for Kurenets residents would arrive in Vilejka, which was 8 km away from Kurenets. Reb Meir was the unofficial postman who would walk to Vilejka every day to bring the letters. He got paid one kopeck for each letter, but his fate was not good since once in a while he would lose a letter along the way. I am absolutely sure that he would be in deep Hasidic thought during his walks and repeat passages of Hasidut that he heard from the Rebbe. It hurts to comprehend what little was given to Reb Meir in this world if you didn't know the pleasure that he had when he studied and comprehended the spiritual world during his deep prayers. On the Sabbath, while the rest of the community was busy with the Shabbat meal, he would still be standing in a corner of our minyan and would pray with a Hasidic tone that would bring deep spiritual awareness that would open his heart and let tears come to his eyes. Reb Meir was blessed to know the Tzemach Tzedek, and to hear from him Hasidic thoughts. I saw how his spirits would lift when he remembered the Tzemach Tzedek and all that he had heard from him. Tears would run down his face when he would remember how the Tzemach Tzedek would explain the passage "Yisa Hashem Panav Elecha – May the Lord lift up his face towards you." I don't know how he earned a living after they opened a post office in Kurenets. Although his wife taught young girls to read and write, it is very hard to believe that this was sufficient for a living. One thing is very clear, that until his last days when he was very, very old, he was loyal to his essence of Hasidut and tried very hard to understand the essence of it. He didn't care about his personal honor. He would even ask much younger men to explain Torah passages. He would also go to Lubavitch every year and would return with a large treasure of learning. Other than new works, he would bring new tunes. Each Shabbat he would come to our minyan to teach and to repeat tunes filled with yearning and love commitment to God.

Reb Heikl Velvel (Zeev) Alperovich

He was busy with Torah and Hasidut, which he studied deeply . Despite the fact that he was a merchant and for his business he would travel through the villages, he would always find time to learn Torah. The Christian farmers would tell that Vulfka would sit all night by the furnace and pray. This is how they understood it. Every day he would have a designated lesson in the Rambam, which he studied constantly. He was also one of the people who went to Lubavitch once a year and was amongst their Hasidim. He had a very important position in the community and would join my father in collecting for the Kimha dPisha. He was a very pleasant man and his heart was open to all generosity. Heikl Velvel was the brother-in-law of Reuven Malisker. It is very strange that in a short time both families passed away. Reb Reuven and his wife and Reb Heikl and his wife. Reb Heikl Velvel passed away all of a sudden: he went to sleep and never woke up. His wife passed away a week before, and shortly after they passed away their home was destroyed by fire.

Another person who did not stand out since he was very modest in his behavior was Shimon Michal, who was a Kapost Hasid. When he was young he lived in Kapost. He was a well-to-do man. He earned his money from selling flour. He was in all his essence a Hasidisher Yid; he would spend all his time in the minyan, and would not leave until he had studied a chapter of Tanya. He also loved to go deeply into Hasidic passages. During Shabbat, he immersed himself in the study of the Torah.

Another respected, well-to-do person was Reb Hetzkl Bina Simhas, the father of Mendel Zalman, and Moshe. He would travel to the Rebbe in Lyadi and also had regular hours for studying Torah. He was very honest and pure in all his ways.

At that time, a person who became important in our town was Yekutiel Meir Hakoen Kremer. He was very God fearing and honest in his ways, and he would teach Mishna to the community of the old shtiebel. His father was Reb Yehoshuah Leib Hakoen Kremer the Melamed. Reb Y. Leib was very knowledgeable in all the Mishna and many times would repeat the Mishna by heart. All his sons were honest and God fearing people. Besides Yekutial Meir there was Nachman Yosef Kremer, Mendel Kremer, and Chaim Zalman Kremer. All of them were businessmen, and Yekutiel Meir was also a merchant. He had a flour store but he was still busy learning Torah. Whenever you passed by his store you could see that there was a book in his hand. He was the son-in-law of Reb Yehiel Yentes and lived in his house. His brothers-in-law were the son of Yakov Mendel Markon, the owner of the flourmill in the village Ivontsevich, near Kurenets. Another brother-in-law was Zishka, son of Shimon Alperovich. Everyone in Kurenets respected the family.

Mendel Kremer son of Reb Yehoshuah Leib Hakoen Kremer and wife Chana nee Eishiski. Perished in Kurenets on 9-9-1942

Amongst other modest Jews in town was Reb Meir Shalom Shulman, the shamash of the central synagogue, the Nyer Shtiebel. He was very knowledgeable in Jewish law and was appointed by my father to the upkeep of the Eiruv[17]. My father, the Rabbi Z-L, relied on him in this matter. Clearly, once in a while he would ask my father a question on this subject, but he knew how to ask a question as a wise man, already giving half of the answer in his question. He was appointed as the representative of the Rabbi in Vileyka, the principal town in the district, to write the births, marriages, and the people who passed away. He also knew the proper way to write all the names of the parties of all the marriages for the Ketuba. I remember that at one time, someone came to my father with a Ketuba written by someone else, and my father was very annoyed and dismissed this Ketuba since the names were not written correctly, and he told this shamash that the Ketuba must be written by Meir Shalom since Meir Shalom was very knowledgeable in grammar and language. I remember that he would read the Torah according to all the rules of punctuation and grammar.

Yoel Nachum the Painter enjoyed his job. His specialty was the dying of cloths. Still, he was busy day and night with the study of the Torah. In the morning, after the Shaharit Prayer, he would stay there long after the prayer ended to study, and each evening, he studied Talmud until the late night hours. I remember that one time he studied Torah in deep pain. Since he didn't want to stop his studies to attend to his pain, he drank kerosene.

Golda nee Shiff of Volozhin
wife of Mendel Alperovich

Footnotes:

1. Head or chief of rabbinical court; the position was usually synonymous with chief Rabbi of a town.
2. The minyan synagogue was for the most learned and devout Hasidic Jews of the town.
3. After the end of the festival.
4. Collection of food for the needy before Passover.
5. The Alter Rebbe founder of the Chabad dynasty also known as Admor Hazaken Shneur Zalman of Liadi 1746-1812.
6. Tzemach Tzedek – Menachem Mendel Schneerson, grandson of the Alter Rebbe. 1798-1866.
7. Referring to the deceased Rabbi.
8. He later moved to Latvia.
9. Rabbi Isaiah Horowitz 1565-1630.
10. Rabbi Shmuel Eliezer Edels 1555-1631.
11. Codes of Jewish Law and Rabbinic responsa.

12. Fifth Rebbe of Chabad 1860-1920.
13. The author.
14. Matza or matza meal that has come into contact with any liquid.
15. The Shabbat before Passover.
16. A government position.
17. To allow the people to carry on Shabbat.

The business people in the community in town were Reb Mendel son of Shimon, who was the son of Meir Freda's Alperovich. Mendel was a very clever and honest man. Before the First World War he had a store in his home that was left for him and his brother Zishka Alperovich by their father. During the First World War he went all the way to the town of Balshov, and I met him there while traveling as a messenger of the Lubavitcher Rebbe to the refugees deep in Russia. I also met there Chanan Itzha's the brother of Mordechai and Shimon Itzha's. After the war, Reb Mendel Alperovich and Reb Zishka Alperovich returned to Kurenets. In the year 1934, when I came to Kurenets he had a hotel where I lodged. A local Polish policeman started bothering me, saying I didn't have permission to stay over in Poland, but Reb Mendel Alperovich quieted him down.

Mordechai [1870- 1954], son of Sarah nee Zimerman and Zalman Uri [son of Avraham Elia] Gurevitz with wife Frada [1870- 1938], daughter of Yehuda son of Meir and Frada Alperovitz

Children and grandchildren of Mordechai and Frada Gurevitz.
Bitzaron, 1936

Left to right [sitting]: daughter, Batia nee Gurevitz Bender z"l.
Grandson Eli Bender of Kibbutz Einat. Granddaughter, Rachel nee Gurevitz Gordin
of Rehovot. Amnon Yaakobi z"l. Daughter in law; Bela nee Shulman Gurevitz z"l.
Top: Son in law, Krolik Bender z"l. Daughter; Luba nee Gurevitz Bardan z"l.
Son in law; Moshe Lehrman z"l. Granddaughter baby Aliza nee Lehrman Rashish
of Petach Tikva. Daughter; Sima nee Gurevitz Lehrman Herbert z"l. Son; Meir Gurevitz z"l.

*The family of Natan,
oldest son of Mordechai and Frada Gurevitz. Kurenets 1935
Left to right: son, Zalman Uri Gurevitz.
Wife, Batia nee Eyeshski, son, Gershon Gorev. Natan. Daughter, Lea Shogol.*

Reb Mordechai Horwitz Gurevich was known in town as Mordechai Frada's (his wife was Frada daughter of Yehuda (ben Meir) Alperovich). He was the son of a Hasidic Jew Zalman Uri Gurevich who visited Tzemach Tzedek and the name of his father was Avraham Elia. By the order of Tzemach Tzedek he became a shohet. Even in his last days (ca. 1920) he served as a shohet in a community near Kurenets. His eldest son was also a shohet. His name was Chaim Israel Gurevich (perished in the holocaust in Kurenets). His son Mordechai, on the other hand, had a business selling iron but his soul burnt with the holy fire. In the middle of market day when his store would be filled with Christian buyers, he would leave the store and run to pray with the community in the synagogue. Every evening he would come to our minyan to study.

When Reb Mordechai Gurevich was young he went to study in the town of Labadowa, and was very influenced by Levik Labadower, who was very pure. He made a few visits with his friends at that time to the Koidanov Rebbe, but when he became middle aged, he turned to Lubavitch Hasidut and became a very devout Lubavitcher. He would pray for a long time on the Sabbath, finishing a long time after the rest of the community. A few times he went to the Admor of Lubavitch even when he was living in Rostov on the River Don. In his older years he was blessed to go to Eretz Israel. This took place about 20 years ago (ca. 1933). He settled in B'nei Brak, and after his wife Freda passed away, he moved to a kibbutz near Petah Tikva (Givat Hashlosha) and lived next to his daughter Batia Bender. Every day he would walk to Petah Tikva to study Gemara together with the Rabbi and a few of his friends. He studied the Mishna intensely, and his deepest desire was to learn all the Mishna 101 times. I am sure that he achieved his goal since he was constantly reciting the Mishna. About two years ago (ca. 1952), he passed away.

Amongst the respected men of the community was Reb Leib Motosov, who had a factory for making tar in the area of Kurenets, and after some years he moved to the town and had a pharmaceutical store. He was also very involved in the community. When I was there he took part in all the public funds and when I came to Kurenets in 1934 he was one of the friends I met and I visited him in his house.

Craftsmen

Rev. Solomon Koor

All the craftsmen were very special in Kurenets. Amongst the shoemakers I must tell about Moshe Kur / Koor the Shoemaker from Dolhinov Street. He was a fervent Jew and would read the Torah with passion. He was also a Koidanov Hasid. His father was Reb Yehoshua, the scribe from Vileyka. The son of Moshe, Shlomo Chaim studied Torah in our minyan, and when he reached the age to be drafted into the army, he escaped and went to London. His last name was Koor and from what I heard he became a Chazzan in one of the synagogues in London, where he later passed away.

*The family of Mordechai Kur
the son of Yehoshua the writer from Vileyka
and his wife Rivka from the Volozhinski / Bunimovitz family of Volozhin.*

*Left to right: son, Eliezer Kur , daughter, Leyka nee Kur Laptzlter died in Israel,
Rivka, daughter of Alexander Volozhinski from Volozhin and Matya nee Bunimovitz,
daughter, Dishka Kur, Mordechai Kur, [brother of Moshe the shoemaker from Kurenets],
Bronia nee Kur Rabinovitz born in Horodok in 1916, lives in Petach Tikva, son Avraham
Kur born in Horodok in 1910. Mordechai, Rivka, Dishka, Eliezer, Avraham [with wife
Frida nee Drashtzki and son Benyamin] perished in Krasne in March of 1943.*

*Nechemia Kur son of Pinya
grandson of Yehoshua the
writer from Vileyka. Perished
during the Holocaust.*

*Malka née Kur daughter of
Nechemia, holding her second
cousin, Mordechai Rabinovitz*

Left to right: Mordechai Rabinovitz born in Volozhin in 1945, his mother, Bronia nee Kur, Chaim Kur son of Nechemia, Luba Kur widow of Nechemia

The family of Mordechai Kur the son of Yehoshua the writer from Vileyka and his wife Rivka from the Volozhinski/ Bunimovitz family of Volozhin

The shomemakers Yerukhmiel were also special people. The son of Yerukhmiel from Kosita Street was called Tanhum and he studied with me in the cheder of Reuven Malisker.

Amongst the blacksmiths, I must write about Leib den Schmidt. Whoever saw him on Shabbat would think that he saw a respected and wonderful Rabbi. He had a long, white beard. His body was tall and strong, and from the top of his head down to his toes was beautiful to look at. He was a Chazzan during the high holy days.

Reb Eliyau the blacksmith was the chazzan on Yom Kippur in the old shtiebel. At one time Reb Shmuel the blacksmith who was a Lubavitch Hasid came to our town. He also knew Torah and was filled Hasidic spirit. In Kurenets there was an old man by the name of Shimsel der Kutler, he was the father of Motke der Kutler. It's hard to describe the charm of his spirit and the essence of his dear soul. Although he wasn't truly knowledgeable in Torah, he would listen to others who studied, but his purity of heart and his spirit were above some who were true scholars of the Torah. In his essence there was the true Hasidic spirit that spread from the well known Hasidic greats of Kurenets down to the simplest people. Once during a Hasidic gathering, Reb Shimshel said, "I deserve to lie on the ground and all the community of the minyan[1] should step on me."

Amongst the carpenters, I would like to mention Zalman der Stoller. Amongst the people who made the furnaces, Reb Yankel der Moller and Reb Yossi der Moller. Everyone who would meet them would recognize that they were Kurenetsers. The influence of the town also reached the small communities in its area, amongst them Radshke, Nyaka, and Oshtkova. They all belonged to the municipality of Kurenets. In Radshke, the shohet was the well-known Hasid, Yosef Meir Halevi Levin, who was one of the students of the well-known Hasid Hillel Paritcher. He used to go to visit the Rebbe of Lubavitch, he was a lively Jew in every one of his bones. It was such a pleasure to sit with him and listen to his tales of the old days about his youth in the shadow of Hillel Paritcher, repeating the Hasidic tales that he was taught.

The butchers in our town were different from other butchers. In Kurenets the butchers were religious Jews with pure souls. Amongst them there was Reb Avraham David Alperovich and his sons Itzhak Mikhail (who was killed before the war), Israel Alperovich [who perished in the Holocaust]. Although Avraham David was a simple Jew, he was pure and God fearing. To give an example, he would never bless the Etrog in the morning of the first day of Sukkot without waking up very early in the morning when it was still very dark and immersing himself in the Mikveh, where he was the very first to dip. He treated all the scholars and Rabbis with respect and love and I must point out that he never got too upset about huge financial losses that were caused because of religious rules. As one can see in this story. When Israel Itzhak the Shohet passed away, my father the Rabbi said that his son, Reb Gershon, had the right to his job. For many reasons that were known in town, many people were against this decision. Particularly against it were the butchers who didn't want a shohet who was so young and with no experience. At that point in time, Reb Gershon only knew how to slaughter poultry, but my father still stood firm that according to tradition the job should be given to the son of the person who passed away. So during a meeting in our minyan, a suggestion was made that Reb Gershon should go to another town to gain experience and then he should get the job. Reb Gershon was a Kapost Hasid and even used to live there. When the Kapost Hasidism moved to Bobrisk, Reb Gershon went to Bobrisk to study for the job of shohet. After three months he returned to Kurenets with certificates showing experience in his job. My father the Rabbi examined him on the rules of slaughtering, the way you should hold the knife, and gave him permission to take the job. The first time that Reb Gershon worked with Avraham David slaughtering meat, he felt something wrong with his knife. After he checked the meat and didn't find anything wrong, he called Reb Avraham David to a corner and told him that he thought his knife was not right. Although it meant a big financial loss, Reb Avraham David accepted this waste of meat without complaint.

Itzhak Mikhail Alperovitz, the son of Avraham David, was killed by some Christians while on the way to Dolhinov. The grandson of Itzhak Mikhail, Zalman, studied in Lubavitch ,was an excellent student and became a well known Chabad Rabbi. He later perished in the Holocaust.

His other son, Israel Alperovich, was an observant Jew and died of starvation during the Holocaust after he escaped to the forest but didn't want to eat non-Kosher food. The rest of Israel's family perished except for one son who moved to Brazil before the Holocaust.

Reb Moshe Binyamin, the son of Hendel the Butcher, was a Jew in whom the Hasidic fire burned strongly. During the First World War, he went as far as Rostov by the River Don for a pilgrimage to the Lubavitcher Rebbe. The brothers, Israel and Itzha sons of Chanan from Kosita Street, were also very pure Jews. In Oshtashkova, lived Mikhail Oshtashkover, a very spiritual and pure Jew. I must also mention the village Narutz with the head of the family Reb Shalom Narutzer. This was a place of Torah. All the brothers, Reb Moshe, Reb Chaim, Reb Itzhak and their father Reb Shalom were learned Jews, deep students of the Torah, and very deep thinkers. When I lived in Kurenets, Itzhak Narutzer moved there and he constantly studied the Torah. He was amongst the visitors who would constantly come to our home.

These few passages should give some impression of the essence of the town of Kurenets during those days, her Shabbatot, her festivals, and other special days, saturated with spirituality and purity and excitement of Hasidic devotion that comes from deep inside the soul. May the next generation see the true essence of the roots that they sprung from.

Footnotes:

1. The community of the most learned Jews.

[Page 35-38]

Grandma (Safta) Marisha

Max Alberts (1955)

(Mendel Son of Feiga Alperovitch)

Translated by Tzafrir "Tzafi" Gordin

"In memory of my great-grandfather, saba Mordechai Gurevitz, who had a zest for life and a passion for bible studies"

Sixty years have passed since the event that I am going to tell you about occurred. It took place on a cold October day. One of those days where the streets were overrun with puddles and the mud was knee deep. At the time, I was a small boy. It was my first year in school. I studied in the Cheder (small Jewish school) of Hertzel, the Moreh, (teacher). Our Cheder was on Kosita street in the house of Yosef Rafael. It was already the middle of Autumn but my poor mother was not able to buy me boots. When walking to the Cheder, she would wrap cloth around my feet, put me on her shoulders and carry me all the way to the Cheder to learn the Torah.

"Chiap, Chiap" was the sound I heard as her feet would sink into the mud of the tiny alley that we called, "Digaslaka." She would hold my feet close to her body and she would place my little hands on her neck. Every now and then I'd feel hot drops fall on my hands. Maybe it was sweat from the brow of my tired mother or maybe it was tears from my mother's eyes. But I was just a little child and I didn't analyze it. I was just delighted that I, Mendele Feigas', was the only child in the whole shtetle whose mother carried him on her back like a sack of flour. "Chiap, Chiap". My mother's feet would drench in the puddles of Dolhinov Street. Here the mud was extremely deep and my mother's back would further hunched over. Fear would come to my heart. It felt like any minute she would trip and we would fall from the weight of the load. But with G-d's help, everything was alright and we reached Kosita Street.

My mother would sit me on the top of the high fence of Cheskel Vellvel house and straighten her bent back, after she'd fix my payas, and clean her face with her apron. She would look at my eyes and a sweet smile would light her sad face. She'd kiss me and her lips would warm my forehead and then she would take me inside the Cheder.

The Cheder was located at the far edge of the street. All the way on the other edge of the street was the place where my mother buried the dreams of her youth. During her spring days. There, across the bridge above the river, near the water mill, amongst the pine trees of the Jewish cemetery lay the man of her youthful desires, the father of her small children… But in this point of the story, my mother's worries were with me. To her I was like a seedling tree sprouting from the ground. She worried and prayed that the seedling would sprout, flourish, and then become a tree of life. This would be G-d's consolation gift to her for all the troubles she endured. Morning after morning my mother would take me to the Cheder, and evening after evening she would take me back, and day after day after day passed…

One day during the market day we sat as usual around the table in the Cheder. The Rabbi was teaching us the chapter, "Veyetzah." I still remember the particular of the moment. We were reading, "Veyetcha Reuven". The Rabbi interpreted it with a beautiful tune. "Ruven went during the days of the harvest and he found berries in the fields and he will bring them to his mother, Leah." Outside it was a cold autumn day, but in our imagination we flew on the wings of the tune to far away fields where the sun is shining and the fruits were ready to be picked off of the trees. while we were still in the world of the fruits, the door suddenly opened and Safta Marisha walked in. She was our favorite. She wore a huge, warm shawl that we called *Patziella*. "Shalom my darlings," she greeted us. "Shalom, Shalom Safta," we all answered in unison. The beloved Safta Marisha approached the Rabbi, whispered something in his ear, and took off her shawl. Can you guess what we saw? A miracle. Like a true shoe maker, Safta held a tiny pair of boots in her hands. It was an absolutely perfect pair of boots. From above they had little ears and from below, on the heel of the boot they had shiny spikes. The smell of fresh leather filled the room. Our sweet, generous Safta told us, " My darling, it must have been a gift from God. When I walked in the market I found these little boots and I want to give them to the one child they will perfectly fit." My heart started beating fast. God knows I wonder, "what if the boots fit me?"

Now it is time to tell you of the way we sat in the Cheder. Usually there was total equality among the kids, especially in times when we played games like *horses, hide and go seek, and Klitklat*. When children play they don't know the hierarchy of their parents' statues in the community and the different classes that exist. But in the Cheder during class time the Rabbi sat the children around the long table and carefully made sure that they sat according to their fathers' status in the community. So here in our Cheder we sat according to this arrangement. At the head of the table right next to the Rabbi sat Shaul Monies'. Next to him was Guttman Denis'. Next to Guttman was Zalman Hetskales', Alperovitch and on and on… and I sat all the way at the other end of the table. I was poor and fatherless. When Safta Marisha started fitting the boot, she obviously started with the way we sit. The first was Shaul Monies.' In the center of the room they put a little stool. Shaul sat on the stool and took off his beautiful shiny shoes. He tried to put on Safta's boots, tried and tried but they were too small. A glimmer of hope flickered in my heart. Who knows the wishes of the God of Abraham, Isaac, and Jacob. They tried the boots on Guttman's feet, but the boot was too tight around the ankle. Zalman tried but the boot is too tight on his toes. They tried to fit all the children in the room but everyone had something wrong with them. Now it was my turn. I sat on the stool, Safta Marisha took the wrapping from my feet and I put on the boots. Safta Marisha felt the fit all around, and pressed from up to down from all sides. The Rabbi checked with her- up and down and from all sides, and I rejoiced as they announced I am the lucky one; I won the boots. Safta Marisha gave me a kiss and a penny for thanks and told me to immediately run home and tell my mother about the miracle that occurred. My mother greeted me with blessings or maybe sorrow. "Nu," my mother said, "now my back will have some rest."

Days passed. I grew and become a little cleverer. I realized that from the beginning the boots were for me and only for me, that our Safta didn't find them in the market, but that the shoe maker had made them to order. Now I understand that the whisper to the Rabbi and the ceremony with the fitting was only pretend so I would not be ashamed in the eyes of the other students, and to avoid making me feel sorry for myself. So were the wonderful deeds and the heart full of pity of Safta Marisha.

"גמילות־חסד" בבית פינטוב
בחצר בית הספר "תרבות"

GMILUT-CHESED - an interest-free loans establishment

[Pages 38-43]

During those Days

From the Memorial Book to Moshe Eliezer Kramer

Translated by Eilat Gordin Levitan

The remote shtetl of Kurenets during the 1860s achieved a significant position in the spiritual life of its neighboring communities. It was well known for its brilliant Jewish scholars and respectable Jews and was recognized as a central headquarters for the Lubavitch Chassids in the Vilna region.

Truly it was a small and fairly poor town, but despite this, it was able to carry four synagogues of Chasidim, and one Beit Midrash of Mitnagdim. It should be noted in her favor that it was amongst very few towns of that time where Chasidim and Mitnagdim lived in harmony with one another… The winds of Haskalah [Enlightenment] that had already spread in the big cities hadn't reached her borders yet. Her Jews lived as their fathers and the fathers of their fathers had lived, peacefully and asking for very little. And the whole shtetl was like one big loving family.

The first that influenced her in the ways of Chasidut was the well-known Gvir, the Righteous Rabbi Zalman Kurenitser. And until today, all the town natives are very proud of him. Adding to his glory were well known scholars as well as other respected men from those days like Rev Yehuda Lev Ephron, Rev Yehuda Zusman, Rev Josef Halevi, and others. Days passed and the magnificence of the spirit of Torah was reinforced by Rev Zishka Z"L, one of the glorious geniuses of the generation and one of his tzadiks.

About the greatness of Rev Zishka, the Chassids would tell wonderful anecdotes of his splendor, and until today, everyone mentions his name with love and endearment. From all the tales that were embroidered about his personality, it becomes clear that he wasn't just a genius, God-fearing person, but he was also blessed with ingenuity and his influence was big over his flock. Rev Moshe Lazar Kramer, who was blessed to study in his youth in the Beit Midrash of Rabbi Zishka and knew him very well and was very close to him, would often say, "If there is a Jewish flame that is burning in me, it's all on account of Rev Zishka…"

Rev Moshe Lazar was born in the year 1867, and his parents at that point lived in Kurenets. After seven years, they moved to the nearby village by the name of Ostashkova. There they leased a farm and a dairy, and there they lived for the rest of their days. The Paritz, the nobleman who owned the village, when he got know Michal, the father of Moshe Lazar, as he found out his honesty and his charming personality, liked him very much and became his confidante. He appointed him as the manager of all his businesses and made him well known amongst all the other noblemen of the area. He made a very good living through numerous, varied enterprises, and endowed large funds for good deeds. Once in a while he would travel all the way to Lubavitch to the Chabad rabbi, at first it was to Rabbi Mendeleh and later Rabbi Shmulke…

… In all the towns in the area, amongst them Kurenets, Ilia, and Ratzke, he was renowned for his generous gifts to Jews that had lost their money, or Jews who were needy. His wife would go every Saturday night to the little town of Ratzke and would give meat, chalahs, bread, and butter to the poor. She had the habit of raising geese every year and she used the meat to give to the poor and the feathers she gave to insolvent brides for their dowry. A guest who came to their house would always find tables laid out with splendid food and beds ready for any guests who were in need of a place to sleep.

When he was still very young, Moshe Eliezer Kramer showed much talent. He had a very sharp mind and a very fresh memory, and when he arrived to the age of Bar Mitzvah, he made a beautiful sermon [drasha]. Rav Zishka was very impressed and bestowed magnificent praise for the lad before his father, and said that he must be sent to study Torah in the yeshiva in Ilia. When he finished two years of study in the yeshiva in Ilia, he returned to his home and started working on the farm. Since in his very essence he was full of energy and a true entrepreneur, no work was too difficult for him. He worked in the fields, he carried tree trunks from the forest, he took care of the livestock, and he grew up to be a strong young man who spread fear amongst the other villagers. At one time the Christian villagers tortured a Jewish traveling peddler who went through the villages with his merchandise. When Moshe Eliezer Kramer came by and saw what they did, he quickly ran to the Christian hoodlums and beat them up to teach them a lesson. He was an absolutely fearless guy, and during the darkest of night he would walk in the deep forest fearlessly. One time the villagers played a prank and when he went alone in the forest they came to him dressed in white sheets, carrying torches in their hands. And like that they surrounded him. When he saw this parade he immediately understood that it was a prank and he ran to them and started beating them up as hard as he could, and since then their admiration for him grew tenfold.

When he turned 17 he wedded. His wife, Rachel Elka, was from a well-known Chasidic family from Dvinsk. She was the only daughter amongst male children who were renowned for their Torah knowledge. One of her brothers was Baruch Hadesh from Vizi. Other than his brilliance in Torah studies, he was also a well-known businessman. One time when he came to Smorgon for business, he encountered Rev Michal Kramer, and after they had a conversation he (Rev Michal) mentioned his son Moshe Lazar. He told Rev Baruch how his son was an excellent Torah learned man and also a good provider, and that he was looking for a bride from a good family. Rev Baruch told him that he had a sister at the age of matrimony, and that he was looking for a respectable groom for her. So they decided amongst themselves that he should come Ostashkova with his sister to meet the family. First, Rev Baruch went to Kurenets to Rabbi Zishka to hear his opinion about this match, and Rav Zishka said glorious things about the boy and his father, recommending the match…

After the wedding the young couple lived in the house of Michal in Ostashkova. The first years after the wedding were wonderful. The house was filled with plenty, and the family lived in harmony and friendship. They saw their daughter-in-law as a true daughter, they respected her good sense, her high taste, and the charm of her ways. Very intelligently, the city girl was busy with teaching her groom the manners of the big city and she tried to change his village boy habits. She made sure that he had regular hours for studying the Torah, and she would sit across from him, listening with pleasure to his studies…

… Until he reached the age of 20, he spent his days in pleasantness, but then came a period of troubles. Since he was a strong person and healthy both in his body and mind, he had no chance of avoiding military service. In order to do it, his only choice was to leave the village and for three years live in hiding until he found a way to be released from his obligation. But as soon as he got out of one trouble, he encountered a second, even bigger problem. This was the issue of the Fravozitlestevo, meaning the permission to live in the village. At that point in time there was an order by the Czarist government that prevented all Jews from living in the village. This order did not hurt Jews who lived in the village prior to that time. They were allowed to stay there with their children until they reached the age of 20. Any children who were above the age of 20 were ordered to leave the villages immediately. So now, Moshe Eliezer with his wife and his three babies was ordered to leave Ostashkova. For a short time they lived in a village near Ilia, and they were able to do it at the mercy of the local official. Except they couldn't stay there for too long since the governor of the region found out about it and he ordered them to leave the place immediately. The Jewish family disregarded the order and stayed there, and when the governor found out, he became very angry and sent an emergency order to the head of the village to immediately kick out the Jewish family and to prevent them from taking any of their possessions other than what they wore at the moment. This order came on the afternoon of the eve of Yom Kippur. Two strong Christian men entered Moshe Lazar's house and ordered him in the name of the law to immediately leave the village. No amount begging or pleading that this should be done after Yom Kippur could help him. He had no choice but harness the horses to the carriage and to put his wife and children there and go on their way. The entire family cried bitterly. Only he held firm and didn't cry. He started putting his belongings on his carriage as much as he could, and when the Christian men tried to prevent him from doing it as their orders had said, he told them;

" Preventing me from doing it would cause me such devastation that I would not be able to control what I would do and You would find yourselves in danger, and you would not be able to get out of here alive."

Hence they left him alone, and they even helped him load his belongings.

Consequently on the eve of Yom Kippur, at a late afternoon hour, the poor family arrived at the little town of Ilia. With difficulty he found an apartment for his family and started looking for some way to earn a living. Since he had a horse and buggy, and since he was a strong man, he started all kinds of hard labor, bringing wood from the forest, rocks from the fields, and any kind of job he encountered. Despite all of it he had little earnings, and if it wasn't for his father's help, he would not have survived.

He would say that those years in Ilia were the worst years of his life. In later years, when his situation greatly improved, he would talk about that time with humor. He would say that there was one good thing that he learned during that time, which was that while he was walking through the forests and the fields, he would say passages from Psalms and for that, all the chapters of the book, he could recite by heart.

After years of toil and poverty, he accepted that there was no sense in continuing such a life and he decided to leave Russia and immigrate to America. At first his father was very much against this plan, but there was an incident one-day when Moshe Eliezer Kramer brought wood from the forest. His carriage drowned in the mud, and Moseh Lazar worked for many hours trying to get it out. By coincidence, his father passed by and when he saw him in his misery he started crying and immediately gave him permission to go to America.

The preparations for travel were made secretly, and no others in the family knew about it. The carriage that came to take him didn't meet him at the house but waited for him outside of the town. To his family members he said that he was going for business to a nearby town for his job. Only his father came to see him of, he walked with him until they were far from the town. There they said their good-byes…

The Kramer Family

… After many years in America, where he became very well off and renowned, Moshe Lazar traveled to his hometown Kurenets in the year 1920. He was 56 years old and during those days there was war between Poland and the Bolsheviks for control of the area. Truly it was many years that his soul yearned to see his hometown and to meet with his relatives, and to go pay his respects to the graves of his forefathers. But this trip, more than it was for himself, was for the sake of other people. He was a messenger of Mitzvah or charity. He had with him more than $25,000 that he planned to divide amongst hundreds of families in Kurenets and the surrounding towns that were devastated and impoverished during the days of the war. Many, many came to see him off at the ship, and he received many blessings from his friends, other Kurenets natives in America. One old man, Shmaryahu Fingerhut, couldn't contain his excitement for the moment, and he immediately made a vow to roll twice if Moshe Lazar would return peacefully from his trip. The old man did complete his vow.

The Cohen Family

Riva Cohen
(born 1846 in Kurenets)

Max Cohen
(born 1845 in Kurenets)

Until he arrived at Warsaw he didn't encounter any difficulties, but here on it was a difficult road. He found out that the Bolsheviks were coming near Kurenets and to travel in such a situation near Vilna, especially since he had 4 million in Polish marks inside a suitcase, was very dangerous. But he didn't bother thinking about all the troubles he might encounter and he went on his way to Minsk. The town was already blockaded, and when they came they stopped him and took him to the commanding officer. He was then imprisoned and the money he had was confiscated since they suspected him of helping the Bolsheviks. But after the officer checked the letter of commendation that Moshe Kramer received from the Polish government in Warsaw that explained that the money was to be used for charity, and after examining the State Department papers from Washington, he returned the money to him and released him. Since he was very brave and he knew the language very well, he was able to get the passport to go to Kurenets and immediately went on his way.

All the train cars were filled with military men and arms. Traveling on those trains was very dangerous. In spite of all this he was able to arrive at Molodetszna, which served as a train crossroads from many places. He arrived that night and was to take a second train to Vilejka. The train was filled with drunken soldiers and he was the sole civilian in the entire station. He had to wait for the next train for a few hours, and this was very dangerous. When finally the train was going in the direction of Vilejka arrived, it contained only two cars, and those were filled with soldiers who wouldn't let him go up. After much pleading the conductor let him stand near the furnace with him.

When he went up on the train one of the soldiers helped him carry one of the two heavy suitcases. He smiled and said, "Oh, you must be carrying a huge amount of gold in here" and ordered him to open his suitcase. Moshe Lazar who was clever and had thought of such a possibility had put the money deep inside the suitcase and covered it with clothes, and on top he put some bottles of alcohol and food. So when he opened the suitcase nonchalantly, in a very good and humorous spirit, he took out a bottle of brandy and offered it to all the soldiers. After one toast after another, all the bottles were empty. As the soldiers were filled with good spirit, they became friendly and offered him a place among them. They didn't bother him anymore.

In Vilejka he got off the train and walked from the station to the town, about 2 km away, holding the suitcases. When he arrived he went to a hotel and invited all the heads of the town. He divided about four or five thousand dollars among the residents and saw him as a sort of savior angel. The way from Vilejka to Kurenets he did in a carriage that was filled with soldiers. He paid them one hundred dollars to guard him.

When he entered Kurenets he immediately realized the destitution. The houses were broken and falling down. The windows were covered with rugs. Many of the doors were locked and the streets were empty of all people. In a short time the town had passed hands nine times from the Russians to the Germans to the Polish. This occurred on Sabbath night, on the P of Balakh. As soon as he arrived in town he visited the grave of his parents. The town stood exactly at the front. The Polish retreated and the Bolsheviks came close. The Rabbi of the town begged that he should not stay here since it was so dangerous, and that he must leave the town with the retreating Polish army, which would respect the fact that he was an American citizen. But he was adamant about staying and all the begging was to no avail. "The first reason," he said, " it is the eve of Sabbath and there was no such danger that would make me disrespect the Sabbath." He continued…"Second, why is my life more dear than the other residents of the town? Maybe it was an order from Heaven that I should die in Kurenets to be buried next to my forefathers."

The next day the Bolsheviks came to town. It took six to seven days for the parade of conquerors to pass through. The soldiers of the Red Army were very poor and didn't have any uniforms. Their clothes were tattered. In the first two weeks they behaved themselves and didn't hurt anyone, but on the third week they started some troubles. At first they took all the food from the residents and only left amount sufficient for one week. After that they printed their own money and they disallowed any of the Czarist or Polish money. But the farmers in the area refused to sell any food for the new money, and the situation became more and more severe. He stayed in the town more than one month without being able to leave. Hard days came for him as well as for the rest of the residents, and he knew a period of starvation. The bread at that point was made from a little bit of flour mixed with hay, and as much as the residents of the town tried to help him, they could not. Sometimes they would share potatoes that they had found in the field. In spite of all of this his spirits were always good and every morning he would get up to say a psalm. And his voice would awake others and make them get up for prayer.

For many days he sat in the synagogue, studying and telling stories to people. Between Mincha and Maariv, he would read before the congregation from the Midrash and Eyn Yaakov. During those days it fell on the fast of the ninth of the month of Av, and later on he used to say he never cried as much as he did on that day.

The Krivitzki family of Kurenets in America

The month of Tishrei was nearing and he really wished to spend Rosh Hashanah with his family in the US so he started taking care of arrangements to leave. After much trouble he received from the commissar permission to go from Kurenets to Vilna, but all the people who owned horses and carriages feared to go such a dangerous route, endangering their horses and carriages. This left him no choice but to buy a horse and carriage of his own, and he paid a large amount of money for them. That person he bought it from endangered his soul and traveled with him to Vilna. The entire town gathered to follow him on the way out of town and they blessed him with love and wishes of peace. When he arrived at Vilna he gave the genius Rabbi Chaim Ozer $102,000 for Kurenets, designated to establish a small yeshiva of Talmud Torah, Bikur Cholim, and a bank. For the Jews of Kurenets his visit was an extraordinary event and for many days it was the main topic of conversation in Kurenets as well as in the neighboring towns.

Eli Zimerman in World War I uniform, c. 1917

Eli Zimerman of Kurenets

Amongst the Kurenetsers in America they also thanked him and wrote him a letter that they gave him as he returned.

A thankful letter:

> If you see him naked, cover him
> Do not deny one who is in your own image.
> And then your splendor will be awaken with dawn
> And your repast will swiftly grew

To our beloved, honored and precious brother, Moshe Eliezer Kramer!

Dear Brother!

Receive from us our blessing, The consecration of your brothers, It is awarded upon you for the magnanimous relief that you secured for our devastated brothers, our beloved who were inflicted by war in our hometown of Kurenets. You speared no money or toil, you endangered your soul and went by water. We will say to you with all of our brothers: May you be blessed You solved with your puissance the destitution of our kinsmen and you became their achi-ezer and achi-semech

And we pray that our brothers will be spared of any adversity and flourish and you will be rewarded for you righteousness. May G-D requite you with lengthy life span and you will harvest in splendid old age filled with blissfulness and affluence, and you will receive enjoyment from your sons and all your family members.

Your brothers who Signed
Max Alberts (nee Alperovitz)
Elyhu Avraham Albert (nee Alperovitz)
Shimon, son of rev Yehuda Leib Bengis
Yaakov, son of rev Aba Dinerstein
Avraham Binyamin Dimenstein
Aharon, son of rev Shlomo Gordon
Baruch Kopilovitz
Pesach, son of rev Eliezer Luria
Kelman, son of rev Eliezer Luria
Mendel son of rev Yehuda Luria
Chaim Peykin
Noach Rubin
Moshe Ze'ev Sapir
Pesach Shafer
Moshe Weiss
Yosef, son of rev Avraham Aharon Weiss
Baruch Zukerman (nee Chait)
Aryo son of rev Yitzhak Zimerman
Eliyau Gershon, son of Yisrael Eisar

Jacob Shulman of Kurenets with his family in Pittston, Pennsylvania
Picture taken during a visit of his two surviving nieces who came from Israel

[Page 44-48]

Images

David Kribitzky

Translated by Eran Gordin

*"In honor of Dvoshel Zokovsky, Michael Gorfinkel, Motik,
son of Reuven Zishka Alperovich and my great grandfather,
Aharon son of Tzvi and Reise Bela Shulman"*

The year is 1880. My gloomy little hometown is a hamlet surrounded by a thick forest and wide, open fields. Her lingering and winding streets converge at the vast, circular focal market. A variety of sizes and sorts of stores, from the "huge" mercantile enterprise of Pini, the metal goods merchant, to a tiny kiosk that belongs to Basha Beyle, the oil merchant, crowd the market. On most days of the week one would find Jews wandering around the market without purpose. The arrival of market day signals the awakening of the sleepy town and affords the poor merchants a flashing glance of prosperity. The hatters repair the hats, the tailors clean the shabby clothing, and the various peddlers prepare bags and sacks to buy all manner of produce: from chickens, to potatoes, to hay. Everyone awaits the farmers that will bring the harvest of their land and toil.

My small shtetl contains 300 families; all together about 1500 souls. Some tailors, a few shoemakers, a number of blacksmiths, a small amount of butchers, three big synagogues, and two minyans. A few *"melamdim"* (teachers), "talmud torah", and many "chadarim". The big world is far from here, and a foreign concept to the inhabitants. They know only the neighboring towns Vileyka, Smorgon, and Molodechno. Of Vilna and Minsk: most townspeople had only heard, very few had actually traveled so far. Most of the people who had traveled had left originally to serve under the Tsar's army. These men tell amazing tales, stories that could not be believed by anybody in their right mind.

There was a young boy named Bentze Dodge's. He was the son of one of the wealthiest families in the region. His father was an agricultural merchant. They had an extravagant home in the middle of the central market. Behind the main house stood their barns and storage rooms. Bentze would never mingle with the town's children. He was a son of the "highest status family" every one else was beneath them. It was not a matter that could be easily overlooked considering that his uncle was the famous Mr. Bitzkovsky from Smorgon!

Bentze had a little puppy, and because he had to keep it a secret from his father, he hid the puppy in one of the barns, and there he would feed and care for him. Bentze poured the affection he withheld from his peers into this little puppy. He would think constantly of new ways to please the little pet. One day he decided that he would begin warming the puppy's food. The boy put a makeshift stove in a hidden corner of the barn, and from then on, he would warm the dog's food.

A day came when Bentze was not carefully watching the cooking. A fire started and spread to the hay that was next to the little stove, the flames grew and grew. The boy was very scared, and instead of running home and getting help to extinguish the fire, he escaped from the barn with the dog, dashed across the adjacent garden, and hid in the "shtable" (the torah study place) of the Chassidim. It took but a few minutes, and the whole barn was engulfed in flames. In only an hour all of the homes and the stores in the central market were in flames. The flames swallowed the little wooden shacks. Like wild beasts, they jumped from home to home, from street to street, gaining might with each new conquest, until they consumed the whole town with a red, burning rage. The little ashes flew to the farthest homes like smoldering black butterflies. Soon the town was covered with a cloud of dark smoke. The central market leapt with flames.

The confused Jews deserted the town and ran first to the fields and gardens behind their homes and then in the direction of the neighboring village of Poken. They carried babies, bags, and dishes – whatever they could save. At evening time, all that was left of the community were the fireplaces and the blackened frames of the buildings that had stood only hours before. The ashes and dust had finally begun to settle. Broken plates and sacks of bedding cluttered the outlying fields. The abandoned bits and pieces appeared to the returning townspeople like open graves. As the smoke disappeared, the totality of the destruction became more and more obvious. Except for Eliyahu Yehosha's mill, and a few homes in the far end of Midel Street, the whole town had surrendered to the fire.

Days passed and the Kurenitz community began regaining its old spirit. Townspeople began rebuilding the stores and houses. When they had finished rebuilding the town was nicer than it had been before. Ringing the markets were modern, two story homes. The new stores were built in the fashion of Smorgon. They had even built shelves in the barns. The new synagogues were larger and more beautiful. How had the inhabitants been able to afford to rebuild a town that exceeded what they had ever had before upon the ashes of their old homes? This was a riddle that no one knew how to answer.

Bentze grew up and was a student in the high school in nearby Vileyka, and when he graduated, he went to the city of Dvinsk to further his education. In the town, amazing stories about Bentze circulated. The people said that he was so successful in Dvinsk, that the governor of the whole province respected him and often invited him to his home for tea time. Others would say that Bentze was leading a movement to abolish the Tzar's authority. Yet others said that Bentze was coming to Kurenitz anytime, and would take care of abusive employers like Asher the haberdasher, that enslaved his assistants, and Eliahu the blacksmith, who spent his days in the house of prayers, instead of working in the smithery, or the shoemaker Yerachmiel. Rumors spread that Bentze was planning to come to town to assist his relative Masha Bitzkovsky from Smorgon in dividing her father's riches amongst the laborers.

One morning Bentze appeared! Pandemonium reigned. No one had seen such a personality before. Bentze was tall, he wore spectacles and a black top hat, and carried a cane in his hand and a fancy shawl over his shoulders. A few young women who worked as tailors claimed they knew the truth about this charming and inexplicable man. This was a prince that pretended to be Bentze and had arrived to search for his lost princess. It didn't take many days until everyone had discovered the true reason for his visit. Bentze had remembered for all of his days the annihilation that had arrived at his hands, and agonized about how to pay for his crime. He swore a vow that one day he'd repay the town for the destruction he had caused. And now he had returned to fulfill his promise.

Bentze gathered a group of children, boys and girls belonging to the poorest families and established a school to teach them Russian and math. His students approached their non-religious studies with the same enthusiasm as they put into their religious studies. People in town began expressing their discomfort with what was happening. The religious people started threatening…But we're talking about Bentze Dodger, who had drank tea with the governor of the whole region!

I don't know if Bentze repaid the town for the destruction he caused, but this I know for sure: Bentze helped to enlighten dozens of boys and girls, and encouraged them to explore the world passed the pale of settlement.

They will remember him with deep love, and I am one of them.

Kurenitz – my beloved, somber hometown! Good, honest Jews were raised on your land. Some were simple, common people that never left the town's limits. Others became well known. Some of them that I will mention are: my Cheder friend Eliahu Golov the Yiddish poet that was well known in Russia, Baruch Zukerman, Samuel Dickstein, and others…

Kurenitz was destroyed at the hands of the wild Nazi beasts. My brother in law, Yosef Zimmerman and my relative Elke Rachel were slaughtered with the rest of the town's Jews. I don't know who is there now in the place that's called Kurenitz, but the earth where I saw my first flicker of light exists. The fields and the forest where I played during my early childhood still exist. The heavens where I heard for the first time the sound of my mother's voice exists. And all this will be kept for all eternity and live in my heart.

Fire in Kurenitz (not the 1880s fire, but in the 1920s)

Nachman, son of Isar

Nachman son of Isar, or as he was commonly known in town, Nachman Isaras' became a legend in his own time. Many tales were told of his heroic deeds and his role in saving the town. We, the children of the Cheder, believed he was the reincarnated soul of one of our legendary heroic figures: Shimshon. But, in our minds, Nachman Isaras exceeded even this ancient hero in deed and character. Shimshon succeeded in killing 1000 of Pleshet people with one donkey's cheekbone, while we were sure that Nachman would have killed 2000!

Here, I would like to tell of one of Nachman's heroic deeds that I not only heard about, but actually saw with my own eyes. Still today, the occurrence is fresh in my mind, as if it happened yesterday. It occurred on market day, a day where thousands of farmers from the villages would gather in the town's market to buy and sell. They brought eggs, cows, chickens, and harvest produce to town, in order to exchange them fir either money, clothes, or tools. Otherwise they'd patron the town's inn and drink away their sorrows, pint by pint. The market day spanned the entire day. Thousands of people, loud sounds and colorful stands filled the square. Here and there, struggle or fight would break out. Two gentiles would hit each other until they bled. Another gentile would be caught stealing. These were the usual occurrences marking market day.

It got worse during the evening, when the farmers began harnessing their horses and leaving for their villages. By this time, the market was full of drunks. The merchants quickly collected their merchandise and locked their stores. The peddlers, with their little stands, hurried away before the hour of curfew arrived.

I would help Noach David the haberdasher sell his hats that were hanging on the wall of a store next to Yuda Zusha's house. On the other side of the market, across from the yard of the synagogue, stood the tiny store of old Basha Beyle selling oil, salt, and sardines. A farmer came to the store, bought some oil, took the merchandise, and subsequently, refused to pay. What could the old woman do? She couldn't take the merchandise by force. Her only choice was to stand there begging and crying. She pleaded that this oil would be her only sale that day. She stood there crying and the drunk farmer stood laughing. More and more farmers gathered, surrounding Basha Beyle, mocking her. Nachman approached the area, and without asking questions, he faced the farmer who had refused to pay. He grabbed his shirt and squeezed the collar until the man's face turned green and he started choking. The farmers had stopped their mocking. Instead, they all jumped on top of Nachman. So, what did Nachman do? He lifted the farmer up in the air like he was a ball, and threw him in the direction of the approaching mob. The mob spread and many of the villagers fell on the ground, but that was not the end of it. Now, more villagers attacked Nachman. Nachman took a metal pen that was sitting on top of a salt bag, and he started striking them left and right up and down with it as if it was a huge crane. Nachman was not selective in his aim. He hit anything in his sight-heads, faces, shoulders, etc., and the villagers were falling in front of him and prevented other villagers from reaching Nachman. Nachman was able to reach them even beyond the falling bodies. Though we deeply believed in Nachman's strength and heroism, it would be hard to guess the outcome of the fight if a policeman wouldn't have come. It was a short skinny gentile that talked in a nasally voice. Not very heroic looking figure. But his uniform and the hat he was wearing with a silver symbol impressed the villagers. They were used to having great respect for the shiny symbols. So when the policeman arrived, the fight came to an end, and the villagers departed.

Old Basha-Beyle immediately locked her store and left, Nachman hung around and looked huge to us, with his wide shoulders. He observed the market plaza with a content look on his face, whispered something in the ear of the policeman, and then they left together. Nachman was a very unusual man. He never showed his strength just for show off, but was always immediately there when the weak needed his help. As I remember him, he was very modest, never trying to be the "front" man. I never heard that Nachman fought with anyone other than for saving the weak. Nachman died during a typhus epidemic that spread in town. And when we heard in America that he died, we refused to believe. For us he will always be a superman that no one could rule.

[Page 49-50]

The Big Boulder

By Yosef Weiss

Translated by Clare Davies

"In honor of my brother James"

On gloomy winter nights, when the Rabbi was praying the Mincha prayer in the synagogue, we, the little children of the Cheder, would gather around the big fire place. The descending darkness would stir our imaginations. We would spend the evening telling horror tales about witches, spirits, and cursed princes and princesses.

The Rabbi's wife would stand, warming herself by the fire, and listen silently to our horrible tales. Maybe she found them interesting, or maybe she only smiled in the darkening room at our naivete. One evening while we sat around the fire place the Rabbi's wife told us, "Today children, I will tell you a tale. But this tale is about an occurrence that didn't take place somewhere far in the world, it is something that people say happened right here. Right in Kurenitz." Our eyes widened in the dark, and our curiosity knew no limits. Our only worry was that the Rabbi might return from the synagogue, and the tale would have to be stopped in the middle.

"Do you know what I am going to tell you about?" she whispered, " I am going to tell you about the Big Boulder; the boulder that you will find far in the field past Mydell Street. Are you listening, children? Long, long ago, there was no boulder in that field. Instead, a huge inn stood on the spot the boulder is now. There lived the innkeeper with his wife and many children. But this man, as you must have heard, was a miser, who was notorious for his many bad deeds. He never gave alms to the poor and banished vagabonds and poor men from his inn."

"Then, one day something happened. A beggar passing through the town was going from door to door in search of alms. He knocked on the innkeepers door and begged for something to eat and a place to eat. The innkeeper kicked him out of his home, and worse yet, sent his huge dogs after the poor man. But this beggar was no ordinary beggar. Oh no, this man was a magic maker and a miracle worker. Immediately, he whispered a magical spell, cursing the innkeeper and his entire family. Only a minute had passed when… the inn with the innkeeper's house with all its occupants inside transformed into a big boulder. And today that very same boulder sits behind Mydell Street. But this my children is not the whole tale. People say that if you come to the boulder exactly at twelve midnight and you say a secret message, when you put your ear to the rock you will hear the rooster's crow and the children cry!"

Of all the children gathered around the fire that night, I was the youngest. And this tale of the Big Boulder awed and haunted me. I wished with all my heart to see that amazing boulder. I started begging my friends to walk to the famous place in order to see the boulder there, with our own eyes. But all the other small children said they would only visit the Boulder during the festival of Lag Baomer. They planned to bring the colorful eggs that they got for the holiday, and break them open on the Boulder.

There were many, many days until Lag Baomer, and I was filled with the urge to see the place at once. Daily I would stand secretly on the roof of our house, and observe from afar this miraculous place. For a while I was satisfied straining for a glimpse of the magical boulder, but soon I fell into my familiar longing to actually visit the Big Boulder.

Every Friday we were let go from the Cheder at noon. The idea soon occurred to me that I escape for long enough on Friday in order to finally make journey to the Boulder. I spoke to two of my friends of my plan and finally convinced them to join me. The next Friday afternoon we were walking through the gardens of Smorgon Street, and on our way. All of a sudden we came across a boy with a huge, hulking dog. Of course, we were very scared. We started sprinting back to the Cheder. My two friends ran swiftly, like leaping deer. But, unluckily, I was wearing big boots and could not run fast. I lagged behind and the dog caught a hold of me.

From then on I didn't dare leave the shtetl. Still, the tale of the Big Boulder remained constantly in my mind. Finally, the day of Lag Baomer arrived. I hardly slept the night before, I was so excited. I awoke at dawn. According to the tradition of our town, the people of Kurenets began taking eggs from the oven where the chickens were kept, and boiling the eggs in onion. I decorated the egg shells with ink designs. As soon as the morning prayer had ended, a large group of children gathered, and we set out our way to the boulder.

My heart was pounding as I walked. Eventually we arrived at the boulder, and stood before it. It rose, hulking and black, out of the middle of the field. It certainly did look like a large house. I stood in front of the boulder, curious and sad. In my imagination I saw the big inn. The owner, clearly, had not been a decent man. Nevertheless, I pitied him and his pitiful family for the horrible punishment that was theirs. I stood there dreaming. All of a sudden, an older boy approached me and said,

"Hey you! Listen, why are you standing there dreaming? If you go around the boulder seven times, and if you say seven times, 'Sits in hiding,' and then put your ear on the boulder, you will hear the sound of crying children and crowing roosters." I did what he told me. I walked around the boulder seven times and then I said with deep concentration and intention, "Sits in hiding," seven times, one after the other. I bent my knees very close to the boulder and I put my ear against its rocky side to hear the sounds. Alas, I hadn't known that the trouble maker was only making fun of me. All of a sudden, he pushed my head into the boulder; my forehead pressed against the smooth rock, my eyes darkened. Instead of the sound of children crying and roosters crowing, I heard a sharp ringing in my ears. I was left with a big bruise on my face.

Those were the days of childhood and naiveté. I traveled to many places: to far away lands, and to the tops of the highest mountains which were scattered with huge boulders. But not one of those boulders left as deep an impression as the Big Boulder in the field of my little shtetle.

[Page 51]

Matia, son of Pesach (Zavodnik)

By Maris Cohen, New Haven

Translated by Eilat Gordin Levitan

Kurenitz was a tiny shtetl; nevertheless, it was greatly diverse. There were learned men, merchants, stores owners, vagabonds, tradesmen and handymen, wealthy and poor. I don't need to tell you that for every wealthy man there were dozens of poor. There were numerous personalities that deserve to be mentioned here; however, I will concentrate only on one person,

Matia Pesach's. Matia did have a last name but we only found out about his last name in the U.S. In the U.S. they called him Max Zavodnick. In the old shtetl, we were not used to last names. It was unnecessary to know last names. There, we called each other by the name of the father, mother, grandfather, or grandmother, or their vocation or craft.

We knew each other as Laibe Mashe's, Yehuda Zushe's, Yechiel Kalman the doctor, Michael the forester, Ara the fisherman, Penia the metal merchant, Shimon the oilman. Asher the haberdasher, Mordecai the tailor, Eliyahu the smith, Yarochmiel the shoe repairman. There were two other Yarochmiels who were also in shoe repair, so we would call them little and big Yarochmiels.

The other was not big and not little. Just Yarochmiel the shoe repairman. The same way as the old people were named, so were the young people named. Yoshka Chaim's, Chaim Zalman Elya Yehoshua's, Baroch Vigdaras' (Zukerman), Mendel Faiga's (Alpert), Havas Rasile's (Shapiro- Alperovitz), Zalman Nachum's (Kastrel?), Leybzke Lea Atka's, Zertel Pinis' and Sara Reyzel Dvora Shlomo Sheyna Feigas'. If you just said Sara Reyzel Dvoras', people would not know the one you are referring to.

In our town, no one knew last names; nevertheless, the generation ties never ended and no one was ever lost.

Matia, son of Pesach, was a very unique person. A simple guy who could hardly read and write, on the other hand he could play various instruments. Violin, flute, clarinet. Matia would write songs and sing them during celebrations. In his nature, he was a comedian and his rhymes were always very original and charming. Why was he given this "gift of music" no one could answer. No one else in his family was a poet or musician.

Matia in his essence seemed to be attracted to far away places. His eyes had the look of restlessness and a deep desire of wondering. He was a tall man, skinny and dark.. His appearance was something of a gypsy. In our town, there was little respect for such people. The people of our town didn't understand or appreciate him, until one day when he did something that changed everyone's opinion. In the year 1890 all of a sudden there was inflation in prices and in the entire region the money lost its value. All the products became extremely expensive and people were starving. We found out that the merchants of the farming products took all the local products and transferred them to a nearby town, Smorgon, to sell them. While we in the shtetl were "sentenced" to starvation.

One day when there were ten carriages full of products on Smorgon's Street, ready to be taken out of town, The drivers were sitting in the inn of Yehuda Zusha's (Alperovitz) drinking alcohol, Matia stealthily went to the carriages and cut the sacks and let all the produce fall to the ground, for the townspeople to use. In this way, he revenged the townspeople's being left to starvation and none of the produce left the town. Everyone was very worried and Matia hid somewhere. However, he couldn't hide for too long. When he came out all the merchants beat him mercilessly. Nevertheless, everyone in town was extremely thankful.

We realize that Matia of all people fought the fight for the town. Everyone respected him for that. Here in America, Matia had many professions. For some time, he was a policeman traveling on bicycles around New York making sure the kosher butchers and restaurants were truly kosher. After a while he became a street musician. He would compose songs and would wander the streets of New York singing. Many of his songs became later songs that other singers sang in entertainment halls. The subject of his songs were usually tragic events. Matia would compose a song for every tragedy that occurred. In 1906 when the earthquake in San Francisco destroyed a large part of the town, Matia dedicated a song to the event.

When General Sarkhoum was burned in the port of New York (a cruise ship with hundreds of kids aboard), Matia arranged a song for the event. Also, when Russia lost the war to Japan, there was an original song for it. What was the root of the choice of Matia to sing about miseries and tragedies? Maybe, his life was very tragic in that he never reached the lofty desires that his soul yearned for. Whatever reasons it is his songs were always sad as his appearance was. Occasionally, Matia would come to New Haven. New Haven was the original settlement of the people who came from our shtetl. The first settlers in 1880 and 1890 chose it as their "haven." Each time Matia reached New Haven, there was immediately a mood of holiday. We all knew that he would generate some excitement in the ambiance that was usually so dreary in our suburban sleepy town. And we were never disappointed.

Matia died in 1925 in New York City. He was 52. He left behind a son, who was an engineer, and a daughter, who lived in Philadelphia. When the daughter was young, she was among the most beautiful girls of Jewish New York City. Let's recall Matia, son of Pesa, a native of Kurenitz with this memorial for our shtetl.

[Pages 53-54]

Kurenitz

by David Krivitsky

Translated from the Yiddish by his grand-nephew Sheldon Rice
With editing assistance by his wife, Rena Rice

Love, joy and pain mixed together,
When I recall my birthplace.
With shingled roofs and soft clay pavement,
With the wooden planks next to the enclosed gardens
With the grand homes in the marketplace
Which I can barely see,
With the mud which no one will ever clean.

Images long forgotten loom up before my eyes,
Playful years, childhood dreams.
Our kheder with its walls of mossy green,
Where the boys used to sit up as if captured.
In summertime and winter when the wind
Wailed outside with frightening sounds.

I see the old rebbe as he
Scolds and smiles at the same time:
"Forgot already you rascal?
Then begin again!"
Letters become birds which
Soar up to the sky,
And carry away my childhood's dream.

I see a gray autumn morning
Accompanied by a tiny, biting drizzle.
In the shtetl the hardship grows,
Worries about work.
When a merchant opens his store,
A woman waits to see if there is
Something to buy on credit.

I see the winter nights,
Sickness and distress.
As they looked in the moonlight
Through the darkened windows
In the homes where sadness lies in wait.
Where there is only silence without joy or sunshine,
Lives lived, sorrow from God.

I see the dark Shabbos evenings,
Empty streets where I see only a goat,
And a woman searching through a
Window for an invisible star, where
Shabbos tranquility has disappeared.

I see the bright weeks before Pesach,
When life awakens in the shtetl.

Everyone kashered and polished day and night,
The chains of slavery have been broken.
In the confusion is heard:
"This is not the time to make money,
It's the holiday and we need to bake and cook!"

Love, joy and pain mixed together,
When I am reminded of the shtetl,
Like a string shivering from the slightest touch,
My heart begins to stir, kindled by flames.
My imagination is transported back there,
Across land and sea.

[Pages 55-73]

Old Images

By Yaakov Alpert

Translated by Eilat Gordin Levitan

Edited by his grandson, Dr. Howard G. Mendel

As if a little Jewish island surrounded by everglade forest and picturesque villages, sat the sleepy shtetl Kurenitz. What was the origin of the name and when was the settlement founded were not concern of the inhabitant. Only the faded Hebrew letters on the graves in the old Jewish cemetery bore testimony of the many generations of Jews who lived and died here. The town circumference was small. In the middle sat the circular town center that contained the market. That was where the town's curvy streets all banded together. In the heart of the market, there was a large square, wood building that contained the stores. Most of the Jewish population's income was derived from the stores. The storeowners would primarily sell to the Christian villagers from the surrounding villages. There was also a factory there that made soda that was funded by my father, may his memory be blessed. It did not contain electric appliances. It didn't have modern plumbing. The soda was made in a very primitive way, the water was brought in pales by Herschel, the well man. The wheel was turned by hand and that was the manner they produced the needed gas.

Life was tough, a mixture of lights and shadows. Only a few families were well off, the rest lived in poverty. The main food source was vegetables, potatoes, salty fish and dark bread. Meat was eaten on Sabbath and holidays. The center of our life when I was a small boy was the Jewish religion. The religious centers were the four synagogues; the Minyan of the Rabbi, the old Shteible, the central synagogue and Biet Hamidrash that belong to the Mitnagdim.

The minyan of the Rabbi belonged to the most devote Lubavitch Hassid's. The prayer there was done with great intent and enthusiasm. Not many belonged to that temple. Those who did belong were very reverent and greatly educated in bible studies.

I remember my first visit to the old shteble when I was a little boy, one cold day when outside it was 'Siberia' as the natives would call it, in the synagogue it was warm. The Shamash, Eliyahu Abba was not cheap with the firewood. He kept putting more and more wood into the furnace. Chayim- Zalman Yuda's (son of Yuda Zushas' Alperovitz), a Jew with a somber, serious face was sitting near the fireplace wearing his talit and tfilin and studying Tnaiya. He was reading aloud and he studied vigorously some passages. He looked very strange, he was shaking and moving back and forth in excitement. He was continuously saying," Omer Hu Tzadik v'Tov lo, Omer hu Tzadik v'Ralo" "omer hu Rasha V'ralo, Omer hu Tzadik Gamor, He tells… My eyes met the smiley eyes of the Shamash Eliyahu. Since I was more then a bit mischievous I couldn't stop laughing. Immediately everyone started yelling at me, "Wild boy, you are making fun of us in a holy place!!!". My lucky break, at that moment the door opened and Chayim Abram Alperovitch entered. He was a tall sturdy man. He looked like he could hardly contain his excitement, his expression was full of delighted and he was holding a huge wine bottle. "Jews," he yelled loudly,

"Drink to life, L'Chaim. My wife Yachka brought to the world a male child and his name in Israel would be Dania." (Dania perished in Naarutz)

The old Shteible was built with red bricks. Near the door in the Western Wall, there was a big sink to wash your hands. On the walls, there were shelves full of books. The people who would pray here were Laibe Masha's, Ykutiel Meir Kremer, Yisrael Micheal the Shochet, my father Eliyahu Alperovitz the Lemonade maker. They were also Lubavitch Hassid's and they would sit studying from early in the morning until late at night too. They would read the bible, they would say Tehilim and converse about social matters.

The central Syasgague was influenced by new concepts. Although the members were Hassidic Lubavitchers too, they were not as devoted. You could see that they took certain freedoms with the prayers. The prayers were short and done in haste. Sometimes during the Torah readings, they permitted personal conversations. There was not true devotion and truly some of the members were unhappy with the way prayers were done and transferred back to the old Shteible.

Biet Hamidrash belong to the Mitnagdim and many amongst the Hassidic Jews looked at that synagogue with a little disrespect. "Look at the way they pray" they would say," they don't even start with Hodu, the start with Mizmor Shir Hanukat Habiet…" In that place most of the members were working class people, the crafts men and handy men. There was hardly devotion or excitement. The prayers were quiet. The prayers were said with sweetness and softly. Often they would have a Magid and the crowd would listen to his speech intently.

I remember that on Saturday before the Mincha prayer I went to the Beit Midrash to hear the moralistic statement of one of those Magids. He was a short, skinny Jew that had big black eyes with a gloomy expression. He stood next to the Holy Ark, wearing his talit and told his sermon in front of the crowd in a weepy voice, he would interpret passages. When he reached the passage, "Halachto ba'derech"he said "One time I went to a specific place and 'eshma Kolkore' all of a sudden while I am still walking I heard a crying begging voice of a man. Veahen Kol V'hor, meaning I began looking around me to see where the voices came from and then I saw, Oy Laanyim Sheko rohot, what do you think I saw? I saw that the angels of destruction pushed a man to the ground, held him by force, and huge cows stepped on him and squeezed his body to the ground. Veshalam Veomar, I approached the angel of destruction and asked, Mahetor Ve ma eashtor, what is the evil deeds of this man that you treat him like that. Veeshma Et Kolam Vecover, I heard the answer, a big sin he did he cut his payas". He was saying his sermon with a sad, expressive deep tone and the whole synagogue was dark and mysterious looking. All of a sudden he yelled with a big shaking voice," House of Jacob, seeds of Israel, immediately return to your old ways of the past, who knows, tomorrow may be too late." The Jews sat with a worried look in their eyes. From the women's section, there was a quiet cry. I was sitting next To Hershel, the water carrier. He was whispering either to himself or to me in a very expressive voice that was full of regret and remorse, "If the barber would once more dare to touch my Payas I will break his bones. This is my vow and if I don't fulfill it, it is as if I am not a Jew."

Shabbat

Other than Shabat, those other days were special in Kurenitz; Sunday was the goyim Sabbath, Tuesday was the market day and Friday there was the evening of Shabat. On Friday women got up very early and prepared the big ovens, then they would run to the market to buy fish. On Friday we (the young boys), would be studying in the Cheder only until midday. Then I would run like a leaping deer from the Cheder, home. It was customary on Friday to eat kugel…

Immediately as we would sit to eat the door would open and Shlomo Hyim would enter. We use to call him the *Nail*, I don't know why. He was a poor Jew and vagabond and would eat at our house every Friday. He was of average build with a dark long beard and sad eyes. When he spoke, he would stutter. He was very spiritual and artistic and would like to draw the holy buildings and the Wailing Wall. He had a beautiful voice and he like to sing Russian songs. Yet something was wrong with him, if you made any movement with your hand, like scratching yourself, immediately his face would wear a melancholy look, he would jump out of his seat as if a snake had bit him and would leave the table, go to my mother and start stuttering. I – Gaverit Hada – Hi – Ta – Hita – Bedal – Hinov – Hita – Sham – Srefa. My mother, a very generous woman would smile and say, "Shlomo Hyim, until you are done telling your story the day will end and I will need to bless the candles, and I still have so much work, so it is better for you to eat now." Shlomo Chayim could not refuse my mother, he was listening to my mothers commands intently and was always ready to eat her delicacies with a good appetite and would fill his dish with food.

Doors would open and close, Jews would go to receive the Shabbat. My father and I would also go to the Synagogue. Everything in the Synagogue was very clean and shining. Yitza Chatzies' (Charles Gelmans' father), was a very handy person he made beautiful lamps and the place had an oura of light blue splendor. The lamps would make a soft murmur sound that sounded like a devotional prayer. The eastern wall was crowded with long bearded Jews. They looked a bit pale standing underneath the blue light. They opened their Siddurs and immediately we would hear the voice of Gatze Dinerstein who was passing in front of the ark. When he would reach the passage; "Arbaim Shana Aku baor imtoeh l'vahem…" I would usually be very hungry and could not hold any longer I would run home early. My quick-witted mother received me with a smile and say to my sisters, " NU my daughters, come quickly, the town crier is here from the synagogue." While talking she would give me baked goods full of cinnamon and raisins. A short time later Father and Shlomo Chayim would arrive. They would take off their Tallits and we would walk quietly around the house. First my father, then Shlomo Chayim behind him and me in the back. We would sing, " Shalom Alechem Malechie Hasharet." The house would be all clean and sparkly and lit. We would wash our hands and sit by the table. Mother usually wearing a green dress with a colorful piece of jewelry in the middle, green was a good contrast to her light brown hair. My sisters were also all dressed up and in their braids little rings and ribbons intertwined. My father would do the Kiddush and give everyone the Hamotzi. Mother would then serve the fish and the feast would begin. Usually Shlomo Chayim would treat the fish like a hungry wolf and would put a lot of Horseradish on it, would start breathing heavily until his forehead turned blue and his eyes would tear. He would stutter with expression of reverence and blame, "Oh, ho the horse radish is like dynamite."

Saturday, early in the morning I am asleep, but father is already walking around the house and singing the morning prayers. Immediately after, they take the big pale from the oven and also the milk pale that now has a brown crust. So we sit and drink tea with milk. Then Jews started going to the synagogue wearing their tallitot. Yonkal starts with the Hodu prayer and when they reached El Adon, Moshe the forester would stand and pray Shaharit. Then it is time for little fights concerning the selling of Aliyot. Many people want Aliyot so they usually sell to the highest bidder. Now it is the turn for my father to go on the Beema to read from the Torah. Then for the Musaf, Yisrael Michal, the shochet would pass by the ark. When the prayers end the Jews would bless each other with friendship, good Shabbas, and our neighbor, Yekutiel Kramer would continue sitting by the table studying. Our neighbor Yekutiel was a perfect example for the big change the Shabbat can make for a Jewish man. Those days he lived in the house of Chyena, in her back yard. It was tiny house the size of a "sigh" as we used to call it. He was very poor and had many young children then. His income from the flower store was very small and six days of the week you would see him running around looking very worried and his clothes would turn white from the flowers. On Shabat you would not recognize him, it was as if he was born again. He was full of excitement and happiness and in his eyes, there was an expression of kindness. He would sit and sing and everyone would listen. "B'zman She Cohien Gadol Nichnas Vhisnashehor." Then he would explain the passage "when the big Cohen would come to the Holy Temple to pray, there were three Cohenim to hold him. One from his right, one from his left and one from the precious rocks. When the one that is above him heard the sound of the foot steps of the big Cohen he would hope he would open the ark". While he would read a holy expression would spread on his face.

After the Saturday rest, My father would sit in the synagogue and study. I can remember the tune even today. He learned the tune while studying in the Ramulous Yashiva in Vilna…

Pinya the metal merchant would study intently from "Tzemach Tzedek" and the tip of his beard he would hold in his mouth. It must be very difficult text that he would usually read, he always read very intently. And then when it seems like has grasped it he would start singing in a Labovitch tune. Fischel the tailor and David the shoe maker would usually sit next to each other and say Tehilim. My Rabbi Yitza Moshe would read from the Zohar, and his eyes would be very red since it was a tradition for him to stay awake all of Friday night. However, not everyone would sit in the synagogues. The youth desired some entertainment. They want to breath some fresh air, so they would take a journey through Dolhinov St up to the Delga all the way to the pear tree. Dusk comes and the Mincha prayers would go home to eat the three meals. But at this time it was usually depressing for me and my appetite would seem to be lacking. Nevertheless, it is a commandment to eat the three meals so I would force my self to eat. Soon after the meals people return to the synagogue in the dark with only one candle usually. In the dark everyone's faces looked somber and depressed. The children would sit around and tell tales about Tzadiks and ghosts that must return to Hell after Havdalla. And then there will be a sudden knock on the table that was on the Beema and then it was time for Ma'ariv service. Vhu Rachoom Iyaher Avon… and then the prayers would end. Jews would bless each other and leave for the streets and for some reason they would walk with heavy steps and a bit sad.

The Charitable Institution: Gmilut Chesed

When I was a young child, I was obviously not knowledgeable of the social affairs in town. There is one thing though that was very clear to me: the poor natives were never neglected and passers by, whom we used to call "guests", on the eve of Shabat would always be invited for a Shabat meal. Considering the fact that our town's Jews were not particularly well off, my father, rest his soul, was known as a well off Jew, but he too needed loans for his business. People were always ready to give a helping hand, and a hand that was begging was never ignored. They would collect money for the brides and the weddings, Achnesad Kalah. For "Albushat Avyonim," meaning to cloth the "naked" and "Maot Chitim," to feed the poor. The money was collected for both the needy from Kurenets and outside of Kurenets. Most people happily gave, each one as he could afford, and some of them more than they could really afford. There was a Jew in Kurenets, a very respectable looking Jew, by the name of Lebim Nashesh. The essence of his existence was to give in secret "Matan Baseter." (So, the poor would not be embarrassed) Often during the winter, he would send a bag full of wood to one of the numerous homes whose residents could not afford buying them. Another righteous woman in our town was Zipah, the wife of Yashe leb Kramer, who knew every detail of the property of every family in town. Nothing would prevent her, not snow nor rain. She was always in a hurry collecting money for charity. One time for a Jewish girl whose time of marriage had arrived;" it's shameful to tell, but she didn't have any underwear to wear". Another time for young child who "reached the age to go to the Cheder, but he sits at home and cannot go study the Torah, since the winter is in its midst and he was still barefoot without any shoes." Another time for "a family who's breadwinner was sick and there was no income". Ever since I remember, my father was the Gabai of Gmilut Chesed, the charity institution. Since that was his job, I was able to experience the difficult financial situation that was occurring those days within the Jewish population. The rules of the institution were so that my father was allowed to lend money only if they gave collateral that had some monetary value. Many times, my father did not keep the rules and it was enough for him that they would just bring something symbolically. If someone would have asked those days to learn and investigate the Jewish economic situation in town, all he needed to do was to climb the ladder to our attic. There he would see a large inventory of the pounded town's possessions. Pots and pans, candle holders, silver spoons, books, hats, and copper containers. It was like a little supermarket. Father's assistant in his work was Abraham Eetzah the teacher, an old Jew, tall, but now from old age all bent. He had a white beard, and his face was very pale. He held in his hand a cane. He was the accountant and the payment collector. This duty was done every Friday in the afternoon when he was done with teaching in the Cheder. In small steps, leaning on his cane, he would enter our home prior to the blessing of the candles. From his pocket, he would take a small cloth bag. With his shaky hands, he would open the ties and, carefully, he would put on the table copper coins of different denominations and start sorting them into organized denominations. After he was done with organizing and counting, he would take from his religious bag a little blue notebook and, since his eyesight was poor, he would ask me to help him. With shaky lips he would read for me and I would write. Sheemunatah Detelah didn't give anything. He had no job. David, the shoemaker, didn't give anything, he had no penny. Or, sometimes, he would say the opposite. Sheemunatah Detelah is done with his loan and David, the shoemaker, paid so-and-so. This blue notebook had the answer to the question: why do the Jews in Kurenets immigrate to far away places. I remember many times a particular woman would come with her fur coat in her hand and beg my father. "Reb Eliyahu," and with embarrassed face she would continue, "The gentile came and gave me the fur coat for sewing but he didn't come to take it back so I didn't give anything to Abraham Eetzah. However, I must have the candleholders to bless the Shabbat. It would be too embarrassing if the neighbors saw me without them." She would clear the tears out of her eyes with her apron and continue. "Do me a big favor Reb Eliyahu, Get the candleholders and take the fur coat as collateral." So father would take her fur coat and bring it to the attic, and from there he would bring the candleholders. On Sunday, the woman would come and bring the candleholders for exchange. One time, Seepah, the wife of Yasha leb Kramer, came running to our house wearing a big kerchief on her head and boots on her feet. She was talking so fast that we could hardly understand what she was saying. She said something like, "Reb Eliyahu we must do something for Mooshah the daughter of Eetzah. She's already ready for marriage. The poor soul is an orphan from her mother. Now we find a Sheedech for her, but she is so poor and has nothing. Her dresses are patch on top of patch. Eetzeh Moshe taught three generations of men. You, yourself, studied with him. Now Yonkeleh, your son, is studying with him. Chesed must do something for her. The women are already doing a lot." While she was telling us that, she shook the coins in a kerchief. When she saw my mother, she jumped towards her and yelled, "Hadah!" then whispered something in her ear. Mother opened the closet where she kept her underwear. A few minutes later, Zeepah leaves our home with a little package. I ran after her and said, "Zeepah! Father sends a sixth small coin." And I gave her the coin that father gave me to buy some candy at Benyah's store. Zeepah understood that the small amount is not from father. She took the coin and pulled me toward her and kissed my forehead and ran off. Father didn't tell me how much the institution gave for Mooshah, but one thing I know not too long after, she was married.

Passover

What energy the women of the town put preparing for Passover! The poorest of them painted their homes by themselves and came to our house to take the paint. The wealthier homes would hire painters but this was not done hastily and simply. In our home, the painters were Stach and Yachmina, a Christian couple. They were average in height, with red noses and watery eyes from being perpetual drunks. The had a run-down house behind the bath-house near the big swamps. They were the town's goyim shel Shabbat. When they would come to work, The first thing we had to put for them was a bottle of wine and salty fish. "Hadah", they would say, "without a glass of wine our hands are paralyzed". After breakfast, they would mix the paint and start to paint the wall. To enter the room was a very scary proposition. If someone dared, he would come out of there covered by paint. They were not painting, they were spraying. "Stach," my mother would ask with a warm smile, "I ask you please to paint the walls, not the floor and windows." When Stach would hear mother's request, he would start laughing and answer, "Ha ha ha. Don't be worried Hadetzkah. We will make your house so so beautiful! And when your holy God will enter your house he will be so please that he will bless you and you bear another son! "(Stach knew a lot of the Jewish customs and knew that in Passover we opened the door, so as he could understand it we were opening it for God who was making a journey from house to house) The house would look like a battle zone. Tables and chairs would be moved. However, ultimately they would arrange things and then everything, all the tools and dishes would be washed. The matzahs in the guest room would be covered with white sheets, and I would hold a lit candle and father would hold a wooden spoon and a goose-feather. We would go window by window and Abbah would clear every gram of Chametz and would say, "Call Chameerah, the Eeshal Belshoodee." On the morning of the evening of Passover, we would get up very early. Since my father was his parents' oldest boy, every year he would do the Seeyum of the Maschitah. We would hurry to pray with the first minion. After the first prayer, we would drink Le Chaim in the synagogue and return home. When we would return, we would find that the last rooms were already prepared for Passover, and Emmah would not let any of us enter. At 10 am we would eat the last Chametz meal. Father would take the wooden spoon that was covered and tied and would burn the Chametz in a little oven would say, "Asher kidshanu bemitzvotav, vitzeevanu al beuoor Chametz." All the town's furnaces would be burning. According to the rules, the furnaces must be so hot that the rocks would glow red like fire and throw sparks. From every chimney, you could see smoke coming to the clear spring skies. The fear of fire was large, particularly in Smorgon Street, where there lived a thrifty misery Jew who never cleaned his chimney. The smoke that came from his chimney was somewhere between black and red. We are all in a hurry that day. We cleared the last dishes in the bathhouse, we took down the Passover dishes from the attic. Now, my mother gives me and my sister, Rocheleh, a new job, Lachtosh Misot, to fix the matzot. This is a difficult job, but I have no choice. Most of the work I have to do. My sister, Rocheleh, who is very tricky always managed to get away. She would say, "Yonkel, my stomach is hurting me awfully," and she would run to the yard. She would return to help for two minutes, then say, "Oh, my hand is tired. You do it Yonkel, in return I'll give you some nuts. I'm mixing and mixing and I'm so tired that I can't feel my hand." Dressed like noblemen, I in a new suit and my new shoes that are a little big for me, my mother put cotton in them, Father in his black and white suit we go to the synagogue. After the Mariv prayer, my father sends me to bring Saftah Gelkah Alperovich to the seder. Saftah Gelkah, tiny and skinny, her face full of deep lines, but her little eyes still sparkling with light, never seems to get old. I dearly loved my Saftah (grandma) Glekah. She always had a present for me. A cucumber from her garden, wild pears, and others. When I would come to Saftah, I would find her all dressed, shining in her black dress and jacket, I would take her to our home for the seder. Father sits at the head of the table, reclining on pillows. Next to the white pillow cases and the white tablecloth, my father would appear a little pale but his eagle eyes shined and his Hertzel beard had a few white hairs was all very groomed. And mother, it's a miracle, she worked so hard, when did she find time to get dressed and look so beautiful! Everything in the house is shiny and clean. The wine in the glasses seems to be winking in the light. Father reads Kalah Machelanah, I ask the four questions, and then we read the Hagadah. We eat and drink from the wine that warms the body. There is one thing that I was never able to do: steal the afikomen. I would watch my sister with seven eyes, but she would always be first and not only that, at the end she would mock me and point at me. The next day, Stach and Yachmeena would get rewards for the painting of the house. They would get the wine that we used for the 10 plagues and call it Makot. My little sister would say, "Stach, Mechnah, makot?" Stach would make a happy facial expression and would tell his wife, "Smatzah! Davie yashtah!" Each home in town had a seder. Many homes couldn't afford real wine and they would use another beverage, usually honey water. In houses that couldn't afford Cheft fish, they would eat the Yazga fish. Nevertheless, matzah was in every home and people would say the hagadah very intently. There was a story about one Jew in town, who came from the synagogue and saw the wine bottle on the table, couldn't wait for the seder and started drinking glass after glass. When his wife begged him to read a little from the hagadah, her drunken husband answered, "What is there to read? We all know that the Pharoh was son-of-a-gun" While I'm telling that story, I must tell the story of Abremel Einbender who, came to the synagogue the day after Passover limping and on his forehead he had a big bump. Everyone was wondering. It was known that Abemel was not a wild man, he would not touch a fly. And his wife, Yonah, is a peaceful person too. So how was he so injured? Mayeebel would not answer the questions but in Kurenets, you couldn't keep a secret and eventually we found out. Since he was a very devoted Lebabovitch Chasid, he had a tradition not to only tell the exit from Egypt, but to" live" the exit from Egypt. He would put a big pail full of water in his house. On his shoulder, he would put a big bag. Moreover, like the fathers of our fathers, he would quickly jump from one side of the pail to the other as if he was crossing the sea. However, that Seder was not a lucky one for him, and his foot fell into the pail and that was how he was hurt.

The first days of Passover the air is usually still, cool, but the sun is shining and the street shines in a golden light. The frost is gone from the windows, but you still see a few drops of shining water from the edges of the roofs. Birds fly in the blue skies. Everyone is dressed in holiday clothes, visiting each other, and the heart is full of hope.

Rosh Hashanah

The synagogues are completely filled since morning. Jews come dressed in white and the Shachareet prayer with the Chazan is very long. Then, they take the Torah out of the ark, and father starts reading with a special tune for Rosh Hashanah. Vedah Beched Etzkarah. After the reading, there is a short break. Then, Rav Noach and Israel Michael Hashochet go to the beema with their talit covering their faces. Moshe Baruch de Shamach hits the table with his hand as if he is warning the crowd. Israel Mechal, under is talit, is praying. Min chametz ebati yeal chamatee beah. He's not finished with the first sentence before everyone in the synagogue answers him and says the passage. When they are done, Reb Noach says quitely, "Shavareem tuat keeyah." I remember that one Rosh Hashanah, I was very sad during the Krieyot. I was reading one of the passages and there was a passage where you have to do it very slowly, carefully, not in one breath, and with great intention. I was not careful, and said it in one breath. That made me so scared that cold sweat came to my forehead. When they are done with the Keyot, they return the Torah to the ark and now it's time for Israel Icha the chazan to pray the Moosaf. Then, his helpers go to the steps that would take you to the ark. One would be Netkah, the son of David the hat maker, a small boy who has black eyes and pink cheeks; his voice is as beautiful as a nightengale. Then a few other kids go up. There is total quietness in the synagogue. Then enters Israel Shedrech dressed all in white. He whispers something to his assistants and they nod their heads in agreement. Then he gives a saying to Rasheb Mabarooch and hits his head on the table. His sweet singing is done in hushed tones "Hee nah nee hee nah nee." And the assistants help with the hum. Then, he will start much louder almost yelling, "I came here to beg for you! To beg for the nation of Israel." From the silence to the loud begging in such a short time, it leaves a huge impression on me. And not just on me, the child, but all the adults are shaking. Their eyes are tearful. Still today, many years later, I shake when I remember this moment.

Yom Kippur

The Meencha prayer on the evening of Yom Kippur was done very early. It was entertaining for me to see respectful Jews with their long beards lying on the floor like cheder boys and the very short Moshe Baruch the Shamas would hit them with a whip to clear their sins. In our house, we would eat our Harucha Mafseket, the meal before the fast, when the sun was still high in the sky. Father would change his clothes and my oldest sisters would wash the dishes. Mother would bless the little children, who were my sister, Rochaleh, and I. When she ended the blessing, she would hug us. She will tell me, "Nu, shanah tovah, my only son. May you grow, my son, healthy and complete and be a good Jew. And may I be blessed so that I can bring you to the Hoopah and have the pleasure to see you grow and become a man, my dear one." Then we will go, my sister Rochaeleh and I, to Saftah Hinda to bless her with… Safta (grandma) Hinda was skinny and bent, she was light and pale and her eyes would be shining with tears of excitement. She would come to close, kiss us and bless us. "Shenah tovah my grandchildren. I so hope that I will be able to be at your weddings. Then I will dance like a young girl."

Eltkah nee Perski with Husband, Eetzah Rabunski

Uncle Eetza Rabunski, tall and strong, his face is fresh and his blue eyes are smart and peaceful. Usually he sits with no kippah on his head. Now he sits with a hat. Next to him sits his young wife, Aunt Eltkah nee Perski (sister to Shimon Peres' father), a very pretty woman with a turned up nose and a beautiful smile. They would hug us and kiss us. I remember one time, when I was ready to leave, my uncle, the brother of my mother, Eetzah Rabunski, said with a smile on his face, "Yonkel did you ever hear how the Russian czar would say Kol Nedre?" I looked at him wondering what the Russian czar had with Kol Nedre ? Then Uncle Eetzah takes out a newspaper that is published in Vilnah and starts singing while reading it in the tune of Kol Nedre. "Kol Nedre, all the promises that I gave concerning the constitution and all the rules that I made prohibiting the hurt of Jews, all of them are canceled. Vosh chelim velot chenin. All my promises our worth nothing. Nadrana voderee nashtanah otmaot. All that I swore with my life is worth as much as a bark of a wild dog." And, while laughing he continues, "Yonkel, remember that tomorrow in your prayer you must ask that the czar, the Vilnah governor, and all the helpers will be brought to a strange death." Aunt Eltkah nee Perski laughed, but Safta Hinda is mad at the lightheartedness and the joking on the evening of Yom Kippur.

The synagogue is full. Everywhere there are containers full of sand and in them there are big candles, medium candles, and small candles. Candles everywhere. They don't wear shoes, they wear _____. Israel Eetzah his assistant and his choir start with Kol Nedre. After the prayer, many Jews stay in the synagogue. Some say preteen. Some Jews stay all night in the synagogue, they just lie for a short time on the tough benches and then return to the prayer.

The Day of Yom Kippur

The sun had just risen. The ground and the grass in the fields were all wet from the morning dew, and there was the mist of early autumn. If Rosh Hashanah appeared as a storm in the synagogue, the day of Yom Kippur seemed like an earthquake. People would pray with their hearts filled with pain. Their lips would move, sometimes in whispers, sometimes in screams of angst. Pity us! Don't discard us now that we have reached old age! The people who came for the prayer of Shah harit would read from the Bible, and Israel Itzha would pray "Musaf". Jews would sway back and forth with fervor, and then they would stand for the prayer of Shmona-Esreh (18). They would beat their fists against the tablets of their hearts (on their breast) for all their sins, and then Leibe Masha's would approach the Ark and bang the table and all the congregation would stand up and say, "Venatna tokef kadushat hayyom…"

The impression that the Jewish congregation left on me as a child was unforgettable. The way they swayed and shook, and the way their voices cracked when praying in ways that would break your heart. " Hayyom norah veh ayom. Ke lo yizkor, beh eneha badim…" (The day is horrible and frightening since they will not receive justice in your eyes). But even deeper and more powerful than that was the impression left in me from the minutes when the entire congregation stood as if frozen without the slightest movement at the moment when Israel Itzha who was the messenger of the congregation and his helpers, would start with Berosh Hashanah Yikatvun (In Rosh Hashanah they will be inscribed). He would stand with his eyes looking skyward, and he would spread his arms upward to the sky, and the sleeves of the kitl which were very wide, made him look like a miraculous bird that was flapping its wings, saying, "Mi l'chaim ou mi l'mavet?" (who is to live and who is to die?). His assistant, in a soft, splendid and clear voice, was joined by other singers whose faces became red from the task. They would sing "Beyom, tsom kippur yakhtemun" (In the day of the fast of Yom Kippur, it will be signed).

From the other area, where the women sat, came down voices and cries that would quickly spread throughout the entire synagogue. I would recognize the voice of Sarah Rifka, the wife of Yekutiel Meir Ha-Cohen Kramer, and truthfully Sarah Rifka had a good reason to cry: not only did they have difficulties in eking a living, but in their house grew up a blind child (David) that the physicians had not been able to cure. Everyone's heart would cry when we would watch how they helped him walk to the synagogue. " Mi bekitzor, mi lobektizor?" (Who is at the end of his days? And who is not at the end of his days?) cried Israel Itzha and the entire congregation would join in crying with him. After this prayer I would watch my father and would see that although he was usually not among the sentimental people, he would also weep, and surreptitiously wipe his eyes with a kerchief.

Many hours would pass, the sun would set in the evening in the west. From the windows you could see the sun's last rays of autumn, and soon you knew that her light would vanish. The colors of the sky would shift at dusk, from blues to reds… Pale fogs would envelope the forest behind Kosita Street. On the train tracks, a loud, fast train would go in the direction of Vileyka. The engine car would billow out smoke and small, fiery explosions. Then you would hear a loud whistle that would shake the heavens! This sound was foreign to the holy atmosphere of the gut-wrenching prayers of the faithful soul-searchers. The synagogue would be shadowed by painful and depressing blackness, only a few little candles would still be flickering in the containers in the sand. The Hazan's voice would already be strained, and the congregation of prayers would be exhausted from both the fast and the emotional prayers. But in the sky, the first stars would appear, and a loud announcement would be made for, "Next year in Jerusalem!" Then Israel Mikhail would blow the shofar loudly. In this darkness it seemed as if a little flicker of hope would be sparked. Everyone seemed to be uplifted and Jews would bless one another for a good year.

Pinya, who sold iron goods, did his entire prayer all the way from early in the morning while standing and he did not sit down for even one second, would start singing with great excitement a tune of Lubavitch Hasids, and many would join him. "In the mercy of our father in the heavens, we overcame Satan the Executioner, may we soon be blessed to hear the sound of the shofar announcing the coming of the Messiah!" Now people would pray, more comforted, the prayer of Maariv. Even when the Maariv prayer was all done, people in the congregation were in no hurry. They would step outside to bless the moon, renewing it. Old Jews would start jumping as if they were little children, babies ready to go to their first cheder, saying to each other, "Shalom aleihem, shalom aleihem, shalom" whiile pointing to different congregation members, being in no hurry to return home.

Kurenets youth celebrating

Simha Torah

Hosheana Raba. Also during that day, the soul would shake for the end of the signing of the good name. Although we didn't wear the white kitls, and no one heard those heartbreaking prayers, and the day seemed to have had some of the excitement of Simha Torah, still it seemed like the synagogues would be filled with all the old Jews and some young children, and everyone would say passages from Psalms. About every two hours they would stop the prayer for a certain period of time, and Shimon Itzha (or Shimon, son of Itzhak) would pass around from one Jew to the next, a basket filled with an apple, and each one would take an apple treat. During the night of Hosheana Raba I would gather all my might and energy so I could ward off any drowsiness since I wanted so eagerly to see that moment where I was told that the heavens would open and the angels would come down, carrying notes for the end of the good signing (Hatima Tova). They would fly to put the notes in the different homes of the people of Israel. It seems like I never could stay awake to reach that moment. I would always be caught in moments of drowsiness and when I would finally awake, I would see that light had come and morning had arrived.

During Simha Torah it seems as though all the Jews of Kurenets were drunk with happiness. Everywhere you saw faces filled with delight. It was the happiness of devotion and the fervor of respect for the Torah. Leibe Masha's would buy attar arait ladaat, and he would transfer some of the passages to his neighbors and comrades who sat on the eastern wall of the synagogue. The synagogue would be filled with young boys and girls who carried flags in their hands. People would be invited to join and everyone would join in the beautiful tunes from the Lubavitch Hasids. The people who would lead the singing would be Pinya the iron goods merchant, Shimon Itzha's, and Moshe the forester. The Jews would gather in circles and start dancing to show their love and devotion to the Torah. Handel, the butcher, would carry a kerchief in his hand, lift it in the air and make round motions with it to encourage everyone to dance with fervor. My very old Rabbi, Itzha Meir, would gather around him all his students and filled with happiness he would yell to us, "Tzon g'dushim!" (A flock of holies!). And we, the children, upon hearing such a reverent description of us coming from our rabbi, had to prove that this description of us was not unwarranted, so we would imitate the sounds of different farm animals like sheep and goats, making loud baas and moos, etc.

Particularly memorable in my psyche was the day of Simha Torah of the year 1913. It could be that it was so memorable for me because it was the last Simha Torah where I truly felt happy. At that point in my life I was already studying Masahet Tuvot and I felt that I was too mature to hold the flag as all the other children did. I stood there listening to how they would give the more respected people of the community the hakafot (a special ceremony), and I heard Reb Yekutiel Meir Ha- (Kramer) was honored with akafa to honor the Torah, and Reb Shimon, son of Reb Itzhak was honored. Then Rav Eliyau son of Rav Pesach (Alperovich), my father, was honored with hakafa for the honor of the Torah. Then all of a sudden… Hakhatan Yaakov ben Rav Eliyau was honored with hakafa for the honor of the Torah.

My mind became confused. Could it be? Could it really be? My father took me in his arms and looked at me, filled with love and said, "Yes, yes my son, they are talking about you." They didn't give me a big Torah. They took out of the ark a smaller Torah, and I was blessed to be holding it and carrying it around. The eyes of all the other children were centered on me. And who could have imagined my excitement at that moment?

During that holy day, Meir the husband of Leah Etkah (they had the only two-story home in Kurenets), was the Hatan Torah. My father was the Hatan Beirashit. After the Filah of Musaf, my father asked all of his friends to come to our home for a kiddush. Shimon Itzha's, who was always in a good mood, now was in a state of much multiplied happiness, since he was aided by the large amount of wine he had drank at that point. He shook his fists on the table and yelled to my mother, "Chada, bring all your treasures to the table! Today is the day of Simha Torah!" Then mother would bring wine and all sorts of cakes, sweets, and all other sorts of baked goods. While mother would keep bringing things from the oven, Shimon Itzha sang, "Sesu yehudim, rigdu hasidim. Halalu vehodu leboreh. Paitya yivorksi l'chaim. Svodanya Simha Torah. Nash bokh, adin bokh. Ein keilenu, ein keadonenu. Altira avdia kov der lubavitcher zan laban shotoy agenalenu." (very roughly interpreted: Sing, Jews! Dance Hasids! Praise and thank the Creator! – then a toast in Russian and in Hebrew: Happy Simha Torah! No one is like our God, our keeper. Don't be fearful, the servants of Yakov, because of the beloved Lubavitcher we will be protected.)

Mother brought to the table a kugel, and all the guests would excitedly devoured and praised her cooking. Then, out of the blue, Leah Etka's, who was Hatan Beirashit, said to my father, "Reb Eliyau, I must admit that maybe in the Gmara you are more accomplished than I am, but as far as filling the heart with excitement for the Torah, here my ability is greater than yours." And my father answered him, with his eyelids heavy and his eyes foggy, "In my nature I am not a true hero when it comes to wine drinking, but if you are talking about respecting the Torah, surely I am not going to be in second place." And Shimon Itzha, when hearing this argument, started yelling, "Let's see now, amongst the three of us who is the true hero!" And the whole vent event ended when the two Hatans and even the third competitor held their heads in their hands and were sighing with exhaustion.

The next day, my father walked around with a pale face and a huge headache. His face was a little embarrassed, but we all knew that it was only for the honor of the Torah that he went overboard.

The Teacher

And here I see you, my little town, one autumn, gloomy and bent from heavy rains and winds. It is as if your homes had huddled together as if fearing some ominous signs. All the holy days have passed, and now came days when the children would fill the time with Torah studies and they would always be running through the streets, holding Gmara books. The children would run to different areas of town, but still it was as if one thin rope went through Myadel Street to the house of Hinda Leah. On one particular day that autumn, all the children, amongst them myself, went to a new cheder. It was a new Rabbi who came to town. His first name was Ben-Zion and his last name Meirovich. His first and last names were very unfamiliar to those of us in our town, a town that didn't use last names. Will he be difficult or will he be easy? Will he beat us as the rest of the melameds used to? Maybe he will beat us even more severely?

As soon as we reached the little house, we started feeling more comfortable. At the entrance stood Hinda Leah, who leased her home to now be a cheder. She was a middle-aged woman of average height, with a face covered by wrinkles, but her blue eyes were very mischievous and happy. With a sweet smile she greeted us, saying, "Bokotov (Good morning), enter children, enter. Does anyone want a glass of milk? Don't be shy. Accept the milk as for your health and for my mitzvah (good deeds)." Hinda Leah, whose dress was very neat and tidy, wore a white apron on top of her dress. Her house itself was meticulously cleaned, and every corner seemed to be shining. Every pot and pan was so clean that could see your image as if you were looking at a mirror.

And here entered the rabbi. As soon as I saw him I breathed a sigh of relief. He was a small person but stood erect and strong. His face was pale with a serious and spiritual expression. His eyebrows were thick and under them there were dark blue eyes that were gave a very piercing look. He had a straight nose that was a little bit wide, and his brown beard was cut neatly and short, unlike the other melameds with long beards. The way he was dressed was very different from the other melameds had dressed. On his head he had a kipa made of velvet. He wore a black jacket that was open, and underneath you could see a sweater. He had a pocket watch with a silver chain. On his feet there were very shiny shoes. After he tested the students and divided them into different classes based on their knowledge, he started explaining to us the method and content of his teachings. Other than Humash and the rest of the Bible and the Gmara, we would also now study grammar according to the Hebrew method devised by Krinsky. We would also learn how to write essays in Hebrew, and from now on the children would have to do homework the way they did it in a regular school.

After he ended telling us what would be the content of the school year, he said to us, "Children, don't call me rabbi, call me teacher. And from this day on we will speak Hebrew." For some of the children in town, this cheder presented the beginning of their salvation. Weeks passed, and from all the children who attended this cheder, there came not a single cry. There was no hitting or spanking. If someone was not paying attention or had done poorly in his work, the biggest punishment was when our teacher would say with almost closed mouth, "Speak to the trees and the rocks." But since he said that very quietly and in Hebrew, it seemed as if the sting was taken out of it and it sounded to us more entertaining than punishing.

The street became shining white, frost covered everything. The snow would pile up and the windows would be covered with the flowers of winter frost, and icicles would dangle from the roofs. On that day I walked from a wintry Myadel Street to the cheder. My spirit was excited and yet at the same time very nervous. It was the first of the month and our teacher had a certain system where every first of the month he would test us to see how well we had retained during the month that had passed. Although I sat til late night hours, past midnight, studying, I was still nervous. While I was studying the night before, a few times my mother went down from where she was sleeping and she hugged my head in her warm hands, and looked into my eyes, saying to me, "Go my child, and lie down. The night is very cold and you could get a cold, God forbid."

Although I was known as having an excellent memory and I retained everything that I studied, but who is smart enough to know beforehand what sorts of land mines the teacher would put on the road for me? I entered the cheder and the floor was just washed and the room was filled with life-saving warmth. There were smells of kamon and fresh bread filling the air. There were already some boys sitting with dark faces that seemed filled with fear of the day of judgment. At that point, the teacher had already tested some of the children and there were a few who failed. I sat there and my eyes wandered about the room, and then my eyes fell on Hinda Leah. She sat on a chair near the wall of the furnace and by her feet stood a white kitten who was dotted by black spots and he licked with his pink tongue milk from a plate. The cat finished licking and his face had a pleading expression. He started quiet meowing, as if saying, "My lady Hinda Leah who is full of mercy, please let me sit on your lap." Hinda Leah said, " Sit already, you wild one! Sit here and be quiet. The children are busying themselves with the Torah." So the cat sat on her lap and Hinda Leah petted him. He closed his eyes and looked so content. And I, watching the cat, felt almost hypnotized. My head fell, and my eyelids got heavy, as if I was about to fall asleep. I was so tired from studying until the late hours. I was awakened by the elbow of my friend Berl Garfinkel, the son of Fega the daughter of Henia.

Berl was the best student in the entire cheder. He was pale and skinny, and had small eyes that were full of excitement. His neck was very long and narrow. He was a quiet boy and very God-fearing. "Yankel," he said as he pushed me. " The teacher."

As if I was sprinkled with cold water, I woke up from my sleep and I heard someone saying, "Stand in front of the teacher."

I stood in front and answered the questions about grammar, "Rahatz, Rahatzta, Rahatzt, Rahatzu, Rahatztem, Rahatzten." He washed, you washed (male), you washed (female), they washed, you (plural) washed (male), you (plural) washed (female). His questions pierced me as if they were arrows from a very competent archer's bow.

"Shvanach, shvana. Hey ashelah, vehey hayadia. Vav hamehapeach, meatid, leavar…" and other obscure questions in Hebrew grammar.

My memory that was already very clear now came to my assistance. It didn't betray me and I stood in honorable standing in this stormy test and answered all the questions. The face of the teacher lit up with pride and contentment. A big smile filled up his face. His dark blue eyes sprinkled and were filled with warmth and affection. He was so filled with excitement and happiness that he started rubbing his hands and words of praise and exaltation came out of his mouth. "Very good, very good!" he said. "You are truly outstanding! Who will give it that all my students can be like you?"

It seemed that from that day on there was some kind of union established between my teacher and I. It was a union of friendship and care that I still feel until today. He was not just a teacher, he was my friend. In his presence, difficult days became pleasant. What he taught me filled us with excitement and made us wait with great anticipation for the next lesson. The way I looked at him was with a mix of admiration and love. To me he was like the big Cohen who came to the holy ark, and his abundance of patience made him like a father who has only one son. He was never tired of explaining and making things clear to us. When he wanted us to learn about things that were very theoretical and on a high level, he would use simple words to bring it down to our level. Things that were very deep he would bring to the surface with simple expressions, and even very complicated passages from the sea of the Talmud or from the gardens of the Bible became clear and attainable for us. What was especially amazing was his revolutionary attempt for that time (the beginning of the 1900s) to have designated hours to talk with the students about the history of the nation and about things that were happening at the time, as well as conversations about well known personalities in Judaism. Sometimes when we were busy with a Talmudic passage like Zeh babekado, xeh nabekorto, Venishbar kado shel zeh bekorto shel zeh. The tune of the gmara would be filling the room, flowing from one wall to the other. Zeh babekado, zeh nabekorto, venishbar kado shel zeh bekorto shel zeh…

And we just finished reading it and the teacher said, "Children, now close your books and I will tell you a chapter from the history of our nation." Outside there would be frost, and if the door would open a white cloud of steam would appear. We inside were so pleased with the warmth, and the blustering wind would be heard howling from the chimney. We sat there with great anticipation. Even Hinda Leah, the owner of the apartment, sat there filled with anticipation. And now the teacher would start speaking Yiddish so all the children would understand. He opened for us large, rolled scrolls with the history of the Jewish nation, about geniuses and tzadiks that in older days were filled with modesty and good deeds. They were filled with holiness and dedication. It was as if they became alive in front of us. Images of Yehudah, Hannesi, Harambam, and Rashi came to us, all well known Hasidic Jews. He would read poems and we would sit very close to one another and it was as if our hearts would be in the east, while we were far in the west.

While we talked like this it seemed all that split us as students and teacher would disappear and we became a group of comrades that had one vision that captured everyone's hearts. Tales of the heroes of Israel and the Jewish daughters who were brought to Rome as hostages and were thrown to the lions in the Colosseum in front of thousands of spectators. And here, caught in the jaws of the lions, met once again the bride and the groom. The wonder of the meeting of their spirits was stronger than the pain of their tortures and death, and here their pure souls left the world with light and love. In a deep, shaky voice, accompanied by the quiet cry of Hinda Leah, the teacher would conclude his story with the passage, "The pleasant and the beloved, together in their lives and in their death."

Sometimes he would tell stories of the martyrs and others who were killed for their religious beliefs. He would see the children who stopped reading and were reduced to short, shallow breaths, their eyes filled with tears, and he would add, " My dear, you must bless yourself and God that we do not live in such bloody times. The flames of the Inquisition were extinguished and will never again be rekindled…"

And who could ever imagine that the times to come would bring a dark Inquisition that would pass by this little room here on Myadel Street. The entire holy community of Kurenets, old, babies, women and children, and amongst them our old teacher, would pass by this room to be taken to their last moments.

Farewell

– Years passed and I experienced many, many hardships – the first World War with all its horrors and disasters – my beloved sister Rochaleh passed away we did all that possible to save her from the death sentence – to no avail. We brought her the best specialists we could find and then my father called three rabbis and this Beit Din of the Living brought their words as a scroll that was signed by witnesses that my father transfers all the years of his life to his daughter Rochaleh. In the synagogue, another name was added to her name, the name Chaia, which means "alive". Fathered hired minyans of Jewish people and they sat days and nights saying passages from Psalms. We went to all the graves of our relatives in the cemetery, and we cried and begged them that they should ask for pity for her in front of the Chair of the Holy. But her fate was not to be changed…

Not many days passed, and next to the fresh grave of my sister Rochaleh, another mound was created. The grave of our wonderful, beloved mother. A bundle of tears choked my throat when I announced in a pitiful, hoarse voice, bitter passages of farewell. "Yit gadal, viyit kadash, shmaya raba…"

A year passed, and in one gray, wintry day, I stood in shock in the cemetery and in horrible fear I saw how Meir Raphael from Chevre Kaddisha (a burial society) put dust on the eyes of my father and covered the grave…

The shining face of our home forever changed – poverty, starvation, being orphaned, and dark depression. At that point there were many epidemics spreading in town, and there was widespread poverty. Our house, which usually was quite lively and had many visitors, now became very desolate. Only a few of my friends still came, amongst them Velvel the son of Basha, and Meir [Gurevich, grandfather of the translator] the son of Frada. Only they would come to visit, and very few of the adults would enter.

Meir Gurevich, friend of the author

But there was one adult who didn't forget me and visited me often. Now, so many years later, when I write these passages, I will see in my spiritual eyes how the door opens and in a cloud of white frost, my former teacher enters the home. His jacket is old and tattered, and his face is red from the cold. He looks at me with his eyes filled care and love and while he rubs his hands to warm himself, he says, "Ah, ah, how cold it is! It is so cold that it is a true Siberia! Yankeleh you must make some tea so that we can warm our dry bones."

I immediately prepared tea and a few pastries made from wheat flour. The pastries were hard, so we sat there dipping them in the tea, and while we drank the tea we started the conversation that many times would last until the very late hours. We discussed many, many subjects, amongst them issues of daily survival, and sometimes lofty subjects like the Kabbalah, Hasidic history, the Enlightenment movement, the Chibat Zion, or literary questions of classical books, conversations and also debates, but all done with love and in a very sophisticated manner. And this, our fresh conversation, helped me a lot to assuage my loneliness and forget my bitter fate…

All of a sudden, like the stories of the 1001 Nights fairy tales, it happened. One morning, a Jew wearing a straw hat and a shiny checkered jacket, with shoes with sharp points, entered our home and asked if this was where the orphans of Eliyau son of Pesach lived. When we confirmed it he said that he had visas for us to go to the US. [Many years before, the oldest sister left the home for America without the permission of her father, though she did receive help from her mother – information from the daughter of Yakov Alpert.] Our house became like a main train station. There was lots of activity, people came to advise us. Amongst them was a native of our town, Motl Leib Kuperstock, a chubby, jovial Jew with a short, neatly groomed beard. He helped me to arrange and tie my belongings. We used heavy rope to neatly tie the pillows and the linens and the covers, and while we were doing this he told me stories about America, the Land of Plenty, where he had lived for a few years. He said, "There I didn't eat any simple fish that we call here yazga, or the dish we call zatzirka. There they will serve on the table pies filled with roasted meat. There I would eat bowls filled to the top with cheese and dip them in sour cream."

Men and women would come in and out. Here my mother's velvet jacket was sold, her dresses and jacket were sold, among them her green vest that I loved so much to see her wear. Towels, underwear, plates and kitchen utensils, all sold very fast. There were only three things that I refused to sell. One was the shabbat tzordot that belonged to my father. This I will give to our neighbor, the best friend of my father, Yekutiel Meir Kramer. Their friendship was so deep that shortly after father died, when Yekutiel Meir had the wedding of his daughter, everyone saw that amongst the chairs standing at the head table, there was one chair that was empty. When people asked why the chair was empty at the best table, he explained, "This is the chair for Eliyau, son of Pesach, of blessed memory, that was my soul friend. I am sure that his soul is hovering around this room to see me in this happy day… And this chair is for him alone."

The second thing that I kept was the tfillim of father. The person who wrote this tfillim was a god-fearing Jew, a very honest man. The man wrote them while he was fasting and dipping, and now they were inside a black velvet pouch that had embroidered on it a Jewish star. This container appeared to me as if it was mourning the person who owned them and loved them as his soul.

The third thing that I kept was my father's books, which were contained in a small black bookcase. Those two things I would give to my teacher, my friend. I took the books, amongst them Mousar books that had shiny, silky bookmarks that my mother had put there so she would know the last page she had read. They were Gmara books and Midrash books, and their pages were yellow from all the years. They were dotted with wax stains, witness to the nights spent studying by candlelight. All of these I neatly put in a big tablecloth that was embroidered with blue flowers, and like this, with two loads, the books and the tfillim, I stood in front of my teacher.

"Moreh," [teacher] I said to him as I was formerly called him, "I wish you will accept from me as a memory these books and the tfillim of my father, and also this little bookcase…"

For one minute he stood before me, quietly, as if he was trying to contain the internal excitement he was feeling, and then he lifted his wet eyes and looked at me and said, "I am very thankful and I am very appreciative with you Yankeleh… but still I think it would be better if you gave the books to the synagogue so that Jews will be able to learn from them. The bookcase, I think, would best serve the minyan of Tiff Eret Bachurim that Israel Mikhail the shohet established. There it could be used as a pillar in front of the holy ark, and it would also be a memorial to the soul of your father, a very honest Jew who searched the truth, was always chasing justice, and very involved in public charity, and not to receive any awards.

"The books Kav Hayashar and Menorat Hama'or I will take for my wife Pela. Also, I will take from you the tfillim and Machzor of Yom Kippur…"

I accepted the advice of my teacher and did as he suggested…

The horses are harnessed and in the carriage the entire luggage followed, some in bundles, some in suitcases. I was dressed in my travel clothes. Standing in my home, saying goodbye to all the corners in the house where a Jewish family grew until it was cut by the storm of the days. I entered our factory, our business of making sodas and other beverages. It seemed to me like the copper containers and the copper tools were whistling to me. They were calling me by name and begging me not to leave. " Where are you going, Yankel? Where? Stay here, don't leave us. We will take care of your earnings as we took care of your father. Stay here and marry the girl you love, and we will be your shelter and your protector…"

The house is filled with relatives, neighbors, and friends. Many kissed me and blessed me with happiness and good luck. My eyes kept running through the room, looking for the one who was not there, my old teacher. But without a doubt I knew he would come to say goodbye… And here he came to me, in his hands he took my hands and looked straight into my eyes and said things about the spirit, the Torah, and belief in God, the strongest fortress that will guide me and preserve me during times of depression and sadness. He told me that treasures of gold and silver would not bring me any security. I must remember the passage that I had learned, "Hashlech al adonai yehavha, vehu yekalkelka… [Put your trust in God and he will protect you and take care of your needs.] And you remember, my dear, that in God is the key to happiness." He held my head in his hands. I felt his tears in my cheek. He kissed me a fatherly kiss and then I heard his last words that were aid with a shaky voice, " Yevarchecha, adonai, veyish mercha…." [God will bless you and keep an eye on you]

… Tell me, a flying flock, where am I going…? Tell me, the waves of the sea, where will my spirit sail to…?

The iron train cars passed swiftly through the dark nights… A ship tosses at the heart of the sea… Huge metropolises, Towers of Babel colored in multiple lights, filled with life and energy, passed around me… Years… years… years… And amongst all this, still alive and will be alive as the day it happened, the picture of the farewell and the blessing that was accompanied by a tear and a shake, "Yevarchecha, adonai, veyish mercha…Yevarchecha, adonai, veyish mercha… Yevarchecha, adonai, veyish mercha…"

Sabina and Aharon Meirovitch, 1937

Family members of Yaakov Alpert's beloved teacher, Ben Zion Meirovich

[Pages 74-80]

Impressions

by Alter Zimmerman

Translated by Eilat Gordin Levitan

Reuven der Maliskai

I studied in many cheders with various melameds during my childhood. At one melamed I studied for two periods of time, at another for three periods, but of all of them, the one who left the greatest imprint on my memory was a melamed who I spent only four months with. It was Reuven der Maliskai in other words Reuven der Malisker as he was known amongst the local population. Already from his appearance you could see he was very special and bore no resemblance to the other melameds.

He was a chubby Jew of average height with a short beard. His face was full and serious. His thick hair was sprinkled with gray, and he was about 60 years old. He was extremely clean and orderly. Reuven der Malisker was also very much a perfectionist. In the pocket of his vest he had a pocket watch attached to a chain that also held a small key. Every day without fail he would pray with the second minyan in the old synagogue where he had a permanent place near the coveted eastern wall. He had very regular habits. At first when he came to the synagogue he would open up the cover of the bench to check what was inside, and then he would take his scarf off his neck and very neatly fold it in a most perfect manner. Then he would take off his snow boots. When I try to remember, I am almost sure that sixty years ago [this was written in the 1950s] there were no rubber galoshes in Kurenets, and for the first time that I saw them, Reuven der Maliskai was wearing them. His galoshes were worn on top of short boots made of soft leather. At that point he would take out the shtender [?] and with it he would go check the clock in the big synagogue that was preserved in a special cabinet. He would go up and would pull on the weights in the clock. He would make a special point to check the time against his pocket watch to make sure that it was accurate and then he would adjust it if it was not. And this job he did daily. My heart is absolutely sure that a more accurate watch than Reuven der Malisker's did not exist in Kurenets in those days.

His treatment of his students was very attentive and demanding, but he would never raise his arm to spank them. In spite of this, the children would always listen to him and treated him with respect and good manners. Only four months I studied in his cheder, and at the beginning of the fifth month I became sick. It was during the winter, so at that point I finished my studies with him.

During the first day of my illness, it was clear that I was extremely feverish, but thermometers were very uncommon in these days and we could not get a hold of one. Anyway, I was given a lot of tea to drink with red berries, malinas, that supposedly had a special healing effect that would bring a sick person to the point of sweating. When all of these remedies didn't help, the next choice was to call Baruch the medic.

On the second day of my illness, on the way to the synagogue, my Rabbi, Reuven der Malisker came to my house. Since he found out that I was sick he decided to check on my situation. He took off his coat and patiently took off his scarf, and then he ordered me to sit down and to my very weak back he put his heavy head and started checking my breathing. "Breathe stronger, much stronger. Hold your breath. Deeper, deeper." He checked me from the right to the left and back, and then he took my wrist and held it with his fingers, and with his other hand he took his watch, and while looking at it he kept counting quietly. The watch was so near me that I became excited from seeing it so close to me. After he finished his check, he took out of his pocket a piece of white paper and folded it in a very exact manner in four equal folds. He then cut one fourth of the paper and took out a very, very narrow pencil and wrote something. But the letters that he wrote were not Hebrew letters, and were unfamiliar to me. He gave instructions that someone should go to the pharmacy and buy this medicine, and I should drink from it three times a day, after eating. He stood up and put his scarf on his neck, took his coat and put it on and left.

There were other visitors in our house during that event and one of them who knew how to read Russian looked at the paper and announced, "This is impossible to read. I am very doubtful that a pharmacist will be able to read what he wrote." However, miracle of miracles, the pharmacist knew how to read it and understood it, and gave me medicine according to what was written. Many days later I found out that Reuven der Malisker knew how to write Latin. Truth be told, shortly after I felt much better, but I was still coughing, so when the Rabbi came to check me again, he suggested I drink milk and honey, and further he suggested, "Since this winter is very blustery, and it's already near Purim, it's not a good idea to send the boy to the cheder until after Passover."

But when Passover ended I didn't go back to his room since my parents decided to send me to a Talmud Torah yeshiva. Many, many years passed from that day, but until today, when I remember Reuven der Malisker I get the sense that I am a sick boy and my back is weak as it was then, and I feel the heavy head of my healer, my rabbi.

Library and a Play

I think fifty years ago [ca. 1900], Kurenets was one of the only shtetls in the area that had a library. However, this was a small library and was established in secrecy… Don't you assume that this was done out of fear of the religious conservatives of the older generation. Most of the population of the Hasidic shtetl were Chabad Hasids, and Chabad stands for Chokhma Bina Da'at. [Knowledge, Wisdom, Intelligence?] It is true that in the town there was a spirit of knowledge and intelligence. It was a pleasant spirit and there was no break in it in the shtetl. When the old generation, as we called them, saw us straying off the path would respond with a sigh but not with fanaticism. So if I said before that the library was underground, it was there only because of fear of the civil authorities, since if we would have come during those days to the Natzalstevo to get a permit for a library, they would surely conclude that the youth of Kurenets was caught up in the wave of Revolution… So for that reason, the bookshelf was constantly on the move from one house to the next. If anyone would raise the suspicion that Uriyadnik had found out about it, or that someone in the Pristavo were informed about the existence of a library, in the middle of the night the devout founders would take the bookshelf to a new location. How beloved and dear was this library! It was like a favorite child, a small only child in front of his mother, and anyone who would exchange books would do it in a most careful way, secretly, so that no buttoned person would see them, God forbid…

And this was the way it was until the year 1906. At that point, there seemed to be some change. Days of temporary and relative openness, and now the library received a permit to operate legally and openly. Now the books would be exchanged in public with no fear. But at that moment we were faced with a new question to solve, and this was also a very important question. As we didn't have to hide the library or keep it small, we wanted to enrich it and to purchase new books. From the amount of money that was received from the membership dues there was no chance to purchase books, so at that point someone suggested that we put on a play and all the proceeds would go directly for this purpose. For myself, during those days, I moved to Vilna and had a job there. I was also a member in the dramatic club Hazamir, which means the Nightingale. In this club, many well-known authors were members, amongst them Numberg who was the head of the club and the writer Anakhi was the secretary. S. Nigal would read his essays, and Peretz Hirshbein would rehearse with us his plays. And Shalom Ash would read to us many times his manuscripts before publishing them.

One summer, when I came home from vacation, all the young people, my friends kept bugging me that I, and only I, would be the man to do it, meaning that I should be the director and I should produce a play to benefit the library that needed to be enlarged. So everyone gathered together and I suggested that we should perform a play by Peretz Hirshbein since I was very familiar with all the characters of this play, and since we already worked with Hirshbein and he instructed us on how to perform it. To my surprise, my friends were not agreeable to my suggestion. The one who was most against it was Nashkaleh Tsipa's, meaning Nathan the son of Tsipa. He was my childhood friend, the same age as me, and he gave me his reasons in very clear messages that a play by Yakov Gordin would be much better understood and be more suitable for the audience that came from the community of Kurenets. An argument ensued but Nashkaleh won and we performed the play by Gordin…

The short of it was that the town became quite excited by the theater and actors were chosen, roles were assigned. We leased the big barn that belonged to Yuda Zusia's Alperovich. We cleaned it diligently and with much excitement and devotion we worked on the play. From a nearby forest we brought branches of fir trees and pine trees and put them on the walls, an on top of the barn's dirt we put down yellow sand. We went to every house and asked to borrow benches and this became a fancy theater. It was fancy and very decorated. Such high style decorations were not known before in Kurenets, and our hearts were filled with wonders and excitement. Now our town was not an out-of-the-way backwoods shtetl. At this point we were becoming more and more residents of the big enlightened world. We even built a stage from wood and a little booth for the soplio [someone to whisper lines to the actors if they forget them]. I am almost sure that during the original opening night of the theater in our town there was not one town resident who stayed home. Many sat inside the theater but even more of them were outside, at the entrance, or by the walls looking for a little crack or hole to peek in and see what a theater was like. The level of performance or the excellence of the play was not at all important at that moment. What mattered was that the actors did their jobs with honesty and dedication, and that evening turned out to be an important occasion in the life of the town…

Since I mentioned my friend who was like a brother to me, my friend who was like a brother to me, Nashka Tsipa's, or as we called him affectionately, Nashkaleh, I must, even if it is in bold lines, draw his image. Nashkaleh was beloved by the entire town. His father was Yasha Leib the Melamed. He was amongst the most respected Jews in town, a friendly, knowledgeable man. Every Saturday he would read the interpretation of Malbim in the old shtabel. As far as his son Nashkaleh, he taught him as much Torah as the boy could handle. The boy was like a vessel that would never overflow or spill over. He retained everything that he studied. Nashka looked very much like his father: he was short, had expressive eyes that would look at you with much love. Eyes that expressed a deep, splendid smile in them. I never saw him depressed or angry. Even when he had reasons to be sad, he had a smile on his face, and I was very envious of him. Here was a person that had no darkness in him, and there was no way you could get him to show anger or hostility. Sometimes we would try to make him mad, but he would conquer us with his generous smile, as if he were saying to us, "So let's see what sorts of energies and stubbornness you have."

Nashkaleh studied much with his father, but this didn't satisfy him and he started studying on his own. The very first thing he was interested in was Russian literature, and he studied it very systematically, and with great attention to detail. When he was satisfied with that, he dedicated himself to Yiddish literature. And when he was done with that, he put all his talents and energy and excitement to Hebrew literature. As we said, everything he did he did with his heart and his soul. And when I would ask him, "Nashkaleh, wasn't it enough for you all that you studied in your father's house? The Tanach, the Gmara, and the other tiny lettering from your childhood days? And secondly, don't you really like the Bund? What is it with you that all of a sudden got caught by Hebrew literature?"

But even in this argument he had the upper hand. He would answer me with his intelligent smile, "Alter, Alter. Do you know the splendor that is found in this language? The expressions and the wonderful passages that it contains? Here, take for example a passage from Psalms: Sas anochi al imratha kemotze shalal rav… [I'm so happy with your sayings as if I had found a treasure?] Listen carefully to the tune! Listen! Wastefully you will try to transfer or translate this passage into Yiddish. No, my friend, you could never accomplish it."

As if he were talking to himself he would whisper with pleasure every word separately. Sas… anochi… al imratha… kemotze… shalal rav…

When Nashkaleh was satisfied with the Hebrew literature he became involved with German literature, and not many days passed before he was fluent in that language. In 1922, Nashkaleh suddenly left Kurenets. He secretly crossed the Polish border towards the Soviet Union and settled in Minsk, and from then on we didn't hear anything about him. In the year 1941, a very short time before the Nazi invasion, I had the first chance to get papers to go to Minsk. In 1939 the area had become part of the Soviet Union. The main reason I went there was to look for Nashkaleh.

I arrived in Minsk and I was able to find him, but alas, in what situation I found him! He was handicapped as one of his legs had been amputated, and he now had a wooden leg. My heart cried inside of me but I didn't ask him about the circumstances of this tragedy. I asked him for his occupation, and he told me that he was a German teacher in the high school. He said that in the past he would write articles for the Yiddish newspaper that was published in Minsk, and that he had also written two plays. One of them was named Gavrahana Tzoymin [Broken Checkpoints] and it was performed in the Jewish theater in Odessa and found great success. It had great critical reviews in the theatrical pages in the newspapers, so I asked him what had been happening with him after all of this. Nashkaleh answered that after all this success, here is what happened: "My wife gave me a son in my very old age [he had married when he was old], and the Jewish heart, you must understand, still beats with Jewishness. So I decided to bring my son into the Union of our Forefather Abraham [he was circumcised, according to Jewish tradition] and you will understand, my friend, that since that day, the Communist authorities prevented any of my essays to be printed in the papers, and the plays I wrote were disallowed on stage… And, my dear friend, if I wasn't crippled, and if I was a person with two legs… yes, yes my dear friend," Nashkaleh kept saying, and from his "yes yes" I heard all the miseries of his life. He ended the conversation by saying, "Surely you will forgive me, Alter, but I have very little time and I must leave now to go school to give the children German lessons. We will still meet and talk. Now we are both citizens of the Soviet Union…" But I would never see him again. Nashkaleh with the pure and splendid soul, was annihilated by the Nazis, whose mother tongue he taught his students…

Once again I return to the days right after the First World War. In our town there was a youth that was enlightened and excited, especially after the Tarbut school was established and in its environs different parties and community activities were involved. They would take part in speeches, debates, and night school… To perform a play became a very common thing. At that time, well-known theatrical troupes would come to perform. Sometimes they would hold a series of performances, evening after evening, and the community of Kurenets would gather to see the plays.

A play written by Yakov Gordin

Performed, directed and acted in a Kurenets playhouse by citizens of Kurenets. Standing first from the right, Zalman son of Moshe-Binia Alperovich. To his left, Eliyahu-Chaim son of Nechama-Risha Nee Gelman and Mendel Zalman's Alperovich. Fifth from the right, David son of Leib Motosov. Standing seventh from the right, Rivka daughter of Rachel and Aharon Shulman. Eighth from the right, Shmuel Spector.

At that point we had teachers who were natives of the town. They were graduates of the teachers' seminary in Vilna, and our dear town was standing in the light of the Enlightenment. This was the situation amongst the younger generation, but also the older generation, the older generation of Chabad participated. During the last two years, we had two rabbis, Rabbi Moshe Aharon Feldman, Z"L, a dear man and a gentle soul, and Rabbi Shlomo Elie Oshpal, Z"L. And how I loved the Sabbaths during winter days between Minha and Maariv. I would enter the new synagogue where Rabbi Oshpal would say Hasidic passages. The congregation was not big, maybe only a few dozens. The synagogue would be enveloped by a gray cloud of the changing sunlight.

Rabbi Oshpal would close his eyes when he spoke. It must have been that he was able to become one with his sermon's ideas. The congregation would listen in serious somberness. Some would slowly shake their heads and bodies, others would close their eyes to try to understand the depth of the ideas. And the Torah passages would come out of the Rabbi's mouth, as if he was a living river, flowing ceaselessly. It was more than an hour that he was giving his sermon and everything sounded so fresh that it would elevate you, bring you farther until you heard the sentence, "Vehu vehum yihaper avon." And the congregation of listeners would awake as if just returning from a wonderful, distant world. And they would start praying the Maariv prayer…

Days and events that happened do not exist anymore… Everything was erased. Rabbi Feldman, Z"L, was martyred and died a torturous death in Kurenets. Rabbi Oshpal became a martyr in the shtetl of Sventzian. My body shakes when I remember how I returned after the liberation of Kurenets in 1944. All the synagogues were burned and on the dust you would find passages from the Torah book, and I walked there, collecting them. Almost the entire town was burned and I thought to myself, "It is very good that you were burned, my town. Our brothers were tortured, killed, and burned. So it is best that their possessions will not become an inherited by people who participated in their tortures and murders."

Everywhere I walked and stood, my feet touched the spilled of my beloved and my heart cried and cried. And it can never be healed…

Natives of Kurenets meet in Tel Aviv after the war

[Pages 80-82]

A Little Bit From A Lot

by Rabbi Yitzhak Dov Oshpal

Translated by Eilat Gordin Levitan

My father and my teacher, the genius Rabbi Shlomo Elie Oshpal Z"L, was a Hasidic Jew. He was born in a small village near the shtetl of Novi Sventzian, in the Vilna Goberneia. His forefathers were amongst the giants of the Chabad Hasids. They were renowned for their knowledge and devotion to the Chabad movement. Ever since his early childhood, my father was known for the purity of his heart and for his special spiritual qualities, his great talent, and his dedication to the study of the Torah. When he was just a teenager, he was accepted in the famous yeshiva in the town of Dvinsk, and there he was respected even amongst the older yeshiva students who studied the Torah and adhered to all the rules of Judaism. During those days, Rabbi Josef Razin Z"L, who was known as der Ragatchaver, was appointed as Rabbi and Av Beit Din in the town of Dvinsk. He was a true genius and a minister of the Torah. His home was filled with committees of the very learned, and amongst them my father, Z"L. My father seemed to have hardly left his tent and the genius rabbi was very entertained by my father, and had a lot of love and endearment towards him. He would have many sessions of questions and answers with him. Pretty often he would say to him, "I am sure that in the future you will be a great teacher in Israel." It turned out to be true. Not many years passed, and my father, Z"L, was certified by this genius of the generation to be a rabbi.

For a few years, my father studied and taught in the Dvinsk yeshiva, and since he was very devoted he was able to acquire a large amount of knowledge about the details of religious studies. But even there he did not abandon the spirit of the Hasidut and its particular style, which he was accustomed to in the house of his fathers. He was very interested in learning the old tales of the Hasids, and he gathered them one by one, as if they were precious pearls. The history of my father, Z"L, and the way of his life through fifty years were one long thread of devotion to the Torah, in the particular way that the Chabad Hasid would experience the religion, and if I would attempt to give details here, there is too much to say so I will just give a sketch of his life.

In the summer of 1926, my father was appointed to be the Av Beit Din in the town of Kurenets and he sat there on the throne of the rabbinut until the year 1941, a period of fifteen years. My father did much for the benefit of the town to improve the physical situation and to encourage and support the congregation in days of rain and wind. Out of his mouth came pearls, and the strength of his sermons would pull the hearts of those listening, bringing them near G-d in heaven. And the congregation would never get tired of listening to his sermons that he would spend some hours in delivering. In a very logical and commonsensical manner, he would discuss the rules of the Torah with regards to business issues and disputes between the people – and it wasn't just the residents of Kurenets that he advised, but also people in the entire surrounding region. He had the special talent of mediating and he would be able to peacefully resolve even the most hostile and complicated conflicts. He did it all with a shining face and with intelligence and knowledge. His wisdom and generous heart during all those disputes and conflicts were renowned in the entire area.

My father was very well connected with benefactors in the US and with his influence they contributed for the aid of poor students and enabled them to study for free in the Talmud Torah of Kurenets. They would also send funds for the poverty-stricken residents of the town. He would devote much of his time to public service. He felt very comfortable with going to the Polish officials, to the ruler of the region in Vilejka, and sometimes he would even go to Vilna to see the minister for the entire province. With his dedication and his pleasantness, he did much for the public and all his requests would be approved.

Here again I can name many, many particular details of his success but I will just mention a few examples about this subject. In one of the neighboring villages, the small community of Ouzla, about 25 km from Kurenets, my father found out that they had buried Jewish soldiers who lost their lives during the First World War. But they had not been buried as customary in Jewish cemeteries, but were put in village cemeteries with Christians. My father could not rest and went through every kind of obstacle so that he could bring them to be buried in the Jewish custom in a Jewish cemetery. It took him a few years to accomplish this holy mission, but finally he was able to transfer the deceased to Kurenets, and to bury them again in the Jewish cemetery. Every Jew in town, men, women and children, took part in the common funeral. My father found out the names and hometowns of each Jewish soldier, and spent much time trying to locate relatives so he could let them know about the impending ceremony. He found that one of these men was a high-ranking officer in the Russian Army and had lived in the town of Lodz. He was able to locate his family and they came to town to take part in the ceremony, and with big, big tears in their eyes they thanked my father for letting them take part in the ceremony.

I would also like to tell about his devotion to save 21 Torah books that fell into the hands of the Soviets. He found out that during the First World War, Torah books were taken out of Kurenets and transferred to Petersburg. The circumstances of that transfer were that during the battles, the holy community that there was much danger, so they were able to transfer the books. At the time when the books were given to the Jewish community in Petersburg, they sent a receipt for the books to Kurenets. My father, who was in Petersburg during the First World War, was given the responsibility by the committee of rabbis there to write down the list of all the books that had come there from different shtetls. All together ethere were 600 books. I will never be able to describe all the troubles and tribulations that my father encountered in this holy matter. Many times he had to go to Warsaw and plead with the Polish religious minister. Finally he got permission from the Polish government, but then there were new obstacles: the Soviets demanded one thousand golden dollars as a tax for sending the books. My father, who was very clever, was able to cancel this evil taxation. He argued that tax was only taken from profitable businesses, and there was no rationale for demanding any taxation for something that is given for safekeeping during dangerous times. This plea was effective and the Torah books were sent to the Soviet Embassy in Warsaw, and from there they were transferred to the minister who ruled the Vilna region.

In 1929, three huge boxes arrived in Kurenets, and in them there were 21 Torah books. It would be very hard to describe the joy in town. Singing and dancing, the entire community came to receive the holy packages. When they opened the boxes, they found a few books that had belonged to other towns in the area, such as Ilia, and all of them were sent to their rightful owners. This event received much publicity, both in the Jewish newspapers as well as in the Polish papers.

Another aspect of my father's personality that I would like to talk about was his dedication to improve the situation of the poverty-stricken residents of the town. He knew each and every one of them, and would often follow their daily situation, and did whatever he could do for them. Many times I would see with my own eyes how he would take from his pocket a few gold coins and would pay for the stamps that they were supposed to put on all the birth certificates that he had to sign for. All that he did was done with modesty, pleasantness, and secrecy. He avoided any possibility of humiliating those who he helped.

My father was a truly dedicated scholar. Daily he would study the Torah, and we greatly enjoyed hearing his voice when he said passages. Sometimes even passers by would stop to listen to him. From early morning until the night hours, he was busy studying the Torah, telling sermons to the congregation, and teaching the Torah to many. Passages would come from his heart and enter the hearts of his listeners. In the large library that we had in our house, there were also very old and valuable manuscripts. There were also some handwritten manuscripts by my father that dealt with revision of the Torah. One of these manuscripts was given to be printed in a publishing house by the name of Ayelet Hashakhar, but my heart breaks knowing that it fell into the hands of the Nazis.

A short time before the destruction of Kurenets, the evil ones sent him to the town of Sventzian. For three days our family, together with 8000 Jewish people, lived in an open field under the sky, with no food or drink. On a Sunday in 1942, they were slaughtered. On that Sunday they murdered all the men, and the next day all the women and children were slaughtered. They are all buried in one huge grave that is three hundred meters long and it is situated near Nevis Sventzian, which is in the vicinity of Vilna. My father walked at the head of the martyrs, enveloped in his tallit. This was told to me by Mr. Tzirtoka. My father gave a sermon in front of the holy martyrs, and his last words were about kiddush hashem [to die as a martyr, to bring glory to God's name]. He did this to comfort them in their last walk…May his soul be melded in the bouquet of the living.

[Page 84]

Self Defense

by Levik, son of Mendel and Gitel Alperovitch

Translated by Nir, Levik's grandson

Levik Alperovitch

The story that I am about to tell you took place when I was still a very young boy not yet studying in the Cheder. From those days, I was left with deep yet imprecise memories of days of fear and tension in our shtetl. I remember that the adults kept saying the word "pogrom". I didn't know what that word meant but that word made me very fearful. Fearful from the sound and the statement people had when they said the word. It was at the beginning of winter, a few days before Hanukkah, the sky was very gray, and the weather so cold that it chilled your bones. In our house we had double windows, although it was very cold, it still wasn't cold enough that the frost would cover them. I stuck my face to the glass, as most kids like to do and looked at the market. In those days, we lived at the house of Israel Itze the Shochet. The market had patches of frozen snow on the ground white spots of snow covered the dark earth hay that were left by the farmers who came with the horses and wagons to sell their produce. I still remember the snow falling covering the dark ground. All of a sudden, a large group of Cossacks riding horses came roaming by the houses. Mixed with that image, I remember that my father Mendel Chetzkales' (Son Of Yechezkel, son of Binia Alperovitz), and my uncle Zalman Chazkeles' Hurriedly left the house. They went to the yard. I swiftly ran to the other side of the room and looked through the window facing the yard, to see what they were doing. Cognizant that they seemed extremely worried I watched them approaching a heap of logs.

Mendel Alperovitz during a visit to Israel in 1938 with son,
Levik and grandson, Amram

They pushed the snow aside, they took the logs one by one and put them against the gate so no one could enter as if there was impending danger coming. Then they returned home and whispered to each other as if they were looking for some solution, shortly after they left our home. I still remember when evening time came. On the table, there was a little candle with flickering light. I remember my father and uncle sitting around the table with other people whispering to each other. I could hear words like "sticks" and "iron gloves" and "rods" to be prepared to "scare off" someone.

Years later when I matured, I was curious about those memories. I started asking questions trying to clear it for myself my frightful memories. I was told that in the year 1905. Many young men and women would gather in the forest near our town and they would plan how a revolution against the czar. There were many Jews from the town amongst them. Some of the Christian people of the town and the surrounding area wanted to harm the Jews who they claimed were all revolutionaries. Just before Hanukkah we always had a huge event called "Hanes" where people from the surrounding town would come to buy and sell, (a big festive Swap meet). The heads of the Jewish community in Kurenets were very fearful since they heard that on swap meet day, some of the villagers planed to harm the Jews. So they sent a committee to the governor of the area and they gave him a "bribe" so he would help. He sent the Cossacks to defend the town, but the Jews still knew not to just rely on the Cossacks. So they organized in secret their own army of self defense. To finance this army, they taxed the Jewish community. Some Jews of the community didn't want to accept the tax and they had to enforce it by using threat and sometimes-physical force. The weapons the mainly gathered were rods with spikes and iron gloves and sticks with nails. They hid the weapons in a large hall that was dug in the cemetery. The same winter, on a Saturday morning, a policeman was found dead. The policeman was found on the highest bench in the steam room and logically people thought his heart weakened from the heat but truly, it was very different. This policeman was known in town as a "Staraznik" someone who works for the czarist government an informant.

He found out about secret army. Therefore, the Jews gave him a lot of alcohol before he entered the steam room. Then while he was lying there, they made the room very hot, so hot that it caused him death. When the swap meet came, the Jewish defense patrolled the town. Each patrol unit had about four people, ready for any trouble. The swap meet turned to be very peaceful other than isolated cases of stealing baked goods from the salespeople.

Argentina c 1923
Bottom row left; Levik Alperovitz on the right; Meir Gurevitz

On the right: Levik Alperovitz, next to him: Meir Gurevitz

*Brother of Levik: Yosef Alperovitz [sitting on the right]
with Ze'ev Kooperstock and Shacna Stole
They all perished in the Holocaust. Yosef was killed
on the last days of the war in the area while fighting the Germans*

*Rachel (wife of Levik) Alperovitz
[daughter of Nechama Risha née Gelman
and Menachem Mendel Alperovitz]
Died in Israel of illness in 1946*

[Pages 85]

From There to Now

by David Motosov, son of Leib

Translated by Eilat Gordin Levitan

As I journey through memories of Kurenets, my beloved town, I will arrive at the year 1912. At that point we lived outside the town, at a distance of about 7 km, at the edge of the big forest. My father Leib of blessed memory owned a factory that processed turpentine, tar, and coal. The name of the place was Palita. I lived in a world filled with wonders and excitement. The deep forest with all its secrets was my playground. I was enveloped by the love of my parents since I was their only male child. And as a youth I had absolutely no responsibilities, I lived a care free life. Once in a while we would travel to Kurenets to pay a visit and occasionally we would have Jews from Kurenets visit us. But the rootstock of my life and its springing point was the Palita, in the forest.

One day I was called by my father and he announced to me, "It is time for you, my son, to enter the world of the Torah." I was close to the age of 7 at that point, and already the next morning they handed a few belongings to me and we traveled to Kurenets. They hired for me a "kasset" at the house of Moshe der Shaffer, and my father entrusted my education to the best rabbi in town. It was Reb Ben-Zion Meirovich. In town they told with awe that he would receive newspapers in the Hebrew language, amongst them "Hatzfirah" and "Hamelitz" on a regular basis. His cheder was located at that point in Myadel Street in the house of Hinda Leah. My father said to Reb Ben-Zion, "I hand you this `jewel in the rough and hope that you will make him a respectable person, educate him to have good manners and do good deeds. He has a good head but he is very, very wild."

The rabbi smiled at me and patted my shoulder and told my father, "Your son is already a decent person and I hope that you will take much pride in him."

I remember some of my comrades in the cheder, amongst them Yakov Alperovich Eliyau den Limanadniks [his family made lemonade, after his parents and sister died he settled in the US], Meir the son of Baruch Mordechai Gurevich [later settled in Israel in Mushav Bitzaron], Levik Alperovich [later settled in Israel], Leib Potropos-Z"l [died in Germany after the war], Zalman son of Itzhak Mikhail Alperovich the Butcher [who later became a well known Chabad Hasid], Shimon Kelman Shulman. It must be that the years in the forest made me very unlike the Jewish kids of the shtetl and deeply influenced my mannerism. The Yiddish I spoke was filled with Russian expressions, and the "R" was very pronounced. The other children in the cheder came from the town, and were very happy to see a strange character like me, and jumped on me as if they had found a treasure for jokes and pranks. They nicknamed me The Goy and The Yeshuvnik [the hick], but I did not sit quietly, and I knew how to fight back, sometimes physically and sometimes by returning their insults and antics.

During Shabbat, my father would take me back to the Palita, and every Sunday we would return to Kurenets. I remember that in one instance I returned to the cheder on Monday instead of Sunday. Obviously the rabbi asked me where I was the day before, so I answered him in immaculate Russian, "Ibaz ednava zidok, kramesh ni budyat?", meaning "Without one Jew there's no market day?"

Everyone started chuckling. The rabbi and the other students all laughed together, and my response became a celebrated adage in town, and this saying would chase me wherever I went.

Slowly I became acclimated to life in the shtetl and rooted amongst my school friends. I started studying Hebrew (only in Hebrew) Hebrew grammar, and discussion about Jewish history, and I also took a great part in the social lives of my friends. We had many so-called "problems" engage. ourselves with We collected decorative covers of candies. We collected lights made from special shiny paper that we used to light the way back from the cheder during nights.

Kurenets circa 1918

We also had fights, fights with children from other cheders and other groups. I remember that one of my most bitter enemies was Yosef Zimmerman-Z"l Yoshka Itzha's as he was named in town, who lived near the bridge on Myadel Street. One very rainy day he hid, waiting to ambush me, and when I returned from the cheder he jumped on me and took one of my shoes and ran with his treasure. I was humiliated and had to return home wearing only one shoe. But luck was with me. On the way I met with Yankeleh Itzhak Pyeshka's, who was the "champion" of the town, and all the children were scared of him. "What happened to you, David?" he asked me. I told him with a voice shaking from crying the awful deed, about how I was jumped on from the back, so he offered in exchange for a little knife that I had, to return my shoe that was taken. I Don't know how he was able to accomplish it, however it didn't take but a few minutes and he returned with my shoe and added to it the hat of Yosef.

I embark on reminiscences of these years and it seems like they were the most beautiful years of my life until the year 1914 arrived and World War I started. The Russians begun retreating from our area and the Germans kept advancing. By 1915, the shots could be clearly heard near the town and all the Jews left their homes and escaped to the village Borodina near Kurenets. Why choose Borodina of all places? To this day I don't know. But the fact is, the next day we returned to town all healthy, and now we were under the eclipse of the wings of Kaiser Wilhelm II, and this surely proved that strategically we were right, even if there was no answer to why.

After about three weeks, the Germans left Kurenets and again the Russians returned. It became a battlefield, and there was even a German plane that arrived and dropped a bomb that killed a Russian soldier that was riding a horse on Smorgon Street. Everyone saw in it the excellent technology of the Germans. My family, joined by other families from Kurenets, left town to go deep into Russia where we lived for seven years, and we only returned to Kurenets in 1922. I left the town when I was still a child and returned as a man of 18. I experienced much during the years and I was very different from the child who left the town seven years prior, but Kurenets also didn't stand still. There was a great change. I found youths filled with enlightenment and erudition. They were contemporary in their attitude. Most of them were members of Zionist organizations. There was a big library and a Tarbut school. There was a headquarters of a Keren Kayemet LeIsrael, which was a funding organization to collect money for Israel. At the head of this organization stood the loyal Gershon Eiyishiski Z"l. Sometimes I think that it was as if I had gone in a full circle and returned to my childhood in a little different sense. I was brought by my father from the Palita to the very different environment of cheder studies of Ben Zion as well as life in a shtetl., and now fate brought me from the depths of the very secular and "goyish" Soviet Russia to the Zionist Kurenets where Hebrew was spoken everywhere, and the dream of Zion whispered from every field, spreading to Vileyka St. to Dolhinov St. to the gardens of Kulik. Kurenets was dreaming and adorning the dreams with beautiful tunes that had just arrived from Israel. To such a Kurenets I arrived, and I was as goy-like as I was in the days of my youth. I could hardly speak Yiddish never mind any Hebrew! But it didn't take long and I became deeply involved in this new environment. I became a pillar of the public service and Zionist spirit.

Creators of Tarbut School in Kurenets 1922.
Holding the picture: (left to right) 1. Shimon Kelman Shulman, 2. David Motosov
Second row from bottom: 1. Unknown, 2. The teacher Shmariahu Dardak; 3. Zalman Gvint, 4. Natan son of Mordechai and Farada Gurevitz, 5. The teacher Berl Dardak, 6. The son of Zalman Mendel Zipilavitz, 7. Gershon Eisheski.
Third row from bottom: first two unrecognized, 3. Yosef Shimon Kramnik, 4. ?(Went to Argentina) 5. Malka Kremer, 6. Ze'ev Shulman, 7. from the Charnas family.
Top row: 1. Son of Mendel Alperovitz, 2. Chaim Kremer, 3. Levik son of Mendel Alperovitz, 5. Meir, son of Mordechai and Farada Gurevitz, 6. Unrecognized

At the end of 1923 we funded a branch of Ha'Chalutz in Kurenets. We established it on Smorgon St., at the house of Moshe Leib Schkalia, Z"L. To be more exact, the house of Chaia Itka. The first committee, contained the following members: Yosef Alperovich son of Mendel son of Yehezkel [Yosef Alperovich perished in the Holocaust], Batia Gurevich [later Batia Bender died in Kibbutz Einat in Israel], Etel Alperovich [died in Israel], Avraham Aharon Alperovich [also died in Israel], and me. With much energy and dedication we opened evening classes for Hebrew instruction, geography of Eretz Israel, and the history of Zionism. Each evening all the members would meet. That year there were about 30 members and we would spend time discussing various topics. We read and sang to bring some more liveliness and to fund the operation, once a month we would sponsor a big dance. The party had certain traditions. We had a band of string instruments, at the head was Ben Zion the Hameraked [Person who makes people dance]. With him were the musicians Yehoshua Alperovich, Itzka son of Netta, and Eliezer son of Racha-Rasha. The band would play and the members would dance and everyone would have a great time. One of the highlights of this party was an awards ceremony at the end where each girl would receive secret letters, and the girl who received the most secret letters would win a prize. To send those secret letters, the guys had to pay. So, clearly if someone wanted to express his affection or to get attention from a certain girl would buy as many letters as he could for that specific girl, and then would send these letters by a certain committee to the girl he cared about. And everyone felt good about it because the guy who sent those secret letters had some hope that the girl would return his affection, and the girl felt very special as if she were the queen of the party. And we had some more funds to run our operation.

After a short time we opened a branch of Ha'Chalutz Ha'Zair in Kosita Street, in the house of three sisters whose last names, I'm very sorry to say, don't remember. I was for a long time the head of Ha'Chalutz Ha'Zair, and I would especially like to point out the very dedicated activities of Aharon [perished in the Holocaust] son of Mendel son of Yehezkel son of Binya Alperovich. I would like to tell about the carpentry shop that we opened as a branch of the Ha'Chalutz in Kurenets. This took place sometime after the headquarters of the Ha'Chalutz in Poland announced that new places of preparing the Jewish youth to work as pioneers in Eretz Israel were being established throughout Poland. Places like agricultural settlements, carpentry shops, and blacksmith shops were being created. Our decision to open such a shop was very courageous in some ways since we needed to do something from nothing. We had no funds to open such a place, but with a very creative spirit that engulfed us and the energy and freshness that a few of our friends were blessed with, we were able to overcome the obstacles and a carpentry shop was established. Reb Mendel Z"L,(perished in the Holocaust) son of Reb Yehezkel son of Binya Alperovich had an empty apartment in the yard of his home in the alley. We ogled this apartment and decided that we should rent it. At first we were very hesitant. We were worried that our request would receive only laughter in response. Should we go to Reb Mendel Alperovich or shouldn't we? At the end we became brave enough. I remember that I decided to use the good name of Gershon Eiyishiski [perished in the Holocaust] who was a very respected person. I asked him to join us in our request. So we went to Reb Mendel and asked him to let us rent the apartment to be used as a carpentry workshop. Mendel Alperovich was a Jew with strong character and keen intelligence, and loved to make everything simple and clear. At first he said that he was surprised and unclear about what we were offering. What was the purpose of such a carpentry shop? Who would be the carpenters? And what kind of insurance against any fires or other possible disasters would we give him? After a short discussion, however, he said, "Children, take the apartment and start working, and we will come to some agreement."

The next day we took the place. The instructor became Ostrovsky, who I think later on immigrated to Argentina. Immediately we established a fund to pay for the upkeep and here it was the Jews of Kurenets and nearby towns like Ilia, Dolhinov, Kriviczi, and Vileyka that we were able to turn to for donations for all the tools and materials we needed. So we were able to open the carpentry shop. And these are the people who studied carpentry in our establishment: Chaim son of Mendel Levin [Perished in the Holocaust], Zaev Shulman [later immigrated to Israel], David Kopilovich from Kriviczi, Natan Shulman from Vileyka, and a guy from Ilia whose name I cannot remember. The girls who were responsible for other activities were Chana the daughter of Naftali Alperovich [later immigrated to Israel], and Tsertl nee Alperovich the daughter of Chaim Avraham.(perished in 1942) Our duties as heads of this enterprise were to get tools, raw materials, and food supplies. We also arranged for cultural and educational instructions here.

The first project was to construct a large bureau, which was sold to the Levin family. We had a big party that day. IT was a spontaneous party, filled with humor and a roast-like atmosphere, where Mendel Alperovich was so excited by our deed that we didn't have to pay any rent. At one point I was sent to prepare for the emigration to Israel in the forest of Magenetza near town Vishnevo. When I returned home after the big fire of 1925, I found that there was a big kibbutz of trainees of the Chalutz in town. Most of them worked on rebuilding the town that had been destroyed in the fire. The first Chalutz (pioneer) who spent full-time in the preparation, which took almost two years, was trained in Solodny near Vilna, was Avraham Aharon Alperovich. He received a certificate to immigrate to Eretz Israel. After he left there was a long list of immigrants, first from Ha'Chalutz then from Hashomer Ha'Zair and so on and so on until our evil enemy, may his name be erased from memory, annihilated all that was most dear to us.

From days of my early childhood, standing in front of me is the lively image of your pure face, my father. Your blue eyes. But at the gates of death, where you stood for many months, I didn't join you. When the killers came near our town, I beg you, that you will run away with me to the Soviet Union, but you said you couldn't leave your daughters, you couldn't leave Chaia, Henia, and Duba and their families, and you stayed in the valley of death. Even today I hear the exciting timbre of your deep voice, its musical quality. I can still feel your hand that held mine when you first took me to the cheder. You made me feel safe and you walked with me through paths of pain and happiness. From all that I heard of you on the days of horror, your image comes to me in a miraculous light that I haven't experienced before. This splendid light must have been hidden in you, and only came out when life became darkened. The Germans were not able to trick you. You had no illusions, as many of the survivors told. Although you were an old man at that point, every day you tried to awaken the hearts. You told them, "You must not sit here aimlessly. You must go to the forest, to fight." And in the day of the annihilation, before the killers were able to touch you with their bullets, you took charge and jumped into the fire and you gave glory to the name of God in every essence of your being. Many, many years passed since you whispered to me the blessing of a safe voyage when I escaped from Kureents. But every day your image will come to my eyes and I am humbled, filled with holy fear and spiritual joy. In my eyes I repeat the torturous occurrence and your last minutes in the day of the awful slaughter, and my lips will whisper, "Avi avi. Rechav Israel Uparashav." And my shut eyes will see you enveloped in a tallit, jumping into the fire…Your soul rising up from the flames…

[Pages 90-94]

Beloved and Unforgettable Kurenets

by Dov Benes

Dedicated to my dear parents,
my father Chaim Zeev son of Shmuel and Ada Benes
and my mother Feiga daughter of Reb Shlomo Itzhak and Henia Kopilovich from Ilia,
and my dear sister Chaia Aada (Only her daughter survived and lives in the U.S)

All of them perished in the Holocaust

Translated by Eilat Gordin Levitan

As if alive you come to my eyes, my hometown, beloved and never forgotten. Many, many years passed since the day I left you, but every day I will visit you in my heart. Sometimes I imagine that it was only a horrible night's hallucination that I experienced, and that one morning I will awake and find you alive and well as when I was there.

Our home that was built with years of toil would be standing in the corner of Myadel Street and the Market. I will enter the home and find my beautiful mother petting her youngest son ["the son of her old days"] Laizarkeh, singing to him songs of Elakim Tsonzer or a tune from a Goldfadden play. I would sit by her and also listen to her stories about the Ger Tzedek from the Potzotsky family, who hid from the fear of the government's informants in the big synagogue in the shtetl Ilia. The stories of her great grandmother, who would bring him food in secret. My mother would tell stories of how he was finally caught and imprisoned after the informants found him and how he was burned alive by the authorities one hour before they received word of his pardon. And here I'll see you, my father, kind and quiet. I do not remember you even once becoming angry. You blessed everyone with your generous and intelligent expression, and humorous anecdotes. Memories, memories!

Melameds (teachers) and their cheders

Some of them were fastidious, others were pleasant, and here comes to me one end of winter. It is almost time for vacation, Passover is approaching… Those were March days in 1917. It was a regular day, like any other day. I was sent by my aunt Yenta to deliver certain things. If my memory doesn't betray me it was flour to bake matzos. I was sitting in their home with the flour and all of a sudden comes my uncle, Shimon Mikhail, smaller-than-average built Jew with a long and splendid beard. He was a very enlightened Jew who didn't blabber away unnecessarily. But this time, he entered agitated and excited. Immediately he approached his wife, Aunt Yenta, and said,

"Miracle of miracles! Miracle of miracles! Did you hear what they are saying in the shtabel? Did you hear who was taken down from his throne? From his mighty perch? The Czar! Czar Nikolai was overthrown!"

My Aunt Yenta who was a true "Eschet- Chayl " Vivacious and very capable, she was a born businesswoman and as soon as she heard it she warned my uncle,

"Look, Shimon. I beg you and warn you not to take any part in it. You must not take any part in it. The result could only be heavy taxation for us."

Clearly at that moment I totally forgot the job that my aunt gave me, and as if my feet were on fire I started running to the synagogue to see with my own eyes what had happened. The synagogue was packed with people. Everyone seemed very excited and words like, "Czar"… "Nikolai"… "Freedom"… "Revolution"… and "Krensky" were thrown in the air, and here on the bimah [podium] stood Pesach the Cantonist as he was known, and with a voice filled with tears he blessed the moment with the blessing of "SheHecheyanou" [blessed that we were alive to see this time]. This blessing he made for this occasion. In his childhood Pesach was caught by the kidnappers and was given for 25 years of service in the Czar's army, and there he was forced to convert to Christianity. Now with the fall of Nikolai he would have no obstacles and he would be free to return to Judaism openly. In the synagogue that day he told of how he was a soldier in the Russian-Turkish war and took part in the battle near Palvana, and there he vowed that if God will save him and keep him alive, he will return to being a Jew, in spite of all the danger that this action would bring him.

I do remember Pesach the Cantonist who always sat in the big synagogue, in the back as the rabbi permitted, saying passages from Psalms and praying without wearing the tallit and fellim…

I remember how Netta the Shamash who was also a Hazan in beit midrash, during holidays or other special occasions. He approached Pesach with much excitement and with vibrating strain in his beautiful and clear voice said, "You were blessed, Pesach. You were able to accomplish your vow!"

The fierce waves of the revolution and its excitement engulfed the streets and the hearts in Kurenets. It awakened the civic movements in the eastern European shtetls with a sort of altered emphasis. It was a Zionist movement that florished. It started with the youths. They established a group named "Tiffeeret Bachurim" ["The Best of the Young Men"]. They would gather in the old shtabel. Their aim was to organize the youths in a sort of society that had some connections to old Jewish traditions and to the new socialist period. I remember that shortly after that day, on a Saturday night, Yosef Shimon son of Hillel Kremnik [perished in the Holocaust] came to me and gave me a note and said, "I ask you, Bere, you must give this note to your sisters Batia and Chaia Ada. But you must be careful not to open it and read it."

Clearly after such a warning my curiosity rose twenty-fold, and I immediately opened the note and read it. I found out that this was an invitation asking my sisters to come to a gathering of the youths that would take part in the house of Chaim Avremel Alperovitz or in the house of Zalman Rashka's Alperovitz. The aim was to organize a Zionist movement in town by the name of Tzeiret Zion [The Youth of Zion]. Amongst other things it was written in the note that at this meeting, Yudel Dardak from Ilia, and Benish Ginzburg from Dolhinov would make speeches. Since the two speakers were cousins of mine, I used this nepotism and entered the meeting bearing in mind my young age. After I promised everyone that I would sit quietly and not disturb the meeting. To tell you the truth it was a very difficult agreement to make for me, but I had no other choice so I made my promise. During this meeting for the first time I heard talk about Zionism, about the living Eretz Israel, and a return to Zion, and establishing a Hebrew nation for the Jewish people. The speeches were filled with excitement, and speakers were talking as if they were breathing fire in the air. The room was filled with echoing sentences. "If the Jewish nation will wish and won't retreat in front of the difficulty, the dream of 2000 years will be accomplished. If you wish it, it will not be a fairy tale." I sat in one of the corners excited and flying on unseen wings. My head was caught in a dream, and only my eyes stayed fixed on the speakers. Could I really disturb such an exciting meeting? My heart widened and was filled with new urges that were awakened in me. When I returned home I couldn't sleep. Early the next morning I left my home and I found the book "Yossefon" by Yosef Plavius. I Remember until today that the book was written in Rashi lettering. I read the book many, many times until I learned it by heart, and since that day there was not one Zionist meeting that I was not present at. Sometimes by permission, but many times in secret. At times when there was no way to enter the place I would stand behind a window, drinking with great thirst every word that came from the speakers' mouths.

I was less than twelve at this point and it is clear that this new interest affected my studies in the cheder. It affected it so much that the rabbi came to my parents and said, "Ayar zon is kilya gavarn. Er ist Zionist." Meaning, "Your son is spoiled, he became a Zionist." My parents started discussing what they should do with me. They decided to send me away from all of the occurrences and a resolution was made that I should go to the town of Ilia to my uncle Moshe Leib Kopilovich, and there I should continue my Jewish studies.

My uncle was a "Talmid Hacham" Jew, very scholarly in Jewish studies. He was a very easygoing person and I studied with him for about a year. But in Ilia there were also my relatives; the Dardak brothers, and using the reason that I was related to them I followed them in every unoccupied minute that I was blessed with, and from their noble spirit they spread to me the love to Israel. I must thank them for the road I chose in the future.

Meanwhile, the Germans conquered Kurenets and I was separated from my parents until one night a villager from the village Kosita came to Ilia to take me back to Kurenets, and I returned home with him. The Zionist activity during the German occupation in the first World War continued in secret, underground. They disguised themselves as a drama club. Also there was a Hebrew school and night classes in Hebrew headed by Yudel Dardak and Yosef Shimon Kramnik. After some time, Natan Gordon, the son of Yasha Leib the Melamed and his wife Tsipa, joined the drama club. Tsipa Gordon, the wife of Yasha Leib, was known in Kurenets as a very able woman. She would do five or six things at the same time. In one hand she would roll the yarn, in the other hand she would churn butter, with one foot she would rock the baby's cradle, with her other leg she would keep pedaling to keep the loom going, and her mouth would say passages from Psalms, and her eyes would watch the students so they would not become wild.

Natan Gordon, or Nashkaleh as we called him, belonged to the Bund. He tried very hard to find new souls for his Bund party but had very little success. For us it was impossible to understand how a Jew could be against the idea of returning to Zion. We kept with the Zionist activities until the Germans retreated and the Bolsheviks entered. At that point all the Zionist activities ceased. During the days of the Bolsheviks, the town was living a sort of double life. On the one hand there was famine, depression, and fear about what tomorrow would bring, on the other hand there was a lot of civic activities by the authorities, and this was expressed in many theatre plays, concerts, and other activities in the community house that they established in the Ungerman Ranch. Many, many meetings, always with bands that played in the central market. They did everything to win over the hearts of the public. I remember one occasion that would sound like a joke, but in my opinion it symbolized those times. It was on a Saturday and a Soviet troop arrived in town. At the head of the troop there was a big band. They all rested in the market. The soldiers were very tired and hungry. They waited there for the arrival of the Kuchnaya, the field kitchen that usually would follow the troops. All of a sudden the soldiers yelled, "Kuchnaya yedit!", meaning, "The kitchen is moving!" And soon after arrived a big container. It was on wheels and was pulled by a pair of horses that stopped in the center of the market. All the soldiers stood in line with their food containers. The cook stood on the podium and opened the cover of a container and started taking things out of it. As it turned out, it was filled with pamphlets and newspapers and other propaganda…

The town after that kept passing many times from hand to hand, between the Polish and the Bolsheviks. At the end the Polish took roots there, the war ended, and Zionist activities returned.

Tzeirei Zion movement was founded. There was a Hebrew school that was established. At first the Yiddish-speakers tried to control the education in town and brought for this purpose a teacher from Vilna, from the CBK. But mainly for the commitment and the blessed activities of Zalman Gvint Z"L [perished in the Holocaust], these attempts to control the education failed, and the school passed to the Tarbut movement. All the subjects were taught entirely in Hebrew. Zalman Gvint was a very special person. He was blessed with all the distinguished qualities that makes a public servant remarkable. He did his job for the sake of doing it, and not to receive any awards. His commitment to the school had no boundaries, and only for his involvement the school survived in spite of all the difficulties and troubles it encountered. One day, after studies, the teacher Berl Dardak announced that a letter was received from Vilna and it said, "Charut Hetria will establish branches in the shtetls in the Vilna district." They suggested that we establish a branch in town. This suggestion was received with great excitement. It was at that point long a dream of ours to belong to an organized Zionist movement, so immediately we established a Zionist committee which was the first in town. The first members were graduates of the Hebrew school. The first meeting took place in the house of Naftali Alperovich on Vileyka Street, and a few of the people who took part in it are now [1950] in Israel. I remember that Efraim Leib Kremer Z" L [died in Eretz Israel] who in Israel changed his name to Ben David, was the first secretary and was the first among us to go to Eretz Israel. The most important cultural activity Charut Vet'chia was the studies of Hebrew history and the history of the laboring in Eretz Israel.

We were busy with collecting money for the different national funds. For these occasions we established certain days of celebrations. We also would go from house to house with a blue box and organize literature parties on different subjects. We prepared ourselves to go to be educated in living in agricultural communities.

Days passed and all the members of Charut Vetchia in the main headquarters went to Israel and the whole movement was almost cancelled. But we didn't give up. We made contact with Gordonia and we established other youth movements like Ha'Chalutz and Ha'Chalutz Ha'Zair. The period of the establishment of Ha'Chalutz was a very splendid period.

Ken Hashomer Hatzair (Socialist-Zionist youth movement)
Kurenets 1929

<u>Sitting right to left:</u>
Sara nee Meirovitz Eizen, Luba nee Gurevich Bardan, Zlata Zimerman, Chana Alperovich,
Bela Meltzer, Batya daughter of Rabbi Oshpol, Chaya Sara Shmukler, Dvusha Kopilevitz,
Daughter of Shlomo Mayzel, Fraydel Zimerman.
<u>Second line sitting, right to left:</u>
Michael Meirovitch, Shlomke Alperovitz, Nechamia Alperovitch, Israel Gvint,
Dvushel Zokovski, Aharon Meirovitch, Yitzhak Gurfinkel, ?, Hirshel Alperovitch,
Eliyahu Zimerman, Standing next: Yechiel Alperovitch, ?
<u>Third row Right to left:</u>
Zev (Wolf) Rabunski, Henya Dimenstein, Chaim Yitzhak Zimerman, Shlomo Mindel,
Shmuel Limon, Yermiyahu Alperovitz, Shimshon Zimerman, Velvel Rodinski,
Aharon Alperovitz, Yakov Dinerstein, Yosef Markman.
<u>Top row right to left:</u>
?,?,?, Rosa nee Chosid Rabunski, Mendel Levins' daughter, Menuchka Kopilovitch,
Chaya Altman, ?,?, Sara Eisak.

My writing would be lacking if I didn't say a few words also about Hashomer Ha'Zair in Kurenets, that came to town like a spring wind, bringing with an intoxicating blossoming. This was in the year 1928. IT was after I returned from my training in Kibbutz Rayuvka that was located somewhere between the towns of Ilia and Krasne. At that point, the Yeshuv [Jewish settlers] in Eretz Israel went through some hard times. After the Fourth Immigration it was very difficult to get certificates for a few reasons. First there were very few being given by the British. Second, it was very expensive to travel. Third, and most importantly, it seemed like the town lost the beautiful dreams. It was as if autumn came. Most of the active members left. Some went to Eretz Israel, others went into serious studies, and a few got busy with jobs. I remember one reading in the house of Shabtai Gordon. We spoke about the difficulties in Eretz Israel and about the difficulties of the pioneer movement. The main thing on everyone's mind was how to renew the old days in town. As a first step a decision was made to commit to improve the situation of the Tarbut school that was having financial difficulties. Clearly, Zalman Gvint took this job, and I was his assistant from a technical point of view, since at this point I had no other job. At that point, Dvozhel Zokovski [perished in the Holocaust] arrived in Kurenets. She had just finished her studies in the Hebrew gymnasia in Vilna, and now she was accepted as a teacher in the school. She, together with others who were visionaries, among them Aharon Meirovich, who was filled with Hebrew culture and traditional culture by his father Ben Zion, who was the first person who established in town so many years ago the teaching of Hebrew in Hebrew. Anyway, Dvozhel Zokovski and Aharon Meirovich established a ken [a local movement] of Hashomer Ha'Zair. My writing ability is too dull to describe the character of Dvozhel and all the special gifts she was blessed with. It's all to her credit that the movement caught the youths with a new excitement that was similar to the good old days.

Kurenets 1929 – Hashomer Hatzair Garden

The working young men: Michail Meirovitz, Aharon Meirovitz, Yizhak Gurfinkel.
Two young girls in front: Nyoma nee Alperovitz Rabunski, Rivka nee Gvint Dudik.

Hashomer Ha'Zair spread to us a wonderful external light and also awoke in us some deep, internal commitment. The activities were filled with the liveliness of youth but it was also tempered by some internal yearning. We had fundraisers and educational meetings about Hebrew literature and geography. We would go on journeys into nature. We would sail on the river. We would put together exhibits of our handcrafts. Once in a while a new tune would reach town and everyone would sing together, and every activity would be done with excitement, as if there was some holiday approaching. It was as if we were in a circle of miracles, a circle that was dancing the hora and a circle that could not be broken. Still, there were moments of good-natured humor that never hurt anyone, but at the same time it sharpened your wits.

I remember that at one time, one of the girls attempted to embroider a swan for one of the shows, but it turned out looking more like a foal [young horse?]. Aronchik Meirovich, who later became a poet, took the piece of art and started singing to a tune of "I hat affafya":

Var hat das gazen
Und var hat das garet
Aza katchka zol oizen vi afrad?

The highlight of our activities was sailing on Lake Narutz, which was 40 km from our town. After this sailing I decided that it was time for me to go to Israel. I again went through preparations, leaving the town her youth came back. Not after a long time I returned from the preparations with my skin all tanned and my body peeling. And my friends from Hashomer Ha'Zair were very proud of me, as if I had gotten the suntan in Jerusalem. A short time later, at an evening hour, the entire unit of Hashomer Ha'Zair walked with me amongst the cedars on Dolhinov Street, and walked me to the train station on my way to Israel. From the departing train I heard their singing, and that was the last sense I received from the town.

Members of Hashomer Hatzair youth movement on top of the "famous" bolder

Standing on the rock from right to left: Shlomo son of Meir Aharon Alperovitz, Michal son of Ben Zion Meirovitch, Leizer son of Chaim Velvel Benes. On the far right Yitzhak Gurfinkel hugging Eiyahu son of Alter Zimerman. Between the standing boys sitting Nechamia Alperovich and leaning on his shoulder Dov the son of Avraham Chaim Reyder the chimney sweeper. Holding the flag is Yosef Markman, to his top left, Luba nee Gurevich Bardan, to her left Chaya Sara Shmukler and sitting on her Henya Dimenstein the daughter of Merka de bakerke. Sitting at bottom right: Sara Eisak, Zlata Zimerman, ?, ?, . Sheina the daughter of Neta Zimerman, Chana Alperovitz and Freydale Zimerman. Above them standing Chaya Altman from Dolhinov Street, sitting far left Bela Meltzer and Menuchka Kupelovitz.

[Page 95-105]

Lost Tunes

by Yehoshua Alperovich

Translated by Eilat Gordin Levitan

To this day I have a great love for music. When I walk down the street and hear an instrument played proficiently, my heart widens. I don't just enjoy hearing others play, I play a few instruments myself. It was in you, my little hometown, Kurenets, that I first heard songs and music played, and this was even before I got to know the professional players of Kurenets, the Kleizmers from Smorgon Street. I was about three years old, we lived on Myadel St. across the street from Hillel Kramnik, the father of Yosef Shimon who perished in the Holocaust [and his brother who moved to the US and changed his name to Kramer and lived in northern NY]. Not far from us, in the alley, lived Gotza (Dinerstein?), and from his house you would hear the sound of a violin being played. These tunes had a great pull on me, making me stop over at that house. And one time, when I walked over to the house with my mother, Z"L, I stopped her and I started crying and begged her that she should let me see what it is in that house that made that beautiful sounds. At first my mother refused, but finally she could not take my cries. She entered the house and apologized. She said to Gotza's family, "A child will stay a child. He doesn't let me continue walking, he demands that we should enter to see what is it in this house that makes that music."

We were received graciously. Gotza was a Jew who knew how to entertain children and the old. He sat me on a high chair and started playing music for me. At first I was very embarrassed since all of a sudden I Became the center of attention and all the eyes were upon me, but slowly I got more acquainted with the place and the people who lived there.

From that day, I would come every day to listen to the music. One day I sat in Gotza's house for a long time and I fell asleep. During my sleep I somehow fell on the floor under the table and no one paid any attention, so I lay there in this sort of hideout and slept for a long time. Nighttime came and I didn't return home so they started looking for me. They went to Gotza's house but they couldn't find me. Gotza's family said that I was there much earlier but I left without them noticing. There was a great worry in town and they looked for me at all the neighbors' houses. Finally I woke up from under the table and started crying, so they took me out with great excitement and brought me home.

When I was about seven or eight, my two much older brothers, Yakov Hirshl and Berl David, came from Harkov, deep in Russia, and brought with them a mandolin. My brothrYakov Hirshl during the First World War was lost and we never heard from him again. Anyway, back to the days before WWI. This was the first mandolin in Kurenets. My brother would play the mandolin and I would listen. Slowly I became more courageous and started playing, and became very proficient, so now other children would come to our windows to listen to my playing and they looked at me with envy.

Many children were envious of me, but I envied others. Who? I particularly envied the Kleizmers on Smorgon Street, who in my eyes were most splendid in their playing. How can someone move his fingers so fast without getting mixed up? I kept wondering that. The Kleizmers of Kurenets were all members of one family (Fidler), and all musicians, an entire family that controlled the town with their music playing. They were blessed with all sorts of talents and specialties. The head of the band was old Itzha Noach. He was known in town also as a humorist or comedian, and it is true that it was like twin sisters for him, comedy and music. During wedding celebrations, he would make jokes while playing music, truly entertaining the audience. They said about Itzha Noach that one of the butchers encountered him in the street and treated him with superiority, so Itzha Noach said, "Hear me, you have no right to disrespect me. My profession is nicer than yours."

The butcher said, "So let's hear why you think your profession is more respectable than mine. Let's hear it."

"Ponder this," said Itzha Noach, "when I go out to the street with my fiddle, who surrounds me? People. People who were born in the image of the holy. They all surround me. And you, when you get out to the street with a piece of meat in your hand? Who is surrounding you? Dogs. Beasts with wide open jaws accompany you."

In the ninth of the month Av [a day of fast], it was a custom in Kurenets to go to the cemetery and cry and beg the people who had passed away to plead with God for the sake of the living that all would be fine in the coming year. Itzha Noach,, his wife Nachama, and all their family members were all healthy, in good shape, but so that the Evil Eye would not take hold of them and so people would not say they were disrespectful of the day, they would also go, this old couple, to the cemetery. Many years before, soon after they were married, their first child died a few days after he was born. The wife of Itzha Noach looked for his grave and found it amongst the trees. She lay on the grave and begged and cried. She asked for his pity, pleading with him to go to the chair of the holy and speak to him on behalf of the nation of Israel, the house of Israel, and all the family members, and make him cancel any troubles and hard times.

When Itzha Noach realized what she was doing, he came behind her and said with a smile on his face, "Nachama, Nachama, everyone says you are smart, but did you lose your mind? Such a huge mission for the Nation of Israel you give to the hands of few days old baby? He will mix up the whole thing. You must stop crying. Let's go home."

When he was in good spirits his specialty was doing magic-like tricks while he was playing. Sometimes he would play Der Pastachal (The Little Shepherd), and he would play the whole story about how the shepherd came in the morning and would blow his horn to announce for the cows to come to the meadow, and all the little details that happened in that story found their expression with his fiddle. You would hear the opening of the gate, the sounds of the cows mooing, and the sounds of the calves, the sheep, the goats, the rooster… And things he could not get out of the fiddle, he would use his throat and his lips. The audience would be roaring with happiness. I particularly remember the wedding of Chanka, the daughter of Nachama Shaina, whose family were neighbors of Itzha Noach. Since the families were close, he did a particularly good job at this wedding. I saw him play the fiddle on his back, Oifen Kleitza. He would put the fiddle on the back of his shoulders and play it on his back while making jokes.

But clearly not every wedding received such a wonderful performance. Here there was the long friendship and good neighboring that affected the party.

In each of the players there was something special, and during a holiday or during a party, you would like them not only for what they played but how they played. The first you would observe would be the very short Avramel, whose fiddle was bigger than he was. He played the batnoon (bass?) and I noticed that many times as if out of habit, for certain tunes he would stand on the tip of his toes. Avramel was an unhappy Jew. He had bad luck and all the bitterness of his life he carried quietly with a lot of internal pain. But what did we, the little children, know of all his suffering? A child who arrived at the age of 10 and became a little taller would stand by Avrameleh and quietly measure himself, and their hearts would usually fill with happiness because they were taller than Avramel. So he was used by the young boys as a measure of the time of passing from children to adolescents.

Avramel had a family and some sons. The glory of the family was his son Chaim Biyenish, a fiddler who studied tailoring and was loved and respected by everyone. One of his youngest sons, Velveleh or Zaev Fiddler, joined the partisans during the war and became renowned for his bravery.

A true artist among the Kleizmers was Leibe, or the way he was known to us, Leibe Der Fiddler. He knew how to play classical concerts and serious music. He always got the role of Batzen Die Kalla, and the women in the audience, when they just saw Leibe starting to tune up his fiddle, minutes before he played, already would take their handkerchiefs out and started wiping their tears.

The son of Itzha Noach, Leibe the Tall, played the flute. There was a time when he was part of the Minsk Orchestra, and for that time he was known not as a Kleizmer but as a modern, cosmopolitan musician. How I loved listening to his soft tunes on the flute in different variations. We, the children, loved him. He knew how to entertain us. We would surround him in big groups and would stand with our mouths open, as if we were swallowing every tune, and we would be in deep, up to the point of losing ourselves in a world of softness and beautiful sounds that the flute magically created. Leibe would trick us, and all of a sudden, as if to surprise us and remind us that there was a world of down-on-earth reality, he would bend all of a sudden and make a circular motion with his flute on our faces. The sounds would be sprayed on us as if we were sprayed by a hose. We would wake up as if from a dream, jumping back, first from fear and later we would start laughing. He would immediately stand straight and serious with an expression almost of severity, as if this was part of the play, and the music and everything was in the notes he had before him.

The fifth among the players was Isar. He was also the son of Itzha Noach. He played the baritone. He wasn't a truly professional player. There was no depth in his playing. The way he played, it seemed like he wanted to attract you with external effects. He was always very cleanly dressed and his instrument was so clean and shiny that you could hardly look at it because of the shininess. As far as we, the children, he would look at us with an expression that said, "Don't be scared by the loud sounds. It's only the instrument that makes those sounds. I feel a lot of love for you children."

His main job was to accompany the other instruments and to fill the empty spaces between the other instruments' playing. He was almost like an announcer for the entire band, as if to say, "People, be ready! A wedding is happening in town. We are coming to you and you should also come towards us."

A big crowd would gather to see the people who had just gotten married, and the "goy women" who would carry water, would come running with their buckets filled with water to receive the young couple and their families, who would be dancing in the market square. At that time, in our eyes music was not something you could learn. We were sure that there was some mysterious way a person would be gifted with musical ability. We knew that someone could study shoemaking, tailoring, carpentry, and other professions, but we couldn't understand that someone could learn how to play, although I had learned how to play the mandolin.

One day, a young man came to town. We called him, Bentze der Tantzer, meaning Bentze who will make you dance. He had a dual job in town: he taught the young people how to dance, and he taught them how to play instruments like the violin, mandolin, and guitar. All the mystery of the ability to play disappeared. All of a sudden the town became filled with dancers and players and the kids were divided as talented or untalented, with a good year and a bad year, as it was customary to divide them in other professions. I was already able to play the mandolin, and became a professional, advising and making decisions for others. I was the one who said, "This child has potential, and this one does not." I was already in my teens when Bentze der Tantzer became famous in town. I would like to also tell you that he was very talented in drawing, especially in making posters.

We would gather in the house of Yekutiel Meir Kremer. They had a son who was blind ever since he was four or five. His name was David. Many of us remember David, who was very involved with people. He would sit in the barn and touch the different things like the wheat, the flour, etc. All he had to do was touch a little bit and he could tell what type of flour it was, what it had been made from, and even what color of flour it was. Sometimes it seems as if he knew people by the way they walked or the way they breathed. His younger brother Chaim Zalman Kremer, would sit by him and read the paper to him. David who had the most wonderful memory, would observe every bit of information. He was like a hole in the ground that would not lose one drop. Everything that was read to him, from important essays on the news to the daily unimportant information, all was kept in his head as if they were papers in boxes.

In the house of Yekutiel Meir, people would gather for Zionist meetings because the young sons were very involved. In all the rooms of the house there was the constant smell of fresh bread that was being baked. One day, when I came to the house, David told me, "Yehoshua I want to ask you something."

His eyes were looking straight up. I answered, "For you I will do anything you wish."

I must say that everyone loved David and everyone wanted the best for him. We would measure the advancement of medicine by the ability to be able to give David his sight back. Many times we would imagine the image of David going to a large city with famous doctors and here he sits at the doctor's clinic, being taken care of, and when he comes out, all of a sudden he is able to see. We kept talking about the big cities in the world, but who would give him his sight back in Kurenets? Sherkvas the goy? Sherkvas the goy who is a doctor's assistant who has a huge stomach and was always conversing with the devil and the spirits?

One day, David was taken to the big city to see some famous doctors, and we were very disappointed with science when they could not find any treatment for him. So obviously now I was ready to listen to his request. "I want you to teach me the mandolin," he said.

When I heard him say that, I was surprised at myself, that this idea never came to me before. I knew that usually blind people had a good ear for music. "I will be happy," I said to him, "I think you will be very good at it."

At that point I found out that this idea had come to him a long time before. His brother Yehiel bought a mandolin for David in Vilna, and brought it back to Kurenets. So David went and brought a case and opened it, bringing out a shiny new instrument. He held it almost fearfully, and his fingers patted the silk of the instrument. I took it in my hand and played a few chords and passages, and David stood across from me with his eyes open and his face, which had a little golden beard, appeared as if he was a holy image. He was about 24 at that point. On his face he had a kind smile, as if he was smiling to the tunes, and I started worrying. What if I couldn't fulfill his request? What if we find that he is not talented with music? It would be such a bitter disappointment I would take part in. For a minute I was quiet and as if he had read my thoughts, he encouraged me. "Don't be worried, Yehoshua. You will see that I will work very hard on this task and you will have no troubles from me."

I started teaching him and after a short time he was able to play perfectly. And now when you pass by their house you can hear wonderful sounds from there and you knew that these are the sounds that David lives in. You knew very well that this was not a matter of fashion, as it was for others. IT was the essence of his life. One of the most beloved tunes of David was The Tears of Israel. It's as if he lived this music in every part of his being's essence, and playing it was as if he was praying. At one time I brought a guitar and joined his mandolin playing, and his happiness could hardly be described. Always he would get a little crowd of children who came to see the miracle of how a blind person could play, and they became also very happy.

Everyone, it seems, was a part of his tragedy. Old and the youth. Even the most wild kids would stand there and listen to him in holy quietness.

Kurenets c 1922

Music playing surrounded the town. Some talents were discovered. One had an excellent ear and one had excellent technique of the fingers, and the town was filled with music that helped the youth express their sentiments and romantic feelings.The sound of the mandolin lifted the urges from the core of your being. Sometimes they would be exciting and happy, and sometimes full of nostalgia, all according to the rhythm of the song and its musical essence. One evening while I was sitting at my home, Yudith Yuda's, the wife of Abba Alperovich the Carpenter, came to me. She told me that her daughters Malke and Zisha, bothered her all the time. They wanted to learn how to play the guitar. She already bought them the instrument, and she was sure that they would be able to put it in their hands and the instrument would play. But there were no bears and no forests. The guitar is not a katrinka (a music box?). The daughters told her that you must learn how to play, and they would not leave her in peace, telling her that she must go to Yehoshua to arrange lessons.

She said to me that her daughters said, "Are we less than Ethel and Minya, the daughters of Itzha Haitza's [Itzhak Zimmerman, father of Charles Gelman]? They play and the heart widens when you listen to them. And look, mother, Batia and Dinka, the daughters of the rabbi are playing. And who is not playing now? Everyone is playing. Dvoshka the lover of Ilia Chaim Alperovich is playing. Leah the daughter of Dvorka is playing, and Chaika the daughter of Marisha Rikla is playing. Why is it our fate not to play?"

"They cry to me every day," she said, "and my heart breaks each day. One day I passed by Itzha Haitza's house and I heard sounds of music and singing, and I was sure there was a wedding happening in town, so I went by the window and saw a group of girls sitting in a circle, playing and singing, and Itzha, who was a very respected Jew in town, stood next to them, listening andsmiling. When they stopped playing he said to them, `Very beautiful, girls. Pleasant and pretty.'

"So at that point," continued Yudith, "if a Jew like Reb Itzha finds it interesting, why should I get mad at my daughters? For this reason now, I come to you. You must test them and give them a lesson, and whatever others are paying, I will pay too."

So on the appointed days I came to their house. Malke was already sitting with the guitar in her hand, playing. She had a narrow, beautiful face, with big black eyes and her curls fell like little bells on her face. The room was very nicely arranged, but despite the fact that the head of the household, Abba Alperovich as well as his son, were very professional carpenters, there was very little furniture in the house. In the corner stood a box covered with a table cloth, and on top of it there was a mirror. On the windowsills stood many little plants. After a short time, Zisha came from the other room. She was more full and sturdy looking than Malke. I started teaching them.

After a few months of teaching, both became members in the band that I organized, and Yudith, their mother, was very, very happy and proud. Not just mandolins and guitars the town knew.

New sounds started coming into town, the sounds of horns and bugles and trumpets. Shmuel Tsipilevich, Z"L, who was the head of the firemen, was a Jew who was busy with many different projects, and he decided that a brass band would be very beneficial for the fire department. During that time, the son of the head of the Polish public school in town, lived in Kurenets. His name was for Foremny. He graduated from the conservatory in Vilna. He was a very talented violin player, a composer, and a conductor, so he agreed to organize an orchestra or a band, and to instruct them. Formeny loved Jews. He did it voluntarily, with no compensation. He was very modest in his ways, and ran away from any publicity and honors. At first 40 people wanted to join the band, but slowly many left and there 12 men who became permanent members. We knew how to play a marching song, and we decided to have a parade of the firemen. Artzik, the son of David Lipa's, who was very tall, walked in front as the conductor of the parade. All the firemen dresed in shiny clothes, and at their head walked the band. Behind them were the water tanks and carts carrying hoses, pulled by horses. The parade went marching through all the streets of the town, and all the little children followed us. But this band was not only for the fire department. We played in the synagogue in different holy days. But here we wouldn't play marching songs, but Hasidic tunes. During Simhat Beit Hashoeva, we played in the synagogue that was filled with lights of the holy days. People were eating apples and enjoying themselves, and old people would dance, and each generation expressed its own way of celebrating.

Sometimes we would have some trouble. At one time we left a party in the early morning hours when it was still dark. One of the guys wanted to check his big horn (tuba?), and it seemed there was some kind of trouble, when all of a sudden there was a huge, loud sound coming from the center of the market. It didn't take but a few minutes when from all the homes people started coming in their pajamas and started taking their cows out to the meadows, thinking that it was the shepherd, who's custom was to call the people to send their herds. We realized it would be very dangerous for us to explain to people who were half-asleep that it was a mistake, so we just ran out of the market to every corner.

And here comes to me the old memories from the fruit garden of the Paritzta [the wife of the local nobleman?]. This was the garden that my father would lease part of, and that's where we made our livelihood. But it wasn't just a way to make a living. We were very drawn to the trees and to being out in nature. Each one of us loved this garden in his or her own way. Zalman and I would build a sukha and we would put some hay on the floor, and with the mandolin and the violin, come there and play. In reality we were supposed to watch the garden, but I swear that we listened more to our tunes than to look out for thieves. So here children would come to listen and to see the sukha where we lived both day and night. Here we would meet Velvel Matta Leiba Kooperstooch's, my friend who was like a brother to me, and Yashka Mendel Heshkeleh's [Yosef, son of Mendel Alperovich]. In the evening we would light a bonfire and would sit around, singing and playing music. Many of the youths of the town would gather here. The beautiful Raiycha, the daughter of Naftali Alperovich, would come and her laugh, with its melodic sound filled with youthfulness, would echo in the woods. Chuba, the daughter of Zalman Mendel, would sit here quietly, deep in thought. Israelke, the son of Yoel Sheffer and Liba nee Gurevitz, would crack jokes. One story I would remember was about a most devout Zionist in town who made a mousetrap with a Jewish star on it. Another was that a certain Jew in town, during the big fire, ran home and the first thing he saved and put away was the ladder that stood in the entrance, and then when he ran back he couldn't go to the attic where the rest of his belongings were. So the bonfire would be flaming and the trees would be filled with fruits, and then Arka the son of Masha Rikla, would sing solo and how could you not listen to the beautiful voice of Arka?

Our home was always open to guests and friends. Near our house on Myadel Street, there was a little tree garden, and I remember that one time we decided to have a party in that garden. There was no electricity in Kurenets, so what did we do? We took bottles and cut off the bottoms, putting candles in them, and hung the bottles with ropes around their necks, and we had the illusion of electric lights.

My father had a great imagination but he always tried to connect his imagination to his actual deeds. My father decided to grow fruits of the land of Israel in Kurenets. Watermelons were very uncommon in our area. Usually we would buy a piece of watermelon that would be brought from far away for Rosh Hashanah, for the blessing of Sheheheyano to make the year sweat. So what did he do? HE collected all the seeds and said, "If God wills it, next year we will have homegrown watermelon."

When spring came, Father put all the seeds in the ground, and before long little sprouts came. My father was extremely happy. At night he would cover them to protect them from the frost, and when the flowers fell and the fruits came, my sister Malke covered them with leaves and hay so that the cold earth would not hurt them, and during that summer that happened to be a warm one, a miracle occurred. Although the watermelons were small, they were sweet like honey. The first watermelon my father gave to Grandpa Hendel and to Zalman Bar the shohet who was his friend. Clearly we also ate the watermelons and were very pleased and we shared them with our friends and our watermelons became a major topic of conversation. Father saw in them the watermelons of the land of Israel, and he said, "We are the seed of Israel who were born in Kurenets, but in all our essence we belong to the land of Israel. Just like those watermelons who grew in Kurenets but belong in the land of Israel."

Days passed, then years passed, and I immigrated to Israel. My heart was very heavy when I did it. It was very difficult to leave the nest of my childhood and youth, to leave my old father and my sick sister. "Don't forget me, my son," my father whispered while clearing his tears. My heart twitched but I didn't show my feelings. I tried to smile a smile that was artificial, and it was immediately overrun by the tears that came from my eyes. Many years passed from that day, and until today, the little town that we so loved lives inside me. Inside me there are the images and the tunes. I see the little homes, the pavement that is cleared every Friday, and the balconies in front of each house. Each house had its own unique balcony. And the divers images; Shmuel Itza the blacksmith, a modest and quiet Jew who would work by the anvil every day. He would be standing there hitting the iron with his hammer, and his head would be covered with a kipa. Under his apron you could see the tallit. And here is Israel Alperovich, the butcher, with his sons Shmuel, Yitzhak, Zundel… each one holding the sedur in his hand on the way to the synagogue. [the family perished, but one brother survived and now, 2003, lives in Brazil] And Chaia, the mother, would be standing at the entrance of their home, and her eyes would be following them. And here I see Velvel der Klashnik [one who makes bicycles], a very smart Jew, tall and with a long, white beard. He was a God-fearing Jew that never strolled off the path of righteousness.

And here comes to me Avraham Shimon and Chana Leba his wife, their son Chaim Ben Zion started learning how to play the violin one day, and I was invited to hear him play. The family of Avraham Shimon was a very special family. Chana Leba was a righteous woman with a heart of gold. She was willing to give her soul for others. In days of rain and frost, you always saw her going in the street from house to house, to gather some donations for different people who were in trouble. People would joke that one time they heard her early Saturday morning in the synagogue saying to the heavens, "Good morning my good one. Here I am, your servant, Chana Leba. I came here to serve you as you deserve. Pretty soon your servant, Avraham Shimon, my husband, and also Ben Zion, my son, will arrive. Don't be worried that they are not here yet. They will not be late for the prayer. They are just finishing to drink tsikoriah with milk for the Sabbath."

There were other women who spoke to their father in the heavens as if he was a real father. One of those was Tsipa, the wife of Yasha Leib. When she would milk the cow and try to give the milk to people who were needy, she would say to them, "What do you think? This is my milk? This is the milk from the cow! Do I give the cow the milk? No, God gives the cow the milk." Then she would look at he sky and say, to it, "Gutenyou!, didn't I tell people the truth?"

They say in 1925 when the big fire took the entire town, Tsipa stood in the middle of the street, shaking her hands up to the sky and yelling, "Be wild you who created all, but you will pay from your own pocket for all of this!"

Who can describe all those dear images and all those sentiments and tunes that were lost? As a final, melancholy passage, always in front of me were the last parting moments in the train station in Vileyka, when my brother Zalman and I stood without words. At that moment I felt so much that I wanted the train to wait for a few more minutes. All of a sudden a sense that there was something very important that I didn't express to my brother. As if only this moment there was something that we both felt and it must be expressed, but there was no time. The cars started shaking, and Zalman went down quietly, and the train moved…

[Page 104]

Beloved Person

by Avraham Aharon Alperovich son of Yehoshua (ben Zalman Noach) and Rivka

Translated by Eilat Gordin Levitan

Avraham Aharon Alperovich

In the year 1918 to 1919, the youths in Kurenets embarked upon the organization of a Zionist movement in Kurenets. At that point I was still in school. I vividly remember how the adults came to us and called for a meeting of all the students in school and made excited fiery speeches. Even before we truly understood what they were talking about, the phrase "the Land of Israel" kept resounding in our heads. Slowly the sermons became clearer and we could follow the speeches a little better, our interest increased. Our intrinsic curiosity was unleashed and our imagination engaged.

During those days, Tzeirey Zion, an organization of Zionist youths was established in town as well as an organization by the name of Cherut and Tchia. Every night, boys and girls from the school would meet and coordinate games and political discussions. As time passed we started visiting the surrounding towns. We would meet with the youths of Vileyka, which was nearby, and we even exchanged letters with the center in Vilna. At the head of the youth movement there were leaders, and amongst them there were teachers from the Hebrew school in town, and they would make speeches about Hebrew literature, the history of Zionism and the history of the Jewish nation. We would have parties that aimed to collect funds for Keren Keyemt and Keren Hayesod (funds for Eretz Israel). We would regularly make the rounds of all the homes in town, trying to get donations for the miscellaneous Hebrew national foundations. We would sell pictures of the Zionist leaders, and once in a while we would put on plays in which we participated as amateur actors. In time we succeeded in getting most of the youths in the area to partake in our activities.

Ephraim Lieb Kramer

In all such activities, Ephraim Leib Kramer (son of David, Later changed his last name to Ben David) was the central figure. He would organize and energize the activities with his charismatic personality. He had a most splendid penmanship. Each letter looked like a pearl. He would also write all the correspondence, and during the meetings, he would many times debate much older people with courage, introspection and acumen. He was chosen as the head of the Zionist committee and with his energetic personality, the local branch was brimming with activities.

In the year 1922, the branch of Ha'chalutz was established in Kurenets. We communicated with the center and followed their instructions from the very start. I remember that year a few leaders from the center of the Ha'chalutz in Warsaw came to Kurenets. Amongst them were Y. Bankover and A. Dobkin. They gathered us and told us about our mission for the future. We all acknowledged the missions that they suggested to us, which would be concluded by immigration to the land of Israel. At the very beginning there were only a few members in Ha'chalutz, but at the end of the year, the branch in Kurenets became a very respected branch and was renowned in the entire region of Vilna.

We chose members to head the organization, and at the top of the organization (the head of the branch) we elected Ephraim Leib Kramer. Other promotions were given to other members of the organization, I amongst them. Each evening we would meet and discuss issues such as how to enlarge the organization, how to teach and promote better understanding of the Zionist pioneer movements among the youths. We started organizing the Ha'chalutz not only in our town but also throughout the whole region. We would go to all the neighboring towns and in time we were successful and managed to involve other youths who were committed to founding branches in other shtetls.

Ephraim Leib gave a lot of time and energy to these activities. Every Saturday, we would meet halfway between Kurenets and Vileyka with the youths in the area. There we would spend hours singing and strolling together. During that time we started organizing Hachsharah (training to live in an agricultural community in Israel), founding farming communities as educational/training places in which to study agriculture in different parts od Poland. We sent some members of our branch to such communities. I was among the first to live there. I went to an agricultural community by the name of Trumpeldoria near Vilna (in Lobodov?). There we lived and worked in an agricultural community. We learned how to clear and plow fields, plant seed, and milk cows.

Hachalutz in Lebodove

I spent almost two years in the agricultural community. Ephraim was not able to go to the farm since his father had died and he now became responsible for the support of his family. Despite his many responsibilities, he spent much of his time volunteering for the Ha'chalutz movement in Kurenets. In the year 1925 he immigrated to Israel together with his mother and his siblings, and after a few months, I joined him in Israel.

[Page 105]

I came to Israel together with a group called Hakovesh. We arrived in Petach Tikva during the very hot summer days. These were very difficult times. There was much unemployment, and most of the agricultural work was done at that time by the Arabs, and owners of orange groves in the area traditionally gave all the jobs to Arabs who were experienced and worked for modest compensations. Since we wanted to get those jobs, we had to work very hard to compete with the Arabs. We had to acclimate ourselves to jobs that were not familiar to us in Poland, in a very hot climate that we were not used to, working many hours for very small rewards.

Every Saturday we would walk to Tel Aviv. There was no public transportation yet. We walked through the sand; there was not even one road. Not only that, but we couldn't even hire a horse and carriage to take us because we couldn't pay for the trip. So, this way we walked in the sand, barefoot, with our clothes tattered, and hungry.

Ephraim, who came with his family, was able to purchase a home in the community of Trumpeldor, which is now the main thoroughfare in Tel Aviv, Dizengoff Street. He worked in the field of music. The house of Ephraim Kramer became like an island of Kurenets in the midst of Tel Aviv. Every Kurenetser who arrived in Tel Aviv would come to him, and he would receive us with extreme warmth. Since we were all new to Israel and everything was so foreign to us, Eprhaim Leib's house where everyone was invited to sleep and to eat was a haven to us. The house was always filled with guests. It seemed like every day there were new arrivals from Kurenets, and everyone would gather at Ephraim's house.

There were times when the new immigrants were not able to find shelter when they first arrived, and they would stay with him for many days. I will never forget our regular visits, every Purim we would come to Tel Aviv and we would feel like a big happy family when we walked together through the streets of Tel Aviv.

Some weeks after Ephraim Leib arrived in Israel he got a good job in Tel Aviv and was able to support himself. Dizengoff, the mayor of Tel Aviv, liked Ephraim very much, and wanted to give him a very respectable job in his cabinet. Ephraim refused to accept the appointment, saying that all the "respectable appointments" he wanted to leave behind him in the Diaspora of Poland. Here he came to Israel to live the life of a hard-working pioneer.

Amongst the family members who came with him was his aunt Nechama Dina, who was like a mother to all of us. She seemed to have unlimited energy. She always prepared our favorite foods for us. She was a pious woman, and in all her actions was dedicated to the youths from Kurenets.

In 1934, I left the area and transferred to Afula, and my visits with the rest of the Kurenetsers became limited because the distance was too great. But still, once in a while I would visit the Kramers. At some point, Ephraim moved to Ramat Ha'Sharon, where he established a most impressive agricultural farm. At that time, Ramat Ha'Sharon was truly an out of the way place. His house stood alone between Ramat Ha'Sharon and Hertzlia. His economic situation was very good and he seemed very happy…

…One day, I opened the newspaper and I started shaking. I read an announcement for the memorial of Ephraim Ben David Kramer in the cemetery in Hertzlia. I immediately went to the funeral and stood in shock by his grave. My heart filled with pain when I saw his mother Sarah Hinda. You could hardly recognize her. It seemed as if old age overtook her because of all her pain. This small Kurenets Island was overcome by waves of grief…

Hachalutz in Lebodove

The family of Avraham Aharon as told by his son Reuven

My father, Avraham Aharon Alperovich was born in Kurenets, his father was Yehoshua, son of Noach Zalman. His mother was Rivka. Rivka was related to the Gurevitz family. My father was one of the first Kurenetsers to come on "Aliah" to Eretz Israel in 1925. In 1927 my father was sent from Eretz Israel to a Zionist congress in Vilna. Commonly, when unmarried Zionist who had passports that allowed them to live in Eretz Israel visited Poland they volunteered to fictitiously marry local Zionist girls so they could bring them back to Eretz Israel (Visas were almost impossible to obtain otherwise). A girl from Moldechno from the Gutkovich family wanted to go to Israel, after they met for the fictitious marriage they fall in love and marriage became real.

*Avraham Aharon
and his wife*

They came to Israel to farm the land. They first settled in Gan Chaim, a community that had others from Kurenets as members (translator' note; My mother, Rachel nee Gurevitz, was born there in 1929). Kurenetsers in America financed the establishment Gan Chaim. The family of my mother (her mother with six of her half siblings) followed my mother to Israel a year later. My mothers' father lived to the age of 105. He had three wives and with each one he had some children. After his first wife died he married a widow by the name Mrs. Axelrod. Mrs. Axelrod had a son from her previous marriage by the name of Max Axelrod who immigrated to America and became very well off. Max who was never married, was a Zionist and philanthropist and gave money for many causes. He was the one who financed the immigration of the third Mrs. Gutkovich with the six kids. Max sent the family many new gadgets from America, amongst them was an electric iron. Electric irons were not common at that time and the Third Mrs. Axelrod never used one before. She misused it (the cord was in water?) and died on the spot. The kids were dispersed amongst family members and boarding schools. She was about 42 years old when she died. The entire family is still very attached to us. In the 1930s Max had a strong premonition of the tragedies that the Jews are about to face in Europe. He went back to Poland in 1938 to beg his half sister (also sister to my mother) to immigrate to Israel. The sister who was married with children and well off refused to go and the family perished in Molodechno three years later. After Max retired he came to live with us in the large farm he purchased for us in Afula. He diligently worked the farm until he died at age ninety. He had a great influence on my life. My brother Amos and I followed in the footsteps of my parents and uncles and we both have farms. My farm is in Nir-Banim. My son Yehoshua (named after my grandfather) runs the big farm while I have traveled around the world as an adviser to farmers. Yehoshua has four children. My son Nir has an important job in the high tech industry in Israel. He is a father of three children. My daughter works as a researcher in pharmaceuticals for the American company Pfizer in their Israeli branch. She has two sons. A few years ago I visited Kurenets and Molodechno. I was joined by my relative Pesach Gutkovich. In Kurenets a local official guided us and showed us a few memorials that were erected for the Jews of Kurenets. One was for the more then 1000 Jews who perished in 9-9-1942. Shalom Yoran financed the memorial. Shalom with his family were refugees in 1939, fleeing the Nazis who took over their hometown in the western region of Poland in September of 1939. They arrived in Kurenets were they lived until 9-9-1942. His parents perished on that day with the Jewish residents of Kurenets. Shalom and his brother escaped with other Kurenetsers and joined the Soviet partisans to fight the Germans.

The Soviet authorities erected another memorial. It is for the "Soviet citizen" who were killed on Simchat Torah of 1941 (it does not say that all 54 of them were Jewish). My fathers' brother; Asher as well as my grandparents; Yehoshua ben Zalman Noach and my grandmother Rivka perished on that day.

[Page 106]

A Few Lines

By Tzvia nee Cohen Even Shoshan,
(1910-1980)

Translated by Eilat Gordin Levitan

Is it possible for me to illustrate in a few lines, a few pale passages, those dear people of my father's and mother's home that are no longer here with us? Many memories passed through my eyes. Each memory will be chased by another and it is such a hard decision which of the memories I should bring to the paper. I remember our home, that stood in the central market in the center of the town. It was surrounded by trees and by green bushes and flowers. My father, Rafael Cohen, was the hazan [cantor] and the shohet of the Mitnagdim in town. He would sit by the table, deeply involved with his notebooks of cantoral music. My father studied to become a cantor with the well known cantor Siroka, Z"L. At home he would sit and sing and review all the different tunes that he was going to perform during Shabbat in the synagogue. My father was a very amicable man. He had a good sense of humor and loved jokes and was always in good spirits. Even in the most difficult of times, when he had worries of his earnings or there was some sort of controversy in the public life of the town, he would never lose his temper.

Mother, Esther Gitel, was a very capable woman. Everything she did she did well. She was an excellent housekeeper. She was always helpful to my father and all day long she would run around, helping her children. Our home was a Zionist home. All of us, my two brothers and I, studied since a very young age, Hebrew and the geography and history of the land of Israel. The sounds of Hebrew words were very often heard in our home.

The biggest imprint on my memory were the nights of Shabbat. We would all sit around the table, and my father would sing Shabbat songs after the evening meal, and we all would answer in a chorus. We would sing Shabbat songs and songs that were filled with yearning for the Israeli nation, and mother would sit across, tired from all the preparation for Shabbat, but her face would be shining with pride and contentment…

Years passed and we all spread out. My oldest brother, Avraham Meir, finished his studies in the seminar Tarbut in Vilna. He became first a teacher and then a headmaster in a few schools in different places in Poland. He taught Torah and the Hebrew language and filled the students with love for Israel. Deep in Yizkor he wished to immigrate to Eretz Israel but worries for the well-being of his parents and to his younger siblings delayed him from doing it. Time passed and I became busy as a teacher in Kurenets and later in Radoshkovicz. My youngest brother, Josef, who was blessed with a beautiful voice like my father went to study in the conservatory in Vilna and became well known. He became a singer in the choir of the big synagogue in Vilna, and also in the opera choir in Vilna. Only my sister Shoshana stayed home with mother and father. She worked as an accountant in the factory of Chaim Zokovsky.

Years passed and I, the lucky one in our family, received papers to go to Eretz Israel So I came home to say goodbye to father and mother. I remember the tears and the blessings of my parents, and the handshake of all my friends who came to say goodbye to me. My brother, Avraham Meir, promised me, "We will not be far behind you. There will be a time when we will all meet in our country, and this time will come soon."

Would it really? I built a home in Israel, a new life. I became a mother to children. [Tzvia married Avraham Even Shoshan, a native of Radishkoviczi who later wrote a well known dictionary of the Hebrew language. They had two children, Yuval and Dafna. Yuval now lives in Jerusalem, Dafna in Tel Aviv.], and the contact with my Kurenets home was only through letters and pictures. They kept hoping to immigrate, but kept encountering difficulties. First they didn't have the financial means and they were very worried about their ability to earn a living in Israel, which at that time was suffering economic difficulties. There was also conflict with the Arabs which caused fears in my parents. So in the summer of 1938, after eight years in Israel, I decided to go for a visit to my hometown. I took my five-year-old son Yuval, and my friend from Kurenets, Emma nee Alperovich Tzivoni with her daughter Edna, and we came for a visit.

Yuval Even-Shoshan
(Son of Zivia nee Cohen who wrote the chapter)
and Edna nee Zivoni
(Daughter of Emma nee Alperovitz)
during a visit from Tel Aviv to Kurenets in September of 1938

Once again I am in my little town. It was not much changed in all the years that I had not seen her. It was the same quiet life, the same houses, and the parents, although they looked a bit older, had the same pleasant light in their face. We gathered all together, all the family members. We sat there for many hours, and I told hem of our life in Eretz Israel. The happy memories and the troubled memories, and they wanted to hear everything, as if their ears could never be filled. "If God be willing, we will all soon join you," my father kept repeating. And my brother Avraham Meir, the Hebrew teacher, announced that he would soon immigrate but he would not be a teacher, but a farmer. He would be busy with building the country. He said, "It is enough for me that all the years I was a teacher here that I taught others the message of love of Zion, so now it was time for me to get up and build my home in Zion. It is time for me to farm the land. And not only for me; Josef and Shoshana and mother and father we will bring after us."

So once again I said goodbye to my family and returned home. At this point my heart was very sure that we would be together in Eretz Israel. Anguish, This meeting was the last meeting with my dear ones…

Not many months passed and the sounds of war were heard through Europe. Years of toil and blood, and all lines of communication were cut. My heart feared what would happen to my dear ones, but deep down there was a glimmer of hope.

Maybe the horrors would pass and I would see them. Slowly the horror of the Nazi Holocaust started to arrive to us. Every day we would find more tragedies. We found out that towns were burning, and Jews were thrown in the fire, and the horrible story of Kurenets arrived. I found out that amongst the shtetls, it was also my shtetl Kurenets. And amongst the martyrs there were my dear ones: my mother and father, my brothers and sisters. They all fell in front of their killers, on 9/9/1942, together with many of the Jews of Kurenets, and the heart cries and refuses to be comforted.

The husband of Tzvia was Avraham Even-Shoshan [Rozenshtein], Even-Shoshan, Avraham. ha-Milon he-hadash; otsar shalem shel ha-lashon ha-`Ivrit ha-sifrutit, ha-mada`it veha-meduberet, nivim va-amarot `Ivriyim va-Aramiyim, munahim benle'umiyim, me-et Avraham Even-Shoshan, be-hishtatfut hever anshe mada`. Yerushalayim, Kiryat-sefer, 726-30 [1966-70] PJ 4830 .E93m [Note: Accompanied by supplementary volume "Kerekh milu'im" (324 p.) issued in 1983.] 7 vols.

He also wrote *My Father, Chaim David Rozenshtein* **in** *Minsk, ir va-em.*

[Page 108-115]

The Tarbut School

by Israel Gvint (son of Sima nee Meltzer and Zalman Gwint)

Translated by Eilat Gordin Levitan

Israel Gvint

Many wrote reminiscences of the Hebrew schools in Kurenets to hail the images of the students and their teachers who were annihilated in the holocaust. Still there are many unrecorded memories that live in the hearts of those that relocated to a safe haven and now find themselves scattered across the world. Although the following lines aim to convey a shared testimonial by many, but to which I know I can't avoid bringing my own knowledge and intimate connections. My father of blessed memory was a person for whom the school was the center of his universe. This fact would be clear in my story, because many of the obstacles that the school encountered somehow intermingled in my personal life.

When was the school established? When I try to answer a question like this I have trouble pinpointing a specific date. Supposedly the school was established after WWI, around 1921. Guided by my old memories, which were validated by others, I seem to remember that during the years of the war there was an attempt to establish a school in town. And what I speak is not in reference to the Cheder metukan were they taught Hebrew in Hebrew which started before WWI, the one I had heard of in tales. Those Cheders of those earlier generations had their own important place in history but they could not fulfill the needs of following generations. The town, which was situated on main roads and near a train track, saw the war face to face. Here settled at one time, battalions from the German army, Kozaks brigades from the Tsar's army, battalions of the Red Army, and battalions of the Polish army. The different battalions exchanged places according to the results of the battles. One would leave and the other would enter, and the town kept changing rulers. Many of the soldiers would live in our homes and that made life very unsettled. Also, many of the town's natives were ordered to serve in the army and were far away from their families. In those days there were many cheders where the children of Israel would receive an education. But this system of education lost its zeal during those days and the war very much affected the spirit of the children. It was as if a sense of lawlessness controlled the streets. The children watched the adults and started busying themselves with their own wars. The battles that the children waged took place on two hills that were situated between Smorgon and Myadel streets. It was in Dysyanka that the children would stand and throw stones at each other. One of the most common games was to light bonfires and to put live bullets that we found in the area and watch as they exploded. Often these mischievous games ended in accidents.

We watched as beaten battalions would retreat. We also saw splendid battalions marching in pristine uniforms to the sounds of drums and army bands. And we, the young ones, would run after them all the way to the edge of the town. The days were tinted by shades of changes. In such an environment, something new easily captured the hearts of the children and controlled them. But it had to be something fresh and something exhilarating, and the cheder was an old tradition, which could not extend this vigor over the children. Opposed to the old system, the new procedure where you had a recess between studies and a bell and youthful teachers appealed to the children and woke the town out of its sleepy educational routine. The days of the Russian revolution initiated a permanent imprint upon the town. The manual laborers of the town, who were the sons of the poor, together with many of the youth, became welcoming candidates for the new ideology. In the central town's market, many ecstatic speeches were made. Also, the Red Army spread their propaganda through theatre troops that traveled to the area. The Bolsheviks confiscated the mansion of the paritsta, where subsequently the army would host plays that the whole town would come to see. To top it all off, there was tidings in the Jewish world about the Balfour Declaration and the return to Zion. All these factors deeply affected the population.

At the same time, these circumstances that offered diverse ideologies affected various people in a different way. Even in the days when the battle was raging around us, there was a female teacher who gave lessons to both male and female students and it was like provisional school.

*During the German occupation in the First World War (1917),
with the German teacher bottom*

*<u>Left to right</u>: Leika Meirovitz, Chana Alperovitz, Batia nee Gurevitz Bender, Rachel Alperovitz, Ema nee Alperovitz Zivoni.
<u>Middle</u>: Henya (Menachem Mendel's) Kramer, ?, The German teacher, Feygel Alperovitz, Frumka Meirovitz, ?, Feya nee Alperovitz Rubin, the boy is the son of Zipilovitz.
Others are unknown.*

For a short time there was a school with one or two classes that was managed by Yudel Dardak, where the studies were done in a combination of Yiddish, Hebrew and Russian. More wonderful memories of the great personality of Yudel Dardak stay with me than memories of the lessons. There was also an attempt to open a night school. The teacher there was the son of Chaim Baruch the Shamash and also Isaac the son of the mill man from the village Khallafi. Different enterprises worked for awhile until the war ended.

The war seemed to sow the seeds to institute a new school and the prior lack of clarity as to whether the school should be in instructed in Yiddish, Hebrew or Russian became clearer. The Balfour Declaration and sons of Eretz Israel that prior to the war were only talked about in hushed tones were now talked about in real and clear statements. Now and then we received letters from the land of Israel and some people were taken with the idea of going to live in Eretz Israel. Once in a while, preachers of Zionism came to town and the entire town would gather in the synagogue to hear their speeches. A Zionist committee was established in town by the name of "Tzeirey Zion", (the youth of Zion). And also for the teenagers there was a committee, "Herut VeTchia" (Freedom and Renewal.) One day someone brought a new song in Hebrew to town and this immediately became the "song of the season". They kept bringing new songs and one of those songs, which I recall

"Shalom Allaychem Yehudi, meayin Yehudi ba LeEretz Israel?/ Peace to you Jew. Where does a Jew come from to the land of Israel?. For the first time you would hear people speak to each other in Hebrew." The words came out hesitantly but with much love.

If it were only the untroubled "detached" environment that the Kurenets residents would look for, the new school would not have been established. To establish the school, you needed people that were entirely dedicated to the idea. I would not be untruthful if I said that my father, of blessed memory, was the most involved in this endeavor. He was one who sacrificed every day of his life for this enterprise. Here I must say that his great involvement was deeply affected by finding me, his only male child, without any proper education when he returned from his service in the First World War.

The beginning was very difficult because my father had to fight much ignorance and many old fashioned ideas. He had to rent a place for the school, get school benches and find appropriate teachers. Many memories come to me from those days. I remember that in the very beginning, the school was not in just one building but in town. There was one class in the house the Shochet; Rafael Cohen, at the back of his house. And the second class was in the house of the mother of Shmuel Spector. At that point the studies would be done in two languages, both Hebrew and Yiddish. The teacher who taught the subjects in Hebrew was Berl Dardek and the Yiddish teacher was Rabinovich. The singing teacher was Yosef Shimon Kramnik, (who perished in the Holocaust ed.). Other than having the most beautiful voice, he also had the most beautiful penmanship and we all tried to imitate him. Many desired to equal his very curly signature. At that point there was still a quiet war between the Hebrew and Yiddish as to what language should dominate school studies. If the Hebrew won this war it was because of the special personality of the teacher Berl Dardak.

At this point, the image of the teacher Berl comes to me. Berl came from the near-by little town of Ilya. He was short, a red head, and wore glasses. He was very easy going and kind. Even when he would get mad it was easy to imagine that he was not really angry. We knew that he wrote poetry in Hebrew, and that made him very respected in our eyes. Some of the poems became songs and they were sung by the youth from the "Tzeirey Zion", and "Herut VeTchia". In their essence they were humorous poems and this was very attractive to us, the young children. Although we knew that these poems were not written for children, and truly we were not allowed to sing them, but somehow we learned them secretly and they were as sweet to us stolen water.

We knew that Berl and his brothers Shmaryau and Yudel Dardak were the descendents of a well-known rabbinical family from Illya. We also knew that they had a deep education in yeshivas and were very knowledgeable about the Bible and religious studies. This fact added to the respect we felt for them because now when we had to argue with people who were old fashioned and wanted to keep the traditional type of education which was essentially religious in nature, we could argue with them that our teacher was not a nobody, he was a telmid khakham . "You must be careful when you speak against him."

When Berl would get mad at one of us he would use biblical sentences to express his dissatisfaction. He would say, "ben naout vemrdut". In the essence of this sentence there was everything we desired, here was a religious language turning to a "real language" where biblical passages contained emotion. Passages from the Bible became material for common phrases of reproach. At that point we had no schoolbooks in Hebrew and Berl would write his lessons on the blackboard and we would copy what he wrote in our notebooks.

Berl lived in a tiny, dark room of Shmuel Spector. In his room there was an oil lamp that burned day and night as an eternal flame. Clearly our hearts were pulled to this room which became inseparable from the school. Here many youths would gather. We sang songs and told jokes and from there we would leave for walks in Vileyka and Dolhinov streets in Kurenets. I remember one journey that some older kids took all the way to the village Retzke and of how jealous I was of my peers that followed the older students there.

Having the school in two homes so far from each other made it very difficult. After a short time they rented a home of Eltka Nee Perski Rabunski (ed. the sister of the father of Shimon Peres). This was a comparatively big house. It had three rooms, a hallway and a large yard to play in. During the holiday of Purim, just before the school was transferred to this place, we held a play there. It was King David. The play was written by Berl Dardek, who was also the director and was responsible for the clothing the scenery. The walls were taken out and the space became one big room. Still the room was too small to hold all the people who wanted to attend. When I arrived with my father, and I was one of the actors in this play, many people stood by the door looking in and all the other actors watched so that more people wouldn't try to come in. Even Batya nee Gurevitz who had the main part as Batsheva took a turn watching the entrance. My father and I could hardly make our way through the people. My father somehow succeeded in getting in and I stayed behind among the people. Since there were so many people the girl who played Batsheva (Batia nee Gurevitz Bender) couldn't see me despite the fact that I was supposed to be her son in the play, I was King Solomon. Finally my father came to my aid and picked me out of the crowd. Besides the play we recited poems in Hebrew and Yiddish and it was a big success and many of the parents in town were so impressed that they began accepting the idea of a more secular education.

During the last months of the first year of the school there was still a silent war between Hebrew and Yiddish but it was becoming clearer that Hebrew would win. By the end of the school year a child by the name of Yitzhak Raykhael visited Kurenets from the big city of Vilna. He was a student in the Hebrew Gymnasia in Vilna and on his hat there was an emblem in Hebrew letters that said 'Gimmel' and 'Ein' For us the students, it was a very special thing, although we had become more accustomed to Hebrew as a living language, a language that came out of holy books to secular books. Still to see Hebrew letters on a hat was very surprising to us and we saw it as a big victory. At the end of the school year there was again a play held in the big barn of Schmuel the son of Yente. The subject of this play was a lesson in school. The role of the teacher was played by Aron Meyrovich. I found myself in trouble and it is a miracle that I emerged unscathed by it. My role in the play was to demonstrate a science experiment to Yokhevet Zipilevich, the daughter of Zalman Mendel Zipilevich. I took a glass filled with water and I covered it with paper and supposedly the air pressure would prevent the water from spilling when I turn it. But to my great dismay, in front of all the community the water spilled on the floor and I felt extremely embarrassed. All of a sudden a thought came to me. I adlibbed and said, "And here I showed you how not to do it. The glass was not filled with water, now I will fill it to the top!" and I tried it again and the water did not spill, and my teacher was very happy with my adjust text.

The second year all the studies were taught purely in Hebrew. The teacher by the name of Kozch'akov taught us. But after some time he emigrated to Eretz Israel there were many thrilling rumors told of how he managed to move to Israel illegally. He was very skilled at forging stamps and with his own hands he made his own stamps and forged to certificates to cross the various borders to get to Israel. In our eyes the image of our teacher Kozch'akov was imprinted as a mythical character that allowed our fantasy to run free with images.

Shmuel Dardek the brother of Berl and Yudel replaced him. He looked very much like his brother Yudell. He was a doer, full of energy and very involved with people. During the lessons he gave, the children were very focused on his words and in their respect for him were elements of worship. He taught us grammar and Bible studies. He was very quick and fresh and had the reputation of being a very brave and strong person. Just about that time Hannah Spector, the mother of Shmuel passed away. In the house during the shiva days there was a gathering of people every day for priers and the minyan. People said that our teacher Shmuel Dardek would read between the prayers of Mincha and Maariv from the book of Job, which elevated his image among the religious people of the town who saw our almost "secular school" in a negative light.

As I mentioned earlier, the hat with the emblem caused great envy among the children. Some of the adults also took this seriously and not many days passed before the children in our school started wearing hats in blue and white. One morning my father returned from Vilna and when I went through his belongings I was very excited when I found shiny metal emblems. On the emblems were inscribed two wings with Jewish stars in the middle and underneath there were three letters 'b' 's' 'h', which means Hebrew School. Who could imagine what I looked like that morning when I came to the school with a true emblem on my hat. It was the first emblem and for that special event I wrote an essay in our school newspaper, "Beit Sifrenu".

Berl Dardek poured much love and toil into the newspaper "Beit Sifrenu". He was the editor. The student who had the best handwriting would rewrite the essays. As I remember the first poems by Ahron Meyrovich were published in this paper. In the first edition there were also poems by a student by the name Leibke, son of Haia Rashkas' who later immigrated to America. I remember a story by him, Anotosh the Drunk, with a wonderful description of how Anotosh tries to catch his rooster so he could sell it in the market and use the money to buy alcohol. During that year a guy by the name of Volkovsky came to town. When he first came he was a photographer, but having quickly become a soul mate of the Dardek brothers he became very involved in the school. Although he believed in Yiddish, he had no conflict with the brothers because he had such a lively personality. Volkavsky was very creative: he wrote poems, painted and made sculpture. He was also the orchestra conductor, played musical instruments and was a P.E. teacher. He wasn't officially a teacher but had great influence on us, the students. (He later married in Vishnevo an aunt of Shimon Peres)

We loved the school and we happily volunteered to come early according to certain role to light the furnace. During recess between classes, we held dances and for the first time boys and girls danced together, and here the first romances were initiated. Anyone who remembers those times would clearly recall the Luria sisters Minoukhka and Mikhla (Louria?). They were twin sisters who came from the Soviet Union with their mother. They were on their way to join their father who had left earlier for the U.S. Minoukhka would dance beautifully the ballet of Swan Lake and Mikhla had a beautiful voice and many of the boys were secretly in love with them.

The studies were very intensive. There was a period where we also studied Talmud. Some of the students were able to read from the gmarrah independently. Still there was something very exciting about these new studies. We studied from the ???. The brothers Dardek once again proved that in this field they were very gifted. When spring came we started taking journeys to the forest. I remember one meeting in the forest in Vileyka, where our school and the Tarbout school of Vileyka met. When the students from the other school arrived one of us made a welcoming speech to the guests in Hebrew. He expressed hope that the Hebrew language would spread like the sounds of the birds chirping in the branches of the trees. It was a very poetic speech and the respect that our school received was tremendous. Just before we parted we sang together the song in Hebrew 'Sham beEeretz Avot' (In the land our forfathers). The town of Vilejka was considered a enlightened, cultural, modern , and cosmopolitan town by us. It was the main town in the district. Her houses were larger and more beautiful and her residents were wealthier. Considering these factors, the children of Kurenetz felt inferior. But during this meeting of the two schools, Kurenetz showed itself superior in education and creativity and we felt that more of a balance had been established.

At the end of the year we were tested both orally and by written exam and the tests proved how much we had advanced during the year. In my memories the third year was the highlight of the school. It had some experience and some of the students advanced farther. One student went to study in Villna in the Hebrew Gymnasia. We had a new challenge. We wanted to prove that we were at least as good as the Hebrew Gymnasia in Villna. We wanted to show that the school life in our town was more interesting and wanted to use this students as a gauge of our progress. The teachers established a club at school composed of three committees: a cultural committee, a library committee, and a judaical committee. In the judaical committee we would hold trials of two natures: one using literary sources, the other drew on disciplinary sources. A student that became a defendant had both a defender and a prosecutor. Once, I found myself a defendant. My crime was that I drew on one of the library books. In this trial Mr. Menachem Rodinski, one of the headmasters of the tarbout school in Villna was present and the speeches and special essence of the school left a big impression on him. The literary trials held at our school became well know in our area, and one of the trials was written about in the monthly magazine Tarbout and was later used a sample for trials in other schools. I remember that our first "literary trial" was based on a poem by Tzernechovski by the name of "Velvele". In this poem Velvele was being pulled in a sleigh by the "Meshulach" during the cold winter on his way to Eretz Israel and he became very sick and for three days was delirious with high fever until he died. Tzernechovski (rightly so in my opinion) did not give the details of Velvele's sickness. One of the children was the persecutor in this trial. He was very, very upset and made a fiery speech about the father of Velvele who didn't bring a doctor for the child, and argued that if it wasn't mentioned in the poem then it didn't happen. He claimed that if a doctor was brought, Velvele would have survived and made it to Eretz Yisrael. After that there was a fiery argument about the poem. During that year the library was filled with books written in Hebrew. There was also a world map and a map of Eretz Israel in Hebrew. We had many fundraisers and parties from which all the money we collected was used to buy tools for science experiments. From then on we studied nature and physics with tools, although there were many accidents while we were experimenting.

Whenever a student would show a special talent, he would be very encouraged. Shmuel Spector showed artistic talent and my father was able during a visit to Villna, to find an appropriate school for him. Many times when students left to school to study a profession, he would stay in touch with us. The school was much more than just a place to study, our lives were deeply rooted in it, spiritually and ideologically. For example, when Shmuel Spector had an artistic success he would send us pictures. In the middle of the school year our teacher Shmoya?? received an appointment to the service and had to leave. He returned after a few months he returned with a higher rank and we were very proud that even the Polish army recognized his superiority. At the end of that year, many of the children at this point came to a crossroads in their lives. Some planned to go to Villna to continue their studies and the older amongst us dreamed of going to Israel. After a year Schmrel Dardek left Poland.

The school moved from the Rabunski home to other homes, amongst them Leib Yaakov Torov home on Myadel Street. It was there that they did the final exam and once again it showed how we had advanced, and how deeply rooted we were in the Hebrew language. These years in school appeared to me as though dream and reality intermingled, and on the horizons of our memory had a unique splendor. The school continued until the outbreak of WWII which brought with it a new period of hills and valleys. A great time was when the wife of the Commander in Chief of the Israeli army was Badana ni Pintov. Badana returned to Kurenets after returning since she knew Hebrew from her early childhood she had no trouble teaching in Hebrew.

The hearts of the children were conquered by her pleasant ways. She only taught us for one year, 1924. And I remember how bitter we were when she left, but there was sweetness in that bitterness since the reason she was leaving was to travel with her family to Eretz Israel. The emigration of the Pintov family was very important to the school. The Pintov family was related to Elemenef Schulman left Kurenets when he was still a young man. He went to the U.S. were he got very wealthy (ed. in the junk business). I remember those autumn days of 1924 when Elemenaf Schulman came to visit Kurenetzs. The days were cold but filled with excitement. The conversation in every house and synagogue was about the large contribution given by (now) Max Schulman. The biggest contribution was to the Beit Nigraf?? the synagogue of the ???. He built a new synagogue with a large bima, a very luxurious, finely crafted dias (?). Max was also the person who paid for the Pintov family's trip to Eretz Israel and their home and big yard in Yaddle Street became the property of the school. Shortly after they left, Max paid to build another building in the yard, and from that day on the school had its own permanent home, which was adjacent to large fields. From here it was not far to walk to the boulder in the Savina forest and also wheat fields and meadows. A special time were the years 1929-1932 when Druvel ni Zikovsky (ed. perished in the Holocaust). She established a unit of Hashomer Hatzairr (a socialist, Zionist youth movement). Her special nature was evident in everything she did. This was the renewal of the splendid first period of the establishment of the school, when the spirit of youth and social commitment melded into one, wonderful essence.

In the year 1938 I returned for a visit to my parents after living in Eretz Israel. The Germans, who later we realized were getting ready for war, brought from Poland a large amount of agricultural products and paid a high price for it. Poland, it seemed, had a financial renewal, and the improved financial situation was even evident among the Jews. At the same time, there was a very clear feeling of anti-Semitism that I experienced everywhere. For me it was clear that this economic improvement was only a sweet pill filled with poison and my visit passed with a very ominous feeling of peril. During one weekend I came to the Hebrew school to talk to the town people about Eretz Israel.

Kibbutz Bamesila, Nes Ziona, 1935
Left to right: Shlomo Mindel, Ahraon Meirovitch and Israel Gvint

Many came to listen to me. There was a new generation of students, but at the core it was the same school of eighteen years earlier - the nucleus school enveloped by a pasture of great hopes that launched the flourishing Tarbut school of 1938. Although it was a year before WWII, Kurenets was already on the edge of annihilation.

[Page 116]

Memories, Memories

by Pesia née Taubes Norman

Translated by Eilat Gordin Levitan

We lived on Myadel Street. The street began in the market and ended in the Shvitzapola. Exactly what is a Shvitzapola we never knew, but we interpreted it as two words, meaning Shvitza, which means "whistling or making a loud sound", and the second word was Pola, which meant "field." When we put the two together, in our imagination we saw a place that was either a street or a field, and the wind would whistle loudly on it. Our house was situated on an incline in the street, across from the post office. To walk all the way to the Shvitzapola required a pretty long journey. It was a house made of wood, and it had a high front porch. My father worked as a wheelwright for carriages and wagons, and for his job he was known as der Kalasnik, meaning wheelwright. We were a big family. I had three brothers, Yankel, Moshe, and Chaim, and three sisters, Yente, Nachama, and Tirtzah. And I was the youngest in the house. I was only nine years old when I became orphaned from both my mother and father, and all my care and education fell on the shoulders of my brothers and sisters.

In town when I was very young, there was a teacher who was a native of the town. He was a bit nervous and lacking in patience. He taught the girls and we that were pretty boisterous recognized his weaknesses, so we sat amongst ourselves and whispered to each other and when he looked at us we would smile innocently. We knew that this treatment made him very mad, however he did not take it stoically, he repaid us with insults. The occupation of our parents became a weapon of humiliating us. If a girl would write a crooked letter "Nun" and her father happened to be a carpenter, he would say, "Look at your letter Nun, it looks like your father's hammer." One time he was very mad at me and said, "Look at your samech, it is as huge as your father's wheels." This made me very mad and I cried. When I told my father what he had said, I immediately cried again, but my father patted my head and said, "Why are you sad, my child? To the contrary this makes me rather happy. I see I have a loving daughter who is so helpful in her father's profession, which is to make wheels."

But at that point he decided to transfer me to another school, and he sent me to learn with Eliyau Abba, Z"L. He was a Jew that had a heart of gold. He had blue eyes that were filled with kindness and were always smiling. He had a nice beard and was very easygoing. The house of Eliyau Abba was small, and was stuck in one of the yards in the market, amongst much bigger homes. The sun would reach that house only a little bit during the morning hours, but despite all that, it was pleasant to be in this house, and it was as if there was some light in it. It was the light of the smiling face of Eliyau Abba that filled the home, even in hours when no sun would touch the house.

During winter, the little windows would be covered by flowers of frost, but the house was still filled with warmth and love. Eliyau Abbawas busy teaching us how to write and would tell us beautiful and enchanting stories. The fathers in town who became worried about the future of their children and were tired of the old system of the cheders, gathered and discussed the idea of creating a Hebrew school. The most dedicated to this project was Mr. Zalman Gvint, Z"L. No difficulty would stop him. He did everything possible until the school became a reality.

I have no idea how the school was funded since the town, which had just recovered from the aftermath of the First World War had no economic resources. I remember that they leased an apartment in the home of Shimshel the Baker. It was a big apartment and here there was no lack of light. The rooms of the school were large, facing southwest, and the sun filled the rooms very generously. We decorated the rooms with different pictures of Zionists. There was a picture of Herzl, there was a picture of the poet Chaim Nachman Biyalik, and Zalman Schneur, and others. The teachers were natives of the town Ilia, near Kurenets. They were the Darduk brothers, and they were very liked by us. At the same time, youth movements were organized in town, and also night classes to learn Hebrew. Berl Darduk would write plays, and the children became the actors and the plays would be performed in front of the entire town.

Years passed and the students and teachers changed. Among the teachers was Badana nee Pintov, (later the wife of the first Chief of Staff of the Israeli Army, Major General Yakov Dori). In all her soul and essence, she was dedicated to the school and the students and the children loved her dearly. During the fall of 1925, the uncle of Badana, Max Shulman, came from the US. He became very, very wealthy in the US (from the junk business?), and since he was a very generous man, he transferred the entire family to Eretz Israel, and their house he bought from them and donated as a Hebrew school that was named for him.

I remember that fall, it was a very cloudy and rainy fall, and the streets were filled with mud and puddles. Despite all of this, people were running all over town, looking to what the next good deed of Max Shulman would be. First he went to the cemetery to pay a visit to the graves of his forebears, and all the town was watching him. Many joined him in his visit so they could tell what had happened, and many, many stories were told about Max. They said that Max Shulman gave the daughter of Tanhum, who had no hand, a lot of money and soon she would go to Warsaw, where they prepare for her an artificial hand. People told that he gave a huge amount of money to build a fancy bima [a stage] in the synagogue of the Mitnagdim. It was a very, very artistic bima. It had pillars that had braid-like carvings on it, and on top of that, there were angelic creatures with their wings covering the ceiling. It also had sculpted lions and tablets, and all sorts of decorations that would bring to your heart the Bible studies that we studied in school.

There was a Jew in our town by the name of Chanan Shlomo from Dolhinov Street. He lived in a tiny house and people said that he was meticulous and orderly, and even every rusty nail he would put in its appropriate place.

There was a time when Chanan Shlomo was a student in the cheder of Max Shulman's father. The people found out that he had an affaer, two passages written in calligraphy by the Rabbi that the students had to imitate to practice their lettering, so in town they told that Max Shulman paid a huge amount of money to buy the affaer from Chanan Shlomo which was written by his father. It was a most dear treasure to him from his father…

Memories, memories come before my eyes…

Some of my very first memories and also the very last memories of my town.

Memories of the nest where I spent my childhood, the nest that we left many days ago as soon as we grew wings. But we returned to the nest, whether it was a physical return, or more likely, a return in our thoughts and our nostalgia-filled hearts until the storm came and all was annihilated.

Kurenets, summer of 1924

The teacher on the left (second line) is Berl Dardak, on the right (second line) is his brother Shmerl Dardak. The teacher in the middle (4th line) is Vilkovsky, a gymnastic teacher who did many other things – was a painter, a photographer, wrote poetry (Yiddish), and married a relative of Shimon Peres from Vishniva. Some other people: First line (top): First left – Avraham Dimenstein; second left – Israel Gvint; first right – Sarah Meirovitch. Second line: near Berl- Rivka Shulman. near Shmerl – Perez Hasid. Third line: First left – Freidale Zimerman. Fourth line: first left (near Vilkovsky) – Ethel Kepelevich.

[Page118-122]

Illustration

by Avraham Dimmenstein

Translated by Eilat Gordin Levitan

Itzhi Chatzi's (Itzhak son of Yehezkel Zimmerman) Each epitaph or maxim must sprout from certain life experience, yet after it germinates it becomes like a lamp that lights the experience from which the epitaph came out of. It brings out the memory or character of an encountering.

There is an epitaph that says "The phrases of the acumen are expressed in a peaceful, pleasant manner", every time I hear this proverb, immediately the image of Itzhi Chatzi's arises in front of my eyes. He will come to me, walking toward me very erect. He walked in a regularly paced, calm manner, dressed in very refined, impeccable clothes, all of his appearance is filled with serenity and self-assurance.

I tried to remember if I ever saw him hurrying somewhere, and I could never remember a single occasion. He was very even-tempered in the way he interacted with people around him, but this was not limited to only the people around him, but in all of his dealings with the creator.

This is the way he approached the ark, during the High Holy Day. It was this manner that he used when he read the Torah with his powerful and crystal-clear voice. Many times when he led the prayers for the synagogue, he appeared as if he was spilling his soul to God. He humbled himself before God, but when these passages would come from his mouth, there was a certain strength that would not ever be heard with any other clergyman. When you heard his prayer you visualized even the most difficult words and they became apparent. His style of explanation was almost pedagogical, as if he was demonstrating to our Father in Heaven in a brilliant voice that he must rescue his nation.

From all that I know, Reb Itzhi never left the town. With great astonishment I would ask myself, "Where did he study and how did he study?" Since his knowledge was so vast and covered so many fields, it was such an inexplicable thing. He was like a sponge that never lost one drop. Not only did he have an excellent memory, but he also possessed analytical sharpness and he would have great insight and ability to clarify difficult topics.

I loved Reb Itzhi very much. There was a time when he was my teacher. I loved listening to him during debates. He would speak quietly and peacefully, and slowly his argument would pierce his opponent. It would cut through the weak spot of his opponent's argument and then take apart the core of his reasoning. Sometimes he would just hint, sometimes he would use analogies, but he would always be concise, pinpointing his arguments. After he had concluded the debate, there would be no questions left to ask.

I remember that on one of these occasions, the rabbi from Lublin came to visit. His aim was to collect donations for the foundation of a Yeshivah. He delivered a sermon in front of a large crowd in the synagogue. If I am not mistaken, the subject was the basic rules of the Torah in the Rambam. All of a sudden, Reb Itzhi stood up and made a comment. I don't remember the comment or the details of the debate that ensued, but I remember how surprised the rabbi from Lublin was by the cleverness and the revealing, insightful statements of Reb Itzhi. I remember him saying to the most respected Jews in the town, "You have a most precious pearl in Kurenets, and you are blessed."

On one occasion, Reb Itzhi saw a man from town, one who liked to pretend he was very scholarly. The young man was reading nothing less than the book "Yeshu hanotzri" (Jesus the Christian) by Kloyzner. Reb Itzhi came to him and looked at the book and simply asked, "Tell me, my dear, is everything from Genesis until Jesus Christ is clear and known to you?"

I remember the days when Germany started the war with Poland in September of 1939. People would stand around in small groups, busying themselves with politics and strategies. Someone stood and proved with all sorts of evidence that in just a few weeks, Hitler would arrive. Itzhi came to him and said, "Why are you scaring the crowd? Hitler will not arrive here; he is afraid of the white bears."

Everyone started talking and found some comfort in the statement since it wasn't anybody who said it, but it was the respected Reb Itzhi. And here Judkah, the son of Hasia Riva, who was a great admirer of the Soviets said, "And maybe he's really afraid of the Red Bears?"

Reb Itzhi knew to win debates without answering. His face had the expression that showed how silly he thought the point was, and though he was left without an answer, Judkah still felt he lost the argument.

Not many days passed and then the Russians arrived in town. They wore white uniforms for camouflage. Now Reb Itzhi found this occasion as a good time to answer Judkah. He met him in the street and said, "So Judkah, red or white?"

I remember that the goy Mishka Takotznik was drunk and he started a brawl, and Reb Itzhi came to him and said a few words. Mishka immediately seemed to sober up and said, "You are right, Mr. Itzhi, you are very right. In God's name, justice is with you." He immediately stopped fighting.

But this event accord in a time when knowledge and light still reigned. With the 32 martyrs the blood of Reb Itzhi was spilled. [1]

The light darkened in the world. The darkest of desires jumped out, and darkened his life as well as the lives of his family members…

A Winter Day at Dawn

The snow came non-stop, and everything was covered with frost. The windowsills were decorated by flowers of frost. White steam would spread from mouths and nozzles, and the road under your feet appeared furious and shrieking… The winter is cruel and you must take care of yourself as well as your home. The furnaces must be constantly fueled… Brutal and relentless.

I would get up at dawn and go to the market to see if the villagers had gathered wood for sale. Outside it was still dark. Very few walked around. A few solitary Jews on their way to the synagogue to pray with the first minyan. The tallit and fellim under the arm. The snow crunching under their feet.

The light in the windows doesn't help to light the street. It appears as an internal light, only lighting the home itself. Only when I arrived behind the house of Yekutiel Meir Kramer would a happy light spill all over me. This caused by the light that came from the minyan in the house of the rabbi.

The first to arrive are already praying, and the light would mix with the tune of the prayer. And the light and the prayer would fall on the road where I walked, and filled it with warmth and hope. In front of me stood the Polish Kosotsyol surrounded by leafless trees, and above the trees all of a sudden a whole flock of crows came up and cut the air with the sound of their call.

I passed Myadel Street and stood at the entrance of the market. The market was still dark and only near the house of Mendel son of Shimon Alperovich, of passersby. A little further you would see wagons filled with wood that would be taken to the market. I would come closer and the shadowy forms became recognizable. They all moved in the start, hitting one foot on the other to warn themselves, their hands were deep in the pockets of their winter fur coats. As I recognized the people I said, "Good morning, Nachman" (Menachem Shlomo Chaim).

He responded, "Good morning, Avraham Aron. What, you also need to come so early to buy cheap?"

"Yes, as you can see, also I. Tell me, what does the goy ask for it?"

"An ocean of money. Five golden coins he is asking for."

Meanwhile, the rest of the Jews came close to see who arrived. Most of them were from the poor population, people who woke up early to receive some discounts. Yitzhak the Shoemaker, David the Shoemaker, Yoshua from Dolhinvo Street, Chaim Reidel from Kosita Street, Shlom the Smith with his blind son who he guides by holding his hand, came to pray and meanwhile stopped to see what was occurring. To bring some life into this dark, sleepy, frosty, pre-morning, I would say in jest to Yitzhak the Shoemaker, "Yitzhak, what would you say to our Nachman who came to shop?"

"No, no, it's not so bad," said Yitzhak, who was kind in his nature.

"He wants me to get up so early to ask for discounts! You must have heard that Lubenska the nobleman sold Nachman his forest, but Menachem has no time to take control of his forest because he's so busy with his passengers that he takes to the train station."

Everyone stands there smiling in a friendly manner. Some laugh and others just smile quietly. "Yes, for you it's easy to make fun," said Menachem, also in good spirits. "The hammer and the nail of the shoe do not ask you to feed them, but my dear, for me things are very different. The children are asking for food, Vaska, my horse, is asking for food, my wife is not a violin that first you play and then you hang on the wall. Today is not a summer day. I cannot send my Vaska to eat in the meadow. If I already took two Jews to the station, you must believe me that I am telling the truth, and if not I am not a Jew. Until this minute I did not see from them even a broken coin. They promised me to give me something only on Tuesday after market day. So for you it's easy to make fun." Nachman ended his speech…

And while they were standing there in the market, all of a sudden, Vashka the horse came by. Maybe she was bored, maybe she was cold, or maybe she just got tired of standing near the porch. Or maybe she heard her name mentioned and became curious.

"You see," Nachman said, "Maybe if you mentioned the name of the Messiah he would arrive."

Meanwhile morning light started piercing through. The frost pushed deeper into your bones and the goy refused to lower the price. Then Nachamka the fisher woman arrived with a variety of fish. "Buy some fish, fresh and tasty fish," she would say.

Yitzhak the Shoemaker again turned to Nachman, "Look at yourself, Nachman, what a sinner you are! What are you missing here in Kurenets? Fish, meat, wood. Everything could be given to you on credit, but you are lazy! You are too lazy to take it." And everyone laughed.

From afar two people arrived from the synagogue. They are Artzik Dinnestein, and Avramil Itza Pesach's Alperovich. "Ah," said Yitzhak the Shoemaker, "Now the goy will give in. Avramil will talk to him."

Avramil first comes to Nachman and says, "Nachman, what is with you? I have already finished praying and you still haven't bought the wood?" He takes off his gloves and extends his hands to the goy, greeting him, asking him how much he wants for the wood. The goy insists on his price, and Avramil argues with him, trying to bargain down the price. He takes the hand of the farmer and squeezes it tightly until his body becomes crooked from the pain. "Three and a half gold coins you want?"

"No," says the goy, "it is five coins."
"Okay," says Avramil, "three and sixty (cents?)", squeezing his hand even tighter this time.

Still there are two more handshakes, and the goy appears resigned to lowering his price. Avramil is a strong Jew and this affects the goy very much. "Only for you, Avramka. Only for you. To anyone else I wouldn't sell."

So now Avramil takes the carriage filled with wood and gives it to Nachman. "So you think 3 gold coins and sixty I have in cash?" Avramil takes the coins from his pocket and says to Nachman, "What are you afraid of? That I will escape from Kurenets tomorrow and you can't pay me back? When you get the money, you pay me back. I can get by until then."

Nachman is very reliable and everyone knows there is no more honest man than him.

"And how are you and the rest of your family?" Avramil asks Yitzhak the Shoemaker.
"My family is written in the prayers, and everyone is beloved. I love my children from the depths of my soul. Everyone is pure and clean. All my children are sweet and cute."

Everyone opens their mouth and says, "Give me bread to eat, give me clothes to wear. Oh, Avramil, this is the way things are, things are very tiring."…

[Page 123]

Dolhinov Street

By Chaya Altman

Translated by Eilat Gordin Levitan

Dolhinov Street originated from the central market. Half of the street was settled by Jews; the second half started with the Christian house of worship that stood on a hill. Directly across from that hill stood a Jewish home with a very shallow roof. It always seemed as if that home shrank with fear from its neighboring buildings. There was a time when the Gvint family resided there. Immediately next to that home stood the homestead of a Christian family, which was surrounded by apple trees that during spring would blossom with splashes of white amidst mottled ivory and streaked fuchsia. Nearby, a small bridge spanned the town river. Here, Jews would come during Rosh Hashanah to perform *tashlich* (the casting away sins into water). On the right side of the street behind the bridge lay a verdant meadow. A bubbling brook there was used by the town people as a source of fresh drinking water. Starting here, most of the homes belonged to Christian families; there were only three Jewish homes, ours included. On the property line between each of the homes were vegetable gardens or fruit orchards. At the very edge of the street, the municipal buildings stood at the edge of the street. There was a public Polish elementary school and across from it, the Polish community center and a statute with a regal eagle astride it, with its beak facing east.

Near the community center, there was a livestock market. This place only bustled on Tuesdays, but each Tuesday, it overflowed with buyers and sellers who bargained over livestock of every horn and hide, kosher and non-kosher. Since the place laid empty the rest of the week, it became a playground for the young boys and girls of Kurenitz. The soccer players would gather here for practice and the bicyclists would ride here. Somewhere behind the elementary school, a path meandered south toward the Ungerman Pool. There, we embroidered our whispered teenage and childhood secrets. When we were members of the youth movement *Hashomer Hatzier*, we would sit here, singing songs of our impassioned desires to go to Israel. Throughout the year, not only in the summer, there was a lot of activity around the pool. Since the pool was frozen in winter, the teenagers would ice skate and sled on a hill that belonged to a non-Jewish noblewoman.

From the edge of Dolhinov Street stretched a wide avenue lined with ancient birch trees on both sides. We called this area the Palisades. When one walked down the avenue, one would first reach the village Bidkovichisna and then the train tracks to the *pulstanak* (semi-train station). In reality, trains would only stop here for half a second. Still, this was a very valuable station for the waggoneers, whose livelihood depended on receiving the visitors that stepped off the trains or the natives who had gone far away. In the days when the young men would immigrate to the land of Israel (*aliya*h), the celebration in this station was very exciting. Many of the residents of Kurenitz would gather in this station to say their goodbyes. There were many tears, songs, and cries of longing.

Dolhinov Street was a street for strollers, especially before sundown. Every Sabbath, I always felt that Dolhinov Street was like the air that we breathed, a necessity. After lunch, the entire town would stroll up and down the street. Our house stood next to the home of a certain Chavitan [?] who had **a Chesnut tree** with heavy branches and large leaves. Underneath the tree was a public bench. Many of the strollers would sit here to rest and often, one would hear laughter and song. Across the street from us lived the family of Michal Alparovitch. Adjacent to their home, they had a factory that made oil. When I was still a naïve young girl, I wanted to rally people's spirits for the Zionist cause. So I began preaching to this family about the need to sell all their property and immigrate to Israel. Among the arguments that they brought before me, they once told me half-jokingly, "How can we leave Dolhinov Street? If we lived on any other street, it would be easier to leave." The street was truly a beauty. There were no large homes and no mansions. The estates were small and the roofs covered with wooden tiles and straw. Everything that grew around the houses burst at the seams with verdant freshness and spaciousness.

1. Three daughters of Ytzi Zimerman perished in the holocaust. (Ethel and Minya Spektor perished in Kurenitz on the same day that their father perished and Sarah with her family, in Volozhin) Ytzis' wife Feyge, perished with

her grandchild, the baby of Mina and Sam Spektor on 9-9-1942. A son and a daughter; Dina survive and they now live in the U.S. The son who changed his name to Charles (nee Yechezkel) Gelman wrote a book "Don't Go Gentle" about his life during the war. You could find excerpts of his book at http://www.eilatgordinlevitan.com/kurenets/k_pages/stories_gentle.html.

"I was the youngest of the five children. My oldest sister, Sarah, was married and lived in the town of Volozin. My youngest sister, Dina, about four years older than I, was also married and lived deep inside Russia, out of reach of the Germans. Also living at home were my two middle sisters, Ethel and Minya. Minya was in the last stages of pregnancy. Her husband, Sam Spektor, had received permission to visit his brother in the city of Kharkov in Russia two weeks before the war started. When war broke out, he couldn't get back. He remained deep inside Russia throughout the war and survived."…

[Page 125-127]

From the Notebook of a Teenager

by Itzhak Arieli [née Alperovich]

Translated by Eilat Gordin Levitan

In the spring of 1925, during the afternoon hours of a certain Tuesday, a weekly market day when all the farmers from the surrounding villages came to Kurenets to buy and sell their products. The market was filled with people and livestock. Fire started at the house of Aharon, son of Zvi Shumlan, or as he was known in the town, Artzik der Biager [the Tanner]. A big flame came from his house, and it took but a few hours and most of the town was burned. Our home was immediately burned since it stood in the market right next to the house of the Shulman family where the fire started. The library with thousands of books was burned. The house of the Hasidim was burned with its clock on top, the clock that would fill us with awe and wonder, and obviously all of our studies from that point were suspended.

The Aftermath of the Fire of 1925

Our family, which had already experienced some tragedies at that point, now became homeless and we had nothing to support ourselves with. We lay down in the field, on top of a few belongings we managed to get out: some pillows and blankets that we risked our lives to save from the burning house. Some officials from the Polish authorities came by, and the help they gave us was only a nod of their heads. And our heads didn't even have a place to lie down! The family of Leib Yakov Torov was filled with pity for us so they let us all join them in their house, which was already filled with children. During the summertime we slept on hay in their barn, and in the winter we slept on the furnace.

The day of the fire became the last day of my official studies. At first I studied in the cheder, and later on in the yeshiva, and at the point when the fire started I was in the Tarbut school. But now I had to start a new chapter in my life, in the "school of the toil of living." I remember how I lay down on the steps of the stores that stood across from the yard where the house of my grandfather used to be. It was the property that belonged to all the grandsons of my grandfather [Binya Alperovich]. I looked at the yard where we started building a new home. We cleaned the yard from the remnants of the bricks and the dust, and my brother and I helped the builders as much as we could. I was shocked that on that Saturday, when a few so-called experts came by, and looked at the frame that was being built for the house, and decided that the frame was crooked and was leaning towards one side. Those experts said, "No wonder the frame was crooked, it is a widow who is the foreman for this enterprise."

At the end of that summer in the year of 1925 I worked in the apple orchard picking apples, and later, my friend Shimon Zimmerman, took me for a month to guard with him a fruit garden near Kriviczi. The days would pass for us beautifully in nature, and the nights were filled with fear when we had to guard from Christians and their dogs and also from thieves. When winter came, our family moved to the house despite the fact that it was not yet finished. There was no floor and there was only one room that was used both for living and for business since we needed somehow to make a living, so we opened a hervatziarnia [a business that sells tea, salted fish, and other such things]. Many times the farmers would come and eat while I was asleep on my corner and they would sit right on the place where I was sleeping to eat their food. This was the most difficult winter for me. I was lonely and far from all my friends and had no warm clothes to wear. I couldn't even walk to the synagogue since I did not have any winter shoes. The vista from my prospective looked very dark. I was an orphan from my father. I was small and weak and many times was on the verge of starvation. Even now, after many years have passed, I still am not able to free myself from the terror and anxiety that I experienced that winter.

As the winter was coming to an end, I heard rumors that Yehiel the son of Yekutiel Meir Kramer was going to open a fadrad, which was a place to bake matozos. He was going to open an enterprise operated in a modern fashion, and he would need young people to help. So with the help of Avraham Dimmenstein, I planned on how to get accepted for work so I could earne a little money for Passover. As a child I was always in awe of those guys, the radelu [?] who stood next to tables covered by some kind of thin metal sheets, and they would roll a special tool to make holes in the matzo.

In my eyes they seemed so capable and cool. Who would not want to do something like this? I was used to the old style of matzo making the way the parents of my friend Shimon Zimmerman did. I loved all the activity in the place where they baked matzos. One would put the flour, another would add the water, and others would mix the dough and on wooden boards they would knead it, roll it out, and then they would make holes in it and put in a big, tall oven that was taller than anyone, and this gave a special holy day atmosphere to life in town. So on that first day, when they started baking the matzos for Passover that year, I got up very early and put on my broken shoes and with excitement I came to the building. But inside I found many, many that needed the job and as the bosses arrived there was a big pandemonium. Each one tried to enter and at that point, my elbows were very weak, and I wasn't able to push my way in. So after I walked around for about 15 minutes I realized there was no place for me here and I walked home disappointed. My mother understood my frustration and tried to console me, saying, "Nevermind, my son, we will survive even without this job."

But I couldn't console myself and the anguish of being orphaned became unbearable for me. It must be that my miserable situation became known to certain people in town, so Chaim Kramer tried very hard to find something for me to do, and he was able to get me a job as a messenger in the bank. This was a very appropriate job for me since I was very good at math and also because I was meticulous. So in a short time I did well in my job and my financial situation improved tremendously.

Small shopkeepers, merchants, craftsmen, and any other money earning Jew utilized the bank in Kurenets. The number of members in the bank was more than 300, and it was almost equal to the number of money earners in town. There was no limitation put on potential members as far as their sex, the amount of possessions or property you owned, to become a member of the bank. The "joint" financed the operation by giving something around 24,000 zloty. Together with the savings we were able to give loans of more than 100,000 zloty in a fair and democratic way.

***Yosef Shimon Kramnik, head of the
bank of Kurenets, with his family***

The bank was not for profit, and the interest was the usual at that time, taking into account the conditions after the war and the inflation. I, as a sixteen-year-old, had some technical difficulties since I had such a responsible job, and sometimes when Yosef Shimon Kramnik [son of Hillel] who was the head of the bank would not be present and then I encountered a lot of difficulties. Also, many times I would see the injustice of the wealthier customers getting larger amounts of money, which was against my beliefs I would protest. Sometimes I would get instructions that I must deliver notices to people who didn't come to get their money on time and that the loan was not authorized. When they would come and bitterly complain to the bank about what was done, other employees of the bank would use me and say I was inexperienced and it was I who had made the mistake. So this situation became more and more difficult. It seemed that as time passed more and more people couldn't pay their loans and they sent me to warn the people who didn't pay and force them to pay something. I was also supposed to go with the person who would repossess belongings, which was extremely unpleasant for me, and clearly my life was not one of milk and honey. Many would complain to me as if I was guilty, although I did what I was ordered to do by people who were above me.

The typical business of the bank was giving loans and taking collateral. Amongst the people who used the bank there were some who were not Jews. The people who signed on the loans were the residents of Kurenets and they signed the loans for other people who bought merchandize on credit from enterprises in Vilna. Clearly the bank had a very important duty in giving them credit and it was particularly important since it was the only institution of such activities in town until they opened Gmilut Chesed [an interest-free loan place] which was managed by Itzhak Moshe Meltzer, but I cannot tell you much about it because I had very few dealings with them.

First the fire of 1925, and afterwards there were financial difficulties that limited the activities of the bank, and Chaim Kramer worked very hard to keep it afloat. Although it did improve in the years 1930 and 1931, some of the loaners couldn't return their loans and they kept prolonging the length of the loan, so obviously the interest kept rising. So many of the loans had to be declared as lost. Since the people were bankrupt, and also the taxes became larger as the Polish government asked for much more from the Jews, and the population, which contained mainly small merchants from the middle class, became poor and unable to earn sufficient money. For the very poor, it seemed like the loans were the only means of survival. When they were not given anymore loans and they had no more means to survive, they stopped seeing the bank as a place for assistance and only saw it as a leech sucking their blood.

The twists of fate and the Nazi killers entered the lives of the Jews in town. But the youth who had a healthy outlook at the future, realized years before that the financial base of the community was falling and that life was very unstable in the shtetl. We loved our hometown but in some way we were feeling like foreigners there, and knew that to add another mercantile business to the market would not solve that sense of foreignness.

From my position in the bank I was a daily witness to the poverty and the difficulties that life in the shtetl presented. This made me wish even more for a very different life, despite the fact that my personal situation (at least from the financial point of view) was fine in this institution. So one evening, quietly, I left the town on the way to the land of Israel. And this came as a great surprise to many, and especially to the few who knew how I felt and kept trying to convince me that I should stay here and describe to me my rosy future in town.

A corner in the Kurenets market
The picture was taken at the end of World War I

The homes from the right:
1. Mota Lieb Kupershtoochs' (father of Zev and Yosef)
2. Aharons', son of Tzvi Shulman (father of Nyomka, Chana, Rivka, Rashka and Bela)
3. Pesya and Moshe Alperovitzs' (parents of Benyamin, Rachel and Yitzhak Arieli from Dan)
4. Reshke and Zalman ÊYechezkel Alperovitz (parents of Meir, Pia, Sara and Moshe)
5. Chaim Avraham Alperovitz, father of Daniel (Dania), Zertel and Chaya
6. Leib Charnas home. After "De Glaska" (the alley)
7. the home of Lea Etka (with the two floors) almost all of the home owners perished in 1942.

[Page 128]

A Miracle of Spring

by Chana Alperovich

Translated by Eilat Gordin Levitan

There are chapters of youth whose imprint remains deep in the soul. With a touch of spring, they appear miraculous and dream-like, even if they took place in autumn or in winter, we keep returning to them in our imagination, to cherish them and to be held and comforted by their shine.

Such a chapter for us was the creation of the youth movement, Hashomer Hatzair in Kurenets. Until today I cannot explain rationally how and why it happened, but we felt a miracle of the creation of something splendid. A feeling that maybe a tree feels during early spring days when his branches fill with flowers, perfume-like smells, and freshness.

The reason that I repeat the images of the miracle and try to explain it with different words is that I don't know the simple, basic way to do it, so I will try now to tell the story as it was.

A family came to our town, the Zukovsky family, mother Pesia, son and daughter. The son, Chaim Zukovsky, was once in Eretz Israel but he returned and built a home in Kurenets, where he owned a mill. The daughter finished her studies in the Hebrew gymnasium in Vilna and came to Kurenets during her holiday to visit her mother and brother. Her name was Dvushel, and in Vilna she belonged to the youth movement Hashomer Hatzair, and she was a troop leader. She was petite, with reddish-brown hair, and big brown eyes. There was something brave about the expression on her face, and when she smiled, her self-confident countenance turned into a appearance of charm and intelligence. In her appearance there was something that pulled you to her, and at the same time there was a calming effect about her. It was very enjoyable to be with her.

Dvushel was very different from the other girls in town. She always wore a green or yellow shirt, and a khaki skirt. On her waist she had a belt, and her shoes were simple, but all her clothing was very clean and pristine. It was simple and not fancy, but still quite charming.

It took a few days until the young girls dared to approach her and asked her why she wore the wide belt, and she explained she belonged to the youth movement Hashomer Hatzair.

Her voice was very special. She had confidence but at the same time it was soft. It was deep and calm. Clearly, because of her we immediately liked the youth movement Hashomer Hatzair…

To tell you the truth, it wouldn't be true to say it was only because of her that we liked the youth movement. The youths felt a need to do something new and different. Our young hearts were already trained by the branch of Ha'chalutz movement that was in town, and also by the Hebrew school, but when Dvushel arrived there was a period of decline, and she awoke a new interest in us.

It wasn't only the very young girls like us who were influenced by her. Also, the teenagers were attracted to her, and all of a sudden it seemed that there was vigor among the youth in town. In the evening there were many who would stroll along Dolhinov Street. People would argue and debate politics, and you would hear voices singing. Soon a few people decided to establish a branch of Hashomer Hatzair in town.

Shortly after, we were told that Dvushel decided to stay in town until she was ready to go to the Haksherah, which was training to become a pioneer in Israel. She also took a job as a teacher in the Tarbut School. This was the autumn of 1928, and in my memory, this autumn felt like springtime.

Looking at it now, our cultural and educational mission was not yet momentous for us 9 the very young), but there was earnest enlightening and cultural involvement. Children of all backgrounds, amongst them even the neglected kids, were introduced to new horizons. How happy, for example, was Dov Reidel, who lived at the end of Kosita Street. He came from a destitute family. How excited he was when he wore the tie of his unit. For the residents of the town, it was a little revolution in the social life, as the rules of Hashomer Hatzair, which stressed equality, simplicity, and love for other human beings, became values that we all held proudly.

During that time, together with Dvushel, Aharon Meirovich became a leader of Hashomer Hatzair. Aharon Meirovich was known in town as Aharonchik. In Kurenets, people predicted that he would be very successful. They said that he wrote poetry, and some of it was published in Vilna. We knew that he was not from a well-to-do family, but he excelled in school.

Some of the older people in town thought that the excitement of the youths was strange. They saw it as regression. They looked at our excitement as childish and without purpose. In their sober and grim world it didn't make sense.

Autumn passed and winter came. There was much more to do and more members enlisted. Dvushel was busy with both teaching and leading activities in our branch. Leaders of the movement came from Vilna and Warsaw. They made speeches, we sang songs, had conversations, discussions, played games, and went on journeys… Aharon was sent to Vilna to one of the conventions of the movement. People became very impressed with him and our branch in Kurenets became well known.

The spring of 1929 was a very special spring amongst all the springs of my life. For hours we sat together, singing with all our souls, with deep yearning. We walked through the fields to the forest of Sabina, to the big rock, and there we would sing songs in harmony, and we sounded even better than the choir of the village Pokken.

The sound of singing could be heard from the town, and the old Jews who saw themselves as very serious and rational would now listen to our Hasidic songs that were heard from afar, and it awoke something in their hearts. Deep down they wanted to join us. Still, we were strange to them and some of them said mockingly that we were "a Baptist cult". But there core feeling of suspicion begun to shift.

I remember our first journey to Narutz Lake. We passed through thick forests, new vista. We slept on hay in the barn, and we met with the youths of Myadel, an isolated town. We danced the horah in the central market to a crowd of people from Myadel. The ties between the youths of Myadel and the youths of Kurenets were established.

Later on we went to a meeting of the entire region of Vilna in the village Rivacki, near Smorgon. Kurenets received many awards for excellence, and Aharon received a high award from Hashomer Hatzair, and I cannot describe how proud we all felt.

There were also comical moments. I remember that once in a meeting 30 km from Kurenets in the village Tzivalki, we stayed in the house of the mill owner. He lived in an isolated home. His son, a large Christian man, would not leave us alone and he demanded that Aharonchik wrestle with him. We were very worried, but a miracle occurred and Aharon brought him to the ground. From then on he treated us very respectfully.

In that same meeting, one of the girls fainted. Ironically, it was during first aid training. Everyone became confused and ran to help her, looking at the pamphlet that explained what to do. While they were looking at the pamphlet, the Christian woman that owned the house entered and took a pail filled with cold water and used the old system to wake the girl up.

One day, one of the guys went to Kurenets to get some bread. He wore short pants, a fashion that had never before been seen in Kurenets, and the entire town became very frightened. "Who knows what is happening in that retreat?" Some traveling [itinerant] Jewish merchants were sent to the retreat to see what we were doing there. They found us living in a camp, in a perfectly organized way, very content. So they returned to town and told wonderful tales, and everyone was very happy.

I remember that one time we went to get donations for the Keren Keyemet, funds for Eretz Israel. We entered one of the houses and explained what the donations were for. The woman of the household didn't understand us. She thought that Keren Keyemet was a specific poor Jew, so she gave a nice donation and with a deep sigh said, "My dear ones, may I always be able to give you donations, but hopefully there will be a time when he would not need any more."

Sometime later, we performed a play that Aharon had written, and Alter Zimmerman was the director. The day before the play opened, two of our friends came riding on horses, dressed as Cossacks. They held big pamphlets and the entire town came running after them, especially all the young children. In the evening there was a huge crowd for the play. All the tickets were sold, but still there were many that looked through the door and windows.

Members of the movement went to training, the first was Dov Benes, and later Dvushel. But when she returned it seemed like she had a different spirit, now filled with depression and disappointment. Days passed and others left for the Hachsharah (training for agricultural Socialist life in Israel). Some members were able to get certificates to go to Eretz Israel, and we would have big parties for their departure.

The branch had periods of blossoming and periods of decline. New generations grew. The ones who were small children when the branch began now became its leaders. During the Holocaust, some of the core members established connections with the partisans in the forest, and a few of them became renowned for their bravery.

For us, the first members, the beginning of this branch would always be like the miracle of spring. A wonderful blossoms by itself, but also a life-changing occurrence for many of the youths…

"Tarbut School", 1933

Hashomer Hatzair Center, 1934

Members of Hashomer Hatzair in Kurenets

[Page 131]

A Journey in Your Vistas

by Aharon Meirovitch

Translated by Jerrold Landau

Every time I close my eyes to see you in my spirit, for some reason your eastern hills appear first, and from there, the full vista of your manifold various details is exposed – every time I seek to see you… I do not know the explanation for this, but I can only surmise: This is possibly because the windows of my house looked over the hill that is over the village of Pukan. Perhaps it is because the wonderful sunrises over that hill that I saw in bountiful fashion during my childhood – sunrises of gold and purple. The colorful images come with thoughts of the heart.

Even now, when I wish to fly over your face, I don't see you first without that hill, from which the sun shone upon me every day, and from which I sail over you southward, westward, and northward – over your fields and pathways, plots of land and plots of dust – changes of times and preparations of the heart.

You had a hill. I saw it through the window – sometimes with the greenery of the fields and sometimes with the gold of the grain, sometimes with the black ploughed fields, and sometimes covered in white snow. On its side a small village spread out, with a strange name – Pukan. Above the village, the place where the skies and the earth joined together, the godly sunrise took place every morning – the creation of the world in miniature. Between the place of the noble sunrise and the holy chambers of my heart, as a stain that has a sort of hole in it, the small village with the strange name of Pukan appeared as dark. In its houses lived gentiles with watery eyes, without depth and without Jewish agony. Their hair was like flax, and there were brazen dogs with strong tongues in their yards…

This is none other than the greatness of the trait of mercy that was in our hearts. Therefore, we did not toughen it up, and we connected the name Pukan with the most precious of all names – the Land of Israel:

"Through Pukan one travels to the Land of Israel," the people of my city would say. This should be light in our eyes, even though it was said with a bit of sarcasm.

The hill of sunrises. It imparted its influence and went westward – over the gardens of cabbageheads, onions, and other vegetables, and finished up over the banks of a small river, over which the willow branches spread their splendor. From the river and onward there was a wide meadow. It became a large pond of water during the days of Nisan on account of the melting snow. During the months of Iyar and Sivan it enthused the heart and eye with a bounty of flowers, of which we only knew their colors, and not their names…

The river flowed southward, crossed Dolhinov Road, and passed over Kosita Street. At times it flowed swiftly, and at times slowly. It moved the wheels of five flourmills along its path, until it reached the town of Vileyka, and flowed into the open arms of the Viliya. There were large bogs and springs of water around the river. The knowers of secrets amongst us thought that the name Kurenets undoubtedly comes from the word *Krynica* (a spring); whereas the jokers amongst us felt it source was from the word *Kurit* (to smoke): i.e. through the smoke of the fires that took place in you, my town from time to time.

[Page 132]

You had six streets, all stemming from your market square. The most heartwarming of them was Dolhinov Road – the street of youths and hopes. However, we never called it by such a rhetorical name, even though we thought about its essence in our hearts… This street continued until the depths of the east, to the horizon adorned with stripes of cloudy purple – the outlines of the forests that spread out afar. These horizons were also a valley of visions for your sunrises every morning.

To this day, many colors and melodies come to me when I close my eyes and recall this street. I see the bridge below which the river hums its constant hymn. Here are the willow and poplar trees, and birds singing songs – trees and trees – but not all of them enthused our hearts. Some of them instilled fear upon us children. These were the trees of the Christian house of worship – a white building, with a long neck, tall, and piercing the holy heavens with it sharp crosses, with great might, broad shoulders, and full of white, open hatred. Their house of worship stood above the trees, and we young *cheder* children could only secretly take revenge for its fear, only in whispers and by reciting verses. We would pass by it in haste – pale, thin, and small, and recite:

"Thou shalt utterly detest it, and thou shalt utterly abhor it; for it is a devoted thing…"[1] This was the sole weapon of disparagement and attack that we ourselves took part in – we pale children, from the seed of Israel… However, it was a childhood accompanied by portents and fears, and many of our dark fears were aroused specifically by that white, lofty building.

To this day, even if I close my eyes and dig deep into my memory, I wonder who it was who revealed to use the terrible secret that with the ringing of the bells of the house of worship in Kurenets, the frightful verse that resonated in the ringing sound: "Golda, Golda, give your son to me! Golda, Golda, give your son to me."[2] During many mornings of my childhood, when I was lying half asleep in the silence of the early morning, and the sound of the bells filled the space of you, o my town, I would inadvertently count the rings, and hear within it the verse that I imagined was connected to a frightening event – a situation where the large house of the cross kidnapped the precious only child of a Jewish mother

In my imagination, I saw the woman Golda spreading her hands over her only child to protect him. However, the sound of the copper did not tire, and it continued to peal out from then and forever: "Golda, Golda, give your son to me." – – Until I would jump out of my bed, wash my hands, recite *Modeh Ani*[3], and overcome the sound of the impure ringing with the power of the holy verses.

This was in the past, in my long-ago childhood. With time, as we grew up, we remembered this with a forgiving smile to ourselves, as a vain illusion from our innocent childhood. Now, the white building does not frighten us.

[Page 133]

We were already pioneers of Israel, and we had with us melodies that were brought from overseas, from the banks of the Jordan and the Kinneret, and they were equal to the ringing and the crosses. Their power was greater than the whispered verse with which we mocked when we were young and pale.

The street of the sunrises now completed the sunrises in our hearts. We came in groups or alone to the large gardens of Kulik, under the shade of his pear and apple trees. We would go on excursions in the boulevards of "The Pathways of Ekaterina the Great" – which are white and ancient, or we would go far out, on the wings of our songs that reached us from the chosen land.

During the spring, the gentiles of Dolhinov Road would go out to the ancient white fields[4], place buckets at their feet, strike the roots with their axes, until the sap would flow into the buckets. The white [pines], the axes, and even the sap of the trees belonged to the gentiles – it was their sap. However, we already knew in those days that the trees were pleasant, that their canopies were pleasant, that their sap was good to drink and had medicinal qualities… Among the white pines of Dolhinov Road, we wove the dream of our own trees, the dream of their canopies and sap.

From the boulevard, some of us would continue along the narrow path to a pond that was called Ungerman's Pond. It was not that Ungerman was a real person. For us, his name was only the name of a pond of water, with thick treetops closing it in like a green wall, with bulrushes padding its canopy, and all together playing in the frothy bubbles in its waters.

Ungerman's pond also belonged to Dolhinov Road, the street of wonders. Indeed, there were also wonders in the pond. There, we learned to swim and to skip small rocks over the surface of its waters. Years later, when our hearts began to feel love, the small bridge next to the pond guarded our secret. The sound of song poured over it pleasantly, until we believed that the wonders only occurred for us, to deepen the glory of our feelings. On spring nights, we would go on this path to the estate of the *Paritzte* [female landowner] to secretly cut bundles of white and purple lilac branches, and place them net to the windows of the house of the girl we loved.

It was the end of the summer or the beginning of autumn. The wagon wheel that a Polish gentile had attached to the top branches of one of the trees to be a nesting place for a family of storks was now empty of its residents. The storks were celebrating very high above the pond, preparing for their journey to warm lands. The storks in flying formation arouse pleasant longings in us, with a sense of melancholy.

Indeed, the longings are many. I recall that you had another street on the border of the street of longings, arousing only melancholy and gloomy soul searching. That is Kosita Street. The turbulent river was on Dolhinov Road. When it reached there, it was like it lost its splendor, its restraint was removed, its turbulence disappeared, and all that was left was gloomy silence. It seemed to me that it whispered a verse from the book of Kohelet [Ecclesiastes]: "All of the river flow to the sea, and the sea is not full – Therefore why do I have to hurry and bustle, for vanity of vanities said Kohelet, everything is vanity…"

At the edge of Kosita Street, a grove of trees casts its shadow – this is the Jewish cemetery. It too confirmed the soul-searching that the river was whispering to itself, the thoughts of hopelessness.

The elders in you, my city, would relate that not far from this cemetery, years earlier, there was an old cemetery that was abandoned with the passage of time, to the point where there is no trace of its monuments and graves. Indeed, the wheel turns – there was once a cemetery and now it is no more…

[Page 134]

At the edge of the river, on Kosita Street, there were large bogs. There, the houses were stooped, and sunk into the ground. No strollers were found in this place. Only horses went out to pasture in the bogs, and if a horse sunk in the quicksand, curious people and experienced people would gather around to save it. It was as if one literally feels the uncertainty, of our lives and of the ground sinking under your feet…

This road was the final journey of your dead, my city. Gloomy, mournful funerals would pass through it. Those participating in the funeral would place the coffin beyond the river to separate it from the town. Those returning from the funeral would wash their hands in the river, and it was if its waters would bear their gloominess and mourning.

Two neighboring roads with different purposes. Each road, with its life experiences. Each road with the emotions of its life.

There was another road in you, my small town. It also led out from the market square. If it had a mouth to speak like a person, it would certainly claim and say:

"It was only for naught that you granted Dolhinov Road importance for glory and splendor, and for naught did you tie crowns to it. Come and let us discuss, if not I will prove, that you have no advantage over me" … -- That is what Vileyka Road would claim were it to have a mouth. Indeed, that street had its own virtues, similar to the virtues of Dolhinov Road. It also went out in a broad path with ancient stones on both sides. A river with points of charm for bathers also passed by it. Only the sun did not rise upon it, and it was never called the street of sunrise. It also attracted the hearts of the strollers. Those who would walk along it for a distance would reach the Jewish town of Vileyka, beautiful and charming, in about an hour. It sparkled from afar with the reflections of the Viliya, and was beautiful with its new houses, its straight roads, and the windows of its houses covered with splendid shutters and decorated with flowerpots.

We loved Vileyka. As we walked, we would dream that if a house was added on the street across the path, we would see in the eyes of our spirit how one house joins the next. From your midst, Kurenets my city, and also from the city of Vileyka, houses on both sides, to the point where they would meet, and you would become one large Jewish city in the future… – – –

If you do not want to walk along the broad path, and you choose the path that extends not far from the river, there too enchantments would await you. At first you would come to Mendel Dinerstein's flourmill – between the trees and the reeds, and a large pond of water, to the place where the frogs croak and grasshoppers rustle, with the sound of the waterfall, the workings of the wheels, and the fresh aroma of freshly ground flour. The pond is large and sparing from that side. However, if you look across from there, it would seem that the mill swallows up the entire abundance of water, with only a trickle remaining through a miracle, flowing between the crags of rocks, evading the place of danger – to the point where you could barely see it. However, your heart should not grieve. The soldiers will overcome. The wellsprings will spread into the river, and would again take up an area of land by the flourmill of the village of Ivontsavichy. It would sprawl out around it to turn into a large pool, and to move other wheels and other mills.

[Page 135]

There are no enchantments around the pond in Ivontsavichy, no tall trees, and no charming corners. The mill is also very old. If you go there and stand to look out, like someone enchanted by the surrounding splendor, it would only be to catch the eyes of the people who will not recognize you, for a different charm is there, a charm that is not to be exposed in public. That is the charm of the daughters of Mordechai the miller. Mordechai the miller had three daughters. Their eyes were blue, their hair was golden, their manner of speaking would attract the heart, and their laugh was heartwarming – Teibl, Sonka, and Henia. They would invite you to enter the house. They would treat you to a cup of tea, and if you were a person of many words, you could sit there for a long time engaged in pleasant conversation. Even as you returned home, you would carry with you the youthful charm of the daughters of the miller.

If you wish to go further, you would go with the river to the village of Volkovshchina. There lived the daughter of Eliyahu Cohen of Kurenets with her family. When you came, she would greet you with true joy, and say, "O, what guests, what guests!" She would give us cold cream with red raspberries, and thin, pleasant cucumbers. Shortly, a wagon would set out from there to Kholopy, the last stop on the Kurenets River. The Kholopy miller was also a Jew… However, it was appropriate to regain one's strength and rest after leaving the wagon. We were free people there, as if we were members of the household. Next to the window stood a large tree, and the sun played between its branches, glancing curiously into the house, as if it wished to see those who were entering. A bird chirps and bounces. O lovely, chirpy bird, please enthusiastically tell the secret to the other birds: Lads from Kurenets came, and they are sitting and eating cold cream with red raspberries…

Next to Vileyka Road, from the place where it leaves the marketplaces, another road spreads out literally westward. That is Smargon Road. There was nothing special about this road other than its name, which is the name of a town that became known as a big city. Aside from your name, you had no other charm – no river and no trees. In the distant horizon there is only the Svina Forest. Smargon is very far, and even if you were to walk for two or three hours, you would not reach its border…

O Smargon Road, this is nothing other than the mercies of Heaven that have come upon you, to also grant you their bounties, the summer rains, for the fell upon you; whereas on other roads, they only hit the roofs and windows. Upon you it is like they desired to play pranks, as a heavy vortex passed over you, with a flood of water flowing from you to the marketplace, and from there on its way to the entire land… The river on Kosita Street, o how we rejoiced, we children, at this flood of water. We rejoiced and even knew that it was from your kind hands, you poor, remote street.

Perhaps from Heaven they saw your poverty, and this was from you that specifically our musician lived in one of your houses. Reb Itzi-Noach the wise-hearted jester came to remove the boredom from your midst and to broaden the hearts of the few passers-by with the melodies of the violin and flute, with shofar blasts and witty words from the veteran fiddler. Even as I walked by you during the day, many years ago, my heart, my heart is to you, to you, and only to you. I will grant you the merit of precedence, and I will walk with you to the large rock, without other people, to Myadzyel Road. Only with you, forlorn Smargon Road, for you are already wiped off the face of the earth, and you only still live in my heart.

Who did not grant honor to the large rock? Those who loved it adorned it with charming legends. It is therefore clear to me that in addition to the legend of the accursed innkeeper, the official, known legend among the masses, private thoughts sparkled in the hearts of everyone regarding your appearance – who could imagine how many hidden ideas came up and were quenched, and nobody ever knew about them.

[Page 136]

I recall one spring day, while I was still a child, and I was walking with my friend Baruch Gedalya's to you, the large rock. Baruch was reliable in my eyes. He was a full year older than me, and therefore I would listen attentively to everything that he told. The spring had only just begun in the land – a swallow was frolicking in the air, going up and down in a rhythm. The fields were plowed, and they had black clods and small stones. Baruch was walking with me and telling me so that I will know and remember that all the small stones in the entire world once belonged to the large rock. We both walked and wondered how large and immense the rock had once been.

When I got older, a new thought entered my heart, that this black rock – the one and only in the midst of the large plain – was not an inn that curses, but rather a shooting star that fell in the midst of the fields many, many years ago, before the Savina Forest and Smargon Road were in the world – a star from amongst the stars of the heavens.

I loved your stars, o my city, the edges and breadth of our streets, even though your market square was round and closed, without an exit to the horizons. I did not like the bustling, noisy market days, full of foreign bounty and grains from outside. The market was clear and sharp, practical, cunning, and calculated. I was a visionary child – and therefore I was not attracted to you.

In your belly, o market, stood a block of shops enclosing a small field, from the midst of which sprouted a tender tree. Its canopy grew year by year until it overshadowed the roof of the shops to see the wide world. In my eyes, the tree was like a prisoner – a bright, green tree surrounded by walls and gloomy partitions.

O market square, you were only open to the sky but not to the breadths. In those days, the sky was not high. Over the chimneys on the rooftops and over the house of Lea-Itka– a two-story wooden house – we measured the distance from the heavens to the earth… O, how moved I was when my sister took me by the hand and brought me to the house of Lea-Itka, to bring me to the second floor – to the gates of heaven…

Your synagogues were also two stories high. They stood adjacent to the square, and hidden in the valley. We wished that they would be tall and high, but we took comfort and said that it was deliberate, to fulfil the verse: From the depths I call out to You o L-rd. [Psalms 130:1]. Therefore, you were low and stood in the valley…

Much taller than them was the white church, which peered out from its green platform with pride and a huge heart. It was on Dolhinov Road, and it sought to fill the entire area around with its essence and awe. Its roof sparkled to the heights of the heaven, but we, the children of my town, believed that they were fleeing from it. It would extend and add on, but would never reach those heavens – which descended like a cloud upon our synagogues.

O my town, you had two more streets. One of them was the alleyway It was also closed off without a continuation, without horizons. It only left the marketplace and touched Myadzyel Road. It was melancholy in my eyes, as if it was pushed off to a corner.

[Page 137]

I lived in one of the houses on the alleyway during my childhood, for a brief time, but it is etched in my heart. That was the first time that I saw death face to face. I saw my mother faint in her calamity, and my father silent in his mourning, with only his eyes weeping quietly. Suddenly, it was revealed to me that I was an abandoned child, without a protector or shelter, for my father and mother were so weak, my house was shaky and broken, and death was sitting in its shadow.

The tragedies of Israel and the exile of Israel – the concept of which would be revealed to me from the breadths of the world ant the times – I also knew first from you, o alleyway. The concept came from a very far-back snowy day: a winter sled stood next to one of your houses, and in the wagon was a Jew who was murdered. His eyes were closed and tormented. His black beard was like a framework of mourning. The name of the Jew was Itche-Michael. He was murdered on his way to a market day. A bloody man named Vasyl came from the village of Litvinki, next to you, o my town.

I knew another case of bloodshed on the alleyway, in which the details were also obscure. My mother of blessed memory told me the terrible story that one night in the past, gentiles entered the house of Gedalyahu the blacksmith and beat him and his wife Freda with fetters, but passers-by interfered and thereby thwarted the efforts of the murderers. After my mother's story, it became completely clear to me why Gedalyahu the blacksmith walked around as if tormented, and there was never a smile on his face.

Nevertheless, aside from the tragedies, the alleyway also had its wonders – that is the new well with fresh water from which everyone came to draw – youth and elderly. For a long time, I was jealous of the lads who had already grown up, and whose strength was already sufficient to be drawers, bearers of the buckets and pole from the well to their houses. This was for many days, until my time came, and I also traversed the entire street with a pole and two full buckets over my shoulders. I secretly bit my lips from the magnitude of the effort. I walked and counted my steps to take my mind off the pain in my hands and shoulders. Your living windows, o alleyway, from the right and left, accompanied my burden of victory. It was a far-back day when I felt that not only had I crossed the street, but I had also crossed the era of my pallid, shaky childhood.

Behold I now reach your last road, the last and the longest – Myadzyel Road. It left the market square, and also turned northward. The sun never shone on it, and never set on it. It led to mysterious forests and to a town situated on a large body of water, called Myadzyel. I traversed it very slowly, and my heart accompanies each and every step. Behold, I am approaching our house. However, now I will not enter its door. I will only stand for one moment and bow. You, o the rest of the houses, do not look begrudgingly at this, for it is my house. My parents built it with toil. Within its walls, one Kislev night, my mother left me; From there my father wrote me his final letter, and with pure Biblical verses, albeit sad and mournful, informed me of the death of my dear parent… I will only bow for a moment, and I will continue on. – – –

Myadzyel Road is very long. Soon I will reach its end. The end of this road was questionably the town and questionably a village. Jews who were people of the land, with fields and furrows, lived there. Here and there, next to their houses, they cleared large bricks. On giant ladders, exactly like in villages, they would dry peas that the Jews had harvested from their fields.

[Page 138]

One day, I stood there in a field and learned the job of harvesting with a sickle. Children gathered about to see me. The children knew that my harvesting was not for an ordinary harvest, but I was rather learning this holy craft for the fields of the Land of Israel. Therefore, the children whispered around me, and they watched my harvesting as if during a silent prayer and as dreamers.

From here, you can see the village of Litvinki very well, and nearby the house of Feishka. This was the only Jewish house, and I looked upon this house in a gloomy fashion during my long-ago childhood years, for it stood next to Vasyl's house.

O, how I wished then to divert my thoughts from Litvinki and Vasyl, to uproot them from my heart… But it was for naught… Their fear pursued me in every place, and even stuck to me on the pages of the Chumash:

"And it was when they were in the field, and Cain rose up against his brother Abel and killed him." [Genesis 4:8]

In *cheder*, with all the children, I read the preceding verse with its trope. The trope did not sweeten the judgement, and it was as if to vex that the image of the murderer from the village of Litvinki pushed its way into our holy book. Instead of Cain, I saw Vasyl, and instead of east of Eden, the location of the first murder, I saw the broad field at the end of Myadzyel Road – between the town of Kurenets and the village of Litvinki. – – –

Behold, I have already traversed you, o my town, and my eyes are closed so that I can see you well. You sat alone in the valley, a weak Jewish town, with Pukan on one site and the village of Litvinki on the other side of you. The church is above you, and its bells disturb your spirit… And you were loaded with great mercy, greater and more numerous than I was able to imagine…

Translator's Footnotes:

1. Deuteronomy 7:26. Translation from Mechon Mamre: https://mechon-mamre.org/p/pt/pt0507.htm
2. Seemingly, an imaginative onomatopoeia from the words *Golda, Golda, teni et bneich li*.
3. The first prayer upon arising in the morning.
4. From the context of collecting sap, I believe this is referring to groves of white pine trees.

Part Two: In Your Shining Face

*Your Youth and the Loveliness of Your Wedding Will Always be Remembered ...
From the Siege I Saw You Soaked in Blood*

[Page 141]

My Hometown

by Aharon Meirovitch

Translated by Jerrold Landau

My hometown, the nest of the spring of my life, how has your good voice become silenced,
That resonated, and aroused healing longing when pain came?
There is no more a letter from father in his refined holy language, not the thought of a letter
Only the worry of the heart regarding what is to come.

Nothing had yet been told to me, my tragedy was still marching in the shadows,
But my heart sensed the echo of its footsteps, which could already be heard.
Shortly he would come, a survivor with singed clothing from my father's house,
Protect me, o L-rd, from the new that he would bring.

My hometown, a sort of hidden world, among silent forests;
Quiet and merciful, but it was not always quiet within you, and not always merciful.
Where peace pervades, and the gift of hidden lights from generation to generation,
And your heart thirsts for every small mercy, and for every caress of light.
I said I would yet return to your source, and compose a great verse of praise to you,
Seeing you strewn with lights and covered with flourishing and strength,
Light up a face of love to every baby within you, and enwrapping innocent childhood;
Stand guard at the top of the slope of graves, shed a tear over them.
Guard the paths that have grown moss, in which I knew sunrise during my youth,
But days have stopped their good, with a song of memory – a song of much apology.

But, alas, suddenly I have seen darkness fall over you,
Covering your surroundings, every path that comes and goes.
Woe, I see you trampled, bowed low and clipped by the enemy,
Broken , with great mercy spread over the elderly and children.
I see you having collapsed, I listen to your cries from afar.
There is nobody who will tell you that you are the head, that your spirit will be returned.

To you, next of my childhood, my path may yet bring me,
After the days of darkness and crisis;
However, who knows whether I will still find a surviving child in you
And whether I will still find a gravestone over a grave?…

5701 [1941]

[Pages 142-146]

My Ravished Home

by Fayga Alperovitch daughter of Gitel and Mendel, son of Yechezkel Alperovitz

Translated by Eilat Gordin Levitan

Kurenitz my Beloved town: Only yesterday you were teeming with babies and old. You awoke at down brimming with excitement and slept with enervation at night. The ground of your allies and boulevards was not yet saturated with the blood of your beloved. Your little children, the children of Israel, played in your avenues. Vibrating in your fields was the tune of synagogue prayers, not the resonance of the last anguished cries of children, men and women underneath the striking axe.

I experienced all your horrors, and survived, and my heart is still firmly attached to you. Each day I will mourn and revisit the horror that could never be comprehended. Day after day, I would ask the inflamed question, Why? Day after day, I would be left with no answer. How can one describe and recount the tales of what had occurred for a period of three years, in the hearts of an entire community? What have transpired in the mind of man and women, young and old? How can one fatefully recite such enormity, when what occurs for one moment in ones soul is impossible for the inscribing hand to account?

A beautiful summer day arises in front of my eyes. It was during the first months of the occupation. We worked at the camp of the Russian POWs on Dolhinov Street. Netka Rodantzki was shoved to the wall of Mishka Takontzik house, for their enjoyment they pointed their rifles at him. They pointed but did not shoot. They enjoyed watching his face pales, his legs shake, his unconscious body drops to the ground. Nobody stopped them from killing him, however it was more pleasurable for them to torture him at that moment. We stood by and our hearts died from fear, but we could do nothing to save him

Here I see you my brother Aharon. You came to me one day and your two eyes were one bleeding wound. All I could do was to secretly cry while putting towels saturated with cold water on your wound. You were returning from your work place, you were just done with cutting wood for your killers. On your way you met with the murderer Shernagovitz may his name be forgotten for eternity. He whipped you with his rod straight on your eyes. Again, he was free to kill you. Your blood was free for all, no judge or justice for you. Nevertheless, he took pleasure in seeing you squirm, he wished to humiliate you.

Another image rises in front of me. A clear winter day, the day of the thirteen – the thirteen martyrs who were murdered that day. – Yitzhak Zimerman was slaughtered in his home. He was studying the Torah when they arrived. The murderers passed by the homes that were designated by the Judenrat as wealthy Homes were they would find valuables.

However, the true desire of the murderers was their souls. They entered Shmuel Zipilevitz home and shoved him to the corner and when he fell on the floor, they took a wooden chair that belonged to Shmuel, and used it to crash his head

On the carriage that stood by the home of Eetzi Chatzis (Charles Gelman's father), they put the victims belonging. Near the wall they arranged a line of Jews and shot them. From the window of the megistrat were I was forced to work as a servant, I watched the horrors in the market.

Your streets were empty my town, behind windows we diligently watched the approaching killers. We made sure that it was not we who were next to be killed. We slept in our clothes. Always ready to hear a message of catastrophe. Behind my room's window I watched our dear beloved rabbi, the towns' rabbi, rab Moshe-Aharon Feldman. They throw him on the market ground, his arms and legs were broken, and the hair of his beard was taken out. Where his eyes used to be, there were only empty holes now.

God o god, was our crime so heavy? Were our deeds so unforgivable?

Another day comes to me, a day between Purim and Passover of 1942. The most hated; Sherganovitz and Sokolovsky were drunk. We paid a heavy tax with the blood of our beloved for their intoxicated condition. Thirty-two martyrs lied dead in front of the killers. They crashed people with axes and penetrated their bodies with knives. They started their murderous parade from Myadel Street. They killed the sister of Chaim- Yitzhak Zimmerman with her two children. They murdered David the shoemaker. Shifra Chadash and her daughter in-law, Frumka were killed. They killed the Minkovitz family. Eetzi Chatzis Zimmerman was murdered. Murdered, murdered, murdered.

Mina Spector the daughter of Eetzi Chatzis was killed, next to her on the snow in a red pool of her blood, laid her baby still alive. Her sister Ethel tried to run, but where was she to run? She was able to run to a street corner and that's where they caught with her, and spilled her blood

A true bastard grew in our town, Belizniyuk the son of the woman who was cleaning the slaughterhouse. Amongst all the bloodsuckers, the killers who spilled our blood, he was the very worst.

They told us that nothing belonged to us. Not our possessions or our toil not indeed our life. They were allowed to take anything they wished. If they let us survive another day, its not because we deserved it. Its only because they can suspend our killing for tomorrow, and in the min time they enjoyed torturing us, they loved seeing us poor, weak, miserable and humiliated.

On cold winter days they would go to all the Jewish homes and confiscate the little wood we prepared. It was not done because wood was difficult to obtain, Kurenitz sat at the edge of a forest, but their aim was not to use the wood for their furnaces. They wanted to see us shivering and freezing.

One cold winter night, at four in the morning I took five logs to warm my parents home. I took them from my work place at the magistrate, Belizniyuk, the policeman saw me. For unknown reason, he did not kill me on the spot. When I came home and told my family about Belizniyuk they started mourning me. Motoros, our town mayor promised to talk for me with Belizniyuk, to beg that lowest of human being to spare my life.

Days passed and a new fear spread in town. Early in that summer, the partisans assassinated Belizniyuk. He was killed in the village Tzavalitkass and his body was brought for burial in Kurenitz. The killer received a stately funeral. Two religious leaders eulogized and honored him. For us, the Jews of the town, it was a long, dark, torturous day. Not one living soul was seen walking down the street, many of us escaped to the fields fearing reprisals. Our entire family (including my brother Yosef's family, my sister Nacha and her husband Yakov- Lieb with their children) – hid in Nuvi Kurenets. We all feared that it would be the last day for the Jewish Kurenets. In the Yard that belonged to Yosef Zuckerman the killers found a headstone, they took it to be used for the slain murderer. (The first thing that Yosef did when he returned from the forest after we were liberated, was to remove the stone from the grave so future generations will never know the murderer burial place – how restrained was our revenge!)

The most horrible day is now ascending to vision, the day of the slaughter. In the town's building, behind a door, standing in the corner of a dark room, I hid the entire day. I heard the cries and the shouts of my Jewish sisters and brothers, the sounds of my beloved taken to be slaughtered. – The cries lasted the entire day, at night I left my hiding place. Stealthily I reached my parents home, I found none, not my mother or father or my brother Aharon. I checked all the hiding places we prepared, I found none, and finally my brother Yosef appeared from one of the hiding places. Together we ran to the forests.

Mendel son of Yechezkel Alperovitz
(Father of the author) during a visit to Eretz Israel
Menachem Mendel, Ami, and Levik Alperovitz

Could I present details of our laborious journey from the town throughout the forests? Already on the first days, when I was left alone in the forest, (my brother was searching for food.) I met with a peck of hungry wolves. With the last of my might, I succeeded in climbing a tree. My entire body was scratched from the tree branches. The only dress that I had, a light summer dress was torn into shreds. Shreds embodying the mourning of our annihilated world.

For two months, we consistently moved throughout the forests of Hob and in the Pushtza. One "lucky" November day, we were able to reach the "Vostok".

One and a half years my brother Yosef and I, with many other Jews from Kurenitz, lived near Polotzchek, for some reason we called the area "the Vostok". My brother and I worked at the headquarters of the partisans, Yosef was renown for his beautiful writing, and people with such abilities were hard to find.

The area was about eighty kilometers by eighty. The Russian partisans controlled the area. Seventeen months past in relative peace, we were all sure that we were going to survive the war. The Germans were losing, and retreating from Russia. May 1944, the Germans decided that in order of turning their withdrawal smoother, they would have to purge the partisan from their zone in the "Vostok". The partisans would otherwise combat them from the west, when they would retreat to the west, and the Red Army will fight them from the east. At first, they sent planes that would daily toss pamphlets. The pamphlets urged the local population to fight the soviets and to kill the Jews and then the Germans would not harm them.

They brought many army divisions to the area to fight the partisans.

Yosef Alperovitz with Kurenets friends
Zev Kuperstock and Shachna Stolar before the war

In one of the most hopeless battles my brother Yosef, Artzik Dinerstien and I were wounded. We were all lying in the same spot, they were both very seriously wounded. My brother Yosef was dying, with his last breaths he whispered to me; "Fayga don't stay with me, go away, please let one of our family survive".

I told him that I refuse to leave him. Anyway I was also wounded, I just lied there amongst the wounded and the dead. At one point, when it turned dark, I fell asleep. One morning I woke up when someone was shaking me, I had no knowledge of how long I was there. When I opened my eyes, I realized that we were surrounded by Germans. A burning German tank was in the vicinity. They put me in a car with many other wounded, and they took us to the schoolyard in Asouatz. There they laid us on the ground. Amongst the wounded, there were many local residents and partisans. I soon realized that from here they were taking the wounded somewhere else.

My will to survive returned to me, I looked for a way to escape. I asked one of the German guards if I could search for my little child that was lying wounded not far from here. I told him that I wanted to die next to him. Since I was covered with blood he must have felt sorry for me and let me go. I walked and walked until I reached a bridge with a German checkpoint. They asked me where I was going, I told them that I am walking to my mother's house that is situated near by. They let me pass the bridge. Immediately I entered the forest, I walked deeper in until I reached the swamps, I sat right next to the swamps and soon fell asleep.

I don't know how long I was asleep in the swamps, I woke up feeling extremely hungry. I walked to a near by village and exchanged extra shirt I was wearing for seventeen slices of dry bread. Those seventeen slices sustained me for three weeks. The slices turned hard and stale and when I would brake them a little green smoke will disperse. Everyday I changed my sleeping location to ensure that no one could find me. The forest wildlife did not touch me, even they must have been scared when they looked at me One night the forest was lit on fire and I had to escape to the fields.

Should I tell you some more intimate details of what had occurred to me during those eight weeks of horrors? Eight weeks of loneliness, deep depression, and lost of all human essence? Would awareness of the horrible details help people to comprehend the general picture? Would it help to know that at one time I was hiding underneath pile of hay and a farmer brought his sick horse to lye on top of the hay to spread concoction on his body?

One day my hiding place was detected by a Christian woman. When she saw me she became so scared that she started crossing herself. She told me to leave the forest, she said the Soviets were here. I begged her to have pity for me and to not give me to the Germans. I begged her to pity me so I could stay alive. She continued crossing herself and assuring me that she was telling the truth.

I came to the village of that Christian woman, my body was covered with open infected abscess. I washed my body and I shaved my hair. I was as skinny as a finger.

On June 6 1944, I slept outdoors by the road. A Jewish officer of the Red army found me there. When the officer found out that I was Jewish he could not rest until he was able to transfer me to the Asouaz hospital. There my condition became critical, particularly when I ate some soup, after a long period of starvation. A decision was made to transfer me to a bigger, more modern hospital in Gorki. It took seven days to get to Gorki.

I was lying in my hospital bed in complete despair, a nurse came to me and said that the head of the hospital, a doctor, wants to see me. There was something important that he would like to discuss with me. I said;

"There is nothing to discuss, I just want to be left alone"

The nurse kept coming with the same request. One day I was told that the head doctor is the cousin of Rabbi Yakov Landau from Bnai Brak, Rabbi Landau was born in Kurenitz and in my childhood, he was the Kurenitz rabbi as his father was before him. When the Doctor saw that my last name was Alperovich, he assumed that I was from Kurenitz. (Alperovich was probably originated in Kurenitz, almost a third of the Jewish population in Kurenitz was named Alperovich) the doctor could not find rest until I let him see me.

The Doctor was about sixty years old, he had a white moustache and his face had deeply spiritual statement. He treated me as if I was is only daughter. Anything I desired was brought to me. The best doctors were brought to take care of me, and the nurses were told to assist with my recovery. I was in the hospital in Gorki for three months. David Motosov's sisters, who lived in Gorki since world war one, would also come to visit.

I recovered but Kurenets was burning inside of me. The spilled blood was calling me and the urge of revenge was boiling in me. One day I received a letter from David Motosov, who had already reached Kurenets, asking me to join him there. I probably could have used some more rest, but I couldn't wait; there was no rest for me. I said goodbye to the Motosov family. I also said goodbye to the dear lovely doctor, the head of the hospital. A nurse took me all the way to Moscow, and from there I left on my way to Kurenets.

On a cold, rainy October day, I returned to my hometown, Kurenets. I came through the road of mourning, Cosita Street. I came to my home to the hills of dust. I found the few survivors. The streets were filled with Gentiles, the bloodsuckers. They were fancily dressed with our clothes, breathing the air as if nothing had happened. How painful it was and how paltry was my revenge.

One day I stood at the house of Kashtuk, a Gentile from the village, Litwinki. He became rich from the stolen possessions of the Jews. I opened his cabinets. I broke the crystals. I screamed, shouted, and handed him to the NKVD (the Russian police), but I truly knew that this was not revenge. This was not reprisal.

248

One day I stood in Vileyka and saw them hang the limping policeman, the leech that could never have enough of the Jewish blood. They brought him from Gomel. The killer escaped all the way to Gomel. He was accepted to a Russian army band, accepted as entertainer. He was found out while playing music. I watched him die and begged that they would let me throw stones at him. Nevertheless, how diminutive was my revenge.

Daily I stood on your mammoth grave, my town Kurenets, knowing that the eradication could never be vindicated. There will never be equal restitution. Every day I'll call upon you in my heart and ask "why?" Likewise, day after day I will have no reply.

[Page 147]

Amongst the Fifty-Four

by Yente née Dinerstein Rudnitsky Baranovitch

Translated by Eilat Gordin Levitan

It was the evening of Simhat Torah 1941. My husband Velvel and I took our baby boy to my sister-in-law's home for a visit. A "visit" in spite of the fact that our hearts were filled with bitterness. My brother-in-law Sina and my sister-in-law Sarah received us with graciousness. We sat and discussed various subjects and blessed every minute that did not bring pain and misery. Being worried had become a second nature to us, so my brother-in-law went outside to see if all was quiet in the neighborhood.

He walked to the far edge of his backyard where he could see the central market. While he was observing the market he saw that from Vilejka Street came a parade of bicyclists and passed rapidly through Dolhinov Street. He found a hiding place and stood there motionless observing the "parade". Soon he realized that they were the German Es de. The entire "parade" stopped next to the house of Asna Limon, which was now the police headquarters. They got off their bicycles and entered. Ten minutes later they left, the same way they had come. My brother-in-law returned home and with great fear in his voice told us what he saw. Immediately, I covered the baby and we left for my parents' home. We walked through the gardens as it was safer and as soon as we entered our home I told my father of what we had seen.

My father felt that since they returned to Vilejka, it was not so worrisome. In any case, we sat by the window so that we could observe the street. After a short time we saw a bicyclist approaching. It was Adamovich, the postman. He came to our yard and hastily approached the window, and clicked on the glass with a little stick. Father opened the window and whispered,

"What is happening?" but Adamovich didn't give him time to finish the sentence. He told him; "Mr. Dinerstein, all men must leave at once. The women can sleep in peace." He looked around to make sure no one saw him talking to us and immediately parted. There was dead silence in the house. We looked at each other in great fear. Finally father said, "Velvel, I will leave right away and after 5 minutes you should leave. We'll go to sleep at Yvonne Gusar's house in Nuvokurenitz. We'll go through the fruit garden of the Ofsisht. And I'll wait for you next to the Christian bathhouse."

Father said goodbye, and, with him, took a pail as if he were going to the well, so as not to create panic amongst the neighbors. He put the pail next to the well and went to the bathhouse. He waited thirty minutes but Velvel didn't show up. Worried that something was amiss, he returned. Velvel was determined to stay at home. He explained to us that he had done nothing wrong, so he didn't expect anything bad to happen to him. There was no convincing him that he must escape, so both men ended up at home.

Dusk came. Jews were not allowed to light their homes, so we covered the windows with a blanket and put on a little light. We discussed what we should do. Mother served dinner but we couldn't eat. At 11 o'clock we went to sleep after telling each other that Adamovich didn't know what he was talking about. By midnight we were all in deep sleep but our sleep lasted for one hour only. All of a sudden we heard loud knocks on the door and just the sound of the rude knocks was sufficient to be an omen for us that disaster was approaching. We tried to ignore the knocks but they got louder and louder someone was knocking both on the doors and windows. Shaking with fear we jumped out of our beds and got dressed. Suddenly we heard a loud noise. Someone had hit the door with a rifle and with a loud shriek said, "Open the door!" Mother was the first one at the door, she asked with most naive sounding expression, as if wondering who it could be, "Who is there?" The killers screamed, "Open the door!" and cursed us. Mother opened the door as if they were common visitors, and tried to appear peaceful in spite of her terror. Three policemen entered the home and some others waited in the hallway. Still others were surrounding the house standing in our yard. The policemen who entered were our gentile friends from school. As soon as they walked in they approached the bedroom. When they saw Velvel, they demanded that he get dressed and go with them.

We all started crying. My sister Rachel approached one of the policemen, her classmate for many years, and begged, "Gintop, leave him alone. He didn't do anything wrong to you. We were friends in the same classroom." The killer pushed her away and screamed, "Get away you bloody Jew! We never were and never will be friends." His blood was boiling as he screamed, "Get dressed! You have 5 minutes." The two other policeman walked around the house with Amused look, they laughed at our embarrassed faces. I was paralyzed. I couldn't get out of bed. It lasted about two to three minutes. Then I recovered and jumped out of bed as if awoken from a nightmare, and walk rapidly all over the room collecting underwear, socks, gloves, sweaters, shawls and hats. In a short time I made a little package for Velvel. Mother also put together a package with food for the way. At the last minute I gave him extra underwear. One of the policemen said that its all unnecessary. They would only take him to work he promised that Velvel will return. We all sensed a great disaster was coming. I was the first person who Velvel said goodbye to. I was shocked from his many kisses and whispering voice. "Take care of the baby and yourself. They're probably only taking me to a labor camp." My tears gave him immense pain and he calmed me down saying, "Don't worry, I'll be warm. I'll take this now, but I'll probably return soon. But just in case I don't, find out where I am and send something." The policeman yelled at us. "No time to make love now. Tomorrow you will make love." Velvel couldn't stop saying goodbye. He said goodbye to mother, father, Rachel, the baby and me. After he made his first step towards the door, he turned back and looked at us again. His face was pale and scared. He stood there for a minute with an embarrassed look until the policemen pushed him out of the entrance. Now the cries got louder. We hurried to window to see him, but we could only hear their footsteps. Then they all disappeared. There was total silence now. At that minute the baby started crying it was a horribly loud cry and our hearts were braking.

The whole night we couldn't rest. Morning came and outside we saw people walking. Mother quickly got dressed and went to the police station that was situated in the market to see what was happening. She entered, went to head of the police and told him that at night, her son-in-law was taken, and that she didn't know why. She asked if it was possible to send him food. Isiavich, the chief of police, answered, "At this point that's not allowed, but maybe later, after we've checked his papers." Mother returned to tell me about it, and then walked back to the police to try to get Velvel released. I stayed home with the baby, who was then six months. Father went to the streets for advice. When he returned I noticed that he looked tired and hopeless, even though he tried to hide his feelings from me. He sat on the sofa and sighed quietly. I put the baby in the cradle and rocked him, not paying attention. Father was now crying. I was confused. My heart was shaking, but before I could ask him if he had found out anything I saw from the window a group of Germans approaching from the direction of the market. They walked in the middle of the street, crowding it. There were ten men. I was extremely scared and I yelled to Father, "Look! The Germans are coming! I think they're coming here!" I stood paralyzed, staring out of the window. They came closer and closer. It was clear to me they were coming to our house. I screamed, "Father run away! They are coming to our house."

Father got up and looked out of the window. The killers were walking confidently, with an air of contentment. Again I yelled, "Father run away!" They're probably coming to take men. You must leave immediately! Leave through the back of the apartment from the window to the garden of Chvayder then to the house of one of your Christian friends.

Father didn't move. His face turned yellow and he started weeping, "How can I leave you, my daughter, without protection?" I saw that the gang already reached Hinda-Leir's house. With full force, I pushed Father and screamed, "Why are you standing? Quickly, run away!" I don't know where I got the energy to push him so forcefully. When father reached the door he stopped and looked at me. I couldn't speak anymore. I saw the soldiers reaching our house. I signaled him to run away and continued rocking the baby very nervously. As soon as Father had left, the gang stepped up to the doorway and entered. A tall officer with glasses approached me and asked, "Is this the house of Rodinsky?" – "No," I answered." "Are you the wife of Rodinsky?" – "Yes," I replied.

He motioned to the rest, and they split up to search the rooms. In five minutes everything was taken out of our cabinets and drawers and thrown on the floor. I stood there surrounded by the soldiers without any protection and had no idea what was going to happen. The commander entered and whispered something to the officer in charge. Then one of the soldiers was ordered to stay. He saluted and kicked his boots together sharply. The other nine killers left the house on their way to a house at the end of street, belonging to Chaim Zukofski. The soldier that stayed with me stood rigidly at attention for a very long time, he was looking at the baby. I gave him a chair and asked him to sit. He just shook is head in refusal. There was total silence. I saw him look at the baby again. I took a chance and asked timidly, "Pardon me, maybe you know if the father of the baby will return." Again there was no answer. The soldier only shrugged as if he had been asked a difficult question that couldn't be answered. The soldier approached the cradle, looked at baby and sighed. I looked at his expression, trying to comprehend his thoughts. I was overcome with fear. I was all alone with him. Still, I was happy that Father had left in time. While I was thinking about it the soldier finally spoke, "Maybe you can give me some wool gloves, a scarf and socks." I was happy that he had finally talked. I told him, "Mother will return soon and she will give you everything." Sure enough she soon came. But he didn't let her move.

After thirty minutes the Germans returned to the house. The lieutenant asked me for my papers. I gave them to him immediately and then the assistant chief of police entered and explained, in broken German, that in this house lives the Dinerstein family and that the apartment of the Rodinsky family was located in the market area. The officer ordered me to take my baby and go to the market. I was sure that he was planning to take me to the apartment, but I was gravely mistaken. I asked mother for diapers for the walk. I left the house certain that they were going to search our house, and then we would be allowed to return to my parents' home. Mother said, "My daughter!" and asked me for a kiss. I calmed her down by saying, "The apartment is empty- it has already been robbed by the villagers."

Outside I started comprehending that something tragic was occurring. Right next to our house stood Pesya Yenta, the mother of Chaim Zukovski, my sister in-law Hinda, and Mulka Thebes's wife with her two children. I whispered, "What's going on?" They said that the situation was awful. We walked very slowly. The gentiles looked at us and whispered. We reached the market and were told by other Jews that the calamity is terrible. But I still didn't know what was going to happen. All the women were weeping and holding their children tightly. I was unable to cry anymore. My heart had become a rock. The other women told me that they saw the men were taken holding shovels. I tried to analyze the situation and decided that the men were being transferred to a labor camp and we were going to say goodbye to them. I was sorry that I hadn't brought food for the baby.

Ten minutes later the police ordered us to walk to Kosita Street now we were surrounded by many policemen and soldiers. We were ordered to go in the middle of the street in one tight and crowded group. I started slowing down and was the very last of the walkers. In a hushed voice, I asked the soldier who earlier had been commanded to watch me at the house who now was walking right behind me if he would let me slip away and disappear into one of the nearby yards. He answered that he could be severely punished for this.

We reached the train tracks. I looked back and saw Kurenets. It looked distant, small and tucked away tightly in the valley. I could see the three synagogues standing next to each other. I thought how even they couldn't help our poor souls. "Will I ever see you again, my dear town?" This was the thought that rang in my mind. Strangely, I was feeling very sad, but not scared. I was pushing away any thought of the awful disaster that was probably waiting for us. Friedka, the daughter of David Lipas, was crying desperately. She asked me, "Yentedske, where are they taking us? And where did they take the men our dear husbands?" I walked right by her, but when I wanted to answer I realized that my tongue was stuck to the roof of my mouth! I felt as if a rock was stocked in my throat, a rock that I wouldn't budge. My lips had no ability to talk, no energy to move. I understood everything that was going on around me, but just couldn't talk. The policeman hurried us up by hitting us with the butt of his rifle.

We reached the Ricolan Forest. At the edge of the forest, we were ordered to stop and to stand inside a trench. All of a sudden we realized that inside the forest there was a clearing and there we could see our husbands holding shovels in their hands. We saw they were barefoot and wearing only their underwear. Their clothes were piled on the side of the clearing and their shoes and boots arranged perfectly in pairs. At that moment I realized that the two holes that our husbands were digging must be in fact two graves, one for themselves and one for us!

We stood at the edge of the forest until the digging had ended. Then the soldiers ordered us to approach the trenches and stand about fifty meters from our beloved husbands. We were ordered to look straight at them. The soldiers arranged our husbands in one line with their backs to us. The killers kept running back and forth, straightening the lines. Behind each person stood a policeman with a rifle and in front of the policemen stood a German with a machine gun pointed at the lines of people. Suddenly we heard the sound of a whistle. Then the sound of rifles and machine gun fire filled the forest. At that moment a huge wind blew through the trees and everything started shaking. Our dear husbands, the fathers of our children, fell like broken trees. The horrified cries of women and children tore the forest to pieces. We pulled out our hair and screamed to the heavens to look down upon us in order to witness the great tragedy that had befallen us. But the wind only carried our screams through the forest. The terrible sound echoed through the woods, but never reached heaven. A few minutes passed and the gentiles that stood in the surrounding area covered our dear ones with earth. The soldiers made us stand in a line to take us to the killing place. At the edge of the woods stood a gentile with a horse and buggy ready to take our clothes. I approached him and said, "Take the baby so he will live." The man started laughing, and scoffed, "Ha, ha, ha, a Jewish baby! That garbage has to be burned so that no memory will be left of you." I stood embarrassed, almost forgetting that there lay only thirty meters between me and death. The whistle again shivered through the woods. The policemen put us in one line, the women and children, and me too. The officer orders us to take off our clothes and pile them in one place. I placed the baby diaper on the heap of clothes and said, "A sacrifice for you, my baby." I placed the other diaper on the heap and whispered, "A sacrifice for me."

I held my baby tightly, pressing him against me with my fingers, digging into his chest. I hoped that when we died we would fall together so when they found us they would recognize us and know to bury us in the same grave, since I was the only mother with a small baby. The killers were busy straightening the line. I looked at the sky and asked God for a miracle. I looked back and saw the killers with their rifles pointed at us. I closed my eyes and acknowledged to myself that all hope was lost. At that moment, when I was sure that there was no hope left a miracle occurred! As if God hadn't left me. He had sent a messenger to spare me from death. The officers were ready to shoot and the senior officer was just about to give the sign, when a policeman came running towards him. The policeman caught the hand of the officer who was holding the whistle before he could give the signal to shoot. The policeman pointed at me and my baby and asked that we be released. The officer pushed the policeman angrily and said that the baby would grow up to be a famous Communist. When the policeman saw that the officer had the whistle in his mouth and was again about to give the signal to the soldiers to shoot, he started hastily explaining. The policeman pleaded with the officer, explaining that he knew me well, that I was a good women and that I wasn't a Communist. The officer gave up and let me leave the line. I didn't see all this. I was told about it later.

The policeman approached me with another man, a Russian POW that stayed in town. They patted my back, congratulating me, "Yente, you are released. Get out of line." I turned my face and saw Minka from Dolginov St., the son-in-law of Resiva. The other man was not familiar to me. Minka said, "Go home quickly. I'll tell you how you were saved later." I couldn't move. I was totally confused. Afraid of myself, my whole body shook with cries and I held my baby to my heart. The officer came to "sympathize" with me. "Don't cry," said the bloody killer. "I now release you, but in the future don't marry a Communist." I lifted my eyes. He stood smiling. He looked tall and sure of himself. He dismissed me with a shake of his hand and told me to go. Again I stared crying but this time, I was able to walk. He shouted for me to come back. I looked back, fearing that they wanted me to return to the line but the officer pointed to the pile of clothes and said, "Take your clothes." With his cane he spread the contents of the pile of clothes and said, "You can take clothes that don't belong to you too," and laughed. I found my coat and took it hastily. As I left I heard him say, "Talk to me," and my blood froze. He offered me a seat with him and suggested that I wait until he was done with his job and promised that then he will take me back to my village. I ran off; I heard the officer give his sign; then I heard the shots.

My heart failed and my knees buckled. I couldn't move a step. I could hear the shots reverberating through the forest as the top of the trees shook. I knew that in no time I'd have fallen to the ground. With the last of my strength I held onto my baby and was able to reach the edge of the forest. I saw a farmer and asked him for help. I placed my baby on the hay in his wheelbarrow and put on my coat. The man said, "You are a lucky one." I didn't answer him. I put my baby under the coat and continued walking. The wind almost knocked me down. Three policeman who left after me, were now ahead of me. One of them looked at me and said, "You are a lucky one." They left singing. My legs seemed to move but I was standing still.

Finally I reached the house of the train watchman. Manka, the daughter of Bougdian, ran to me from the house and took the baby, who was half unconscious. She brought me inside the house where they had some food on the stove. She tried to give me something to eat. I begged her to just let my mother know I was alive. She sent her little sister, and then I took my baby and left. I walked to Cositta St. There was not a living soul in the street. Fearful, I looked in the yards, but there was a deadly quiet all around. Near the house of the Neshka Copels, Avraham Meir Kaygan came to me greatly agitated, and cried, "God! Oh God! How did you get here? How is it that you're walking all alone in the street? How did you get away from the murderers?" He showed me where to walk so as not to get caught again.

I stumbled through in the alleys and when I reached the house of the Zushibebes I saw my mother from afar, running toward me with open arms. We ran hastily towards each other, and when we were just few steps away, we fell into each other's arms, fainting. From one of the houses someone came and took the baby and I was taken to house of Smallshaness. When I came to and opened my eyes, I saw my two sisters-in- law: Sarah and Hannah. They asked me where Velvel was. I could not tell them, so I replied that I had returned in the middle of the march to the forest. I went to my parents' home, but I was incredibly restless. I felt like I was going to lose my mind.

At dusk, Viera, the daughter of the obieshtzik, came to the house and whispered to me, "My heart is with you Yente, in your tragedy. I know that in this house you won't find peace. Come to my house for a few days until you feel a little better. When it got dark I went to her house. She took me to a dark room that was lit only by a little furnace. Now I was separated from my mother and I didn't know what had been the fate of my father. I cried quietly until I was drenched with tears. I whispered my thoughts to Velvel. I felt as if he was standing there listening. All sudden I heard footsteps, soft and careful. The door opened and Viera came in and told me that my father came, and wanted to see me. She asked me to keep our voices hushed during our meeting so that no one could hear us. Father entered the room. I clung to him like I was still a very little girl. He hugged me to his heart and cried and whispered, "My little girl my little child." He stroked my hair, kissed my eyes, and held me in his arms for long hours. We sat at the edge of the bed. Father took the baby, held him and cried. For a long time we sat crying, not wanting to separate. Then Viera came and said it was very dangerous and that father must not leave the yard too late at night.

Father said goodbye and left. The first night after the tragedy and I was lying there feeling as if I am lying at the edge of a great, steep cliff. The horrors that I encountered during the day were too heavy to carry and every moment I was worried that I was going to lose my mind.

Dinerstein family members in Kurenets before the war

With the partisans
Yente née Dinerstein standing first from the left, her sister Rachel is in the center

[Page 155-192]

The Struggle to Survive

by Wolf (Zev) Rabunski

Translated by Ari Solly Gordin

*"In honor of my grandfathers, Dr. Sali Gordin and William Burk,
both possessed a noble and generous spirit, and are greatly missed"*

On the Road

Wolf (Ze'ev) Rabunski
[first cousin of Shimon Peres]
son of Eltka nee Perski and Yitzhak Rabunski

Three days after the Germans invaded Russia, my family, like many other Jews in town, ran away east toward the old USSR border. After encountering many difficulties on the road and being turned away at the border, we decided to return to Kurenets. My wife and child returned directly with other women and children. My good friend, Leib Putrpas and I, decided not to return immediately because we believed that the women and children would be spared by the Nazis, however the young men would be castigated. We decided to return using a longer, more secluded route. During the late afternoon, we reached the little town of Krivitz. We entered at a fateful moment, immediately after the gentiles from the town and the surrounding villages raided the Jews and their homes. As soon as we entered the town, we were caught by some Polish police who were now working for Germans. They beat us severely; their punches were brutal and exact. As soon as they were done with us, they were planning to take us to the German authorities to be put in a POW camp. They continued to beat us mercilessly as a group of German soldiers came to the area, looking for people to clean some barns nearby. One of the soldiers approached me and asked me to identify myself and explain what I was doing there. I made up a hasty story that we were imprisoned by the Russians and that we had quickly escaped and wanted to return to our homes, and that we didn't know why the townspeople were beating us. He ordered us to come with him. As he was taking us to the stable, he noticed one of the town homes where all the doors were open. He entered and stole a record player and some records, ordering me to carry the record player and Leib Putrpas to carry the records. As we continued, he saw another home and decided to steal something there too. We were ordered to wait outside. We decided to run away. We set the stolen goods on the ground and quickly made our way to the fields behind the house.

Evening came and it was growing dark. After a long walk, we asked one of the farmers where we were and he told us that we were near Neyaka, a small village about 10 kilometers from Kurenets. Many of the Jewish residents of Neyaka were involved in business with and had relatives in our town. We decided to rest for a bit until we felt better. We were badly injured and we hadn't eaten for awhile, and we were exhausted. Leib Putrpas knew an old man, named Valah, who lived in Neyaka. He wore a long, white beard, and walked with a limp. Valah was well known all over the region as a most gracious host and as a man of noble spirit.

The village, Neyaka, was small and we found Valah's house with no difficulty. Frightened and in pain, we heard of what was happening in Neyaka. Valah told us that a few days earlier the Germans had come to the synagogue and thrown out the Torah books, and now the Jews are sitting on their luggage ready to run, but nobody knows where to go. The Christian villagers avoided them like the plague, and at best, they treated them as if they were total strangers.

"Don't worry children," Valah said, "God will not desert us. The main thing to concern us with right now is your safety. Go in the barn and sleep on the hay. Tomorrow, we will see what we can do for you."

Only then, when we lay on the fresh hay, did we feel the extreme exhaustion and horrible pain that the beatings from Krivitz had caused us. The wounds burned like fire, and it was impossible to fall asleep. Our clothes stuck to our open wounds and we turned from side to side trying to alleviate the pain until the morning came. At the break of dawn, we heard the birds chirping and we smelled the wonderful scent of freshly cut fields.

Valah couldn't sleep either. He was very concerned about us and got up very early to see how we were. We heard the sound of someone walking with a limp, and realized that it must be him. "Good morning!" he greeted us cheerfully, and announced that we would get porridge to satiate our hunger. We were very excited, for it had been days since we had last eaten like normal human beings. Now that the morning light came, Valah saw that we were hurt. He saw our bruises and immediately ran home. He brought his daughter, who carried a pail of hot water, back with him. They peeled off our bloody boots and shirts. The pain was unbearable since the clothes were sticking to our bodies. They then started washing and feeding us as though we were babies. Valah would encourage us in good spirits, "Eat, children, eat! We must gather our energy so that we can dance when the enemy is annihilated. You know that they took the Torah's from the synagogue and desecrated it. You will see that God will not take it quietly."

We asked him if he knew anything about what was happening in Kurenets. He said that it was impossible to have any contact with other towns as no one could come or go anywhere. "You need some more courage, my children," he said, "Big troubles have come to the nation of Israel; we must stay strong to overcome them. Lie down and get your strength back for a few days, and then we will see what you should do."

He covered us in more hay, and we started feeling more energetic and rested.

Through that time, other Jews started coming to visit us, asking what was going on in other towns. We told them about the troubles in the neighboring towns. Nevertheless, Valah told us not to worry, and kept saying, "We must fast and ask for forgiveness. In the history of our nation, we have known bigger troubles than this and we still see miracles and salvation." The Germans, who were camping in the train station in Kanahanina, started coming to Neyaka to scare and rob the few Jews who lived there. We realized that there was much danger here too, and one of these days we would get caught and receive a similar reception as we did in Krivitz. Thankfully, we were able to escape from there, but we felt that now we were out of miracles.

In the Homes of Israel, there is no light

It had been months since we had left our town, and it seemed like the Germans were winning one victory after the next. We kept asking ourselves, "Is there no force that can stand up to the Germans? Where are the Russian Katyushas, Vanyushas, and all the other renowned weapons that the public constantly heard of?"

After consulting each other and Valah, we decided to leave for Kurenets. We left at night with heavy feet and heavy hearts. A heavy rain fell and drenched our clothes. Finally, we reached the hills of Belashi. From afar, we could hear the sound of the carpentry mills of Zokofsky. From another direction, we could hear the dogs barking in the village of Poken. There in the valley was our town. Occasionally you could see light in one of the windows, yet not one light from a Jewish home. In the homes of Israel, there was no light.

Our hearts were beating fast with excitement. Soon we would see our dear ones; my baby boy, my wife, and the rest of my beloved family. But how difficult it was to return to our hometown crawling on barbed wire as if we were some kind of criminals escaping prison! The farmers had already cut and stacked the hay, as if no war was happening at all. All this excitement made me forget my wounds and pain for a while.

I approached the alley and waited for the German patrol to distance themselves before I crossed the street. I reached my in-law's window and knocked on the shutter quietly. My mother in-law woke up and asked, "Who's there?"

I answered her, whispering, "It's me, your Velvale". She woke up my father-in-law and asked him to go see.

All the commotion woke my wife, and she approached the window and said excitedly but controlled, "Mother, Volvol is here!" After receiving many hugs, kisses, and tears, I went into the bedroom. I stood next to my son's bed. Through the illumination of a candlelit bottle, I saw my sleeping baby. He was sleeping with a little smile on his face, as if he were greeting me from his dreams. We decided that I must not be seen, and that even the child shouldn't see me fearing that he might tell someone of my arrival through baby talk.

There was a Christian man in town who was called the Parifa, since all of his torn clothes were connected by parifas, instead of patches. After we left, he had become the governor of Kurenets, and we had to be very careful.

I hid in the basement, amongst the many healing herbs that my father in-law used to deal with. The next morning my mother came from her home in Myadel Street to visit the baby, and was very excited to hear of my return. She fell on me crying, saying, "My son! My son! The only son who is still left in town!" Her cries woke up the baby and I had to immediately run back to the hiding place.

I looked at my son from a hidden corner and I heard him talk to other children outside the door. He said, "My daddy will come and bring me a little horse."

From then on, mother came to visit me daily and bring news. She was very sure that God would not leave us. She said "Rosh Hashanah is approaching, and God would bless us with a good year." My little sister, Chanaleh, started coming every evening after a day of hard labor, and she tried to cheer me up. I also kept in touch with my friend, Leib Patrapas, by writing letters to him. Life continued peacefully until the week of Simchat Torah.

A few days prior to Simchat Torah, I decided to start sleeping in my own bed every night. The town had settled to a certain routine, and it seemed relatively quiet. This was during the time that most people worked in labor camps, thinking that by doing so, the German authorities would spare them. The baker, Abraham, would come to visit me in my hiding space once a week. He would sit on a haystack and smile to me, saying, "People are telling me that this German business will last for a few hours, or days at most in my opinion, it's a matter of weeks." Abraham told wonderful tales, and I enjoyed listening to him. He told me "fairytales" and I wanted him to continue with the stories because the tales he told me encouraged me and encouraged him. Mother would pat my back and say, "You see, my son? You are so depressed. Cheer up and have faith like Abraham has." She told me this every time she left our house, encouraging herself that good days were still to come.

One time, my son, who still didn't know that I was there, laid in his little bed, I kissed him and immediately left for the hiding place. The child woke up and said, "Who kissed me?" My wife answered that it was Grandpa. My two and half year old answered, "It couldn't be Grandpa. Grandpa's beard is not prickly. Maybe it's daddy." I heard him from my hiding place and tears came to my eyes. My wife continued trying to make him go back to sleep while singing a lullaby of hope and happiness. One morning while I was sleeping in the house, the boy asked to sleep with my wife in my bed. He immediately recognized me and we met for the first time since I'd left town. He hugged me tightly and clung to me. We all cried with happiness and he said to me, "Now I know that a few days ago it was you who kissed me and not Grandpa. You have a prickly beard and Grandpa does not."

All of a sudden the child jumped up and said, "Daddy, run away, the Germans are coming." My wife got scared and told me, "Little children are very sensitive. There is light outside. Take your boots and hide." In just a few minutes, we heard knocks on the doors, windows, and everywhere. I was trying to get out of the house through the window that was facing the yard. Pelvic, Parifa, and Beetah from Vileyka Street, who now worked for the Germans, saw me, therefore now there was no way I could run.

The Rabunski / Chasid family

Simchat Torah, 1942

My father in-law opened the door and let them enter. My son started crying, begging me to carry him. They ordered me to immediately get dressed and go to the police station. They said, "You never registered with the police and you are escaping from doing your share of hard labor."

All the begging and crying didn't help. They only gave me enough time to put some healing pads on my ear, which was still hurting a lot from the beating I got in Krivitz. The police department was very close to our house. It was located next to the house of Eetzah Chaizes (Yitzhak Zimerman) where the stores of Eetzka the husband of Lea and Hirsha- Mendel the tailor used to be. When I entered the police station, I saw a policeman taking Zalman Kasdan, the husband of Chaya-Tzertel. Zalman himself was from Globoki. We greeted each other by silently shaking our heads. From the expression on his face, I could see that he was very surprised to see me there.

Sokolovsky, the assistant to the head of the police from Vileyka Street, had yellow hair that stuck out like a porcupine. He greeted me mockingly, "How are things in Moscow? You must have just returned from there." While talking, he started hitting me hard right in the head.

I told him, "Kasick, what are you doing? You're hitting me? We went to the same school, we sat on the same bench. What troubles did I ever cause you? I always gave your father jobs to take supplies to Vileyka."

He answered, "I am not the same friend from school. Go to the next room and wait for the policeman, Ezaivitz. He has many many things to talk to you about."

Ezaivitz was a farmer. His farm was located a short distance from Kurenets. He was a one-eyed man. He lost his other eye in a drunken brawl. They took me to a room with a window, next to which was a big piece of plywood that was used to darken the room at night during the bombing. After a few minutes, they brought Kasdan back through the room on the way to a third room that was now used as a prison. When they opened the door to let Kasdan in, I saw that there were many Jewish people in the room. This looked very ominous to me. The movement amongst the police was very rapid. They kept running from one place to another, bringing more and more people. They brought Velvel, the son of Asher the haberdasher, they brought Zalman Gelman from Kosita Street. Here to my room, they brought Esther Charnas and David Kapilovitz, the tailor. They brought the father in-law of Moshe Markman and then they brought Nachum, the son of Michael and Pesia Alperovich. Everyone who they brought after Esther Charnas they left in the first room, Sokolovsky room.

Next to me stood a policeman, it was the son of Zusya, the one who brought water to the town's homes. All her days, she worked for us and her son was almost raised in our house. I was waiting for the officer to come. Meanwhile, I saw that many Christians were standing in the market as if they were waiting for something to happen, watching the police headquarters. I saw the son of Yadviga running in haste and bringing shovels. I saw the prior head of the post office that was very friendly with us at one time. When he saw me, he said to the son of Zusya, "Watch him very carefully. This bird is capable of escape and can fly through the windows."

Next, they took out from the prison room Shimon Lieb, Baruch Kremnick, and Asher, the son of Yehoshua Alperovich. We greeted each other, and they all looked at me with amazement. They thought I had escaped to Russia long ago and didn't understand why I would come back. All of a sudden, I sow the Christian mob outside running in panic. A big group of Germans riding on motorcycles was approaching the police headquarters. One German, tall and nervous, with many badges that I did not recognize, entered the room. From his manners, I knew that he was a high officer. He asked me if I was a Communist. I answered that I had nothing to do with Communism and never had anything to do with Communism and that I was simply waiting for the head of the police to return. The German officer left the room and the two watchmen, who did not speak German asked me what the German officer had told me, I said "he asked me to stay for now, but he will let me go soon." This must have left some impression on them because they left me and went to the front room. Outside there was some commotion. They brought a lot of shovels and axes and other tools.

Another German man entered the room. He was fat with a flat nose, he wore shiny boots with skulls on them. Right behind him, entered Mataras, the mayor of Kurenets. They were going to discuss something privet and didn't want me there so they put me in the third room, the prison room where many people from Kurenets were crowded in. The heat in this room that was only two and one half meter wide was unbearable. I stood right next to the door. The people in the room immediately asked what I had seen outside. I answered, "My dears, whoever knows what to say will say it." Still I was persuaded to tell them about all the commotion that I saw through the window, I spoke about the German officers who came, and about the shovels, they carried. Zalman Kasdan interrupted me saying, "Why are you spreading unneeded panic here? It must be that the partisans blew up some bridge and they will take us to fix it." Shimon Leib said, "How could anyone comprehend such horrible idea that they will take, just like this, innocent people and murder them?" Chaim Zukovski, who was totally exhausted and could hardly stand on his feet, said in a broken voice, "My dear people, David Motosov once told me of what he had seen when he ran away from the occupied areas of Poland prior to June. I will believe anything. I believe that the Germans are capable of the most evil crimes." Asher, the son of Yehoshua, said, "If they will really take us to be killed, we must try to escape. Maybe someone will be saved." Others were sitting and reciting passages from the Bible. A few were sitting quietly with a frozen expression on their face.

I felt that I was going to choke so I started banging on the door saying that I need to go to the bathroom. Betar from Vileyka Street came in. He took me outside and held his rifle pointing at me ready to shoot if I try to escape. I was taken to the yard next to our house. I looked if someone from my family is around. Thinking that at least, I can look at them for the last time. I started begging Betar, "You must let me run. I know you are going to kill us. Take the thousand rubbles that I have and release me. I had never hurt anyone." He refused, but still took my money. I kept begging him "please let me run and shoot after me and explain to the Germans that I ran and you were shooting" but he would not be convinced.

It was a beautiful day, a sunny day, and the morning of Simchat Torah that always filled our town with singing and dancing. Now, I was walking right next to my home with a death sentence hanging over my head. There was no place to escape to. Everywhere we were surrounded by barbed wire. Now Betar was taking me back to the police headquarters. Betar wanted to take me back to the prison room. I told him, "Why are you doing this? I am supposed to wait for Ezaivitz and the German officer." No talk helped. With a kick, he threw me back in the room. After a few minutes, I started banging on the door again. A different policeman came. I immediately put my foot in the open space between the door and the frame so he couldn't close it. I said, "Please permit me to go out and get some water. I must take my valerian pills. I am dying." He refused, I pushed my way out of the room while begging. "You must let me take my pill and then you can put me back in this room."

Now I was in the room where I had stood before. The policeman accepted the fact and brought me some water. All around was commotion, and the policeman did not return. Through the window, I saw him walking with a German officer holding a box. Now I was in a room with the people who came with Esther Charnas. Many thoughts and ideas came to my head. I thought of tricks and ways to get out of there, but I couldn't find a real solution. Again, I looked at the big plywood and decided to hide behind it. I asked everyone in the room to stand next to the plywood to hide the opening between the wood and the wall and they all did it. I made myself very little sitting behind the plywood. I heard the sounds of the steps of the Germans entering. The door of the prison opened and I heard them counting eight people to take out. Again, they counted eight people and took them out. Each time, they counted eight. Nachum, the son of Pesia nee Kastrel and Michael Alperovich, who was standing at the edge of the plywood whispered to me that they took out Ruben, the tailor, Asher the son of Yehoshua Alperovich, and Zalman Gelman amongst other. Then he told me that they gave them shovels and they took them to Kosita Street. He said they were surrounded by many German guards. After a few minutes, Nachum said that they were taking the families of the people who were imprisoned in the room. They took their Parents, wives, and children. I quickly glanced out of the window fearing that some of my family would be there, but I did not see them. I prayed that they would have run away in time. Once more, the Germans entered and took the rest of the people from the prison room. First, they took them to the market, then they took them to Kosita Street. I hid behind the plywood wondering what my end would be like. Soon, I thought they would come and get me. I kept pondering about the tragic fate awaiting me.

All of a sudden, I heard the tone of Ezaivitz voice. He announced Esther Charnas's name, and ordered her to go to the front room. There he ordered her to lie on the bench. She begged for pity but to no avail. She was thrown on the bench and they started hitting her with a whip. I heard the counting of the Germans and her screams, first very loud, then very mute. She must have fainted. Soon afterward, I heard them throwing her outside the building. They did the same to almost everyone in the room. I decided that it would be much better to be whipped than to be killed. Therefore, without much thinking, I stood at the end of the line to be whipped. Next, they thrashed another man who fainted immediately, and was thrown out. All of a sudden, Ezaivitz who had only one functioning eye managed to recognize me. He started screaming, "What are you doing here?" He gave me a powerful kick and threw me back in the prison room. Locking the door behind.

Extraordinary luck

I was alone in the room. Now I knew that my fate had been nailed. Soon, they would kill me. From afar, I could hear shooting. It was perfectly clear to me that right now the people who had sat in this room half an hour ago, the residents of Kurenets, my neighbors and friends, were lying in their own pool of blood. I heard echoes of what they had said in this room. I heard Kasdan saying, "They are taking us to fix a bridge." Shimon Leib saying, "How could it be that they would take innocent people and kill them?" Chaim Zukovski saying, "They are capable of anything." I could still hear the passages from the Bible and Asher son of Yehoshua saying "lets try to escape". Most of these people were raised together with me, we were like one big family since early childhood and now they were lying there lifeless. I was so worried that my family was with them. Could my little boy who warned me, "Daddy run away the Germans are coming," be with them? I was looking for something in my pockets to commit suicide with. I wanted to die by my on hands, but I couldn't find a thing. I decided to use my belt. I tried to reach the window, but the window was very high, almost to the ceiling. So I closed the door from the inside and tried to connect the belt to the door handle. The other side of the belt I put around my neck.

All of a sudden, I heard knocks on the door. I didn't open it, but I couldn't commit suicide without opening the door. They broke the door and saw me with the belt around my neck. They brought with them more prisoners. Yechezkel Zimerman (Charles Gelman), Chaim Yitzhak Zimerman, Tuvia Sosensky, Shmuel Blinder (son of Pisel), Moshe Mordechai Peretz, and a few more who's names I cannot remember. They were just brought there from Luban, where they worked in the agricultural farm.

When the police left, the new comers told us that Arka the son of Ruben, (Revka Teiba's Alperovich) from Myadel Street attacked one of the policemen taking them and ran to the fields. However, the Germans shot after him and managed to kill him. We all agreed that it was a much better way to die than to wait for them to kill us. Shmuel Blinder, the son of Pesach, took out a small Sidur. He read passages from it. We all repeated it after him. We excepted that any minute they would come to take us but we had waited there for a long time and we could see that dusk was coming. Finally, we heard heavy steps. The door opened and Sokolovsky, the assistant to the head of police, came in. He had red eyes from years of being drunk, he said, "Today you are the lucky ones. For now, you are all staying alive." He looked at me and said, "You are particularly lucky. You have escaped death for now. But you won't escape forever." He told us to leave. He asked if we have any valuable things to give him. However, we had nothing.

We all hastily left the death room. Outside it was getting dark. We went through the fields. There was total silence around us. There was not one lit window, one other person walking. I hid behind the houses of Shmuel Eetzi and Artzik the son of Gutza Dinerstien. Moshe Mordechai Peretz joined me, we hid there until there was total darkness. I entered the house of Yosef Alperovich, the son of Mendel Chezkales'. His wife, Leah, the daughter of the Maizel family, was my wife's best friend since early childhood. She fell on my neck kissing me and crying and told me while sobbing who was killed today. I asked her nervously what had happened to my family and to my great relief she told me that the police came to take them but they managed to run away prior to their arrival. Leah couldn't stop sobbing. She wanted to give me something to eat but I could not eat anything I just wanted to go see my family. They didn't let me. Yosef said that he must go first to check the road to my house to make sure it is safe. He went through the gardens and when he returned he said that my family had just returned home. Crawling all the way, I managed to reach my house. I found out that my son was hidden behind the cowshed of our Christian neighbors covered with branches and bushes and like that, he lied there the entire day. My wife hid in the fields. My mother, when she saw me, fainted from excitement. Everyone was sure that I had been taken to my death. Again, days of hiding came.

Usable Jews

Mendel Chasid

The winter of 1942 was extremely cold but that only made us feel happy imagining the troubles that the Nazis were having in the frozen battlefields. Therefore, although it was very difficult for us, considering we didn't have any firewood for our furnaces, we still prayed to God that more snowstorms would come. Rumors started that the killers had retreated from the battlefields. The Jews who worked for the train station would bring us the good news. They would say that large amount of supplies are going west, meaning they are retreating. The villagers were ordered to clean the snow from the roads and to put yellow sand on the ground. All the Jews were ordered to do this even during the night. They would work nonstop. The police were very cruel. They would beat them mercilessly. Still, in our hearts we were full of hope reasoning that like Haman, that was destroyed in Purim, this would be the fate of our current enemy.

This was how the very religious among us thought. Many of the orthodox Jews would fast every Monday and Thursday reciting Tehilim passages and waiting impatiently for Purim to come.

There was a big letdown and dreadful sadness when Purim had finally arrived, that was the day that the Nazis killed the residents of our sister town Vileyka, the few who survived the first actzia. Many of the Jews from Kurenets that were taken there to be used as forced labor in the train station were also murdered. Now, Jewish Vileyka, our young beautiful sister town was erased from the Jewry map with hardly a survivor.

When people found out that the rumors of the inhalation were based on facts, they all started to look for hiding places. They started making tunnels and underground hideouts inside fireplaces, between double walls, in basements, and in attics. Everyone was looking for a hideout knowing that the day of slaughter of our own town Jews would come soon. The day after Purim, it was unbearably cold but we ignored the freezing weather. We kept running from one person to another in attempt to find out if anyone we knew survived the killing in Vileyka. Through gardens and fields amid homes, we reached each other. No one had any fences--the fences were used as wood in our fireplaces. The streets were empty of Jews. It was just too dangerous to use them.

A rumor spread that all the "professional people" will be taken to work for the Gveent Commissar in Vileyka and all the usable Jews were to be kept alive for the duration of the job. Therefore, everyone tried to become a "usable Jews". We all wanted to stay alive. I didn't have any usable profession and I was very depressed. It had been eight months that I had been escaping hard labor. Now, I had to find a profession that would keep me alive. I really didn't trust the promises, but still, as if I was a drowning man looking for a stick, I was hanging on this opportunity. After a lot of pondering, I had an idea. I would register as a tanner.

My father in-law, Mendel Chasid, had supported me in this idea. He said that he would also register in the Judenrat as a tanner and together we would be able to learn the profession. I had no knowledge of the job but I knew that my father in-law, prior to the First World War, had a workshop for leather goods and he knew some information about the profession. Therefore, I was dangling on this profession. I went to the Judenrat in the house of Yechiel Kremer, the son of Yekutiel Meir, and I registered. The crowding in the house was unbearable. Everyone was looking to be saved. They all came to register as professionals. Merchants, shopkeepers and teachers, became carpenters, glassmakers and any other handy profession. Shotz, the head of the Judenrat registered all of them. He was a Jewish survivor from Austria. He knew German fluently. Now, he controlled the miserable Jewish community. I didn't envy any person who Shotz didn't like. After crowding in lines with the rest of the people, I reached Shotz. My face was completely new to him. He registered me as a tanner and told me that at three in the afternoon, they would take all of the registered people to Vileyka.

I ran home to take something for the road and to say good-bye to my family. I cried when I came home. I knew that shortly I would have to say goodbye to my son, my dear wife, my mother, and my mother in-law. Abruptly, I decided not to go and to stay here. If it were our fate to perish, we would perish all together. Every corner in my house was dear to me. I was married only three years ago. Mother started crying, and I joined her. "My son, my son," she said, "Don't forget your lonely poor mother. Don't forget son that all my days as a widow, I only gave for you my children. I already lost my dear Yankeleh to this war, don't forget me my child." My wife and my mother in-law joined her crying. I decided that no matter what, I would not go to Vileyka. My father in-law said, "You cannot let go of an opportunity to be saved. Maybe someone will be saved. God is full of mercy. We must stop the crying in the name of God. Collect something for the road and let us go." Here, the cries became louder. Everyone was hanging on me and we couldn't separate.

Then, Israel the tailor came, he separated us and said, "It's getting late and we must depart. Later will be too late." Hence, my father in-law and I left the house. We all met next to the Christian prayer house. We left like soldiers in lines. All around us stood our relatives to say goodbye as if it was a funeral. Some of the Christian town natives were dressed in black suits with gray ribbons on their sleeves, with shiny boots and rifles on their shoulders. They were watching us. These people grew up with us; they went to the same schools with us. Now, they became collaborators, killers of the town's Jews. They took us in long lines through the empty town's market. It was freezing and the snow was making loud noise under our feet. The wind was whispering as if it was crying for us. Our guards kept hitting us with the ends of their rifles. We were walking as if we were sheep ready to be slaughtered. The closer we got to Vileyka, the more they hit us.

We entered Vileyka. The doors and windows of most of the Jewish homes were all broken. Broken furniture and dishes were thrown all over the streets. The wind blew parts of clothes. This was what was left from the beautiful Jewish Vileyka. The only people we saw there were the German police in their light green uniforms and their shiny helmets with skulls on their uniforms.

A tanner and the painter

Our guards wanted to please the German rulers, so they started beating us harder and they made us run all around Vileyka so we could see the destruction of the Jewish quarter. Then, they brought us to the Gveent commissar. We stood near the main building and here came one of our most fateful moments: would they accept us as professionals or would they turn us back to Kurenitz? There were just a few more Jews left in line when my time came to stand in front of the Germans scum. He was dressed in a uniform with many medals. He held a stick in his hand. "What is your profession?" he yelled in my face. I tried to give myself an expression of confidence and I answered, "I am a tanner." I saw that everyone who was present from my townspeople, were very surprised that I had lied, and they looked at me with sorrow. "How old are you?" he asked. I said, "Twenty-six." "How many years have you worked in this profession?" "Twelve years," I answered. "I know how to prepare leather for fur coats and for shoes." To the right, he screamed so for now I got a sentence to live. Next, was my father-in-law. He asked him the same questions. When he answered, "Fifty-six," he said, "To the left." I was shocked. My father-in-law looked at me from afar signaling me with eyes full of tears. Nevertheless, we were not allowed to say anything.

This is how Hendel decided the fate of the entire community. Standing on the side trying to be seen as little as possible, I didn't know whether it was good or bad that I had lied to Hendel. What if tomorrow I would have to prove my knowledge in this profession? In front of Hendel stood a huge man, a survivor from the slaughter in Rakov. He was dressed like a villager with a rope around his waist. When he was asked, he also said that he was a tanner and obviously he was immediately chosen as a professional. All my hopes and thoughts were with him thinking that he was a real leather man. As soon as they sent him to the right, he approached me as a member of the same profession, and, at first, I was very happy. He immediately said that he would assist as much as he could. He told me how strong he was, that he was as strong as ox and that he could help me with anything if he were next to me, the professional! When I heard that, it was as if my world as darkened. All hopes with him were lost. One liar meets another liar.

When evening came, it started getting very cold. The police collected us and took us through the alleys to a broken building. They announced that all the people who were not selected would be returned to Kurenitz the next day.

Here, I met again with my father-in-law. We would separate this night. We sat in a room corner on the cold floor and my father-in-law started teaching me the secrets of the profession. The names of the processes, the chemicals that I had never heard of, what tools to use, what to do first and next. I was totally depressed and ready to give up. I didn't think that there was any purpose in this. It was clear that I didn't know the profession, but my father-in-law would not let go. Like a teacher with a student, he was announcing things, testing me, and asking me to repeat everything, checking to see if I understood. Everyone else was lying around, thinking that we had lost our minds. This was a sleepless night, hardly anyone slept a wink. The night lasted as if it was a whole generation.

Morning came. The police shouted and everyone who was found useless were put in lines and returned to Kurenitz. At the edge of Vileyka, not far from the Jewish cemetery, a big wooden building was built by the Russians as a school for the children of the laborers. The wooden building was partially destroyed as most of the homes in Vileyka were. The furnaces were broken the doors and windows were taken out, and inside the rooms was snow that came through the broken ceilings. Very near the building there was a kitchen. Right next to the kitchen was a huge dog, probably put there on purpose. Every time we went there to get water, we would feel his bites. The first thing Shuts gave us was sharp barbed wire and told us to put it all around our area. I was put in the same room as Yosef Zuckerman, the brothers Kopel and Eliyahu Specter, Hershel Zimmerman, Yechezkel Zimmerman (Charles Gelman), and Yermiyau Alperovich. Yermiyau had a heart of gold and hands of limitless capabilities. He could fix anything, he was a miracle worker. He was always ready to help anyone. He would go through fire and water to help us. In a short time, Yermiyau built in our room a furnace, and at the first night there was already wood warming in the furnace and we could use it to boil water. He was like a merciful mother to us.

Shortly, all the professionals' people started working. The carpenters were making furniture, the shoemakers were making boots, the tailors were working, the blacksmiths were working, and everyone was busy except for me and Gershon from Rakov. We were walking around aimlessly. I approached Shuts and explained that for our job we needed a separate area. The smell of the leather is very strong and the process of the leather was very slow. It would take a long time until we could produce anything. Therefore, I asked that he would arrange for us a separate house where I could mend the leather according to the rules of the profession. Shuts, the director, understood my explanation and said that very soon I would get the raw materials to fix the leather for fur coats. While he was talking, he said that making fur coats were not as difficult of a job and the smell was not so bad and could be done in one week. Immediately, I told Shuts that I did not want to wait and be idle until the raw material got there, so maybe I could meanwhile be a painter. I knew much more about painting. My request was transferred to Hendel and, with the help of God and my good friend Yosef Zuckerman who tirelessly talked to the other painters and asked them to help me, I became a painter. Gershon from Rakov, who was such a strong man became a woodcutter and would do any work that required strength. At first, we were told to paint the house of one of the heads of the camp, Graveh, a Latvian killer who killed many of the Jews of the towns in the Vileyka district. His apartment was very near the jail.

One time, I was sent outside to get water from the well to be used for mixing the paint, I looked for the well and all of a sudden I saw near the jail a big bon fire. From the direction of the fire, I smelled burning bodies. Right next to the bon fire, I saw a man who I could not recognize with a long stick. He would push the burned bodies into the bon fire and pour gasoline on them. I ran as fast as I could to tell this to the rest of the painters. We went to the back window, and from there, we could see this awful site. We stood there shocked and paralyzed. These bodies were leftover from the Purim killing of the Vileyka and Kurenitz Jews. All of a sudden, we heard the footsteps of the killers coming towards us, consequently we had to leave that scene of horror and return to our job.

My friends, the painters, put a large amount of paint on my clothes to make me look experienced, and I continued painting with them. However, the Jewish head of the camp never forgot my original profession. One day, he brought me two foxes to be used. When I saw the two dead foxes, my heart plummeted. I was sure that my end was near. My friends, the painters, started looking at me with eyes full of pity saying, "What else can we do for you that we didn't do before? Now our hands our tied."

I started thinking very hard trying to remember what my father-in-law had tried to teach me when we laid on the cold floor that night. Trying to remember names of chemicals, the order of the tasks, and the tools that I should use. I decided that if I would not be able to do the job, I would try to escape. First thing, I brought water and put the two fox bodies in it. There was still meat stuck to them and the smell was horrible. I remembered what my father-in-law ordered me to do. I squeezed the carcasses, massaged them, and cleaned them until one could see the white leather and the fur did not fall off. To my surprise, Shuts liked my job, and, again, I prolonged the arrival of the angel of death using chicanery and lies.

The Bathhouse

The sanitary conditions in the camp were very bad. We had no place to wash ourselves and we didn't have clean underwear. The "third Egyptian plague" started bothering us. Day and night it bothered us and we could not find rest. Finally, the Germans decided to take us to the bathhouse. I will never forget that bathhouse. We walked under heavy guard outside of town. We were taken to a big auditorium that was not heated. The glass windows were covered with ice. We were ordered to strip naked. All our clothes were taken and put in a boiler. We were divided into two groups. I was among the first group. The cold weather pricked our skin and we stood there naked. We started hitting one hand with the next, running in place, and kicking with our feet--anything to keep warm. The killers looked at us and started laughing with enjoyment. It was even worse when we entered the next room. There, was ice water. In this room stood a German, next to a pail full of black soap. Each one of us was ordered to go to the pail and there the German would use a paintbrush on every inch of our body. The soap was very stinky and caused a burning reaction. Therefore, the cold and the burning sensations made my body feel as if I was hit with many iron whips. While standing like this, naked, ready to leave the showers, all of a sudden we heard screaming, "Fire! Save us! Fire!" The panic spread all over. People were jumping on top of each other to get out. There was a cloud of black smoke that burned our eyes. The German police kicked us all out to collect snow to put out the fire. Later, someone told us that the one responsible for the cleaning of our clothes was new at the job and put the clock that controlled the water temperature on too high, and this was the reason for the fire. Many of us thought he did it on purpose.

All of the clothes of first group were burned, so now there was a question of how we would return to the camp. There was no choice but to use some of the clothes of the second group. A few gave pants, stayed with their underwear, some gave shoes, and stayed with socks, some gave sheets. This is how we returned. Evil ghosts would look nicer. Covered with black soap, frozen and stinking, we walked through the streets of Vileyka. All through our walk, people gathered and laughed. Little children ran after us throwing snowballs and cursing us. From our eyes, there were tears of blood. We walked hunched with no will to subsist.

Together with our families

We were there for more than three months with very little contact by our families. Occasionally, they would send us food or short letters that we read breathlessly with our hearts pounding. The usual news was about punishments, killings, and tortures. The Jews of all the shtetls in the district were killed at this point. Would our town Jews survive?

All of a sudden, there was an announcement by Shuts that he would give us permission to transfer to Vileyka all the families of the useful Jews. They already had made the same announcement in Kurenets, and the wives and children prepared for the move. It was as if they were going to embark on a voyage to a golden beach. The rest of the town's Jews who were tortured and depressed saw them as the luckiest of people. On Sunday morning, the governor of the district sent us with guards to Kurenets so that we could bring our families. At the head of the group walked the bloody killer, I can't remember his name, but we used to call him, "The Limped." The oven maker, from Vileyka, his cruelty knew no boundaries. When we saw him, we almost fainted. After the war, I was privileged to see him hung near his home.

How difficult was our entrance to our hometown meeting the Christian inhabitants walking around freely, dressed with the clothes that they stole from the Jews, and in their eyes was a mean mocking look of superiority! Can I ever describe both the meetings and the good-byes from the relatives that came to meet us for the last time? The mocking of the gentiles, the screaming of the police, and the deep, dark depression of the Jews who were standing in the market, broken and displaced. I can never forget the last words of my dear mother, "My darling children, we are giving to you the rest of the years of our lives. You must survive, at least when you will be saved you must tell others about our destruction."

The two grandmas and the grandpa clung to their little grandchild crying. The site tore our hearts, but the Christian inhabitants and the police were watching the pitiful site saying words of mockery and cursing. The police started yelling and ordered us to hurry. We started moving and behind us, we left weeping and broken hearts.

In Vileyka, the women were also sent to work. Each morning, they would get up very early to clean the streets, shovel the snow, clean the toilets, and bring firewood to the German homes. In the winter, they would harness them, like horses, to the buggies. In the summer, they would harness them to sleighs only to torture and mock them. Our children were hungry and dirty wearing torn clothes. They would stay in the barracks all-alone and would regularly go to the barbed wire fence to see if their parents were returning. Shuts announced that again we would be classified and the ones who would be found suitable for jobs in the camp would live in a different barrack closer to the head of the unit. Also, they would bring some new workers from Kurenets and other places and their camp would be headed by Zsinstand, a Kurenets native. Shuts, at this point, knew that I wasn't a painter or a leather man, so I was sure that now he would get rid of me. After bribing him, using my good connections to plea for me and a lot of begging, he decided to let me be classified as a useful Jew.

Next to the public hospital was an abandoned home whose inhabitants were sent to Siberia by the Russians in 1940. There were about eight rooms in the house, and now they put there 150 people – men, women, and children. The living conditions were unbearable, but, for some reason, they didn't watch us very carefully. Therefore, through the yard, occasionally, my little sister, Hannah, would sneak in to see me. She belonged to the children workers camp of Zsinstand. During those days, sometimes a smile would come to our face. The carpenters told us that lately the Germans ordered a huge amount of coffins, the amount of which was getting bigger and bigger. They said, "Das machen dee maradee rash partisanan. Ze marden un zara saradaten." How happy we were to hear that! A new spirit of hope spread amongst us. We decided that we must escape to the forest as soon as possible. The situation in the Zsinstand camp was horrible. That is where they took children, mostly they were from Kurenitz There were a few from Ilya, Myadel, Smorgon, Keblenek, and Dolhinov. Hendel decided that he could not live without a sport court. He coerced the Jewish children to build him one. Every day the children would break rocks. From early in the morning to nighttime they made gravel to be later put on the ground. They put the gravel in a huge tank, the little children were harnessed to it, and they would take it from one side of the yard to the other. There was a horrible watchman by the name Gadi, who caused a lot of blood and tears to spill by the young children. Still today, I can remember the lines of blood on my sister, Channaleh's back from the whip of the watchman who used it while she was washing his floor.

The Slaughter in Kurenets

Three days prior to Rosh Hashanah 1942, the Christians people came by and told us the most horrible news. They told us about a slaughter of the Jews who were left in Kurenets, they said it occurred at the end of Myadel Street. At first, we refused to believe them. We had heard rumors like this before, and later the rumors would be disproved. However, to our horror this time, it turned to be the bitter truth. We still had with us letters that we had received from our relatives and friends in Kurenitz from a day or two prior to the slaughter. We took the pages out and cried. We kissed the letters that were written by our dear ones, and we could not continue working. We were shocked and deeply depressed. A short time later, they brought carriages full of clothes and other belongings of the Jews of Kurenets. Our wives were ordered to separate them into men's clothes, women's clothes, children's shoes, etc. Occasionally, they would recognize clothes that belonged to their beloved relatives. Nevertheless, the watchman did not allow the women to show any signs of depression or desperation while working. How they were able to continue their job? Where did they find the spiritual strength? The little children also found out about the horrible occurrence.

On that night, no one slept. It was a night of mourning. We cried and we tore our clothes. We pulled the hair out of our heads. We sat on the ground and mourned our martyrs. People who were left single with no families said, "We must escape immediately. Now, it is very clear what the Germans are planning, and anyone who refuses to escape will stay here to be hung." Nevertheless, some of us said, "winter is coming. Where will we escape to with little children?" Others tried to console themselves by saying that the Germans were building a big theater and that they would need us for at least six months so we should stay here until spring and then try to escape.

It was a night of tears and desperation until the morning came. We went to work, but we were like human shadows. A few survivors from the slaughter in Kurenets came to Vileyka. They stealthily hid in the Zsinstand camp. It was more complicated to reach our camp inasmuch as it was watched carefully.

One day, around noon, I entered the barn to take some water to boil. All of a sudden, I heard a strange noise from the roof. At first, I was sure it was a cat. However, when I kept hearing the sound, I guessed that it wasn't a cat, but a person. I called, "Who's there?" I thought that someone was trying to commit suicide so I went out of the barn to let other people know. Gitel Kapelovitch, the wife of David the tailor, stopped me and said, "Don't run anywhere." She started whispering to me that her sister, Dvushka, the wife of Eliyahu Chaim Alperovich, was brought here a few days ago by Ingeleh Byruk, a gentile from Kurenets who saved many Jews. He hid her in his carriage under a pile of hay for a few days, and now she was concealed here and no one knew of it. Dvushka came down from her hiding place crying and begging me not to tell anyone. Maybe later she said she would convince Shuts to let her stay. Dvushka was beautiful, with all the prettiness of a Jewess. She sounded so naïve when she said this. I said, "Dvushkaleh, don't stay here. Run to the forest. Find people who will help you and you will survive. For the love of God, don't stay here." My heart was crying inside. As if to mock, she was blossoming in her beauty. After a while, Shuts took her to work as a cleaning woman. A short time later when she left to work outside the camp, some of the Kurenets inhabitants recognized her and immediately informed the Germans that she had escaped the slaughter and that she was with us illegally. One evening, two killers from the SS entered the camp. They found her and took her, the next day she was released. We were very happy to see her among us. We said, "Dvushkaleh, you must run out of here immediately." "Where will I run," she begged with tearful eyes, "My face will be a testament that I am a Jew anywhere. I must stay near my sister. I am already lost." The next day, the two killers returned. She cried and begged for mercy. She was held in prison for two weeks, where she was tortured by every killer. Later, together with Itka Chadash, she was shot by the killer, Gravah, behind the jail.

Kurenets 1937
***Standing second from the left; Dvushka nee Kopilovitz, the wife of Eliyahu Chaim Alperovich
(standing next to her) with his parents, sister and niece.***

The gun

To pretend that we were gentiles was almost impossible for most of us. Most looked Jewish. Despite that, I decided to take my chances and to take off my yellow tag of. To conceal the Jewish star that were sewed on the front of the clothes and on the back, to dress in typical clothes of farmers in our area. To secretly leave the camp and get in touch with some Christian acquaintances. Whenever I would plot it and start getting apprehensive of the idea, I would consider the aim of my mission and then my fear would subside. Finally, I was able to accomplish it. I left the camp in attempt to get weapons in preparation for the escape to the forest. I knew the roads very well. I was able to reach the home of one Christian acquaintance of mine who lived in Vileyka and he promised me to buy me a weapon.

Many times I returned to his home and each time I returned to the camp very depressed because he would delay giving me the weapon. Every time he would raise the amount of money, he wanted for it. Finally, he took me up to his attic and gave me the "supplies". With excitement, I started kissing his hands. He was not satisfied with just kisses and asked me to give him some leather for boots, the only break he gave me was that I could give him the leather on a later occasion. He put the gun in a rag and tied it around my leg in case someone would check me. My heart was beating with happiness and excitement and in great spirits, I returned to the camp.

Of my secret, I only told my friend Yosef Zuckerman, and his eyes lit with happiness. However, both of us had no knowledge of weapons. I knew that Hertzel Alperovich used to serve in the army, so I was sure that he would know something about weapons. How shocked I was when Hertzel told me that you could not even try the gun because it locked the barrel with bullets.

My heart broke. My spirit was lifted again thanks to Kopeleh Specter who was an absolute genius and in his hands, the gun became lethal. He fixed the gun according to the exact rules. Now all I needed were bullets. Therefore, again I started running around looking for the correct bullets amongst my Christian acquaintances. Finally, I got three bullets.

The annihilation of the Zsinstand camp

*Chanale Rabunski,
sister of the author*

A short time prior to the slaughter in Kurenets, the governor of White Russia, Koobah, came from Minsk to "visit" our camp. He was the one who was responsible for the destruction of the Jews in Belarus. He came on a foggy, rainy day. All of a sudden, we were surrounded by Belarussian police, and they took us back to the camp. At that point, we were all sure that they were going to kill us. It was impossible to run away – running was a sure death. Each one of us started counting our sins to ourselves. All of a sudden, Shuts announced, "Everyone go to work. No one stays in the camp." Hastily, everyone started running to their workplace – the carpenters to the carpentry, the shoemakers to the shoe shop, etc. Only I and my brother to the lie, Gershon from Rakov walked around aimlessly not knowing what to do. All of a sudden, I remembered that there was still one dead fox in my sleeping place, so immediately I ran through a side alley to my room, took the leather, and tried to return to the work area. When the women saw my face and my fearful running, they suspected that I took my weapon and was planning to kill Koobah. All the women stood in the door front and prevented me from leaving. They started checking me and begging that I must not do it, they feared for their children's life. It took a lot of explanation to calm them down and to prove to them that I had only returned to fetch the leather for my job.

When I returned to the work area, the group of killers entered. Amongst them were Koobah and the commissar for our area, Schmidt. They were followed by guards. Everyone was armed as if ready for a battle. At once, I turned the fox around to the inside and the smooth skin to the outside. I put it on a piece of wood and with a knife, I started working the skin. Our nervousness became fear when we heard the sounds of their creaking boots. All the workplaces were very busy. You could hear the sounds of hammers, saws, iron, etc. I was the last one to be visited. Koobah looked at me and at what I was doing with a look of great disrespect. He listens to my explanation of what I was doing. My heart died inside until we finally reached the blessed moment and they left. Now I could sigh with relief.

The results for our camp were only our great fear, but Koobah gave an order to eliminate the camp of Zsinstand. A few months later, on Saturday in November early in the morning before we even left for work, two young girls came to us running. One was the sister of Shalom the tailor from Kribitz, the other was Hashka, the daughter of Israel David from Kosita Street. Their hair was all messy and their eyes were turned around and strange with fear. They were talking in very confused order and crying hysterically. They told us what had happened in their camp. The night, when it turned dark, the killers had taken all of the children out of the camp on trucks. They were taken to the forest near the Jewish cemetery and all the children were murdered. Again, everyone in our camp started crying.

I had a particular part in this tragedy. My only sister, the baby of our family, Chanaleh. We could hardly walk to work. The carpentry was on the second floor, they could see through the window the black smoke from the direction of the Jewish cemetery. Again, people talked about escaping. The people who were single announced, "We are going to escape, we are getting out of here immediately. Today we are going to run. We are not going to perish because of the families here who believe the Nazis. Look at the smoke," they yelled, "Look and see. This is your own blood burning here. What are you waiting for? Very soon, they will bring their clothes for us to sort. Who is going to sort your own clothes? Who?" Some of the family people said that they were right, but still among us were true professionals who believed that they were needed at least until Passover.

The Germans were building a theater and our work was necessary they said. These people would not let us run. They threatened us that they would stop us by force saying that if we escaped, everyone that stayed would be annihilated. Secretly some people managed to escape on that Saturday since that day the watch was not very careful, the guards were busy preparing for Sunday celebration. So on that day, about twenty escaped, amongst them Chetskel (Charles Gelman) Zimmerman, Tuvia Kopelovich, Moshe Lazer Torov, Chalvina Torov, Shimon Zimmerman, and Riva Gordon Zimmerman. Everyone thought that the German revenge would come soon. Women started calling to their husbands, "What are you sitting for? Run and escape with them. We must save whoever we can." We dressed the children with the few clothes that we had and stood ready as if we were standing in the train station with our little bundles. All of a sudden, Shuts came and said, "It's fine, the governor said that nothing bad would happen to us since we were useful Jews." Shuts continued saying that he thought we would manage to save ourselves through this war. We didn't really trust those promises. We knew that those were lies, but we were very fearful to escape on a winter day with little children. Therefore, for now we decided to stay.

On Monday, all the women were sent to take the clothes, the shoes, and other belongings from the Zsinstand camp. They came back from their work destroyed emotionally. We felt as if the gates of pity and the gates of revenge were forever locked for the Jews. We were broken people and had no means to do anything to control our fate.

We become gravediggers

Many days past since the annihilation of the Zsinstand camp. Time seemed to crawl very slowly. However, in our heart we started feeling a slim hope that maybe we would be lucky enough to see Spring, and then, if God wishes, we would be able to escape. The news from the front was encouraging. Now, the Germans were busy with the killing of their own collaborators, they were killing Polish and other the German sympathizers. They would even bring priests to the Vileyka jail and there, they would kill them and put them in a common grave. Other "important people" who saw themselves as German patriots and who continuously killed Jews now were being killed by the Germans. Therefore, now some of the Christian citizens started feeling that the Germans were treating them as "Jews" and they must do something against them. Still, we were very depressed with only a slim hope.

One day, I with seven other men was called by Shots, it was a very early morning hour. I did not have any time to say goodbye to my wife and son. I could find no way of escaping. We were surrounded by Belarussian police, who were armed with machine guns, dressed in black clothes with gray straps tied to their sleeves. They ordered us to take shovels for digging. We were sure that our end was coming that they were taking us to dig our own graves. As usual, they made us work in pairs going in the direction of the Jewish cemetery. We immediately realized that that is where they were taking us, and Yitzkale, who was my partner, could hardly walk. I whispered to him, "Itzka, if they ordered us to dig our own graves, we must escape. When they shoot us, at least we will be running. We shouldn't just accept our death quietly." We all told each other to do this whispering to each other. Gershon from Rakov, my business partner, said, "With my shovel, I will kill at least one of them. I will cut him into two from up to down. And then I will die." Clearly, he would have been able to do this even without a shovel, just with his hand since he was so strong.

The local Christians were looking at us smiling and the Belarussian police were laughing saying, "Say hello in heaven to the rest of the Jews." They brought us near the Jewish cemetery where they had killed our sisters and brothers, the citizens of Kurenets. Two of the police walked away to look for something and they ordered us to sit on the ground. The three other police stood around and said, "Anyone who tries to escape will be immediately killed." Our teeth were shaking although the day was not cold and there was little rain and fog on the ground. They ordered us to get up and start to dig. One of us said, "Why are you torturing us? If you wanted to kill us, do it right away." A policeman from Vileyka, someone, who used to be a shoemaker and learned his job with one of the Jewish shoemakers, started cursing us very dirtily. He ended his "speech" saying " first you must put in the ground the bodies of the Jews from the annihilated Zsinstand camp. Now, there is a danger of disease spreading to Vileyka", then he continued, "Your turn to die would come later."

The horrible sight is very difficult to describe. I don't think anyone has the strength to describe the details. Still today, I see it with all its horror constantly. There was a broken bathhouse in the area. In the chimney, which was all broken, there was a skeleton of a man that must have tried to hide there and was shot right there? All around the field were torn parts of bodies eaten by dogs and wolves. There was a cloud of black crows that covered the area. It looked like the plague of locusts had arrived. We had to fight them to get to the area. The smell was unbearable. The police let us tie something around our noses and mouths. There was no way we could work but the police said that they would kill us if we did not work. "We will bring other workers and they will bury you too," they said. They started hitting us with their rifles so we returned to the job. Deep in our hearts we knew that our horrible job was a "mitzvah" since we were bringing to Jewish burial our dear ones. With our last might, we started collecting whatever was left of the bodies and put them in the hole that we dug. Here and there, we could identify from the clothes that were left some of the bodies. I could recognize Velvel Markman from Smorgon Street. He was saved from the slaughter in Kurenets and later reached the Zsinstand Camp. He begged to get a job there. I recognized him because he was a big man and I knew his coat and his color. I knew that my darling sister, Chanaleh, would be there. I thought that maybe I would find her body and I would bring her to a Jewish burial. I looked among the clothes. I also recognized another Jew from Smorgon. His name was Simon Danishevsky. At one point, he had worked with me as a painter. I recognized him by his short fur coat and his rubber boots that were full of paint. I buried him and continued looking.

All of a sudden – Chanaleh, my Chanaleh – her body was without a head or arms. I recognized her from her blue coat. The coat was torn and full of blood. I also recognized her belt. I couldn't control myself anymore. I fell to the ground and held to what was left of her body. I started tearing my clothes and ripping my hair out and cried with horror. My friends tried to separate me from the body. The police knew what was going on and understood that I was going insane so they took me away from the burial area and put me lying on the ground. My friends continued without me. I was so destroyed that when we returned I could not walk. They had to support me. This is how we returned to the camp. The news that we brought that day was like salt on our open wounds.

The escape

There were many arguments among us. Opinions were divided. Some of us wanted to force our manager, Shuts, to discontinue his career working for the Germans and together with us to find the means to escape to the forest. It was very difficult for us "employees" to convince him that the killers were not going to keep us alive for our hard work. The truly professional people supported such opinion that they will be saved and refused to escape. (All of them did perish one day prior to the Russians freeing the Vileyka district. They left a note inside a wall where they begged us to say the Kaddish after them). After horrible arguments, we managed to elect a committee for the escape. The members of this committee were Mordechai, son of Havas Alperovich, who now lives in Israel; Hertzel Alperovich, may he rest in peace; Yosef Zuckerman, who now lives in Israel; Kopel Specter, may he rest in peace; our manager Shuts; Yonah Riar, from Ilya, both live in Israel; and I. The mission seemed very difficult. How would we be able to get the women and children out? Some had ideas, but they seemed impossible to accomplish. At that point, we got a message from the people who had escaped on the day that they annihilated the Zsinstand Camp. They told us that we should immediately try to escape, that to stay in the camp means to wait for death. They also said that we must get weapons. In the forest, we would need weapons. They sent the messages through a farmer from the village Neyaka, 20km from Kurenets. We called the farmer "The Beard". He had a long brown beard that was much groomed. He wore laptzas on his feet. He would usually wear a huge coat, and on his neck, he wore many crosses. He was very calm and relaxed with a generous face. He had sparkly blue eyes. For us he was a saving angel. He would bring us news from the battles in the front, and would give us hope telling us stories about the partisans. His motto was, "You must escape. In the forest you will survive."

We kept sending with him things that we wanted to safe keep. For us this was a miracle. This rare occurrence to find such a Christian man. He would sneak into our camp endangering his life each time. Danger could come from anywhere for him. We started preparing to go to the forest in full force. We prepared double souls for our boots we made them from the blankets. We started sewing warm clothes and underwear and we made duffel bags with sewing kits and anything else that could help us for life in the forest. We were preparing as if we were going on a long journey. Through that time, we were constantly worried that someone would leave prior to the set day and then the rest of us would be annihilated. People were particularly worried that I would go prior to the set day. Even my little three-year-old son would beg me, "Take me to the forest. I also want to survive." He would say that every time I would wear my jacket to go to the Christian homes to talk to one of them about our plans. My heart was crying inside when I heard him beg. Each time I had to convince him that I was leaving but that I would also return.

Shuts was now convinced that hard labor would not save us. He knew very well that most of the people in the camp were planning to escape. Still, I was worried to let him know that I had weapons. However, I knew that he had good connections with a German native that hated the Nazis so I talked to Shuts and he talked to the German man. Eventually, the man sent me through Shuts sixty bullets for my gun and another gun for Yosef Zuckerman. To find a German behaving like this was unheard of. He was always telling us, "Escape to the forest. The time of defeat for Hitler and his murderers is coming soon. Escape to the woods. Here, you won't survive." Yonah Riar from Ilya also got a gun, but when we finally escaped, he had no time to get hold of it.

Spring was approaching and the air was getting warmer and our hearts filled with good hopes. We all watched the tree branches to see signs of blooming. After a day of hard labor, hunger and fear, we would all gather at nighttime and all we would talk about was escaping and planning how to get the children and women out. The main thing that working against us was the fact that Vileyka was situated in a geographic area that was very hard to escape. A large portion of the town was surrounded by the river Vilya. From the north, the train tracks were constantly watched by the Germans. Moreover, that was the only way we could the large forests surrounding Kurenets.

During the slaughter in Kurenets, Gravah collected some Jews and brought them to the yard of the jail were he was living. There, he arranged them according to their profession to work in a big wooden barrack. With them were some laborers from the towns of Ilya, Krivitz, Smorgon, Oshmena, Voshenva, and other towns. There were professionals he brought to be used for his project. There were about thirty people, all single with no children. Among them were a few women. We knew of them being there, and they knew of us. They wanted to get in touch with us therefore occasionally they pretended that they did not have tools and they came to our camp to borrow tools. This way we knew of what was going on with them.

I remember at one time on Sunday morning the bell rang for us to go to work. We were all prepared for inspection. We were all sure that Shernogovitch was coming. His terrible name was known to every Jew in Kurenets. He was responsible for dozens of killings. When we saw that he was approaching, we all ran. However, when he came close, we realized it was not Shernogovitch, but it was Meir Alperovich son of Zalman and Reshka daughter of Yuda Alperovich. When he saw us running, he started yelling to us in Yiddish. We surrounded him and started asking, "How is it that you are wearing Shernogovitch clothes? How could you be a policeman for the Nazis?" Meir told us that yesterday the Germans murdered Shernogovitch, the collaborator, and for some reason, they ordered him to take the clothes off the body and to wear them. He ended his tale saying "maybe we would be lucky and revenge all our killers. Hopefully, I would be lucky enough to also bury Gravah the Horrible."

Gravah was eventually killed by land mines while he was strolling in his carriage with his wife and child. The mines were put there by the partisans. Just like our connection with Meir, we met other Jews who wanted to escape. They also waited for spring. Their situation was much more difficult than ours. They had less freedom, less food, and more torture. Still, some of them managed to survive. At one point, they brought to Vileyka huge number of Jews from Branovitz. They were all men who were survivors from many different slaughters in the area of Branovitz. They told them that they were taking them to Russia for productive work but they brought them here and they all lived in one big barrack near the train station. The barrack was originally built as a barn for produce by the Russians. They only put a little hay on the ground and that was how they lived. They gave them very little food and no sanitary help. Many diseases spread amongst them. People died every day. The Germans would also kill a lot of them. Their main job was cleaning the tracks, putting supplies on the train, and taking supplies off the train. We had some communication with them, but it was very difficult. We could only meet them when we were sent to the train station to take some coal. There we would have a minute to tell them, "Escape to the forest." We quickly told them the forests and villages where they could find Jews and partisans. We tried to help them in any way we could, giving them cloth to bandage their wounds. They also, like us, had different opinions. Some thought that they should continue working, and others thought that they should immediately escape. However, every day some of them would die. At the end, only very few managed to escape to the forest. A few of them survived.

The fate of the professionals

In Vileyka, itself, outside of the camp, there were a few families who were useful Jews. There were three brothers with their families. There was Malahshekvitz, who was a soap maker; Shmookler, who used to sell metal but now became a glass blower; Shimshelevetz, a dentist who survived the war and lived in Russia; Yashteshev the veterinarian, with his wife, sister, and child. They lived in their own homes with their possessions, but they had no illusions. They knew that their day would come. They helped us as much as they could. If it were not for Malahshekvitz, we would not have had one piece of soap to wash. The brothers gave us leather, and the veterinarian also helped us. They were in touch with many Christians and they would tell us of what was happening in the world.

Other than these professional people, the Gentiles did not know some professions. On that account some Jewish people who were herbal medicine makers worked for the Germans. From Germany came merchants who established a factory for pharmaceuticals. Among those people were people who were saved from the Kurenets slaughter. Among them were Gershon Ayeshevsky, his wife and children; Cantor and his father-in-law Mendel Canterovitch. Originally, they all escaped to the woods but they could not withstand the difficult conditions there so they returned to Vileyka. We were very bitter when we thought about that. For us, the forest was the ideal, the aim of our desires. Here they came and destroyed the image of our idea. We still kept in touch with them. The letters that The Beard would bring us from the Kurenitzers said one repeated thing, "Bring weapons. Bring bullets. Go the forests and save your lives." When we would read the letters, we would shake from excitement. Everyone was looking for bullets. Each time, prior to The Beard's arrival, Hertzel Alperovich would take two pieces of wood with a deep space between them, and there we would hide bullets. Once the bullets were in, we would cover the sides and put dirt on it with mud so that no one could see that it was recently disturbed. Then, we would take it to a place in the yard of the hospital that was next to our camp and put it on the ground. The Beard would go all over the yard, as if he was looking for junk and he would take our wood with the bullets together with other junk to bring to our brothers in the woods. We would call the wooden plaques, the Tablets of Revenge. We did not have much chance to send such merchandise because it was very dangerous and it was hard to get bullets.

Spring was coming and we sat there as if we were sitting on hot coals. Each day seemed to us like a generation. The three brothers from Vileyka knew that their end was coming. The students already knew their jobs, so they decided to escape to the woods. They left with a lot of possessions, clothes, money, and valuables. They had many acquaintances in the villages around and we all were very envious of them. We were very worried that day, thinking that the Germans would punish us for their escape. However, the incident passed with no problems. To their homes their assistants entered. The fear subsided. Now we were very happy that they escaped and we were telling each other how they had weapons and how they were so strong and that they contributed a lot in the fight since they knew the villagers.

Not many days later, we were all shocked. The oldest of the brothers came to our camp dressed as a farmer so no one would recognize him. We found out that he came as a messenger for his brothers to beg the killers to let them come back. He came to beg for forgiveness for him and his two brothers saying, "We did a foolish thing. The police told us that they were going to kill us, but now we know they were joking, we are sorry for what we did and come to ask for forgiveness and to let us be come back". We saw him as totally insane and we would have done right by his brothers and family if we had killed him immediately before he went to the authorities. If we had done so, we may have saved the rest of his family.

Although there was some truth about the difficult life in the woods, to us it was nonsense. We spit in his face and warned him not to do it. Despite the difficulties in the woods, he was better off there. However, he refused to listen. This was used as a big enforcement to the people who were against going to the forest. They said, "Look. Those strong brothers with their connections could not withstand the conditions in the forest, so how could the rest of us do it?" We answered that the day of death would come here and that we would not stay here waiting. We would escape to the forest. The Germans were very happy with this incident saying that the Jews would not be thinking anymore about going to the forest.

They let the three families return to their jobs. When the three families left, they took with them Yosef Norman, but he did not return with them. He had found connections with Jews and partisans in the forest. He survived and now lives in Israel. Some days later, Shimshelevetch, the veterinarian, was taken out of his home to be transferred to the Zsinstand camp, but he succeeded in escaping and survived. After a few weeks, the Germans killed the brothers who returned with their families.

The day of escape

It was Wednesday, 18 March 1943. It was a clear and crisp day. At noon, the sun was very hot and some of the snow started melting. Drops of water melted off the roofs, and the ground was full of puddles. You could see some of the dark earth and this was a sign of the approaching spring. Good smells of spring were all around us, which healed our hearts and filled us with a renewed will to survive.

We watched with envy the local Christian citizens walking around freely enjoying the splendor. Here we were imprisoned waiting to be slaughtered.

Some urge, I did not know where it came from, made me not go to work. I stood strong against Shuts and did not go to the train station to put the coal for the hospital as he ordered me. I stayed only in the hospital yard to help with taking down some things. For some reason, I just could not be useful that morning. All I could think about was our "Tablets of Revenge" (the wood planks with the bullets) that were lying at the edge of the yard of the hospital. I was intently waiting for The "Beard" to come and take them. I was looking all around searching for him, and the rest of the workers did not understand my nervousness. Only Shmuel Ashkenazi, the son of Sipka the widow, knew the secret and would answer the people who were questioning my strange mood saying, "Leave him alone. He is not healthy today."

Finally, at noon, I found The Beard inside the camp. I did not know how he entered the camp without me seeing him. He brought a letter telling us to be ready to escape this coming Saturday. The letter said that across the train tracks their would be carriages to take the women and children, and a young Christian women would come and help us escape. Our hearts were filled with excitement and we wanted to dance with happiness and to kiss the feet of our savior. Grandfather, may he rest in peace, would say he was the spirit of Elijah. We kept blessing him and thanking him, but we knew that he should not stay for long. I said my goodbye and told him I would see him in his home next time. He got out using a side alley and I returned to the job. My heart was beaming with excitement. I could not wait for evening to come to let the rest of the people who were working in other areas the good news. The Beard was walking around the yard taking all kinds of junk, among them the Tablets of Revenge. It seemed like everything was fine so I returned to the camp through a hole in the fence. With me also Shmuel Ashkenazi. We were ecstatic, but very quickly everything turned upside down.

The tale goes like this… There was someone in the camp that knew the secret of the tablets, and he told the secret to his wife. Naturally, she told another woman about the secret. When The Beard took the junk and left the yard, they saw that a Belarussian policeman approached him and took him in the direction of the German police. Here in the camp, people were sure that The Beard was arrested. The woman who knew the secret of the tablets could not control herself. Full of fear, she ran to her room, gathered her children, and started screaming that any minute the Germans would come and kill us. Not only this, but she ran to the area where the carpenters were working and told them the awful news. Immediately, everyone panicked. When Shuts heard this, he got his gun and suit and ran. Shmuel Ashkenazi and I were paralyzed. We did not know what to do. At first, I wanted to tell them to calm down, but soon I realized it was like a big wave that was going sweep me with it if I did not save myself. I ran to my wife and yelled, "Rosa! Quickly take the child and run to Navashevah." Navashevah was a Christian woman who promised to help us in our time of need. Her family was very helpful to us prior with encouragement and helped us getting weapons. I took the weapon and had no time to take all the bullets, only the bullets that was in the weapon. I put the new boots and the short fur coat on, but the rest of the clothes that I had prepared, I had no time to take. I could not forget my loyal friend Yosef Zuckerman who helped me so much, so I quickly ran to his wife and told her to run with my wife to the Christian woman. Yosef was at that point busy painting not far from the camp. I was afraid to run to him using the regular road, so I jumped over the fence to let him know.

In the paint shop, I found Eliyahu- Moshe the painter, and he told me that Yosef went to get paint. I told him to immediately escape. I returned to the camp to see if Yosef was there. There, my wife Rosa told me that Yosef, his wife and son, had already escaped. They wanted to take her but she waited for me. I said for her to take the Jewish signs off herself. While talking, I started taking all the signs off her clothes and ordered her to immediately run. My little son was begging me to take him with me. I was surprised at my decision for them to run alone, but I realized that this was the best way since if we went together on a working day it would cause more suspicion. Soon, I said to myself, we would meet at Navashevah's house. I walked on the sidewalk with my hands inside the fur coat holding the gun. I thought that if someone stopped me I would immediately shoot him. The people of the camp spread all over. While walking, I met Yitzchak Alperovich, his wife Batshevah, and the two children. Yitzchak was walking holding a shovel as if he was going to work, but how foolish it looked going to work with two babies! I walked by them and without stopping I said, "Are you taking a leisure journey or are you escaping? Hold each child and run to separate areas. Don't walk together." I walked by our first living space where I had been so tortured. The place where my sister, Chanaleh, was taken to her death. From afar, I saw a group of German soldiers doing some physical exercise. Should I return? No, I decided to continue thinking that they would be too busy with their exercise to pay attention to me. I arrived at the house of Navashevah, the Christian woman. I stood by the gate at her yard but to my surprise, it was locked from the inside. From the house, I heard the pleading voice of Navashevah. She told me that there was no way she would let my wife in when the Germans were standing across from her yard. This could have caused death to her home. She suggested running to the forest and surely, she said I would find my wife there. While saying this, she locked her shutters.

By the train tracks

I had no time to consider each moment seemed fateful. I was walking and my heart beating in pain from all the horrible failures, from all the plans that did not succeed. I reached the forest, it was getting dark. As night was approaching, the snow became hard again. I was walking amongst the young pine trees looking at the snow that maybe I would see footsteps. I was walking from one place to the next. My heart was bitter and feeling guilty. Why did I separate from my wife and son? Why was I so relying on the Christian woman and her promises? Still, I was hoping that they reached the forest and the Germans did not catch them. All of a sudden, I heard footsteps. I hid behind a bush, listening, with the gun ready to shoot. I heard Yiddish. It was David Kapelovitch and his wife, their two daughters, and their son Natchkah. They were happy to see me that they finally found someone else.

I asked them if they saw my wife but they saw nothing. Gitel, David's wife, was a very clever and energetic woman. She said, "We must run now past the train tracks. If we pass the tracks, we will laugh at the Germans." From afar, we could hear the sounds of explosions and shooting. I told her that I was not planning on running but that I had to find my wife and child. In my opinion, it was too dangerous to run now since the Germans probably had found out that we escaped and had put more patrols. However, Gitel would not listen to what I was saying. There was no convincing her. They said their good-byes and I was questioning at that moment, "What if they are right? What if my wife also went across the train tracks?" I decided to go with them. I ran and caught up with them. The train tracks were not far, at the edge of the forest. By the area around the train tracks were trees and bushes that were cut, so now you could see everything. The Germans did it for the guards so they would have an easier time spotting the partisans. I heard shots from the direction of the train tracks and I said to Gitel, "Listen Gitel. There are many shots." Nevertheless, she was very sure in her opinion saying that this was an illusion and that the shots were coming from another direction. The children looked very scared like little fawns. Their clothes were too short and too tight. They had grown up in the camp. Their teeth were knocking from fear. I saw a shadow of a person walking on the train tracks. Quietly I pointed out the shadow to Gitel, but she refused to pay attention. Her husband, David, said, "How good it would have been if we were on the other side of the tracks already. At least 150 meters away from here." The sounds of the shots stooped and everything quieted down, Gitel said, "Now is the moment to run and cross the train tracks." She did not wait a minute. She spoke and ran. She was first, walking as if she was the main officer. Behind her walked her son Natchkah. Again, I explained to her that if she wanted to cross the tracks, she must crawl. Nevertheless, she walked erect because it was hard to crawl on the frozen ground. Unexpected, there was a shot, and Natchkah started crying. "Abbah, Eemah!" Immediately, I fell to the ground in a puddle that was slightly frozen. With my hand lifting the gun so that it would not get wet. I yelled to them, "Lie on the ground!" No one listened to me and everyone ran to save the son. Now the killers had a clear aim. I could not see anything, but I heard voices saying, "Save! Save!" With the rest of my strength, crawling, I returned to the forest, hurt and wet. When I reached the forest, I started running away from the place. Now it was getting much colder and my wet clothes started freezing. I ran from one bush to the next. All of a sudden, I heard a sound of someone running on the snow. I listened and I heard a voice of a child saying, "My hands are very cold daddy. Will we find Mommy and Ruben David?" When I approached them, I saw that it was Yitzchak Alperovich. He was digging with a shovel. What was he doing? I don't know. When he saw me, he was so shocked that he threw shovel, took his child, and started running. I yelled to him, "Yitzchak, why are you running?" He recognized me and came to talk to me. I asked him about my wife and child and he asked me about his wife and child. We stayed under a bush whispering questioning what we should do. I told him what had happened to David the tailor and his wife.

I warned him not to go to the train tracks. All of a sudden, we heard the sounds of German voice, "Rashkas Slinchas." We started running and I lost Yitzchak and his child. I did not hear any more German voices but I could hear many shots that were getting closer and closer. I lay there all by myself and a thought came to me. I never shot my gun. What if the gun does not work? I must try. Among all the shots, no one would hear my shot. From all the ammunition that I had collected through time, I was only able to take seven bullets. I pulled the trigger and shot. The gun worked. From near the train tracks, I heard sounds someone walking and someone saying, "God, what did you do to us? Mommy and daddy, your situation is better. You already live in a better world." I tried to see who it was. At first, I saw a shadow on the snow and slowly I saw a short person wearing boots with a dark coat and messy hair. It was a woman who was limping. All of a sudden, I recognized Dinkah Spektor. She stopped, confused, and scared. She fell on the ground saying, "Where am I?" The snow around her was red from the blood coming from her leg. The blood kept coming, so I took my shirt and tore the sleeve and put it on the wound. I started covering her bloody footsteps and transferred her to another location. She told me that together with many of the camp workers, she already passed the train tracks and on the other side, they met German soldiers who shot all the escapees. She told me who ran with her and who she knew was killed. How she survived, she did not know. Instead of running to the Kurenets area, she somehow returned to the other side of the tracks back to Vileyka. She did not see my wife and son. I put some snow on her wound. Quietly, she twitched from pain. I thought that I should take the other sleeve and put it on her wound. Unexpected, I heard more steps, quick steps. I peeked from the hiding place, it was Doba Alperovich. Her jacket was open and her hair was messy. I yelled to her and she stopped but couldn't see me. I yelled to her again and she saw me and started crying from excitement. She also thought that she was on the other side on the way to Kurenets. Lacking any energy and depressed, we decided that when night came we would cross the tracks. From the bushes, we could see the road. I saw some people riding bicycles. I crawled closer to the road and saw that it was a farmer that I knew from the Soviet days. He greeted me, "Hello," and told me that I must quickly go to the other side of the forest since the Germans were coming to this side. He blessed me and quickly departed. I returned to the girls and told them. We decided to somehow go near the road to Molodetchna. Dinka had horrible pain. Doba and I supported her and walked toward the road. All of a sudden, we heard horses running, and the sounds of Belarussian and Latvian voices. We fell on the ground in the bushes. I held my gun ready. We could see them. They were policemen. We all decided that we would commit suicide if they caught us. Dinka was begging that she should be shot first since she was wounded anyway and would not survive. Doba was begging that she should be shot first. Dinka was shaking so much while talking that she sounded as if she was stuttering. We were all watching the killers' every step hence we would not fall in their hands alive. I was almost ready to use the gun, but Dinka stopped me, "Maybe you should wait a minute." Doba said, "They are coming right by us. What are you waiting for?" unanticipated, I saw the police going in our direction turn to the right. They continued looking for people in a further direction from us, so now we had some hope of escape. Finally, we could not hear their talking. It was getting much darker and the air was getting colder.

A meeting at midnight

We waited for the late night to come so we could pass the train tracks, but we were not lucky. The night was very clear, the moon was shining, and the snow was very bright. We stayed lying on the ground and our clothes froze and became hard. I looked at my watch, it was 10pm. I decided that we must leave. I was also starving. I helped Dinkah get up. She was lying on the ground and it was impossible for her to move. I tried to encourage her to get some strength telling her that we must go to the other side of the tracks, because if we stayed here until daytime, we would be dead. From among the trees, we could see the lights of the houses where other people sat safely in their homes. We walked and the snow was making a swish sound beneath our feet. This made us very upset. We were very fearful. We thought that someone was waiting behind every tree. We reached the edge of the forest. We hid under a bush, looking at the train tracks that were about 50 meters away from us. All of a sudden, we saw red flares then green flares then other colors. The Germans were busy watching. They were not going to sleep. We went to another area and we saw shadows of people on the train tracks. We heard sounds of talking but could not understand. It was already midnight and the watchmen were busy patrolling. Without warning, we heard the sound of breaking snow as if someone was running.

We were lying on the ground quiet and scared. Could the Germans be searching so late at night or could it be Jews? We were very fearful. From afar, we could see the barracks with the red flag and swastika. We could see two shadows going toward the barracks. It must have been the watchmen returning from the patrol. Then we saw the running people returning to where they came from, stopping in certain spot and searching for something. For some reason, in my heart I was very sure they were Jews who were lost like us. I started running and the girls tried to catch me being fearful that they would lose me in the dark. The two shadows must have heard our sounds. They stopped, as if they hesitated, I stopped and waited too. A woman's voice started calling, "Don't shoot!" It was like an electric shock going through my body. I recognized the voice, I could not talk for a second. I then yelled, "Rosa!" My son immediately recognized me and yelled, "Abbah!" He ran to me and we all started hugging and crying from excitement. The second shadow was of Batshevah, the wife of Yitzchak Alperovich, with her children. Doba and Dinkah started hugging Batshevah and her children. I told Batshevah that around 5pm, I saw in the forest her husband with her son but I had lost them. I carried my little son. He hugged me very tight and said, "Now we won't leave you daddy. Now we will be with you." Somehow, he felt much safer now, believing that I could protect him. Life seemed much dearer now, I had a reason to live and fight and try to get out of here. The tracks, the tracks. How could we pass the tracks to the other side? It was already 1:30am. I tied my son on my back using a big kerchief that my wife had. My hands were free so I could use them if I needed to. While we were walking, my son whispered to me that the Germans caught his mother and him but somehow his mother convinced the guy that they were not Jewish and he let them go. They went to Navashevah's house, but she did not let them in. We crawled all around looking for a way to cross, but they watched the tracks everywhere.

The double floor

Chavi Sarah née Babiniyar and husband,
Yermiyau Alperovich

We lay on the snow not knowing what to do. All of a sudden, an idea came to me. It seemed stupid at first. I told it to my little group. We must return to Vileyka. They all looked at me as if I was insane. "Kill us right here before you take us to Vileyka," they said. I explained to them that we must not stay here until daytime to cross the tracks. Tonight there was no chance. Since we were not very far from the barracks that used to be the Zsinstand camp, which was half destroyed and was empty, we could hide there during the day. I also reminded them that in the wooden barrack, there was a wooden floor and between the two floors, there was an empty space of about 30-40cm or slightly more. Therefore, we could hide there in the open space. Furthermore, tomorrow they would stop watching the tracks so carefully and we would be able to pass. I explained that I knew the hiding place well since I had used it on occasion. The women said, "Do as you wish. Without you, anyway, we are lost." Time was getting short and we had to quickly do something. Immediately I tied my son on my back and I walked in front of my little troop. I held the gun in my hand and we walked quietly. No one made a sound. We reached the main road. I lied in a ditch looking. I saw no one so I signed to my group to pass across the road. We reached the Jewish cemetery. I looked at the graveyards, jealous of the dead who died a natural death, had stones on their graves, and had a Kaddish said. Among them was also the burial place of my dear friend Yermiyau Alperovich. Yermiyau, my dear friend, with the heart of gold, committed suicide not being able to take the torture. He drank poison and died with horrible torture. We tried to save him by taking him to the hospital but he begged to die. I could still hear the cries of his wife Chavi Sarah nee Babniyar with her two children and one more on the way. On his grave was a wooden plank that we put as a memorial.

We knew we should not stay there. The distance from there to the barrack was about 50 meters. All of a sudden, we heard a loud bark, it was the horrible dog that many of us were bitten by. We ran and we somehow managed to get to the wooden barrack. We found the opening in the floor. We entered the hiding place. Now, I had time to think and I realized that the children were hungry and tomorrow they might cry from hunger and we would be found out. I decided to leave and find some food. Next to the barrack was a home of a Christian woman that many times helped me, therefore I decided to go to her house and give her my watch in exchange for some food for the children. I left the hiding place. The sky was full of stars and it was freezing. Slowly, I reached her house. I stood behind the window and I could hear someone coughing. Again, I had a pang of envy of people who could sleep quietly in their home. I started knocking on the window. No one answered. I knocked louder.

All of a sudden, I heard steps of people walking on the road. They stopped and I heard them talking German. They said, "Where was the knock?" I was frozen. I stuck my body to the wall and stopped breathing. When they moved, I entered the yard and, in a little storage area without a door, I hid in the hay. The Germans came in the yard. They lit the place with an electric light. They quickly looked everywhere but finally left. I decided to return to the hiding place. I took two ice balls so people could drink. Everyone was very happy to see me and said that somehow we could withstand the hunger. We lied there hugging each other and we fell asleep.

I kept having nightmares seeing pale tortured children surrounded by SS with rifles. I saw fires on Myadel Street. I saw a woman running with a baby inside the fire looking for a hideout. I saw my mother and my mother-in-law coming to me saying, "Don't run in this horrible time. Hide." I saw my mother-in-law lighting a candle saying, "Good week to you. Good week. May you be blessed." The sounds of wooden planks being taken up woke me up. Not far from here were Christian homes and residents would come to the barracks to take pieces of wood for their fireplace. We lay very quietly hardly breathing. Even the children knew the danger and they put their little hands on their mouths so no one could hear their breathing. We layed this way without food and drink, only snow.

My wife did not let me leave to get food. She also had a dream where she saw her mother who told her that we must wait until Saturday and then we will succeed in our escape, consequently that is what we did. I held the watch in my hand deciding that exactly at 11pm we would leave. I took the children out of the hiding place like a cat taking her kittens. They could not stand on their feet from lying there for so long. But, their behavior was exemplary. They waited patiently with no food for days. Much worse was the situation of the women. When they finally got out of the small space, they fell on the ground and almost fainted. I put snow on their faces to wake them. I knew that in the condition they were, we could not proceed far, so I decided to try my luck again.

I left them there and went through the cemetery to the house of Navashevah. They were not asleep yet in the house. I was afraid to enter the house thinking that maybe they had guests, I stood at the corner of their home waiting for them to close the gate. When Navashevah saw me she instantly crossed herself as if she saw a ghost. From fear, she fell on the ground but quickly controlled herself. She hugged me with excitement and started kissing me. She took me to her barn and entered her home to tell her husband to put the children to bed so that they would not see me. Her husband was very happy to see me. He let me enter their home as if I was their son. I told them that I could not stay long and must get something for the children to eat. When they found out that my wife and child were safe, they could not hide their excitement and they started crying. They apologized and said that there was no way they could let them hide in their house, but it had caused them a lot of guilt. They put bread, butter, eggs, milk, soap, and underwear in a little bag. I wanted to give them my watch, but they were insulted. They told me that almost every one of the escapees who ran to the tracks was killed. We kissed and said our good-byes.

After the war, they told me that the neighbors saw me when I had come to the house and told the Germans. The Germans beat them very badly, and their daughter was sick for many months because of the beating. I brought the food and everyone jumped on it like hungry wolves. Quickly, I tied my son to my back and gave him two pieces of bread to hold. Like this, we left. A train passed the tracks. We waited for a short time and quietly passed the tracks. It was another cold bright night. We quickly moved away and we passed a body of a Jew with a child of about six all naked with their hands on the ground. Until today, we still do not know who those people were. All night, we walked around looking for familiar roads by using the stars for direction. All of a sudden, we saw from a hill the white brick home with a little window slits and we realized that we were once more near Vileyka and this was the jail.

At the edge of the forest

I knew that we must not be too close in the farms. We must hide because the farmers might report us to the Germans. I found a big, thick bush under which we lay and I cut some branches and put them all around us so nothing could be seen by passerby's. We heard the sounds of bells. Some young people must have gone to a wedding. We could hear harmonicas playing and the sounds of drunkenness. At one point, a farmer came to the forest and started cutting trees with his saw. We lay quietly in the bush listening intently. All day long, I looked through openings in the bush. When night came, we started walking away from the farms. We passed through a village that was about 5km from Vileyka. Instantly, I smelled smoke and the smell of burning bodies. From afar, I saw a bonfire. This was the bathhouse where I later found out that they took all the escapees that they found alive and burned them. I was told this when one night I came to a farmer and using my gun, I demanded that he give me bread and show me the road.

After walking all night, we passed by Kurenets from afar. I only saw the sharp top of the church. We could also hear the sounds of the carpentry that used to belong to Chaim Zokofsky who was killed with the 54. We passed there as if we were smugglers. This was the town where we were born, the town that had a lively Jewish community for many generations. I knew the names of the villages where I could find some survivors from Kurenets. It was Katlovetska, Naviky, Starinky, and Rusuky. They were about 15-25km from Kurenets. If we would have used the main road, we would have quickly reached the villages, but we had to use fields and the forest path and at no time used real roads. Our feet were beat from the strenuous walk. My son's feet, who I was carrying the all time, were frozen from lack of movement.

Finally, we approached the village Starazi. We stopped at the edge of the village next to the Christian cemetery. We decided to rest there amongst the gravestones. I left my group and went to find out information from the villagers. I found a little home at the entrance to the village. I could see from the window that the only light was from a kerosene lamp. Around the table sat two children and their father. A woman was giving them dinner. I knocked on the door. When they opened it, the heat almost shocked me. The farmer immediately recognized me as a Jew and said, "What do you want Jew? We have not bread for you. The Kurenets Jews do not give us any rest. They beg us for bread all night. Where are we supposed to get so much bread? How long will you bug us like this?" He told his wife to give me a few potatoes. I told him that I did not want food but that I wanted to find the way to the other villages. The goy was surprised. What Jew does not take food offered to him? At that point, I did not know that the Jews in the forests had become beggars.

I had thought the forests were full of partisans armed with ammunition. We were sitting in the Christian cemetery waiting for late night when the villagers go to sleep and maybe some of the Kurenets Jews would go there. Suddenly, we heard footsteps. Quiet and unsure footsteps. We saw two men walking cautiously and stopping every few feet. I was lying with the gun in my hand, wondering who these people were.

I heard Yiddish. I was excited. When they saw me, they became very scared and started running in different directions, leaving their bags there. I yelled to them, "Jews don't run! Jews don't run!" They came back. I could not recognize them at first, though when they started talking, we recognized them at once and we hugged them. One wore a hat with no brim. His hair was very messy. He had a dirty messy beard. They both wore short torn jackets tied with ropes and their feet were covered with rags. One was Dania Sosensky. He was dressed a little nicer. On one foot, he had a laptza and on the other foot, he had a boot. But Daniel Alperovich, the son of Chaim Abraham, (who was later caught alive by the Germans on May 1, 1943 when he was sick with typhus. He was then taken to Vileyka and they cut him with a saw into two). At this point, Daniel Alperovich looked awful. Who was saved? We asked. Both of them told us that they would immediately go to the village to get some food and get something for us too. Later, they would take us to the forest and we will find out who was saved. "You must be very hungry," they said. Daniel Alperovich took out of his bag a frozen latkah. He divided it into two parts and gave it to the children. After a short time, they came back very angry. The villagers did not want to give anything. They carried the children and the rest of us followed to the forest. "Very soon, we would be there," they encouraged us. After walking 10 km, we reached with our last energy the forest. The yearning of so many Jews that the killers got before they were able to complete this journey.

Ze'ev Rabunski with others from Kurenets after the war

An unknown Rabunski family member who visited Kurenets in the 1950s
[he was a high rank official in the communist party]

[Pages 193-197]

One Month

by Yosef Zukerman

Translated by Eilat Gordin Levitan

Our escape from the Vileyka labor camp took two days. My wife, my one and a half year-old baby, and I felt a sense of safety when we finally reached the village Andreika. During the escape, we were surrounded three times by the Germans and two-thirds of the escapees were killed. Some were murdered on the road, others were caught alive and taken to a village near the labor camp in Vileyka. There, they were locked up in a barn and burned alive. We were told about this by the farmers of that village. Our route of escape was extremely difficult. We were forced to run through forests and fields and distance ourselves from any paved roads. The earth was covered with snow. We spent a full day hiding in a forest near the Kurenets train station beneath a bush. Miraculously, our little baby remained quiet during the entire day, as if he understood the grave danger of the situation.

One incident I will never forget: during the second blockade as we were surrounded by the German police, we were almost facing The Belarussian soldiers whom we called, "Crows," since they wore black coats and tied gray ribbons to their sleeves. At that point we were in a thick forest, not far from the bridge that connected Vileyka and Molodechno. The "Crows" opened fire with machine guns and rifles. I had a gun in my hands and returned fire. I was carrying my son on my back as if he were a piece of luggage. It was impossible to put him on the ground since there was snow and he might have gotten lost in the dark. At one point when we were running away from the killers, my son raised his arm and turned his face toward the Germans and screamed in their direction, "Hei, hei!" It sounded as if he was saying, "Stop shooting, you sons of bitches, and let us pass!" Still today, I cannot explain how we were once again saved. Immediately, as we lost them, we hid behind a very thick bush.

Our escape started at exactly four o'clock in the afternoon. We went together with Kopel Spector, his brother Eliyau, and his sister, Sarka, may they rest in peace. I want to tell you about them for all the good they had done for us. The escape was very difficult for me and my wife. We had to carry our baby and I asked Kopel,

"Don't desert us at this time. Please help us. It is very difficult for us with the baby."

He immediately answered,

"Yosef, we will never desert you. We remember all you have done for us."

He was talking about the time I helped him buy a gun. Since our escape from the Vileyka camp was unplanned, he didn't have time to take his gun. Until Kopel, Eliyau, and Sarka were killed, they ran with us, and every few minutes, we switched who would carry the baby in their arms. The snow was very deep, and we were running and falling, running and falling. The road was full of bushes and spikes that stuck out of the snow, so the journey was a truly thorny one.

Two days later around midnight, we reached the *pushta*, the depths of the forest where only wild animals had gone before. When we reached the depths of the forest, we met Leizer from Kurenets. He had gotten some food from the village Andreika to sustain his family in their hideout. At this point, we had no idea what life in the forest was like, (if one can even call it life). Leizer took us to the *zemlanka* (an underground hideout) of Zundel, the son of Israel Alperovitz. "Zundel" was the hideout's "address" in the forest. This hideout was used as a central gathering place in the forest. Since Zundel was a relative of my wife, we decided that it will be the first place we should visit. When we reached the place, I was shocked to see the state of people who lived there: they were in tatters, they had long hair and beards, and their faces had become yellow from sitting all day around a smoky bonfire to warm themselves. I couldn't recognize some of them even thou I have known them all my life. How we looked in their eyes, I don't know. But I remember one thing: our spirits fell tremendously.

When I escaped from the camp, I was wearing boots and galoshes, but when I reached the forest, only one of my feet still had a boot and the other had only a makeshift sock. Zadok Shavetz, the husband of Rushka, saw my situation and gave me another boot. Although it was old, it saved me. I was thinking how we were preparing for the escape from the camp, we gathered clothes and what we thought would be necessary for life in the forest. But our escape was sudden and unlucky and I was not able to take anything. When I heard the Jews' shouting "we were discovered we must escape now" I was at my workplace, I immediately ran to our room, where my wife and baby were, took my family and my gun, and we quickly made our way to the forest.

Zundel's hideout was really a hole in the ground that was covered with branches. There was a storage area that was used for both sleeping and sitting. From the outside, the hideout was covered with dirt. Though originally, the hideout was built by Israel Alperovitz and his sons, now Israel was no longer there. He died in the forest because he refused to eat food that was not kosher and, thus, only ate potatoes. Eventually, he starved to death. I was told about this by Zadok, Rushka and a few other Jews from Kurenitz. We sat together and talked about all that had happened to us during the escape. They gave us something to eat but what was considered food there, I still don't know. They let us sleep on the storage area next to them. One of the daughters was badly wounded during a blockade by the Germans. They (Germans and collaborators) came in large numbers to the forest (shortly before we arrived there) to kill the Jews who were hiding there. They told us that some people were caught when they went to beg for food and were killed. I sat with them, looking around, feeling very depressed from all that I heard. Still, I felt that we were much safer here than we were in the camp.

The next morning, we awoke early. It was difficult to sleep that night because during that night we were covered by lice and we knew we had to be ready for any disaster to happen. The experience of the forest was new to us. As I arose, the first thing that I was told "You have to help us with burying the body". I looked very puzzled so they explained that the wife of Shmuel, the son of Yohoshua, died that night. We buried her nearby. When I came out of the hideout, I looked around and told Zundel that I did not like the location that they have chosen for their hideout. It was sparse with trees. Though they were old pines, they were far away from each other and if you walked through the forest, you could easily be spotted from faraway. As I explained the danger in this situation, he agreed with me but insisted that at that point, it was too difficult to reroute the families. He said "I would wait for two weeks and then transfer them to safer location". I decided to leave immediately.

Since I was new to the forest and didn't know my way around, Zadok told me that he would help me and take me to another hideout in the deeper forest that belonged to Natke Charnas. As he was walking with me, I looked at him in amazement: how was he able to find his way? All the trees looked alike to me! He took me right and left, and again, right and left, as if he was walking through boulevards in our hometown. A few days later, I learned the ways of the wood. Every few meters, we put young branches in the ground so one could find his way. First, we walked through the forest and when we reached the edge, the forest became very thick. In the very thick area was a hideout.

We went inside Natke Charnas's hideout. Natke received us very graciously. He was happy to see us and took our little son in his arms and led us to his "inn". The hideout was very deep in the ground and from the outside, you couldn't see a thing. There were stairs that took you down into the ground and inside, there were even fires on which to prepare food, upon which pots of water were boiling. There was a sleeping area and at the corner of the room, there was a small window. This looked like a very decent living space.

The inside of a Zimlanka, a hideout in the forest that Jews and partisans built to hide from the Germans during two winters. Yehuda Cheres spent his early childhood there.

During the daytime, we rested and at night, Natke invited us to go with him and his wife to the village to ask for food. My wife left with them and I stayed with the baby. After two days, I also went to beg for food and started my "new line of business". About two weeks had passed in the same routine. Before we left for the village, we would bless each other, "Go in peace, and return in peace." But returning in peace was not as sure as leaving. Going to the villages was a very difficult job. First you had to go a long long way through the forest and you could never use any of the roads. For your safety you had to go through fallen trees, rocks, and boulders, and once you reached the village, you would carefully approach a farm and from the side of the window (never directly in front), always ready for trouble, we would knock on the window and say, in the most pitiful of voices,

"Kazain dai fokoushet." Some people would use the word, "Podari." To tell you the truth, I always had trouble with the word, "podari." But after they gave something, I would bless them and thank them.

This was a very difficult way to sustain ourselves. They would give us potatoes and a few pieces of bread and we would return at dawn and immediately start cooking. Salt was a rarity that the farmers refused to give us–they themselves lacked it. Many times, at the end of the meal, we would start feeling extremely hungry, the amount of food was so pitiful. We would sit there for hours, waiting, not knowing what to do or how to spend our time. Sometimes, someone would say, "Be quiet, I think I hear a shot." Our hearts would then fall. "Here! I think I hear another shot!" Sometimes returning from a trip, someone would say that there were Germans in the villages. Other times, someone would say that there were Germans in Kurenets with dogs, getting ready to search the forest. We could find no rest from these horrible rumors: we slept in shifts, someone standing by the beds and someone by the stoves. The hideout was built months ago and couldn't contain all the new comers. As my wife and baby slept, I stood by the stove. Then, my wife would take my place. Sima nee Melzer and her daughter, Rifka Gvint, were very kind to us. Many times, they would give us their sleeping space. The baby would wet the sleeping areas, and we felt bad because of that. But they always dismissed our apologies and said, "This is what babies do normally."

Time passed. We reached Passover 1943 and we wanted to keep kosher. We went to the villages and took some vegetables, but didn't want to take any *chumetz*. Our hideout was a gathering place for "public prayers". Jews from Neyaka came, Weiner from Lebedove came with his wife Rachel, the daughter of Mendel Kanterovich from Kurenitz. The prayers were done with such intent and emotion. We were celebrating the day of our nation freedom from slavery in Egypt. So many tears were poured during the prayer. One would think that all the tears would have stopped the madness and cruelty. Every one of us said the Kaddish, because everyone was in mourning for someone that year. Oh, how horrible this event was! It will never be forgotten from our hearts. Jews in torn clothes who had almost lost their human image, stood in the dark forest saying Kaddish and the tears spread like a river, begging with their prayers. I thought," God, oh God, hear us I am begging you, but don't just stand there listening, look at us from the heavens and see what has happened to us! " Can any artist paint this picture?

1998
Gershon Gorv son of Batia nee Eisheski and Natan son of Mordechai Gurevitch (second from the left) with two of his sons, Eran and Benny (on the right) next to a hideout like the one Gershon and his family hid in 1942- 1944

One night, two Jews went to a village. One was Natan son of Mordechai Gurevitch from Kurenets and the other, I can't remember his name. They were neighbors from the same hideout. When morning came, they did not return. Everyone was very worried. Some of us couldn't sleep. Finally, during the day, they came back. They told us that the Christians were very happy to see them and invited them to their homes. They were also celebrating, it was Easter. That is why they were so late in returning. Since many of us didn't sleep well, we decided to go back to sleep. My wife and my son fell asleep immediately and I was awake since it was my turn to stand by the stoves.

All of a sudden, the door opened wide and our contact from the partisans came in and screamed, "Schreize passe …," which means, "Quickly, save yourselves! The village is full of Germans!" The village he was talking about was one and a half kilometers from where we were. Everyone jumped out of the sleeping quarters. I immediately took the baby in my arms, did not hesitate for a second, and started running toward the swamps that were located near our hideout. We would always build a hideout near a swamp, first for the water and second, so we could hide there during trouble times assuming that the Germans would be afraid to enter the swampy area.

We heard shots and we went deeper into the swamp. The shots became more and more frequent and we ran to distance ourselves from them. We ran like ducks in a line for about an hour and all of a sudden, the shots came from the other side. The bullets rang out and the ground thundered under our tramping feet. Some fell on the ground but most continued to run.

While we were running, one of the women running next to us told Rivka Gvint, "Let's get away from this family! They have a baby who might cry and we will be discovered!"

Rivka immediately answered, "I will not desert them. If it is our fate to survive, then the baby will not endanger us." Rivka stayed with us until we reached safety.

My wife at one point was confused and ran toward the bullets. I was crawling with the baby in my arms. Quickly, I ran after her, caught her, held her hand, and immediately took her away from that area to another route and finally we got farther away from the shooting. We continued running further and further and we managed to evade the blockade. Dusk was coming. And for us, this was the moment between life and death, because we knew the Germans would leave the area when it grew dark.

We sent a few people to check the area. They went into the village to find out what had happened. The villagers accepted them "warmly", shouting at them, "Bloody Jews! You are to blame for of all of this! Because of you, they had burned our homes, stolen our things, and sent our sons to Germany! All this because of you!" But did we have any choice? We wanted to survive, so we returned to the villages to ask for bread. Truly, the villagers of that area were greatly tortured during the blockade. The Germans burned their homes, took their cows, and many of their sons were sent to work in Germany. When we found out that the killers had left the area, we decided to find out what had happened to our hideouts.

At that time, the snow was thawing so it was very difficult to walk. All of the lower areas were flooded. We had to trudge through freezing water and we were chilled to the bones. Our teeth were chattering and our feet would get stuck in the mud. We walked for hours till we reached our old hideouts. We found that all the hideouts were destroyed by explosives. From our hideout, there was a long tunnel to be used during dangerous times. That tunnel was also destroyed and all of our belongings were burned. In the hideout of the people from Neyaka, we found bodies, they were not able to escape in time and all except for the daughter of Valah from Neyaka were killed. Valah's daughter was miraculously saved. She held her young boy in her arms when the Germans entered and sprayed the hideout with bullets. One bullet hit the boy's face and his blood spread all over his mother. She lay on the ground with her face covered in her baby's blood. The Germans walked by her and thought that she was dead, but she was only in shock.

During the blockade, everyone who was living in Zundel's hideout was killed. And with them, some other Jews.

The story that I have told here is just a little sample of what had happened to us in just one month in the woods. After that month, we stayed another seventeen months in the forest and experienced blockades, a typhus epidemic, many pains and troubles, and every horror and deprivation that no written words can truly describe.

[Page 198-229]

Three Years

Yitzhak, son of Nethka Zimerman

Translated by Eilat Gordin Levitan

Like Lost Sheep

June 24, 1941. It was the third day of the German-Russian war. The Soviet authorities had begun retreating from our area, and to us it appeared that the Red Army troops were in total pandemonium. We too, the Jews of Kurenitz, were panicking. We watched the Red Army turning to the east. "Where would we go?" we asked desperately, running for advice from one neighbor to the next. Each one of us knew of the impending disaster. But still some Jews consoled themselves and others by saying, "It is impossible that the renowned Red Army would be defeated so easily". They said, "This must be part of their tactics to win the war. You will see, tomorrow or the next day they'll get reinforcements and the whole situation will change."

Other Jews would console each other announcing "the Germans only hate the wealthy Jews. Since there weren't any rich Jews amongst us in Kurenitz after the period of Soviet rule, which had made everyone of us equally poor". So, they reasoned, "we had no reason to worry". Kurenitz buzzed with these kinds of conversations as the German army entered the town.

The same day, on Tuesday afternoon, we saw the troops of the Red Army rapidly fleeing from the advancing German army. Wounded Russian soldiers, lost and confused ran around, trying to find shelter. German planes flew very low, almost touching the roofs of the houses. The Germans planted seeds of death in the midst of the running troops. They also killed peaceful shepherds and their herds.

All of our reasoning and calculations ceased with the sounds of the slaughter. The Jews searched frantically for a place to hide themselves. Many went east with the retreating army, but only a few managed to cross the border. Most of them were stuck in the little shtetls east of Kurenitz, such as Dockshitz and Dolhinov. The ones who stayed in town prayed for pity from heaven.

We started gathering a few families together like lost, lonely sheep. We felt the danger was all around us, so we clung to each other. We believed that if we all huddled together we would be safer.

I remember a Saturday morning a week after the war had started. It was a beautiful, clear June day, beaming with natural splendor. All the cedar trees at the end of Mydell Street were covered in bright green aura, as if they were mocking our dark fears. Then the first Germans arrived in Kurenitz. They were known as the 'Spearheads' and it was their mission to scout out the area before the actual army was brought in. (In reality, there had been Germans in Kurenitz on the fourth day of the war, but they were paratroopers disguised as members of the Red Army.) The scouts came from the fields near the Savina Forest. They crossed Mydell Street and continued toward Poken. A few of them saw my father and asked him mockingly, "Nou, harasha tasiviatsa?" (Do you live comfortably?).

My family and I lived on Dolhinov Street, near the center of Kurenitz. When we learned of the Germans' arrival, we left our apartment and moved to Sweshtchefola at the end of Mydell Street. We had always thought of Sweshtchefola as the end of the earth, the area was on the outskirts of the village and was largely Christian, but now we felt more hidden there, and safer.

I remember that Saturday well indeed. Our family gathered in Uncle Yesha's yard that afternoon. The yard was big, and open to the surrounding roads and the fields, including the road to Balashi.

Suddenly, as we stood there, discussing what to do, I saw an armed car coming from the direction of Mydell Street. At first we were hopeful, and thought it was a Soviet car, but as the car approached, we saw the white and yellow flag and the black swastika of the German army.

"The Philistines," I said, and everyone froze.

'This is the end,' we thought, but a miracle occurred. The soldiers said 'hello' respectfully and greeted us politely. The unexpected attitude of the German troops improved our spirits and bolstered our hopes for the future. Uncle Yesha was very excited and a passage from Tehilim (Psalm) came to his mouth.

"The ones that sow with tears, harvest with happiness, " he recited. The family began discussing the situation. Uncle Yesha was convinced that we were still safe and that the future would be bright. He believed that we would be awarded despite the fear that was haunting us. Our imagination, he claimed, allowed us to get carried away.

The German tank drove to Mydell Street and across the market, and a short time later, we saw it returning and going to Balashi in the direction of Kribitz

The town was left without any rulers, a situation that left us at the mercy of thieves and pillagers. The villagers from the surrounding farms attacked the town. They came with sacks, saws, and axes and began robbing and looting. This was our introduction to the impending disaster that would soon sweep us away. The biggest mobs came from the villages of Starazi, Karutoca, and Zuriych. Desperation was everywhere, but still we worried that much worse was coming. Lieba Gotzes' and Sharel Berman put up a fight, but they were cruelly beaten by the robbers.

In some cases, the gentiles tried to protect us. We must remember Mishka Tkatzonik, who walked out of his house with an axe in his hand and wouldn't let anyone rob the Jewish homes in his neighborhood: the home of Mikhail Alperovich from Badonova, the homes of the daughters of Chaim Michael and my home. He continued to treat the Jews with equal kindness and honor throughout the war.

Later, a temporary police squadron was organized to "keep the peace". The most despicable and cruel of the town's citizens became participants in this squadron. They retained their duties under the leadership of Doctor Shestokovitz throughout the duration of the German oppression. However, at the moment of its creation, the police squadron consisted jointly of gentiles and Jews. A watch patrol was organized to protect the towns' Jews.

Already, on the first day of the Germans' arrival, two people had died. They were my relatives and shared the same name of Shimon Zimmerman. One of them was the son of my Uncle Yesha. Uncle Yesha, who had so recently hoped that the future would bring a harvest of happiness… The other was the son of my brother, Yermiyau. The two cousins were killed while on their way to return the weapons they had carried during their shifts as members of the temporary police. As they walked towards the makeshift police station that had been recently established, the Germans caught them and took them to the nearby village of Horidovich, which lay two kilometers from Kurenitz. There they murdered the two young men. None of the townspeople knew where they had disappeared to. The Jews didn't dare leave their homes; German troops were moving east and it was extremely dangerous to cross the streets. It was only a few weeks later that two villagers from Horidovich came to town and reported that they had found two bodies and had guessed their identities from their clothes. The parents of the boys went to retrieve the bodies with one of the gentiles. It was a very dangerous mission, but eventually, they were able give the cousins a Jewish burial.

On the day that the two boys were murdered, the top German officer in our area ordered all male Jewish residents between the ages of sixteen to sixty, to present themselves at the market at exactly one in the afternoon. Anyone refusing would be killed wherever they were found.

Torture and Killing

All the male Jews of the town, fathers and children, grandfathers and grandchildren, were forced to stand in the middle of the market surrounded by German soldiers with machine guns, waiting for their fate. Women with little children in their arms and men older than sixty stood at a distance and cried for their townspeople, but they were not allowed to approach the area. We stood like this for three hours on a hot summer day. We were frozen with fear. We didn't even cry when Shatzs came out of the police station and let us know that the high officer would soon come and we would know when we would be taken from there.

A few moments later, the head of the Gestapo came out and gave us a 'beautiful speech'. He listed all the wonderful things that had befallen us being under the wings of the Third Reich. Now, he reasoned, we had one duty!-- to obey their orders and work for the German army. Also, he demanded that we put special signs on our clothing to show that we are Jews. In addition, he ordered us to elect a Jewish committee that would serve as the official connection with our new rulers.

This was the first month. Later, the German army moved east and the front moved far away from us. Jews were forced to work for the Germans with no pay. People somehow got used to the situation and now what they wished for most was for the Germans to lose the war soon, and for the difficult period to pass with relative peace.

The Germans began transferring Soviet POWs through town. The Soviet POWs would be rounded up together in the meat markets at end of Dolhinov Street as soon as they arrived. The Jews would cook food for them and give them water. They used the barrels belonging to the fire department, filled them with water, and the Jews would be harnessed and carry the barrels like horses on their backs. But we got used to that too.

One day, a few Jews from the town of Sventzian came to town and told us a horrible tale. They said that by some miracle they had survived, but that the rest of the Jews in their town had been killed. People asked each other how could an entire community be slaughtered for no reason. We couldn't accept the idea of such a monstrous occurrence. And when we finally found out that the story was true, some of us continued to reason that there was hope for our town. They said:

"Sventzian, after all, was part of Lithuania in the days of Soviet rule, and during that time many residents of Sventzian had developed a stereotype image of the Jews as Communist supporters". Others said, "In addition, the Lithuanians are known as having a very cruel nature". "And so," they said, "it's hardly surprising that the Sventzians had decided to 'avenge' themselves against their Jewish neighbors." But here, we believed, that could never happen.

A civil town committee was elected headed by Polish people who had been chased out by the Communist Authority during the Soviet days.

The lowest class of the mob that now joined the police force frequently caused troubles for us. They demanded that the Jews make them clothing. They wanted boots and hats, and often even those demands that we promptly met wouldn't appease them. Once in a while, they would come to our homes and take whatever they desired.

Weeks passed and it was time for Rosh Hashanah. Many of the previously non-religious Jews experienced a renewal of their ancient faith. They fasted and read the Torah and prayed. I remember my sisters, Sheina and Myna, who had previously been non-practicing Jews, now became orthodox. They would fast twice a week, and read the Torah, now they found emotional aid in the Jewish religion. They said that if we returned to God fully, our punishment would subside. Myna would stand for many hours next to her baby's carriage with a kerchief on her head, and say passages from the Torah, with tears flowing and a spirit of true conviction. There were many others in town just like her. Hardly anyone went outdoors, except for those who had to be part of the forced labor troop. Some Jews were sent to Vilejka, others to Poken. The people that didn't join the forced labor troop tried to hide in their homes. If anyone wanted to go to a neighbor's home, he would go through the yards and gardens in secret. To go into the street was to take your life in your hands.

The head of the police was a gentile named Aazevich from the village Kolbaszina. He was a one-eyed villager who'd had the nature of a murderer from the day of his birth. His assistants were Sherangovich, a Polish killer from a small village next to Kasziniavitch, and Belzniyookthe bastard son of a cleaning lady at the slaughter house. All three were the worst humans to be found in the area.

Motoros, the head of the town committee, was a Polish gentile that was very good to the Jews. He gave us permission on Rosh Hashanah to go to the synagogue. Prior to the Russian invasion he was the principal of the school.

On the day of Rosh Hashanah, Rabbi Moshe Feldman stood before the congregation. How can one describe the prayer that day? The pain and the tears flowed… Most of the people that came to the synagogue lived close by. I remembered that this was a sunny day and that my neighborMikhail Alperovich and I couldn't walk through the fields as we usually did at those times. Instead, we decided to go through the streets, though not on the sidewalk (Jews were not allowed to walk on the sidewalk). The streets were empty and seemed to us as dangerous to cross as a dark, never ending forest., Rabbi Moshe Feldman cried even after the prayer, as we left the synagogue he blessed each one of us and said, "Shana tovah my dear shana tovah. You must hope until the last minute. Even if a sharp sword is held to your throat, you must not despair. God will not let go of his people."

On that day Motoros, the head of the town committee, sent us a message warning us that we must not go to synagogue on the second day of the holiday because the police were planning to interrupt the prayers and cause havoc. So, on the second day we all stayed in our homes, praying separately. This is how the holidays passed.

On Shminit Hazerets, seventy members of the Gestapo came to town. We were very scared no one knew the reason for the visit. They went to police headquarters, stayed for a few hours and then they returned to Vilejka. During the night, the local police went to different homes, and arrested Jews that were suspected of being Communists.

The next day, on Simchat Torah, the Gestapo came to town again. They took the prisoners out to the market and had them joined by their families: wives, children and parents. They handed them shovels and transferred them through Kosita Street to the forest across from the Jewish cemetery. There they were told to dig two holes. Then they were ordered to strip. Then they killed them. First they shot the men, and then the women, a total of fifty-four in all. We mourned these men and women who were pure, and innocent and yet, had been killed, but we continued with our sad life knowing there was no authority we could protest to.

I will never forget the night of that massacre. It was a dark night. We sat in our house sad and scared. Suddenly there were knocks on the door. I went to the door carefully, in fear, and whispered "Who is there?" I heard the voice of a child saying, "Open the door for me. Don't be scared- its me the little child of Yankel, the shoemaker. Let me just get warm."

We opened the door and let him in. He looked pale and skinny and he was shivering from the cold. He told us that he had been taken with his father and mother to be slaughtered, but he had escaped and hid in bushes until darkness had descended.

"The Germans," said the child, "are big liars. They said that they were taking us to work. But I knew that a little child like me couldn't work with such big shovel. I knew that they were going to kill us. I prayed that maybe God would watch for me and that I'd survive." We all sat there crying.

Months later, the child and his sister were murdered in the Vilejka camp.

The homes of the murdered families were robbed by the Germans and their helpers. Their houses were left without doors and windows, screaming for a reason why, for answer, or an explanation. But the heartless world was deaf to their screams.

Reason told us that we were lost. We had no escape, so people started trusting and believing irrational beliefs: dreams and miracles, deeds and signs that would console them. Some people started believing in numerology. When the number of the murdered reached sixty-six, I heard Mendel Zalman say that in psalm, passage number sixty-six reads, "hosienou adonai ki bau mayim ad nefesh …God save us because water came up to our soul" …in conclusion he said: "and now G-d will save us"

We had no connection to the outside world: no newspaper or radio. We weren't allowed to talk to the Christians. There was a strict law forbidding Christians from getting in touch with any Jews. Once in a while, a Christian would come to us and whisper something, but we never knew if what they told us had any substance. The Saturday after the fifty-four were killed, the Christians that worked for the telephone company came and told us that they saw with their owns eyes how the Germans took the Jews of Molodechno, men, women, and babies, and murdered them all.

A Bloody Winter

The Jews of the town were planning escapes. Outside of the town the dangers we would face seemed much bigger. We were surrounded by human wolves demanding our souls. They wanted our possessions and anything that would be left over after we perished. So we started looking for a hiding place in the town itself. People started building hideouts in double walls, in fireplaces, and in basements. Each one of us became an engineer and many people showed great creative inventive skills. Meanwhile, winter had arrived. This year it had come early.

Some time passed and we didn't hear of any killings in the area. This was interpreted as a good omen, and people started hoping against hope. Some said that Hitler had forbidden any more killings, and people that worked diligently for the Germans believed that they would pass the wartime peacefully.

Many Jews believed they would be spared until February 1, 1942 came. On that day the Gestapo came to Vilejka and moved into the courthouse that was next to the prison. They immediately ordered some Jews to report for work. Ten people were sent to do labor. They only worked for one day, and in reward they were cruelly beaten. Many returned with no teeth. Immediately after this incident, the Germans started annihilating the Jews in the Vilejka district. Almost daily, refugees from other towns who escaped death came to our town. We waited for our turn.

On March 15, a few Gestapo men came to Kurenitz. They played a bloody game. They killed thirteen people, and left. I remember that bloody day in the month of Shvat. It was a Sunday and the weather was unusually cold. Suddenly we saw Merill, the wife of Ortsik Alperovich, running in panic. On her head she wore a kerchief like the villagers do and she looked as if she were being chased by a monster. We yelled to her from our door, "What happened Merill?"

"Don't ask," she said as she ran, "The murderers have come to town!"

We panicked. What should we do? Where should we run and hide? My wife said we should hide behind the house. We went to the doorstep of our neighbors.

As we hid we heard and saw Egoff. He wore a Kosak's' hat and a long black fur coat, and in his hand, he held a whip. He was a famous killer whose name alone, could inspire fear. He called to Fredkin, the husband of Zelda, and asked him something. Fredkin showed him our house and Mikhail Alperovich's house. A few minutes later, he entered our home. My wife Mina returned home. He greeted her politely and asked if Jews lived there, and where there were other Jewish homes. She pointed to Fredkin and Mikhail's house. Then he went to Michael's house and asked questions, but even then, he was not satisfied. He went to Christian homes and asked questions.

We knew something was going to happen, and decided to go to our hiding place. We were once told by a Christian woman who cleaned the Polish school, that there was a huge basement under the school, and she suggested it as a good hiding place when trouble arose. She also told me that Nahum Alperovich and Nyomka Shulman had stayed there many times.

I took my children and hurried to the Christian woman's home. This was on Sunday and the street was full of Christians that came to pray. After we stayed there for a short time, we had to leave. One of the policemen that knew us came by and although he was not outwardly hostile, the woman was very worried. The policeman told us to not concern ourselves needlessly, that the Gestapo came to Kurenitz but they were just mugging the Jews not killing them. But from his expression I thought it better not to go back home. We left the house and decided to walk along the train tracks toward one of the neighboring villages. A Christian woman who saw us went to town to report that Jews were running away. The police came after us. On that day the SS killed only people that tried to run away. They were most likely going to catch us had not coincident saved us. A Christian villager from Lipnivitz went to doctor Shostokoviz and in his sled he brought some harvest in exchange for his visit. When he reached Kurenitz he found out that while he was riding, the harvest sack fell from his sled and so he hurried to find the lost sack. On his return he took us in his sled and all the time hurried his horse. The German chased us and after many troubles we reached Ratzka, a little village near by safely. We stayed there for a short time and then returned.

On that Sunday the Germans killed 13 Jews, amongst them the town rabbi, the dear Moshe Feldman. He suffered many tortures till his death. They threw him in the central market and broke his arms and legs and there he was left to die. It was a few days before they let us bring him to Jewish burial.

Shatz, the head of the Judenrat arranged that the ghetto that would be inhabited by professional Jews would be under the German governor of the region, Shmidt. About a hundred people were registered as professionals and after a few days, they were transferred to Vilejka and a month later joined with their families.

On 3/27 the policemen of Kurenitz played a bloody game and killed 32 people amongst them: Yitza Chatzties'(Charles Gelman' father) with two daughters, Minzikovitz and his family. We risked our lives and we took the holy martyrs to Jewish burial in Jewish cemetery. It was a very cold winter and Artzik Gutzes(Dinerstein), Chaim Sozkover, Sara-eshkas' husband, and I took the bodies and brought them to the cemetery. For two days we had to burn the frozen ground till we could dig graves and we buried them separately men and women.

Other then the killings by the Gestapo there were separate killings of single Jews by the local policemen. One policeman that was particularly cruel was the one that lived near Kasinevitz. He was a detective during the Polish days and was in hiding during the soviet days. He was the one that killed the two boys; one was the grandson of Leib Motosov, the other was the son of Natan son of Meir-Shalom Shulman. Both were sixteen and were sent to work for the Germans. He also killed the 32 Jews and later he killed my sisters.

In the months of Shvat and Adar all the shtetls in our district were annihilated. Vilejka, Ilya, Krasna, Volozin, Redshkovich, Rakov, Evia, Eivnitz and more.

Any plans that we had about hiding in the forest were postponed since the winter was such a tough one. Even the partisans were not in the forests yet. After every "actzia" (action of systematic killing) the Gestapo would lie to the Jews and say that this is the very last massacre. After every killing the killers were ready with the reasoning and stories. They would say that this time the Jews were killed for using a radio that was connecting the townspeople with the partisans, the next killing the Germans came with another story like finding a gun.

At the month of Shvat and Adar there were killings everyday. So all hope was lost. Many thought that death was better than living in such fear.

There were some Christians that pretended to be Jew lovers and told us that they'd keep our belongings to help us during bad situations. I remember that one day when I went to the well for water I met one of my friends, a Christian villager. When he saw my water container, all shiny and new, he liked it and said "Itzka what do you need this kettle for? Instead of letting the kettle fall in hands of stranger why don't you give to me? I answered, "Don't wait so impatiently for my death. I'm still hoping to survive." The Christian stood there embarrassed. He was after all a friend, so he apologized. "I don't think of you badly. God bless you and you'll stay alive. I was just saying rather than let a stranger take your kettle its better that a friend takes it". Some Christians would come and tell us they heard from an official source that the slaughter would be on that date or another and suggested that the Jews hide in another town.

The Fate of the Escapees

Sheina Zimmerman
(daughter of Neta, sister of the author)
Perished with her baby in Vileyka on March, 1942

Myna Bartz
(daughter of Neta Zimmerman, sister of the author)
Perished with her baby in Vileyka on March, 1942

My two sisters Myna and Sheina were both married and had babies. One had a one-year-old and the other a nine-month-old baby. One day a Christian woman came to them and said that she had heard from official sources that two weeks before Passover of 1942 they were going to slaughter the Jews of Kurenitz. She suggested running away. My two sisters went to the village Litvinki, they hired a carriage and paid with good money to be taken to Dolhinov since there it was quiet at that point (relatively speaking).

They left at nighttime. The Christian villager took them in the direction of Kribitz through the village Nieka. Unluckily for them that was on the same night that the killer Sherangovich took the Jews of Nieka to Vilejka to be killed. While he was transferring them, he ran into my two sisters and demanded they join the group. When the group came near Kurenitz the villager with the carriage left the group and went on a side trail that led to Litvinki so my sisters managed to escape. When Sherangovich reached Vilejka and checked the group he realized that my two sisters, their babies and the villager were missing. Immediately he sent police to start the search. First they found the villager and threatened that if he didn't tell where the women were, he and his family members would be hanged. The villager was brutally tortured but did not say. The rest of the villagers from Litvinki looked for my sisters all day, wanting to save their village from punishment, and just before dawn they found my sisters. One was hiding at the Doba Zife house and the other at the house of Sarah Shifra Torov. They took my sisters with their babies half-naked. Doba and her four children were taken too. They made them run in the deep snow holding their babies underarm. The whole way they hit and tortured them. When they reached Vilejka, they put them in a cold prison cell with no food. The bigger torture started the next day. The babies were torn to pieces in front of my sisters' eyes. Then they took their teeth out and broke their arms and legs till their pure souls went to heaven.

I was told of this by one of the policemen that witnessed the horror.

Three days prior to Passover 1942, we gathered in Mikhail Alperovich's house to bake matzos. It was absolutely impossible for us to celebrate the holiday according to the usual tradition. We baked the matzos in secret. Someone was watching the house from the outside. Inside, we cleaned the oven for Passover and from eight kilograms of flour that I had, we baked "poor bread" to remember the Jews in Egypt. While we were getting ready to celebrate, the wife of Chaim, son of Elchanan and Chana Alperovich, came to our house and told us a horror story about the slaughter of the Jews in Dolhinov, that she had miraculously managed to escape. The next day, we saw a truck full of the furniture and belongings of the Dolhinov Jews. Our celebration for the freeing of the Jews from slavery in Egypt was very very somber that year.

At about the same time, three families from Kurenitz decided to escape the town for the deep forest. Amongst them were Zishka, son of Shimon Alperovich, his wife, Bashka Chana, and their son Yechiel, Faybush, son of Chaim Shulman, with his wife and two children, Menucha Payken and Burl Chadash. They all managed to get fake documents saying that they were travelling to the forest to work for the Germans. They were able to reach the woods safely and found a place to settle. But a villager that lived near the forest brought the Germans to their hiding place and they were killed right there. Just around Passover the Germans brought their bodies to town to show us that any escapees would be found and killed. The horrible fate of the escapees caused others who were planning to escape to the forest to re-think their plans. Right after Passover, Zev Kupershtooch, who worked at the wheat mill, was taken straight from work to Vilejka and there he was tortured and killed.

We Dream of the Forest

Spring came. Everything around us was teeming with life. Weeds were sprouting, trees were flowering, and once again we started thinking of escape. But to accomplish this was very difficult and dangerous, and in the back of our minds, we remembered the fate of the three families, and that was preventing us from making a serious attempt at it. Some people also warned us that if a few of us escaped, it might cause the killing of the rest of the Jews in town.

We had a friend, a poor Christian widow by the name of Anna. She was from the village Lipnovich. Prior to the war, she would come to me for advice and help with her legal documents. She was still loyal to us, and very deeply wanted to help us. Often, she would secretly enter our house, even though the deed was punishable by death. When she came over, she would tell us about what was happening in the outside world. One day, right after Passover, she entered our yard and brought a big container full of sour cream. She tried to comfort us.

"My dear," said Anna, "the Germans will be annihilated. Their heads will break. Do you know what happened last night? In the little village Retzka, the Partisans came to the mill that belonged to Kundra. They took everything he had in the mill. They didn't just come as ordinary people. They wore Red Army uniforms. When they left, they burned the mill and left a letter. The letter said, 'We, the partisans, took everything for our army.'" Then she continued, "Well, Itzka, they are not merchants, they're not going to sell the flour. If they took such a large amount of flour, it's a sign that they have a huge army. People say that the forests are filled with them. You will see, my dear, the Germans will have their heads broken. They will suffer a great defeat. My dear, you must escape to the forest." We knew that she was highly exaggerating, but she did it out of good will, wishing to comfort us and make us happy. We were very excited about her news.

The summer of 1942 came. The Germans announced that their army was going deeper and deeper into the Russian territory. As usual, they announced the news from the war front on huge posters that they hung all over the town's walls. They told us that the whole Red Army was destroyed, but we had other signs to tell us what was going on. In our hearts we followed our own signs, and not the German posters. Each night we saw hundreds of Soviet airplanes going toward Germany. They blew up German bases all around us. Every night we heard explosions. Terrorist attacks by the Partisans were usually aimed at railroads. We interpreted this event as a sign that there was some hope for us.

Many others amongst us continued putting their trust and hope in tales of miracles and dreams. I remember that Fayga Rivka, the wife of Mendel Kanterovich, had a dream that became the main subject of many discussions in town. In her dream, Fayga Rivka saw the most despised killer Sherangovich come to town and all of a sudden the Gestapo members jumped him and killed him right on the spot. Many believed that this was an omen that the Day of Judgment would come to the killer Sherangovich from Karsinievitz. Sure enough, sometime in May or June, a group of Germans entered the town. They caught Sherangovich and killed him. Everyone saw this as a sign from God.

Yeshaya Shmukler also had a dream. In his dream he saw all of his relatives who had departed this world. They came to him and said, "Your wife is ready to deliver a boy. You should call the boy `Yehoshua' because aid is coming soon." Yeshaya's wife did deliver a boy, and on a suggestion of Mendel Zalman Roshkas', the boy was named Yehoshua.

One day, we got an order that all men and women must take part in the labor force. We were all told to clear the forest around the train tracks, 150 meters from each side, so that the Partisans would have a harder time reaching the tracks without being seen by the German guards. Each morning, at seven exactly, we had to show up for work. The place we had to meet was by the apartment that was used as the headquarters for the Judenrat. From there we were taken to work. This job lasted for three weeks, and ended on September 9, 1942, three days prior to Rosh Hashanah.

Almost all the Jews from towns in the area were annihilated at this point. It seemed as if only our town survived. Daily, the killers would give us stale compliments. They would say, "The Jews of Kurenitz are useful Jews, and nothing bad will happen to you." We heard it everyday until the day the Holocaust reached our beloved home town.

The Day of Slaughter and Escape

It was Wednesday, very early in the morning, around five o'clock. I heard the loud noise of trucks going back and forth on the street. It was absolutely obvious to us that something was going to happen that day. My heart told me that this was the day of slaughter. I approached my wife and told her about my dark fears, and immediately returned to the window to watch. A few minutes later, I saw cars full of Gestapo men drive through the street. Outside it was still dark. Light would come at around six o'clock. We dressed our two children so that we would be ready to escape. For a moment, a thought came to me. Maybe my senses are betraying me, and my assumptions are wrong. Still, we sat nervously, listening to the sounds from outside. I went out to the yard to listen. I could hear shots from a machine gun. All around there was a thick fog that prevented me from seeing more than a few meters ahead. I returned home and told my wife, "We must not wait. The fog will aid us with our escape."

So we took our children in our arms, and started running through our garden into the direction of Poken. Our aim was first to get to the Segovitz Forest. While we were still in the garden, our Christian neighbor (the one that, you might remember, had a big tree in his yard, and right next to his wall there was a bench that people used for rest while walking on Dolhinov Street) stepped in front of us, preventing us from continuing. He forced us to return. He never said anything. Until today, his aim is still a mystery. Was he trying to hurt us or save us? Whatever his intention was, the result was in our favor.

The town was tightly surrounded by German guards in a ring formation. If we had continued running, we would surely have fallen in the hands of the Germans. Anyway, we had to return home. Light came, and we didn't know what to do. I walked to the house of Mikhail, our neighbor. In his home he had a little factory for oil, and on the wall there was a big sign saying that this was a factory, so a few families gathered there. We all thought this sign might confuse the Germans and that they would assume that no Jews lived there. There was the Rugbin family from Vilejka, and the family of Yosef the son of Motel Leib Kopershtook. Sometime earlier, Zev Kopershtook had been murdered. So now Yosef would go to sleep at his parents' home in the central market, but his wife and children would sleep at Mikhail's house. On this particular morning, Yosef didn't return and his wife, Rachel, was very worried. While we were standing at the entrance to Mikhail's house, we saw from the market-side, Mishka Takchonik's sister, a Christian woman, approaching. When she came near us, she yelled at us, "Why are you standing there like that, stupid Jews? Didn't you hear what is happening in town? Quickly, hide! Half of the town's Jews are already murdered, and you are standing here as if nothing has happened."

We started running, looking for a haven. In moments like this one, the quest for life increases greatly. We started saying our good-byes to each other; we kissed one another and asked for forgiveness. Each one of us assumed that this was his last day on Earth. It was already 9:30 in the morning, when we entered our homes. We sat there waiting. We assumed that any minute the murderers would come and take us. All of a sudden an idea occurred to us. We told our child to go outside, and to hang our key on the outside door, and then lock the door. Our boy did it, and we helped him get back in through the window, closing the shutters after him.

We had a hiding place under the floor, right under the bed. We lifted the loose planks of wood and entered the hole. We all got into our hideout and lay there for an hour or two. Then we heard sounds of voices and steps from the outside. We heard people speaking German and Polish. Someone said, "The door is locked here. There's nothing to look for." The sound of the steps seemed to be going away. Quietly, I left the hideout, and approached the window to look. I saw a car loaded with planks of firewood. It was driven by the Gestapo. I returned to the hideout, and shortly we all fell into a deep sleep. We woke up at four in the afternoon. There was total silence surrounding us. Once in a while, we heard loud steps. When my wife woke up she said, "Maybe it was all a bad dream."

Once again, I got out of the hideout and approached the window that was facing the yard of our neighbor, Mikhail. I saw that his house had been ransacked, and all his belongings were thrown into the yard. I left that window and went to the window that faced the street. There, I saw a horrible image. Two Gestapo men were holding Rachel, the wife of Yosef Kopershtook, with her two children. She was crying and begging, asking for pity, but they kept hitting her and the children with the butt of their rifles and pushing them toward the market. Then I saw them taking Mina, the daughter of Chaim Michael, her face pale, full of anger and hate. She was fighting the Germans, screaming insults in their faces and refusing to walk. Finally, they shot her on the spot and she fell down in the middle of the street, bleeding. This sight paralyzed me. I felt as if it were impossible for me to move. I felt that any minute, they would come here and take us.

When I was able to move, I returned to the hideout and told my wife what I saw. I knew that time was running out. We must leave. It was September, and the days were already short. The dark evening shadows were enveloping the last day on earth of the Jewish Kurenitz. Dusk was coming, and I told my wife, "Soon it will be dark. We must leave immediately." It was the last day of the Jewish month, and it was very foggy and dark. We got out of the hideout, dressed warmly, took our children, and left for the dark and the mysterious world outside. We had no clear plans and no aim. At that minute, we had one prayer in our heart: let us cross the road to Poken village peacefully. When we approached the village, dogs started barking and immediately there was shooting. They started throwing flares in the air. We lay down flat on the ground among the cabbage and plants that were in the garden. We lay there for a long time, until it quieted down. Then we crawled to the village, which only had one street. We crossed it, and hurried to reach the Sekovitz forest.

When we were three hundred feet past the village, we heard more shooting, but now we were past the danger zone. The night was very dark, and we walked through fields of potatoes. For a few minutes we stopped and looked in the direction of Kurenitz. We could see a big bonfire at the edge of Mydell Street, and we could smell burning bodies. We thought that we were the only survivors: four souls, mother, father and their two children, the last of a holy and renowned community. We stood there crying quietly to the dark, but pretty soon we remembered that this was no time for crying and eulogy. We had to distance ourselves from where we were. We continued on our way until we reached the forest. We started discussing our situation, and we reached one conclusion: we were sentenced to death. The winter was approaching, we didn't have appropriate clothes, and we had no food. We were being chased, and death could come from the cruel winter, with its storms and snow, from hunger and disease, from wild forest animals or, most likely, from the human wolves. Everywhere we might go, death awaited us. This was our rationale and reality, but our urge to survive didn't allow us to analyze our situation. It ordered us to stop thinking, and to start fighting… fighting with any means possible. We walked deeper into the woods, about half a kilometer. We were hungry and exhausted. We lay down on the cold ground to rest, and had a short nap.

All of a sudden we heard someone walking near us. My wife whispered to me, "Itzhak, are you asleep? Someone is walking here. Could it be the Germans? How could it be that they would chase us at night in the forest?"

I whispered to her, "We must not move. If we lie down, they won't see us in the dark, but if we move and try to escape they'll see us."

So we lay there quietly listening intently. We heard sounds of steps, and then a voice of a child, "Mama, mama." Immediately we understood that these were our brothers, and I cried out, "Jews, come here." It was our neighbors Mikhail Alperovich from Badanova, his wife and two children, and the husband of Zelda, the daughter of Chaim Michael. We sat together discussing the situation, suggesting where we should go. They were all very happy to see me since it was well known that I was, since my teenage days, a traveler. I used to join my father in his travels around the villages and forests, and my experience, they realized could be very useful now.

Deeper in the Forest

We rested a bit, but since I was chosen as the guide, I encouraged them to move ahead rapidly. To sit here, next to town, was extremely dangerous. We had to distance ourselves from any populated areas and go deep into the forest. Our assumption was right. Many days later, I was told that on the same day the Germans had caught Herschel, the oven-maker, and his family, eight souls, in the forest not far from Kurenitz, and killed them all.

I didn't have a compass, but my senses guided me in finding trails that would take us to the deepest woods. When we got about five kilometers away from the town, the woods became very dense and it was almost impossible to walk. We were scratched and hurt from the tree branches, and we had to carry our young children in our arms. That's where we were at dawn, when rain came down and drenched us. It was our second day without food. When we left home, we only had one piece of bread, and we'd given that to our children. All that day we stayed in that area, and at night we decided to go to the Sakovitz village to ask for food. Mikhail had a Christian friend in Sakovitz by the name of Ivan, who used to work for Mikhail in the days of Polish rule. Earlier, Mikhail had given him many of his possessions to store in his house for safekeeping. Now Mikhail wholeheartedly believed that if he came to Ivan, Ivan would be very happy to see him, and would do whatever he could to feed us with the best that he could offer. But Mikhail didn't know how to get from where we were to Sakovitz, so Rugbin and I joined him to show him the way.

For a long hour, we walked through the thick woods until we found the village. We walked through the fields so that the villagers wouldn't see us. We knocked on Ivan's door. When he saw us, he looked extremely scared, as if we were ghosts that had come from the grave. He murmured, "Have pity. Quickly run away from here. In God's name, run away and saves yourselves and me. There are many Germans in the village. If they see you in my house they'll kill me and you together." Mikhail and Rugbin were ready to run, but I was not so easy to trick, so I just stood there and said, "We have no reason to save ourselves, and you must give us bread. We have nothing to lose. Better we die from a bullet than from starvation." Knowing the soul of the beast, it was clear to me that begging would not suffice. So I continued, in a threatening voice, "If you won't give us bread, we will burn your home and your possessions. We are people with a death sentence hanging over our heads. We have nothing to lose. You must know that we intend to keep our threats."

Ivan the Christian farmer looked at us in terror. He brought a huge loaf of bread. It could easily have weighed as much as eight kilos. We left to return to our families with the supplies. We trudged on for miles and miles through the forest, we got lost for a short while, but finally, we found the women and children. We also brought water in bottles, and we divided the food and the drink amongst the group. This experience was an important lesson for me. It was like a candle that lit my steps through our journey in the forest. We had to be strong in spirit. We couldn't afford to give up or to be depressed. Even the shadow of defeat could kill us.

We spent that night in the forest. The next morning, which was the eve of Rosh Hashanah, we decided to move forward. My plan was to reach the Pelita, a place were Leib Motosov had a factory prior to WWI. While we were walking, Mikhail decided to separate from us and to go to the village Kalin. There, he said, lived a gentile that he had given the rest of his belongings to, and who had promised to help him whenever he needed aid. So Mikhail and his wife went to this man's home. We were later told that when the man saw them, he murdered them with his own hands.

We continued without them. It was about ten in the morning. The sun slanted through the tree branches, and a deep silence filled the woods. The towering pine trees swayed with the wind from side to side. The sound resonated like the hum of a devotional prayer. The sounds of birds were heard everywhere, echoing in the woods. How we envied the birds that were free to sing and call each other, while we were here, whispering, walking on our tip-toes, lost and fearful, not knowing what danger zone we might reach next.

All of a sudden, I smelled smoke. In panic, we leapt into the bushes, fearing that there were people nearby who might see us. Our eyes were searching, our ears were listening, and our minds wondered what the origin of this smoke could be. Could it be shepherds from the neighboring village that made a bonfire in the woods? Or maybe it was Jews who had escaped? All of a sudden, I saw a group of people, gathered a short distance from the road. It was Israel Alperovich, our town's butcher, his wife

Chaya, their son Yosil, and the wife of Zondil their other son. They must have heard us approaching, because they ran into the forest. I wanted to calm them down, but I knew it was dangerous to yell, so I waved my hands and gave them signals saying that they should lie on the ground. They recognized me, and lay down on the ground, sighing with relief.

When we reached them, we asked them why they had chosen a rest place so near the road. Not only were they resting there, but they had started a bonfire that could easily reveal their whereabouts. Israel replied that they were afraid to enter the deep woods. The women asked desperately, "What will happen to us? Who will be with us? Where will we go?" I was very familiar with the surrounding area and I said, "First we must go to the deeper woods, in the middle of the forest, as far as we can from the road. " I was still full of energy, and eager to fight against our bitter fate. My senses were sharpened, and in my heart I had many ideas and thoughts about how to survive. But they looked so defeated. We walked towards the deeper woods for about an hour. When I thought that we were a good distance from the road, we sat down and built a small bonfire. Israel brought out from his bag his talit and tfilin, and said, "Look, Yitzhak. God bless, I succeeded in taking this so that at least I will have a talit at the hour of my death." We sat on the ground and Israel told us how he was saved, and how he succeeded to leave town on the day of the slaughter:

Early in the morning, he had walked to the minyan to pray. He made his way through the empty lots amongst the homes in the alley. While he was walking, he ran into some Jews who told him that the Germans had come into the town and were kidnapping Jews. Immediately, he ran home and led his family to their hiding place under the floor, where they sat the entire day. At night they abandoned their hiding place, and walked to Poken village, to the home of the gentile Kashtzook, who was extremely gracious. He took them under his wing, gave them a loaf of bread, and walked with them all the way to the forest. Israel was a very religious Jew. He didn't touch the bread. All he ate were the potatoes he had baked in the fire.

Around three in the afternoon, a young village girl who looked about seventeen, came from the woods. When she saw us, she waved as if she were giving us a signal, and then she ran away. We still don't know how to explain the signal. A few minutes later there was a barrage of gunshots that seemed to come from the side of the road. We stomped the fire out, destroyed any signs of our having been there, and ran into the woods. I ran first, and everyone else was behind me. We ran for five kilometers, until we found a niche hidden between two small hills, where we lay until darkness came.

Where Are We Going?

We were three families traveling together. The Rugbin family, Israel Alperovich family, and my family. We all wondered where exactly we were. The children were lying quietly, saying nothing. They were not a burden. It was as if they understood that we were in a world of horrible occurrences, and that they had to be responsible and acclimate themselves to the situation. We were thirsty and hungry. I estimated that we were somewhere near the village Hob. I remembered that near the village there was a little river, named Maentenna. From my estimation, we were also about three kilometers from the village Stidiyonka. The villagers from Stidiyonka were known as very cruel gentiles. So where should we go, to Hob or to Stidiyonka? In Hob I also knew there were many isolated farm houses, and that lessened the danger, so we chose to go to Hob.

We held hands as we walked so that we wouldn't get lost in the darkness. It was the middle of the night by the time we reached the river. We didn't have any cups or anything else we could drink from, so we all fell to the ground and drank directly from the river.

From there, we walked through the fields and headed towards the first farm we encountered. There was no light in the house. When we knocked, the farmer asked, "Who is there?" I answered, "Itzka from Kurenitz, the son of Netka from Shvashzapole". He knew me before the war. He approached the window and gave me half a loaf of bread and some onions. We went on, to another farm, and there they also gave us half a loaf. We took some vegetables from the garden, as well as a big gourd that was next to one of the fences, and with all these supplies we returned to the women and children that were waiting at the edge of the river. It was getting very late. We didn't have a watch, but we knew it was after midnight. We entered the woods, but couldn't find our original spot. For three hours we roamed around.

All of a sudden Israel said, "My dears, I have no energy to continue. I'll stay here." He was much more tired than the rest of us because he didn't eat the bread, so we stopped and lay down on the ground, bundling up with each other. When we woke up, it was already light. A plane flew over the woods, and the sound was unbearable. We realized that today was Rosh Hashanah. Israel put on the talit, stood next to a tree and prayed. He announced that we must pray for all of our townspeople. When he said this, we all started to cry, and we couldn't console ourselves. This was the first big cry after fifteen horrible months. We cried for all that had occurred to us.

When the sun set, we continued our journey. We walked towards the village Tzavolitkes. When we were about three hundred meters from the village, we met with more of the town's surviving Jews. To my surprise, my sister Rivka with her husband and children, my brother Hilka with his wife, and the daughter of my other brother were among them. I never imagined that anyone of my family survived. They, in turn, had never imagined that I had survived. They lived on Mydell Street, at the spot where the murderers started the killing spree. Once again, we stood there crying, and then continued our journey. Now we had twenty-seven people among our ranks.

We entered the village. It was clear to us that as Jews, we belonged to the night. The night, from now on, would be our day. The gentiles didn't dare leave their homes at night. They feared the dark. In this village, we got some bread and onions. That night, we rested in an area between the villages Varoniyatz and Tsavolitzkes, in the middle of the forest. The night was cold, the forest was very dry, and we were dying of thirst. We squeezed plants and sucked their juices.

All of sudden, Rugbin remembered that in one of the farms there was a villager that owed him some money for a sewing machine he had bought. We searched for the house of this gentile, and he gave us bread and a pail of milk. We went to him before nighttime. He refused to let us in, telling us to wait outside, and after a short time he brought out the food. He suggested that we never come again, in the daytime, only at night, and he was very astute in his suggestion. We brought the bread and milk to the children, and lay down on the ground to sleep.

It was very cold and we couldn't sleep well. We heard the howling of a pack of wolves. They came closer and closer. We were not really scared, but we wanted to get rid of them, so we took some dry branches and lit them with a match we got from the villager. It was a small bonfire, but sufficient to make the wolves disappear. It also warmed us, and made it easier for us to fall asleep. At dawn we awoke, and put out the fire, erased all signs of human population, and traveled to another area.

There we ran into a villager from Veronietz who was searching for his horse, which had run away at night. At first we were very scared. Could he be a German agent? But as we continued talking to him, we realized he was an honest and righteous gentile. He told us that we must not stay there. He urged us to go to the Pushtcha, an area deep in the woods, where we would find Jews from the village Nyka who had escaped, and had been hiding there for two months. He started crying and said, "What do they want from you? What do they want from you?" He took bread out of his bag and gave it to the children. He showed us the road to the Pushtcha, and told us that we would also find some Partisans there. "Go there," he said, "and God will be with you." When I think today about this meeting, it warms and encourages me. But on that day, we were cold and suspicious of him, and when he left us, we were scared that he would send the Germans to catch us.

In the Deep Pushtcha

The Pushtcha was an everglade in our area, measuring about twenty kilometers long, and twelve kilometers wide. There were huge pine trees crowding the area. No man had ever walked in the deepest areas of the Pushtcha. Hundreds of trees' limbs lay on the ground where they had fallen during storms, and had been lying there for dozens of years. It was a strange world, dark and wild, a habitat for wolves and wild pigs, foxes and snakes. Not even the villagers of the surrounding area dared to enter the forest. They would travel only to the edges of the forest. There were areas of swamp that one could only walk through in winter, when the swamp froze over. But we were now drawn to the deepest part of the forest.

We stood fearfully at the edge for a moment, and wondered, "How could we live here, how could we come and go and find our way?" But even that night we had to stay in the Pushtcha with the children and wives. We walked to the villages Bodka and Talets to obtain some food. Those were the closest villages. When we returned we made a bonfire. We felt much safer, now. We assumed that the Germans would not come there to look for us, even if they knew that Jews were hiding there. They would assure themselves that we would die anyway from starvation and disease. Still, we didn't want to rely totally on our assumptions, so we decided to go as deep as we could, and to watch our step. For now, our main goal was to meet up with the Partisans.

On our second day in the Pushtcha, we did just that. We looked at them with tremendous gratitude, as though they were angels from heaven. They greeted us warmly, and joined us. They were dressed very poorly and carried old weapons from WWI. They didn't have much ammunition, only a few bullets. They gave some bread to our children, and were curious to hear of our situation. It seemed to us that they meant well, but they could hardly help us. They had a radio and they told us about what was happening in the world. We sat with them for two hours. They told us about the battle of Stalingrad, they explained to us how to survive in the woods, and they told us in no uncertain terms, that we must never stay in one place for too long, we must change our location a few times a day. They also suggested that we speak quietly because there was echo in the woods, and that we had to whisper and learn signals. They also taught us how to whistle like a common forest bird, and said that if we lost each other, we should use that whistle.

We started our long journey in the Pushtcha. We went all around, lengthwise and widthwise, so that we were never in one place for more than a few hours. Throughout our journey, we met many surviving Jews, and they told us details about the slaughter in Kurenitz. From there on started our daily struggle to survive in the Pushtcha, a struggle full of trials and tribulations, a struggle that our horrible fate forced us to face, a struggle that had no comparison or precedent in anything we'd ever heard of, read of or even imagined in our worst nightmares.

Generally, the Belarusian villagers in the surrounding areas were sympathetic to us. We received handouts, both from the ones that were behind us ideologically, and the ones that weren't. Some gave out of pity, others gave fearing that we would burn their homes. As time passed, we realized that asking for pity was not as effective as scaring the villagers. We took long pieces of wood and made them look like rifles and, in the dark of night, we went to the villages and threatened them with our "weapons." We also used rough voices and harsh language so that they would think we were Partisans. Our journeys to the villages were ridden with danger. Even the villagers, that we asked handouts from, might have murdered us. Any gentile that would bring a Jew to town, either dead or alive, would receive a bag full of salt as a reward. Salt was a very precious commodity at that time.

Sometimes, on our way back from the villages, we weren't able to find our resting places. One family, returning from the village, couldn't find us for two days. Finally we ran into them and brought them back with us.

There were many men that acted as policemen for the Germans who lived in the villages around the forest. Among them were included some true murderers. In one "charming pair" were the two sons of Karibi from the village Hob. One was twenty-five and the other, twenty-three; both bloodsucking leeches. There were horror tales told all around the villages about the cruel deeds they'd done on the day of the slaughter in Kurenitz. They grabbed little babies, and threw them into the fire. They tortured and slaughtered many people. I want to tell you about how we were almost caught by these two killers:

One Saturday night in October of 1942, Shoal, son of Abraham Yitzhak Gordon, his wife, my wife and I, approached one of the farms. As usual, we stood near the window, but not facing it. We knocked on the window, but there was no answer. We knocked again, and still there was no answer. We were just about to leave, when we heard from afar someone walking. At first I thought it might be the homeowner, but I could just make out two young men walking in the night. Our eyes had become accustomed to the dark, like those of forest animals. They approached us and said in an almost polite tone, "Kurenitzki Zashidki. What are you looking for here in the middle of the night?" Shoal Gordon, who was encouraged by their friendly tone, answered, "We came to ask for bread for our families and children." They responded, "Come in, please, enter the house, we'll give you bread and other food for the soul". I recognized from the tone of their voices that these were the Karibi sons, the killers. I leapt out of the yard. I knew that a moment of hesitation would mean our death. As I escaped, I whistled like a Partisan to scare them. One of them was already holding my wife by her coat, but when she heard me whistle, she jumped too, and all he had left was her old coat, that ripped to shreds when she jumped away. Shoal also realized the danger, and ran out of the yard with his wife. The German collaborators were very afraid of the Partisans, and that explained why they didn't try very hard to chase and catch us.

When we returned to Hob a week later, we were told by some sympathetic gentiles that, after we left, the Karibi sons looked for us in the homes of almost every villager and threatened everyone in the village, telling them that they would kill them like dogs if they aided or fed the Jews. We stopped going to Hob until one day, with the help of the Partisans, we burned the Karibis' home, and the entire family, fearing the Partisans, left the area.

One day, the Partisans were told to leave the area for a different camp, much farther east, in the former USSR. When they left, they took a few young Kurenitzers in order to train them as Partisans. Our living situation was much more difficult after they left, but luckily for us, two weeks later a new unit came to our woods. They numbered four hundred, and we were extremely impressed by them. They had new weapons, and they arrived riding horses. The name of the troop was Revenge, and amongst them were Jews from Minsk, Dolhinov and Kurenitz. The Jews of Kurenitz included Yankel, the son of Orchik and Maryl Alperovich. The year before, Yankel was taken to be killed with the fifty-four and saved himself and his brother when he demanded an answer from the Germans: Was he receiving a death sentence for being a Communist or a Jew? Also, when the war ended, he got many commendations and medals for his bravery. Others from Kurenitz were Nyomka Berman, the son of the barber, and Velvel (Zev), the son of Abraham Fiddler from Smorgon Street.

The troop had just returned from a mission to save the Jews of Mydell, who the Germans held captive in a ghetto. They were successful in their mission, and they brought some of the Jews they had rescued to the forest. During the mission, however, the leader of the troop, who was known to be very heroic, and always walked in front of the troop in dangerous times, was killed in action. One of the families that was saved from the Mydell ghetto and brought to the woods was Yosef Blinder with his wife and children.

Realizing that the snowy season was approaching, we feared that our footsteps would be noticed in the snow, and would lead the Germans to our camps. The Partisan headquarters decided to collect all the Jews from the forest and transfer them to Russian territory in the east, where the Russians still held some control. The Germans didn't dare enter those forests.

We are Going to the Vostok

Sometime around November, the Partisans collected all the Jews that were in the woods, some from Mydell, from Kribitz, Nieka, Kabilinik, and other places. All together, there were three hundred souls. Amongst them there were two hundred Jews from Kurenitz. Many were entire families that had been saved. The political commissar gave us a long speech, explaining that there was no choice but to leave and walk east. He drew a picture for us of all the difficulties we were going to encounter. We would be walking by foot, never using the main roads, only fields and forests, and never walking during the day. Despite the gloomy picture he drew, we were very excited. We all prepared for the journey. The main ingredient that we were told to collect was salt, since salt was unavailable in Russia. We were able to get it in small quantities from the villages, but it cost a lot of money. The commissar also told us to get laptzas, a kind of shoe made from cloth. Everyone's shoes at that point were totally destroyed from walking in the woods. We bought those and other clothes form the villagers, and everyone was busily preparing.

We left on a Saturday. We were divided into units of ten people, each with a head leader. I was chosen as a head of a unit. They took everyone to the edge of the wood, where we waited for darkness. There were three Partisans guiding us. Amongst us were little children and people that could hardly walk from exhaustion, so the healthy people were supposed to take care of them. The three Partisans were wonderful. They helped us enormously. They wore leather jackets, blue pants and boots, and they were armed with the best weapons. They carried the children, and helped in any other way they could. When we reached five kilometers away from the train tracks, the Partisans entered the village Paskovishtsizana and confiscated three horses with buggies. They put the young children and the sick people on the buggies, which is how we reached the train tracks. Here we waited while the Partisans returned the horses and buggies to the village. Now it was time to cross the train tracks. Later, we crossed the main road between Kurenitz and Dolhinov. The road, which we called Yakterina's Boulevard, was famous and was bordered by old cedar trees on both sides. We were told to cross it near Kastsiniavits. This was the way the Partisans came and went, and it seemed like a safe way.

The train tracks were at that time guarded in many spots by the villagers. We traveled until we were one hundred meters from the track, near Niyaka. There was complete silence. We all crawled on the ground, which was wet, but not frozen. We lay down and waited for orders. The Partisans whispered for us to cross immediately, in one big group. We crouched and quickly crossed the tracks. Our mission was to cover forty kilometers through the night, until we found a place to rest the next day. The area where we were nearing was very dangerous. We were close to Kanahahinina, where there was a large group of Germans in the train station. In addition, many Germans and police were stationed in Kastsinievitz. The mission was almost impossible.

Three men were sent to check the area, amongst them Zalman, the son of Maisie Alperovich, and two others that I don't remember. We lay down, awaiting their return. We waited and waited, but they didn't appear. The night was getting shorter and shorter. We didn't know what to do. We were waiting in a very dangerous spot. We realized that there was no reason to wait anymore. Later, we found out that they had returned and had taken fifty people, thinking that the rest would follow. But, there was a miscommunication, and we never knew that they had left.

We knew we had to find a forest to hide in during the day. We did have the three Partisans, but still, we felt we were in incredible danger. We found a tiny forest, surrounded by open fields and isolated farms. Very close to it was the main road from Kasanivits and Kanihahinina. All day long, we saw cars full of armed Germans, crossing the road. We lay close to the ground, as if we were part of it, all day long until darkness came. When it was completely dark, we organized ourselves into units, and continued our journey. We had to cross thirty-five kilometers to get out of the danger zone and into a forest where the Partisans had control. Now we could see how difficult our mission was. The older people were exhausted, the children were tired and thirsty, all day we lay in one spot without drinking, and we had to walk five kilometers to reach the village Davidki. There began to be more and more space between the different units. We were carrying a lot of baggage, the children started crying, and the metal food containers in our baggage were making noise which, in the quiet of the night, could be heard from a great distance. The noise was getting louder and louder.

But maybe that was our lucky break.

The Failure

In Davidki, there was a blockade in our anticipation. The Germans were going to kill us when we entered the village. But, when they heard the loud noises that was coming, they thought we were a huge Partisan troop, so they opened fire with everything they had and lit the area with flares much earlier than they originally planned. As soon as they started shooting, everyone ran with no guidance. We spread all over the area. Parents lost their children and men lost their wives. I tried very hard to control my group of ten. I ordered them to lie on the ground, and while still in lying position, to crawl and try to get away from the main road. The shots continued for about an hour with small breaks. At every break, we got further away from the main road until we reached a small forest that was more bushes than trees. The shots stopped. I counted my group and realized that, instead of ten, we were thirty five. We didn't know where the rest of the people were. So what should we do now? And where were we? From my estimation, we were still between Kastsinievits and Kanihahinina, at the mouth of the lion, with no real protection. Amongst the people with me were Natan Gurevitz and his children, Leah, Zalman and Gershon, the Vexler family, Rachel from the town of Kribits with her two children, Yoel and Michael the two children of Israel Shaefer, the daughter of Meir of Mydell, the wife of Chaim Zalman and her daughter, and women and children from Mydell. We decided to find a bigger forest. We walked all around. We knew that the Germans would look for us when daylight came, so we had to find a good hideout. All we could find were fields and bushes and thorny areas. We got more and more exhausted until we finally found a forest, where we lay down and fell asleep. In the morning we woke up hearing shots. The Germans were going through the main road looking for us. When we opened our eyes, we got very depressed. We were in a tiny forest in the middle of a field, and there were farms all around us. Not far there were shepherds with their flocks. It seemed clear to us that the Germans would find us shortly. We lay on the ground, observing the Germans who looked through the farms, but never approached the forest. It seemed that the rest of our group returned to our old place during the night with the help of one of the Partisans, and that the Germans followed their footsteps, so they were after them and not us, never imagining that we were lying so close to them. We lay like that all day. When evening came, we heard a lot of shots, we discussed what to do, how to get away, and return to the Pushtcha. We knew we were about twenty kilometers away from the Pushtcha, but we didn't know which direction to go. We decided to enter one of the farms and ask someone. This was a very dangerous mission since in that area, there were many Poles that were known as anti-Semites. Zalman Gurevitz and I endangered our lives and went to the village.

When we reached the window of one of the houses, we heard whispers. The residents would not light their home fearing the Partisans. I pretended to be a Partisan, and asked in a rough tone where the main road was. From inside I heard the voice of an old woman. She claimed that she was all alone and too tired to greet us. We told her that all she needed to do was tell us which way to go. She reached the window and showed us here and there, and was all confused, so we saw that there was no help from her. We decided to try and find our own way. We found a little path, and took our people through the path. I knew that a path must somewhere join a main road so, after we walked for a short time, we found a main road. Still, we didn't know which way to go. Zalman Gurevitz and I found another farmhouse. Everyone waited in the bushes by the road. Lucky for us, there were no dogs to bark since the Partisans killed all the dogs. We reached a farm that looked like a wealthy farm. Since it had a big barn and storage areas, we knew it was a Polish home but despite this fact, I came to the window and knocked on it, asking in Russian, "How do I get to Kasetsinievits?" An old man came to the window. The young people were hiding, fearful that the Partisans might take them. He explained how to get there. We returned to our people, and started our journey.

Clearly we didn't go to Kasetsinievits. We went in the other direction. The night was very long, and we walked about twenty kilometers. We were very thirsty. We hadn't drank in twenty-four hours. Near one of the villages we found a drainage system. We lay on the ground and put some water in the palms of our hands and rank it. We didn't go into the village. I recognized it. It was Zukavitsa, three kilometers from Niaka. From there on I knew the road. We approached the tracks. The villagers, as usual, were watching the tracks, but three hundred meters from there was a German patrol. Once in a while the German patrol came with flashlights and checked over the villager guards, who didn't have any weapons. We stopped near the tracks. Mikhail Vexler, Zalman Gurevitz and I checked the tracks and realized that there were no Germans. We gave a sign to the rest of the group and they all quickly passed across the tracks. It was around eleven at night. Now we could breath a little easier. We passed Nayeka, which seemed to be in total slumber, and then we reached the edge of the Pushtcha. We slept there. the next day we reached the area that we had left just a few days before.

Our Bonfires and the First Snow

The earth was already frozen, our clothes were torn, and the men were all ragged looking and unshaven. Fear of the approaching winter was enormous. Till now we'd lived next to the bonfires that burnt day and night. The bonfires had many advantages. The fire warmed our bones, we would bake potatoes, and boil our clothes. Each bonfire was a center for a few families. One family was incapable of taking care of the bonfire, since one needed many trees to keep it burning. There was no lack of trees in the forest, but it was impossible for us to cut them down. We didn't have the appropriate tools. It was also dangerous to hit the wood with the axe since it would make a loud sound that would echo in the woods. Even when we talked we whispered so that we wouldn't be heard. So we used wood that was already cut a few years back by the Soviets. They had put it at the edge of the woods prior to the Germans' invasion. We lived in the deepest of the woods, so we had to carry the firewood to our hiding place, a very difficult task. Only a big group of people could do it. For this reason, we had to live in bigger groups. The disadvantages of bonfires were that many of us got burned since the trees that we used were the kind that sent sparks flying out, in turn burning our clothes. It was especially dangerous while we slept. We lay on the ground in ring formation around the fire, foot to head. One person had to stay awake to watch for any fire that might get out of control. In our group, we had an organized guarding and since I needed very little sleep, I passed many nights watching the bonfire. We were so used to sleeping like this, with one person's head on another's legs, that we hardly felt the roughness of the earth. We lay at a distance from the fire where we could put our hand in and warm it. The side of our body that was near the fire was almost baked, but the other side suffered the cold. We knew that any minute the snow would start. We were extremely worried about it. Where would we hide in the snow? We knew we wouldn't be able to lie on the ground, and we knew that the bonfires would not last. But still, our worst fear was that the Germans could see our footsteps in the snow.

The first snow came when I, my wife and a few other Jews from our group went to one of the villages to get food. It was very wet snow, pouring constantly, without pity or consideration. Our shoes were destroyed. We were left barefoot. When we saw that the snow was not stopping, we left the village and, with great difficulty, reached the Pushtcha. We were still about ten kilometers away from our hiding place, where the rest of the group was, but it was impossible to continue. We didn't know what to do. We started looking in our pockets to see whether someone had a match and a miracle occurred! Dania, the son of Chaim Avremil Alperovich, had one match. So how were we going to light a bonfire with one match? The fear that the match would go out was huge. We knew we must prepare the wood to that the match would not fail. We started looking in the dark for dry brush, anything that the snow had not yet reached. We took any dry twig that we could find and broke pieces that were try, and prepared the bonfire. Who can describe the moment prior to lighting the match? It was a fateful moment. The match came alive and lit the wood. The fire took a long time, but finally it spread, one minute red one minute blue, from one twig to the other until, finally, we had a bonfire. We sat there for a long time warming ourselves and we rested. When we returned to our hideout, we found that our bonfires were almost all out and that the children were frozen. We spread out all over to find twigs and bushes for a new fire.

We knew that the arrangements that we had for the last few months were not going to work, and we decided to make "zimlanka" (a deep in the ground hideout). We didn't have tools like shovels, and there were many children without parents and women without husbands that couldn't contribute to the job. We divided ourselves into groups, and started digging. Some families were unable to dig into the ground, so they made a hut out of foliage. Inside their huts they had constant fires. I remember that Yosef Blinder had a hut and one night the roof caught fire while the family was asleep, and they barely made it out. Yosef was gone, getting food in one of the villages at the time and when he came back, he found a burned hut and his family without a place to live. This new arrangement eventually caused the loss of a lot of lives since now we lived in a more permanent hideout, and there were paths that led to it which the Germans found.

Life in the forest started affecting us. The cold, the anger, the filthy conditions all started killing our people. Israel Alperovich, who kept to the Jewish rules till his last breath, only ate baked potatoes. On days when he couldn't get potatoes he just fasted and, finally, he died from starvation. The wife of Mendel Kramer died. The sons of Israel Shaefer, Yoelke and Michael, who were left without parents died. The daughter of Yerachmiel the shoemaker died, as well as some Jews from other towns. We didn't have funerals for the dead. We didn't sew appropriate clothing to bury them in. Only Israel, who had the talit that he kept like a treasure, was buried with his talit. We dug the ground with our bare hands, and there we put the bodies of people that we were so closely attached to now. The ones that survived, tried to improve the situation. Someone brought scissors and razors, which was like a treasure for the citizens of the woods. The owner of the "treasures" was moved from place to places, and treated with great respect. We used potatoes to soap our faces, and with great pain we shaved.

Bigger problems were the ticks and lice. Our skin was full of bites. Eventually, typhus spread. The disease took the life of Yechiel, the son of Yekutiel Meir, the son of Faybush the Shochet, and many others. We used to joke about the typhus calling it the Crazy Typhus. Even if they got past the disease and fever, people were half crazy, and many lost their hearing. About the many that recovered without doctors and medicine, we used to say that the climate of the Pushtcha was a healing one. We had very little means of fighting the lice. Sometimes we would go to the villages and secretly use their bathhouse and steal wood to warm the water, but the smoke from the fire sometimes got in our eyes and we walked in pain for days. This practice caused the death of quite a few. People would fall asleep from the heat in the water, and sometimes they woke up the next day, falling into the hands of the Germans. The bathhouse was only a small room about two hundred meters from the farms. There was an oven with no chimney and on top of it were many rocks. There were two big barrels of water, one with cold water and the other warm. The practice was to put the water on top of the warm rocks, which gave us steam.

At one time, a father with three sons, survivors from Svier, went to the village Stranika to use their bathhouse. After they took a bath, they fell asleep. When they woke up, it was already daylight. They left to return to the woods, not realizing that there were thousands of Germans in the village. This was on November 2nd, 1943, and they were preparing for the first blockade. When the family left they were all caught and shot. The three sons died immediately, and the father was wounded in his head, but survived and reached the Pushtcha in the next evening.

Blockade

That was the day of the first blockade. The Gestapo used spies in the neighboring village. They found our hideout and now they brought the Germans. The Germans surrounded the forest and started searching. Into every hideout that they found, they threw grenades; this continued from morning through the night. They took many lives. Our hideout was in a more isolated place and that probably helped. Altogether we were 32 people in our hideout. About 75% of the survivors who lived in the woods were centered in one location. They made something that looked almost like a settlement. From there were many trails you could see in the snow. I always told them that there were great dangers having a central community, that we must spread everywhere in the forest but people didn't listen. At 2am I returned from gathering food at a village about 15km away. I was exhausted, it was a very successful trip I got a lot of supplies and it was heavy to carry, my wife greeted me saying, "Now you can rest and not go to the villages for a while because you got so many supplies." I immediately went to sleep and in no time was in deep sleep. My little four-and-a-half-year-old daughter woke up very early in the morning and went outside to relieve herself. She immediately came running back very scared. She said, "Why are you all lying here? There are shots in the woods. The Germans are coming!" She woke up everyone and we quickly became ready. Someone said that it was her imagination and it was just the crackling of the forest from the frost. But it no time, we realized it wasn't her imagination. The forest became a battlefield. We could hear shots from every kind of weapon – rifles, machine guns, grenades, etc. The German used army tactics and army strategy to kill the small remains of the Jews of Kurenitz. In our hideout there were 14 people, and 200 meters away from us there was a group of 18 people. They immediately came to us and asked for advice – could we survive? By that point, we were all surrounded and we could hear the screams of the Germans. The screams echoed all throughout the woods. We had no time to think. A few suggested that we might be better off joining the other Jews, as if we could fight the Germans. I said quietly that in my opinion we should go in the direction that the Germans came from, meaning in the direction of Katilovetska. Thinking that the Germans would concentrate on the deep woods it would be smarter to escape through the edges. David, the son of Namancha, came running from the woods. The Germans shot at him; he threw his fur coat and boots as a decoy and the Germans shot them thinking that they had killed him. He ran barefoot. When it got dark, the shots quieted and the Germans left the woods. We returned to our hideout. The next day we left the hideout again thinking that they would continue with their blockade but they didn't return. So we left the forest to see what happened to the rest of the Jews. There were 9 Jews killed and 3 that were caught and tortured to death. Three of the hideouts were destroyed by grenades. Now we decided that we must build our hideout inside the ground. In case there was another blockade, we would not have to find another hideout in the forest. This was a complicated job since we didn't have the tools or the capability. In our group the main workers were Eliah, son of Shimshel Specter, and I. We built a hideout deep in the ground that was very hard to find. The hideout was connected to our living space and there was a tunnel from the hideout that was about 15 meters long. The end of the tunnel was in the middle of a thick part of the forest. In case they discovered the tunnel, we felt we could run out of it. Right after the first blockade, in March of 1943, Yetzkaleh "Yitzhak" Einbinder came to see us. He was a member in a partisan troop and was already involved in many dangerous missions. Although he was still a teenager, he appeared very serious, courageous, and melancholy as if he became an adult under tragic circumstances. He was wearing a short fur coat and boots and he had a Russian hat that the partisans used to wear. On his waist, he wore a rifle and a gun. He heard of the few Jews from Kurenitz who lived in our hideout so he came to see us. Here in the woods he found out that his parents and his entire family had been killed. When he saw us near the fire, he approached us and hugged and kissed each one of us crying. He sat somber on the ground as if he was eulogizing. Finally, he said, "There is only one thing left in my life. To revenge and to revenge." He sat with us for about two hours and then left alone. His name was renowned all over the forest. He took upon himself the most dangerous missions and his name was feared all over the villagers. They would call him Bezesmitnee, which meant the courageous, the one that death cannot take hold of. In the mean time, Passover came. It was our first Passover in the woods. I remember Feige Lea Shmiraz and Migallee the wife of Shmirnah had a few metal containers and a broken pot so they washed their "treasures" to make them kosher for Passover. All through the Passover holiday we didn't eat bread – only potatoes. The second blockade came on April 30, 1943 four days after Passover. Just two days prior, the partisans came to Luban and killed some Germans. Among the partisans were Yankale, son of Archik Alperovich, and Zev, the son of Abraham Fiddler from Kurenitz. After they killed some Germans, they took a herd of cows and brought it to the woods. They gave one cow to each of two hideouts for slaughter. It was already Spring and mud was everywhere because the snow was melting and there was much rain. I and my brother and law and another of our group went to receive our cow. When we returned with the cow, the cow got stuck in the mud and it was impossible to get her out. While we were trying to get her out, all of a sudden we heard a few shots. We left the cow and ran to our hideout. The next day started the second blockade. In the second blockade, many survivors who didn't have hideouts were killed. Altogether, there were 19 people from Kurenitz and many others from other towns. One woman was caught and tortured to death at Vilejka. Danya, son of Abraham, was caught alive. They cut his body with a saw. Spring passed, and summer came. Night life was more comfortable. The hope that we would one day leave the woods and be saved- increased. In the fronts, the Germans kept losing. We heard that the Russians won the Stalingrad battle, but at the same time, more people among us died. Some were killed by Germans, and others by disease, particularly typhus. In September 1943, a few days prior to Rosh Hashanah, which was the first anniversary of the day they killed our town, the Germans went to the forest with a big army. Some were between 30-40,000 soldiers. Unlike the other blockades which lasted only a day, this blockade lasted for two weeks. Many of the villages that they suspected the residents for helping the partisans and the Jews were burned. The residents were taken to Germany. Fayga Lea Sorrel's was caught by the Germans in one of the searches. She was brought to the village Sterenski where there was a German headquarters. They tortured her very severely and tried to make her admit that in the villages the Jews of the woods were getting food. The villagers watched her be tortured and were very scared. They knew that their lives were dependent on what she said. For three days they tortured her with everything, but she denied everything. She kept saying that the gentiles beat her mercilessly in the villages and they ran us out of their homes and everything that we have to eat is only from what we managed to steal from the fields or what the partisans give us. When they saw that the torture was not going to get them anywhere, the Germans started a new tactic by promising all sorts of things. They even tried to trick her by bringing her to a gentile who already confessed that he was giving food to the Jews of the woods. But she claimed right in front of the gentile that he was lying, that he was one of the cruelest villagers and that he caused many troubles to the Jews. A few days later, she died from torture. When the villagers heard that she died, they were unusually emotional. They couldn't understand how one woman had such spiritual powers to withstand that much torture. They claimed that she must be one of the holy saints that took a shape of a human being. They secretly took her body and buried it in the graveyard in Sterensky and they would go to her grave and pray as if she were a saint. The partisans left prior to the German entrance of the woods, so hardly any partisans were killed.

Our situation improves

A large partisan brigade came to the woods and our situation improved greatly both financially and safety-wise. They established small workshops for sewing, shoemaking, baking, and other crafts. Many Jews started working for the partisan since most of the Jews were not trained to fight and could not join the other brigades. We joined the work troop. We dug in the ground for new hideouts that were now used as workshops. The Jews who joined the work troop were from different towns and many started coming after they escaped from Vilna. We didn't have any new materials so what we did was mainly fix old clothes and old shoes. Underwear we sewed from parachutes that the Russian Red Army had used to parachuted weapons down. The partisans brought the sewing machines from the villagers. As it turned out, most of those sewing machines had belonged at one time to the Jews of Kurenitz and were stolen after the Jews were killed.

So we started dressing a little better with patches, but everything had no holes. Also, our cleansing situation improved dramatically. We made a bathhouse so we would no longer need to go secretly to the villages to bathe. Our bathhouse was made from an oven with rocks on top. We even managed to get some soap. We started producing soap too. Natcha chanas from Kurenitz established a soap factory that was very primitive but he managed to produce real soap. So now we were much cleaner and we looked almost like human beings. All the Jews eventually left the Pushtza and moved to the Zazarious wood near the community called Oozla. The reason was that, in that area Zoomitel there were big partisan troops and brigades. So this was our situation at the end of 1943 and the beginning of 1944. Large areas were in that point in the hands of the partisans. In the woods, they even made a small secret airport. Planes landed and took the wounded from amongst the partisans to behind the line.

Winter passed and Passover came. This Passover we baked matzos from our flour and we even made everything according to the rules and we had a seder. Immediately after Passover, there were rumors that the Germans were planning a big blockade in the woods so we started preparing and built many hideaways. On the one hand, we were seeing the end of the war, but on the other hand we were very worried that the Germans would kill us as the war was ending. We knew that in some areas the Germans started using dogs and they were able to find every hideout so our hearts were full of fear. The Germans started the blockade in forests that were about 180 km east of us. In this forest, there were many survivors from our town that were hiding there and we lost 15 souls out of them. What saved us was that the rapidly approaching Red Army had prevented the Germans from entering our forest. On June 29, 1944 the first Red Army scouts came to the edge of the woods. We waited for that day for 3 years, but few of us were able to see it.

The day we returned

Only when we were finally free, we truly realized how alone we were. Where should we go? That was the question that we all asked. Our town was burned, the Germans totally destroyed it when they retreated. How could we come to that place? How could we look at the faces of the gentile residents of the town who had assisted in our destruction? But something was pulling us. We had to go to the graves of our beloved. We needed to lie there and put our heads in the earth and cry. So we returned to our broken homes.

I will never forget the day we returned. When we approached the town, it looked like a war-zone. All around there was a barbed-wire fence and the town was full of tunnels and holes. There was no true battle there, but the tunnels were where the "Superior Race" had hid from the partisans. We entered Mydell Street and walked by the first house – Fiyashka's house. We walked crying, and with each step our hearts beat faster. These were moments where we didn't want to believe what occurred really occurred and that everything around us was taken from the land of the living. That we will never again meet anyone. Did everything really die? Could it be? Here in Mydell Street are we not going to see Leib Yakov, the glass-maker, with his smiley face and his shiny eyes? A little bit farther would my mother, father, brothers Yermiyau and Hillel, and my sisters Shaine and Myna come running as usual to greet us? And now we reached the huge cedar tree, our childhood playhouse. Will I not see the darling little Jewish kids of Sheveeshtzefole playing under his shade? I only had a few seconds of those memories, just a few seconds.

Very soon, we reached the two huge holes at the end of Mydell street, the valley of the killing… A burial for our beloved brothers and sisters. And here we stood on top of them on the day of victory – all depressed and broken.

[Page 230-233]

A Little Drop

by Yosef Friedman

Translated by Eilat Gordin Levitan

**Arka Alperovich, son of Reuben and Chiena nee Turov
with his grandmother and his great grandmother**

*The Torov family, in laws of the author,
Yosef Friedman, before the war
Rivka (Turov) Alperovich, Rachel, Arka Alperovich, Chaia-Fruma, Chalvina Turov*

The Red Army entered town and all the large homes were confiscated. The house of Nachama Risha (nee Gelman) Alperovich, and the house of Zalman Mendel (son of Cheikel Velvel) Alperovich, and also the home Shmuel (son of Yente) Spektor were among those confiscated, as well as the house of Ziskind (son of Shimon Alperovich), and the synagogue for the Mitnagdim.

A few of the town's residents were arrested by the Soviets and sent to Siberia. Dark shadows, but there was also some light during the rule of the Soviets. And we lived like this for more than a year and a half until the German invasion. This occurred on a Sunday. The Soviets immediately started conscripting the young people to serve, but they didn't have enough time to send them to join the battle. By Tuesday all of them were sent home. Since the main train station in Molodeczno had been bombed, from that day until Saturday there was no ruling authority in the area and some of the Christian villagers came to town to rob and loot. The most notorious were the villagers from Studyonka, and Starazi. This situation lasted for some days. The skies were filled with Soviet planes and German planes that chased them. I remember one Soviet plane that flew by, on fire, and then fell near the Baraseif, by Vileyka.

The Germans arrived and gathered all of us in the market. They made us stand in two lines, and they pointed their weapons at us. We thought our end would come here, and that we could not come out of this alive. Many of the non-Jewish residents of the town stood around and laughed, but then the German commander came out of the house of Rashka (daughter of Yehudah Alperovich and widow of Chazkel, son of Binia) Alperovich, and ordered us to choose a Judenrat. He gave some other instructions, such as that from then on we should put on our clothes a white patch in the middle of which we would have a letter J for Jew. From then on, every day brought new punishments, humiliations and new rules to make our lives more miserable.

We had to perform forced labor and to pay a ransom every day for our survival, in the form of gold, money, and other goods. During one of the coldest days, the Germans arrived from Vileyka. They kidnapped many Jews and ordered them to take their clothes off. Wearing only their underwear, they put them on a truck and drove them back and forth through the streets of the town. In order to save their lives, we had to give large sums of money. Otherwise, we were told, everyone would be killed.

At another time, Agov and Shernagovich, may their names be erased, decided to play a bloody game which ended with the murder of 13 Jews. Seven of them I later brought to a Jewish burial. Shmuel, son of Pini Tsipilovich; Yitzhak (Esther Zimmerman's son or husband?); Yoshua Limon; Baruch Kremer;, son of Mendel son of Ashka, the youngest brother of Nathan Zalman Alperovich (son of Reuben); Mendel Levin; and the last to be killed was our genius rabbi, the pure soul and pious Rabbi Moshe Aron Feldman, who suffered a horrible torture. They broke his arms and legs, and his whole body was covered with wounds. [Others that were killed that day: Shimon Gelman, wife Gita and their daughter Chana, Avramil Alperovich, Zisha the daughter of Abba Alperovich, and one other.]

On the eve of Purim of 1942, the last massacre of the Jews of Vileyka [the town neighboring Kurenets] occurred. Schatz, the head of the Judenrat in Kurenitz was ordered to arrange a forced labor camp for professional people to be taken to Vileyka. They came to me and told me that I should go there so I could put some furnaces in the barracks of the camp. I didn't want to go, but Schatz promised me that after I had completed the job he would let me go home. He didn't fulfill his promise and I had a difficult time in leaving Vileyka. It took many months, and it was only sometime in August, two weeks before the massacre in Kurenets, when I finally was able to escape from Vileyka.

It was three days before Rosh Hashanah when the massacre of our beloved town's residents occurred. I was with my wife and child, and we hid inside a deep hole that we had made in the garden behind our house. Above it there were rows of vegetables growing and you would never recognize that we had dug a hole there. When night came, we gathered together with Lazar Rod's, Yakov Kiva (Katz) and his wife and four children, and two grandsons of Shalom the Blacksmith. We ran through the meadow in the direction of Poken and arrived at the house of a Christian man in Novi Kurenets. He gave us half a loaf of bread and some onions and we entered the forest near Skabbe.

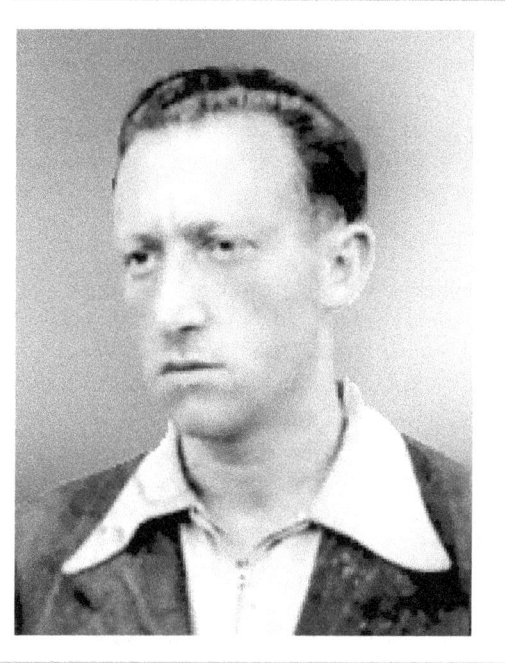

Moshe Alperovich

The next morning we encountered Yankel son of Orchik Alperovich, and Moshe son of Rashke Alperovich. We continued deeper into the forest and there we encountered the son-in-law of Mendel Dinnestein, Zadok Shevitz, his wife Rashka and their daughters Perla and Sarah. Late at night we arrived in the village Studyonka. We left the women and children in the forest and came to the first house and forced the residents to give us a basket filled with eggs, a little bit of cheese, and half a loaf of bread.

The next day we met Dania, the son of Chaim Avramil Alperovich, and together we entered the putzcha [a very thick forest] of Katlovtza. The men decided to return to Kurenets so we could bring some clothing for us and our children. Among the people who came with me were Lazar Rod', Yakov Kiva Moshe Alperovich (son of Rashke Alperovich), and Dania the son of Chaim Avramil Alperovich. We left late at night. We arrived in Pokken, but there the Germans were guarding the lumber mill that used to belong to Chaim Zokovsy, (killed with the 54 on Simhat Torah of 1941). The guards became aware of our presence and started shooting rockets to light up the area. We kept walking and falling on the ground. None of the rockets hit us and nothing happened, but we had to retreat and go to Novi Kurenets, in the north, in the direction of Halinova. We had to go on a very long detour, going north, then west near the village Litvinki in the direction of the big rock, near the big slaughterhouse. Finally we arrived at our homes…

When we returned to our houses we found them all destroyed[1], but some of the belongings that we had hidden very cleverly were not found and we were able to take them and return to Novi Kurenets, where we all met up as planned from the beginning.

I knew that there was a Christian man by the name Ramanovsky who had a pistol. I entered his home and asked him to give me his pistol but he lied to me and said that he did not have it and only a Pugatz (not a real pistol, something just to scare a person?), and he gave me that. We left and arrived at the forest. On the way we met with Israelke and his sister, the children of Netta Itza son of Chanan. We went through the village Varomnya and from the water well we took a bucket that was on top of it. When we arrived at Patlovka we filled the bucket with water and carried it on a pole until we were deep in the forest.

That evening we transferred to a new location near the village Budka. One day we started building huts to settle in, when all of a sudden we heard someone yelling. "Ketta tem" We became very scared and started running, but immediately we came back because we said to ourselves, "If we are to be killed it is better that we are with our families."

When we returned we realized that it was the partisans. One of them was Ivan from the village Andreyka. The second was from the Soviet Union. He was a very good-hearted person and he started consoling us, telling us that soon they would take all the women and children to the Soviet Union, while the men would stay here to fight the Nazi animals.

Shortly after, the partisan brigade "Revenge" arrived in the forest. I helped in some of their combat missions and also in getting food to the forest. The partisans collected all the Jews in the forest and most of them were sent east, but our group stayed in the area. Most of the hundreds of Jews who were sent east were not able to continue, and they returned to the forest in our area.

Winter came and we started building underground places to live. The ground was already frozen, which made the job very difficult. Shortly after we built the underground shelters, my two brothers-in-law (the brothers of my wife) arrived. They were Halvina Torov and Moshe Lazar Torov. They had just escaped from the Vileyka Ghetto. One night, they left for the villages Halinova, Litvinki, and Kuzmit, and took from the villagers all the cows that used to belong to the Jews of Kurenets. They slaughtered the cows and brought the meat to the forest.

Meanwhile, Yankel Orchik Alperovich joined the partisans and became a scout. He was an excellent soldier, he would come around riding a horse and scaring all the Christians in the area. After some time his brigade transferred farther east.

The day of the first blockade arrived. The Germans surrounded the forest. They swept back and forth and killed many of the Jews of Kurenets who were hiding there. Two of the women were caught alive. They were my sister-in-law (my wife's sister), Shaina Liba nee Torov Cheres[2], and also the wife of Avraham the Butcher.

Photograph taken in Natanya in 1957

From left to right: Efraim (son of Reuven Alperovich and Cheyna, daughter of Yakov Leib and Chaia-Fruma Turov),
Pesya (Peshka) Friedman (daughter of Chaja-Fruma), and
Yehuda Cheres (son of Shalom and Sheina Liba)

Pesia nee Turov Friedman (the second wife of the author): She was the only offspring of the Turov family who survived. She married the author, who lost his first wife, her older sister, during the holocaust. She helped him bring up the kids of her older sister. Here she is with the sons of two of her other sisters.

Yehuda Cheres wrote a book about his memories "The town is burning"

On that day, Israelke the son of Netka, and Yakov the husband Feyga Leah the daughter of Cyril, Chaim (the son of Chana nee Gurevitz and Elchanan Alperovich the Butcher), his wife and their little daughter were all killed. But their little son Leyzerke, who was only five years old, survived in the forest[3]. Moshes' mother; Rashka the daughter of Yehudah Alperovich, was found dead a few days later. She was sitting on a tree branch.

As the days of the blockade ended, a Christian villager came to the forest and pretended to be insane. Every question we asked him he said, "I don't know" and started making sounds of insanity. Eventually two partisans came to the area and started interrogating him. They found out he wasn't really insane and that he had been sent to the area by the Germans as a spy, so they executed him immediately.

After many days we transferred to the forest Zezaria. There were about 30 people with us. The forest was terribly cold and we had to build underground shelters once more. The location was next to a partisan brigade base, and amongst the partisans there was a guy from Glubokie named Yitzhak Blat. He had a heart of gold, but tragically he was killed during one of the missions.

The commander of this unit was a Russian by the name of Lonke Kozak. Lonke was a very dear man. He loved the Jewish people.

On one of the missions that took place near Kurenets, two of us joined them as scouts. Together with me was Shimon the son of Hilka, son of Netta Zimmerman [today Shimon is the head of the Kurenets Society in Israel]. When we returned from that mission, we heard the sound of gunfire. We entered Drucy and when the villagers saw us they looked at us very strangely. We went to the blacksmith so that he could adjust the horseshoes. He said that he had no materials to do it, and we felt again that there was something going on. The village Drucy was a long village, and when we arrived at the other side of the village, a Christian woman came out of one of the homes. She was the contact of the partisans. She told us that just a few minutes ago there had been German troops there and that they had left Sherematshitz. Immediately the partisans left and came to the forest to set up ambushes for the Germans. Shimon, a villager, and I went to the Hutarz (village homes) near the river Uzla to wait for them.

When evening came, some of the partisans returned. One of them had been killed. Shortly after the Germans established a police station in the village Talit, and this made us very worried. During that time, the commander of the partisans talked with one of the Christians from the village Startzi, and this Christian agreed to go to Vileyka and to bring information from the forced labor camp that still existed in Vileyka, where many from Kurenets were working. The Christian man kept going to Vileyka, where he'd get information and also bullets that Jews in the camp had stolen from the Germans and put inside a hollowed-out piece of wood.

One day, shortly before the Jews in Vileyka planned to escape, our Christian spy took the wood pieces with the bullet, and one of the Polish collaborator policemen came to him and told him to go with him. When the Jews saw that the Christian was walking with a policeman, they were sure that he had been discovered and that he was being led to jail. They panicked and everyone started to run away in the middle of the day. Only a few survived and were able to escape; most of the others were killed. Later on they found out that the policeman only wanted him to take his wife to the hospital.

These are just a few lines and a small drop from the ocean of blood and horrors that we experienced.

[Photograph – A naming ceremony for a street in Herzliya to be named for the Jewish community of Kurenets: Arie Fishbein, the grandson of the author with his cousin, Yehuda Cheres]

Translator's footnotes:

    1. I talked with Moshe Alperovich (first cousin of my grandfather, Meir Gurevitz) shortly before he passed away. Moshe told me about their escape and how his sister, Sara, left her two young boys sleeping in their beds. When he returned to Kurenets to check on them he found the beautiful boys dead. One was shot in his bed the other must have opened the door for the Germans, he was shot at the entrance to the house. When Moshe returned to the forest his mother made him promise that he should never tell about it to his sister, Sara. Moshe kept his promise and never told his sister. Moshe came to Israel in 1946 and his sister came to America about the same time. She lived near Los Angeles in an agricultural community (Chico or Chino) with other survivors from Kurenitz. She married and had one son. Sara and Moshe died a few years ago.

    2. Shaina Liba nee Torov Cheres was the mother of Yehuda. Her husband, Shalom and her four children survived. You could find their pictures at http://www.eilatgordinlevitan.com/kurenets/k_pages/cheres.html.

    3. The son of the brother of Chaim, Israel Alperovich, survived and served with the partisans and the Red Army. I called him in Israel to ask about his cousin Leyzerke . He told me that the child was put in an orphanage after the war. Before Israel left the Soviet Union he met with his cousin who was by then an adult.

[Page 234-243]

In The Luben Farm

by Nathan Alperovich son of Reuven ben Natan Zalman's

Translated by 17-year-old Jared Fleisher for his grandfathers.

1941

Our house stood at the edge of the swamp that spread near the back of the town's synagogues. We were a hard working family, with meager means of support. We owned a tiny house and one white goat that managed to sustain itself by chewing grass growing in the swamp. My youngest brother's chore was to ensure that the goat did not run away. Father was sent to work in the carpentry mill that prior to the war belonged to Chaim Zukovski. Although I was not yet sixteen, I had to partake in the forced labor, morning after morning I would arise proceeding dawn, put on my tfillin and pray. Next, I would eat something, usually porridge that my mother would boil for me in a little pan. Soon afterward, I would hastily go to the assemblage place for Jews who participated in the forced labor.

My initial assignment started immediately following the German's setting foot in Kurenets. I was sent to the old meat market and told to fix it so it could be adapted to contain the Russian POW's while they were being transferred to the West. We surrounded the yard with barbed wire, dug a deep cavity in the ground, and put immense barrels of water in the earth, to be later utilized by the POWs.

The first days passed in relative peace and father, who knew German due to the time of the German occupation in WWI, would discuss politics with the German soldiers. He would try to debate moral issues. though, their typical response would be, "Jew – shut your mouth. This is not World War One."

Eventually the POW's arrived. They came in colossal numbers. They pull in walking from Dolhinov, through the old avenue lined on both sides by ancient pine trees. They kicked up clouds of dust all surrounding them. They appeared like a gigantic herd of people. The Germans soldiers who were guarding them rode horses; they brandished whips and would constantly strike the POWs to dispatch them. The POWs clothes were torn and they could barely walk. They were completely exhausted. We were not aloud to make any contact with them. Even the trees of the old avenue seemed to be bowing as if to eulogize the POWs. We looked at them with eyes full of tears and with fearful hearts. Whenever one of them would bow to get an item from the ground, he would be immediately shot. The POWs that walked slowly or fell on the ground were also instantaneously murdered in the spot where they fell. The Jews would dig holes along the road to bury them. Most were buried on the side road directly after their assassination.

There were tables on both sides of the entrance to the temporary camp, on which was arranged a meager amount of aged bread. There were large pails abundant with stale concoction they termed "soup". For every six POWs, they would prepare one small loaf of bread. No dishes or utensils were given to them, therefor they were compelled to use their hats to scoop the soup. We tried to bring them canned foods and containers to eat the soup, when the Germans were not watching. The soup would be served to two people at a time, and the POWs would push each other to get to it. This provided a good opportunity for the Germans to strike them on their heads with their rifles.

On the outskirts of the camp stood many Christian villages, mostly Belarussian women who were trying to recognize relatives amongst the POWs. The village women brought food to give to the POWs, but the Germans would not let them approach the POWs. Consequently they stood from afar, looked on and cried.

Amongst the POWs, there were a great number of Jews, who served in the Red Army. The commander of the camp would walk around with his gun ready, and every POW he did not approve of, would be shot on the spot. I remember on one occasion, a POW kissed his feet, cried and begged for his life, all to no avail.

I was ordered to use a horse that was harnessed to a large pail of water, take it to the river and fill the pails with water. One time on my way back from the river, when my pail was full of water, I asked one of the villagers to throw the food she carried into the pail, promising her I would pass it to the POWs. The idea appealed to her and to the other Christian women who were standing there. They started throwing cheese and bread in the water. Twice I succeeded in transferring the food to the POWs, however on the third day the POWs pushed each other to get to the food and created a pandemonium. The German in charge realized it was my doing, he ran toward me yelling, "You bloody Jew."

He grabbed me by the collar and started shaking me. He brought me outside the gate to where a huge crowd of villagers was standing. I managed to slide out of his hands onto the ground, and when I was separated from him I crawled into the crowd and succeed to mingle and escape.

Instantaneously I went to the other side of the street and through the garden of Kuilic I ran to the forest by the river and there I hid until evening came. Then I stealthily returned home.

Following that day, I did not return to work at the POW camp. A short time later, I was reassigned to work on the Luben Farm. I was among approximately one hundred and fifty Jews. Luben was a vast agricultural farm that was famous in the area for the apple and pear orchards that the Jews used to lease prior to the war. One day, we were taken there in long lines by the local police. I walked in the same line as; Yankel, the son of Orchik Alperovich, Asher, the son of Yehoshua Alperovich, Pesach, the son of Finka Alperovich, Chanan, the son of Risha. During the walk, many of the villagers, who stood on the side of the road, holler insults at us. They would call, "It's time that you Jews stop being merchants, finally you got what you deserve! Its about time!"

It took us about an hour and a half to trudge to the farm. The main building in the farm was called "the castle" and was encompassed by enormous trees. There was a portal made of massive wrought iron and there was a school there. The homes around were sparkling in the sun and the trees were bright green, in contrast, we were in a very dark mood, in spite of the fact that we were still very young. Once we reached the gate we sat on the grass, we were told by the Germans what to do. The head of the farms was Kalashnikov and his assistant was Shilak. We were divided into small groups and sent to do miscellaneous jobs. There were German troops in the area, however at this time we had no contact with them.

One Jew from Kurenets, by the name of Dania Sosensky, was an acquaintance of the managers of the farm. He used to lease land from them prior to the war, therefore at this time they chose him to be our leader.

Chaiale Sosensky [daughter of Dania] and her brother

These were the last days of the summer, and the weather was starting to cool off. The heavens were clear and beautiful. Here below, amongst the medley of trees and gardens, summer remained in its perfect splendor. The trees were abundant with fruits, the harvest season had just ended, and forthwith was the season for potatoes.

I was placed with a crew that resided in a small oil factory. They brought us straw mats to lie upon at night. The next day we were awoken early and worked until dark. We had a short break for lunch, officially they only gave us a small amount of bread. However, the Christian people who worked in the yard brought us potatoes and milk. Donia Sosensky always managed to get us extra supplies.

I worked with Yisraelke the son of Nata Eetzi ben Chanan. Our job was to bring the potatoes from the field to the little factory to be formed to a raw material. I worked for one week and on Saturday, they took us back to Kurenets. On the second week, I stayed home and my father replaced me. A week later, I returned to work. When I returned, I remember that Chaim Yitzhak Zimerman walked next to me. He seemed extremely depressed and said, "We cannot hope for anything good from the Germans. Do you see the bushes here? This is where our bones will roll and there will be no one to bring us to burial. We must escape from here. We need to escape but I don't know where to. Yet of one thing I am certain, we need to escape soon."

From then on, he would urge us to escape. One day when we arrived in Luben, the Germans sent a troop of executioners to the farm. They demanded that Kalashnikov, the head of the farm, give them some of the workers to be murdered. They wanted to show us that they ruled us. Kalashnikov argued with them, saying that all workers were needed as it was the middle of the busiest part of the season. He told them to go to Kurenets where they could find "useless people."

The troop of executioners came to town in the afternoon. That day I returned to Kurenets and I was taken by the troop to shine their shoes. In town, there was a great fear. At nighttime, the police spread around town and imprisoned Jews that were suspected as communist sympathizers. The next day, four of the policemen went to Luben and took Pesach and Tevel, the sons of Finka Alperovitz, Arka the son of Reuven Alperovich, Chaim Yitzhak Zimerman, Tuvia Sosensky, Charles Gelman, and others. While they were walking, Arka Alperovich told the rest, "We are taken to be killed. We must jump the police and take their weapons."

Arka Alperovitz in the middle of the middle row

The rest of the people thought that it was too dangerous and they still held out hope that they didn't seized them to be killed. Particularly since the policemen who took them were friendly to them. Thus, they refused to join him. When they reached Myadel Street, across from the house of Tayba, the grandmother of Arka there was a small bridge with a little tree growing next to it. At that point, Arka jumped on one of the policemen, hit him on the head, and started running to the fields behind the homes. Another policeman ran after him and eventually killed him. That was the day that they killed the fifty-four Jews of Kurenets, accusing them of being Communists.

That day I was cutting wood. As we returned to Kurenets, at the distance of two kilometers from Vileyka, we met with the band of executioners returning from Kurenets. They were riding bicycles, their sleeves were rolled up their arms. Each one was holding clothes and other belongings of the murdered Jews. They looked at us strangely and we immediately realized that something horrible had happened in town. Our hearts died inside.

We quickly returned home. When we entered Vilejka Street, there was deathly silence all around. There was not one breathing soul to be seen. Finally we met a Christian woman and she told us about the slaughter in town. I continued thorough the gardens. When I reached home, I found my mother crying Gitel Kopelovitz sister and Shacna Stoler were sitting with her. Sobbing they informed me of the entire barbarous event.

After Simchat Torah, I went back to Luban. At first I worked at the potatoes field collecting potatoes, Policemen would watch us while riding their horses and if they had found that we left one potato on the ground they would whip us mercilessly. Beatings were daily occurrence. On one occasion Shilak ordered Yisraelke (Nata's son) to restrain a horse. The horse succeeded to escape, Yisraelke was whipped, and shoved to the ground, Shilak stepped on him and kicked him until he fainted surrounded by a pool of his blood.

When we were finally done with the fields I was sent to work in the cowshed, I was strong and fast and most of the time the managers were happy with my work. Time past and partisans started organizing in the district, the Germans were very concerned and sent a lot of reinforcement to guard the area. One time when they walked their routine patrol around the farm, they met with a partisan blockade. Two Germans were killed and there were many wounded. We were very worried that the Germans will take revenge on us, the Jewish farm workers.

A few days passed and reinforcement of thirty soldiers was sent to the farm. They came to visit all the farming projects, a few soldiers with an officer came to the cowshed were I worked, the place was sparkly clean and very neat. They greeted us with respect, complemented our job, gave us some cigarettes and left.

During that winter, my youngest brother was murdered with twelve other Jews by the drunken Kurenitz policemen. After the calamitous event, I would visit my distressed family whenever I got permission. Shilak gave me permission to go with him in a buggy on the last evening of Passover, 1942. I spent the night at my house in Kurenitz and very early in the morning I started on my way to Luban, I was suppose to start work at 6 am. I took with me a supply of latkes, the only food we ate during that Passover. (We had no matzos that year)

It was a splendid spring morning, the snow melted and the earth was black and seemed to spread forever. Here and there, it would be sprinkled with shiny white dots of snow, every thing was teeming with life; birds chirping, trees flowering, but my heart was so sullen and melancholy. I was thinking of my beloved brother, How I so missed him, how dispirited was my family now. I took off the boots I borrowed from my father, they were too big and made my walk difficult. I tied the boots to one side of a stick and my food to the other side. My yellow Jewish star was dirty and could hardly be distinguished.

I was already out of the forest, almost in Luban, when I saw German soldiers riding bicycles, coming toward me. I was walking in the middle of the road as Jews were suppose to, there were villagers that were going in the same direction as I was, when the German reached them they started yelling "Jew, Jew". They pointed at me and since they could not speak German, they made signs with their fingers showing curly pias'.

The Germans observed me and continued on their way, I was very surprised that they did not stop me. (Jews were not allowed to leave their homes without supervision) I continued on my way, when I was fifty meter distant from them I heard the sound of a whistle, I pretended I did not hear it and continued walking. Both sides of the road had wide-open fields and nowhere to hide. I kept thinking of the Jews that a few days earlier were riding with a farmer from Litvinki and when the Germans encountered them on the road, they ordered the Jews to get off and killed them on the spot. I was certain that my destiny is to be killed here and now.

I heard a second whistle, I knew it makes no sense to ignore it. I turned around facing the Germans, they had stopped on the road and were waiting for me. They stood in an area adjacent to the forest. I started walking towards their direction, As soon as I came close they hollered "Are you a partisan? What do you have there, food for the partisans?

My heart was beating hard and fast. Somehow I gathered the courage to reply, I said with a wavering voice; "I am working at the Luban farm, last night I went home to get some clean clothes and now I am returning to my job"

They asked for my working card and after I showed it to them. They started interrogating me about my job, however luck was with me that day, one of the German soldier remembered me form a visit to the cowshed. He asked; "are you the child who is working with that red head guy?" then he turned to the other Germans and assured them; "the kid is doing a very good job, the child does a nice job"…

At that point, we were surrounded by local Christians who were looking at the scene with exited expression on their face. One village woman yelled to her friend that was leaving "don't go, wait a minute very soon they are going to kill a Jew, you must come here and see!" The German officer said " if he is a good worker we must release him, he needs to hurry to work"

I arrived to Luban, my body was shaking all over and my teeth were shattering. From that day on I made a decision to never walk alone.

The next weeks passed somewhat peacefully, One day a partisan troop arrived in Luban, the first thing they did was to seize the flock from the pasture. They tied the shepherd loosely so he was able to free himself and return to the farm. He was immediately arrested because the Germans suspected that he collaborated with the underground. Rumors spread in the farm that the Jews would be sent to dispatch the herd, they said the Germans were afraid of the partisans, however they knew that the partisans would not combat the Jews. We were both worried and exited, as it turned out the Germans must have realized we would stay with the partisans in the forest, so they changed their mind.

At the end of August, 1942, I was transferred out of Luban back to Kurenitz, the partisans were terrorizing the Germans by putting explosives on the train tracks. Both sides of the tracks bordered thick forests, which made it difficult and dangerous for the Germans to patrol the area. The Germans decided to cut all the trees that grew by the tracks. They brought immense number of Jews to do the job. I worked with a crew from Kurenitz, in the same section worked a very large group of men, Jewish survivors of annihilated shtetls in the Baranovitz district. The Germans brought them here to be utilized as slaves. Their predicament was horrible, they resided in the labor camp in Vileyka and received extremely meager amount of food. They would be shot on the spot whenever they would attempt to talk to any one of us. They worked from early in the morning until late at night and had very bad sanitary condition in their camp, many died from starvation and disease. Our hearts were crying inside seeing the miserable situation of our Jewish brothers. All we could do for them was to give them some of our food, food that was not plentiful for us either. Truly we could not even give it to them; we just left it on the tracks in hope that they would grab it while working. Usually they would come to collect the wood after we cut it, so with the wood they would collect the food we left for them, and it sustained them for a while.

At the beginning of September 1942 I came to Kurenitz, the purpose of the visit was to argue my mother's case with the Judenrat, who's duty was to dispatch the Jews to different jobs. I worked in the Luban farm, my father was sent to work in the carpentry mill, my sister was sent to work in the Vileyka labor camp. Now, my sick and spiritually crushed mother, who was in deep mourning for her youngest son who was murdered that year, was sent to work. They demanded that she would remove brush from the train tracks area.

I felt deep resentment toward the Judenrat, so now I decided to let them know how I feel. I approached Sina from Myadel, who was a very vocal member of the Judenrat. I told him "it's unfair that many families don't partake in the forced labor at all, they just sit idle in Kurenitz, yet my entire family is working like slaves". I continued, "farther more, my mother needs to stay home so she will cook dinner for father when he gets home after a long hard day of work". When I saw the negative expression on Sina face, I immediately suggested that I should replace my mother at her job by the tracks.

Sina completely rejected my plea and started yelling at me. I became very upset and said; "If this is the way you see things, I refuse to participate in the hard labor force- I will not go to Luban!"

He yelled; "if you won't go to Luban, we will take you there by force, you super man! We will bring the police and they will take you!"

"Fine" I said, "send the police to take me, I have nothing to lose anyway! I just want you to know that I am not going to work there out of my free will!

I went on my way and stopped at the house of Shachna Stoler, Shachna had a bathhouse on his property. Moments later Sina came running, he was screaming "You must immediately depart for Luban. The rest of the people left already!"

I replied "I will only go if you release my mother from the forced labor troop." At that moment mother returned from her forced labor duties. She started crying and told me "go my son, go. Don't look for justice in times like these. Anyway, it would be better if each one of us worked in a different area, this way maybe one of us will be lucky and will survive!"

I spend the night at home and the next morning I left for Luban together with Yisraelke the son of Sarka from Kosita Street.

I hugged my dear mother and said goodbye, never imagining that I would not see her again.

As soon as we arrived in Luban, we were sent to work in the fields. We worked there the entire Monday and Tuesday. Wednesday morning I was sent with a horse and buggy full of hay to deliver it to the barn that set on the main road. It was extremely foggy morning I could not see a thing in front of the horse. I worked together with a guy from Smorgon. We were done taking off one load of hay and I was just about to depart for the fields to get a second load when a child approached us.

The child was a son of a farmer from Luban, he asked me if I wanted to buy some tobacco, I answered that I had no money, he appeared perplexed, as if he was considering telling me something. After a short while he asked in a hesitant voice; "Are you from Kurenets?" the way he was asking, his voice and even the way he stood made me very anxious, it was as if he was keeping a horrible secret.

"What happened in Kurenitz?" I yelled in anguish. "Nothing happened " he replied in a frightened tone. I held him by his collar he seemed scared, he quickly said; "My brother walked to Kurenitz this morning and he was not allowed to enter, all around the town there were policemen and Germans. From afar he could see something was burning".

I immediately knew that this was the day of our town slaughter, the day that we all so feared would come. I did not know what to do, I wanted to scream, I wanted to run there. All I could do was to cry. For one minute, I considered taking the horse and escaping to the forest, however I realized that I must tell the other Jews from Kurenets about the tragic event. I returned to the farm and saw Donia standing outside our living quarters, he was cooking lunch on a fire pit, for the entire crew. I told him of what I have heard, however he refused to believe my story.

By lunchtime, we found out that it was true, none could eat, we just sat there and cried, we all decided to escape that night. We returned to work to not arise any suspicion that we are planning something. The Christian workers looked at us while whispering to each other, their eyes were full of pity.

At nighttime we returned from work and planed to escape but soon realized it was impossible since the Germans brought extra people to watch us.

Early in the morning two Jews came running from Kurenitz, one was Chava, the daughter of Sara- Elka, she told us that she hid in the storage building that Kanterovitz used for his enterprise of "shmates". She hid there for twenty-four hours. The other person was Nachum Raginholtz he was originally from Rakov but moved to Kurenitz during the war. Nachum hid with other Jews in the attics of the synagogue. They told us of what they knew about the calamity.

We were all moved from our living quarters at the school to the attic at the factory. That evening the policemen came from Kurenitz, they set with us and told us detail of what had occurred in Kurenitz during the slaughter. Some times, they were somber and serious, other times they were mocking and making fun of us. They told us about Chaiale Sosensky, Donia's daughter. The policemen knew her well, she used to work at the restaurant that they ate at. They claimed that they gave her a choice to save herself, however she answered that the town's fate is her fate. They told us of the speech she made. She cursed the German murderers and she prophesized that judgment day will come soon and then they will have to pay for their evil did.

Chaiale Sosensky

They told us about Zusia Benes and his wife lea Gurevitz Benes, an older couple that when they realized the Germans were coming to get them, they burned their home and jump in the fire.

They told us of the Jews who were dressed with their talits, they jumped in the fire saying a prayer before the Germans had a chance to shoot them.

They said that Chaim Sozkover jumped on the policeman that came to get him and started choking him but the other policemen shot him on the spot.

We sat there all broken, we could not stop crying.

The next day Yankale, the son of Artzik Alperovitz, came to the farm area with other partisans. While the other partisans were waiting in the forest, Yankale looked for his younger brother Shmuel who was a shepherd, Shmuel was with the cows in the pasture. When he found him, he told all the Christians who worked in the fields near the pasture that the partisans would kill them if they'll tell anything to the Germans. He took his brother with him. The Christian shepherd, who worked with his brother, kept the secret the entire day. And when he returned with the cows that evening he told the Germans that Shmuel just walked away, saying he was going to Kurenitz to look for his mother.

Now I should tell about Yankeleh heroic stand that occurred a year earlier.

Kurenets, 1960
Artzik Alperovitz [middle row on the right]
with some of his surviving children and grandchildren

Yankeleh's father, Artzik Alperovitz, was a horse dealer. He was a minor dealer buying and selling or exchanging one horse at the time. When the Soviets came to our area in 1939 they declared him a "merchant" (merchants were considered to be enemy of the 'people"). As a punishment, he was sent to Siberia.

On the day of the slaughter of the fifty-four, a day that the Germans claimed was solely to be rid of communists in our town, Merrill Alperovich (Artzik's wife), and all her children were taken to be killed. When the parade of the Jews, who the Germans took to be slaughtered, passed trough Kosita Street, Merrill and the younger children managed to escape and hide in one of the gardens. Yankeleh and one brother were taken to the killing field near the Jewish cemetery. While Yankeleh was already standing in the pit and the German officer was ready to yell "fire!", Yankeleh ask the officer that was in charge of the killing if he can ask a question. The officer allowed one question, Yankeleh said; "before my execution I have a final request, I would like to know for what crime have I received a death sentence? Is it because I am Jewish? Or is it because of a suspicion that I am a communist?"

Yankeleh brave stand in his grave, surprised the officer, he answered; "you are about to be killed, as the rest of the people here, for being a communist!"

"If this is the case against me" said Yankeleh "I would like you to ask the many Christian villagers who are standing here, to bear witness. They can all testify that in the Soviets' days the communist broke our family and sent my father to Siberia. Having had such bad experiences how could I be a communist? The officer turned to the villagers that were standing there with a shocked look on their faces, they all nodded their heads in agreement.

The officer said, " if this is the case you are free to go"; Yankeleh said, "I ask that my sick young brother who is as innocent as I am should be released" – The officer must have liked Yankeleh stand, he let both of them go. Shortly after the brother died of natural causes and Yankeleh joined the partisans and became renowned for his bravery and commitment. When the war ended, he received many high commendations and medals.

Back in the Luban farm, after Shmuel's escape I was assigned to take Shmuel's job as a shepherd. Shortly after a Christian man from Studyonka by the name of Ivan, came to us (Jews) he gave us a letter from Yankeleh in the letter he urged us all to escape and come to the forest.

We liked the idea of escaping, but to accomplish it with the entire crew seemed impossible. Single people could have escaped easily, however we all felt responsible for each other. We knew that the Germans would take revenge on the Jews that stayed.

Some of us were reluctant to leave a place that had relatively decent conditions for a life of fugitives in the forest. Still most of us knew that we are not safe here, so we all came with ideas, we decided to jump the policemen who routinely came to visit us during nighttime. Some of our guys were very strong we could easily disarm the police and take their weapon with us to the forest. Our plans of escape kept being delayed.

One day I received a package from my sister who worked in the Vileyka camp. A Christian woman brought the package. In the package, I found a shirt, one pair of pants, a jacket that the police would wear, it was missing all the buttons. In addition, I received a note. The note said that father was in Vileyka but she (my sister) is not able to see him. She asked if I knew where our mother was. At this point, I did not know, later I found out that my mother ran to our designated hiding place in Shachna Stoller's bathhouse on the morning of the slaughter. She was shot while running. Father who was a strong man was taken that day to Vileyka to work for the SD.

While I was working in the pasture two Christian men kept urging me to escape to the forest. One was an old farmer from Luban who kept asking why I was still here. He pointed out the way to the Pushtza, the deep in the forest hideout of the partisans and many Jews. He gave detailed instructions how to get there, I said nothing but I kept repeating to myself the information. The other Christian man was the shepherd who worked with me, he was always very concerned for me, and he was constantly telling me I should escape.

The rainy autumn turned to winter, the ground had frost in the morning I had no shoes and I was walking around barefoot, a Christian man felt sorry for me and gave me a pair of shoes with wooden soles.

One freezing Sunday morning, Donia Sosensky stood outside our living quarters, cooking lunch for the crew on a fire pit.

*Dania Sosensky with wife, Chana
and their surviving children after the war*

Kalashnikov, Shilak and the gardener passed by, they were drunk and in a generous mood typical of people who just started drinking and the wine had soften their hearts. They asked Donia why he was cooking outdoors. Donia realized that this was a great opportunity to help the cause of escape. He said that in our quarters there are no facilities for cooking. He immediately asked if we could be moved to the "inn" since it had a few empty rooms and cooking facilities. They were first hesitant, but after a short time gave him permission. Donia immediately notified us. We took our meager belonging and moved. There was no watch during the day on Sunday since the policemen were sleeping after their nightly watch. We knew that we must escape tonight for two reasons; The inn was ideally located outside the farm near the main road, in addition, the Christian people seemed drunk, and a bit confused on that day. We arranged the rooms in the inn as if we were planing to live there for a long time, so no one would suspect that we are planing to escape tonight.

Donia's wife, Chana baked bread the entire day to be later taken on the road. Motka from Molodechno worked every night in the factory until almost midnight. When he found out that we were planing to escape that night, he refused to go, fearing that we will leave without him. He said that he was sick and he could not go to work.

Donia approached me, he explained the situation, and asked me if I would replace him. I knew that I would have to work until eleven at night, then a policeman will take me to the Christian mechanic sleeping place in the farm. If I were to walk alone in the farm after it turned dark, I would be most likely shot. I agreed to go with one condition, that under no circumstance were they to leave without me. Donia agreed.

I went to work, I cut wood and put it in the furnace, I brought water from the well and put them in the boiler. A few moments before 11 I fell to the ground holding my stomach curling up, shaking and screaming as if I was in great pain.

The two policeman who were watching me, asked; "What is the matter with you?" As if with the last of might, I whispered that, I have horrible stomach pains.

One of the drunken policemen said mockingly "I will shoot you with a bullet and then the pain will subside". I begged them to let me walk to my room to get medication, and to not force me to sleep at the designated place where I would be in pain for the entire night, unable to get medication. They said; "Go to your room if you want to, anyway you would be shot on your way there". It was a very dark night, a rainy and snowy night. I crawled all the way to the fence. I jumped the fence by the road to Vileyka and ran across the road and hid in a ditch, waiting a few minutes, to make sure that no one was following me. When I realized that no one was pursuing me, I decided to check the place to make sure there was no German patrol in the vicinity. I got out of the ditch and walked in the fields in a distant of a few dozen meters, then I returned to the main road and walked towards the inn. I carefully checked that there was no watch, patrol or blockade around the inn. When I found out that there wasn't, I entered the inn.

It was close to midnight, our room was pitch dark. I felt in the dark, I soon realized that everyone was asleep, they all woke up when I touched them. The windows were covered with blankets so we would be able to light a match without being seen from the outside. Everything was already packed. We had saws, axes and other tools that we used in our jobs. We took everything with us. I carried an ax and a package that belonged to Donia and we started walking.

It took us three hours to reach the house of Ivan the Christian man from Studyonka who was helping the Jews, when we got there, we felt much freer.

He took us to the forest. Months past, and one evening we came to the village Tallatz. When we entered one of the homes, we met the Christian mechanic from Luban. He immediately recognized me, he joyfully kissed and hugged me saying, "You tricked the police. You truly tricked the police". He told me that immediately following our escape, early in the morning, many SS policemen arrived from the Vileyka headquarters to capture us to be killed.

[Page 244-253]

By the nails of the Eradicator

by Rivka Gvint
daughter of Sima nee Meltzer and Zalman Gvint

Translated from Hebrew by Gil Gorev

*In honor of his grandfather Gershon Gurevich and his family
who spent two years with Rifka hiding in the forest*

When the Bolsheviks entered Kurenitz in 1939, I submitted an application to become a nursery school teacher. I had just graduated that year from a Seminar for teachers in Vilna. The board of culture and education in Vileyka turned down my application. The reason for that was that at the time, there was a tremendous shortage of upper grades teachers, consequently I, as most other teachers in the area, was sent to a crash course of Russian and Belarussian studies. As soon as I was done with my studies, I was appointed the temporary school principal, in a four grades school, in the village Kalin, three and one half kilometers away from Kurenitz.

The farmer who had taken me in his carriage for my new job started a conversation with me. When we were nearly in Kalin, he enlightened me of what was awaiting me in Kalin. He told me that the village residents were extremely distressed with the idea that a Jew would be responsible for the education of their Christian children. Furthermore they did not accept the appointment peacefully; they sent a committee of the village citizens to protest to the board of education. They demanded that the Soviets send a Christian replacement.

Therefore, I started my job in a hostile and mistrusting environment. However, I came to work with an abundance of energy and with utmost commitment. After a short time the students flourished and greatly advanced in their studies. When the students became attached to me, the parents changed their attitude towards me too. By the end of the year, our bond was so strong that they suggested that I teach permanently, in spite of the fact that the old teacher had come back. Now they sent a letter to the office of education demanding to designate me a permanent teacher in their village.

I was a teacher in Kalin for one more year. In June, when the school year ended, I went to my parents' house in Kurenets to acquire some rest during the summer vacation. As it turned out, I didn't get any relaxation that summer.

On June 22, 1941, the Germans invaded Russia. Fear and hysteria spread rapidly amongst the Jewish population. We understood well the extent of the war, since Kurenitz was a central gathering station for the Red Army in the first few days. The town was teeming with soldiers day and night.

Rumors spread that the Germans were very close. Minsk was exploding and soon the Soviet workers, who were sent from Russia to Kurenitz two years prior, (before 1939 Kurenitz was part of Poland) started running away east, toward the Old Russian border.

It took one night for them to collect their belongings and run.

My parents' home was divided after the Soviets came, in one part lived a clerk with the NKVD and his family, in another part lived the head of the police. His family at that point was vacationing in Minsk, he was so busy with police matters that when he received the order to leave, he had no time to gather his belongings.

Many left town toward the east. Some went by foot, others by transportation. They used trucks, trains that departed from Vileyka, carriages, riding horses and bicycles, – anyway they could distance themselves from the approaching enemy.

The town's streets were awash with action and pandemonium. Young people carrying luggage scurried from one street to the next looking for some means of transportation. All around you would hear cries of good-byes and words of desperation. I wanted to run east, however my heart did not let me leave my parents behind. I considered taking them with me but I knew that this was an impossible journey for them. I consulted with the head of the police who was leaving that day, he assured me that he would return the next day and inform me of the situation on the road. Meanwhile he said that I should not panic, I should wait in town for a few more days. He did return the next day and told me that there were rumors that some Germans dressed as Red Army soldiers parachuted in the area and we should be careful when we talk to strangers. Minsk was already occupied by the Germans, the head of the police left and didn't return. In fact, the town was left with no ruling authority.

Most of the Jews, who ran away, returned to town, some found the roads blocked. The Germans preceded others. Great fear spread amongst the Jews. We all remembered the scary days prior to the Soviets' entrance to town in 1939, days where the town was left with no one who governed, and the villagers came to rob. And if it happened prior to the Soviets, we were sure it would happen on a much larger scale when the anti-Semite Germans were approaching.

To our surprise, the Christian inhabitants of our town decided to help the Jews; they organized a patrol to prevent the villagers from entering town. They asked us to join them in the effort to save the town from the approaching pillagers. We soon realized that they were doing it not for the love of 'Mordechai", when the Soviets ran away, they left a lot of supplies behind. The Christian inhabitants did not want to share the supplies with out-of-town pillagers. Therefore at the town outskirts there were voluntary citizens patrol, some were armed with rifles. They let none enter town.

The Germans already entered most of the towns in our area; we were amongst the last. Most of the Jews hid in their homes but some were curious, they stood outdoors when the Germans arrived. The first to reach town was a unit riding motorcycles. They opened the potrebsyoz storage buildings and the cooperatives and distributed the merchandise amongst the local residents. Right behind them, a large group of soldiers entered the town. An order was immediately announced; "all weapons that are held by local citizens must be brought to the field police at once". When two Jewish cousins (both named Shimon Zimerman), who were just done with their watch as the Germans arrived, returned their weapons, the Germans imprisoned them. We were all very fearful for them since they had just vanished! Two weeks passed and then a villager told their family that they were murdered on the day they were arrested.

Jews who held high positions during the Soviet days were now very fearful of reprisals. The men, who did not succeed in escaping to Russia, searched for hiding places. My father hid Leib Charnas above our room in the attic right next to the Rabbi minyan. He was in hiding there until his family was able to arrange something else for him. The Germans ordered the Jewish men to gather in the town center, there they were told of the new rules and limitations. All Jews had to partake in the work force without any monitory compensation. We were from now on, as livestock, only allowed to walk in the middle of the road, no sidewalks for us. Every Jew older then sixteen had to put a sign that he was a Jew on his clothes. The sign had to be seen and recognized from afar. First, we had to tie a white ribbon on our sleeves with the letter "J" for "Jew". Then a patch replaced it with "J" on our chests. Later it was a patch with a Jewish star. At the end, it was a yellow Jewish star on both the front and the back. Any gathering of more then three people at the time was disallowed. No contact with the Christian population was permitted. Disregarding any of these rules would cause very harsh punishments. Of the kind of punishments they were talking about we had a clear idea. Shmuel Gurevich and Zalman Mendel son of Cheikel Velvel Alperovich were amongst the well to do Jews in town in the Polish days. When the Soviets entered Kurenitz in 1939, they confiscated their properties. Both men and their families moved to the shtetl Sol. When the Germans invaded the men decided to return to Kurenitz, the men came first to check the situation. They arrived and decided to go back to Sol and transfer their families to Kurenitz. On their way the Germans caught them and killed them on the spot. Travel by Jews was not permitted except for the places that the Germans were ordering them to go.

Particularly devastating for us was the order prohibiting any contact with the Christians. Since we were not being compensated for our work, we needed to barter for food. The farmers didn't need us now; they were well off from the properties that the escapees (both Soviets and Jews) left behind. The homes and rooms of the escapees were broken. Locks, doors and windows were destroyed; all their possessions were stolen. Even the door handles were taken. This was the fate of the part of our house were the former head of the police used to live.

There were farmers who disregarded the threats and continued, out of friendship, to help the Jews. My family also had such righteous Christian friends, and amongst the kindest of them was the Smetinko family that we knew from the days of Polish rule. At the time of the Soviet rule, I met them again in the village Kalin, where I worked as a teacher. So as soon as the Germans entered the town, Mr. Smetinko and his daughter came to our house with food and were very concerned for us. When the situation worsened, especially after Simhatoa killing, Smitenko put his own life in danger and came to our house to comfort us. One day he came with a suggestion that we move to his village in his new apartment, where I used to live when I was a teacher. He suggested it without asking for any valuables in return, which was so unusual at the time that most Jews gave their valuables to friendly farmers, and many of them were later turned over to the Germans by these same farmers. But Smetinko, who received nothing from us, tirelessly tried to help us through all the days of the German occupation.

The only food we were able to obtain was a little bread that we received for our hard labor. Two hundred and fifty grams was given to each soul. My first job was at a community center, where the German POW patrol lived. The camp was situated on a yard that had previously been the meat market. Pokenn village on one side, and the fields of Dr. Schostekowitz on the other side bordered it. The yard was fenced in by barbed wire, and watchtowers with searchlights were at each corner. There were 30 of us who were sent there to clean and wash clothes. When the German soldiers left for training or to receive new POWs, we would clean their rooms and clean their laundry. Then we would peel potatoes and prepare bread for the POWs. Originally we didn't know who was going to eat the bread and we did as we were told, cutting the bread into five equal pieces, which meant two hundred grams for each slice. But when we realized this bread was given to the POWs, we were full of pity and we wanted to do something for them. So we disregarded the rules and we started cutting the bread into four pieces, so that each would get a little more. But most of the time we would get caught and were forbidden from doing this. From the potatoes we would make soup that was very watery and tasteless. Sometimes we managed to put a few pieces of dry fish that we found in the Soviet storage area, but this was a very rare occasion.

The Germans would beat the POWs with rubber sticks till they bled. Germans that were not able to find sticks would hit the POWs with their rifles, knives, or whatever they could find. The POWs came through the little town of Retzka, the rest in the meat market for one night, and in the morning they would continue on their way to Vileyka. At the entrance to the camp, the German soldiers stood in two lines and each POW would be beaten till he bled. If there was a sick or wounded POW that would fall on his march or would lean on his friend, they would double the beatings, and many times they would kill them on the spot.

We, the Jews, stood near the POWs. We were very closely watched and were told to give each POW a piece of bread. If we noticed that the Germans were not paying attention, we would give the POWs the breadcrumbs that we collected after the cutting of the bread, or we would gather the breadcrumbs at the edge of the table so the POWs could take them themselves. When we were caught we were blamed for our negligence and we were beaten very severely, but even more so they beat the POWs that were caught doing this. In two boilers that were standing outside, other people made soup for a few hundred people. Altogether they would put in three to five containers of potatoes.

Some prisoners had little empty cans, but some didn't have even that, so they had to forego the soup. Some would take their hats and put the soup in them, eating from that. Each day they would march from 50 to 80 kilometers, lasting for weeks. They were tired and depressed, and many died on the way. The Germans murdered those who were weak and malingering. The nights were cold, and many of them did not have anything warm to wear. Many of them threw away their coats when they had originally attempted to escape imprisonment, or during the long marches as their coats made the walk more difficult. The reason why many of them let go of their coats was that you could see their rank insignia. Some who had high rank did not want the Germans to know about it. Most of their shoes were torn from their marches, and they could hardly sleep at night from the cold. Sometimes, before night came, the Germans would give them a few pieces of wood to make bonfires, and those few pieces of wood caused big fights among the POWs. Sometimes it even made them kill one another. A few POWs tried to escape during the night, but they almost always failed. When the Germans caught them they were killed on the spot. Early in the morning they were kicked out of the yard and make them march to Vileyka. When they left, the Jews of the town would bury the dead and clean the yard for the next transport.

After a while I was sent to another place, to the Luban farm. Prior to the war the Luban farm was a model farm. When the Germans entered, they sent us to work in the cowshed and in the fields. This work was not too difficult, and the farmers treated us well. But, after a while the situation of the women worsened. There was a troop of German soldiers in Luban, and during the day they didn't interfere with our jobs, but at night they would bother the women. They slept in a separate house, when it turned dark we locked the doors and the windows and tried to look dirty and ugly. We slept in shifts, some slept and some stood guard. In the morning we would all be tired from the fearful, sleepless night.

I only worked there for one week, but it left a memorable impression on me because during Simha Torah, the Germans came to Luban and took a few healthy, strong men to be killed with the 54 martyrs of our town; killed because the Kurenets police identified them as Communist sympathizers.

In the police force were the trash of the Christian community; especially infamous was the policeman Berzinjuk. Before the Germans entered the area, we hardly knew him. He was illiterate, a slob, cruel and completely ignorant. During the Soviets' time, despite the trend of lowly members of society receiving high positions, he remained a lowly watchman. But now was his chance to take revenge, especially on the Jews. In a very short time everyone reviled his name. He made every Jewish heart fearful.

One day, during early morning hours, a woman entered our home. She was dressed like a villager and with her came a boy about fourteen or fifteen. I came to greet her and I realized that it was Karlova, a Christian woman and the wife of the police chief during the Soviet days. She had lived with us back then. The boy was her brother. When the war started, she was visiting her parents in Minsk and was left there penniless. Now she came to Kurenets to see whether anything was left of her belongings. We had a long talk during which she told us of the situation of the Jews in Minsk, locked in a ghetto. I told her of the situation in Kurenets and informed her that her Christian neighbors Yolka and Melvina had robbed all her belongings. While we were talking, Berzinjuk entered the house. He recognized her when she passed by the police station and without saying anything to anyone he came to arrest her. She begged for pity, but to no avail. I approached him and begged him to let her sleep in our home and to let her return to Minsk the next morning. In return I promised to give him suits that belonged to my father. After a little bit of bargaining he agreed and left.

The next day, early in the morning, Karlova left Kurenets. Many days later, the partisans murdered Berzinjuk. Another bloodsucker was Shernegowicz. He was from Kasinjewitz village. He was the very first to look for hiding places that were used by the Jews. Every Jew that he met in the street he would beat up, and sometimes for no reason he would kill him. The blood of many Kurenets residents stained his hands. Whenever we found out that he was approaching, all the Jews would fear for their lives and run to their hiding places.

My father and Nathan Gurevich had a factory that made soap, shoe polish, ink, and other chemicals. For that reason they didn't have to do hard labor, as the Germans needed them. They were allowed to continue factory production. One time, the factory in the next town, which made similar products, produced defective ink, so they ordered my father to go to Vileyka and correct the problem. On his way, he met Shernegowicz. Although my father had licenses and permits to go to Vileyka, Shernegowicz was unable to read the documents so he tore them up and beat him mercilessly. Still, when he came back alive, we were very happy.

There were almost no Jews left in Vileyka; most of them had been killed by that point. So the Germans had no laborers. Now they took Jews from Kurenets and made them live in Vileyka. At the beginning everyone in Kurenets was fearful of moving to Vileyka, as it was known that this was the town where the killing started. But slowly we realized that danger was coming from every direction, and some felt it would be better to separate the family to many different spots so someone would survive. I still remember Pesja Nee Kastrol Alperovich, the wife of Mikhail, she would say, "I prefer that some of my children be in Vileyka and others in Kurenets. Maybe we will be blessed that someone will survive. We kept hearing about slaughters that occurred in the neighboring towns, we heard that a few survivors had reached our town, and heard that others who were in hiding sent letters via Christians to their relatives in Kurenets. We realized that our chances of survival were minute, and we knew that the destruction of our town was coming.

Our Rabbi, Moshe Aron Feldman, the pride and glory of our town, his poor soul left his body after many tortures. His body was found in the market with broken arms and legs. Each day, there were new punishments and tragedies of Joban proportions. One Jew was killed because he didn't have gold for the Germans, and another Jew was killed because they found that he was hoarding gold. One day, old Leib Matosov came to my father and demanded that we leave Kurenets. He said that he knew of secret places in the forest near his old factory that the Germans would never find. He said that we must not sit here idly. We must go to our Christian friends, get rifles and wait for summer to come. Maybe by then the Russians would return.

My father decided to join Leib Matosov, but just at that point, a horrible thing occurred. Ziskind Alperovich, the son of Shimon, with his wife Bashka Hannah, and her son Yikheil, Fabish Shulman with his wife and son Hannan, Berka Hadash, and Joshua Kremer, the son of Mendel and Ashka, were found hiding in the forest near Andreiki. There bodies were brought to Kurenets. In the town, no one knew they left. They had left secretly but someone reported their hiding place. The Germans wanted to make sure that we knew we would be caught if we tried to escape. So now there was a deep depression and many of those who had planned to escape now changed their minds. There was only one group of young men whose spirits did not break, and they continued to plot their revenge. Sometime in the summer, we found out that Elich, the son of Ziskind Alperovich, was killed during a battle between the partisans and the Germans. And we all found out that a group of young men from the town, mostly members of Hashomer Hatzair, boys aged 17 and 18, kept in touch with Russian soldiers that managed to escape the Germans and hid in the villages. Together they planned guerrilla attacks against the Germans. In one of these battles, Eliau was killed. From the boys who took part in this partisan movement, the ones who survived were Zalman Gurevich, Nachum Alparovich, Yankale Orchik Alparovich (who later received many commendations). Amongst the group was Iskelin Einbender, who received many posthumous commendations.

When my father gave up on the idea of escaping, he started turning to religion. Every day he would go to the Minyan and pray. Every day there were new mourners and the line to say the Kaddish was getting longer and longer. When it turned dark people would gather for the Minyan and they would pray. With the first morning light the worshippers would disperse. Each family started building hiding places and kept this information to themselves. They would not tell of their hiding places to their dearest friends, so no one, even if tortured would be able to tell of others' hiding places. Some built hiding places under their homes, and the entrance would lead through a cabinet. Some would be under beds, others inside ovens, some in attics, in holes in their gardens or yards, and some still would hide in sheds. I knew that everyone had hiding places, but I only knew where our own hiding place was. At first it was very simple, kept between the oven and the wall, in a room near the synagogue. It was very difficult to enter and the place was very narrow; you could only stand there. Once Shernegowicz started hunting for Jews not only in the road, but also in their own homes, everyone realized that they must have hiding places to survive.

After several days passed, we decided to build our hiding place above the furnace. For that we had to discontinue the use of the furnace, but we still made it look like nothing had changed. We built a new wall and closed the furnace and had a hiding place inside the chimney. We made a little hole in it so we could have air, and the entrance to this place was through the range top. My father always avoided this hiding place, saying it was as if we were buried alive. Only one time did he use it, when one of the killers by the name of Egov entered our home. We knew from survivors of neighboring towns that the slaughters always started in early morning hours, so we kept surveillance to see if the Germans were surrounding the town.

The night before the slaughter, 9/9/1942, between 3:30 and 4:00 in the morning, my father realized that there was a lot of movement in the market, and that many cars approached the town. That night the town was surrounded by thick fog, and he woke us up and told us that this movement looked very ominous, since he observed that these cars and trucks were loaded with large barrels. Later on we found out that these barrels were filled with incendiaries used to burn the victims. At that point, the Minyan of prayers in our yard was crowded with Jews. Father quickly ran there to tell them that they must escape. The Jews spread all over to return to their homes. My mother and I stood in the window waiting for his return. Daybreak came and we could see him leaving the synagogue. All of a sudden came Germans in uniforms. They caught him and took him with them. His desire to help others lasted till his final moments on earth. When the Germans took him he lifted his head to look at us, and this was our last goodbye.

During the winter of 1942, the Germans made a Christian man the head of the factory. Prior to that, the man was a teacher and we knew him. His name was Tkatchuk. When we saw the Germans take my father, my mother approached Tkatchuk and asked him to save my father as a professional man. We entered his room through our yard. He was already awake and said nothing to us, but only sent us to his attic to hide. The attic was big and originally two families, brothers Ziskind and Mendel Alparovich, used it. The one window in the attic was very high and we couldn't see anything, but we could hear horrible shrieks and screams and cries of children and women, and many shots and sounds of cars going back and forth. And this occurred through the entire day. Every moment of that day we feared that the door would open and they would catch us. We also heard familiar sounds of different Christian inhabitants that spoke Belorussian and were walking from home to home to look for hiding Jews. The apartment of Ziskind Alparovich was empty since the Germans killed the last of the people who lived there, the last residence was Matarosz, a Christian Polish man who used to be the head of the public school. During the German time he became the city mayor, but when the Germans found out that he was involved in underground activities, they killed him with his entire home.

Now only the watchman lived in the house. His name was Stach the Short. He knew nothing of our hiding in the attic and we were very fearful that he would decide to search the area and search the area. We lay like this for two days. On the second evening we heard the Christians yelling while they were looking for Jews. We practically stopped breathing. We could hear Stach telling them that he would with pleasure give up any Jew to the Germans if he caught one, but here there are no Jews and there is no reason to look for them. The house, he continued, was under his watch the entire day and he saw no one coming. He must have convinced the Christian mob that there are no Jews because they left shortly to go to other homes while screaming, "kill the Jews!" For three days and three nights we were hiding in the attic. Each night Tkatchuk would open the door and give us bread but he never gave us anything to drink. Probably since he was so fearful and confused he forgot that we were thirsty. On Saturday evening we heard Tkatchuk and his girlfriend fighting. His girlfriend had just arrived from Vileyka and had found about our hiding in the attic and didn't like it. We knew that we had to leave the place immediately. Later that night, Tkatchuk explained that although the day of the slaughter was long gone, some of the Christian population was continuing to look for Jews, so there is really no reason for us to endanger ourselves and him too. We had to leave. I wanted to leave the day before but my mother was very weak and refused to leave, but now we had no choice. We decided to leave at 1:00 AM to the village Kalin. We asked of one thing from Tkatchuk: to put a pail full of water in the yard to quench our thirst. We said our goodbyes and drank. Stealthily we went to our yard. Our home was locked. We crossed our yard and then to the yard of Netka Charnez and then to the ally and to the market near the house of Itzhak Zimmerman (Charles Gelman's father). From afar in the pharmacy we could hear the sounds of German soldiers. We walked barefoot and very quietly to Kosita Street. We had to cross the train tracks without the guards detecting us. This was the only road to Kalin. We crawled to the other side of the road near the house of the track watchman and quickly crossed the tracks. We were still nearby when all of a sudden a train began to a approach and the whole area was lit. We quickly lay on the ground until the train left. We continued going by the cemetery envious of all the people that had died naturally. When we reached Kalin it was 3:00 AM. I approached the window of the school where the Smetinko family now lived. I knocked on the door and the door was immediately opened as if they were waiting for us. They were very happy to see us and were very warm and understanding and encouraged us. They thought that if they would not invite us to the apartment we would be insulted to they invited us. But we refused. We asked to hide in the barn, which was some distance from the house. The barn was big and full of hay and had a pleasant smell of fields. So now after three sleepless nights, we quickly fell asleep.

I can't describe the beautiful way that the family treated us, and the way they encouraged us and felt sympathy for us. They would say "Remember. You are heroines. You didn't let them kill you. You survived. And this is truly heroic. You must remember that you are heroines. You are not victims, you are heroes." Every night at midnight the old man that was seventy years old got up and took us out to breathe some fresh air and to relieve ourselves. Three times a day our daughter would bring us food using baskets or pails so none of the neighbors would realize that we were hiding there. She brought the best of foods. The old man would sit with us and tell us how during World War I he helped eighteen people hide under his barn, and they all survived. Every few days he would go to Kurenets to see what was going on there. He kept in touch with the Jewish pharmacist Lunya Shnayorson and his wife, Riva, the only remaining living Jews in Kurenets. He told us the good news that many survivors were going to gather in the forest. He also told us some tragic stories. He told us about Meyir Tzirolnik from Dolhinov Street. A Christian inhabitant of the town found his hiding place a few days after the slaughter and took him to the Germans. He also said that a Christian, Vlodka Stenkivitch, the son of Mishka murdered the entire Sandler and Bevinar family when he found them hiding in the attic of the synagogue. He used his ax to kill them. It was getting cold and rain began to become a frequent thing. Smetinko and his daughter kept telling us, "Don't worry. You have a place to stay. We will provide for you and you will be with us until the end of the war". We saw how they risked their lives from pure desire to save us. Daily they were fearful that the Germans would come looking for Jews. Smetinko's wife had heart disease so they didn't tell her about our hiding there. Smetinko was not the owner of the place. There was a woman that he had rented the place from. This woman didn't know about our hiding there. Although she knew me from the time I was a teacher at the school there and we had a good relationship. After staying there for three weeks, the Harvest day came, and they needed to use the barn where we were hiding. So the evening before, they took us to the attic of the house, since they knew some strangers would come to the house.

The next morning we were awoken by the sounds of policemen and German soldiers saying, "Where are the Jews hiding? Get out of there." We lay in the attic quietly until they left. As soon as they departed, the homeowner came to the attic. We were primarily frightened and didn't know what she wanted but she explained her delight in knowing that we survive, and that she also wanted to help us. We asked Smetinko to communicate with the other surviving Jews and tell them that we want to meet with them. Although we really appreciate what he had been doing for us, we couldn't risk his life any longer. Meanwhile, the police went to the other side of the village. We used the momentary sangfroid to run to the forest that was 100 meters away from the house. We decided to hide in the forest until nighttime and then we planned on walking to the Bordina forest, where we knew the Jews were hiding. Smetinko left for Kurenets. There he talked with Lunya Shnayorson, and they arranged for a Christian man by the name of Ignale Birok to wait for us in the field across from the Christian cemetery, and from there he would take us to the forest where the other surviving Jews were staying. In the evening, Smetinko's daughter and the homeowner, Mrs. Charivitz came to us and dressed us in laborer clothes as if we were village girls. This was the season of collecting potatoes so they gave us baskets filled with potatoes as if we were returning from work. We were supposed to leave the village at 6:30 pm, which is prior to the time when the Germans watch the train tracks. We tied kerchiefs to our heads. We put our shoes in our baskets that were also filled with food. We said our goodbyes and thank you's and left. I was very fearful of meeting someone who was a resident of Ivonovitz since they all knew me from the time I was a teacher there. But we passed the road and train tracks safely. It became dark when we finally arrived to the road between Kurenets and Vileyka, which were across from the graveyard. This was the spot where we were supposed to meet Ignale Birok. We heard the sound of approaching horse and buggy. We put our baskets by a tree and hid behind it. All of a sudden a second carriage arrived with many passengers. They saw us and started yelling at and chasing us. We ran to the fields, hiding behind bushes. All of a sudden we heard our code words and saw Ignale Birok. We ran behind him in the fields till we reached the forest of Bordina, and there he took us to the family of Natan Gurevich, Rashka Alperovitz, Shoyl Gordin, Shimon Alperovitz, the son of Zishka Alperovitz and Baska Chana, and a refugee family that lived in Kurenets [Shalom Yoran's family]. The next day we all left for the big pushtsta, a hiding place in the big forest, where we met the rest of the survivors from the Kurenitz slaughter.

Hungry in the Forest…

When we arrived at the forest, we found a few, very miserable, Jews, hungry and dirty from the fires that were lit at night. The world into which we came was very harsh, we had to drag our feet through the forest, go in the middle of the night begging for bread or potatoes from peasants. Given the fact that we didn't know the roads, we were afraid to fall in the hands of hostile villagers or the police. Here the advantage of being a man was evident. A man can demand and threaten, he can put a stick on his shoulder instead of a gun, and in the dark of night, the peasant would give him, because of fear or mistake, some food. This scheme couldn't work for us women, and we didn't have gold or other objects to exchange for food and other needed supplies. We looked for someone who would guide us at least for the first time and take us to the village and in return we would share with him the food we would receive. To our aide came Moshio and Salim, who were the first ones to take us to Margi village. We decided to start walking from both ends of the village, and to meet in the nearest exit to the forest, going back together from there. When we left our hiding place in the forest I paid attention to the paths, trees, and special bushes for use as road marks on the way back, incase we lose Moshio and Salim. Luckily we met as scheduled and got back safely to our camp. Since we started to know the terrain well we no longer needed a guide and this ability helped us a lot.

In the first few days we didn't dare to light a fire in fear of the shepherds. At nights the fires warmed us only in front, and the back was already cold. Right from the start we walked barefooted, since our shoes were lost during the first night, when we ran from Klini. We baked the potatoes in the burning ashes under the fire. One evening, when one of the girls who sat with us tried to take the potatoes out of the fire, unintentionally she moved the hot ashes right on my bare feet. The burns were bad; there were no medical supplies, and thus no way to put a bandage on. Mom had to walk alone to the village to gather food. During one visit to Noviki village one of the peasants recognized my mother and became very excited. He told her how, many years ago, my father returned him a financial loss, and therefore he fed us and promised to weave some sort of sandals for us. For our sorrow these sandals didn't last long, and in the first winter in the forest I walked on the snow with bare feet wrapped with old rags. During that time mom got a pair of boots she used up to the liberation.

In that winter partisans came to the forest, and among them was one from our hometown, Yakov Alperovitch. He offered to help us organize, and with the help of the partisans to cross the front to Russia. This plan seemed to us like salvation. We knew that the road east was be tough and that we'd have to move in a big group, on damaged roads, and mostly at nights. In addition, we had to equip our selves with food, but I couldn't go to the village, being so badly burned, and so, we left with little food only. On the way we passed a railroad and were ambushed in the first night. Some members of our group managed to go through, but the majority, us included, stayed in the forest, we were hiding in it all day long and didn't know that we were under the Germans' noses. After a day of tension we went back to the poshtza from which we left a day earlier.

The fear from the oncoming winter was great. The questions that bothered us were: what will we do after the first snow falls and our tracks will give us away to the local farmers when they come for wood, or the shepherds or the Germans? From where will we get food for the winter? How will we build a shelter for the cold nights to come? We had to find answers to these questions. We had to make a permanent place for the winter. Some people started planning for those measures. We lacked the tools and therefore were hungry most of the time. We joined the Gurevich, Charnas and Shogol families that were already equipped with working tools and started digging. The ground was made from frozen clay, and the work went on slowly. I did my best to put a shoulder in on the work. After the digging was done we needed logs to build the inside of the hole. We learned to chop wood, saw it, and move to the site. We needed clay, bricks and covers for oven, which will be used for cooking and heating. The rest of the group without our help built the stoves. After the zimlanka, measuring 3 on 3, was done, 18 people lived in it. The part that was above ground level was covered with thin logs and moss, on top was a layer of dirt for camouflage. Inside it was divided in two, in the entrance stood the oven, and next to it the women were cooking potatoes and the second part was made of double bunks. On top it was very warm, and below it was very cold. The main food eaten was potatoes, but we didn't have anything to cook it in until we received a small can. We also lacked a knife, and it made it very difficult for the entire group, because they had to share theirs with us. Finally the biggest problem was hygiene since we had no soap, no combs, and spare clothing we could change into.

During one of the evenings we left, mom and me, to the village and came back bruised and frightened. It appeared that Jews came into the village at night and stole from the fences some laundry and tools and we paid for their actions. On the way back in the forest we encountered a pack of wolves, and saw their shining eyes. The sight was terrifying. The hunger made us crazy, we had no people like Byelski, who helped and guided Jewish people.

Each time we entered a peasant's hut while they were eating, we blessed them "beteavon", and hoped they would invite us in. During the winter we were attacked and Jews from Kurenitz and the surroundings, who were hiding but a few kilometers from us, were killed. It was our luck that the Germans didn't reach us during that first winter in the forest. On the dawn of Passover 1943, while we were sleeping, a partisan came from the nearby village and informed us the Germans were coming. In a short distance there was a swamp and by preplanned strategy we started running towards it. The German gunfire was soon heard, we didn't know where to go, or even where we were, we were like wild animals escaping a hunter. During our escape we discovered suddenly that we were exposed and that the German dogs were on our trail. We changed direction, doing our best to stay away from the shooting, and realized that Leah Gurevich was with us. To ease her run she had to throw away her coat and by that saved her life.

With night fall the barking of the German dogs faded away and we understood that the Germans had left the forest. After recognizing the spot where our hiding place was we found that it was all ruined and that one of our members was taken alive by the attackers. In another hiding place, a few hundred meters from ours a four-year-old girl was killed in her mother's arms and the mother was left alive.

Life becomes a Living Hell

Our life became a living hell. We were too afraid to go to the village even during nighttime. We had no food. We had to switch hiding places very often in fear of the shepherds. After a few weeks we settled on the edge of the swamp and from there started slowly to go out to the villages. In the villages we heard that typhus was diagnosed among them, but the need for food was stronger than the need to stay healthy, and so, one day, I was the first one to catch the disease and bring to our camp. Not only did we lack doctors and medical equipment, we were even short of drinking water by living in that foul swamp. When my temperature had risen and I became unconscious, a wooden mat was made for me. After a couple of days a message that partisans or cops were coming scared everybody. They all ran for their lives and only my mother and I stayed. A group of partisans did show up, but after seeing I was infected with typhus they quickly took off. The last of them approached my mom and gave her six slices of bread with butter and boiled eggs, and poured some sugar to her hand, asking her not to tell anyone about this. (A long time after this event we were invited to a family relative in Israel and told this partisan story, and suddenly, one of the guests, named Berel, turned very excited and said he was the partisan who helped us). After that my mom caught the disease as well, and so did the rest of our camp, but luckily none of us died of it.

In the end of our first year in the forest my mother got very weak and couldn't go to the villages any more. In those days the partisans became very strong and we could walk in daylight to the villages. They were practically controlled by the partisans and the Germans were afraid to enter them. Then we moved to Zaziria forests. One day Salim came to our camp, after a long absence. He brought us a leather gun pouch and a piece of flannel, from which I sewed my mom some underwear. With time my boots were repaired with the piece of leather, and held on to the end of the war.

A short time after moving to Zaziria forests came the youth from Vilna. Some members of our group were accepted into the partisans, and us, the fires left the women, old men and children, again.

Then, one morning, a rumor started that Germans equipped with many weapons were coming from the fronts to fight the partisans and the forest inhabitants. The siege started in surprise, and we could see everybody running away. We started running as well, without knowing where to. In the general rush we managed to see Shogol with a group of partisans signaling us to follow. The partisans didn't let us, the Jews, to go near them, but we followed in their path into the huge swamp. In wintertime, when the ground was covered with a thick layer of ice, we would use a certain trail to go in the swamp, but the locals knew about a different way to enter the swamp during the summer. This path was the escape route of the partisans. Our feet sank deep in the mud and walking was very difficult, the two kids in our group had great difficulties to move on and we just barely made it to the rest place. The partisans stayed away from us and we sat on the wet moss, hungry and tired. In the first night we were afraid to put on a fire. The day after showed up in our place a Jew from the town of Uzla, named Shulman. He had a rich experience in life, after spending years in a Siberian camp in Russia. During the 30's he was sent back to Poland and ran a mill over there. When the Germans conquered the area he and his family hid in the swamp with the help of a Christian friend. They built their camouflaged tent so well that even we, who were right next to them, didn't notice it. They lived off their old property that was partially hidden with their gentile friend. The following day Shulman brought us a bucket of soup made of flour and water, and some bread for the kids, and we were happy. During the next few days we heard shooting and explosions from afar, but the Germans didn't get to our spot. After an eight day siege the Germans withdrew, leaving their casualties behind as well as Jewish and partisan casualties.

Later we were told that many of the Germans drowned in those swamps. My friend who had come from Vilna only a short while before the siege had also been killed along with many others.

After the siege the partisans started regrouping in the forest where we were hiding. The peasants were afraid of the partisans, and dared not expelling us without giving us some supplies. Life was held out in daylight and we were much eased. Once I went with a boy from our camp to Brusi village, and suddenly noticed a group of cops sitting around a table laid with vodka and food. They started interrogating us about our camp and of the partisan brigade in the area. I told them that we only came to seek a piece of bread and that we know not any partisans. My answer didn't satisfy them and they started shouting and demanding information, threatening to kill us "like dogs" if we didn't answer. Since we told them nothing, they put us against the wall, held a gun at us and started counting: "one, two… well guys, it's good you didn't say anything about the partisans, we heard you Jews will give them away for a piece of bread and there you stood honorably in the test." I started crying from the insult and the fear and we took off to the forest.

In that same time we started planning a hiding place for our second winter in the forest. This time the work was much easier. Now we choose the spot in soft ground, thus making it easy to dig in. We also had sufficient tools with us. With Haya Gurevich and her relatives we built the bunker and together got hold of a horse and wagon. We drove to the burned village of Loje to disassemble ovens that were exposed after the big fire and use the bricks to build our shelter. With the iron we found we took the ovens apart and put the bricks on our wagon, and suddenly the horse refused to move on. And so we went on by pulling the wagon until we got back to our camp with the precious bricks.

The final result was that our shelter was satisfactory, we were only nine inside, and with time we gathered enough wood for the winter.

I got a new needle as a gift and started repairing our worn out clothes. In our free time we sat on the mat or near the oven, and I would tell stories to the two kids and practicing mathematics with them. To the adults I told the contents of movies and books from before the war, and singing songs in Russian, Hebrew and Yiddish expressed the sorrow and nostalgia.

With the "Repatriation" Movement to Poland on the Way to Israel

To our aid came the new law in those days about sending Polish citizens from before the war back to Poland. We were among the first to enlist in Kurnitz, with the fear of being led to the "white bears" in our hearts. The news about the end of the war caught up with us in the train station of Bialistok and from there we were led to Lodj. I started looking for a connection to the Zionist movement. There I also met Haia and Shimon Plevski, and Lible Auigenfeld. Shimon instructed me how to make contact with those in charge of sending people to Israel. Knowing Hebrew opened many doors for me, and I was accepted immediately for a group, under the condition that my mom would be sent after a while, when the roads will be safer. It was during the days when those left in the concentration camps were liberated. I didn't agree of course to the offer of going out without my mom and thus we were joined to a group of 10 and with faked red cross I.D. traveled to southern Poland towards the border with Czechoslovakia in coal trains. This happened after the first riots of Polish people against Jews, in the end of the war. The fear of being murdered after being so-called liberated escorted us on the roads. In the border we exchanged our documents with others, proving us to be Greek citizens going back home. We went on through Czechoslovakia, onto Hungary and then to Romania.

In our next stop, Urdia-mara, we stayed for a month, because the road to Israel via the black sea was blocked. The Russians were already in Romania. After a month in Romania we came back to Budapest, and from Hungary to Gretz in Austria. We stayed in the luxurious "Vitzer" hotel, which used to host Goebbels. The hotel was luxurious but we didn't have any food, and so were transferred to the international refugee camp in Lankovitz. After staying there for a week we were returned to Gretz. Here was the main headquarters for the Zionist organizations taking care of the illegal immigration to Israel. We received an order as partisans to cross the border to Italy. This border was closed for a month and all the trains carrying refugees were sent back to Austria. The British liberation forces, posted in Italy and Austria at that time, got hold of the connection with the Jewish soldiers from Israel, and found out that they were helping in moving the remnants from the Holocaust to Israel. That was why the border was closed for us. Following an order, we moved on to Vylech in a train and from there on to the border on foot. We had to cross the border on a rope bridge through the Alps. We got to the bridge by daylight, but the guard in charge sent us back to Austria. During that day we hid in a nearby forest, and at night when we got back to the bridge there was no guard. We passed the border without any problems to Italy. A light rain was falling and we were in total darkness. We could not advance and waited for the morning to come. When dawn came we recognized by a description we received prior to leaving our whereabouts. We stayed all day long in the mountains, and at nightfall were about to descend towards Terevizo without entering it. We assigned into couples when suddenly a guy from our group arrived with the message that a car from the brigade is waiting for us in the exit from Terevizo, and indeed it did. We were put inside enclosed pickup trucks and drove on to Puntebe, where was situated an Israeli unit from the brigade that took care of the illegal immigration to Israel.

Since the border we crossed was closed for a month, family members who passed were cut-off from their relatives in Austria. When they found out our group managed to pass, many of the refugees came to see us. An acquaintance I met gave me rejoicing news. He told me that my brother from Israel is a soldier in the British Army and is in Milan, He knows we're saved and is looking for us. This knowledge struck us numb. My brother was in Israel since 1933, but since the war broke we lost contact with him. The excitement was in its peak. In the morning we found a letter from my brother, where he asked us to wait for him in Puntebe, if we reach it before he does, given the fact he's looking for us in Austria. When my brother, who was equipped with British Army authorization, couldn't find us in Gretz, he came back in a train to the border. On the way, in Clegenport, he met Rivka Alperovitch and the others, and found out from them that we were about to cross the border on that day. On the train he met a group of partisans who tried as well to cross the border, like us. For a bribe, which was paid to the train worker, the partisans were loaded into an enclosed wagon and my brother sealed it from the outside. When they passed the border my brother opened it up and let them out, and thus all were witness to the exciting meeting with my brother.

My brother took us to Milan, where his unit was stationed, and for two months he and his friends, among who was Hertzel, my husband to be, tried to make our stay as pleasant as possible, but then my mother had a heart attack. On October 25th 1945 we left Milan. After my mom's recovery we traveled to Rome and Venice and on November the 8th we arrived in Israel due to my brother, with a legal status. After 62 hours in rough sea, in a military boat carrying 800 people; we reached the shores of Israel. From the port of Haifa we were transferred to Atlit, and the day after received permission to leave. We had taxis put up for us, and since my mother had a sister in Tel-Aviv, we drove there. On the way we enjoyed the orange groves we saw for the first time in our life. It was a Friday, and from the windows of every house we saw candles lit for Shabbat. The reunion between my mother and her sister, as well as our reunion with the rest of the family was hearty and joyous.

These were our first steps in Israel.

[Pages 254-255]

The Day of the Massacre

by Tuvya Sosensky

Translated by Eilat Gordin Levitan
(granddaughter of Bela nee Shulman, cousin of the author)

Tuvya Sosensky

We hid in the house of Lazar Shlomo Shulman at the edge of Myadel Street. The house was filled with people. Other than the family of Lazar Shlomo, there were young men and women who escaped the massacre from Dolhinov, as well as my wife and my little baby girl.

During that evening, the daughter of Lazar Shlomo arrived in the house. She was about 17 or 18 years old. Before this she had hidden in the village Litvinki, but they brought her home since she had a horrible infection in her leg. I don't know exactly what she had, but she was in terrible pain. Her entire leg became black and the girl wailed in agony, saying, "Kill me! Give me some poison. What value does my life have?" Then all of a sudden would beg and cry, "Save me! Have pity on me. Save me!"

No one could help her. Her mother sat near her and hit her head on the wall, and her father, Lazar Shlomo sat all evening, crying like a little boy. Most of the night the girl cried, and no one who lived there was able to sleep a wink. Only after midnight, the girl fell asleep with exhaustion and with her the rest of the people of the house fell asleep.

On the floor there was hay to sleep on and everyone slept in their clothes. My wife and my baby girl slept on a bench. I couldn't sleep. I had dark premonitions in my heart. I stood by the window and put my forehead on the cold glass. Frozen and dejected, I didn't move. The night was facing against me, a chasm without an end….

Tuvia Sosensky on the left with brother during better days c 1930

All of a sudden I heard the sound of a truck coming nearby. It stopped about 20 meters in front of the house, and German soldiers jumped out of the truck and spread out to the fog. Immediately I woke up all the sleeping people. Everyone panicked and went to the underground hideout.

My wife and daughter and I did not stay in the house. We looked for another hiding place, entering the home of the neighbors. I went outside to check on the situation. I saw the Germans coming by with flashlights in their hands. I jumped above the fence and entered the home of Netta Zimmerman and waited there.

All of a sudden, the door opened and Yankel Orchik Alperovich came running, and in a panicked manner announced, "Jews… very bad. I was running together with Chaim Itza. They shot at us and Chaim Itza was killed."

He ran to a hiding place in the back of the house, and I stayed in the front of the house. The door opened and three Germans with drawn guns entered the house. They searched with their flashlights and they only found me with an old Jew who stood near me. They took us out, and when we came out we saw that the house of Lazar Shlomo Shulman was burning.

Outside stood a group of six people, including Dvoshol Zokovsky the teacher, Yakov Leib Torov, and four others. They ordered us to go in the direction of the market. I walked near Dvoshol. When we walked near the house Paikon, we saw that in a puddle of blood lay the body of the rabbi's widow (Moshe Aron Feldman's wife).

Dvoshol was limping, so she walked slowly. The Germans kept pushing her, but she begged them, saying that it was hard to walk fast. A soldier slapped her.

Dvoshel said to me calmly;

"On the day that I am to be killed they slap me"
When we entered the market we saw that the house of Zusha Benes was lit on fire. The Christians kept poking their heads out of the yard, but the Germans warned them not to be in the street. We arrived in the market, where we saw very many Jews. They all sat lined up on the ground, shaking from the cold and fear. Every moment, a new person came. My wife and baby daughter came. I sat facing the pharmacy. All of a sudden, Lumia Shnerson (the pharmacist) came to the window. He was wearing his white apron, and he was as pale as a ghost. For one minute he stood by the window, shaking his head as if he was lamenting his fate. After a short time they brought the baker Shabtai Gordon, and then Avraham Meir Cohen, his sister Soshka, and their parents, and then a Christian woman appeared from the edge of the alley. She held a little Jewish kid, about five years old, and she took him to one of the Germans and said, "Here, another Jew for you."

The German commander announced all of a sudden that some professional people would be taken away. He collected 27 people, and I was amongst them. Others were Tabel Markon and her husband and two children. They took us in a truck and brought us to Vileyka…

- Tuvya Sosensky was not originally from Kurenets. He was from a small village near by but had many relatives in Kurenets, and would visit them many times. Tuvya's wife; Tamar and their daughter were killed on that day, 9/9/1942. Tuvya escaped from the Vileyka work camp and arrived in the forest. He went east when many of the Jews in the forest moved to the partisans' area. There he survived and married a Jewish widow (Bela?) and adopted her daughter. After the war he searched for relatives but found none. He came to Israel to his only surviving sister; Tamar nee Sosensky Wolf, in Kibutz Glil Yam (she left Poland before the war). In Israel he had another daughter. His youngest daughter Ariela, and her three children live in Raanana.

1933, Tuvia Sosensky in the middle between his cousins;
Rashka and Rivka Shulman
Sitting on the bottom Tamar Wolf (his sister), cousin Nyomka Shulman, ?
On the right; the Shulman family. On the left ?

[Page 256]

In the market on the day of the slaughter

By Avraham Bergstein

Translated by Eilat Gordin Levitan

I was new in Kurenets. I wasn't a Kurenets native, I recently arrived in the area and lived in the house of Shabtai Gordon, the baker, and worked in his bakery. With me were my wife Rachel Leah, and daughter Fruma. 9/9/1942 was a very foggy morning. At five in the morning we heard shots and pandemonium. We immediately realized that this would be the day of our slaughter, so we decided to put all the families who lived there in the hideout. Its entrance was through the closet. Since this hideout could not keep all the people who lived there, Aharon Gordon (shaptai's son) and I stayed outside and continued the baking.

Shabtai Gordon and family
Only oldest daughters, Michle (wife of the son of Alter Zimerman)
and Riva (wife of Shimon Zimerman) survived.

At six o'clock we heard many more shots and also screams. We decided to escape. In the yard, the head of the police, Adamovich was standing. Aharon said he would go home and get his pistol before leaving, and then we'd decide what to do. He didn't return. The Germans saw him and ordered him to halt. When he didn't stop, they shot him and killed him.

The windows of the house faced the windows of the pharmacy. I spoke with Lunia Schneiorson, the son of the pharmacist. He was the one who told me how they shot Aharon. He also told me that in the market they were taking all the Jews they could find, and it must be today that they would slaughter them.

The Shneirson (related to the Chabad Rabbis) pharmacy

Only one of the Shneirsons' kids survived. The Shneirsons were kept alive for 10 months after the slaughter of the Jewish community since the Germans needed pharmacists. They were used as contact between the escaped Jews and the partisans and help many to survive and were asked to stay in Kurenets for gathering information. They planned to escape and join the partisans but the Germans killed them before they had a chance.

At eight in the morning, the manager of the bakery came to work. He was a Polish man from Vileyka. He didn't enter the bakery. He stood outside. When he saw me he greeted me.

At 8:30 the Germans entered and they asked me who I was. I told them I was a Jew. They asked me if there were any other Jews, so I told them no. They took me out to the market. I was wearing an apron, and my white cook's hat. Many of the town's residents were already in the market. Many of them were taken out of the prayer house. There were also wounded people there. They kept bringing more Jews.

At nine o'clock they brought the family of Shabtai Gordon as well as my wife and daughter. I found out that the manager of the bakery from Vileyka showed the Germans our hiding place, and that is how they were found.

The head of the German SD, Grava , arrived and chose professional people and also strong people. Amongst them he chose me. He ordered us to go on the truck. For ten minutes the truck stood in the market, and I looked at the town's Jews. I heard them talking about running away. Leib Motosov said, "Let's organize and run. Maybe someone will survive. We have nothing to lose, anyway they're taking us to be killed."

After ten minutes they shut the trucks, and they took us away. When we arrived we saw we were in the Vileyka jail.

[Pages 257-266]

In the Vostok Territory

by Abraham Aharon, son of Naftali Alperovich

Translated by Eilat Gordin Levitan

Abraham Aharon Alperovich

September 1942

We arrived at the big Pushtza (deep in the forest place) and continued our "traditional living arrangement" form our shtetl. Once again, we were neighbors of Zadok and Rushka Shavetz and their two daughters, Sonka and Perla. The members of my family who survived the slaughter in Kurenets and managed to escape to the forest, were my sisters, Raicha, Relka, and I.

Now, we lived in huts, deep in the forest, and the Shavetz's hut was right next to ours. During the night, we would go together to the villages at the far edge of the forest to beg for food. One night, we reached the village Villeivitz. We passed through there and we were able to receive bread, vegetables, and a little bit of salt. Some of the residents told us that a son of one of the villagers works for the German police, so we had to be extremely careful from now on when we come for food. It was already after midnight when we finally decided to return with the food to the Pushtza. It was during autumn, so it was already very cold and that night there was a rain storm. We were still extremely tired from the long walk to get to this village. So after a short walk Zadok suggested that we find a bath house in the village and spend the rest of the night there and return to the forest during the early morning hours.

Zadok volunteered to look for a bath house to sleep in and we set in hiding to wait for him. We sat just outside the village, waited and waited, and Zadok did not return. An hour passed, two, three hours. We sat there through the cold night with the wind blowing upon us. We sat as if we were sitting on burning coals. We said to each other, "What happened to Zadok? Could he be caught by someone?"

Abraham Aharon with Zionists friends in Kurenets before the war

I was feeling particularly guilty. Why did I let him go alone? I suggested that we should go and see what had happened to him. We returned to the village. This village was extremely long. The first villager we saw, we asked, but he said he knew nothing. Dawn came and we knew that it would be very dangerous for us to stay there so we quickly left for the Pushtza without Zadok or any information about his fate. When we got to the Pushtza, we met with some partisans who had just returned and we told them what had happened. To our great surprise, they knew all about it and the head of the partisans informed us that Zadok was wounded by his partisans by mistake. A bullet hit his calf and the partisans put him on a horse and took him to the village of Asneivitz near Neyaka.

There they carried him to one of the villagers door and informed the villager that they brought a wounded Jew. They ordered the villager to hide him in his barn and warned him that if he gave him away to the Germans, his house would be burned and he would be murdered. They promised the villager that they would come to take Zadok the next day and bring him back to the forest, and once again warned him that he should tell no one, not even his own wife, about the wounded Jew.

At eleven at night, some guys from Neyaka and I went to Asneivitz to fetch Zadok. The villager took us to his barn and there laid Zadok, his leg covered with blood, but his wound was bandaged So we carried him all the way to the forest. On the way to the hideout, he asked us to go to his wife Rushka and his girls and let them know that he is fine. He was in extreme pain, but he was very brave. We took him to one of the huts and the Jewish doctor Zrinski who lived there took care of his wound.

This occurrence happened while the Jews of the big Pushtza were planning to go to the Vostok. Rushka knew that they now had no chance to be among the people who would go to the Vostok and that she and her family would have to stay at the big

Pushtza. She cried for days, during that point of time, we all saw the Vostok as a haven from the brutal life in the forest, here in the forest we were hiding from the Germans and their collaborators, we had been living in little huts exposed to the elements, while winter was approaching. The Vostok we were told, was controlled by the Russian partisans. People prepared for the departure for days, both emotionally and physically. The partisans gave each group a few guides and the Jews stated preparing bread, toast, salt, shoes, and especially lapses (type of Shoes the farmers wore). The ones that could afford the lapses prepared two or three pairs for the very long walk. There was a Jewish shoe maker from Krivichi, he was sitting in his hut in the forest all day preparing shoes.

I was among the very first group to depart the Pushtza. With us, there were fifty-four people, most of whom were from Kurenets. Some were also from Molodetchna. The Shochet from Krivichi, the Rogovin family from Vileyka. We had a guide, a partisan with a rifle. We came to say good-bye to our dear neighbors, Zadok, and the girls. That proved to be very emotional parting.

Among the people from Kurenets who I remember going with us, were Michail Gurfenkail, Yoshka and his sister Feiga Alperovich, the children of Mendel, Hilka, son of Netta Zimmerman and his wife Freidl., Reuven- Zishka and his wife Marka and their children, Motik and Abraham, Shimon, son of Zishka Alperovitch, Yenta and her sister Rachael Dinerstien, Archick, son of Gutza Dinerstien, Chetskel Zimmerman, (later changed his name to Charles Gelman), my sisters Raicha and Relka, and myself.

Avraham Aharon as a teacher before the war

During the days of the Soviets, 1939-1941, I was a teacher in the little town of Kriesk that was located between Ilya and Dolhinov, I was very familiar with the area that we were going to go through, so I took upon myself the mission to guide our group. When we crossed the train tracks near Neyaka, all of a sudden, we saw five rifles pointing at us. They pointed but did not shoot. It turned out to be the partisans. I asked them how they knew not to shoot. They said that our language saved us. "We heard that you were speaking Yiddish and by now we can clearly tell Yiddish from German."

There were five partisans. They were waiting for the German train to come by, so they could plant explosives. They said that when they were done with their job, they would meet us in the forest near Sosenka and help us. We passed the way peacefully and reached the forest by Sosenka and I must confess my "crime". During a few minutes that the group took for rest, my two sisters and I fell asleep. When we woke up, we saw that everyone had left. It was around three in the morning. I was supposed to be the guide! We quickly ran and somehow found the rest of the group in the dark.

Light came and we sat in the forest to wait for the partisans. Around three in the afternoon, only two of them arrived. They told us that during the mission, the three others were killed. When nighttime came, we crossed the river Viliya in the most shallow area that we could find and reached the village Zabalota. This was one of the villages where I used to teach. I knocked on the door of my old landlord and he received me very graciously. This area, was clear of German at that point. The Germans were patrolling only in specific central locations near the train tracks but in the village itself, there were no Germans. I walked across the village, remembering the days when I would be greeted as a very respected person. They'd harness their horses for me and treated me like I was an important personality. And now, I crossed the village secretly and in fear.

Avraham Aharon as a teacher before the war

My landlord agreed to come with me to greet the rest of the people in my group and he told all of us that at that moment, there were no Germans in the area, but that we should be very careful and watch our steps. He told us a horrible story of what happened a few days prior. Seventy Jewish people, escapees from the town Mydell, walked across one of the villages in the area and had stolen two lambs from a farm. The Christian villages reported the incident to the Germans who were patrolling the nearby area and during a time when the group was resting in the forest, the German police surrounded them and killed almost everyone. Only a few had managed to escape. He once again warned us that we must go only at night time and very quietly at that.

We were dressed very poorly and if these days were like the regular old days, it would have been very funny. But at this moment, we were surrounded by a world of horror and tragedy and humor was hard to come by. Still, there was one person who received his fate with good spirits, at least outwardly. This was Michail Gorfenkel. He had a towel tied around his head and another towel tied to his waist. He carried a small bag for putting the goods he begged for into, but he was always in good spirits. His good spirit helped not only him, but the rest of us. I remember him saying was, "One thing that I wish for myself right now, is for someone to take a picture of what I look like at this moment. After the day of victory, if I survive, I will enlarge it and put it in my bedroom, across from my bed." But Michael did not get either wishes. He never got a photograph and he did not survive.

I also remember Artzik Gutze's Dinerstien. He had a huge fur coat that he never separated from. When we were walking through the forest, we felt very sorry for him. He kept tripping over his coat. But we were very jealous during the cold nights. After many, many troubles and wandering, we passed the old Russian-Polish border, the border prior to 1939. We passed near Pleshentznitz, about 10km from Poloshnitz. A few days later, the first snow fell. We didn't dare go to the local homes. We slept in the forest. The weather was very cold and only one person had the appropriate clothes: Archick, the owner of the fur coat.

I still remember the suffering of the children of Zishka and Rogovin. During the night, we would go to the villages. I always chose Michael as my partner. I would leave my sisters in the forest. The area we arrived at was almost all at the hands of the partisans and villagers were very scared of them. Michael would tie a stick to his shoulder and in the dark, the villagers thought he was a true partisan. This was not the only tactic that Michael used to get food. He used to sing songs to the villagers. He would sing the song, "Katyusha" or "Yasili Zvatra Vyana" so the "rifle" would scare them at night and the songs would soften them and even get them excited, so they would usually give us good items. I liked Michael a lot. Even in the darkest hours, he was in good spirits. And in songs and jokes, he could overcome the difficulties and spread joy to his surroundings. Sometimes we would even forget our troubles.

One night, when we crossed a village, Michael told me, "You know, Abraham, I am really getting tired of eating only bread. Let's go catch us a chicken and prepare us some chicken soup." So we went to a chicken coop and tried to get a chicken. As it turned, there were more geese then chickens in the coop, and in the dark, we caught a goose and he started making very loud noises and woke the entire village. Michael had no choice but to let go of the goose and run. We both ran for our lives. When we reached the forest, Michael said, "I could never imagine that a chicken and a goose could live in the same room. During this war, all order and life rules had changed. But I would never give up and one day I will bring back a chicken to the forest, although I really crave a goose at the moment , but geese don't know the rules of danger and can bring disaster."

Two weeks passed since we left to get to the Vostok. We reached the partisan area near Oshuetz. Matrina and Gomel near Polochek. Here, we were much freer. The Germans were headquartered in Polochek and Matrina and the rest of the area was free of them so our situation improved tremendously. We slept in the houses of the villagers, staying here for three weeks. Then we decided to continue toward the Vostok, going east eventually we planned, to cross the front and reach the USSR area passed the fighting. Our guide was the partisan Vanya. The road was almost impossible. The snow was very unstable and our lapsas, the shoes we wore, were extremely wet. So every night and day when we were resting, we would spend hours trying to dry our lapses and our shoes. We would try to dry them next to bonfires and using the fireplaces of the homes of the villagers. The villagers here treated us very nicely. Some of them even gave us their beds and they slept on top of the furnaces. They would repair our shoes and warm their bath houses so we could wash ourselves.

In the village, Voloki, I once walked with Michael in an area that turned to be a river that froze. The frozen layer broke and we fell in the water. Lucky for us, it wasn't too deep and we managed to get out. Michael said, "This world is very confusing. Everyone goes to the river during the summer and we are swimming in the winter, as if we are professional sportsmen! I never imagined that I would turn into such a sportsman!"

Finally, we reached the frontline. We met the local partisans and they told us that it was almost hopeless to try to go through the front. There were some groups of Jews that succeeded in passing, but in the meantime the Germans had found out about it and started putting blockades, and every trial might be defeated. They told us that a few days before, a big group of Jews tried to pass the border and everyone was murdered. So they suggested that we should return to the partisan area from where we came, and the young people would join the partisans, and the older people would find work at the farms. We were very disappointed. Was it really worth it to go through all this trouble to get here? We remembered the Pushtza near Kurenets and we felt bad that we left. So we returned to the Ashuatz area. When the Christians there saw us coming back, they started complaining. "Our blood is spreading all over and you are sitting with nothing to do!"

They totally ignored the fact that most of the blood was the blood of the Jews in this war, and without weapons, we were not able to be accepted as partisans. Just about that time, a Christian man came to us and told us that near Polochek, there is a big barrack that used to hold weapons and the Germans burned it but some of the weapons were still there. If we were to repair them, we would be able to use them. He told us that if we paid him, he would take us to the place. We started arguing. Some of us believed him and some of us thought he was lying. The ones who believed him went there and brought the weapons. They started repairing them and everyone was very busy. Just for that, we must bless those weapons.

One villager who knew about weapons looked at the rifles and said to me, "You know what you can do with such a rifle? You can watch rabbits, but only rabbits that are locked in cages. That's what you can guard with these!"

But truly, after repairing the weapons, there were some rifles that were able to shoot. But when we came to the partisans and tried to join the troops, they found our rifles lacking and we looked lacking as well, in their eyes. Still, some of us were accepted. One of them was Motik, the son of Moshe Alperovitz. He was young and very likeable. In a short time, he became a real partisan. Our group was divided and we spread into different villages and started looking for jobs.

In the village, Papovichzina, near Gomel, lived my sisters Raicha and Relka. Hilka and Freidl Zimmerman, The Shochet, from Kribitz, Tuvia from Mydell, with his daughter. In the village Mirakova, lived Reuven- Zishka with his wife Marka and his young son, Abraham. The women were sewing dresses and knitting sweaters for the villagers. In exchange, they got bread. The young men of the villages, were fighting with the partisans, so many of the farms needed workers. So Michael, Chetskel Zimmerman, and I, started working as tree cutters for families whose men were serving with the partisans. We worked from early morning until night and in exchange, we got food.

Michael would check the homes, and, according to the shape of a home, would guess where we would expect to find good food and a decent amount of it. One day, he chose a beautiful, large home. He said, "Here, there must be wealthy people."

After a hard day of labor, we received only potatoes. When the homeowner saw how disappointed we were, she "gave" us a saying: "You cannot judge a book by its cover." She suggested to go to one of the small homes and there she said, they would probably give us bread. Michael went to one of the homes she suggested and returned with a huge loaf of bread that consisted of eighty percent potatoes and the rest, wheat. This was a great feast. Once in awhile, we would mow the fields. Chetskel (Charles Gelman) was a very good looking young man, with easygoing spirit. During the days of the Holocaust, he would say, "You know, everything that we are going through will surely impact our personalities. So much, I would like to see our people after the war. What kind of lessons are we to learn from our experiences? Could it be that people will forget those hard days and continue to go with the flow as they did in the past?"

This was around the spring of 1943. The Russians started winning some battles. Among the Jews in the area there were also some changes. Many of us were accepted by the partisans. Even the issue of weapons was not so important any more. Shimon son of Zishka Alperovich, Artzik son of Gutza Dinerstien, Yoshka (Yosef) and his sister, Feiga children of Gitel and Mendel Alperovich, were accepted by the Malinko brigade. I was accepted by the Voroshilov brigade. Chetskel (Charles Gelman) was accepted to the Zelazniak brigade. Motik son of Reuven -Zishka Alperovich continued with the Vorovsky brigade.

Jewish natives of Kurenets as partisans

At one time, when I was getting ready for a mission with my brigade, we met with another brigade and one of the people there was the very young Zalman (Zalmanka the brother of Rivka) from Kurenets, the son of Moshe Alperovich. I was excited to see him and suggested that he would transfer to our brigade so we can be together. The officer of his brigade said that there was no way he could let go of Zalmanka. He was a young man, not even seventeen, and he was very well liked both by the soldiers and the officers of his brigade. His commitment was limitless. His officer said, "You will meet him after the war."

When we reached the village Vyozana near Polochek, there was a big battle between our two brigades and the Germans. This was in the afternoon and we were surrounded by German tanks. I was together with Zalmanka. He kept trying to run in front of the tanks and it was very difficult to stop him. I told him, "Don't be a hero. Stop yourself. What sense does it make to do this?"

In that battle, Moshka Shulman from Molodetchna was killed. We were very upset. He was the very first person to be killed from our troop…

…Many days and months passed and we reached the month of May, 1944. We came to the town of Viyanitz, about thirty kilometers from Globoki. This town was part of the Soviet territory before 1939 (Kurenets was part of Poland at that time). The population of the town was purely Jewish. Now we found it empty. There was not one Jew left. In the homes, we found torn Talits, Tfilins and pages of Torahs and prayer books. Gentiles came to the town and used the Torah books to replace the broken glass in the windows. We went to the Jewish cemetery and we found it intact. All the graves had Hebrew writing on them. The gentile partisans, friends from our troop, would bring me names and pages from the prayer books and ask, "What is written here?"

In this town, I experienced my first revenge. Two years before, after the Germans murdered all the Jews, there was one Jewish woman left. She was very light and she looked like a Christian. But one of the villagers that lived in the surrounding area told the Germans that she was Jewish and they killed her. Syomka Perlman, the son of this woman, was now an officer with the partisans. He came to look for his mother and when he found out what had happened, he vowed to revenge the blood of his mother. We found the house of the Christian villager and entered but only found his wife and the children at home.

Syomka broke everything in sight and then waited for the man of the house to enter. When the man entered, Syomka told him, "You made a grave mistake. You made a bitter mistake. You were very sure that no one was left of our family, and now, look at me! I am still alive and now I can tell you exactly who the woman was that you gave away to the Germans. She was my mother. Look at me! I am the son of the woman that you murdered!" He took the man to a bridge near the river and there, he killed him.

At this town, we were prepared to celebrate May 1. The victories of the Soviets in the battlefields were huge. In our hearts, we believed that we would survive. But all of a sudden, instead of a big celebration, we got an order to retreat. Those were the days where Vilna was already in the hands of the Red Army, and so was Kovna. Only the Vittebesek front was still in German hands, and that included our area. The Germans started retreating from our area, but on their retreat, they decided to purify the area from partisans so the retreat would be easier. They put all of their force into this battle. They brought the army from the front, from Smorgon and Vileyka, full divisions came. This area had about sixteen partisan brigades, about forty-thousand people. The Germans surrounded the entire area and each day, they tightened the circle around us, reaching for the center. For the first time, we felt a true battle. We, the partisans, were fighting an army. And not only did we feel the battle from the German side, even our partisan friends were bothering us, since they were afraid that if they fell into German hands together with Jews, they would suffer greatly. I was the head of the transport unit. We passed through the villages where the Jews from Kurenets were hiding. I tried to help them. I tried looking for my sisters, but couldn't find anyone. Everyone had left the villages, along with the inhabitants that were following the partisan troops. There was no organization or plan. The only person I found was Archick Dinnerstien.

The Germans blockaded us in three rings. The rings were concentric and it was impossible to escape. The first ring consisted of Belarussian and Ukrainian soldiers. The second was Polish and Latvian soldiers. The third was German. Thousands of partisans were killed. It was a hopeless war. The partisans started drowning the heavy weapons into lakes and rivers, and we were left with only automatic rifles. All the villages were burned by the Germans. In areas where the residents didn't have enough time to leave, the Germans burnt them, along with their homes. The night sky was red with flames and fires. It was the red of horrors, an inferno. During the daytime, there was so much smoke and confusion of people, livestock and the sound of planes dropping bombs and explosives, that the air was permeating with fear. From the planes, Germans also dropped pamphlets which said, "You are fighting for the Jews and not for Russia. Kill the Jews! Put your weapon down and nothing bad will happen to you!"

The fear among the partisans was great. The rings grew tighter and tighter. Near the village, Mattriyene that's next to Assouaz, I met with Shimon son of Zushka Alperovich from Kurenets, the pharmacist from Radoshkovich, and his wife. The pharmacist told me that he had poison pills and suggested that the three of us kill ourselves. I said that I would consider it and later I was told that they did poison themselves.

The battle lasted the whole day. We kept running from one area to another, looking for a way to break through the line, but to no avail. One of the places was around Lapeil. We were trying to cross the German lines. Here, I met with Motik, the son of Reuven- Zishka Alperovich. Here, we had a horrible battle with the Germans. A grenade blew off his legs. He was beloved by everyone. We wanted to carry him away, but he begged us, "Leave me here. Don't take me. I am lost already." After throwing the grenades on the approaching Germans, he took the last grenade he had and used it to kill himself.

We regrouped to troops that would run in front and I was among them. I knew that this was our only choice. It was during the night and from afar, we could see the shadows of the Germans warming next to bonfires. They let the first ten-thousand people pass, only to trick them and as soon as they were in the center, they would open fire from the front and the back. The battle continued the whole night. The Germans and the partisans were mixed. We could see the Germans with the police in their black uniforms. We knew we lost this fight. We were certain about it. The officers started destroying their IDs. We were waiting for our death to come. Then, a Russian captain came to us and said, "Friends, there is only one choice. We must attack them. Most will be killed, but some will be saved." This was around nine in the morning.

Yankel, the son of Archick Alperovich

We jumped up to their bunkers. Many, many were killed. A few were saved and I was amongst them. I returned to Kriesk. Here, I met Yankel, the son of Archick Alperovich from Kurenets. He was well-known among the partisans. Very courageous and renowned everywhere. He told me that in the big Pushtza, there were blockades and many of the Jews were killed. Yankel came riding a horse, one of the villagers rented his horse and for that, we got two chickens, bread, milk, and a meal. We decided to return to the Pushtza of the Kurenitzers. We managed to get to Bogdanova, the little town between Kurenets and Retske. Here, we had to cross the train tracks and we were not able to do so. The Germans opened fire and we had to return to Kriesk. From there, I left Yankel. He stayed with the partisans, and I continued east to look for my sisters, but could find no Jews. A gentile friend of mine told me that they were all killed by a German during an ambush near the village, Matriyana.

Reicha,
daughter of Naftaly Alperovitz

Just about the same time near Asouatz, we heard the sounds of the approaching Soviet front. Soviet airplanes passed by us and bombed Molodetchna. Around three in the afternoon, we were blessed to see the entering of the first Russian tanks. A few days later, I had a most memorable meeting in Asouatz: while I was standing in the street, I saw an image approaching me. I was scared and started retreating back. The person approaching me was covered in bandages from head to toe. On her back, she had a sac and she was carrying a stick in her hand. She said to me, "Why are you running away? Don't you recognize me? Don't you recognize Feiga, the daughter of Mendel son of Yechezkel Alperovich?"

My eyes filled with tears. It was now that I could see the horrors that we had experienced. She told me what had happened to her and her brother Yosef. She was badly wounded and her brother was killed during the blocade. She was lying among the dead bodies. At one she got up and asked a German Guard to let her look for her son who was killed and she now wants to die next to him. The German let her go to look. Meanwhile, she escaped and entered the forest and hid there for many days, alone and wounded, eating grass and other plants. One day, a Christian woman came to the forest and found her. She told her that the Red Army conquered the area and that she now could get out of the woods.

At first, she didn't believe her. But finally, she left the woods and lay on the road. A Jewish officer from the Red Army found her and when he realized that she was a Jew, he stayed with her and took care of her. He took her to Asouatz and there, the Jewish doctor Zirinsky, from Kurenets, took care of her. Later, she was sent faraway to Gorki to a hospital and there she was able to recover.

In that area, I also met with Chetskel Zimmerman (Charles Gelman). He had gone through the same horrors as I did. The partisans gave me a month of leave and I went to Kurenets. I wanted to go to my family's tomb. But when I got to Kurenets, I realized that I couldn't handle it emotionally. After a short time, I moved to Krivichi, where I got a job working for the government.

One day, I got a letter from the Soviet government. This letter was in gratitude for the heroic deeds of Zalman Alperovich, son of Moshe. The letter was sent to me because they thought that since my last name was Alperovich, I must be a relative. The letter bestowed honor upon the young Zalman Alperovich, who originally was not accepted in the Army because of his young age. He volunteered nonetheless, to revenge the enemy of the people. He died in East Germany as a hero of the Soviet nation. After his death, he received two medals of high honor. The letter ended, saying that his behavior and his courage is an example to the other soldiers of the Red Army. I read the letter many times and my eyes filled with tears. The letters were jumping from the page. I remember what his officer had said to me: "You will meet after the war." And here the war has ended, and only in his death, I meet with his memory…

[Page 267-296]

Resistance

by Zalman Uri Gurevitz

Translated by seventeen year old Ron Levitan

*"In honor of Benjamin Nyomka Shulman, my great-grand-uncle
who believed that a young boy from Kurenitz could fight the Nazis and was able to accomplish
that mission, but died fighting for Russia"*

*The Gurevitz family near their Kurenitz home were the Jewish
members of the underground hid their printing press and weapons
Left to right: Luba née Gurevitz Bardan, Zalman Uri Gurevitz, Batia née Eishiski Gurevitz,
Gershon Gurevitz Gorev, Natan Gurevitz, Lea nee Gurevitz Shogol*

I was born on 8/10/1924 in the little shtetl Kurenets, Vileyka Uzed, Vilna Gubernia, west Belarus. In 1920, the area passed to Polish hands, after more than hundred years of Russian control. Most of the district population was Belarusian, but there were many Poles, Jews, Russians, and even two German families. Kurenets itself was predominantly Jewish, and its population numbered about 1800. Most Jews spoke Yiddish amongst themselves, while the higher class spoke Russian. The majority were poor merchants and tradesmen; few were well off, and none were rich.

During the era between the major wars, there was a strong Jewish Zionist sentiment around town. Many subscribed to Yiddish newspapers like "Mament" and "Haynt". We had a library with some of the best books that Yiddish, Hebrew, Russian and Polish literature had to offer. All the Zionist parties and youth movements were very active and some people were bondist or communist. Townspeople with different ideologies fought daily wars.

My father was a political activist, belonging to "Zionim Claliym Alef." He would make speeches during elections to the Zionist congress in all of the synagogues in the area. He was doing the same prior to local elections and elections to the Polish parliament. The town's commitment to education, culture, youth movements, and politics was typical of the area and was strongly influenced by Vilna. But there was something unique about the shtetl. In the dark days, there was a group of young people that demanded action and revenge. They wouldn't be discouraged or apologetic and tirelessly worked for rebellion.

The Gurevitz Family
Standing Sima née Gurevitz Herbert, her youngest sister,
Luba née Gurevitz Bardan is sitting in the middle, on her left is her niece,
Lea née Gurevitz Shogol, on the right: the author, Zalman Uri Gurevitz

We were students of the daily Hebrew school, Tarbut and members of the socialist Zionist youth movement, HaShomer Hatzair. We spoke Yiddish and Hebrew fluently and dreamed of Aliyah to Eretz Yisrael. We were affected by Hitler's rise to power and information about the sad situation of the Jews. Poland also saw a rise in anti-Semitism in the thirties and we were closely watching the Spanish Revolution. All of these factors affected us. We believed in the justice of socialism and desired to accomplish it by living in an Israeli kibbutz. But we were young boys, still a long way from being able to make this a reality. Most of us were born between 1922 and 1924 and our troop leader, Kopel Spektor, was our strongest influence.

That was the state of affairs at the dawn of World War II. Immediately as the war started, in September of 1939, the Soviets invaded our areas and we became part of the USSR. To our disappointment, they closed our Hebrew school, and made it a

Yiddish school. They announced that all the Zionist movements were imperialist and they canceled our youth movement. We wanted to be active but didn't know how since our troop leaders weren't around anymore. So we agreed to continue our activities in secret. We were a determined group of people. Amongst us were Benjamin (Nyomka) Shulman, Shimon Zirolnik, Yitzhak Einbinder, Mordechai (Motik) Alperovitz, Nachoom Alperovitz, and me. Our original troop leader was Kopel Spektor, a man of all seasons- an athlete, a bookworm, a mathematician, and a generous and dedicated person. He was like a father to us. During the days of the Soviets, he was a technician and a cartographer in the central train station in Molodechno, 30 kilometers from Kurenets. He was graduate of a technical institution in Vilna and an extremely capable man.

His job compelled him to travel throughout the USSR. When he came back from his trips he was very disappointed. He asked Benjamin Shulman to congregate in his house. It was the winter of 1940. We sat in the dark and listened to his sad statements. He told us about Minsk, the capital of Belarus, that had a large Jewish population. He only found one Jewish school there, and when he went to the one Jewish Theater to see "Fiddler on the Roof", they had changed the essence of Tuvia and made him a fighter against Czarism. He found a lot of mixed marriages there and people pulling away from Judaism. Our dream that the Jewish problem would be somehow resolved in the Soviet Union and that the Jewish entity will be recognized as a separate minority was abolished. In conclusion Kopel said, "The Jewish population in the Soviet Union will mix with the general population and in no time there will be no independent Jewish entities".

Nyomka Shulman and Shimon Zirolnik were devout Marxists and hoped that the Soviets would comprehend the nationalist desires of our youth movement. Since both ideologies were so similar, both based on Marxism and with an emphasis on the betterment of society as their first priority, they could not accept the Soviets' rejection.

At the end of the evening Kopel passed the flag to Nyomka Shulman and suggested that we should find a way to get in touch with the movement headquarters in Vilna. Nyomka was an excellent theoretician, a leader type full of energy and zest for life; a short, intelligent guy who was always ready for action. He approached Chaim Yitzhak Zimmerman, an adult that used to be very involved with the youth movement, and asked him to go to Vilna.

Chaim happily agreed. This was not a simple trip. Vilna passed hands from Polish to Lithuanian hands in 1939 and Chaim had to pay large sums of money to border smugglers for an opportunity to travel. In exchange they let him crawl on his hands and knees across the border. He came back five days later and what he told us was very encouraging. The Aliyah to Eretz Israel was continuing. However, the pace was slow and the route was strange (through the USSR and the Far East). But to us teenagers, it sounded very romantic, with a hint of danger, and it filled our hearts with hope, and renewed our sense of commitment.

We had two meeting places. One was the dark room of Nyomka's blind grandmother. The other was the town hall that the Soviets built on Dolhinov Street. There we would meet at the library reading room. First we would collect the daily newspapers like Pravda and Esbastia (you could only get them at the library and you had to read them right there). We then pretended that we were young comsomols (communists). We would crowd the room so there would be no sitting space for anyone else and argue very loudly. Once we established that no one was listening we would talk Zionism. Ironically, this part of the room where we were usually seated was called "The Red Corner". The daily planner in our group was Shimon Zirolnik. He was the oldest and already had a job in the train station. Everyone in town saw him as a strong follower of the Communist Party. He had only finished elementary school, yet managed to educate himself and was very well read, sophisticated, and open minded.

In February of 1940 we had a contact with HaShomer Hatzair from Warsaw. Yosef Kaplan came from Vilna as an ambassador to encourage the Jewish youth in the area. He visited many other shtetls (Globoki, Dunilovitz, Dockshitzi). When he got to Kurenets, he went to Kopel Spektor's house. Since Kopel left town, his family sent Yosef to Nyomka Schulman. Nyomka called us all to gather at his house. The people that came were Chaim Yitshak Zimmerman, Shimon Zirolnik, Motik Alperovitz, Yitzhak Einbender, Nachoom Alperovitz, Ilia Spektor, Ishayau Kramer and me. Yosef told us that there was still some communication with Eretz Israel. We also learnt that the training camps to become Chalutzim moved to Vilna, and that there was some immigration to Israel. He reminded us to retain our commitment to Zionism and most importantly, to maintain the bond we had with the other members. Finally, he ordered us to destroy all of the paraphernalia of Zionism, except for the flag. This was the last communication we had with the Youth Movement abroad. Yosef slept over at Nyomka's house, and the next day walked over to Vileyka- a town 7 kilometers from Kurenets. I never saw him again.

Soon after, Lithuania became a republic of the Soviets. And for now, our hope for Aliyah to Eretz Yisrael was lost. We continued our studies and our close friendship. In 1941, for Laag Baomer, we convened as a group by the boulder in a field outside of town. It was a quiet, beautiful night. We sat in silence and despair. Spring was all around, but our hearts were lonely. Nyomka took out our special flag and spread it over the boulder. He spoke about the symbolism of the flag and the connection that we all must have. He read from a book of the Youth Movement, and then we sang songs. One of the songs was "Anu Olim V'Sharim". Tears filled our eyes. We were young, sentimental, and melancholy, we lost all hope for Aliya to Eretz Israel . We spontaneously started hugging. We felt as if we were friends for life and death. And that's the way it was.

Motik Alperovitz, his brother Elik,
Shimon Zimerman and Avraham Alperovitz
Motik and Elik were partisans they were killed while fighting the Germans.
Their parents, Reuven Zishka Alperovitz and Marka and youngest brother
were also killed during a German blockade.

What to do

It was June, 1941, and a beautiful summer. We had just finished taking our last test at the high school. My mother, who had a lung disease, was in a nursing home. My father, Natan Gurevitz, was both a mother and father to us. He worked very diligently. An active Zionist prior to the Soviets' invasion, he was also a merchant, and was very worried that he would be sent to Siberia. As a result, he decided to walk to Vileyka with his friend and coworker, Zalman Gvint to work at a Soviet soap and shoe polish factory. He never missed a day of work, even if he had to walk in the snow or in the heat of the summer. He did anything to look productive in the eyes of the Soviet authorities.

Leah, my older sister, had just graduated from the high school in Vileyka, and my younger brother, Gershon was studying at the Yiddish school that the Soviets had established. And then…

The war started on June 22, 1941. Panic spread though the population. The belief that the renowned Soviet army would swiftly destroy the German army was abolished in two days. Vilna and Molodechno were constantly bombed. The Germans were rapidly approaching and the Soviets were even more rapidly retreating. The confusion and panic was grave. For our family, the worries intensified because we lost touch with our mother.

The Soviet politicians and their families were the first to escape east. Trains, trucks and horses pulling buggies full of crying children and housewares left for the east. I asked my father what I should do. He advised me to stay so that mother would have a place to find us. I ran to our meeting place at Nyomka's house. Yitzhak Einbender and Shimon Zirolnik were already there. Riding on our bicycles, we left town, heading east.

Benjamin [Nyomka] Shulman
with his much older sisters, Rashka (left) and Rivka

As I looked back to our little shtetl, I wondered if I would ever see my parents again. We arrived in Ratzke, a small town that was 8 kilometers from Kurenets. We saw many of our townspeople there. We ran into the head of the Kurenets police. He said that there was no need to panic, and that we must return to town. We ignored him and kept going. People crowded the road . Pandemonium was everywhere. Fear was particularly strong in the eyes of the Easterners. They had lived with the Soviet authorities for many years, and were accustomed to obeying orders. Now, there was no one to give them orders. On the evening of June 25, we reached Dolhinov. I wanted to rest there for a short while. I had relatives and friends from the Youth Movement who lived there, and I particularly wanted to see a pretty blonde girl named Bushka Katsavitz that I had met in a Zionist summer camp.

In the central market area I met a Soviet worker name Timsok. He knew my father well. He told me "Son- You are a child, but don't listen to others. Don't procrastinate. Go east." So that's what we did. We wanted to reach Pleshnitz, which was on the other side of the old Polish-Russian border. The situation there was total chaos. That night, only residents that were former Soviet citizens were allowed to go east. The rest were ordered to turn back.

Extremely disappointed, we slept in a field near the border. Early in the morning we saw German planes going to Poloczek. There was a great panic, and we decided to go back to our town. Everywhere on the roads we saw people going east with hope in they eyes, and people returning west with disappointment and a quiet acceptance of the bad situation. All through the ride, Belarussian farmers who were standing on the side of the road, kept mocking us, but they didn't physically hurt us.

On June 26, we arrived in town. The Germans hadn't entered the town yet. The Jewish population was very fearful. The gentiles gathered in the center of the town, and we were afraid that they had come to raid us. But we soon realized that they wanted to prevent the farmers from entering the town. They took a barrel and used it as a podium. The son of Bazil the Footless stood on the barrel and shouted, "We will be with you, Jewish residents of Kurenets. We won't let them touch you." They called us to take part in the congregation, and we all decided to arrange watch groups. Mendel the son of Henia Motosov, marched us to the house of Reshka Alperovitz, the former headquarters of the Soviet police. We found rifles and ammunition there. The rifles were divided among the young people who knew how to use them. Shostakovitz the Belarussian doctor that was later a German sympathizer, was at that moment on the side of the Jews. He organized patrols of gentiles and Jews to patrol the town. I was stationed at a watch point near the railroad, together with Eliyahu Spektor. The farmers started coming with horse and buggies. We told them that they couldn't enter town and that if they did, we would shoot them. They all left, and for two days, there was silence in the area. But then the town's gentiles started robbing the Soviets' storage areas and a few of them also robbed some Jewish homes.

That was the situation until the 28th of June. And then, the German army paraded through the town on motorcycles and cars. The gentile citizens of the town held flowers in their hand, and gave them bread and salt. Immediately, the Germans ordered to return all weapons, and told us that whoever refused would be shot to death. We returned our weapons.

Among the people who returned the weapons were two Shimon Zimmermans. One was the son of Yosha, and one was the son of Yermiau (they were cousins). The Germans took them to a nearby village and killed them. They were the town's first victims. The Germans announced that every Jewish man from ages 16-60 had to be in the center of town at 1:00 PM sharp. Anyone that didn't attend would be shot immediately. So from 1:00, to 3:00, Grandfathers, fathers, and teenagers stood in the center of town surrounded by the German army and police, who had machine guns. Then a German officer came and gave us a speech about the wonderful thing that had befallen us: life under German authority. We were ordered to obey all instructions, and anyone that would not do so, would be shot to death.

They told us to immediately choose Jewish representatives, or Judenrat. The Jews started calling names of prior representatives, like my father, (Natan Gurevitz), Zalman Gvint, Shabty Gordon, Gershon Oyeshisky and Dov Einbender, but they all declined the offer. They chose Shotz, a Jewish refugee from Austria as the head of the Judenrat. We were told we must participate in forced labor, we must wear a Jewish star, we weren't to walk on the sidewalk, and we were not supposed to congregate with or talk to gentiles, and…!!!

Some members of the
Kurenets underground in 1939
1. Yitzhak Zukerman; 2. Kopel Spektor

Kopel Spektor had just returned to Kurenets, so we asked him to secretly meet us in a hideaway on June 30. This was our first meeting since the German occupation. The main question on our mind was "What are we going to do?". We all came to the same conclusion: we must fight the Nazis. We were only 17 and 18, and we were still naïve enough to believe that there was something we could do. We believed in the slogans of the Youth Movement about our collective and personal responsibilities. Kopel knew that the situation was grave, but didn't try to stop us. All he said was "I so hope that you will succeed".

We devised a practical plan. Firstly, we were to collect weapons and organize a Partisan group. Secondly, Shimon Zirolnik suggested that we print flyers urging people to fight the Nazis. Nachoom Alperovitz, who prior to the 'Soviet time', had worked in a printing office, decided to organize this. Lastly, and most importantly we would try to find other people that could join us. We hoped, in particular, to contact the Russian resistance.

As we were leaving we ran into Yosef Zukerman he told us that during the Russian retreat he noticed a soldier throwing his gun in the marshy area next to town, we went there and found a gun with three bullets- we had our first weapon!

At the end of July a transportation camp for war prisoners was established in Kurenets. Every evening thousands of POWs would come walking from Dolhinov, and at night they would sleep on the ground at the meat market. The next morning the Germans would force them to walk to Molodechno. Most of the POWs were in horrible shape: wounded, sick and starving. The road between Dolhinov and Kurenitz was filled with corpses. We all wondered how ten German soldiers could lead two thousand young Russian soldiers through thick woods with only a few, isolated attempts at escape. We asked ourselves, "How could that be?"

Just around that time, we found out that all the Jewish men of Vileyka had been killed. On July 12, 1941 signs were put all over Vileyka notifying them that all Jews age fifteen to fifty must report at the 'big synagogue' at ten in the morning. These Jewish men and boys were told that they would be taken to work. Instead, they were taken to the woods, slaughtered and buried.

Seeing death all around us was unbearable. We wanted to help the POWs, so we arranged, through Shotzs, a job for ourselves at the transportation camp supplying water to the prisoners. If the Germans thought that we gave them too large an amount of water, they beat us severely. Our fate was worse, if the Germans suspected that we had talked to the prisoners. However, we managed to point some of the prisoners to a pile of clothes which they put on while laying down pretending to sleep. And when we left the camp, they mixed with us and managed to escape. One of the escapees, Vlodia, later became one of the leaders of our resistance group.

One day Chaim Sozkover approached Eliyahu Alperovitz. He told him about a rifle he had hidden deep in the woods and said "You young ones will need it."

My aunt Fiska Kastrel Alperovitz, Nachum's mother, was a woman in her fifties. She was different from most women: full of energy and extremely brave. During the time of German occupation, her slogan was, "We must do something." She encouraged her son to fight the Nazis anyway he could. She immediately volunteered to bring the rifle.

The next evening, Fiska, Nachoom and I started walking toward the area were the rifle was hidden. Fiska walked ahead, and we followed a few steps behind. Suddenly she stopped and we could see her walking down to the river, trying to hide behind the trees. She took a huge hay sack off her back and she started pulling something very long. It was the rifle. She put it in the hay sack, but it was too long and you could see the tip of it sticking out of the sack. She started walking towards the woods and we followed her to the front yard of Moshe the woodsman. We did not know what to do. We continued, with our journey planned in two stages. First, we ducked through the pigs alley. Pesia carried the knapsack all by herself. From there we took it to our hiding place. She was fearless. We walked right next to her to hide the rifle from view. We safely crossed the market place and immediately hid the rifle in Nachoom's cow shed, next to our house. Now we had a gun with 3 bullet and a rifle with no bullets.

יוסף נורמן, חבר המחתרת היהודית בקורניץ, לחם בשורות הפרטיזנים ביערות נארוץ'.

Yosef Norman

We decided to make fliers to encourage the population to fight the Germans. Shimon Zirolnik made a primitive printing press. Our problem was how to get the printing letter stencils. There were no letters in Kurenets so we decided to steal them from the printing house in Vileyka that was now used by the Germans. We found out that Nachoom's friend Yosef Norman worked there. We visited Shotzs from the Judenrat and demanded that Nachoom be taken with the first labor group of Kurintzers to be sent to work in Vileyka. Shotzs agreed. Nachoom went to the camp. There he met Yosef Norman, and Yosef agreed to be a member of our underground group. Three days later a little package was ready for Nachoom, and in it was the whole alphabet, and everything else we needed. Yosef acquired the package of printing letters under very dangerous circumstances. He knew that he would be shot on the spot if revealed, but he continued transferring printing material. Pesiah, Nachoom's mother sewed an apron with little pockets, each contained a different letter so Nachoom could put it on without it looking suspicious and also it could be quickly hidden. We made a printing room in the cowshed and next to it we built a hiding area deep in the ground. We started printing. Shimon Zirolnik planned our first flier but soon after he was imprisoned with other Jews with the suspicion that he was a communist. He was immediately taken and no one knew where to. A few weeks later his parents got a letter from Grodno from a prison camp for communist. In his letter he asked his parents to say "hi" to his boys and this is how our older friend was taken to his death.

Our house became the center of underground activities. My father was very worried about the Jews' fate and many times would quarrel with me. He said " I don't want the shtetle to be annihilated because of my son." But when he said it I could see some pride in his eyes. He never forbade me to participate in the resistance, just begged. So in the end of August our first fliers were posted. It read, "Farmer, keep your bread for yourself and for your heroic brothers that fight the horrible Nazi invaders. Not one seed to the Germans! Death to Hitler!" Shimon Zirolnik managed to post the flier just before he was arrested. We made hundreds of fliers and posted them in the villages next to Kurenets. The fliers made deep impressions on the communities around Kurenets. The rumors were that there was a large group of underground fighters in the area. Some of the Jews in town knew we were behind the resistance movement and saw us as saviors. Others denounced us as crazy and believed we would cause the annihilation of the shtetle. Politically being seen as a united group improved our relations with the Judenrat. We appeared as an organized entity, and they sent us wherever we requested.

The mayor of the town at that time was a Polish man named Matorose. Some years earlier at the time of the Polish rule he was the head master of the elementary school in Kurenets. Nyomka Shulman was then his favorite student. Nyomka approached him and asked to get a job as a official delivery man and assistant to the mayor. Matorose gave Nyomka the keys to the storage areas where there was supply of salt, gasoline and other goods. Nachoom got a job as a janitor and they both got official papers showing they were allowed to be around the restricted areas.

Nyomka told me to try to contact the non-Jewish residents in the district that were communist sympathizers and to find out if there is organized resistance. The first person that came to my mind was a relative of our housekeeper, Vera. He was the director of a factory at the time of the communists. Luckily, when I went to Vera and explained to her that I was looking for a hiding place for our family, she said she had a relative Andre Volinitz, who was also hiding from the Germans. I knew he would not betray me because we had the same enemy. I went to meet him in the little village Zoletki. He was sitting in a barn holding a rifle and a gun . He told me about himself. He was born in that very village. In 1934 he joined the Communist Party in Belarus and was eventually arrested for his communist activities he was imprisoned for five years. When the Communists took over they made him the director of a factory. Now he was in a similar situation to ours, hiding and trying to connect with the underground resistance in the area. When I told him about our group he was hesitant at first. I was the son of an owner of a store and he could not believe I would want to fight for the Soviets. I explained to him that our common enemy the Germans made all Jews want to join the Soviets in their fight against them. Anyway, in the end he agreed to head our group and to help us become underground fighters. We made an arrangement to meet again at the house of Ivan Shirutzin from Volkoveshtzina. The next day I went to Ivan Shirutzin and asked him how we could get weapons. He told me we could get weapons in exchange for salt and kerosene.

Farmers that were connected with the communists started coming to town and Nyomka that had forged the signature of Matorose gave them big bags of salt. In exchange we got rifles. The problem was how to bring the rifles to Kurenets. The first rifle was delivered by Motik and me. At night Motif Alperovitz and I snuck out of town ignoring curfew hours. we took the very large rifle from the house of a communist farmer, and put it in a nap sack and at 3 in the morning we started back to Kurenitz. The gentiles could not believe seeing us Jews walking during curfew It was a miracle we were not caught. The next day the farmer brought us 80 bullets for the other rifle we had.

Sometime after we distributed the fliers Nachoom had a visit from a young woman, she looked like a typical farm girl. Although she had black hair she spoke and looked like a shiksa. Her name was Berta Dimenstein. She was a Jew from the village Kolofi. She had some underground connection with Ivan from Volkoveshtzina. Prior to the war she was a member of HaShomer Hatzair. She said that she would be our main contact with the underground. She asked to print some fliers for her troop. She told Nachoom that she would come back the next day to get the fliers. Nachoom immediately called Eliyahu Alperovitz, Yitzhak Einbender, Nyomka Shulman and I to get together because he was worried that this arrangement was a trap. We argued a bit and then decided to take a chance and make the fliers. The next day when she returned I was present and immediately recognized her and knew everything was fine. Many years later I found out that Yosef Norman sent her to us.

From then on she met us every few days, she connected us with Motyokavitz, a communist youth we knew from our school. In September there was a meeting of the underground in Volkovishtzena. Nyomka insisted that we attend. The code word was "Vlodia." Nyomka took the gun that he had just exchanged for four salt bags with the main dealer in the area, Kostia from Litvinki. The meeting took place in the small chapel in Volkovishtzena. Commissar Vlodia the POW that we helped escape was the main organizer. They were planning to go to the woods at the end of 1941.

[Click here to enlarge the picture]

*A newspaper article written in 1990 in Molodeczno
about the Jewish underground members from Kurenets*

Now we belonged to a real organization and we were part of the collective fight against the Nazis. We were ecstatic. We were too naive to realize that these were individual resistance groups that at this point were not connected to the USSR.

We continued with the fliers and searching for weapons. Itzka Rider told us that Bogdanyook, the guard of the train station in Kurenets had a "Browning". Nyomka Shulman was becoming our leader. He decided that we would take Bogdanyooks' gun. Afraid to be recognized we sent one of Vlodia's men, Soborov to go Bogdanyooks house. Soborov entered the house and threatened Bogdanyook and was able to get his gun. All the weapons that we acquired were hidden in our house.

The whole month my father was depressed, he could not get in touch with my mother. Then Kopelovitz, a Jew from Kurenets, told us that after the Germans invaded, on their way back to town from the nursing home. Mother died of starvation. They buried her in Ivia. Our beloved mother had joined the group of victims of the Nazi occupation.

My father started walking around the house in deep depression. After we heard the news of 54 Kurenitz Jews killed for being Communists, my father and I had a conversation. He said, "Son who knows maybe your way is the right way, they will kill us all. Neither G-d nor the Judenrat can save us, all we are left with is revenge."

Going from Kurenitz to Volkovishtzena and back became more and more complicated and dangerous. Berta who looked like a Christian, took it on herself to distribute the fliers that Nachoom printed and Nyomka Shulman and Vlodia edited.

Noach Dinerstein from Vileyka

In the beginning of Autumn a new member joined our group. His name was Noach Dinnerstein. He was an alumni of HaShomer Hatzair in Vileyka. In 1939 he was a soldier in the Polish army, When the Germans invaded, he was a POW and managed to escape and return home during the Soviet times. Just before the German invasion he became a soldier in the soviet army and was sent to Bialistok. Once again he was POW, he managed to escaped from the Germans and returned to Vileyka. When he returned he stayed in hiding. One day he went down from is hiding place and learned that all the men were taken by the Germans. He then left to stay with relatives in Kurenets. Finally we had a man in our midst that was trained as a soldier. He taught us how to take a rifle apart, how to oil it, put it back together and to use it. Later Noach Dinnerstein became a renown partisan who was eventually killed in action.

We decided to add some more people to our troop; Chayim Yitzhak Zimmerman and Yankale Alporevitch, two brothers; Salim and Moshe Shnitzer, sons of a family of refugees from Poland who in their escape from the Nazis somehow ended in Kurenitz. Later on we added Shimon, son of Zishka Shimon Meirs' Alperovich, one of the most educated men in town, Shimon became a great fighter but to our regret he was killed just before liberation. Vlodia asked us to see if the Jewish doctor Sorinski would join our group. He agreed and later on he became a doctor for the partisans in the forest.

After the Actzia, where the Germans killed 54 Jews saying that they were killed for being communist the Judenrat warned my father and other parents of our underground members, telling of the threat we posed to all the town Jews by our activities. When we heard about it, we stormed into the meeting with two drawn guns. We threatened to kill whoever threaten our families. This helped and they never directly approached us again. The head of police, Adamovitz though, told my father that he saw me outside of town past curfew hours and explained how this behavior could cause both mine and my father's death. We decided to be less conspicuous and to use more covert tactics.

On November 1, nine members of Vlodia's troop all of whom had once been POW's, left for the forest. They called the troop "Sovietico Belarus", which means for Soviet Byelorussia. The highest officer was Volinitz and the commissar was Vlodia Betinov. They had seven rifles, two machine guns and 3 automatic weapons. Occasionally this group would carry terrorist actions. But at that point, mostly they distributed fliers and communicated with other groups.

The winter of 1942 was a rough, harsh one. With the help of Michael Basilic, we attained a radio and we started getting information from the Soviets. We printed the information and distributed it around the villages. The German EsDe looked every where for the printing place. They never guessed it was 100 meters from the local police and was being generated by Jews. On December 20, 1941 we got the order from Berta to come on the 26 to Kolofi. This was the first general meeting of everyone that was connected to Vlodia.

One of Vlodia's men dressed as a policeman and took Noach Dinnerstein, Eliyahu Alperovich, Yitzhak Einbender, Nyomka Shulman, Yankale Alporevitch and me . We pretended we were prisoners going to work in the Vileyka camp, the partisan was very convincing in his roll as a cop. When we arrived we had to hide for many hours till night time came. All together there were about 40 people at the meeting. They pretended that it was a dance party. Inside everyone was armed. Berta introduced Vlodia as the commissar of the partisan Otriad. Vlodka said we must forget each others names, each one will get a nickname. we would work secretly, and most importantly make sure that no traitors infiltrated our group. We were told to learn how to fight in the same way the red army fought at the gates of Moscow. We elected representatives for Vileyka and Kurenitz. They were Uri Bolshov, Berta Dimenstein, Nikoli Motyokavitz, Vladimir Sovitz and Vlodia Betinov. Assigned to the terrorist missions were Motyokavitz, Sokolov, Bolshov, Zalman Gurevitch (me), Yakov Alperovich and Vladimir Sovitch. For the flier printing and distributing, Berta Dimenstein, Nachoom Alperovitz, Noah Dinerstein and Yitzhak Einbinder and Ivan Shirutzin were assigned. The radio was the responsibility of Michael Baslik. Benjamin Shulman, Vladimir and Uri Bolshov, would be responsible for food clothing and supplies and transferring them to the woods and to also organize a secret youth resistance troop.

On January 20, 1942 Nachoom printed fliers saying, " Fellow Belarussian brothers, farmers and teenagers, the red army destroyed the Nazis in the gates of Moscow and threw them west. The fairy tale of the undefeatable Nazis is a lie. The partisans are doing everything to help the red army with its fight against the Fascists. We call unto you to refuse the orders of the Nazis, blowup the bridges, destroy the telephone and electricity, clean the soviet land from the Nazi filth. Death to the Fascist Occupant." Meanwhile Nachoom got a job in the printing press in Vileyka and under the nose of the head of the printing house he was able to print fliers and to steal printing materials. These materials were all transferred to Ivan in Volkovishtzena.

On Feb. 3, 1942 I got an order to blow up the bridge near the grain mill that belonged to Mendel Dinerstein. Yitzhak Einbender, Nachoom, some non-Jews partisans and I crossed the street Vilyeka and continued across the forest and the frozen wet lands and approached the mill. At eleven at night we met with the Kolofi underground members, gave them the explosives and continued to the train tracks. Sokolov connected the explosives to the train tracks, I lined the wire across the trucks to the other side, went down the hill and pulled the wire about twenty meters. We lit the wire and a few minutes later there was a huge explosion. We immediately left. first we went to the synagogue and from there we all separated to our homes. When I got home my father was at the door standing there crying. He asked if I was there I shook my head and said nothing. Another group that was headed by Noah Dinerstein and included Nyomka Shulman and Motik Alporevitch was supposed to do the same operation to another bridge in the village of Ratzke. Both missions were scheduled for exactly 11 o'clock. I didn't hear an explosion from Ratzke and was very worried. But at two in the morning I heard a huge explosion. The next day Nyomka said that the string was not dry enough so they went to a farm and took some shavings of wood to dry the string and that is why the mission was delayed. The Germans never suspected the Jews, they searched the villages and killed some farmers and some ex POW's that they found working for the farmers.

On Feb. 15 we met with Vlodia and a decision was made that on the 23 of Feb, the day of the red army, we would blow up the main storage house of the Germans. Nyomka insisted at first that we take part in that mission. Vlodia objected using the same reasoning as the Judenrat did, that if they catch one Jew belonging to the underground they will immediately kill all the Jews. He said "I will agree that you will join us at missions in the fields and villages, but not in town". On Feb. 23, Volinitz people blew up the main storage area that was also used to gather cows to later be sent to Germany. 1000 cows were burned to death. The fire lasted all night and Volinitz people also succeeded to steal a lot of flour, rice and other supplies and can goods. They brought it all to the partisan base.

Noach Dinerstein and I were sent to look for a suitable place for an underground base. We went to Soroka, a Christian friend of my father from the village Ob. We told him we would like to find a base and he promised to talk to a friend of his who was a woodsman. Meanwhile we walked to the next village, Nieke. We approached Old Mullah, Noah Dinnerstein's uncle and asked him to arrange a meeting with the young Jews of the area. We hoped that they would join the underground because they grew up in the woods and knew every trail. Mullah was thrilled and shortly he gathered some young men. They immediately wanted to help. One of them Yerachmiel suggested that he would also talk to some Jews from Kribitz and Dolhinov who worked in the train station Kanahanina.

The forester looked for a suitable place for the base. He went to Nyomka and got some salt for payment for his search but soon after the German's killed the woodsman. Someone must have informed the Germans.

Yerachmiel did go to Kanahanina and he told us how the Jews there were practically starving so we asked Shots from the Judenrat to send them some food. We also encouraged them to escape. Some of them did and later they joined the partisans in East Belarus. Some years later I met two of them. On was Bushka Kalkovitz that I knew from Dolhinov. The other was Motka Bengin who I met at the end of 1944 at the Minsk University. He was a professor of Rhetoric in the low faculty where I was later a student.

Meanwhile, we were collecting weapons and warm clothes in preparation of our departure to the forest. On May 3, 1942 Noah and Berta left for the woods. At the same time they took most of our weapons with them. On May 5, 1942 we were contacted by Xina Bitzon, she was our new intermediary. She said that at this point only three people could go. We decided that Nachoom with his printing press, Eliyahu Alporevitch and I would go now and the rest of the troop will stay under the command of Nyomka Shulman. At night we hid in the woods and only early in the morning, Berta and another partisan met us and took us to join the rest of the partisans. To a camp between Tzintzivi and a little village Zlotki. The forest was very misty and all the zimlankas, (deep in the ground hiding places) were used so we just lied under a pine tree and immediately fell asleep. When we woke up we went to Volinitz and demanded that he give us our weapons. He explained that the Otriad (troop) numbers 30 people and that there are not enough weapons for everyone. Meanwhile he gave us rifles that were not nearly as good as our rifles. At night 16 people went on a mission but they didn't let us join because we were too new. Still while I was guarding the camp I felt great. for the first time since the German occupation I was free. The woods were beautiful. I was not a "nobody" any longer and now I could revenge…

One day Motyokavitz voluntarily went to work for the Germans to be a double agent. He told us of a German patrol of policemen that goes everyday between Vileyka and Luban riding bicycles. We put a unit on the road and when they went through we shot them and took 11 rifles and 4 hand guns and police clothing. The head of the underground was becoming more ambitious and decided to destroy a bridge on the river Villia on the main road to Molodechno. Motiyokevitch situated himself as a guard on the bridge. On the 13 of June everyone in our base but our guards went to the Villia river. We watched as three policemen, Motiyokevitch, Volinitz, and Shetonov, all connected to the partisans, left their posts. Motiyokevitch tipped his hat as a signal and from a hiding place two partisans walked out and they were dressed with German uniforms. They walked directly to the bridge. The two policemen from the Molodechno side of the bridge approached the impostors and left only one policeman guarding with a machine gun. Shetonov lifted his rifle and hit him on his head. The two partisans continued walking from the Vileyka side and joined Motiyokevitch. Motiyokevitch and Volinitz killed one of the German guards and threw him to the river. Shetonov jumped the German next to the machine gun but he started screaming. When the rest of the Germans and policemen heard the screams they jumped out of the building. We immediately started shooting. The partisans on the bridge started throwing grenades. We took a lot of weapons from the wounded and killed Germans. We lit the wooden bridge an fire. 15 Germans and Policemen were killed.

We knew that the Germans would not forget that and we should plan for a counter attack. On the 27th of June we heard shots from about ½ a km from our camp and knew an attack was coming.

*Kurenets 2000, Zalman Uri Gurevitz
with a non Jewish partisan who helped to save many Jews*

The First Battle

Everyone was in a panic. The head of the brigade Volinitz immediately gathered us. We were 37 in total, ready for battle. One of the guards came running and told us that the Germans had surrounded the camp and it seemed that someone who knows us had shown them the way. I had one gun and two grenades. Volinitz ordered us to separate to four groups. Nachoom and I were in Vlodia's group. The other groups were commanded by Volinitz, Brazovbiski and Novogin. Each group split in a diameter of about 70 meters from the camp and crouched on the ground. Our group had one machine gun and ammunition and some rifles. Meanwhile the shots stopped, the guards joined the groups.

Only half an hour later we started seeing Germans. They walked in a chain formation protected by heavy fire attack. Then they laid down and waited for shots in response. They did the same three times. They were very close to Volinitz's troop and after awhile we heard our guys shooting. Immediately as the Germans heard the firing they began throwing grenades. They kept advancing, reached Norvitz group who also began firing at the Germans. Then the Germans approached us. When they reached about 30 meters away we were given the orders to fire. We saw some Germans fall down but others kept advancing closer and closer. Then they were quiet. The Germans were digging trenches. We knew we could not fight them so Vlodia gave the order to retreat. All the other groups retreated as well. We all separated and hid in different areas. I was with Vlodia and Nachoom until the evening came.

When it got dark we returned to the camp. The German's had left the area. The hiding places were left alone but the kitchen was burned, the food destroyed and the printing press thrown away. Near the radio we saw a body. Vlodia turned his lamp and we saw that it was our dear friend Eliyahu son of Reuven- Zishka Alporevitch with a bullet in his head. We couldn't find anyone else so Vlodia decided to retreat in the direction Krelietza. He was sure the Germans would return the next day to clear out the base. From far away we heard shots so Nachoom went to see what was happening. We waited ½ an hour and he did not return. We did not know what to do. Vlodia told me that I must return to Kurenitz and he would return to Volkovishtzena and after he finds out more information he will send Berta or Xina to get me. I returned to Kurenitz with one gun in my pocket. My family was ecstatic. They told me that Nachoom arrived earlier. My father told Nyomka that I returned and he came over with Yitzhak. He decided that we must be seen in town.

The first thing I did was to go Reuven-Zishka Alperovitz and tell him about his son death. We sat together and cried. Reuven-Zishka never forgave me for taking his young son to the woods. The Judenrat paid some money to the woodsman Silak so he would not tell the Germans that the deceased was a Jew from Kurenitz. Silak told Sina from the Judenrat that Eliyahu was wounded during the battle and the Germans investigated him about the partisans. Elik told them that there were hundreds of partisans with a lot of weapons. After a short time they shot him in the head. Silak never told the Germans who Elik was but he was the one that brought the Germans to the area for which he was punished later. But that is another story I will tell you about later.

Nyomaka and sister, Chana Shulman
Nyomka was killed while fighting the Germans in 1943.
Chana was killed with her father; Aaron and mother Elka, on 9-9-1942.

After that Tzintzivi battle our partisan head quarters realized it was not logical to put our base so near German bases. They decided to move east near Plaschesnitz. There they first joined the Otriad Brava and eventually with Otriad Distival they became part of Diadia vasia. Meanwhile we were waiting in Kurenitz for some communication. Most of the weapons we collected went with the Otriad. We did have some weapons that Nyomka managed to keep, not fully trusting the gentiles as to let go of our entire collection. He also purchased some new guns from Kostia. On July 5 Nikoli Shirotzin's wife came to me and told me that the Otriad went East and at this point they had to leave about 40 people in our area. She promised that in about 2 weeks they would collect the rest of us and take us east.

Every week we would go to Volkovishtzena to see if there is news from the Otriad. One time Nachoom went and he run into Berta with another partisan named Vorbviov. Vorbviov told Nachoom to join them at once to go east. Nachoom refused, he said he must get the rest of the guys. Nachoom returned and sent his mother to Nyomka. Meanwhile Xina Bitzon arrived to take us, Nachoom, Nyomka Shulman and Yitzhak Einbinder looked for me but couldn't find me so they left a note to meet them in Volkovishtzena. In the evening as soon as I got the note I went to meet them. But it was too late. They had already left.

So now from the old troop only Chayim Yitzhak Zimmerman, Motik Alporevitch and I were around. It was already the middle of August and there is no communication. Most of the Jews that were left in the area were killed and we knew that Kurenitz' turn was approaching. On Aug. 24 Motik and I went to Volkovishtzena hoping that we could make some communication with the resistance. Ivan said that Berta did come once looking for us but she had not returned. We decided to do something on our own. We went to Soroka in the village of Hog, and he told us that in the woods there were some Jews from Nieke. He also heard that there were partisans there but he never saw them. We decided to leave for the Pushtza (deep in the wood area that the partisans used for their bases) on the 20 of Sep. We were all prepared and then…

Lately I was sleeping in a hide out and I was doing the same on Sep. 9. At two in the morning Moshe Alporevitch our neighbor came to our house. He was very frightened, he told us that from his window across from the police station he saw a few hundred police men in cars and from what he understood today was going to be the day of slaughter. My father and sister and brother and the family of Moshe Alporevitch decided to hide in that sacharon (hiding place). I said I was not staying and would go at once to Volkovishtzena or the woods. I took my rifle and a gun, dressed very warmly and carried a few thing I prepared ahead for our departure to the forest. I left from the vegetable garden to the direction to the fields that would take me to the forest Savina. The fog was thick. At the edge of the field I saw many shadows running. Some of our troop members joined me; the two brothers Salim and Moshio Shnitzer, we were also joined by Chayim Shletzer, Chayim Alporevitch and 16 years old Zalman son of Moshe Alporevitch that later joined the Red Army. They all begged me to take them with me . They thought they would be safer because I know my way out. We started towards the fields, we crossed the roads circling the town and when we were two hundred meters away there was a bombardment of shots from all sides. From afar we could see the shadows of policemen circling the town. There was a distance of 20 meters between each. We immediately laid down and started crawling to the direction of Savina. But there was no chance to cross the ring of soldiers. Luckily for us the fog was very thick so we started crawling towards Vileyka street where only Christians lived. I hoped that there I would not find so many policemen. But I was wrong. It was clear now that the whole town was surrounded and that there was no way out. So I decided to go to one of the Christians barn hoping they would not search there. Three of the barns were locked. The fourth one was open. As I found out later it was Ingale Biruk's barn. We went on top of the hay that was all the way to the ceiling and we hid deep inside it. When I reached the barn I realized that Zalman was lost. Many hours past and we had heard shots from everywhere and that was the way we passed the night. At 8 in the morning we heard the sound of footsteps. Someone came inside, walked on top of the hay, but then left. We heard him lock the door.

All day long we heard shouts, cries and shots. The air was filled with the smell of burned bodies. We wanted to scream but we had to be quite. We waited for night to come to try to escape. At 11 o'clock at night we heard the door open and then close. We heard whispers but we could not make out what was said. It lasted a long time. At the beginning I thought it was a couple making love. I decided to leave the barn. We started rolling form the top of the hay and all of a sudden I heard Yiddish words and people running to the direction of the locked door. I understood they were Jews and I yelled to them in Yiddish, "don't run." They stopped and to my surprise they were my mother's brother Gershon Iyashivski, his wife Etta and their two children, Yochevet, Etta's sister with a child and their father Zalman Mendel Zipelevitch who was lying on the hay dying. They told me that the gentile Ingale Biruk knew about their hiding place and helped them as he promised and brought them here. Ingle knew that there were some other Jews hiding in his barn so he locked the door after us knowing that the Police would not look in locked barns. I didn't know what to do. Little children and sick men. I offered my uncle to join us. He answered, " No Zalman, you are a partisan, but where would I with little children go, how could I leave Zalman Mendel in such a state." We kissed and while crying he said sounding very fatalistic, "My dear you will be saved but we are lost, say Kaddish after us. " We broke the door and left towards the woods. We heard shots but they were not after us. After 1 km we started running. The forest was 50-600 meters away. Then I saw a man running towards us, it was Shimon son of Zishka Alperovitz, he was a member of our group.

*Members of HaShomer Hatzair
(and later the underground) in Kurenets in 1938
Standing on the left: Yitzhak Einbinder, Elik Alperovitz and Shimon Zimerman on the right*

*Spring of 1990 at the former headquarters of the
Varshilov Brigade in the Naarootz forests
From left: Zalman Uri Gurevitz, Danilotzkin (Vlodia), Yakov Alperovitz and his son*

In the Deep Woods

My father and I had an agreement that if anyone would be saved from the Actzia the meeting place would be at his good friend the Christian Yoshekevitz from Borodino. I took the whole group to Yoshekevitz. I knocked on the window and sounding like a partisan I demanded to open the door. He recognized my voice and told me that he heard they killed Kurenitz' Jews and he was waiting for my father the whole day but so far he had not arrived. I asked him to go to Kurenitz and find out what had happened to my family. He gave us food and showed us a hiding place in the small forest not far from his house.

In the morning he went to Kurenitz and later returned with horror stories. Concerning my father and my family he said he couldn't find them but the gentiles told him that Natan Gurevitch family was not amongst the dead. He told us a little bit of what he heard of the day of slaughter. How they took the beautiful girl Sarah, daughter of Bat-sheva and smashed her head against the wall. He told us of our teenage friend, Chiale Sosonoski that fought the German who took her, scratched his face and shouted, "The day of revenge would come." He said that many Jews escaped and he saw many gentile residents of Kurenitz going from house to house taking out the floors and looking for hidden treasures. I decided to stay for a few days in the little forest until I find out what happened to my family. The rest of the group decided to wait too. On the third day Shimon went to get some food from Yoshekevitz and found out that my family was alive and here in the woods. And they were with Moshe Alperovich family. I started looking for them and immediately found them. We were all ecstatic, kissed and cried. The whole family was saved.

I stayed in the woods for another day and then walked with Salim to Volkovishtzena to see if there was any news from the partisans. We couldn't find any of our connection. The Germans and the police were searching for suspects in all the villages and all the men escaped. Ivan's wife was arrested.

Salim and Shimon left us to check the situation in the deep forests, they promised to return and take the rest of the group to the deeper woods in Hog. At night I returned to Volkovishtzena and I found Berta. She told me what had happened with the Otriad. about Noah Dinerstien who was fighting with the partisans in the east. She also saw Nyomka Shulman going east. She said that Nachoom Alperovich, Nyomka Shulman, Yitzhak Einbinder were sent east through the gate of Surez. A place that through it the partisans and refugees crossed the German lines to the Russian side. There they sent my friends to learn terrorist's techniques and explosive management.

I told her of my dilemma, that my whole family was safe and was now about 4 km from Kurenitz, what should I do?!. Berta said, "Wait, you are so lucky for your whole family to be saved, that is a present from God, don't leave them. Take them to the Pushtza and then join the Otriad." We agreed that on the 10 of Oct. I will come to Volkovishtzena and wait for her until the 20th. Meanwhile I would transfer my family to the woods. I returned to the Borodino forest and saw that Simah and her daughter Rivka Gvint joined us. A few days later Salim returned from the pushtza and together we transferred everyone to the big pushtza in the vicinity of Hog.

The situation of the Jews in Pushtza was bad, very bad. About 300 Jews including old women and babies escaped from the Kurenitz slaughter and were now in the Pushtza. The men and the women walk to the neighboring villages and asked for bread, potatoes, flour or soup., A few of the men received the food after they threatened to light the farms on fire. A few times when they refused they stole from the fields. They stole laundry that was hanging in the yard. What could they do? they had to survive.

Even harder was the situation of women who escaped without men. They were victims for every Christian, every man. The fight for survival was very cruel. So the lucky ones that were left from the slaughter from Kurenitz, nyake, Kribitzi and Mydell had their own hell on earth….

The Departure to Vostok

In the forest I met Motik Alperovich, Eliyahu's brother. He was also a member of our troop. I told him about Berta's promise to meet up with me in Volkovishtzena. We went to Volkovishtzena and we were told that if any of our troop members want to join the partisans they must come to some meeting place in Harstintzitz. And from there they will be taken to the Otriad. We returned to the pushtza and there we found Yankale Alperovich. He joined the partisan Otriad Mastetal, (meaning the revenged). I rested for two days and then went to the headquarters of the Otriad. The guard went inside to ask if they would allow me entrance. They let me in and immediately I saw a familiar person. It was Timsok, the now commissar, who I knew from

Kurenitz and the day I left Kurenitz for Dolhinov I met him in the market and he told me to go east. He knew all of our deeds as a troop and asked us to join his troop particularly because I had a weapons.

I told him about my family that was saved and how I want to transfer them east. He told me not to worry, that they were planning on moving all the Jews east to the Soviet Union through the gates of the Surez. So he decided to make me one of the coordinators of the transfer unit and he said that when I reach Plashntzenitz I would join the Brova Otriad and my family will continue deep into Russia. I consulted with my father, Motik Alperovich and Shimon Zishka Alperovich, and they all were very happy with the news because some of their family members were saved and we could now take care of them. I didn't find the Shnitzer brothers and heard they were somewhere in the Pushtza. I returned to Timsok and told him that we all agreed.

The Jews started preparing for the journey to the Vostok. They prepared lapstot, a kind of boots that are made from clothing material. Among the Jews in the woods there was a shoe maker from Kribitz and he repaired everyone's shoes. They also gathered some bread, salt, and crackers. This was the middle of November 1942. On one Saturday, 300 people from all over the Pushtza gathered. 200 of them were Jews from Kurenitz, the rest were from Nyeke, Kribitz, Molodechno, Vileyka, Mydell and Kobilnik. The camp was divided to groups of tens. At the head of each ten they put a captain and every group had partisans as guides. The first group included fifty men with one partisan. When night came we started walking.

At the beginning everything was fine. But parents with little kids and old people suffered. Slowly the distance between the groups grew larger. The young people held the children and carried them on their shoulders. The partisans also tried to help and they were extremely nice to everyone. A few started slowing and the partisans told them they must hurry to cross the train tracks before light. 300 people spread around one km, many just could not keep up with the rest. The partisan decided to get some horse and buggies because they were so slow. 4 km from the train tracks the partisans went to the village Peskovitch Tzizana and they took three buggies with horses and they had the little children and old men sit in them. When they reached 200 meters from the train tracks they told everyone to rest and they returned the horse and buggies. When they returned they ordered everyone to cross the train tracks. Everyone got up and quickly crossed the tracks.

We still had to cross the Kurenitz Dolhinov road and not far from there were two German camps. This was the most dangerous part of the 40 kilometers that we had to go that day. We sent three people to check the road. We waited and waited and they did not return. Later we found out that a group of 50 people crossed the road safely and they wrongly assumed that the rest of us were following. Somehow there was miscommunication and we did not follow. When hours past and night time was almost over we decided to look for some forest to hide during the day and at night we would continue east. 250 people rested in the forest joined by 3 partisans. The danger was unimaginable but everyone was extremely well behaved. They hardly talked and even the babies were quiet. All day long we saw German cars on the road and farmers walking here and there. We kept quite and in extreme worries we passed the day. When it got dark we continued east. We left the clearing and went into the forest. The next village was 5 km away. From there we had another 20 km to the next partisan stop.

Very quickly we realized that in theory this was a good plan but in reality the people could not accomplish the mission. Everyone was very thirsty having not had anything to drink all day. The children could hardly walk, the line became longer and longer and the distance between the groups grew larger. The belongings and the metal food containers were making a lot of noise and along with the crying children and the parents trying to calm them down the noise could be heard all around.

All of a sudden we heard shots being fired and machine guns shooting from the direction of Dividki. Our being so loud saved us. As we later found out the police put a barricade and were waiting for us to arrive. They thought it was a small partisan group that was arriving. But when they heard such laud sounds they thought is was a big partisan army and that scared them and they opened fire sooner than originally planned. They started lighting the night with flares and kept shooting at us. Everyone panicked and ran to the direction of the forest. I knew that they were not going to touch us because they were too far. About forty people reached the forest with me. We lay on the ground. I had no idea what happened to the rest. From afar I could see people crawling to the forest. I could see 13 year old Yishayu Kramer who looked like a ten year old falling and getting up. Crawling and on his shoulders he was carrying his three year old sister Marishka. What a nightmare.

The shots stopped. I couldn't find the partisans and we were in a tiny forest. I didn't know the area but from my calculations we walked about 3 or 4 km east so we were still between Kastivonitz and Kanihinina. I knew that the Germans would look for us at the first day light so we looked for a bigger forest. We found one and exhausted we fell asleep. Early in the morning we woke up to the sound of shots. The Germans were going though the road looking for partisans. They didn't come near us. We laid down the whole day without movement. When evening came again we heard some more shots. We decided to go back to the Pushtza where we originally came from.

I was happy Yitzchak Zimmerman was with us. He was a village man, smart and even tempered. I had someone to consult with. We both knew we must return to the woods we came from. But first we had to find out where we where. Yitzhak and I left the group and went to look for a farm. We found one and knocked on the window. An old woman answer but she gave us no help. We decided to find the road on our own. We managed to find a road and while walking we found a rich looking farm. The farmer told us the way to a town that was the opposite way from which we wanted to go. We didn't want him to know our real plans. We returned to the group. We didn't have anything to drink for 24 hours. We started walking and reached a village. We saw dirty water in the drainage system. We all drank from it using the palm of our hands. Yitzhak knew of this village and knew it was close to the train tracks.

Once again Yitzhak, Wexler and I left the group and went to check the train tracks. This time we were luckier it was not watched. We motioned to the rest of the group to follow us and we crossed the tracks. Everyone was very thankful but we had no time to rejoice. With Yitzka's help I hurried the group. We walked all night and in the morning we reached the village Margi at the edge of the Pushtza we left earlier.

Now I was all separated from my original troop. Motik Alperovich and Shimon Zishkas' Alperovich were with the first group of people to successfully reached the Vostok. I never saw them again. Both were killed in action during battles in the east Belarusian Forest in 1944 as heroes of U.S.S.R.

Meeting of former partisans from the Naarutz forests
in Petach Tikva 1957
Middle row second from the left: Morbatzik, Rala Bogin, ?, Shura Bogin, ?, Moshe Yudka Rodnizki.
Top row, first on the left: Moshe Shotan, fifth: Zalman Uri Gurevitz, Yaakov Shafran

Part Three: On Hills of Dust

[Pages 299-303]

A Small Remnant

by Daviv Motosov

Translated by Eilat Gordin Levitan

As soon as Germany invaded Russia in June of 1941, I left Kurenets and joined many others in the waves of the storm to escape the Nazis until I reached a town in Siberia by the name Novosbirsk, where I settled during the war years. After some time, we started hearing horrible rumors from refugees who arrived from the occupied areas. The rumors were about bloody massacres and annihilations carried out by Hitler's thugs against our people. My heart was filled with worries about the fate of my tortured brothers and particularly my dear family members who stayed in Kurenets, trapped in the jaws of the predatory beast. Everyday they came to my heart, and images of their bitter fate kept coming to me. These images were very disturbing, so disturbing that I couldn't get any rest. I knew very well what the Nazi monsters were like. I experienced their cruelty personally during the days when I was a POW of the Germans in 1939. I could hardly wait for the day when the evil rulers would be annihilated. Though my heart was filled with worries and anxiety. Despite all the rumors and all the news I received, I still had some hope that one day I would see the town of Kurenets with its Jews the way I wanted to see it, but to my great sorrow it was never to be. Finally the war reached an important point. The Russians had their first victories in battle and the Nazis started retreating from the Red Army, which took control of the situation, going from victory to victory and town after town was freed from the hands of the invaders.

At the beginning of June of 1944, I went to the town of Gorki. This was a time of summer vacation for me and I wanted to spend it with my sisters who lived in Gorki ever since the first World War. Everyday I sat by the radio and listened with great anticipation to every bit of news from the front. And here, on one summer day, the announcer, Levitan, announced in Russian, "Today, after bitter, cruel, and prolonged battles, our splendid army freed from the oppression of the Nazis, the towns Ilia, Kriviczi, Kurenets, Dolhinov, Vileyka…"

My excitement and anticipation kept increasing, and in my imagination I was already back in my Kurenets. Despite the fact that I knew very clearly that my brothers, the sons of my nation were annihilated almost entirely, I still hoped in the depths of my heart, that maybe someone from my large family in the area had survived. The thought of returning to Kurenets would not let go of me, not even for a minute, and after a sleepless night I woke up early in the morning, determined to go there. My sisters tried to stop me from immediately leaving since the war still going on. Maybe they were right. The entire area knew that Kurenets was still in a war situation and there were pockets of fighting all around, but all their reasoning could not prevent me from going.

A day later, with a small suitcase in my hand, dressed in a Red Army uniform, I left on my way.

I experienced an unbelievable journey embarking on the very extensive and intricate road from Gorki, which was situated Far East from Moscow, all the way to Kurenets. Renowned diaries of adventurers that I used to read in my youth were nothing by comparison to all that I experienced during that journey, where the roads were destroyed and many of the trains never reached their destinations, consequently I had to rely on every kind of transportation, including my feet.

After eight days and nights I arrived in Vileyka. From Vileyka it was impossible to find any transportation, so in the usual tradition of the Kurenetsers, I walked to my hometown by foot. It was a beautiful summer day. With each step closer to Kurenets, my heart beat faster, and my head would spin. Would I find amongst the ruins, which I was told about on the road, any of my family members alive? While I was walking the ancient cedar trees, I saw from afar, an image of a man coming towards me. When he came closer I recognized him, it was a goy by the name of Kasia Siamka's. He was our neighbor in previous years. He also recognized me. With all the excitement, we kissed each other. At that point, I didn't know that Kasia was a collaborator with the Nazis and that his hands were stained with the blood of the Jews. I asked him, "Kasia, who is alive from my family?"

Kasia didn't answer anything, he only bowed his head, not looking at me. I didn't ask anymore. I understood the tragedy in its entirety. I said goodbye to him and continued walking ahead, but without any excitement and with no anticipation. I knew now that I would not find any of the dear ones alive, and soon I would enter a huge graveyard that was named Kurenets.

Here I reached the first homes on Vileyka Street and as a person who is walking inside a horrible nightmare, I approached the market square. And all of a sudden... Empty space... Only the tall chimneys came up from the ruins. All the houses that used to be in the central market and the nearby streets had disappeared... I didn't meet one living soul. I stood in silence at the middle of the market, not knowing where I should go from here, the empty market.

Suddenly I saw two figures walking from afar, near the ruins of the house of Zalman Gvint Z"L. Those two figures were coming close to where I was standing. They were two Jewish girls. I recognized them as Freydl the daughter of Mendel Alperovich, and the other was Hana, the daughter of Chaim Avraham Alperovich. They didn't recognize me. I introduced myself and together we started walking towards the few houses that remained intact.

The first remaining house was in Kosyul (?) and until the edge of Myadel Street. We sat on the front porch of the house of Ruven Dimmenstein Z"L, and one by one, the few Jewish remainders started coming there. The Jewish residents of my hometown who had stayed were broken, lacking any energy. They were all in shock and depression. They came to me and greeted me. The entire evening, until midnight, we sat there and I listened to their stories of grief and mourning for the annihilated town and its people. Now, when I think of it, I can hardly remember what I felt that moment. All I can remember is that I couldn't say a word. IT was as if I became frozen. The images of the tortures of the martyrs and the pain of their last moments kept coming to my eyes, but as much as I tried to really comprehend what happened, I could not help but ask, "Is this a nightmare? How could this be true? No, no, it is a nightmare."

Reality, reality, reality. The conclusion was very cruel. From the two thousand souls that our Jewish town contained, only about 100 survived. The family of Natka Hana's invited me to stay with them, and I couldn't sleep that night. At early morning hours I lay down for a few minutes, but as soon as the sun came up, I left the house to see the place where the town's Jews were annihilated. It was a small field near the house of Dov-Bar Shulman Z-L.

On the graves of the martyrs of Kurenets
<u>*Standing from right to left*</u>*:*
Atta Harnas, Nachamka Zimmerman, Ruven Alperovich and David Motosov

A beautiful summer morning, filled with excitement was teeming around me The sun came up with all its glory as I experienced many days before. And there I stood, like a pillar of stone, on that piece of land that was saturated with the blood and the dust of all those who were once the people of my town, my friends, my relatives, and my dear family. My dear ones, what were your crimes and your sins that such a horrible punishment was given to you? Weren't your lives a life of honest toil?

The life of people who day and night worked for the welfare of your families? To educate your children, and to keep the rules of God and the rules of the state of which you were citizens? Why were you given such an awful penalty? What did you feel when you knew that you had reached your last moments and cruel death that the wolf-like people prepared for you? My dear and honored father, did you forgive me for saving myself while leaving you there? I fell on the wet meadow that already grew on top of the huge grave of the martyrs and tears streamed unstoppably from my eyes to the land.

On the graves of the martyrs of Kurenets

Left to right:
Yankle Alperovich, Yizhak Fidler, Meir Mekler, Zelig Liberman, Aba Naruzki & Moshe Liberman

Left to right: Leizer Shulman, Gutel Gordon, Zelig Liberman,
Moshe Liberman, Aba Naruzki, Akiva Levin, Meir Mekler,
Yitzhak Fidler, Yankle Alperovich, Orzhik Alperovich,
Moshe Mordechai Dinerstein & David Zimerman

Family and friends returned to Kurenets in order to relocate the remains of ones they had lost. This mission was carried out in secret for fear that the government would disallow their efforts or that people living in the surrounding area would return to search the remains for riches as they had done before the surviving Jews of Kurenets in the 1950s' taking the bones of their slaughtered brothers and sisters to a Jewish burial.

Already that day, after I paid my respects at the cemetery of my dear mother, Z-L, I was ready to leave Kurenets forever, but the remnants who were left there didn't let me accomplish my decision. They begged me to stay there so that together we could get revenge on and bring to justice all the Christians that robbed the victims and spilled their blood, and collaborated with the Nazis. Twenty-one months I sat in Kurenets. Every day I heard from the remnants as well as a few righteous Christians testaments of the annihilation of the Jewish residents of Kurenets. I heard and recorded testaments of each of the more than one thousand people who perished in Kurenets. I was told that there were about four minyans, among them also my father's, who would meet and pray during the Nazi era. My father prayed in the minyan of Rabbi Zishka Z-L that was situated in the yard of Zalman Gvint Z-L. On the day of the annihilation, 9/9/1942 (the Hebrew date is Kafzain in the month of Alul, Taf Shin Bet, three days before Rosh Hashanah), my father and others were praying in the minyan and from there they were taken to the locale of the annihilation in the central market. When they started with the action, my father and Leib Dinnestein Z-L, covered themselves in their tallits and jumped into the fire, yelling, "Shma Israel!" In this act they brought glory to God's name.

A Christian man by the name of Bakatz, a very dear person from Vileyka Street told me that on noon of that day that the action took place in the midst of the most active moment of the killings. He decided to go there, to the killing field, so that one day he could tell the next generation of the details of what he saw and heard. He walked through the fields and gardens and the Stiyenka, and when he came near he heard the yells and the cries that reached the heavens. Here and there he saw bodies all along the way. He kept seeing bodies all along the road, Jews who mostly likely tried to escape, but the killer's bullets had caught them. Bakatz told me that in the yard of Ruven Zishka Z-L, there was the naked body of a young Jewish girl, and all of a sudden there was a storm and a big leaf flew in the air, and fell on the young girl's body and covered her intimate parts. Bakatz continued saying, "It seemed to me that the heart of Mother Nature filled with pity for the martyred girl, and Mother Nature was ashamed to watch her miserable nakedness." Yet not far from here, people who lost all resemblance to human beings, amidst bestial ceremony, killed without any shame. Bakatz told me that he couldn't be there anymore. The smell of the burning bodies was unbearable, so he returned home. No, no, I cannot continue recounting the details. I don't have the spiritual force to continue with the details.

A few words on a little wooden plaque that we put on the killing field told that here were buried such a number of people, women and children, and here the fate of almost two thousand people that once were the holy community of Kurenets perished. Days and weeks passed, and Rosh Hashanah and Yom Kippur came, and we decided to have ceremonies during those days, ceremonies of public prayer. The people who came to pray were very different than the usual we'd see in the Jewish synagogue. Most were very young. There were a few older people, but you could hardly find one Jew that looked respectable enough, having a long beard, for example, to walk in front of the ark. Despite all of that, we celebrated everything as Jews were accustomed to. We started with a prayer. They gave me the assignment of going in front of the ark during the minha prayer of Yom Kippur. Filled with emotions of fear and excitement and nervousness, I started praying. I remember the old Hazans and leaders of prayers in Kurenets. I remember Reb Itzhak Zimmerman Z-L, Itzi Hatzi's [father of Charles Gelman], he had the most beautiful voice. His Hebrew was lively and his diction was pure and perfect. I remember Reb Mendel Alperovich [father of Rachel Alperovich, Emma Tzivoni, and Eliyahu], the husband of Nachama Risha, that had such a sweet voice, filled with sentiments and would reach the depths of your heart. He would pray the morning prayer of Rosh Hashanah and Yom Kippur and the last I remember was Zusia Benes, who prayed with dedication and excitement and with Hasidic fervor, and until this very day I remember his beautiful kaddish prayer. So then, while I was praying, I tried very hard to imitate his beautiful kaddish prayer.

Many times I prayed in my life, but I do not remember any other prayer that had such tragic sentiment and such a broken heart as my prayer that day. Depressed and in shock, shadows of men, we stood there, the remnants of our town. Tiny remnants from a splendid holy community, and our tears flowed like a river…

[Page 304-306]

The Broken Limb

by Sima Gvint

Translated by Jason I. (Yos'l) Alpert

In memory of his parents, Isaac and Dorothy Alpert

The Russian front is reaching our area. Soon we will be free! Is this really going to happen? We are overcome with fear. We are sure that at the last moment, we'll be murdered. For years our most intimate reality has been the close whisper of fear, and the tight grip of hunger. After all this, the Germans cannot leave without a party! They launch a massive final blockade, far worse than any we've ever encountered before. This is their final salute. We tuck hideaways in the most remote corners of the forest. We doubt. Can this Russian victory really be a fact or is it just another rumor?

The forest offers us plenty of shadows and gloom to hide in. We prepare red flags with which to receive the approaching Red Army. But when the front reaches us, we hardly feel the war. Instead, we cheer on ranks of tattered-looking Russian boys. They battle the Germans on the main road. We watch two German soldiers running away from us, the dying people. The partisans bring them to the headquarters to be investigated.

We are preparing for our return to Kurenitz. Our emotional state is very difficult to describe. Only now do we begin to understand all that we have gone through – and it is impossible for us to accept everything that has happened. Yesterday, our hunger for life filled us with a determination to fight for survival. Today, we find ourselves in a barren land. We are free now. Our lives are no longer motivated by the sheer will to live and our hearts have a chance to remember and reflect on the tragedy that has occurred. Now we wonder, "What did we stay alive for? Why did we fight so hard? What was the purpose of all this? Where, and to whom, will we go tomorrow?" Our hearts still cling to the reality of the past. Now, the present and the future have no meaning.

The memories come to me in sharp, jarring fragments. They are jumbled in my mind, and I can't foretell what memory will arise at any given moment. For some reason, I keep hearing the terrible echo of Balzinyouk's voice, "Palzili vasimanast selovieck – We lay them down! We killed eighteen Jews in one place". He struts around – proud and excited with his accomplishment. Thirty-two Jews were killed that day. Balzinyouk was referring to the eighteen souls he had found in the house of Chaim Zukofsky, and whom he had killed on the spot.

More memories flood my mind. They are broken with no real chronological order. I remember the day of the slaughter. Zalman, my husband, the father of my children, is being dragged away by the Germans while on his way to warn the Jews praying in the Minyan to escape. We hid in the attic, but knew we had to leave as soon as we could. We fled to the village Kilin, and then to the forest. What are we going to do in the forest? How can we sustain ourselves here? I asked Rugbin's wife when I met her. "You must collect handouts from people. Go from door to door like beggars. Knock on windows, and in your most pitiful voice you say, `My world has darkened. Please give me a helping hand.'"

Can you hear, my daughter? Do you know how low we've sunk. We were in desperate need and we've walked all this way crying.

The forest rises again before my eyes. My daughter Rivkale is sick with typhus and she is lying on the damp forest floor. I have covered her with tree bark. She must stay warm!. Everyone has run away and left us. They are afraid of the coming German blockade, but I am staying with my sick child. Soon enough I hear the soldiers coming. I cannot breathe. I think, `How can my heart still be beating?' By the time I realize that the "soldiers" are in fact partisans, I am certain of death. The partisans' hearts are with us and they ask me, "How are you healing her?". I recover enough to answer with a sense of humor and irony: "I heal her with cold water." Full of pity, they give us bread and butter, some medicine, and six eggs – and then warn us not to tell anyone. None of us in the forest can brag. As I continue through the forest, I see Rachel Kanterovitz. She's lying dead among the fallen leaves. On her face, there is an eternal frozen smile.

Horrors – horrors! Was this all a nightmare, or were we really awake?

And today, they tell us that we are dismissed! Where will we go from here? What will we do now that our freedom has been returned? What can the broken limb do – drying and lifeless?

The head of the partisans, a Jew named Sernack, arrives. He arranges for the people going in the direction of Kurenitz to be taken there by horses and wagons – the partisan troops' only means of transportation. He gives us supplies for the first few days, because he knows we won't find any in Kurenitz. When we enter Kurenitz, we find some Jews who have arrived ahead of us, My daughter and I were invited to live in the house of Tzirka Alperovich. We had been living in the same hiding place since last winter, so she invites us in. The house has been destroyed and the gentiles have ripped up the wooden floor. But compared to our hovel in the forest, this is a luxurious apartment.

Our first move is to go to the graves at the end of Mydell Street. There, we find huge holes at the site, which has not been covered well. Next to them are smaller holes. Handkerchiefs are thrown onto the ground. The place is not fenced off. According to the villagers, it had been used as a place for pasture until the last few days. We stand here and cry, overcome with emotion again. Our sense of loss is renewed. We realize just how empty life has now become. Even so, we have not fully lost our instincts for survival. As I cry, the intensity of pain reminds me that there still exists a hunger for life within the dry limbs.

Some gentiles – the bloodsuckers – are not pleased to see us. As we stand on the steps of Tzirka's house – on our very first day back in the village, a few pitiful women, gentile women, pass by us and exclaim in amazement: "Boze myee yeshtang asta alas – God! Oh God! There are still many of them left!" But there are other gentiles, who honestly respect us and sincerely share in our sorrows. They come to console us and name the people who have taken our possessions. Statoayudviga told us that many days after the slaughter, she had seen our stamped books, encyclopedias, and picture albums circulating all over the market, but she was too scared to take them.

I couldn't live with myself if I didn't mention the names of Ingaly Birook and Bakatz. They were two virtuous gentiles who did all they could to save things. "You see, I too stole and robbed from you," Bakatz told the Jews. And with this he returned to us a large Torah-scroll, which he had kept hidden in his basement for years.

On one of these senseless days, I forced myself to visit the wife of the Organizer to see if they had any of our stolen belongings. I am forced to enter the house of these thieves, and to talk politely. She is fearful of my being there. I recognize one of our blankets and point it out to her, but she denies that it is ours. She says that when her husband and daughter ran away with the Germans, they took everything with them. She claims that this blanket was one of many that she had purchased in a store.

A few years back, we had left some of our more expensive belongings with Shostakovich, the doctor, for safekeeping. I visit his house to ask that they be returned. I find that Shostakovich, being the head of the Belarussian committee, had been imprisoned – along with the other committee members – for signing the request for the Jewish slaughter. His wife, always the obedient law-abider, claimed that all our possession now belonged to the new rulers…

One villager, a woman, returned the iron she had taken from us a few days before the slaughter. And I succeeded in getting back our bed, which I had hidden in a special location.

The whole town had been burned down. Behind the old home of Mendel son of Yechezkel Alperovich, there used to be fields that belonged to the Jews. Now some gentiles had planted potatoes in the lot that had previously belonged to us. Many of the gentiles have now run away, fearing Communism. So we, the survivors, have taken all the potatoes. This is what we eat, and this is the way we live. We are free and ravaged. Before the war, Kurenitz was known for the outbreaks of fire that destroyed sections of the town. Afterwards, the streets would come to life, as everyone gathered together to help erect new buildings among the ruins. Now, there is only earth and dust. And on this dreary surface we walk like shadows – void of life and of the will to survive.

[Page 307-311]

After the Liberation

By Zev Rabunsky

Translated by Eilat Levitan and Kevin Chun Hoi Lo

Where are we going and whom will we find when we arrive there? Only the Christian town natives, most of the Jews perished in 1942. Now the Christians were the new heirs of our possessions and their only interest was that nothing be left of the true owners so they could receive their belongings without any disturbance. Amongst the town residents we only encountered a few that expressed goodwill – a few even endangered themselves by assisting us. Well-known were Konstantin Bakatz and Ignali Biruk (there were two Biruk brothers; Vladia Biruk was most evil to the Jews. Iganli Biruk saved many Jews) and maybe another two or three Christian residents. The vast majority took an active part in our destruction; some killed with their own hands and others used their words to incite our annihilation. Among them the best known was the Pap, the Belarussian priest with the yellow beard and the little fox-like eyes. He used every opportunity to give dirty salacious sermons in the Christian prayer home.

How could we return to Kurenets and even look at these people's eyes? We did. I was among these returnees. We, the broken vessels, approached the town.

I passed by the last house in the first street on the way back from the forest, which had belonged to the Pieshka family, which had perished in its entirety. We came near Miadel Street and this big silent fear prevented us from walking there. We had a strong desire to choose another road because we were all acutely aware of what was at the end of the street: the common grave of our townspeople. Our hearts were filled with fear but in some unexplained way, we were pulled there. All around us we found huge weeds and bushes that messily covered the area since the time of destruction. We walked through there crying, some weeping to themselves and others screaming in anguish. We were finally free to express our pain, to cry from the depths of our hearts. When I reached the beginning of the street, I saw that our home had been burnt to the ground. I said to myself, "This is very good." I only felt bad that the storage area in the basement survived. This was the place where we had held ice for our soda factory. Life in the last few years taught me to comprehend things in the most suppressed, rigid and emotionless manner. I stood at the center of Kurenets' market, which had been burnt to the ground and choked by weeds. I walked to the home of my father-in-law, Mendel Chasid, who had perished, and I saw the same picture. We entered the home of Moshe Benyamin and we lived there. During the war, a shoemaker had lived there. He had escaped with the retreating Nazis, fearing the punishment that he would get from the Soviets for collaborating. The house was filled with children's shoes and we knew very well to whom these little shoes used to belong. After we entered, my wife and I arranged the room and then went outside to see the celebratory parade of the splendid Red Army. It came from Dolhinov Street and Kusita Street toward Smorgon and Vileika. Tanks with long cannons shook the entire town. Heaven and earth were trembling with this strong army. The children of Israel that in previous wars would run behind the tanks with excitement were now all dead. Now only Christian people stood on the side of the street looking. From afar I saw huge posters ordering all the male residents age 55 and under to immediately enlist in the army in order to break the head of the Nazi snake. The Christians stood around looking and I felt that I was not part of this world anymore. This earth rejected me, scorned me, purged itself of me. A big wall came between me and this earth. All of the sudden, as if coming from within the earth, the murderer who threw Jewish babies into the fire, Vladia Biruk, rose from Vileika Street. Upon seeing me he greeted me with a wide "Shalom Aleichem." Seeing his smiling face, I thought about how before the war he was the head of the fire department in Kurenets. He probably learned from his appointed job that you do not extinguish fires; you feed them by throwing in Jewish babies. My arms and legs shook when I saw him and I spat in his face, calling him a murderer to his face. "Your hands are covered with blood. How dare you greet me? You will pay for all your bad deeds." The farmers looked at me as if they had seen a messenger of bad news. How dare a Jew have such chutzpah? At this moment I was too weak to do the murderer any harm. All I did was scream at him that he will pay for it all.

I was still standing in the market when I saw two people riding horses. One of them greeted Vladia Biruk. I wanted very much to know who had come. To my surprise I realized that the person who greeted Biruk was my manager Romankov from the tax department. He knew Biruk very well since he paid the allowance for the fire department. I came near and as soon as Romankov saw me he started screaming with excitement, "You are alive!" He hugged me and started kissing me. My self-assurance began to return and I told him a short version of all of the bad deeds of Vladia Biruk. My first request was that Romankov shoot Biruk on the spot. He started asking Biruk if what I was saying was true. I did not wait for an answer. I tried to take Romankov's weapon to do justice myself, but Romankov tried to calm me down and said that too much assertiveness now could harm me in the long run. He said that once the Soviets took over, they would put Vladia Biruk on trial and every culprit would be punished. At that time, Biruk escaped, but his escape was temporary. From what I know, he was later sentenced to twenty years in prison and killed when he tried to escape.

Romankov asked me if anyone had survived from my family. When I told him that Rosa and my son (Jay, he now lives in Florida) had survived, he became very excited. He patted me on the shoulder and told me that I was truly amazing for surviving against all odds. He pulled his horse closer, told the ediotant to wait and walked with me to where the house of Nechama Risha Alperovitz used to be (she perished with her husband Mendel son Eliyahu and some grandchildren from the Gordon family). We went to see my family and Romankov cried like a child when he met my family. He took my four-and-a-half-year-old son in his arms and pulled him against his heart, sobbing. My wife joined him and started crying, incapable of comforting herself. Romankov finally stabilized and told us that he himself did not know the fate of his family because he spent the entire time in battle. He had been appointed the governor of the town Postov (Postavy). At first they wanted to appoint him to be the governor of Kurenets since he knew Kurenets from before the Nazi occupation and was very attached to the people there (during the Soviet time 1939- 1941). However, he could not accept this because that would be too depressing since most of his friends and their children had been killed there. Romankov said to me, "A horrible war is now taking place, but you, the Jews, have given too much already and since I know you and your capabilities as an administrator, I will find you a job near me so you do not have to enroll in the army. I am sure that much good will come from appointing you." I immediately told him that Leib Futerfas, who had worked for him, and his wife Ethel Sepelevitz had also survived. (Leib Futerfas died of a heart attack in Berlin in 1948.) He was very happy to hear this news and told me to fetch Leib. I took Romankov's horse and quickly arrived at Dolhinov Street at the one surviving home of Meir Aharon the builder, which had now become the home of Leib and Ethel. I told Leib that Romankov had summoned him and that he must return with me. The meeting between Leib and Romankov was also filled with sentiment. Romankov had little time, though, as he had to do something more concrete for our situation. He took out a pencil from his backpack and told me to write something. I said that I had forgotten to write since in all the years of the war I never had a pencil in my hand. Romankov immediately wrote two permits of travel for us to be workers in the tax department in the area of Postov, where a new department was to be organized. He told us to leave Kurenets the next morning and to go to Postov. There was no way to get to Postov other than by foot. Romankov departed sentimentally and told our wives that he would send for them as soon as possible.

The hour of parting was very difficult. I had to say goodbye to my family, but there was no other choice because this was a great opportunity that would not be repeated and therefore had to be taken advantage of. The next morning we walked a distance of eighty kilometers by foot. The road was very dangerous at that time since instead of being filled with hiding Jews, the forest was infiltrated with remaining soldiers of the defeated brigades of Germany and their assistants in the local villages. It took us three days to get to Postov and the story of the walk itself could fill a few chapters in another book.

We were very afraid to meet the Christian population that resided in the area. We found a run-down abandoned home that used to be a carpentry enterprise and slept there. In the morning when we came out, the local population looked at us as if we were animals that had escaped out of a circus. It was not difficult to recognize us since we had just came out of hiding in the forest and we were still barefoot and our clothes were tattered. We found Romankov sitting in a nice looking office. He was very happy to see us and immediately ordered one of his people to find appropriate clothes and shoes for us. We washed and we had the opportunity to look in a mirror to see our own faces, the faces we had transformed into, for the first time in years. Since the roads were filled with marching armies we could not even send word to Kurenets to inform our wives that we had arrived.

Slowly, the few surviving Jews returned from hiding to Postov and took possession of their broken homes. After a few months, I had the opportunity to bring my wife and son to Postov and we began a routine life in the Soviet Union.

Almost a year passed. It was the springtime of 1945, the day after we took out the double windows of winter. I was busy with work and suddenly I sensed someone walking nearby. This person was dressed in black and he had long hair in the back. Without asking questions this shady creature went into the manager's office. Since the manager was not there, it was my duty to greet any arrivals in his place. I stood up and entered the room. When I opened the door, I felt as if my hands and arms had become paralyzed. Sparks began flying out my eyes. Across from me I saw the person who during the Soviet days had been my Russian teacher. This was the Pap, the Kurenetser from Dolhinov Street. This was the infamous Pap that during the Nazi occupation was not famous as a Russian teacher. Rather, he was famous for being one of the darkest enemies of Israel. Every Sunday he would give a sermon in the Christian prayer house, telling Christians to take their axes and anything else they could find in their homes and kill the Jews. He forbade his parishioners from exchanging any food with the Jews and from being involved in any commerce with them since he declared that all Jewish possessions would fall into Christian hands anyway.

These sermons were no secret to the Jews since all the Christians would talk about them openly. Once in a while I would see this Pap in the labor camp in Vileika. He would come to the head commissar of the Nazis and would express his wish that they would quickly annihilate all the Jews of Kurenets. Here, this criminal fell into my hands.

The Pap immediately recognized me as his old student. He extended his hand to reach me but instantly realized his fate. I caught him by his hair and started knocking his head against the wall with all of my strength. I did not care that this could get me in trouble for becoming an official government worker who could not control his need for revenge. I could not stop myself. Only one thought filled me, that I must kill him with my own hands as payment for the spilled blood of my mother (Etka Nee Persky, sister of former prime minister; Shimon Peres' father), my sister, my in-laws and my Jewish brethren. Other clerks who came into the office after hearing his painful screams thought that I had lost my mind and tried to separate us but failed at doing so. Leib Futerfas, who also heard the screams, ran to the office. When he saw that it was the Pap from Kurenets, he became even more enraged than I was. Now the other clerks realized that this was not a simple matter since both Leib and I had both lost our minds. They soon understood the situation since we were the only Jews. They finally separated us and the Pap was covered with blood. He was put in an ambulance and sent away to the Narodnyi Komissariat Vnutrennikh Del (NKVD). The next day we were sent to the NKVD for investigation so we could tell them all that we knew about the Pap's bad deeds. Leib's wife Ethel, who now lives in America, begged the head of the police to let her at least scratch out the Pap's eyes as retribution for all the spilled blood that was caused by his incitement. Such a reception he must have not have seen even in his worst nightmares. The Pap had not been successful when he attempted to escape with the retreated Germans. He knew that he could not retreat to Kurenets since the Soviets would put him on trial. He thought that in Postov he would be able to hide out. However, it was the Pap's bad luck that two surviving Jews of Kurenets happened to meet him here. The head of the police comforted us and said that the Pap would receive his due punishment and that he in a short time "he would become a shepherd with a whip and that he will wear slippers, walking behind the white polar bear at the edge of the north".

One day I found out that the Pap had been released from the jail at Vileika and he was walking free in the area. I could not find rest in my soul. I traveled to Vileika and after much tribulation I stood in front of the head of the NKVD asking how this could be. He calmed me down and told me that "this bird will not fly away" since "there are hundreds of eyes watching him." He was released so he could lead to other collaborators in hiding. After some time I found out that they had captured the Pap, as well as Vanka, the son of Shorekvas, and Doctor Shastakovitz, the heads of "the committee of the liberators of White Russia from the Communists." I had the special privilege to be invited to Vileika during the investigation. I could not spit in their faces anymore as I did to Biruk and the Pap. An armed policeman stood and watched the prisoners. In my testimony I did not spare them and I told all that I knew. Each one of them received twenty years of imprisonment.

May all the enemies of Israel appear the same way as these three did during this investigation.

[Page 312]

Bakatz

by Aharon Meirovitch

Translated by Jerrold Landau

I do not recall Bakatz directly,
I did not know of his soul and its goodness
Only several survivors from my destroyed home
Gave over this painful testimony to me.

He was a gentile, inobtrusive in my former city.
Nobody knew his secret,
Nobody would have imagined that this gentile
Had his foundations in the righteous of the gentiles.

Until we felt the realities
Impetuous days, times of tribulations

Thus did they tell me, in their weeping,
My brethren, the survivors of my city.

In front of them, memory demanded
A heavy shadow, the story in their words.
Only with Bakatz, when they mentioned him positively
Did I see a ray of light over them.

And it was – so did they relate – at the time of the spilling of our blood
When every son of iniquity swallowed them up.
Only he, when Jews were set up for slaughter
Did support them and weep over their deaths.

And this man risked his life
He cast his soul before him
To comfort a tormented Jew and heal him
And to be a support and pillar for him.

However, the glory of this man and his extra spirit
Became exposed later on –

[Page 313]

And we ask you to preserve their testimony and its candle
As an eternal light never to be extinguished.

The matter was when the news came:
Our enemy had reached the day of reckoning,
And it happened – when you shall go from darkness to light
The survivors of the plundered Israel.

Then we survivors returned from the forests and the distant places,
But there was no ray of light for the returnees,
It was not like those who go in praise of the battles –
Bodies and extinguished brands.

Gloomy, degraded and in transit
Only ashes, no glimmer of salvation
Mounds of desolation, ruins upon ruins
The traces of the holy community.

And upon the dust of the dead community
Sat the bent over survivors.
Then Bakatz quietly approached the remnants
And sat mourning in their midst.

He sat silently low down and held his silence
And he was like the community, like its spirit:
Until that man began to speak
From the lowly dust:

I know that the netherworld sinned against you
Very much, your beating was severe,

For my heart is filled with comforts for you to bear,
But I have a matter of holiness for you.

Give me three Jews,
Elderly, high in years,
For the matter is very pure and holy –
It has many agonies, blood.

We answered the man with our words:
O, turn and look at the survivors,

[Page 314]

There is no longer a difference between young and old
When they emerged from the frightful cauldron.

For we have returned, see, from destruction and the forests
There is only one remnant from destruction,
And in it, the remnant, there are also children and lads
Very old people, with hoary heads.

For you merge the souls of the survivors, and grant them merit
Very much from their paths in the fire.
Every holy, pure child is like an elderly person,
Choose whom you wish.

Then he took three into his council and covenant,
From amongst the surviving remnant, as he wished
And they walked, feeling their way, and went with him,
The three went with Bakatz to his dwelling.

And they were very curious about what would happen.
The three sat in his house,
And saw that he took out a sheet and covered
The picture of the Holy Mother [i.e. Mary].

And they saw that he approached one of his pitchers
Filled with drawn water
And with that water he washed his hands,
And their hearts did not understand any of this.

O, what is this service that is not understood
And what is this ceremony hinting at.
And why did he take out a white cloth
And cover the top of the table?

With two candles he lit a flame,
He placed them on his table opposite them,
And bowed to the ground, and showed them a hiding place
He descended to the cellar with a ladder.

They were still sitting astounded and silent
About what was transpiring around them in the house

[Page 315]

And they saw that the cover of the cellar again rise up
However, o, how moved was their hearts.

They saw the man, but not alone
Emerge from the dark cellar;
He carried a Torah scroll in his hands
And their eyes they covered with tears.

He placed it on the white cloth
Their souls now understood and knew,
And Bakatz then spoke slowly
His voice trembling:

Perhaps you will consider this a sin
If I place my hand on the holy book,
But my witnesses are on high, that in purity and awe
I guarded your book with me.

I knew that some of you would return
And I guarded it for you,
For the time your hearts wish to supplicate regarding it
Without anyone to answer you.

I knew you would return very forlorn…
But Bakatz did not continue his words
For tears came over him, and trembling.
And his voice disappeared in his tears. – – –

Over the Torah Scroll that remained as a monument
The three wept incessantly.
With them also wept in a sad corner
The most righteous Bakatz.

My brethren told me all this with tears.
They told it and asked with you,
That you place the memory of this man with a breath
Sealed upon the tablet of our hearts.

5706 [1946]

Part Four: A List of the Martyrs

[Pages 315-335]

A List of the Martyrs

For these I weep …

Transliterated by Shalom Bronstein and Haim Sidor

Family name(s)	First name(s)	Gender	Marital status	Father's name	Mother's name	Name of spouse	Remarks	Page
TOROV	Leib Ya'akov	M	married			Chaya Fruma	[1]	321
TOROV	Chaya Fruma	F	married			Leib Ya'akov	[1]	321
TOROV	Sarah	F		Leib Ya'akov	Chaya Fruma		[1]	321
TOROV	Moshe Eliezer	M		Leib Ya'akov	Chaya Fruma		He perished in the forest	321
RABONSKY	Yitzhak	M	married			Leah	[1]	321
RABONSKY	Leah	F	married			Yitzhak	[1]	321
RABONSKY	Shmuel	M		Yitzhak	Leah		He perished in Wilejka	321
RABONSKY	Chaya	F		Yitzhak	Leah		She perished in Wilejka	321
FIEDLER	Mina	F		Yitzhak			She is the daughter of Yitzhak FIEDLER; she perished in Wilejka	321
FIEDLER		M		Yitzhak			It is not known where the unnamed son of Yitzhak FIEDLER was murdered.	321
ALPEROVICH	Cheina	F					[1] Maiden name TUROV	321
ALPEROVICH	Devushal	F			Cheina		[1]	321
ALPEROVICH	Teibel	F			Cheina		[1]	321
ALPEROVICH	Elka	F			Cheina		[1]	321
ALPEROVICH	Ya'akov	M			Cheina		[1]	321
ALPEROVICH	Arka	M	married	Reuven		Nechama	he attacked the policeman arresting him and was killed while attempting to escape[3]	321
ALPEROVICH	Nechama	F	married			Arka	[1]	321
ALPEROVICH	Zelda	F		Arka	Nechama		[1]	321
CHERES	Sheina Liba	F					She perished in the forest Maiden name TUROV	321

Surname	Given name	Sex	Status	Father	Mother	Spouse	Notes	Page
ROITSTEIN	Avraham	M	married				He, his wife & their 3 children, all unnamed[1]	321
ROITSTEIN		F	married			Avraham	She, her husband Avraham & their 3 children, all unnamed[1]	321
SHULMAN	Eliezer Shlomo	M	married				He, his wife, 2 sons & their daughter, all unnamed[1]	321
SHULMAN		F	married			Eliezer Shlomo	[1]	321
SHULMAN		M		Eliezer Shlomo			The first of 2 sons of Eliezer Shlomo SHULMAN[1]	321
SHULMAN		M		Eliezer Shlomo			The second son of 2 of Eliezer Shlomo SHULMAN[1]	321
SHULMAN		F		Eliezer Shlomo			[1]	321
SHULMAN	Feibush	M	married			Henya	He perished in the forest	321
SHULMAN	Henya	F	married			Feibush	She & her unnamed mother perished in the forest	321
SHULMAN	Chanan	M		Feibush	Henya		He perished in the forest	321
SHULMAN	Rivka	F		Feibush	Henya		She perished in the forest	321
SHULMAN	Sonia	F		Feibush	Henya		She perished in Wilejka	321
ZIMMERMAN	Aidela	F					[1]	321
ZIMMERMAN	Yosef	M					He was one of the 32[3]	321
GELBERSTEIN	Ita	F					She was noted as an outstanding partisan and perished in the forest	321
GELBERSTEIN	Zev	M					He died in battle	321
ZUKOVSKY	Chaim	M	married		Pesia Yenta	Shifra	[3]	321
ZUKOVSKY	Pesia Yenta	F					[3]	321
ZUKOVSKY	Shifra	F	married			Chaim	[1]	321
ZUKOVSKY		F		Chaim	Shifra		[1]	321
ZUKOVSKY	Devushal	F	married				She, her husband and daughter, both unnamed[1] Maiden name ZUKOVSKY	321
ZIMMERMAN	Nuta	M	married		Devushel	Elka	He, his wife and unnamed granddaughter[1]	321
ZIMMERMAN	Elka	F	married			Neta	She, her husband and unnamed granddaughter[1]	321
ZIMMERMAN	Yirmiyahu	F	married	Nuta		Chasia	[1]	321
ZIMMERMAN	Chasia	F	married			Yirmiyahu	[1]	321

Surname	Given name	Sex	Status	Father	Mother	Spouse	Notes	Page
ZIMMERMAN	Shimon	M		Yirmiyahu	Chasia		He was one of the first two victims to perish in the town (cf. Yizkor Book)	321
ZIMMERMAN	Chaika	F		Yirmiyahu	Chasia		She perished in Wilejka	321
ZIMMERMAN	Etel	F		Yirmiyahu	Chasia		She perished in Wilejka	321
ZIMMERMAN	Elka	F		Yirmiyahu	Chasia		She perished in the forest	321
ZIMMERMAN	Hillel	M	married	Nuta		Freidel	He perished in the forest	321
ZIMMERMAN	Fraidel	F	married			Hillel	She perished in the forest	321
SHMUKLER	Nechama Racha	F					[1]	321
SHMUKLER	Yishayahu	M	married				He, his wife and daughter (both unnamed)[1]	321
SHMUKLER		F	married			Yishayahu	[1]	321
SHMUKLER		M		Yishayahu			[1]	321
SHMUKLER		F		Yishayahu			[1]	321
SHMUKLER	Chaya Sara	F	married			Berel	[1] Maiden name SHMUKLER	321
	Berel	M	married			Chaya Sara	Wifes' maiden name SHMUKLER[1]	321
		F		Berel	Chaya Sarah		The first of two unnamed daughters of Berel & Chaya Sarah (nee SHMUKLER) [1]	321
		F		Berel	Chaya Sarah		The second of two unnamed daughters of Berel & Chaya Sarah (nee SHMUKLER);[1]	321
ZIMMERMAN	Yosef	M					[1]	322
ZIMMERMAN	Leah	F		Yosef			[1]	322
ZIMMERMAN	Shimon	M		Yosef			He was one of the first 2 Jews murdered by the Germans in June 1941	322
ALPEROVICH	Chaim	M	married	Hevess		Mariashka	The son of Hevess[1]	322
ALPEROVICH	Mariashka	F	married			Chaim	[1]	322
ALPEROVICH	Ya'akov	M		Chaim	Mariashka		[1]	322
PEIKON	Menucha	F					She perished in the forest	322
HADASH	Barka	M					He perished in the forest	322
HADASH	Sarah	F					[1]	322
HADASH	Itka	F					She perished in Wilejka	322
FEIGELSON	Yitzhak	M	married				The grandfather of Nisan RAIZ[1]	322
FEIGELSON		F	married			Yitzhak	The unnamed grandmother of Nisan RAIZ[1]	322

RAIZ	Nisan	M					The grandson of Yitzhak FEIGELSON[1]	322
FEIGELSON	Moshe Chaim (Fima)	M	married			Duba	The name Fima in parenthesis appears after his personal name; it is not known where he perished	322
FEIGELSON	Duba	F	married			Moshe Chaim Fima	[1] Maiden name MATOSOV	322
FEIGELSON	Miriam	F		Moshe Chaim Fima	Duba		[1]	322
FEIGELSON	Sarah	F		Moshe Chaim Fima	Duba		[1]	322
ALPEROVICH	Moshe	M					[1]	322
ALPEROVICH	Rashka	F		Moshe			[1]	322
ALPEROVICH	Dishka	F		Moshe			[1]	322
ALPEROVICH	Yitzhak	M		Moshe			He perished in the forest	322
ALPEROVICH	Batya	F		Moshe			It is not known where she died	322
ZAMOSHCHIK	Lipa	M	married			Elka	He, his wife and their 4 unnamed children[1]	322
ZAMOSHCHIK	Elka	F	married			Lipa	She was killed with her husband and 4 unnamed children[1]	322
ZEIF	Shlomo	M	married			Duba	He perished in Szarkowszczyzna Nowa. 4 children	322
ZEIF	Duba	F	married			Shlomo	She and her 4 unnamed children perished in Wiliejka	322
KRAMER	Menachem Mendel	M	married			Chana	He was one of the 32[3]	322
KRAMER	Chana	F	married			Menachem Mendel	She perished in the forest	322
KRAMER	Mosheka	M		Menachem Mendel	Chana		[1]	322
KRAMER	Gershon	M		Menachem Mendel	Chana		[1]	322
KRAMER	Henya	F		Menachem Mendel	Chana		[1]	322
KRAMER	Yishayahu	M		Menachem Mendel	Chana		He perished in the forest	322
KRAMER	Baruch	M	married				[4]	322
KRAMER		F	married			Baruch	She perished in Maladzyechna	322
MEKLER	Meir Shmuel	M	married			Pesia	He, his wife and unnamed daughter[1]	322

Surname	Given name	Sex	Status	Father	Mother	Spouse	Notes	Page
MEKLER	Pesia	F	married			Meir Shmuel	She, her husband and unnamed daughter[1]	322
MEKLER		F		Meir Shmuel	Pesia		Their unnamed daughter[1]	322
MEKLER	Hillel	M		Meir Shmuel	Pesia		It is not known where he perished	322
ZISKAND	David	M	married			Nechama	He and two of his unnamed daughters[1]	322
ZISKAND	Nechama	F	married			David	She and one of her unnamed daughters [3]	322
ZISKAND		F		David	Nechama		[1]	322
ZISKAND		F		David	Nechama		[1]	322
ZISKAND		F		David	Nechama		She was one of the 32[3]	322
ALPEROVICH	Reuven Zishka	M	married			Marka	He perished in the forest	322
ALPEROVICH	Marka	F	married			Reuven Zishka	She perished in the forest	322
ALPEROVICH	Eliyahu	M		Reuven Zishka	Marka		He perished in the forest	322
ALPEROVICH	Mordecai	M		Reuven Zishka	Marka		He perished in the forest	322
ALPEROVICH	Avraham	M		Reuven Zishka	Marka		He perished in the forest	322
SHKOLNIK	Meir	M					He perished in the forest	322
ROITSTEIN	Eliezer	M	married				He, his wife, 2 sons and 1 daughter (all unnamed) [1]	322
ROITSTEIN		F	married			Eliezer	[1]	322
ROITSTEIN		F		Eliezer			[1]	322
ROITSTEIN		M		Eliezer			[1]	322
ROITSTEIN		M		Eliezer			[1]	322
ZIMMERMAN	Rivka	F					[1]	322
ZIMMERMAN	Chaim Yitzhak	M			Rivka		[1]	322
ZIMMERMAN	Sheina Chaya	F	married				She & her unnamed son [3]	322
ZIMMERMAN		M	married			Sheina Chaya	It is not known where he perished	322
ZIMMERMAN		M			Sheina Chaya		He was one of the 32[3]	322
ZIMMERMAN	Nechamka	F	married				She, her husband and son (both unnamed) [3]	322
ZIMMERMAN		M	married			Nechamka	[3]	322

Surname	Given Name	Sex	Status	Father	Mother	Spouse	Notes	Page
SHULMAN	Sarah	F					[1]	322
SHULMAN		F			Sarah		The unnamed daughter of Sarah SHULMAN perished in Wilejka	322
ALPEROVICH	Pesach	M	married			Rivka	[1]	322
ALPEROVICH	Rivka	F	married			Pesach	[1]	322
ALPEROVICH		F		Pesach	Rivka		The unnamed daughter of Pesach & Rivka ALPEROVICH[1]	322
FRIEDMAN	Chana	F					She perished in the forest Maiden name TUROV	322
	Yoel	M	married				He and his wife[1][1]; it is not known where his son died; neither his wife nor his son are named	322
TOROV	Avraham Shimon	M					He, his daughter and unnamed grandson [1]	322
	Sarah Shifra	F		Avraham Shimon			She and her unnamed son [1] Maiden name TUROV	322
TOROV	Chaim Ben Zion	M	married				It is not known where he or his unnamed wife perished	323
TOROV		F	married			Chaim Ben Zion	It is not known where she or her husband perished	323
KRAMER	Ya'akov	M					He and his family, number and names not given, perished in the town of Swir	323
DINERSTEIN	Yehuda Leib	M	married			Sarah	Wrapped in a Talit he jumped into the fire before he could be shot[1]	323
DINERSTEIN	Sarah	F	married			Yehuda Leib	[1]	323
DINERSTEIN	Moshe	M		Yehuda Leib	Sarah		He perished in Lublin	323
DINERSTEIN	Ya'akov	M		Yehuda Leib	Sarah		He disappeared	323
BLINDER	Avraham	M	married			Bluma	[1]	323
BLINDER	Bluma	F	married			Avraham	[1]	323
BLINDER		F		Avraham	Bluma		The unnamed daughter of Avraham & Bluma[1]	323
TAUBES	Moshe	M					He perished in Wilejka	323
TAUBES	Ya'akov	M					He and 6 of his unnamed children perished[1]; it is not known where another unnamed son perished	323
TAUBES		M		Ya'akov			It is not known where he perished	323
ALPEROVICH	Zvi	M					[1]	323

ALPEROVICH	Zev	M		Zvi			[1]	323
ALPEROVICH	Moshe	M		Zvi			[1]	323
ALPEROVICH	Yisrael	M		Zvi			[1]	323
	Chana	F	married	Zvi		Mordecai	[1] Maiden name ALPEROVICH	323
	Mordecai	M	married			Chana	Wife's maiden name ALPEROVICH[1]	323
	Shifra	F		Mordecai	Chana		Maiden name ALPEROVICH [1]	323
TOROV	Chalvina	M	married			Rivka Hinda	He perished in the forest; his wife & 2 children perished[1]	323
TOROV	Rivka Hinda	F	married			Chaloina	She and their 2 unnamed children[1]	323
SUTZKOVER	Chaim	M	married			Sarah Ashka	[1] It is told that he jumped the soldier who came to take him and began to choke him; soldiers came to the rescue of the policeman and murdered him	323
SUTZKOVER	Sarah Ashka	F	married		Shasha Raiza	Chaim	She, her mother, her husband and their unnamed son[1]	323
	Shasha Raiza	F					The mother of Sarah Ashka SUTZKOVER; [1]	323
SUTZKOVER		M		Chaim	Sarah Ashka		[1]	323
TZIROLNIK	Chaim	M	married			Chaya Itka	[1]	323
TZIROLNIK	Chaya Itka	F	married			Chaim	She and her unnamed daughter perished in the forest	323
TZIROLNIK		F		Chaim	Chaya Itka		She perished in the forest	323
ALPEROVICH	Moshe Binyamin	M					[1]	323
ALPEROVICH	Malka	F		Moshe Binyamin			[1]	323
ALPEROVICH	Zalman	M	married	Moshe Binyamin		Chana Tzipa	He perished in Wilejka	323
ALPEROVICH	Chana Tzipa	F	married			Zalman	She perished in Wilejka	323
ALPEROVICH	Reuven	M		Zalman	Chana Tzipa		He perished in Wilejka	323
ZIMMERMAN	Tanchum	M					[1]	323
ZIMMERMAN	Sarah	F		Tanchum			[1]	323
RODNITSKY	Nuta	M	married			Riva Zlata	He, his wife and their 2 unnamed children[1]	323
RODNITSKY	Riva Zlata	F	married			Nuta	She, her husband and their 2 unnamed children[1]	323

Surname	Given	Sex	Status	Father	Mother	Spouse	Notes	Page
KATZOVITZ	Shalom	M	married				He, his wife, 2 childen and his sister, ALL unnamed, perished in Wilejka	323
KATZOVITZ		F	married			Shalom	She perished in Wilejka	323
KATZOVITZ		F					The sister of Shalom KATZOVITZ, she perished in Wilejka	323
	Ben Zion	M	married			Sarah Gitel	He, his wife and 2 unnamed children perished[1], surname not given	323
	Sarah Gitel	F	married			Ben Zion	[1]	323
FRIEDMAN	Yehezkel	M	married			Hinda	He, his wife and their 3 unnamed children[1]	323
FRIEDMAN	Hinda	F	married			Yehezkel	She, her husband and their 3 unnamed children[1]	323
ALPEROVICH	Bila	F	married			Moshe	[1]	323
ALPEROVICH	Chaya Stirel	F		Moshe	Bila		She perished in Szczucyn	323
SOSNESKY	Fruma	F					The grandmother of Chayala, she[1]	323
	Chayala	F					The granddaughter of Fruma Sosneski; she scratched the faces of the Germans who came to murder her predicting that they would have a very bitter day; she was brutally tortured before they murdered her[1]	323
KOZNIETZ	Mordecai	M	married			Leah	He, his wife, 2 unnamed sons and a daughter perished[1], one son perished in the forest	323
KOZNIETZ	Leah	F	married			Mordecai	She, her husband, 2 unnamed sons and daughter[1], one son perished in the forest	323
KOZNIETZ		M		Mordecai	Leah		First of 3 unnamed sons of Mordecai & Leah KOZNIETZ	323
KOZNIETZ		M		Mordecai	Leah		Second of 3 unnamed sons of Mordecai & Leah KOZNIETZ	323
KOZNIETZ		F		Mordecai	Leah		[1]	323
KOZNIETZ		M		Mordecai	Leah		Third of 3 unnamed sons of Mordecai & Leah KOZNIETZ; he perished in the forest	323
KOZNIETZ	Yeizha	M	married				He perished in the forest	323
KOZNIETZ		F	married			Yeizha	She perished in Dalhinov	323
RACHA-RASHA'S	Eliezer	M	married			Racha Rasha	He perished in the mass murder[1]. His wife and child (both unnamed) perished in Dalhinov	323

Surname	Given	Sex	Status	Father	Mother	Spouse	Notes	Page
ZIMMERMAN	Yitzhak	M					[4]	323
ZIMMERMAN	Shimshon	M		Yitzhak			It is not known where he perished	323
ZIMMERMAN	Feiga	F					She perished in Wilejka	323
ZIMMERMAN	Yosef	M	married			Leah	He, his wife and their 2 unnamed children [1]	324
ZIMMERMAN	Leah	F	married			Yosef	She, her husband and 2 unnamed children [1]	324
	Mirka	F	married			Eliezer	She (nee ZIMMERMAN), her husband and their unnamed child perished in Glebokie Maiden name ZIMMERMAN	324
	Eliezer	M	married			Mirka	He, his wife and unnamed child perished in Glebokie	324
GORDON	Shmuel	M	married			Chasia	[1]	324
GORDON	Chasia	F	married			Shmuel	[1]	324
GORDON	Ya'akov	M		Shmuel	Chasia		[1]	324
FORMAN	Avraham Moshe	M	married			Chana	[1]	324
FORMAN	Chana	F	married			Avraham Moshe	[1]	324
FORMAN	Levi Yitzhak	M		Avraham Moshe	Chana		[1]	324
FORMAN	Liba	F		Avraham Moshe	Chana		[1]	324
FORMAN	Tzipa	F		Avraham Moshe	Chana		[1]	324
ALPEROVICH	Chana	F	married	Elchanan		Elchanan	The wife of ElcChanan the butcher; she[1]	324
ALPEROVICH	Chaim	M	married	Elchanan		Mariashka	He, his wife and unnamed daughter perished in the forest	324
ALPEROVICH	Mariashka	F	married			Chaim	She, her husband and unnamed caughter perished in the forest	324
ALPEROVICH		F		Chaim	Mariashka		She perished in the forest with her father & mother	324
ALPEROVICH	Hershel	M	married	Elchanan		Dishka	[1]	324
ALPEROVICH	Dishka	F	married			Hershel	[1]	324
BENIS	Zusia	M	married			Leah	[1]; they set their own house on fire and hanged themselves in the attic	324
BENIS	Leah	F	married			Zusia	[1]; they set their own house on fire and hanged themselves in the attic	324

Surname	Given Name	Sex	Status	Father	Mother	Spouse	Notes	Page
ZISKIND	Mordecai	M					The brother of Itka he perished in the forest	324
ZISKIND	Itka	F					She is the sister of Mordecai ZISKIND; she perished in Wilejka	324
GURVITZ	Chaim Yisrael	M	married				He and his unnamed wife perished[1]; their daughter Sonia, her husband and 3 children (all unnamed) perished in Dalhinov	324
GURVITZ		F	married			Chaim Yisrael	She and her husband perished[1]; their daughter Sonia, her husband and 3 children (all unnamed) perished in Dalhinov	324
	Sonia	F	married	Chaim Yisrael			She, her husband and 3 children (all unnamed) perished in Dalhinov Maiden name GURVITZ	324
		M	married			Sonia	The wife of Feivish the Shochet, their son and daughter perished[1]; one son perished in the forest and a daughter perished when she returned from the forest; none of their names are recorded.	324
ALPEROVICH	Yisrael	M	married			Chaya	He perished in the forest	324
ALPEROVICH	Chaya	F	married			Yisrael	She perished in the forest	324
ALPEROVICH	Zundel	M		Yisrael	Chaya		He perished in the forest	324
ALPEROVICH	Yossel	M		Yisrael	Chaya		He perished in the forest	324
ALPEROVICH	Chana	F		Yisrael	Chaya		She perished in the forest	324
ALPEROVICH	Itka	F		Yisrael	Chaya		She perished in the forest	324
		F				Feivish	The wife of Feivish the Shochet, their son and daughter[1]; one son perished in the forest and a daughter perished when she returned from the forest; none of their names are recorded	324
ALPEROVICH	Shmaryahu	M	married	Yisrael			The son of Yisrael the butcher[1]; his wife and 2 children perished in the forest	324
ALPEROVICH		F	married			Shmaryahu	She and her 2 children perished in the forest (all unnamed)	324
DUBIN	Yosef	M	married				He, his wife & unnamed daughter[1]	324
DUBIN	Malka	F	married				She, her husband & unnamed daughter perished[1]	324
DUBIN		F					The daughter of Yosef & Malka DUBIN[1]	324
KOPILOVITZ	Gedalyahu	M	married			Freida	[1]	324

Surname	Given	Sex	Marital	Father	Mother	Spouse	Notes	Page
KOPILOVITZ	Freida	F	married			Gedalyahu	[1]	324
KOPILOVITZ	Yosef	M		Gedalyahu	Fraida		[1]	324
KOPILOVITZ	Tevel	M		Gedalyahu	Fraida		He perished in the forest	324
KOPILOVITZ	Devosha	F		Gedalyahu	Fraida		She perished in Wilejka	324
KOPILOVITZ	Baruch	M	married			Frumka	He, his wife and their two unnamed children perished in Wilejka	324
KOPILOVITZ	Frumka	F	married			Baruch	She, her husband and their two unnamed children perished in Wilejka	324
ASHKENAZI	Tzipa	F					[1]	324
ASHKENAZI	Avraham	M			Tzipa		[1]	324
BAT NOACH	Liba	F		Noach (?)			She, her husband and son perished in the forest	324
BAT NOACH	Shifra	F			Liba		She perished in Wilejka	324
ALPEROVICH	Nechama	F	married			Itza Michael	[1]	324
ALPEROVICH	Tzirel	F		Itza Michael	Nechama		[1]	324
ALPEROVICH	Liba	F		Itza Michael	Nechama		She perished in Wilejka	324
ALPEROVICH	Herzl	M					He was killed escaping from Wilejka	324
ALPEROVICH		M		Herzl			He was killed escaping from Wilejka	324
ALPEROVICH		M		Herzl			He was killed escaping from Wilejka	324
ISAK	Shmuel Yitzhak	M	married			Shosha	[1]	324
ISAK	Shosha	F	married			Shmuel Yitzhak	[1]	324
	Fraidel	F		Shmuel Yitzhak	Shosha		She and her 2 unnamed children[1] Maiden name ISAK	324
	Chaya Racha	F	married	Shmuel Yitzhak	Shosha	Nachum	She, her husband and 2 chidren (unnamed)[1] Maiden name ISAK	324
	Nachum	M	married			Chaya Racha	He, his wife and 2 children[1]	324
ISAK	Eliyahu	M	married				He, his wife and 2 daughters (unnamed)[1]	324
ISAK		F	married			Eliyahu	She, her husband and 2 daughters (unnamed)[1]	324
ISAK		F		Eliyahu			The first of 2 unnamed daughters of Eliyahu ISAK; [1]	324

Surname	Given	Sex	Married	Father	Mother/Spouse	Notes	Page
ISAK		F		Eliyahu		The second of 2 unnamed daughters of Eliyahu ISAK;[1]	324
BERGER	Feiga	F				The words di Lioviker (from Liov) appear in parenthesis after her name; her daughter Chaya and her husband[1]	324
	Chaya	F	married		Feiga	The daughter of Feiga BERGER; she, her mother and her husband[1] Maiden name BERGER	324
		M	married		Chaya	The husband of Chaya nee BERGER[1] with his wife and mother-in-law	324
BERGER	Isser	M	married			He, his wife and unnamed children perished in the town of Dokszyce	324
BERGER		F	married		Isser	She, her husband and unnamed children perished in the town of Dokszyce	324
BERGER	Zev	M	married			He, his wife and children (all unnamed) perished in Smorgonie	324
BERGER		F	married		Zev	She, her husband and children (unnamed) perished in Smorgonie	324
DINERSTEIN	Aharon	M	married		Esther	He perished in the forest	325
DINERSTEIN	Esther	F	married		Aharon	[1]along with her children Yosef & Yenta	325
DINERSTEIN	Yosef	M		Aharon	Esther	[1]with his mother & sister	325
DINERSTEIN	Yenta	F		Aharon	Esther	[1]with her mother & brother	325
BRATZ	Mina	F		Nuta		The daughter of Nuta ZIMMERMAN, she and her infant daughter were tortured to death in Wilejka Maiden name ZIMMERMAN	325
BRATZ		F			Mina	The infant daughter of Mina ZIMMERMAN BRATZ, she perished in Wilejka	325
ZIMMERMAN	Nachum	M	married		Sheina	He perished in Wilejka	325
ZIMMERMAN	Sheina	F	married	Nuta	Nachum	She perished in Wilejka Maiden name ZIMMERMAN	325
ZIMMERMAN		F		Nachum	Sheina	The unnamed daughter of Nachum & Shina ZIMMERMAN; she perished in Wilejka	325
GEVELMAN	Chaim	M	married		Gita	He, his wife and their 3 unnamed daughters[1]	325
GEVELMAN	Gita	F	married		Chaim	[1]	325

Surname	Given	Sex	Status	Father	Mother	Spouse	Notes	Page
GEVELMAN		F		Chaim	Gita		The first of the 3 daughters of Chaim GEVELMAN[1]	325
GEVELMAN		F		Chaim	Gita		The second of the 3 daughters of Chaim GEVELMAN[1]	325
GEVELMAN		F		Chaim	Gita		The third of the 3 daughters of Chaim GEVELMAN[1]	325
ALPEROVICH	Zisha	F		Abba			[4]	325
ALPEROVICH	Malka	F		Abba			The sister of Zisha; she perished in Troki	325
ALPEROVICH	Nuta	M	married	Yitzhak Elchanan		Chaika	[1]	325
ALPEROVICH	Chaika	F	married			Nuta	[1]	325
ALPEROVICH	Sima	F		Nuta	Chaika		[1]	325
ALPEROVICH	Yisrael	M		Nuta	Chaika		He perished in the forest	325
ALPEROVICH	Yocheved	F		Nuta	Chaika		She perished in the forest	325
ALPEROVICH	Rivka	F		Nuta	Chaika		She perished in Wilejka	325
ALPEROVICH	Zalman Mendel	M		Yitzhak Meir			[1]	325
TZIROLNIK	Zev	M	married			Leah	He, his wife and their 2 unnamed children perished in Krasna	325
TZIROLNIK	Leah	F	married			Zev	She, her husband and their 2 unnamed children perished in Krasna	325
ZIMMERMAN	Uri	M	married			Braina	[1]	325
ZIMMERMAN	Braina	F	married			Uri	[1]	325
ZIMMERMAN	Nachum	M		Uri	Braina		[1]	325
ZIMMERMAN	Nechama	F		Uri	Braina		[1]	325
STOLIER	Hirsh Mendel	M	married				He, his unnamed wife and 3 unnamed children [1]	325
STOLIER		F	married			Hersh Mendel	[1]	325
TZIROLNIK	Zalman Moshe	M	married				[1]	325
TZIROLNIK		F	married			Zalman Moshe	She perished in the forest	325
ALPEROVICH	Chaya Leah	F					She perished in the forest	325
PERETZ	Yisrael	M	married			Baila Itka	[1]	325
PERETZ	Baila Itka	F	married			Yisrael	[1]	325
PERETZ	Moshe Mordecai	M		Yisrael	Baila Itka		[1]	325

Surname	Given Name	Sex	Status	Father	Mother	Spouse	Notes	Page
PERETZ	Chaim Zevulun	M		Yisrael	Baila Itka		[1]	325
PERETZ	Reuven David	M		Yisrael	Baila Itka		[1]	325
PERETZ	Raicha Devorah	F		Yisrael	Baila Itka		[1]	325
ALPEROVICH	Esther Mariasha	F					[1]	325
WEISENHOLTZ	David	M					He was one of the 32[3]	325
NAROTZKI	Ya'akov	M	married			Leah	[2]	325
NAROTZKI	Leah	F	married			Ya'akov	[2]	325
NAROTZKI	Shimon	M		Ya'akov	Leah		He perished in Wilejka	325
NAROTZKI	Sarah	F		Ya'akov	Leah		She perished in Wilejka	325
HASID	Mendel	M	married			Sarah	[1]	325
HASID	Sarah	F	married			Mendel	[1]	325
BLINDER	Sheina Dova	F					[1]	325
	Tzipa	F	married		Sheina Duba		[1] Maiden name BLINDER	325
		M	married			Tzipa	Wife's maiden name BLINDER [1]	325
		M			Tzipa		Maiden name BLINDER [1]	325
		F			Tzipa		Maiden name BLINDER [1]	325
DINERSTEIN	Chanan	M	married			Serel	He perished in Wilejka	325
DINERSTEIN	Serel	F	married	Chaim Berel		Chanan	She perished in Wilejka	325
DINERSTEIN		M		Chanan	Serel		He perished in Wilejka	325
TILLIS	Rivka	F					[1]	325
TILLIS	Dov	M			Rivka		[1]	325
TILLIS	Zalman	M			Rivka		[1]	325
TILLIS	Shimon	M			Rivka		He perished in the forest	325
ALPEROVICH	Reuven	M		Chaim Berel			The brother of Chana, he perished in Dalhinov	325
ALPEROVICH	Chana	F		Chaim Berel			The sister of Reuven[1]	325
FRIEDMAN	Leib	M	married			Tirtza	It is not known where he perished	325
FRIEDMAN	Tirtza	F	married			Leib	[1]	325
FRIEDMAN	Berel	M		Leib	Tirtza		[1]	325
FRIEDMAN	Velvel	M		Leib	Tirtza		[1]	325

Surname	Given	Sex	Status	Father	Mother	Spouse	Notes	Page
FRIEDMAN	Yosef	M		Leib	Tirtza		[1]	325
ZIMMERMAN	Yitzhak	M	married		Chatzi	Feiga	He was known as Itche Chachis and was one of the 32[3]	325
ZIMMERMAN	Feiga	F	married			Yitzhak Itza	[1]	325
ZIMMERMAN	Etel	F		Yitzhak Itza			She was one of the 32[3]	325
ZIMMERMAN	Sarah	F		Yitzhak Itza	Feiga		She perished in Wolozyn	325
SPECTOR	Mina	F		Yitzhak			She was one of the 32[3] Maiden name ZIMMERMAN	325
SPECTOR	Shimshon	M			Mina		The infant son of Mina SPECTOR [1]	325
DIMNETSTEIN	Reuven	M	married			Marka	[1]	326
DIMNETSTEIN	Marka	F	married			Reuven	[1]	326
HADASH	Henya	F		Reuven			She perished in Postawy with her 2 unnamed sons Maiden name DIMNETSTEIN	326
HADASH		M			Henya		The first of 2 unnamed sons of Henya HADASH; he perished in Postawy	326
HADASH		M			Henya		The second of 2 unnamed sons of Henya HADASH; he perished in Postawy	326
DIMNETSTEIN	Tzira	F					[1]	326
DIMNETSTEIN	Sarah Malka	F					[1]	326
DIMNETSTEIN	Relka	F			Sarah Malka		[1]	326
SHAFFER	Yisrael	M	married			Etel	He perished in Postawy	326
SHAFFER	Etel	F	married			Yisrael	[1]	326
SHAFFER	Yoel	M		Yisrael	Etel		He perished in the forest	326
SHAFFER	Michael	M		Yisrael	Etel		He perished in the forest	326
MEIROWITZ	Ben Zion	M					[1]	326
MEIROWITZ	Michael	M		Ben Zion			He perished in Postawy	326
VARFMAN	Fruma	F					[1] Maiden name MEIROWITZ	326
VARFMAN	Beshinka	F			Fruma		[1]	326
VARFMAN	Perla	F			Fruma		[1]	326
LEVIN	Yosef Leib	M	married			Gitel	It is not known where he perished	326
LEVIN	Gitel	F	married			Yosef Leib	She and her unnamed son[1]	326

Surname	Given name	Sex	Status	Father	Mother	Spouse	Notes	Page
LEVIN		M		Yosef Leib	Gitel		[1]	326
BECKER	Nachum	M	married			Perla	He perished in the forest	326
BECKER	Perla	F	married			Nachum	She perished in the forest	326
BECKER	Zelig	M		Nachum	Perla		He perished in the forest	326
BECKER	Etel	F		Nachum	Perla		She perished in Wilejka	326
KOPILOVITZ	David	M					He perished in Dokszyce	326
KOPILOVITZ	Yehoshua	M		David			It is not known where he perished	326
	Fraidel	F	married	David		Ya'akov	[2] Maiden name KOPILOVITZ	326
	Ya'akov	M	married			Freidel	Wife's maiden name KOPILOVITZ [2]	326
		M		Ya'akov	Fraidel		Maiden name KOPILOVITZ [2]	326
		F		Ya'akov	Fraidel		Maiden name KOPILOVITZ [2]	326
	Chaya Sarah	F	married	David			It is not known where she and her family (names & number not given) perished Maiden name KOPILOVITZ	326
KOPILOVITZ	Arieh	M	married	David			He and his family (names & number not given) perished in Smorgonie	326
MATOSOV	Leib	M					On the day of the mass slaughter of the town, wrapped in his Talit he jumped into the fire before the murderers' bullet struck him	326
KRAMER	Chaim Zalman	M	married				He, his unnamed wife and their unnamed children [1]	326
KRAMER		F	married			Chaim Zalman	She, her husband and their unnamed children [1]	326
KRAMER	Yechiel	M					He perished in the forest	326
KRAMER	David	M					[1]	326
KRAMER	Avraham	M					It is not known where he perished	326
MARKMAN	Yehezkel	M	married			Nechama Racha	He, his wife and their 4 unnamed children perished in Parafjanowo	326
MARKMAN	Nechama Racha	F	married			Yehezkel	She, her husband and their 4 unnamed children perished in Parafjanowo Maiden name KRAMER	326
EISHISKY	Mordecai	M	married			Musia	It is not known where he perished	326
EISHISKY	Musia	F	married			Mordecai	It is not known where she perished	326
EISHISKY	Yehoshua	M		Mordecai	Busia		It is not known where he perished	326

Surname	First Name	Sex	Status	Father	Mother	Spouse	Notes	Page
EISHISKY	Cheina	F		Mordecai	Busia		It is not known where she perished	326
RABONSKY	Alta	F					[1]	326
RABONSKY	Ya'akov	M			Alta		It is not known where he perished	326
RABONSKY	Chana	F			Alta		She perished in Wilejka	326
BENIS	Chaim Zev	M	married			Feiga	He, his wife and daughter (both unnamed)[1]	326
BENIS	Feiga	F	married			Chaim Zev	[1]	326
BENIS	Chaya Hoda	F		Chaim Zev	Feiga		[1]	326
GEVINT	Zalman	M					[1]	326
SVIRSKY	Devora	F	married	Yona Chaim		David Yona	She perished in Ponary Maiden name SVIRSKY	326
	David Yona	M	married			Devora	He perished in Ponary	326
ALPEROVICH	Mendel	M	married	Shimon		Golda	[1]	326
ALPEROVICH	Golda	F	married			Mendel	She perished in Wolozyn	326
ALPEROVICH	Shimon	M		Mendel	Golda		He perished in Wolozyn	326
ALPEROVICH	Ziskind	M	married	Shimon		Batya Chana	He perished in the forest	326
ALPEROVICH	Batya Chana	F	married			Ziskind	She perished in the forest	326
ALPEROVICH	Shimon	M		Ziskind	Batya Chana		He perished in the forest	326
ALPEROVICH	Yechiel	M		Ziskind	Batya Chana		He perished in the forest	326
RODNITSKY	Velvel	M					[2]	326
RODNITSKY	Zalman	M		Zalman			The infant son of Velvel RODNITSKY[1]	326
CHARNEY	Shmuel	M	married			Chana	He, his wife and their 3 unnamed children perished in the forest	326
CHARNEY	Chana	F	married	Asher		Shmuel	She, her husband and their 3 unnamed children perished in the forest Maiden name RODNITSKY	326
ALPEROVICH	Shmuel	M	married		Taiva	Hinda	He, his wife and their unnamed son and daughter[2]	326
ALPEROVICH	Hinda	F	married			Shmuel	She, her husband and unnamed son and daughter [2]	326
ALPEROVICH		M		Shmuel	Hinda		[2]	326
ALPEROVICH		F		Shmuel	Hinda		[2]	326

MEIZEL	Shlomo	M	married			Chana Chaya	[1]	327
MEIZEL	Chana Chaya	F	married			Shlomo	[1]	327
SOLOMINSKY	Yisrael	M	married			Esther	He, his wife and 2 unnamed children [3]; their 2 other innamed children[1]	327
SOLOMINSKY	Esther	F	married			Yisrael	She, her husband and 2 unnamed children [3]; their 2 other unnamed children[1] Maiden name MEIZEL	327
MEIZEL	Shmuel	M	married				It is not known where he perished	327
MEIZEL		F	married			Shmuel	It is not known where she perished	327
GEVELMAN	Henya	F	married			Zelig	[1]	327
GEVELMAN	Faigla	F			Henya		[1]	327
GORDON	Meir	M	married				He, his wife, 4 daughters and one son (all unnamed)[1]	327
GORDON		F	married			Meir	[1]	327
GORDON		F		Meir			[1]	327
GORDON		F		Meir			[1]	327
GORDON		F		Meir			[1]	327
GORDON		F		Meir			[1]	327
GORDON		M		Meir			[1]	327
TZINSTANG	Yitzhak	M	married			Rachel	He perished in Wilejka	327
TZINSTANG	Rachel	F	married			Yitzhak	She perished in Wilejka	327
	Hinda	F					The sister of Rachel[1]	327
	Chana	F					The sister of Rachel, she & her 2 unnamed daughters[1]	327
CHARNES	Leib	M	married			Asna	He perished in Krivitch	327
CHARNES	Asna	F	married			Leib	[1]	327
CHARNES	Avraham	M	married			Racha Batya	He perished in Krivitch	327
CHARNES	Racha Batya	F	married			Avraham	She perished in Krivitch	327
CHARNES	Eliezer	M					He and his family (names & number not given) perished in Troki	327
CHARNES	Menachem	M	married			Rachel	He, his wife, son & daughter[1]	327
CHARNES	Rachel	F	married			Mendel	[1]	327

CHARNES	Chaya	F		Menachem	Rachel		[1]	327
CHARNES	Moshe	M		Menachem	Rachel		[1]	327
ALPEROVICH	Daniel	M		Chaim Avraham			He was caught in the forest & was tortured to death	327
ALPEROVICH	Tzertel	F		Chaim Avraham			She perished in Wilejka	327
	Chaya	F		Chaim Avraham			It is not known where she & her family (number & names not given) perished Maiden name ALPEROVICH	327
ALPEROVICH	Menachem Mendel	M	married	Yehezkel		Gitel	He, his wfe & their son[1]	327
ALPEROVICH	Gitel	F	married			Menachem Mendel	[1]	327
ALPEROVICH	Aharon	M		Menachem Mendel	Gitel		[1]	327
PIASTONOVITZ	Arieh Leibchik	M	married			Necha	He perished in Wilejka	327
PIASTONOVITZ	Necha	F	married	Mendel		Arieh Leibchik	[1] Maiden name ALPEROVICH	327
PIASTONOVITZ	Mina	F		Arieh Leibchik	Necha		She perished in Wilejka	327
PIASTONOVITZ	Pesia	F		Arieh Leibchik	Necha		[1]	327
PIASTONOVITZ	Yehezkel	M		Arieh Leibchik	Necha		[1]	327
PIASTONOVITZ	Zalman	M		Arieh Leibchik	Necha		[1]	327
ALPEROVICH	Yosef	M	married	Mendel		Leah	He perished in the forest	327
ALPEROVICH	Leah	F	married			Yosef	She perished two days after the mass murder of the town Maiden name MEIZEL	327
ALPEROVICH	Shimon Motel	M		Yosef	Leah		He perished two days after the mass murder of the town	327
ALPEROVICH	Rashka	F	married			Zalman	She perished in the forest	327
ALPEROVICH	Meir	M			Rashka		He perished in Wilejka	327
	Zalman	M					The grandson of Rashka[1]	327
	Moshe	M					The grandson of Rashka [1]	327
RUBIN	Pia	F	married		Rashka	Shimshon	He, his wife and 2 of their children perished in Dalhinov Maiden name ALPEROVICH	327
RUBIN	Shimshon	M	married			Pia	Perished in Dalhinov. Wife's maiden name ALPEROVICH	327
RUBIN	Zalman	M		Shimon	Pia		He perished in Dalhinov	327

Surname	Given Name	Sex	Status	Father	Mother	Spouse	Notes	Page
RUBIN	Ya'akov	M		Shimon	Pia		He perished in Dalhinov	327
ALPEROVICH	Pesia	F	married			Moshe	[2]	327
ALPEROVICH	Binyamin	M			Pesia		[2]	327
	Rachel	F	married		Pesia	Eliezer	She and her unnamed son[1] Maiden name ALPEROVICH	327
	Eliezer	M	married			Rachel	The husband of Rachel (maiden name ALPEROVICH), it is not known where he perished	327
SHULMAN	Frada	F	married			Aharon	[1]	327
SHULMAN	Aharon	M	married			Frada	Great grandfather of Eilat Gordin Levitan	327
SHULMAN	Chana	F		Aharon	Frada		[1]	327
SHULMAN	Binyamin Niomka	M					A Partisan, he perished in the forest	327
	Batya Raiza	F					The grandmother of Binyamin [1]	327
SOSENSKY	Mara	F	married	Unknown	Unknown	Unknown	Name of husband and children are unknown. Sosensky was her maiden name.	327
SANDLER	Yosef Zev	M	married			Rachel	After the mass murder of the town, they hid in the attic of the synagogue, they were caught and tied to a wagon that dragged them to the cemetery	327
SANDLER	Rachel	F	married			Yosef Zev	After the mass murder of the town, they hid in the attic of the synagogue, they were caught and tied to a wagon that dragged them to the cemetery	327
SANDLER	Osnat	F		Yosef Zev	Rachel	Leah Malka	After the mass murder of the town, they hid in the attic of the synagogue, they were caught and tied to a wagon that dragged them to the cemetery	327
ALPEROVICH	Zalman Mendel	M	married	Haikel Velvel		Zalman Mendel	It is not known where he perished	328
ALPEROVICH	Leah Malka	F	married				She was murdered in Pokan the day after the mass murder of the town[1]	328
ALPEROVICH	Hanoch	M		Zalman Mendel	Leah Malka		He was murdered in Pokan the day after the mass murder of the town[1]	328
ALPEROVICH	Haikel	M		Zalman Mendel	Leah Malka		He was murdered in Pokan the day after the mass murder of the town[1]	328

Surname	Given	Sex	Status	Father	Mother	Spouse	Notes	Page
ALPEROVICH	Rachel	F		Zalman Mendel	Leah Malka		She was murdered in Pokan the day after the mass murder of the town[1]	328
LEVIN	Mendel	M					[4]	328
LEVIN	Elimelech	M		Mendel			[1]	328
LEVIN	Chaim	M		Mendel			He perished in Wilejka	328
LIMON	Yehoshua	M	married				[4]	328
LIMON		F	married			Yehoshua	[1]	328
LIMON		F		Yehoshua			[1]	328
LIMON		M		Yehoshua			He perished in the forest	328
LIMON	Osna	F					She perished in Kobylnik	328
LIMON	Asher	M	married			Chaya Ashka	It is not known where he perished	328
LIMON	Chaya Ashka	F	married			Asher	It is not known where she perished	328
LIMON	Shlomo	M		Asher	Chaya Ashka		It is not known where he perished	328
LIMON	Batya	F		Asher	Chaya Ashka		It is not known where she perished	328
LIMON	Chana Rivka	F			Asna		[1]	328
COOPERSTOCK	Mordecai Leib	M	married			Chana Esther	[1]	328
COOPERSTOCK	Chana Esther	F	married			Mordecai Leib	[1]	328
COOPERSTOCK	Yosef	M	married			Rachel	[1]	328
COOPERSTOCK	Rachel	F	married			Yosef	[1]	328
COOPERSTOCK	Avramel	M		Yosef	Rachel		[1]	328
COOPERSTOCK	Raizel	F		Yosef	Rachel		[1]	328
COOPERSTOCK	Zev	M	married			Sheina	He was tortured and perished in Wilejka	328
COOPERSTOCK	Sheina	F	married			Zev	[1]	328
GORDON	Shabtai	M	married			Sonia	[1]	328
GORDON	Sonia	F	married			Shabtai	[1]	328
GORDON	Aharon	M		Shabtai	Sonia		[1]	328
GORDON	Zalman	M		Shabtai	Sonia		[1]	328
GORDON	Chaim	M		Shabtai	Sonia		[1]	328
GORDON	Golda	F		Shabtai	Sonia		[1]	328
	Rivka	F	married			Mordecai	The sister of Shabtai GORDON, she her husband and their 2	328

Surname	Given	Sex	Status	Father	Mother	Spouse	Notes	Page
							unnamed children[1] Maiden name GORDON	
	Mordecai	M	married			Rivka	He, his wife and their 2 unnamed children [1]. Wife's maiden name GORDON	328
SHULMAN	Natan	M	married			Sarah	[1]	328
SHULMAN	Sarah	F	married			Natan	[1]	328
SHULMAN		F		Natan	Sarah		[1]	328
SHULMAN	Zalman	M		Natan	Sarah		He perished on the way to Wilejka	328
TZEPLEVITZ	Tzipa	F					The sister of Zalman Mendel TZEPLEVITZ[1]	328
BRONSTEIN	Pesia	F	married			Zalman Asher	The wife of Zalman Asher[1]	328
SHULMAN	Zalman	M	married			Rivka	[1]	328
SHULMAN	Rivka	F	married			Zalman	[1]	328
SHULMAN	Ya'akov	M	married				It is not known where he perished	328
SHULMAN		F	married			Ya'akov	[1]	328
SHULMAN		M		Ya'akov			[1]	328
SHULMAN	Zvi	M	married				[1]	328
SHULMAN		F	married			Zvi	[1]	328
SCHNEORSON		M	married				A pharmacist, he was murdered in Kurenets ten months after the mass murder of the town[1] with his wife (both unnamed), their son, his wife and his daughter	328
SCHNEORSON		F	married				She was murdered in Kurenets ten months after the mass murder of the town[1] with her husband (both unnamed), his son, his wife and his daughter	328
SCHNEORSON	Lyona	M	married				He was murdered in Kurenets ten months after the mass murder of the town[1]	328
SCHNEORSON	Riva	F	married				She was murdered in Kurenets ten months after the mass murder of the town[1] Maiden name ANTZILVITZ	328
SCHNEORSON		F		Lyona	Riva		She was murdered in Kurenets ten months after the mass murder of the town[1]	328
TZEPLEVITZ	Shmuel	M					[4]	328
TZEPLEVITZ	Duba	F	married			Moshe	[1]	328
TZEPLEVITZ	Chaim	M			Duba		[1]	328

Surname	Given	Sex	Married	Father	Mother	Spouse	Notes	Page
MELTZER	Rachel Leah	F					[1]	328
SUTZKEVER	Ya'akov	M	married			Sarah	[1]	328
SUTZKEVER	Sarah	F	married		Rachel Leah	Ya'akov	[1]	328
SUTZKEVER	Binyamin	M		Ya'akov	Sarah		[1]	328
SUTZKEVER	Avraham	M		Ya'akov	Sarah		[1]	328
FELDSHER	Ya'akov Mendel	M					He perished in Lida	328
GURVITZ	Shmuel	M	married			Henya	It is not known where he perished	328
GURVITZ	Henya	F	married			Shmuel	[1] Maiden name MATOSOV	328
GURVITZ	Avraham	M		Shmuel	Henya		[1]	328
GURVITZ	Yitzhak	M		Shmuel	Henya		[1]	328
GURVITZ	Meir	M		Shmuel	Henya		[1]	328
GURVITZ	Sarah	F		Shmuel	Henya		[1]	328
EINBINDER	Chaya	F					[1] Maiden name MATOSOV	329
EINBINDER	Zev	M			Chaya		[1]	329
EINBINDER	Rachel	F			Chaya		[1]	329
EINBINDER	Mendel	M			Chaya		He was murdered on the way to Wilejka	329
ALPEROVICH	Sarah	F					[1] Maiden name ZUCKERMAN	329
ALPEROVICH	Bluma	F	married			Yisrael Monis	She and her 3 grandchildren Shifra, Isser & Neta[1] Maiden name ALPEROVICH	329
	Shifra	F					[1]	329
	Isser	M					[1]	329
	Yenta	F					[1]	329
ALPEROVICH	Rivka	F	married			Reuven Nathan Zalman	[1]	329
ALPEROVICH		M		Reuven Nathan Zalman	Rivka		The unnamed son of Reuven Natan Zalman [4]	329
ALPEROVICH		F		Reuven Nathan Zalman	Rivka		The unnamed daughter of Reuven Natan Zalman perished in Wilejka	329
KOPILOVITZ	Zvi	M	married			Feigel	He perished in the town	329
KOPILOVITZ	Feigel	F	married			Zvi	Feigel was alive in the forest; she was severely tortured but did not reveal that the villagers gave the	329

								Jews food; she perished in the forest	
KOPILOVITZ	Ya'akov	M		Zvi	Feigel			He perished in the forest	329
KOPILOVITZ	Leah	F		Zvi	Feigel			She perished in the forest	329
KASHDAN	Zalman	M	married			Chaya Tzertel		[2]	329
KASHDAN	Chaya Tzertel	F	married			Zalman		[1]	329
KASHDAN	Ya'akov	M		Zalman	Chaya Tzertel			[1]	329
KASHDAN	Leah	F		Zalman	Chaya Tzertel			She perished in the forest	329
SHEFFER	Shalom	M	married			Leah		[1]	329
SHEFFER	Leah	F	married			Shalom		The sister of Menucha PEIKON[1]	329
ALPEROVICH	Menachem Mendel	M	married	Zalman		Nechama Risha		[1]	329
ALPEROVICH	Nechama Risha	F	married			Menachem Mendel		[1]	329
ALPEROVICH	Eliyahu Chaim	M	married	Menachem Mendel		Dvusha		It is not known where he perished	329
ALPEROVICH	Devushal	F	married			Eliyahu Chaim		She perished in Wilejka	329
ALPEROVICH	Michael	M	married			Pesia		[1]	329
ALPEROVICH	Pesia	F	married			Michal		[1]	329
ALPEROVICH	Rashka	F		Michael	Pesia			[1]	329
ALPEROVICH	Henya	F		Michael	Pesia			She perished in Wilejka	329
ALPEROVICH	Rachel	F		Michael	Pesia			She perished in Wilejka	329
MELTZER	Yitzhak Moshe	M	married			Tzirel		He perished in Wilejka	329
MELTZER	Tzirel	F	married			Yitzhak Moshe		She perished in Wilejka	329
MELTZER	Akiva	M		Yitzhak Moshe	Tzirel			He perished in Wilejka	329
MELTZER	Chaya	F		Yitzhak Moshe	Tzirel			She perished in Wilejka	329
CHAYIT	Shasha Minia	F						[1]	329
COHEN	Rafael	M	married			Esther Gitel		He was a Shochet (ritual slaughterer)[1]	329
COHEN	Esther Gitel	F	married			Rafael		[1]	329

Surname	Given	Sex	Status	Father	Mother	Spouse	Notes	Page
COHEN	Avraham Meir	M		Rafael	Esther Gitel		[1]	329
COHEN	Shoshana	F		Rafael	Esther Gitel		[1]	329
COHEN	Yosef	M		Rafael	Esther Gitel		He perished in Estonia	329
WEXLER	Zalman Nuta	M					[1]	329
WEXLER	Yisrael Leib	M					He perished when he returned from the forest	329
CARMAN	Zvi	M	married			Sarah	[1]	329
CARMAN	Sarah	F	married			Zvi	[1]	329
CARMAN	Bracha	F		Zvi	Sarah		[1]	329
ZIMMERMAN	Shimon Leib	M	married			Leah	[2]	329
ZIMMERMAN	Leah	F	married			Shimon Leib	[1]	329
ZIMMERMAN	Moshe	M		Shimon Leib	Leah		[2]	329
ZIMMERMAN	Rasha	F		Shimon Leib	Leah		[1]	329
ZIMMERMAN	Gitala	F		Shimon Leib	Leah		[1]	329
ZIMMERMAN	Avraham	M		Shimon Leib	Leah		[1]	329
KREMNIK	Baruch	M	married			Gitel	[2]	329
KREMNIK	Gitel	F	married			Baruch	[2]	329
KREMNIK	Itka	F		Baruch	Gitel		[2]	329
KREMNIK	Yisrael Michel	M		Baruch	Gitel		[5]	329
KREMNIK	Rachel	F		Baruch	Gitel		She perished in Wilejka	329
DINERSTEIN	Moshe Mordecai	M	married			Rasha	It is not known where he perished	329
DINERSTEIN	Rasha	F	married			Moshe Mordecai	She & her 2 unnamed sons[2]	329
DINERSTEIN	Yochka	F	married			Mendel	The wife of Mendel the miller[1]	329
SHEVETZ	Tzadok	M	married			Rashka	He perished in the forest	329
SHEVETZ	Rashka	F	married			Tzadok	She perished in the forest	329
SHEVETZ	Perla	F		Tzadok	Rashka		She perished in the forest	329
SHEVETZ	Sarah	F		Tzadok	Rashka		She perished in the forest	329
HADASH	Shifra	F					[3]	330

Surname	Given Name	Sex	Status	Father	Mother	Spouse	Notes	Page
HADASH	Yehuda	M			Shifra		It is not known where he perished	330
HADASH	Ya'akov	M			Shifra		It is not known where he perished	330
HADASH	Yishayahu	M	married			Frumka	It is not known where he perished	330
HADASH	Frumka	F	married			Yishayahu	She was one of the 32[3]	330
HADASH		M		Yishayahu	Frumka		He was one of the 32[3]	330
HADASH		F		Yishayahu	Frumka		She was one of the 32[3]	330
ALPEROVICH	Naftali	M					[1]	330
ALPEROVICH	Raicha	F		Naftali			She perished in the forest	330
ALPEROVICH	Relka	F		Naftali			She perished in the forest	330
ALPEROVICH	Zvi	M	married	Naftali		Rivka	He perished in Postawy	330
ALPEROVICH	Rivka	F	married			Zvi	She perished in Postawy	330
ALPEROVICH	Mina	F		Zvi	Rivka		She perished in Postawy	330
GORDON	Shaul	M	married			Mina	He, his wife and their 3 unnamed daughters perished in the forest	330
GORDON	Mina	F	married			Shaul	She, her husband and their 3 unnamed daughters perished in the forest	330
GORDON		F		Shaul	Mina		The first of 3 daughters of Shaul and Mina GORDON; she perished in the forest	330
GORDON		F		Shaul	Mina		The second of 3 daughters of Shaul & Mina GORDON; she perished in the forest	330
GORDON		F		Shaul	Mina		The third of 3 daughters of Shaul & Mina GORDON; she perished in the forest	330
ROITSTEIN	Shifra Hinda	F					She perished in the forest	330
MINDEL	Gershon	M	married			Nechama	He, his wife and their son perished in Dunilowicze	330
MINDEL	Nechama	F	married			Gershon	She perished in Dunilowicze	330
MINDEL	Avraham Aharon	M		Gershon	Nechama		He perished in Dunilowicze	330
MINDEL	Batya	F	married				It is not known where she, her husband & their 2 children (all unnamed) perished	330
MINDEL	Paya	F					She and her family (names & number not given) perished in Dunilowicze	330
SPERBER	Yisrael	M	married			Feigel	He perished in Wilejka	330

SPERBER	Feigel	F	married	Gershon		Yisrael	She & her 5 children[1] Maiden name MINDEL	330
SPERBER	Chaya	F		Yisrael	Feigel		[1]	330
SPERBER	Rachel	F		Yisrael	Feigel		[1]	330
SPERBER	Henya	F		Yisrael	Feigel		[1]	330
SPERBER	Tzipa	F		Yisrael	Feigel		[1]	330
SPERBER	Yosef	M		Yisrael	Feigel		[1]	330
TOROV	Nachum	M	married			Devora	He, his wife and 3 of their children[1], an additional daughter perished in the forest	330
TOROV	Devora	F	married			Nachum	She, her husband and 3 of their children(unnamed) [1] an additional (unnamed) daughter perished in the forest	330
TOROV		F		Nachum	Devorah		She perished in the forest	330
TZEPLEVITZ	Zalman Mendel	M					[1]	330
TZEPLEVITZ	Aharon	M		Zalman Mendel			It is not known where he perished	330
RAIZ	Yocheved	F		Zalman Mendel			She and her 2 children [1] Maiden name TZEPLEVITZ	330
RAIZ	Pinchas	M			Yocheved		[1]	330
RAIZ	Feigela	F			Yocheved		[1]	330
EISHISKY	Gershon	M	married			Esther Henya	He, his wife, son & daughter perished in Wilejka	330
EISHISKY	Esther Henya	F	married			Gershon	She, her husband, son & daughter perished in Wilejka	330
EISHISKY	Devora	F		Gershon	Esther Henya		She perished in Wilejka	330
EISHISKY	Moshe	M		Gershon	Esther Henya		He perished in Wilejka	330
FELDMAN	Moshe Aharon	M	married				The rabbi [Harav Hagaon][4]	330
FELDMAN		F	married			Moshe Aharon	The rabbi's unnamed wife[1]	330
LEVINSON	Pesach	M	married			Malka	He, his wife & their 3 children[1]	330
LEVINSON	Malka	F	married			Pesach	She, her husband & their 3 children[1]	330
LEVINSON	Ya'akov	M		Pesach	Malka		[1]	330
LEVINSON	Devora	F		Pesach	Malka		[1]	330
LEVINSON	Rivka	F		Pesach	Malka		[1]	330

FIEDLER	Freida	F		Isser			She & her brother perished in Opsa	330
FIEDLER	Reuven	M		Isser			He & his sister perished in Opsa	330
KANTOR	Yosef	M	married			Sheina Chaya	He, his wife & 3 of their sons (2 unnamed) perished in Wilejka	330
KANTOR	Sheina Chaya	F	married			Yosef	She, her husband & 3 of their sons (2 unnamed) perished in Wilejka	330
KANTOR	Binyamin	M		Yosef	Sheina Chaya		He perished in Wilejka	330
KANTOR		M		Yosef	Sheina Chaya		He perished in Wilejka	330
KANTOR		M		Yosef	Sheina Chaya		He perished in Wilejka	330
SEKLIAR	Chaya Itka	F					[1]	330
CHAYIT	Nachman	M	married				He, his unnamed wife & their 3 of their sons (unnamed) [1]	330
CHAYIT		F	married			Nachman	She (unnamed), her husband & their 3 their sons (unnamed) [1]	330
CHAYIT		M		Nachman			[1]	330
CHAYIT		M		Nachman			[1]	330
CHAYIT		M		Nachman			[1]	330
CHAYIT	Bezalel	M					It is not known where he and his family (number & names not given) perished	330
MEKLER	Malka Feiga	F					She and her sister[1]	330
MEKLER	Raina	F					She and her sister[1]	330
MEKLER	Mordecai	M	married				It is not known where he, his wife and children (all unnamed) perished	330
MEKLER		F	married			Mordecai	It is not known where she, her husband and children (all unnamed) perished	330
		F				Baruch Itsche Gedaliahs	Identified only as the wife of Baruch Itsche Gedaliahs[1]; it is not known where her 3 sons perished	330
	Alta	F					Identified only Alta together in listing above[1]	330
FIEDLER	Avraham	M					[1]	330
FIEDLER	Masha Menucha	F		Avraham			[1]	330
FIEDLER	Zev	M		Avraham			He excelled as a partisan and perished in the forest	330

Surname	Given Name	Sex	Status	Father	Mother	Spouse	Notes	Page
FIEDLER	Chaim Beinush	M	married			Rachel Leah	He, his wife and unnamed daughter perished in Molodeczno	331
FIEDLER	Rachel Leah	F	married			Chaim Beinush	She, her husband and unnamed daughter perished in Molodeczno	331
FIEDLER		F		Chaim Beinush	Rachel Leah		She perished in Molodeczno	331
MARKMAN	Zev	M	married			Chana Eta	He perished in Wilejka	331
MARKMAN	Chana Eta	F	married			Zev	She perished in Wilejka	331
MARKMAN	Yosef	M		Zev	Chana Eta		It is not known where he perished	331
MARKMAN	Moshe	M	married			Rachel	He, his wife and their unnamed son perished in Wilejka	331
MARKMAN	Rachel	F	married			Moshe	She, her husband and their unnamed son perished in Wilejka	331
MARKMAN		M		Moshe	Rachel		He perished in Wilejka	331
ASHKENAZI	Rasha	F					She, her son & daughter, both unnamed, perished in Wilejka Maiden name MARKMAN	331
ASHKENAZI		M			Rasha		He perished in Wilejka	331
ASHKENAZI		F			Rasha		She perished in Wilejka	331
ZENDEL	Yitzhak	M	married			Rivka	[1]	331
ZENDEL	Rivka	F	married			Yitzhak	[1]	331
ZENDEL	Meir	M		Yitzhak	Rivka		He perished in battle	331
ZIMMERMAN	Masha	F	married			Alter	The wife of R' Alter, she perished in Vilna	331
ZIMMERMAN	Sima	F		Alter	Masha		She perished in Vilna	331
ZIMMERMAN	Eliyahu	M		Alter	Masha		He perished in Vilna	331
FIEDLER	Leiba	M	married				He, his wife & their 2 children (all 3 unnamed) perished in Ilja	331
FIEDLER		F	married			Leiba	She (unnamed), her husband & their 2 children (unnamed) perished in Ilja	331
KANTROWITZ	Mendel	M	married			Feiga Rivka	He perished in Wilejka	331
KANTROWITZ	Feiga Rivka	F	married			Mendel	She perished in Wilejka	331
KANTROWITZ	Shlomo	M	married				It is not known where he perished	331
KANTROWITZ		F	married			Shlomo	She with her 2 children (all 3 unnamed) perished in Dokszyce	331

The Scroll of Kurzeniac

Surname	Given Name	Sex	Marital Status	Father	Mother	Spouse	Notes	Page
KANTROWITZ	Reuven	M					He and his family (names & number not given) perished in Glebokie	331
WEINER	Dov	M	married			Rachel	He perished in the forest	331
WEINER	Rachel	F	married			Dov	She perished in the forest Maiden name KANTROWITZ	331
KOPILOVITZ	David	M	married			Gitel	He, his wife & their 4 unnamed children perished in Wilejka	331
KOPILOVITZ	Gitel	F	married			David	She, her husband & their 4 unnamed children perished in Wilejka	331
ALPEROVICH	Moshe	M	married	Chaim Zalman		Sonia	He perished in the forest	331
ALPEROVICH	Sonia	F	married			Moshe	She perished in the forest	331
ALPEROVICH	Zalman	M		Moshe	Sonia		He perished in the Red Army	331
EINBINDER	Dov	M	married			Perla	He perished two days after the mass murder of the town[1]	331
EINBINDER	Perla	F	married			Dov	She perished two days after the mass murder of the town[1]	331
EINBINDER	Nechama	F		Dov	Perla		She perished two days after the mass murder of the town[1]	331
EINBINDER	Sima	F		Dov	Perla		She perished two days after the mass murder of the town[1]	331
EINBINDER	Zalman	M		Dov	Perla		He perished two days after the mass murder of the town[1]	331
EINBINDER	Yitzhak	M		Dov	Perla		He perished as a Partisan and after his death he received extraordinary recognition for his daring activities and outstanding service	331
SOSNASKY	Mara Shosha	F	married				She is listed by her maiden name; she, her unnamed husband and their son[1] Maiden name SOSNASKY	331
		M	married			Mara Shosha	He (unnamed), his wife (maiden name SOSNASKY) and their son[1]	331
	Dudel	M			Mara Shosha		Maiden name SOSNASKY [1]	331
ALPEROVICH	Yehoshua	M	married	Zalman Noach		Rivka	[2]	331
ALPEROVICH	Rivka	F	married			Yehoshua	[2]	331
ALPEROVICH	Asher	M		Yehoshua	Rivka		[2]	331
ALPEROVICH		F	married			Shmuel	The unnamed wife of Shmuel, she and their 2 unnamed children perished in the forest	331

Surname	First Name	Sex	Status	Father	Mother	Spouse	Notes	Ref
KRAMER	Yishayahu Zev	M	married			Sarah Hinda	[1]	331
KRAMER	Sarah Hinda	F	married			Yishayahu Zev	[1]	331
KRAMER	Rivka	F		Yishayahu Zev	Sarah Hinda		[1]	331
ALPEROVICH	Musia	F		Yitzhak Moshe			[1]	331
ALPEROVICH	Mirel	F	married			Ortzik	The wife of Ortchik, she perished with an unnamed son & daughter & a named son[4]	331
ALPEROVICH		F		Ortzik	Mirel		[1]	331
ALPEROVICH	Chaim Isser	M		Ortzik	Mirel		[1]	331
ALPEROVICH		M		Ortzik	Mirel		[1]	331
SHMUKLER	Feiga Michla	F		Meir Aharon			She and her unnamed daughter[1]	331
SHMUKLER		F			Feiga Michla		[1]	331
ALPEROVICH	Shlomo	M		Meir Aharon			He perished in captivity	331
NORMAN	Rashka	F		Meir Aharon		Zusman	Listed by her maiden name, she, her husband and daughter perished in Wilejka Maiden name NORMAN	331
	Zusman	M				Rashka	He perished in Wilejka	331
	Nechama Itka	F		Zusman	Rashka		She perished in Wilejka	331
ALPEROVICH	Yirmiyahu	M	married	Meir Aharon		Chaya Sarah	He perished in the Wilejka Ghetto	331
ALPEROVICH	Chaya Sarah	F	married			Yirmiyahu	She and her unnamed son and daughter perished 2 weeks after the mass murder of the town[1] in the synagogue's attic Maiden name BEVINER	331
ALPEROVICH		F		Yirmiyahu	Chaya Sarah		He perished 2 weeks after the mass murder of the town[1] in the synagogue's attic	331
ALPEROVICH		M		Yirmiyahu	Chaya Sarah		She perished 2 weeks after the mass murder of the town[1] in synagogue's attic	331
ALPEROVICH	Michael	M	married			Gita	He & his wife were in hiding with a non-Jew in the village of Klyn who turned him over to the Germans who murdered them	331
ALPEROVICH	Gita	F	married			Michael	She & her husband were in hiding with a non-Jew in the	331

						village of Klyn who turned him over to the Germans who murdered them	
FREDKIN	Zelda	F	married			She and her unnamed son[1]; her unnamed husband perished in the forest	332
FREDKIN		M	married		Zelda	He perished in the forest	332
FREDKIN		M		Zelda		[1]	332
WEISENHOLTZ	Mina	F		Chaim Michael		[1]	332
RODINSKY	Tzipa	F				[1]	332
WEINSTEIN	Sarah	F				The sister of Hinda, Shosha & Bluma; [1]	332
	Hinda	F				The sister of Sarah, Shosha & Bluma; [1]	332
	Shosha	F				The sister of Sarah, Hinda & Bluma; [1]	332
	Bluma	F				The sister of Sarah, Hinda & Shosha; [1]	332
TZIROLNIK	Yitzhak	M	married			[2]	332
TZIROLNIK		F	married		Yitzhak	[2]	332
TZIROLNIK		M		Yitzhak		[2]	332
TZIROLNIK	Shimon	M		Yitzhak		It is not known where he perished	332
TZIROLNIK	Meir	M	married			He, his unnamed wife and their 3 children (unnamed) perished a few days after the mass murder of the town[1]	332
TZIROLNIK		F	married		Meir	She, her husband and their 3 children (unnamed) perished a few days after the mass murder of the town[1]	332
ALPEROVICH	Rachel Leah	F				[1]	332
ALPEROVICH	Avramel	M		Rachel Leah		[4]	332
ALPEROVICH	Shifra	F		Rachel Leah		She was one of the 32[3]	332
ALPEROVICH	Charna	F		Rachel Leah		She was one of the 32[3]	332
ALPEROVICH	Mordecai	M	married	Abba		He, his wife & their 3 children (all unnamed) perished in Wilejka on the day the town was liberated; he left a note where he wrote "They are taking us out to	332

Surname	Given name	Sex	Status	Father	Mother	Spouse	Notes	Page
							be killed, I hear the Russian tanks, say Kaddish for us"	
ALPEROVICH		F	married			Mordecai	She perished in Wilejka on the day it was liberated	332
ALPEROVICH	Yisrael	M	married	Zelig		Batsheva	He, his wife & their 3 daughters[1]	332
ALPEROVICH	Batsheva	F	married			Yisrael	[1]	332
ALPEROVICH	Rachel	F		Yisrael	Batsheva		[1]	332
ALPEROVICH	Devora	F		Yisrael	Batsheva		[1]	332
ALPEROVICH	Zelda	F		Yisrael	Batsheva		[1]	332
KUSHNIR	Ya'akov Moshe	M	married			Huda	[1]	332
KUSHNIR	Huda	F	married			Ya'akov Moshe	[1]	332
CHESLER	Reuven	M	married			Chaya Sarah	[2]	332
CHESLER	Chaya Sara	F	married			Reuven	[2]	332
CHESLER	Malka	F		Reuven	Chaya Sarah		[2]	332
BEVINER	Arieh Leib	M	married			Rachel	He, his wife & daughter were killed in the synagogue attic after the mass murder of the town[1]	332
BEVINER	Rachel	F	married			Arieh Leib	She was killed in the synagogue attic after the mass murder of the town[1]	332
BEVINER	Rivka	F		Arieh Leib	Rachel		She was killed in the synagogue attic after the mass murder of the town[1]	332
GELMAN	Shimon	M	married			Gita	[4]	332
GELMAN	Gita	F	married			Shimon	[4]	332
GELMAN	Chana	F		Shimon	Gita		[4]	332
GELMESON	David	M	married			Sarah	He, his wife, 2 daughters & an unnamed son[1]	332
GELMESON	Sarah	F	married			David	[1]	332
GELMESON	Esther	F		David	Sarah		[1]	332
GELMESON	Masha	F		David	Sarah		[1]	332
GELMESON		M		David	Sarah		[1]	332
ALPEROVICH	Pinchas	M	married	Yitzhak		Shoshana	He perished in the forest	332
ALPEROVICH	Shoshana	F	married			Pinchas	She was one of the 32[3]	332
ALPEROVICH	Tuvia	M		Pesach	Shoshana		[2]	332
ALPEROVICH	Pesach	M		Pesach	Shoshana		[2]	332

Surname	Given	Sex	Status	Father	Mother	Spouse	Notes	Page
ALPEROVICH	Fruma	F		Pesach	Shoshana		[1]	332
ALPEROVICH	Chaim	M		Pesach	Shoshana		[1]	332
ALPEROVICH	Bella	F		Pesach	Shoshana		[1]	332
ALPEROVICH	Chaya	F		Pesach	Shoshana		[1]	332
RAIDER	Avraham Chaim	M	married			Marisha	[1]	332
RAIDER	Mariasha	F	married			Avraham Chaim	[1]	332
RAIDER	Dov	M		Avraham Chaim	Mariasha		It is not known where she perished	332
RAIDER	Yitzhak	M		Avraham Chaim	Mariasha		It is not known where he perished	332
RAIDER	Yishayahu	M		Avraham Chaim	Mariasha		It is not known where he perished	332
	Rachel	F		Avraham Chaim	Mariasha		It is not known where she and her family (names & number not given) perished Maiden name RAIDER	332
VINIK	Avraham	M	married			Rachel	He, his wife & their 5 children[1]	332
VINIK	Rachel	F	married			Avraham	[1]	332
VINIK	Michael	M		Avraham	Rachel		[1]	332
VINIK	Chaya	F		Avraham	Rachel		[1]	332
VINIK	Eliyahu	M		Avraham	Rachel		[1]	332
VINIK	Meir	M		Avraham	Rachel		[1]	332
VINIK	Tzipora	F		Avraham	Rachel		[1]	332
	Leah	F		Zelig			[1] Maiden name ALPEROVICH	332
KRAVITZ	Zev	M	married			Chana Sarah	[1]	332
KRAVITZ	Chana Sarah	F	married			Zev	[1]	332
KRAVITZ	Liba	F		Zev	Chana Sarah		[1]	332
CHESLER	Zalman	M	married			Chana	It is not known where he perished	332
CHESLER	Chana	F	married			Zalman	She and her unnamed son[1]	332
CHESLER	Perla	F					[1]	332
CHESLER	Bila	F			Perla		[1]	332
VINIK	Noach Nuta	M					[1]	332
KRAMER	Devora	F					[1]	332

KRAMER	Chaim	M	married			Malka	[1]	332
KRAMER	Malka	F	married			Chaim	[1]	332
KRAMER	Sima	F		Chaim	Malka		[1]	332
KOPILOVITZ	Elka	F					She and her 2 sons[1]	333
KOPILOVITZ	Yehuda	M				Elka	[1]	333
KOPILOVITZ	Yerachmiel	M				Elka	[1]	333
ELISHKAVITZ	Mordechai Motka	M					Known as "Motke the Katler - the Coppersmith," [1]	333
ELISHKAVITZ	Yerachmiel	M	married			Shoshana	[1]	333
ELISHKAVITZ	Shoshana	F	married			Yerachmiel	[1]	333
ELISHKAVITZ	Meir	M		Yerachmiel	Shoshana		[1]	333
SPECTOR	Natan	M	married			Rivka	[1]	333
SPECTOR	Rivka	F	married			Natan	[1]	333
SPECTOR	Esther	F		Natan	Rivka		[1]	333
SPECTOR	Sarah	F		Natan	Rivka		[1]	333
SPECTOR	Koppel	M		Natan	Rivka		He perished in Wilejka	333
SPECTOR	Eliyahu	M		Natan	Rivka		He perished in Wilejka	333
SHULMAN	Hinda	F					[1]	333
SHULMAN	Aharon	M	married	Meir Shalom		Chana	[1]	333
SHULMAN	Chana	F	married			Aharon	[1]	333
SHULMAN	Elka	F		Aharon	Chana		[1]	333
GORFINKEL	Michael	M					The brother of Batya Rivka, he perished in the forest	333
GORFINKEL	Batya Rivka	F					The sister of Michael GORFINKEL[1]	333
GELMAN	Zalman	M	married			Sheina	[1]	333
GELMAN	Sheina	F	married			Zalman	[1]	333
GELMAN	Yitzhak Moshe	M		Zalman	Sheina		[1]	333
BLINDER	Shmuel	M	married			Feigel	He perished in Wilejka	333
BLINDER	Feigel	F	married			Shmuel	She perished in the forest	333
BLINDER	Pesia	F		Shmuel	Feigel		She perished in the forest	333
GELMAN	Velvel	M	married			Chasia	He, his wife and their 2 unnamed children[1]	333
GELMAN	Chasia	F	married			Velvel	She, her husband and their 2 unnamed children[1]	333

Surname	Given Name	Sex	Status	Father	Mother	Spouse	Notes	Page
GELMAN	Zalman	M	married			Michal	He, his wife, his son Dov and an additional unnamed son[1]	333
GELMAN	Michla	F	married			Zalman	[1]	333
GELMAN	Dov	M		Zalman	Michla		[1]	333
RUBIN	Shimka Dina	F	married	Moshe Leib			The daughter of Rabbi Moshe Leib LANDA and her unnamed husband perished in Dalhinov Maiden name LANDA	333
RUBIN		M	married			Shimka Dina	He perished in Dalhinov	333
LANDA	Meir	M					The grandson of Rabbi Moshe Leib LANDA and his family (names & number not given) perished in Wilejka	333
	Peshka	F		Moshe Leib			The daughter of Rabbi Moshe Lieb LANDA and her unnamed daughter perished in Kojdanowo Maiden name LANDA	333
		F			Peshka		The unnamed daughter of Peshka perished in Kojdanowo. Maiden name LANDA	333
LANDA		F	widow			Avraham Zalman	The unnamed widow of Avraham Zalman LANDA perished in Wilejka with her unnamed daughter	333
LANDA		F		Avraham Zalman			She perished in Wilejka	333
	Devora	F		Elyakim			[1] Maiden name DINERSTEIN	333
	Sarah Pesia	F			Devorah		[1]	333
SOSNESKY	Leib	M	married			Yenta	He perished in Sosenka	333
SOSNESKY	Yenta	F	married			Leib	She perished in Sosenka Maiden name TAUBES	333
SOSNESKY	Chaya	F		Leib	Yenta		She perished in Sosenka	333
SOSNESKY	Chana	F		Leib	Yenta		She perished in Sosenka	333
DINERSTEIN	Masha	F	married			Ya'akov	She, her husband & their 3 unnamed children perished in the forest Maiden name DINERSTEIN	333
	Ya'akov	M	married			Masha	He, his wife (maiden name DINERSTEIN) & their 3 unnamed children perished in the forest	333
EINBINDER	Yehoshua	M	married			Devora	He perished in Postawy	333
EINBINDER	Devora	F	married			Yehoshua	She perished in Postawy	333
EINBINDER	Leah	F		Yehoshua	Devorah		She perished in Postawy	333
SOKOLINSKY	Zisel	M	married			Rishka	He perished in Postawy	333

Surname	Given name	Sex	Status	Father	Mother	Spouse	Notes	Page
SOKOLINSKY	Rishka	F	married			Zisel	She perished in Postawy	333
SOKOLINSKY	Avramel	M		Zissel	Rishka		He perished in Postawy	333
SOKOLINSKY	Sarah	F		Zissel	Rishka		She perished in Postawy	333
SEKLIAR	Chaya Itka	F					[1] Maiden name FIEDLER	333
	Shoshana	F	married				She, her unnamed husband and their family (names & number not given) perished in Swir Maiden name FIEDLER	333
		M	married			Shoshana	He perished in Swir. Wife's maiden name FIEDLER	333
	Esther	F	married			Hirsh Getzel	She, her husband and their family (names & number not given) perished in the forest Maiden name FIEDLER	333
	Hirsh Getzel	M	married			Esther	He perished in the forest. Wife's maiden name FIEDLER	333
KREMNIK	Yosef Shimon	M	married			Slava	He perished in Wilejka	333
KREMNIK	Slava	F	married			Yosef Shimon	She perished in Wilejka	333
KREMNIK	Pira	F		Yosef Shimon	Slava		She perished in Wilejka	333
ZUCKERMAN	Risha	F		Meir Rafael			She & her daughter were killed in a hiding place in the synagogue several days after the mass murder of the town[1]	333
ZUCKERMAN	Badana	F			Risha		She was killed in a hiding place in the synagogue several days after the mass murder of the town[1]	333
ZUCKERMAN	Elchanan Shimon	M			Risha		He perished in Wilejka	333
ZIMMERMAN	Hinda	F		Yitzhak			She was burned alive in the Wilejka Ghetto	333
ALPEROVICH	Feiga Leah	F					She was killed in Wilejka 3 or 4 days before liberation	333
BERGSTEIN	Rachel Leah	F					[1]	334
BERGSTEIN	Sarah Bluma	F			Rachel Leah		[1]	334
OSHPOL	Shlomo Eli'	M	married				Listed as 'Harav Hagaon' - Rabbi & Scholar - he perished in Swieciany	334
OSHPOL		F	married			Shlomo Eli'	The unnamed wife of the Rabbi, she perished in Swieciany	334

Surname	Given Name	Sex	Marital	Father	Mother	Spouse	Comments	Page
OSHPOL	Mordecai	M		Shlomo Eli'			He perished in Swieciany	334
OSHPOL	Dina	F		Shlomo Eli'			She perished in Swieciany	334
OSHPOL	Batya	F		Shlomo Eli'			She perished in Swieciany	334
OSHPOL	Mina	F		Shlomo Eli'			She perished in Swieciany	334
ALPEROVICH	Zev	M	married				The brother of Bentcha Haminagen (the musician), he perished in the forest	334
ALPEROVICH		F	married			Zev	His unnamed wife & their 2 unnamed children perished in Ilja	334
TUNIK	Avraham	M	married			Teibel	He, his wife and their 2 unnamed daughters perished in Wilejka	334
TUNIK	Teibel	F	married			Avraham	She, her husband and their 2 unnamed daughters perished in Wilejka Maiden name MARKON	334
TUNIK		F		Avraham	Teibel		She perished in Wilejka	334
TUNIK		F		Avraham	Teibel		She perished in Wilejka	334
MARKON	Mordecai	M					He perished in the forest	334
MARKON	Sonia	F		Mordecai			She perished in Riga	334
MARKON	Cheina	F		Mordecai			She perished in Bialystok	334
SHAPIRA	Sarah Frada	F					She perished in Wilejka	334
	Batsheva	F	married		Sarah Frada	Moshe	The daughter of Sarah Frada, she and her son[1]	334
	Moshe	M	married			Batsheva	He perished in Wilejka	334
	Eliyahu	M		Moshe	Batsheva		[1]	334
WEISENHOLTZ	Mordecai	M	married			Ita Rachel	He perished in Wilejka	334
WEISENHOLTZ	Ita Rachel	F	married			Mordecai	She perished in Wilejka	334
LAPKIN	Yosef Eliyahu	M					He perished in Smorgonie	334
LAPKIN	Baruch	M		Yosef Eliyahu			He perished in Smorgonie	334
LAPKIN	Natan	M		Yosef Eliyahu			He perished in Smorgonie	334
LAPKIN	Marka	F		Yosef Eliyahu			She perished in Smorgonie	334
GEVELMAN	Rasia	F		Zelig			[1]	334
GEVELMAN	Gensia	F		Zelig			[1]	334

Surname	Given	Sex	Status	Father	Mother	Spouse	Notes	Page
TZODIKOV	Zalman	M	married				He and his unnamed wife[1]	334
TZODIKOV		F	married			Zalman	[1]	334
TZODIKOV	Gutel	M		Zalman			It is not known where he perished	334
AIDELMAN	Manya	F		Yishayahu			[3]	334
AIDELMAN		F			Manya		The first of 2 unnamed daughters of Manya AIDELMAN, she perished a few days after the mass murder of the town[1]	334
AIDELMAN		F			Manya		The second of 2 unnamed daughters of Manya AIDELMAN, she perished a few days after the mass murder of the town[1]	334
RABONSKY	Rachel	F					She & her 2 unnamed daughters[1]	334
RABONSKY		F			Rachel		The first of 2 unnamed daughters of Rachel RABONSKY[1]	334
RABONSKY		F			Rachel		The second of 2 unnamed daughters of Rachel RABONSKY[1]	334
GURVITZ	Batya	F					She perished in Zdzieciol Maiden name EISHISKY	334
ALPEROVICH	Sarah	F					She perished with her 2 unnamed sons in the mass murder of the town Maiden name EISHISKY	334
ALPEROVICH		M			Sarah		Maiden name EISHISKY [1]	334
ALPEROVICH		M			Sarah		Maiden name EISHISKY [1]	334
ALPEROVICH	Hershel	M	married	Avraham			He, his unnamed wife and their 2 children (unnamed)[1]	334
ALPEROVICH		F	married			Hershel	[1]	334
ALPEROVICH	Sarah	F	married			Uri	The wife of Rabbi Uri, she perished in Wilejka	334
ALPEROVICH	Rivka	F		Uri	Sarah		She perished in Wilejka	334
TZIRINSKY	Fanny	F					She, her unnamed mother-in-law and two children (unnamed) perished in Wilejka	334
TZIRINSKY		F					She perished in Wilejka	334
EINBINDER	Zalman	M	married			Miriam	Perished, date and place not given	334
EINBINDER	Miriam	F	married			Zalman	Perished, date and place not given	334
ZIRTZIS	Pinchas	M					[2]	334

Surname	Given Name	Sex	Status	Relation	Spouse	Notes	Page
COOPER		M				Originally from Smorgonie, the father of Grisha, he perished in the forest	334
COOPER	Grisha	M				Originally from Smorgonie, he perished in the forest	334
SCHNITZER	Shmuel	M	married		Chana	[1]	334
SCHNITZER	Chana	F	married		Shmuel	[1]	334
SHUGOL	Anna	F				Originally from Vilna, she was caught in the first roundup in the forest, brutally tortured & died while being tortured Maiden name KRONIK	334
GREEN	Adzia	F				[1]	334
GROSSBEIN		F				Two unnamed sisters, perished in Pokan on the day after the mass murder of the town[1]	334
KAGAN	Arieh	M		Eliyahu		He perished in Sol with his family, names and number not given	334
KATZ	Yenta Chaya	F				She and her two unnamed children perished in Dokszyce	335
KATZ	Alter	M				[1]	335
KATZ	Avraham	M				[1]	335
SESENSKY	Tamar	F				She and her infant daughter[1]	335
SESENSKY	Golda	F		Tamar		An infant [1]	335
LIFSHITZ		M	married			He and his unnamed wife[1]	335
LIFSHITZ		F	married			She and her unnamed husband[1]	335
STOLER	Shachna	M	married		Malka	He, his wife and their 3 unnamed children[1]	335
STOLER	Malka	F	married		Shachna	She, her husband and their 3 unnamed children[1]	335
ROGOVIN		M	married			He, his unnamed wife and their 2 (unnamed) children perished in the forest	335
ROGOVIN		F	married			She, her unnamed husband and their 2 children (unnamed) perished in the forest	335
LANDA		M	married			Originally from Wilejka[3]	335
LANDA		F	married			The unnamed wife of LANDA from Wilejka[1]	335
LANDA		F				The unnamed daughter-in-law of LANDA from Wilejka; she and her son [3]	335
ZIMMERMAN	Mosheka	M				It is not known where he and his unnamed daughter perished	335

Surname	Given Name	Sex	Marital	Father	Spouse	Notes	Page
ZIMMERMAN		F		Mosheka		Perished, date and place not given	335
BARON		M	married		Esther	He (unnamed), his wife and their 4 unnamed children perished, date and place not given	335
BARON	Esther	F	married			She, her (unnamed) husband and their 4 unnamed children perished, date and place not given	335
REITSTEIN	Elia Meir	M	married			It is not known where he, his unnamed wife and their 2 sons (all unnamed) perished	335
REITSTEIN		F	married		Elia Meir	It is not known where she, her husband and their 2 sons (all unnamed) perished	335
REITSTEIN		M		Elia Meir		The first of two sons of Elia Meir REITSTEIN, it is not known where he perished	335
REITSTEIN		M		Elia Meir		The second of two sons of Elia Meir REITSTEIN, it is not known where he perished	335
	Avraham	M	married		Chaya	He, his wife and their 2 unnamed children [2]	335
LIEBERMAN	Chaya	F	married	Zelig	Avraham	She (the daughter of Zelig), her husband and their 2 unnamed children[2]	335

1. Perished in the mass murder of the town 27 Elul 5702/Wednesday, 9 September 1942
2. One of the 54 killed by the Gestapo round-up on Simchat Torah 5702/Tuesday 14 October 1941
3. One of the 32 killed in the random murder in Adar 5702/27 March 1942
4. One of the 13 murdered by Gestapo in Shevat 5702/15 March 1942
5. Michael, son of Gita and Baruch Kremnik, was presumed by his family to be dead but actually survived the war. It was not discovered until the 1990s that he had actually survived. Michael served for many years in the Red Army, starting as soon as the war ended in the area of Kurenets. He knew that none of his relatives in Kurenets and Volozhin survived and he never returned to the area. After he married, he told his wife and children about his first cousin Bela Kramnik in Israel but did not know her married name. He passed away before the family immigrated to Israel in the early 1990's. The wife and children found his first cousin Bela Kramnik Salitarnik in Israel.

Part Five: Supplement

The day the war started in Grodno, 1941

by Shimon Zimmerman

Translated by sixteen year old Oren Levitan

*In honor of his great-uncles,
Benjamin (Nyomka) Shulman, Zalman Uri Gurevitch, and Nachum Alperovich,
who as teenagers fought the Germans*

I was 17, a student in the technicum for economic studies in Grodno, on the shores of the Nemun River. I did well in my studies and received a scholarship in Stalin's name. I was the head of the school's student body and was very involved with the communist party. Full of plans and dreams for the future, I was absolutely sure that the communist rule that two years prior had replaced the radical anti-Semitic Polish rule was heaven on earth for us, Jews. This idyllic fantasy didn't last long.

On June 21, 1941, I finished my finals with high marks. In good spirits, my friends and I went to see the choir of Yordnah. The next morning, I was planning to go back to Kurenitz to spend my summer break in my hometown. What happiness I was anticipating, seeing my parents, girlfriend Riva, my good friends, and having a good time every minute of my summer vacation.

Instead of leisurely getting up and going to the train station, exactly at 4am I was awakened by sirens from the dorm alert system, then the sounds of aircraft, German messerschmitts, and explosions everywhere. At that moment I had no idea of the tragedy that befell me, and I never imagined that my days of youth were over. That teenage celebration of life, schoolwork and having casual fun with friends would be replaced by a daily struggle to survive. I was sure that everything would be like the songs we sang – Stalin would give the orders, and our pilots would clean the skies of the messerschmitts. Marshal Voroshilov, the head of Russian army, would take the Red Army to swift triumph and knock down the German infantry like a samurai from Japan, and I would come home only a few days late.

*Riva née Gordon and her husband to be,
Shimon Zimerman
as Partisans in 1943 in the Varshilov brigade in Naarutz (Belarus)*

But as high as the expectations so were the depths of the disappointments. Already in that first day I knew it was not like the songs we sang. Grodno shared a border with Germany at that point in time, and now was heavily air attacked, the bombing growing in intensity. The Soviet planes that just managed to take off, as Skidal airfield was destroyed, were chased and hit by the German messerschmitts, and fell out of the sky like paper toys. The Germans had absolute control of the skies. The bridge that connected the city that was parted by the Nemun River was the only way to go east, but it had a huge traffic mess, and nothing could move because of the innumerable out of order vehicles.

In the afternoon, we got an order to gather in small groups and leave Grodno. Carrying our packages on our backs, without instructions as to where to go, no food, and no information about what was going on, we chose partners. Our group included 8 guys and 2 girls. We took off from the largest synagogue in Grodno; prior to the war it was used by our school for lectures. We started walking toward Skidal-Lida. The whole town was girdled with traffic, broken army vehicles, and torn telephone wires; the communist authorities left the city hastily in great panic while German aircraft were continuously attacking and pushing inland…

Encountering hardship and danger, we finally managed to leave Grodno. We were tired, hungry, and lost. The roads were filled with civilians and soldiers who ran in a frenzy. The German planes flew very low, almost touching the ground, shooting at everyone below with machine guns.

We reached a forest and decided to rest. At dawn we saw horrible images. The road was filled with wounded and dead and no one took care of them. The Russian soldiers didn't know where their officers were. They took off their uniforms, got rid of their weapons and ran for their lives.

Hundreds of prisoners of all nationalities – that were mostly imprisoned for being late for work – were supposed to go that day to Skidal to build an airfield. Instead they left the prison camp half-naked and mixed in with the crowds going east.

Because of all this pandemonium, the second day, I was left only with one friend of the entire group; the rest were lost. On the third day, four prisoners from the Skidal camp joined us; we were on the road to Dolhinov, 30m km from Kurenitz. We ate fruit and vegetables we found in the fields, and drank from every dirty puddle. The heat was unbearable and the flies wouldn't leave us alone. On top of it all, I had new shoes and my feet were all swollen and when I took my shoes off the skin came with it.

Hungry, in a daze, and bare-foot we continued east. The train did not work and every kind of public transportation was destroyed. There was no private transportation because gas was not available. We reached Lida and took a longer route; circling the burning town, we continued to the direction of Ilya. We came close to the road that would take us to Minsk, the capital of Belarus.

We were sure the Red Army would stop the invaders from coming there, but that didn't happen. The Germans' strategy was to put units in the back of the Red Army; they put small units everywhere and that helped them to create demoralization and panic in the Russian army and local authority. Later on, we found out that the general of the Minsk front was a German collaborator and helped the Germans capture the city. Everything around us was destroyed and an enormous marching German army, extremely organized and prepared with every equipment and supply you could imagine, continued going ahead like it was a never-ending army parade.

I understood that all was lost. I dug a hole in the ground and made a mental note of where it was and put my party membership and professional cards in the hole, hoping to retrieve them one day. In no time we were in the hands of German soldiers who took us to the German headquarters. A young German soldier with a baby face asked me where I was going, I explained I was a student and was going home, I showed him my student ID (I didn't even remember that it said I was a Jew). He left and came back with a higher authority officer and explained to him that I was a student and pointed to my long hair, then they both left. Later the baby-faced soldier came back and gave me a sandwich with jelly and egg. He gave me my ID card back and let me go.

My friend and the other guys with buzz cuts were taken blindfolded. The Germans suspected that they were soldiers in the Red Army. So in the heat of the afternoon of June 24 1941, I stood shocked and confused after my first meeting with the Germans. I was 20-km from Radeshkovitz. The town where the poet Mordechai Tzvi Maneh, who I admired so, was born.

Before I was let go by the Germans, I was sure this was my end; just thinking about it brought tears to my eyes. I was an only son and could imagine what my parents were going through. My girlfriend, Riva and my parents would have never known where I was buried… The sound of what turned out to be two German planes chasing a huge Soviet plane brought me back to reality. I saw them hit the plane and tons of papers and maps dropped from the sky. The Russian pilot parachuted not far from me. I just lay there frozen with fear. A few minutes later pastoral quietness took over. I first stood, and then ran, not knowing where to go. Not far from there, I saw a little farmhouse. I knocked. The farmer was scared to let me in, but he gave me a piece of bread and cucumber and showed me the way to Ilya, a town where my uncle lived.

When I arrived in Ilya, I learned the Germans had not entered yet. At the Soviet headquarters of war, I saw many armed soldiers. A policeman hung warnings on the street that two people had been executed for stealing something from a factory. At my uncle's home, there were a few Jews, merchants and businessmen during the time of the Polish control, and they were happy about the defeat of the Red Army! I was shocked and couldn't understand. Despite their knowledge of Hitler's views of the Jews, Jewish people were sitting so content, not even considering what was to come. The poor people truly believed nothing would happen to them, that they would manage!

At dawn, the German army approached Ilya, marching in the direction of Dolhinov. With help of relatives, I left Ilya for Kurenitz. The Germans entered Ilya. I immediately crossed the river Vilya at a hidden place and took the forest way to continue. I saw the Red Army taking groups of prisoners from Vileyka, handcuffed with barbed wire. The family members were chasing after the prisoners. I couldn't explain to the families that 20-km away the Germans were approaching.

My legs were cramped and full of cuts from walking barefoot. I arrived to Kurenitz. Across from the train tracks on Costa, I saw Dishka, daughter of Zalman Mendel, strolling around with a basket in her hand collecting mushrooms in the forest. When she saw me, she threw her basket in the air and ran to my parents to let them know I was alive. A few minutes later, my parents and girlfriend came running to kiss me. For a moment we forgot the impending madness all around us.

Riva née Gordon Zimerman with her father,
Shabtai Gordon and the rest of the family
Other than Riva and her oldest sister, Michla,
the entire family perished on 9-9-1942 in Kurenets

1923 Kurenets

Riva with her grandparents, Nechama-Risha née Gelman and Mendel Alperovitz perished in Kurenets, 9-9-1942 [sitting in the middle] on their right; their daughter [Rivas' mother] holding Michla. Above her: Shabtai Gordon holding Riva.
Left of Shabtai and Riva: sisters of Rivas' mother, Emma née Alperovitz Zivoni [died in Israel c 1996]. Rachel née Alperovitz wife of Levik Alperovitz died in Israel c 1947.
To their left: their brother in law, Zalman Pinchas Alperovitz. Under him, his wife, Helena née Alperovitz Alperovitz holding her son Jaime.
Bottom from left: Two of the children of Zalman Pinchas and Helena Alperovitz, Benjamin and Maurico A. [the family lived and died in Argentina]. Sitting on the right: the youngest and only son of Nechama-Risha née Gelman and Mendel Alperovitz; Eliyahu Alperovitz [perished in the Holocaust].

My time in Kurenitz

On the 25th of June, 1941, the Germans hadn't arrived in Kurenitz yet. The Russian authorities left, and the town that was almost exclusively Jewish, was left without official control. The goyim farmers from the town's neighboring villages started coming toward the town with horses and buggies. Their aim was to take all the supplies that was left from the Soviet times. All the hooligans, criminals, and Jew haters lifted their heads with pride and newfound presence. One of the Christians from the town organized with the help of the Jews a line of defense for the Jewish homes. A group of Jews, amongst them, my two cousins named Shimon Zimerman had a watch patrol, and everyone armed themselves (in other shtetls the Jews were rubbed out as soon as the Russians left). When the Germans came to town and saw my two cousins they killed them. Only a few days later, we found out about it and gave them a Jewish burial.

Shock and fear spread among the Jews, and they locked themselves in their homes. Two days after their arrival, the Germans collected all the Jewish men from 16 to 60 in the center of town. The German commandant said that all Jews had to wear a yellow star, everyday they had to participate in forced labor and make themselves useful, they couldn't walk on the sidewalk, only in the center of the road like horses, they couldn't gather more than three at any time, and they were only allowed out during certain hours. They had to choose Jewish representatives (Judenrat) and they had to obey the Judenrat's orders.

We didn't want to believe that this was the beginning of the end of Kurenitz as the end of the rest of the Jews in eastern Europe. The Germans' first step was taking away all our rights not only as citizens, but as human beings. Our self-respect was walked all over. We were demeaned and humiliated in front of our friends and neighbors. Gentiles that were once our friends stopped talking to as if they never knew us. The shame and lack of control over our own lives made some of us not want to live anymore. Every month a new group of Jews would be executed; the first group for being communist, the second for being loyal to the Polish ways of old. But still people held on to hope, thinking of miracles that would keep them alive. People became very religious. On a regular basis the rabbi would announce another fast. We simply didn't want to believe that a cultural nation like the Germans could be so cruel and insane. When rumors spread about the annihilation of neighboring Jewish communities, many refused to listen. People refused to believe that all the males of the neighboring town of Vileyka, only 7 km from Kurenitz, were executed on the second week of the Germans arrival. People of our town sent them food and clothing, The Christian merchants pretended they were still alive so their relatives and friends would continue buying and sending supplies. Only after the war ended we found out they were all buried next to the Vilya River.

The Judenrat on the one hand wanted to please the Germans and on the other had to encourage the Jews to comply with the rules. They thought that if the Jews made themselves useful, the Germans would keep them alive. But they didn't always do their jobs perfectly and favoritism was rampant.

At the beginning, I worked with the prisoners of war; they were transferred through towns towards Germany and their situation was horrible. When they came to town they would sleep on the ground at a field that belonged to Chaim Zukovski (Zukovski was executed two months later with 54 Jews of Kurenitz – they were taken to the woods and dug their own grave and then were shot and thrown into them with their wives and children). Later on I worked in Luban farm and my last job was in the labor camp of Vilyeka as a carpenter even though I had never held a saw in my hand prior to the war. With the agreement of Shotz, the Jewish head of the camp, my girlfriend Riva got a job as a printer in the printing press in the same camp. She was put to work with a printing press so she could secretly send printing material to our Jewish friends who joined the resistance and were printing fliers telling the local residents not to support the Germans and to fight.

For a few months I worked for Foster, the infamous head of the German army in the area. After every actzia (a planned action where the Jews would be systematically killed), he would come to me and say, "Today we annihilated the Jewish residence of the town. I brought a few usable Jews, get them a job." (In 1958, I went to Germany to give a testimony against the Nazi criminal, he was then a successful industrialist from the Ruhan region, who excused his deeds by saying he was only following orders and that in the war with the underground he lost an eye. In spite of my testimony that made people cry he got a symbolic punishment because of his top-notch lawyers.)

They escape to the woods

Immediately after we heard that the Jews of Kurenitz were killed, on 9-9-1942, we, the young people of the camp decided to escape to the forests. The plans were complicated and difficult to achieve: first the danger of crossing the train tracks that were watched constantly by the German patrols and then to cross the Vilya River and the German troops. And more importantly each of us had a difficult time leaving our relatives with no hope. We also were worried that if we escaped and saved ourselves the rest of the Jews in the camp would be killed, but we still decided to go. Since I knew well the roads in the forests, I was the head of the first escape unit. One Saturday afternoon the Germans gave us an order to go to the train station to take down the cargo. Marching in one straight line, wearing the yellow stars, we walked in the middle of the street in the direction of the train. We came through a checkpoint and one of the Germans asked us where we were going, I said, "to take the down the cargo." He hit me with his rifle and said, "That is the way Jews go to work? Run." We ran like crazy to the other side of the train tracks and minutes later we were in the forest. From far away we heard shots. But the night came and we knew the Germans would not search at night. After an hour we met up with the rest of the groups, and we started going deeper into the woods, hoping to meet the other escapees from the town along with the underground fighters.

Just prior to dawn, when we exited the village of Viloci, we saw two Jews from Kurenitz who had just returned from a night mission to get food. They took us to the thickest part of the woods near Andrieky, where most of our shtetl's Jews who had managed to escape on the day of slaughter stayed. Also some of the underground fighters under Didia Vassia hid there. It was a morning in late autumn of the year 1942. The frost had already frozen the top layer of the earth, and it sent chilling shivers through our spines.

In the woods there was total quiet. We saw a very depressing site. Sitting around little camp fires dressed in rags, sat families of escapees from the slaughter of Kurenitz. Their faces were black from thick smoke. Only their eyes were shining and it was hard to recognize them. I found out that a few days before my parents had fled to the east with a few other families.

We came full of excitement, we succeeded, and we escaped from the German camp to freedom. Now we realized we must confront the difficulties of every moment's survival. The winter, the snow, and the cold were coming. The underground fighters were going to go east for the winter, and they would not take us. Where could we go? Where could we live? All around us we saw families with little children, old men and women, single survivors of entire families, people who saw the woods for the first time in their lives with no knowledge of the area. They go to find wood for the fire and can not find their way back.

The branches of the pine trees were our roofs, the fire pits our homes, and the ragged clothes our blankets. There were a few families that were luckier. They escaped Kurenitz with their entire families and with some supplies. They knew the area and knew farmers that lived near by that would help them. So, even here people were not equal.

A relative of mine, Nechama, and a few of her cousins, invited Riva and me to their fire pit. They shared baked potatoes with us. I was extremely tired but could not go to sleep. I wanted to study the situation so we would have the best chance of survival. I tried to join the underground but failed because I didn't have a weapon. They wanted to take Riva, but she wouldn't go without me. Riva had a watch that they wanted, so we reached an agreement that they would take us to the East in exchange for the watch, but this plan fell through because my feet were in too bad of a condition to go.

Winter was coming so we decided to prepare. There were two ways to go about it, first to prepare food for the winter months, and , to stay in a hole in the ground, losing all contact with the outside world until springtime. Although this was the best chance to stay alive, we chose the alternative, to build a concealed hiding place (zimlanka) with a few other families, get food and information at night. Particularly during snow storms, so no one could see our foot steps. The main reason we chose this route was because we were hoping we could join the underground.

We were 7 families, including 9 children, with the help of Roman, who was our underground contact. We built a Zimlanka (deep in the ground hide out) in the woods between Jazerio and Liaznitzi. I have to tell you about Sina, a Jew, member of the judnerat of Kurenitz, who joined our group, who even in the woods had a horse, a sled, and a rifle. He was afraid to leave the hiding place so he used us for what he néeded. Yosef, son of Yunkele Kiva and I would go to the Kurenitz area during every snow storm, and right under the German's noses. We would enter a farm holding Sinas' rifle, and scare the farmers so we could take whatever we néeded. We never actually used the rifle though. We lived like this for two months. We had food, water from the snow, and potatoes that we had stolen from the farms. To combat the ticks we used fire. Moshe, the son of Yunkel Kiva from Kurenitz, was very handy and made us Lutinutz, little pieces of wood used as lamps and lapses, which are boots made of parts of the woods with a rubber sole. He also built two fireplaces made from a special material he found in the woods. Each family had one cooking tool and we took turns cooking. We had more than enough wood.

After two months this idyllic stage ended. One morning our contact, Roman, with his son, came and told us that the Germans knew of our hiding places and that we must leave immediately. We had no choice, we took our belongings and put it on our two sleds, one of which I had bought from a farmer, and went to the more hidden away woods and fixed us a place to sleep. With the first morning lights we were awakened by shots. The Germans surrounded us. This was the first blockade. From the shots we understood that they were closing in on us. We had no time to think. We had to try to go through the ring of the Germans or go across an area that was clear of brush that was approximately 500 acres in size. We guessed that the Germans had come from Andreiky and surrounded the woods from three sides. The fourth side that was the part clear of trees was also clear of Germans. The Germans did not believe that anyone would try to go there. Despite the clear danger I decided to cross that area, thinking that since the Germans were at least 600 meters away they would have a hard time catching us. Riva and I were the first to cross the clearing crawling. The snow was melting and in some areas its height was one meter. Above our heads the bullets whistled. But we had no choice, we had to continue.

We were already in the middle of the clearing and could see a wooden area with no Germans, and then a bullet hit me in my left knée. My boot was filled with blood. I couldn't move and I begged Riva to go on without me. I lifted myself up praying that the Germans would kill me and not catch me alive. But Riva caught me and pulled me to the direction of the woods. Exhausted, we reached the woods. There we met some people that succeeded to cross the prairie. I tore my clothes to stop the blood. We had no medicine or first aid kit. The sun went west and the Germans stopped shooting. All of a sudden I saw in the path made by me being dragged across the snow, a very tiny image slowly walking towards us. This was four year old Lazerke, son of Chayim Alperovich. From far away he saw us and followed behind. We waited for him to reach us. His father, mother and little sister were killed and he was the only one left from his entire family. We didn't have enough time to recover and we heard a horse with a sled coming. Everyone ran away but Riva and I stayed because I couldn't move. The horse came right next to us. Riva caught the horse that the Germans must have lost. Inside the sled we found furs that must have belonged to a farmer. We called our friend Itzka Londers, and he took us back to our hiding place.

The Germans destroyed all the underground hiding places except for ours. After a while the partisans started bringing the wounded. Among them was the head of Spats Grofa, Major Orlov. We found out that everyone who tried to cross the German line was killed. Many Jews who were saved from the slaughter of Kurenitz found their death in the first blockade. I knew where the troop of Commissar Shebetznko stayed. They put me in the sled, and Riva, Itzka Londers and I went to get help. Major Orlov gave me his gun. We had to cross some villages. We couldn't go around them because the snow was very high. Before we entered a village Riva and Itzka would knock on a window of a more secluded home to find out if there were Germans in the village and then we would continue. At dawn we reached the front line of the partisans. They would not let us go ahead but immediately let Shebetznko know of our arrival.

Half an hour later, five sleds with partisans approached us. They gave me primitive first aid. They only had cotton but that helped a little. We went back to our places, but we found the Major dead. His partisans joined Shebetznko and together they all left this part of the woods. They didn't feel any obligation to help the wounded Jews. They didn't seem to have any sympathy for the Jews they left behind (Later we found out that Vanka, the head of this group was a Jew hating German spy, and when the partisans found out about his true identity they executed him.)

After the blockade our spirits were very low. We started looking for other survivors. We only found dead people and we buried them where they were killed. At night there was a very heavy snowstorm, so most of the dead were not found. They didn't even get a burial. The Jews that were left form the Kurenitz slaughter and were able to escape to the woods were greatly reduced in number after the first blockade. Most of them left to the woods like Yazni, Jazerio and Lods, in horrible condition. Most that were left behind were single women who couldn't move by themselves. The people who shared our hiding place collected all their belongings; they put me on the sled and returned to our old hiding place in Jazerio.

On both sides of the road the snow was higher than a meter. There was a fierce snowstorm. Two people pulled the horse and the rest pulled the sled. I lay on the sled, frozen and in horrible pain. Finally we arrived at our hiding place and to our dismay we found that it was totally destroyed. We were in despair but we had no choice, the struggle for life must continue. We were tired and hungry; we built a new shelter. It took us two days. Six families lived there, all together eighteen people.

A few weeks later, without medical help or medicine, my leg started to get better. Later, with Riva's help, I started to stand on my leg. We had no information about physiotherapy, but I knew that if I wanted to be able to walk, I must force myself to use my leg. So in spite of the pain I started walking.

The Failure of the Escape from the Vileyka Camp

One day, I met a Jewish partisan from Kostov. His name was Blat, and he introduced me to the Shebetznko, the head of a partisan brigade. Shebetznko, it turned out, was politically involved with Kurenitz prior to the war, and he wanted to know what happened to the Jews. When I told him about the labor camp, where some of the surviving Jews of Kurenitz were prisoners, and how they wished to escape and fight against the Germans, he decided to do something to get them out of there.

The men, women and children in the camp had to get weapons to survive in the woods. I dressed myself like a Christian and secretly went to the camp and met with the Jewish head of the camp Shotz. I gave him details about the plans of the escape and talked to him about the ways we could get weapons, especially ammunition from the camp to the woods. We made plans to meet again in two weeks. The Jewish camp inmates argued a lot about the issue of escape. Most of the ones that had a good profession refused to escape, they truly believed they would be spared. The main voice against the escape was that of the carpenter, Motka Avis. But the majority of the prisoners and their representative, Hertzel Alperovitz, tilted the balance towards escape. In the next meeting Shotz told me that they elected a committee to prepare for the escape. The committee members were Shotz, Motik Alperovitz, Hertzel Alperovitz, Yonah Riar from Ilya, Kopel Spektor, Yosef Zuckerman, and Velvel

Robonsky. They prepared for life in the woods. They studied the details of how to get weapons and ammunition out, and how to connect with us.

The instruction and connection between the camp and us were done by an intermediary, a gentile from the village Noykee. He had a long brown beard and a huge cross around his neck. When he would go to Vilyeka, he would wear a thick fur coat and wear lapses. Secretly, he would give them our letters and instructions, and on the way back in the yard of the hospital next to the camp he would get wooden blocks that Hertzel made holes in to transfer bullets the Jews stole to the woods. Everyone in the camp was preparing for life in the woods. They got shoes, clothes and other necessities. Most of the men succeeded in getting weapons in spite of the difficulties and danger to acquire weapons and ammunition. The intermediary continued coming to the camp and taking the ammunition to the woods. Even the leader of the partisans was amazed with the heroism of the Jews who risked the lives of their families to steal the weapons and ammunition so needed by the partisans.

In the beginning of March 1943 we decided on March 21 as the day of escape. We were so close to making this dream reality. Everything was ready to the last detail. On the other side of the railroads we were supposed to wait with sleds to carry the women and children. And a few partisan women were supposed to help them cross the town. We were sure this was going to succeed, but fate took us somewhere else. On Wednesday March 18, the intermediary came to take ammunition from the camp. We have already put the wooden pieces on the sled when a local police man stepped on to the sled and took the reins from the guy and he and the guy went away. One of the Jewish women that saw it screamed in panic and everyone started running away in fear that their plot had been exposed. Men and women left their places of work, swiftly rushed to their homes took the children and run. Most of them didn't know where to run. The Germans had no idea what had happened and started chasing them and shooting them. Only a few dozens survived. The rest were shot by the Germans or killed on the way to the woods. How painful it was the next day when we found out that the policeman took the horse only to bring his wife from the hospital, later returning the horse and ammunition. For three days, Riva, Blat and I tried to find survivors. I had relatives among the escapees. But the search results were tragic. We only found bodies.

At the same time we were joined by Yaakov Shafran, Baruch Kotavitzky, his brother Libu, Avrasha, Moshe, Mordechai Posner and his daughter Hanna. We lived in a commune. At night the men would go to collect food in the nearby villages. We had plenty of mushrooms and potatoes. Riva and Hanna cooked very tasty food and we would all share it from the same pail, with everyone getting equal portions. For dessert we would eat some kind of berries that were plentiful, and in the evenings we would sing Russian war songs. Hanna would be the song leader. Our connection with the partisans became much stronger and we would take missions under their command. We would go to transfer explosives from the woods to their bases. Each one would take 20kg of explosive and put it on their back, and like this we would walk 40 km.

The Attack on the Workshop in Kurenitz

To be accepted to the troop called Masteltle (Revenge), we had to carry on some military missions to show our capabilities. One of the missions we received was to go to Kurenitz and burn the German storage area that was holding their provisions and their carpentry workshop. This mission was for 8 men with no weapons, with one partisan that had a gun. We were skeptical about it working. With this one killer weapon we were supposed to go into the mouth of the lion that was carefully patrolled by the Germans. From the West there was the bunker of the Germans, from the East there was another bunker. From 2000 m next to the school where the workshop was, there was another German bunker.

At night, after walking 30 km, we reached the area. We split into two groups. One went to the storage and the second one, including Salim and I, went to the workshop. We looked through the window. We couldn't see anything. Salim forcibly opened it and jumped inside. The guard screamed, so Salim grabbed him by his neck, threw him to the ground and stuffed a gag in his mouth. We poured gasoline all over and lit the shop. Once we saw the building was on fire we retreated. When we left we saw that the second building was also on fire. Salim decided to also knock down some phone poles. The next day everyone in the area was talking about the event. The rumor was that a big group of partisans burned Kurenitz and killed many Germans.

In the spring of 1943 groups of Jewish people from Ghetto Vilna escaped to the woods. The Russian headquarter decided to organize an all Jewish Unit. The unit was constantly evolving. The first leader was Botianitz, and then he was replaced by Bomka Bialsky. The last one was Vlodka Salovitz. Vlodka was not Jewish, He was an anti-Semite who took all the jewelry from the members saying that it would be sold and the money would be used to fight the Nazis. We saw his true face in the second blockade he didn't help the large group of Jews that just escaped from the Vilna Ghetto. The troop was involved in many dangerous missions, but it did not last long. The Soviets did not encourage separatism by religion.

Three days before the second blockade, Vlodka asked two partisans and me to collect information in the villages of Natzki, Shomki and Lintopi. During the third day of mission, we ran into a group of Jews that escaped from the Vilna ghetto. We arranged a dinner for them and we found them a sleeping area in one of the farmers' fields. The next day we brought them to the base. It was clear to everyone that the Germans were going to search the woods soon. We reported this to Vlodka and I said we must do something about these Jews as they were not familiar with the forests. He said everyone that had a weapon could join the unit. The rest had to go to a separate area. My girlfriend Riva had a new weapon with a large amount of bullets. Vlodka approached her and said, "This weapon can be used by someone more skilled than you." "At the end of the coming blockade, you will get it back". Riva held her finger to the trigger and said," you will have to kill me to get this weapon" so Vlodka let go.

Our group consisted mainly of Jews that came from the Vilna ghetto. We all left in small units to look for hideouts, My unit went towards the marsh areas between Donilovitz and Mydel. Before we left the base Vlodka gave us huge machine guns that were half full with ammunition. He showed me how to use it and said good luck. Our mission was very difficult. The road was complicated, winding through wet lands and hills. Some of the wet lands could only be passed by walking on rotten pieces of wood. Often we would fall into the water. Mira Glasser, one of the partisans was very sick and could hardly stand on her feet anyway. The area we had to reach was an island. After a few days we realized that the Germans had left the area. We went to a village nearby to look for food. We found out that the Germans had punished the farmers and burned all the villages. But we were able to find a lot of potatoes.

We started walking back to the base and we rested in the village Niknipi. All the farmers ran away when the Germans came and still had not returned. In one of the barns I found a pig, so we slaughtered him and had him for dinner. This was a real treat for us and made everyone happy. The next day we all got very sick. We returned to the base from all corners of the woods and wet lands, All units returned from their different hiding places during the second blockade. Riva and I were accepted to a new troop, Soborov. The head officer there was Jewish, Shura Katzenbogen.

My main job during this period was spying. Once in a while we would be sent with explosives to destroy the train tracks. One mission was in an area that went through the woods. To prevent terrorism, The Germans would cutoff all the woods near the tracks. They would keep German patrols close-by the train tracks. We watched the patrols for two days until we realized that there was a very short window of opportunity to put the explosives in when the soldiers were far enough away. Late at night, Kopol, from the shtetle of Shofan, crawled to the tracks and made a hole in the ground. He hid some explosives, then connected the wires to light the explosives. He erased his foot prints and quickly crawled back as we watched with our weapons drown from a far. It was important that the Germans not know of the explosives. We all hid few hundred meters from the tracks, waiting until morning when the train was expected to arrive. The Germans were standing right next to the explosives. One of them lit a cigarette. We were hoping nothing would happen then because we aimed for more than just a few Germans. Luckily, the Germans did not discover the explosives. When the train came, Kopol lit the wick. There was a huge explosion and the train derailed. We quickly escaped. The Germans started shooting everywhere. All the supplies being transported by the Germans were destroyed and they couldn't use the tracks for many days.

Kopol was later killed while trying to retrieve ammunition. He was buried in the village of Salutiki and after the war I wrote on the stone, " Buried here is a heroic partisan, Kopol." I never knew his last name.

In the middle of 1942 Markov decided to record the history of the partisans brigade. They built a large hiding place, Zimlanka, for the writers and I lived with them. My job was to collect all the necessary supplies for the printing press. At one point we found out that a unit of Germans from Vileyka would have parties on a regular basis at one of the houses in the area. We decided to capture them and bring them with their weapons to the partisan brigade. We were four partisans with some sleds. We stationed ourselves close to that house. An hour later six German soldiers with weapons came to the house. We waited a while. When we heard the sound of singing we knew they were getting drunk and that was the time for action. Avner Feygelson,(Riva's cousin) and I broke the door down and entered with our guns drawn. I announced in German that the house was surrounded by partisans and ordered them to put their hands up and face the wall. They immediately obeyed and we took their weapons that were standing against the wall. We took the soldiers on our sleds and two hours later we gave them to the head of the partisan brigade.

During the final days of 1943, when the Red Army started getting closer to our area, a small airplane, bearing precious supplies, landed in the makeshift airport the partisans build in the woods. Upon returning, they took some of the Jewish partisans (including the wounded Mira Glazer) with them. On June 1944 the Red Army reached the Vileyka area. At that time Riva and I were involved with an underground newspaper. The whole staff of the paper left the woods to the village Polsa near Vileyka. We watched the Nazis running for their lives. In all the panic they forgot to destroy the bridge on the river Vilya. The colors of battle still hung in the sky, but huge undisturbed Russian army was approaching. Red Army tanks supplied by the Americans, crossed the river Villya and continued toward Molodechno, the main cross roads between Minsk and Vilna. We immediately drove to Vileyka. We found the city destroyed by fire. The Jewish school Tarbut and the synagogue were still burning when we got there. We quickly ran to the building of the Es De. We knew that until the last days, a few dozen professional Jews that worked for the Germans were alive. We found no Jews, but I did find a letter written in Yiddish which was written in poem style. It was written by Motke Aves. In the letter he wrote, "we hear the sound of the tanks, to us they are the sounds of the bells announcing the coming of the Jewish messiah, but we know that they are not ringing for us, we would not be saved. I ask for forgiveness that I didn't consider escaping from the ghetto and shout with bitter cries, revenge the blood of your brothers." Later I gave the letter to the local newspaper and it was printed in Russian translation.

We found out that the Jews, together with other prisoners from the Vileyka prison, were taken on trucks in the direction of Tzintzivi. We quickly drove there. Just a few kilometers from Vileyka, in a big field next to the road, we saw smoke and smelt the stench of burning meat. We knew that smell well from the time we were in the Vileyka camp. The smell was familiar to us since after every Actzya (action where the Jews were gathered and massacred), bodies were burned. As we approached the area we were greeted with a horrifying scene. A large group of semi burned bodies had been thrown in a giant pile. A constant stream of Red Army soldiers passed us on the way to Smorgon and Vilna. One of the Soviet officers put a huge sign saying, "Stop, look at the horrible deeds of the fascist Nazis. Revenge these victim's blood." The next day we buried the murdered as brothers, in one huge grave. Amongst them were a number of Jews from Kurenitz who had believed even until their last days that they would stay alive. One of them was Motke Aves.

The next day we returned to Kurenitz. Most of the homes were burned. All the survivors started leaving the forests and returning to Kurenitz. The gentiles looked in amazement that there were still a few Jews left. It seems like most of them preferred that there would be no one. The local authorities were not sympathetic either.

For awhile I got a job as the manager of a storage building that was full of provisions and supplies that came from the US. I had two helpers, Riva and Rivka Alprorvitz. We slept on top of the tables. Riva was also working for the partisans newspaper that was no longer underground. A short time later I found out that many of the supplies had gone missing . I was not able to stop the politicians from taking the supplies for themselves. I knew that the punishment would be a few years in jail.

I had no choice but to run away and join the Red Army. So started a new stage in my fighting the Germans that lasted from June 1944 to February 1949. First, I took part in horrible battles against Germany in East Prussia in the area of Keningsburg. Later I had to fight the national partisans of Latvia, Lithuania and Estonia. Partisans from these areas were carrying on a cruel battle with the Red Army with the support of Sweden and Norway. My important job allowed me to get permission to bring Riva over. Together we went from place to place as we helped to fight the war against the Lithuanian partisans. Our first daughter was born during this time.

In February of 1949 I was released from the army. We missed our turn to leave the USSR. I went to the university and after graduation I got a good job. In general I was treated very favorably. However, I quit my job, let go of my communist party membership, sold my house. I left for Poland on the way to Israel as soon as I got a hold of the néeded papers.

The Escape from Ghetto

by Yeoash Alperovitch, Israel. (April, 1982)

Last week we watched on TV a movie "The Wall", which showed the resistance of the Jews in the Warsaw Ghetto. This movie reminded me of how my family and I escaped from our Ghetto in 1943.

The Germans occupied our area in June 1941. After several months they organized a Ghetto in the city of Vilejka, about 5 miles from the town (Kureniec) where I was born.

The Jews of Vilejka were killed a short time before, but we were sure that they were evacuated to a work camp in another area, exactly like the Jews from Warsaw, according to the movie.

In the Ghetto there were about 300 people, most of them women with children. After a short time the Germans divided the Ghetto in two: one – for specialists and the other – for people without defined specialties. Our family (father, mother, my young brother and I) was enrolled in the list of the specialists Ghetto, because my father and I became "Carpenters"

We were sent to another place, about a mile from the common Ghetto. It was a big hut near the workshops where we worked. We were about 100 people including the specialists and their families. I was at the time 15 years old.

Yeoash with parents
Liba [daughter of Yiza Michael Alperovitz]
and Mordechai Alperovitz [originaly Shapiro]

About one month later the non-specialists Ghetto was liquidated and burnt down. We could see it through the windows of the workshops. Now, all we could do is wait for our turn and it was only a matter of time till our turn would come.

During the first two weeks, six young boys escaped from our Ghetto and they looked for a connection with the partisans, who only recently began to be active in our area. They needed guns and ammunition badly.

Most of us intended to escape from the Ghetto in a short time, but we had two big problems.

First of all: the Ghetto was guarded only at night, so we had to go out from the Ghetto in daytime. But in the daytime all the men were in the workshops, which were guarded. At noon we had an intermission for about a half-hour.

There were a lot of German camps around the ghetto, including the Gestapo, so we decided we must escape at noon, and during that half hour cross over, with the families and children, about three miles of snow without being seen by Germans. Three miles from the Ghetto was a big forest, and we hoped to hide there until night. This was the first problem.

The second problem was even worse one. Some families had many children and they objected to the idea of going out of the Ghetto. Those people had a good reason for the objection. It was winter, snow and very cold. To go into the woods with little children in winter meant hundred percent death for the children. They said that if they would waited, may be the Russians will return to this area and the Germans would not have enough time to kill them.

Furthermore the Germans have threatened to kill all of us if somebody would escape, so they objected to anybody escaping and even observed at night over suspected people. This was a real complicated problem, which did not have a clear solution.

In the meantime we found a way to get guns and ammunition, we arranged a connection with the young boys who escaped and sent to them guns and ammunition. We also got guns for ourselves.

The method to send ammunition was organized this way: We made two thick wooden boards, which had holes along them. We filled the hole of one board with ammunition and closed it very carefully. The boards had the same measurement as regular boards of a wagon.

A farmer who lived near the woods would come once a week to Vilejka and leave the horses with the wagon near the hospital, the wall that was adjacent to the Ghetto.

One of us would come to the wall and take out the board from the wagon and put in our board with the ammunition, which was exactly the same. The farmer would return to his horse and wagon and ride home. The boys from the woods would come at night to this farmer and take out the ammunition.

It was March 1943. The Germans still needed us, so we were still alive. But rumors arrived from all over the area about liquidations of Jewish communities of our area. We knew that the time we had at our disposition was not long any more.

We made preparations and plans how to escape, we even got guns. But the problem with the big families remained. Those families didn't like the whole idea of escaping and they made every effort to prevent it. The solution of this problem must come, may be, from heaven, and it actually did.

It was the beginning of the spring. At daytime the sun would shine, but the nights were still very cold. The snow began to melt, but at night the surface would be covered with ice.

We had been waiting for the farmer, who would take the "board" once a week. We looked through the window and saw the farmer coming on time. Then we saw one of our people taking the farmers board and putting ours into the wagon. Ten minutes passed and we saw the farmer come, he took his horse and wagon and went away. Everything was perfect as usual.

But five minutes passed, and somebody in the workshop shouted, "We are lost! The farmer with the "board" was caught by the Germans".

Everybody ran to the window and saw the farmer with his horse going along the street and a policeman was going behind him. The direction was to the Gestapo.

It was about 20 minutes before the lunchtime. We consulted quickly what to do and decided to run out of the Ghetto at once.

We went out of the workshops and told the families what has happened. We told them to prepare themselves and the children to leave the Ghetto in five minutes.

We took down the yellow stars, which we wore constantly, we took the little bags, which were prepared and went out of the Ghetto. According to our plan (which was prepared for an occasion of escaping) every two-three persons went in a different direction in silence.

I went with my father and held his hand. My young brother went with our mother and held her hand. We agreed to meet each other at a certain point in the woods and then continue together.

On our way we met some Germans, but they didn't recognize us as Jews and didn't pay attention. First we went along the street and the road. Later we turned across the field.

We knew exactly that in twenty minutes (when the intermission in the workshops is over) the Germans would be behind us and hurried on.

We were about a half-mile from the forest when we heard the noise of the German cars and motorcycles behind us. They jumped down from their vehicles and ran in our direction shouting and shooting. The distant between the Germans and us got shorter and shorter.

When the Germans were about 150 feet from us, some of our people took out their guns and began to shoot at the Germans.

The Germans stopped for several minutes, apparently to organize their pursuit according to the new circumstances. This short stopping allowed us to reach the woods.

The Germans continued the pursuit us in the forest, shooting from the machine guns and using dogs. Many of us were killed or caught by the Germans.

Needless to say that each one of us has a different story of this day. To finish the story briefly I will tell you the results of this action for our family.

My father and I arrived at the Partisan's Zone after four days. My mother was killed in this action. It is not clear why the German, who killed my mother, let my brother go (he was then 9 years old). Somehow or other my brother remained alone in the woods.

After rambling for four days in the cold woods and without food he was only about one mile from the city of Vilejka. A good farmer found him and gave him to a Jewish partisan from our town. He brought him to us. His whole body was swollen and he was unconscious. Nobody even believed that he would live. After several weeks he recovered, but only physically.

For years he shouted at night and held our father's hand even when he slept. He shouted "Don't leave me alone!" (My brother died in Israel in a work accident, when he was 24 years old in 1958, before I came to Israel. I didn't have an opportunity to see him after 1944).

To conclude I would say that the escaping, generally, was the least of the evils we could choose. Despite all that had happened, deaths of many people and suffering of many others, there were positive results of our escaping.

First of all about 60 people out of 100 succeeded to escape in this action and about 50 of them survived at the end of the war. It was a lot, relative to other Jewish communities of our area.

Secondly, my cousin and I had the opportunity to be witnesses in a court at a trial of the chief of the gestapo of Vilejka and tell to hundred of young Germans who were present in the hall, what had happened there.

Being in the Ghetto we didn't believe that even one of us would have the chance to do it.

Finally, the Germans didn't kill a part of the specialists of the Ghetto after our escaping. They continued working up to the time the Russians liberated the region. But just before the Germans left, they killed all of them. After the liberation we found a letter from one of the victims, which said: "We can already hear the cannonades of the Russian cannons, but we are sure that we will not be alive when the Russian army comes." The same fate was waiting for us.

Yeoash as partisan

One more question of this story requires an answer: What has happened with the farmer and the board with the ammunition?

The answer of this question is very simple. – Nothing.

Yes, nothing. A policeman asked the farmer to take his wife to the hospital. So he brought her to the hospital and then he went home safely with the ammunition.

After our arrival to the woods, we adapted ourselves to the conditions of the new life. It is hard to describe how we could sustain ourselves in such conditions in general, but I want to note one interesting phenomenon, which has a connection with our topic.

A short time after our arrival in the woods my orientation in the forest was incredible. The same was with some of my other friends. Now I often hardly find the way driving in Tel-Aviv, but then, just in the woods, I was able to find the way from one point to the other without apprehension. Can you imagine that we went for ten miles and more looking for food in a certain village, and return "home" in the middle of the night through the forest and came exactly to our base. Maybe we recognized the trees, the plants, the ground, but in addition to this, we developed a special sense, something similar to a sense of an animal, who was born in the woods and lives there. The first Partisans came to our area from the eastern district in beginning of 1942. They began to organize bases to stay, and until the end of the year they already became a serious force. The Germans knew about it, but they didn't realize how serious the situation was. They thought that they were just a little group of criminals. So they decided to "finish" them before they became a serious force. But it was already too late.

The Partisans were already organized in real military units, equipped with serious weapons, and they were ready to fight the Germans. The main forces of the Germans were far to the east, so they collected people from the gestapo, the S.D. the gendarmerie and other small units, which took up position in this area. Together they were several hundred soldiers. The commander of this action was the chief of the gestapo of the city of Vilejka.

The villagers around were ordered by the Germans to come with their horses and sleighs (it was winter) and take the Germans to the Partisan Zone. The Partisans knew exactly every step of their action and were waiting for them and prepared for them an excellent reception. Shortly there was a short battle between the Partisans and the Germans. About 40 Germans were killed and wounded. The chief of the gestapo was wounded in the head, was taken to a hospital in Berlin and returned after several months with only one eye. (That was why I recognized him easily after the war at the court in Bochum).

At this time I was still in the Ghetto and I had the pleasure of participating in repairing the coffins for the dead Germans. After this action the Germans didn't dare to come into the woods for a long time.

Meanwhile the Partisans organized a whole "Partisan Zone". First, they attacked the Germans who stayed in some villages of the area, which was close to the "Partisan Zone", they killed many of them and forced the others to escape. The Germans fortified themselves in the main city of the district and a few other points and abandoned all their camps in the "Partisan Zone". The Partisans built a small airport, so Russian small plans landed there and brought weapons and ammunition. They had even their own hospital, a mill and a bakery in the woods. The farmers who lived in the Partisan Zone "paid" taxes to the Partisans. (It was grain or other agricultural products). It was a "country within a country". And what was worse for the Germans, the Partisans organized a net of units, which attacked the Germans almost every day. They blew up trains and other military vehicles, killed soldiers and officers. When we arrived to the woods the Partisans were in a process of organizing and all young people made every effort to be accepted in a partisan unit. For me it was a very hard problem. First of all I was too young, and second I was a Jew. It was funny, but even the Partisans (most of the MzAzzz1units) refused to accept Jews. In the summer of 1943 a Jewish unit of Partisans was organized. This unit didn't exist long, but after it was dissolved, other regular partisan units received most of us. I personally was accepted by a unit called "Tshpajevsky Otriad" and stayed there till the end of the occupation of this area.

Yeoash in 1945

More than a year passed from the time when the Germans came prior into the woods and we knew that sooner or later they would come again. This time they would bring a big force. They had done it already in the eastern areas. But at this time the German army was busy near Stalingrad, where they just began to feel the true taste of real war.

Their opportunity came later when the German army began to withdraw from the eastern areas and they were nearer to us. Now they had two important reasons to "finish" the Partisans.

First of all the army was already near the partisan Zone. And they had an opportunity to attack the Partisans with a real unit from a regular army. What was more important, the Germans understood very well where the wind blew from, and they could imagine what the Partisans would do to the German soldiers, when the army would withdraw from the positions across the Partisan Zone. Anyway in summer of 1943 the Germans organized a blockade around the whole Partisan Zone in our area.

On the sketch below you can see a part of the Partisan Zone. The Germans occupied only one point, the city of Myadel. The Partisans would later surround this city and not even one German would escape till the Russian army arrived in summer 1944. The circle "P" indicates the center of the partisan forces. About 15 partisan units were concentrated in one brigade called Markov's Brigade (later it was called Voroshilov's Brigade). At this time I was in the Jewish unit. Like others, our unit sent people to explore the area determining where the Germans were located. My friend and I were sent in the direction of Gatovichi road. We went along the road in the direction of the village of Gatovichi, which was near the lake Narotz. Near the point "M" where we were stopped by machine-gun fire. Every one of us jumped into the woods in a different direction. After a couple of hours everyone arrived separately to the camp "P". Meanwhile other emissaries, who were sent in other directions, returned and the picture of our situation became clear. The Germans surrounded us from three directions. The fourth direction was closed by an impassable swamp, which continued till Narotz Lake. Briefly we were cut off from all sides. We knew that a short time before, the Germans organized a blockade around partisan zones in the eastern area. The Partisans were not organized to lead a frontal fight against a regular army. In such a fight they didn't have any chance. So these units decided to break out of the blockade through the German positions. They concentrated all their forces and attacked the Germans in one point. They broke out of the blockade, but there were many victims among the Partisans and the civilians, who stayed in the partisan zone.

In the meantime German airplanes began to fly over the partisan camps and the artillery opened a fire over the woods. Since we had moved out from the camps the shooting didn't bother us; it was very easy to hide ourselves in the woods. But we knew that in a short time the Germans would come into the woods with their whole force.

Our Brigade chose a solution that was different from that, chosen by the partisan from east. We decided to divide our people into small groups of 5-10 each, to spread ourselves in the woods, especially into the impassable swamp. After this every group would act independently. Our commander decided also to send a part of us, especially those who had families into the woods, to our relatives to help them pass the blockade. At this time the Jewish partisan families were near the camps. Since I was competent in finding my way through the woods I became a guide of about eight people, who included my father and my young brother.

When I returned from Gatovichi road, the evacuation of the people from the camps was in full swing. I knew that my people went to the swamp, so I went to look for them. When I reached the swamp I saw a horse drowning slowly into the swamp. Apparently somebody tried to take things on its back, but it didn't get very far. I had already seen people dying, or getting killed, but I couldn't forget the eyes of the poor horse, which went down little by little into the swamp. When I left the area I still saw the head of the horse.

Anyway I found my people in a terrible situation. They hadn't much food, water or clothing. We moved deeper into the swamp in order to advance as far as possible before nightfall. I supposed we passed over about two miles. We went ahead five more miles the next day, found a relatively dry area and decided to stay there till the end of the blockade. All the time we heard the cannons from the direction of our camps and from time to time airplanes crossed over us, looking for victims. We were sure that the blockade continued. I don't remember how many days we stayed there, I supposed three-four, but our situation got worse. We didn't have any food or water. We drank from the swamp, it was disgusting and many of us were ill from it. In short we decided to try to get out of the blockade. Of course we could sit and wait for the end of the blockade in the swamp, we were sure that the Germans would not dare to come into the swamp. But we could not bear it without food and water and we didn't know how long the blockade would last. Our plan was very "simple", cross the swamp and during one night try to cross Gatovichi road. We knew the forest, which lay over Gatovichi road very well. We wanted to reach point "C". There was a house in the forest and we knew the man who lived there. He was a friend, and we were sure that there we would find food, water and clothes.

But we had two "little" problems: First to get over the swamps to the road, and second, we were not sure that it would be possible to cross the road. Anyway we began our "voyage". It is impossible to describe how we advanced. There were small trees, like shrubs, which had some roots, and we jumped carefully from one tree to the other. The soil was like a mattress with springs and it cradled our feet. It was a miracle that none of our group sank down into the swamp. From time to time somebody shouted for help, when he fell into the swamp up to his waist. To pull out a person from the swamp was a very complicated operation, and we did it several times a day. We also found a partial solution against our hunger. In this area there was a lot of cranberries and they became our main food during our "voyage". We advanced very slowly, maybe 1-2 miles a day (at night we rested).

My trouble started when the people became anxious about whether we were moving in the right direction. They were sure that they already passed 20 miles, much more than the distance to the road. "Who decided to take a child for a guide" – they said. They were sure that they had no chance of getting out of the swamp. The fact was that we advanced more and more slowly because we were exhausted and hungry.

Somebody even suggested "killing the child, who will bring the death of the whole group". But that wasn't a serious suggestion, because they knew very well that nobody, but I had any chance to lead the group out of the swamp.

After two or three days (I don't remember exactly) I told the people that we were about 2-3 miles from the road. I was sure more than ever that we were near it. The reason was that we passed forest-glades with piles of hay. I knew that in these places the villagers used to chop grass during summer, leaving it there till winter. When the soil froze they came with sleighs and took it home. I was sure that this must be near the road, because the villagers wouldn't go far away deep in the swamp. I saw many such piles going many times along Gatovichi road. Our people didn't believe me even then, and I was very sorry about it.

As the people were tired and exhausted, I suggested that the group remain on a relative "dry island" which we found, while I and another young boy would try to get to the road. When we will find the road we will return to the group and take them. The tired people liked this idea and agreed to wait. That afternoon we left the group and got to the road in 3-4 hours. We lay down near the road and could see German cars passing along the road. We returned in the middle of the night and told the people what we saw. Now the people began to believe that we did go in the right direction. We decided that during the next day we'd reach the road, and at night try to cross it. We got within 200 feet from the road, and lay there until night. We watched the Germans, collecting the villagers. They took them to work to Germany. Their only "crime" was that they lived near to the Partisan Zone. During this time we learned how often and when the German patrols passed along the road. It became clear that the Germans didn't keep big forces here. Certainly because they were sure that nobody could come out from this swamp. We waited till one of the patrols passed along the road and quickly went across it. Now we knew very well the way to achive our goal. We were out of the blockade! The blockade continued on for one more week.

Most of the Jews passed the blockade sitting in the swamp. They remained alive, but they suffered hunger for a very long time. We already had food and clothes. We prepared a tent and stayed there until the blockade was over.

Yeoash Alperovitz

In conclusion, several sentences about the results of the blockade. During the blockade the Germans burned down most of the villages which belonged to the Partisan Zone. They took many of the people to Germany to work there. This made some difficulties for the missions of the Partisans. But there were also many villagers who escaped to the surrounding forest and returned after the blockade to their villages. The Germans didn't kill many Partisans, only a few, and after the blockade all units were complete again as before the blockade.

"For Capturing Berlin"

All the fears of the Germans, regarding to the Partisans, came true. Before the Germans withdrew from the occupied territories in Belarus, the Partisans blew up the railways and bridges for hundreds of miles. Escaping from the Russian Army, many of the Germans were killed, or were taken prisoner by the Partisans. During about a month, our unit, as did many others, took part in "purification" of the area from Germans. When they were gone I joined the Red Army, and took part in chasing the Germans out from the very last part of Russia that they still held. Then we chased them out of Poland and finally pursued them to Berlin. But this is already another story.

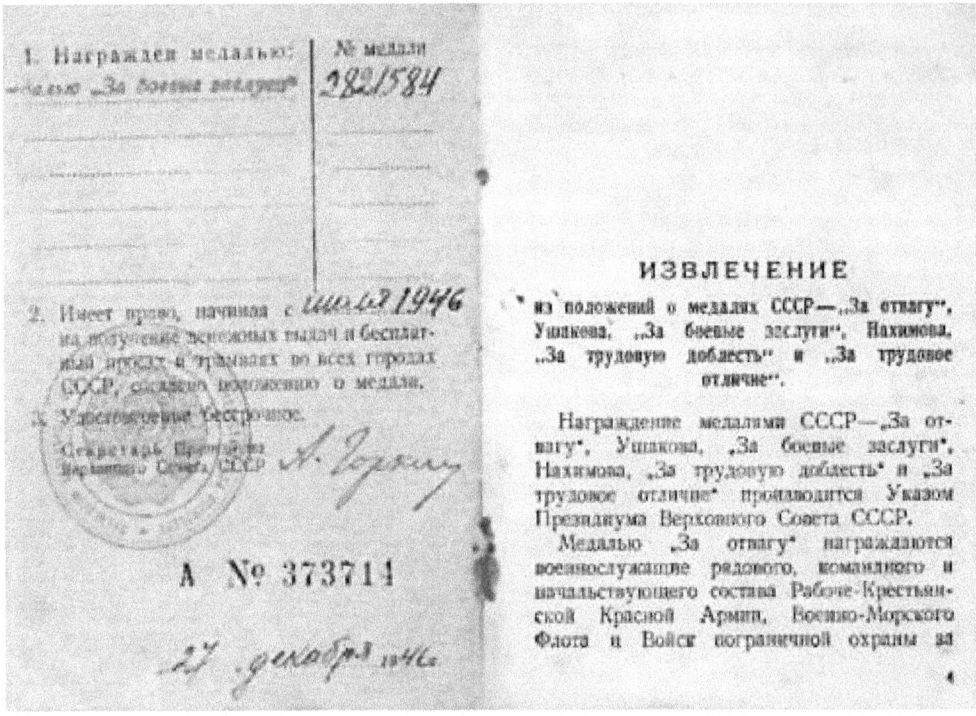

A medal "For Achievements in Battle"

Zira née Schulman
(1929-2000)
wife of Prof. Yehoash Alperovitch

Perez Schulman (1900-1987) – The blacksmith from Vileyka
Chaya Schulman (1904 -1993) – his wife
[in laws of Prof. Yehoash Alperovitch the author]

A document for serving in partisan unit Tshapajeu (Brigade Voroshilov)

Memories of Solomon, son of Orchik Alperovich
Jewish Life in Kurenets After the Holocaust

Written in English by Shlomo Alperovich

Edited by Sandra Krisch

I was born in "shtetel" Kurenets (Belarus) in 1948, and I wish to share my own memories and stories that I heard and remember from Jewish natives about Jewish life in Kurenets and its surroundings.

After the liberation of Belarus (including Kurenets) in 1944, Jewish people started returning to the area. Kurenets was almost completely destroyed and burned by the retreating German Army. Only a few houses were left standing. Most of the surviving Jews immigrated to Palestine and the United States in the next few years.

*Shlomo Alperovich near the memorial for the
1050 Jewish people from Myadel street, Kurenetz (2001)*

My father, Alperovich Aaron Abramovich (Orchik son of Abram, grandson of Chaim Isar; born in 1896, died in 1974) returned home to Kurenets from Saransk (Mordovia), where he had been sent in 1939 (when the Soviets came to the area). He was sent there by decision of Stalin's court for 5 years of hard labor. When he returned he found neither home nor family. His wife Mirel and 3 of his children (Chaim Isar, another son, and a daughter) had been murdered.

*Kurenets (1945)
Miron Meckler and Aaron Alperovich*

From local residents and Jews who returned from the forest, he found out that his older son Yakov (Yankel) joined the partisans during the war. He was informed that he was recruited to Belpolk – a Red Army unit that was supposed to search and clean the Belarus forests of Nazi soldiers and local collaborators (*politzais*) who were now replacing the Jews and hiding there. Father finally found Yakov near Minsk. He was very skinny and very tired. He learned from him that Yankel's sister and brother, his daughter Lisa, and his son Shmuil survived, and that during the war they also joined the partisans' ranks.

In the Red Army
Above: Benjamin-Yosef Sosensky, Yakov Alperovich (from Kurenets).
Sitting: Levi Koton and Dov, son of Chykel (lives in Minsk)

Yankel Orchik's story is well known and told in many books. On Simchat Torah of 1941 his family was taken to be killed. His mother was able to escape with the younger children while they walked to the forest. Yankel and his brother Chaim Isar were taken with the other Jewish men. The men were put in groups of ten and killed, while many of the local population were watching. Just before it was Yankel's turn to be killed, he said that Yente (nee Dinerstein) Rodanski was let go by the Germans and was told to never marry a communist again (they had just killed her husband, Velvel Rodanski). Yankel realized that all are not equal, and he demanded to speak before he was killed. The German officer let him talk. Yankel said in broken German "Before I am to be killed I would like to know if my sin is being a Jew or being a communist." The officer answered, "Clearly, being a communist." Yankel said, while turning to the local people, "They could all tell you that my father Orchik was sent to Siberia for being an enemy of the Soviet people; why would I then become a communist?" The officer liked what he [Yankel] said, and maybe it was the broken German that made him laugh–he told him to stand to the side. Yankel said that his sick brother should be let go first, and they let Chaim Isar go.

Yankel did not trust the Germans, and together with the sons of Pinia Alperovitz he escaped to the woods. They [the others] were killed. Yankel survived and later joined the partisans and saved many many Jews from Kurenets and Myadel and also his brother Shmuil.

In 1944 my mother, Botwinnik Evgeniya Samuilovna (Zelda daughter of Shmuil Botwinnik, born in 1920 in Rakov) came to Kurenets. After her release from the partisans she looked for her relatives. She found out that all of her family was killed in Rakov. She moved to Kurenets, following some of her Jewish friends from the partisans. And that is how two lonely people met each other and established a family. At first they lived in the house of Aaron's brother Hirsh, who was killed with his entire family (wife and two children). Here, in August of 1946, their first son, Abram, was born. At that time Arye Leibe (Lior's grandfather), the brother of Aaron [Orchik Alperovich] returned from evacuation to Russia; their two sisters, Hava and Feiga, also returned after being partisans during the war. They all married and started their own families. My father moved to a new house of his own, which he built with his own hands; he left the old house to his brother Leibe and sister Hava.

In July of 1948, in the new house, a new citizen of Kurenets was born – that was me. About my birth I will tell you the following story: My mother felt that she was about to give birth, so my father took her to the Vileyka's hospital, which was 8 km away, riding on a horse. However it was too early, and after one day in the hospital she asked to be taken home because she had a lot of work to do there. And so my father brought her back. A few days later he had to set the horse again to take mother to the hospital. This time she was left there for several days, while my father had to return home to take care of the housekeeping chores. A few days passed and then a fellow Kurenets resident by the name of Nikolay met my father and told him, "Vorchik, I've visited my wife in the hospital and saw your Zelda. You have a boy." Father took a horse and went to meet us. Mother asked to go home right away, so father took off his jacket, put me inside, and brought me home. That is how my life in Kurenets began.

Alperovich family – Kurenets, 1959

At that time almost every Jewish family in Kurenets had a newborn. About 15 Jewish families remained in Kurenets after the war. On Saturdays and at Jewish holidays Jewish people gathered at the old Leizer Shulman house. There they had their prayers, and after the religious ceremony they were drinking *L'chaim*. We kids played outside the house and never forgot that Leizer had an apple orchard. We, all the Jewish kids, were raised together among the other gentile kids – together we went to the river and to the forest. Sometimes we had our fights. During the winter we would build snow forts and have snowball battles. Starting at the age of 7, every kid in Kurenets would attend school; there we met with new duties and challenges and made new friends.

In 1955-56, many Jewish Kurenetsers started moving to Poland in order to continue on their way to Israel. Since Kurenets was part of Poland before 1939, the Soviets let the old Polish citizens cross the border to Poland. The first family to take that step was my father's sister Hava and her husband Boris, with their 5 children. The oldest child was 7 years old and the youngest, Sholom, less than a year. I still remember his *brit milah* ceremony: all the Jews of Kurenets gathered together in the small room and then came the rabbi. All the Jews raised the money to pay for his services. That is how the last Jewish child was born In Kurenets, and that happened in 1955.

Surviving Jews from the area of Vileyka meet in Naarch'

Many families followed that path, moving directly to Poland or to the larger cities in order to arrange the needed papers and then move to Poland. So in 1958 only two Jewish families were left in Kurenets: Levin's and ours. But Jewish life didn't stand still. At every holiday the older children of my father would visit us with their children. Also we kept in touch with the Jews in nearby villages: Dolginovo (4 families), Lyuban (7 families) and Vileyka (about 15 families). The spiritual leader of the remaining Jews was Mironovich (Finkelshteyn-Tewel) the head of the Lyuban *sovhoz* [state farm].

In 1958 a new school director arrived in Kurenets – Catznelson. He lived in Kurenets till 1963. The head doctor of the Kurenets regional hospital was Dr. Nasis. He lived in Kurenets from 1960 till 1966. They both had children younger than school age.

At the Kurenets public school between the years 1958 and 1966, only two Jewish kids studied: my older brother, Abram, and me. Despite this, we never felt excluded and participated in all kinds of social activities; along with the other students we went dancing and training. Abram even won a regional championship in throwing the discus. We participated in all-night parties in the nearby villages and hung around with boys and girls of our age, but what we were missing were Jewish friends.

Alperovich family in grandfather's house (1960)

Kurenets (1961) – childhood friends
Left to right: Petya, Tolik, Abram and Shlomo Alperovich, Lenya

Abram finished school in 1964 and went to Brest to study pedagogy. I finished school two years later in 1966 and went to Minsk to study engineering, but it didn't mean that we left Kurenets. Every holiday we returned to visit our parents.

Kurenets soccer team, champions of the Vilekya area (1964)
Abram Alperovich is 5th from left

Kurenets (1964) – Abram Alperovich jumps

After finishing my studies in 1971 I returned to the Vileyka region to work. I was the head engineer of Kolhoz, and later a regional agriculture machinery engineer. At that time my brother Abram was already a math teacher in Vileyka's school. Almost all the Jewish kids of the Vileyka region received a higher education.

Estony, Tallinn (1971) – Abram's wedding
Left to right: Zelda, Shlomo, Samuel, Lisa, Misha, Aaron and Yasha Alperovich, Victor and Bunya Kempin

Soon Abram got married and moved to Tallinn (Estonia). In 1974, my father passed away. It happened in January and it was very cold outside, but still many Jewish and also local (gentile) populations came to pay him their final respects. Among the locals he was a well-known authority. Everyone who had to buy or sell a cow went to Aaron ("Vorchik") to ask for help in [the form of] advice or even in [case of] a shortage of money. I still remember how some of our Russian neighbors cried at the funeral and kissed his legs.

At the funeral of Aaron Alperovich (1974)
All the Jews of the region came together

My mother and I, in 1975, sold our house and left Kurenets and moved to Tallinn. I would still come to Kurenets for visits. One time, it was in 1981, I went there after getting married; just after the wedding ceremony, my wife and I flew to visit my father's grave. At that time I learned from local non-Jewish citizens who still remained there that they [the Jews] are all called "Vorchiks" by the nearby villagers—that's how deep and lasting was the memory of the last Jewish family that lived in Kurenets.

Vileyka (1984) – Wedding of Taisa Alperovich and Jenya Hayet

After us, there was only one Jewish family left in Kurenets – Issak and Jeniya Levin. Issak passed away in 1990 at the age of 90, and his wife moved to Svetlogorsk to live with her sister. Before leaving the USSR and moving to Israel, in 1989 my brother Abram and I visited Kurenets and our oldest brother Jacob (Yankel), who lived in Molodechno and worked not far from Kurenets in *sovhoz* Lyuban with Mironovich. He organized the placement of a memorial at the graves of those who died in the Holocaust. At this visit in Kurenets we met our old neighbor Felsher Shuberty (born in 1918). While talking to him we found out that he was a Jew, something that we didn't know before. We lived near him from 1956 until 1975, went to school together with his children, and didn't know of his being a Jew. So, since 1990, he is the last Jewish settler in Kurenets, he is the one who welcomes visitors who come to Kurenets, and he is the one taking care of the Jewish graveyard.

My brother Abram and I have lived happily with our families in Israel for 10 years already. Our brother Yacob also immigrated to Israel, but he passed away in 1996. My other brother, Samuil, is still living in Belarus.

Shlomo and Lev Alperovich by the grave of Miranovich,
Vileyka (2001)

Belarus, Hoyniki (2001). Samuel Alperovich's family

Shlomo Alperovich near the house he was born in
Kurenets (2001)

At Abram's house after the funeral of Yasha Alperovich
Israel (1996)

Alperovich in Israel – Afula (1994)

Thus It Began

Chapters from the Underground

by Nachum Alperovich

Edited (in Hebrew) by Aharon Meirovitz

Translated by Eilat Gordin Levitan

(Granddaughter of Nachum Alperovich's first cousin, Meir Gurevitz)

Edited by Sandra Krisch

There is strong evidence that during World War II many Jews fought the Nazi annihilator and did not go to their deaths like sheep, as has commonly been thought. Considering the hardships the Jews encountered, the hostile environment, and the methods the Germans used to trick and control the Jews by consistently promising to "let them live" if they were "useful and obedient," the evidence of courageous resistance becomes obvious. As someone who experienced the evils of those days as a teenager in my hometown of Kurenets and afterward in the forests with the Resistance, I can present many examples of heroic stands by Jews. Even if the Resistance was not always physically present, they treated the enemy with open hatred and contempt.

I was told about our town's residents, Zusia Benes and Leah (daughter of Chaim Yisrael Gurevitz) Benes, an old couple. The day the Germans came to seize them to be slaughtered, they burned their wooden home and jumped in the fire; consequently, the Germans did not get to touch them.

Leib Motosov and Leib Dinerstien encountered similar fates. They jumped in the fire wearing their prayer shawls saying, "Hear, oh Israel!" before the Nazis had a chance to shoot them. All the examples I have used so far are of people who were old and could not physically fight the Nazis; I have no doubt that if they would have had the chance, they would have fought them fiercely. Moreover, if I mention the older townspeople, I must mention Chaiale Sosensky, a teenager of about fourteen or fifteen. When the Germans came to get her, she scratched the faces of the policemen with her nails and prophesied the day of revenge. I was told that she was severely tortured but continued to curse the killers.

During those days of horror, the Jews of the town were not allowed to have contact with each other, so we don't even know the extent of revolt, particularly in the cases of families who did not survive. However, even the little that we do know makes me feel deep respect for my townspeople. Another tale I must tell is that of Israel Alperovich.

Israel was a deeply religious Jew. When he escaped to the woods with his family, he continued keeping kosher. He starved for many days but did not allow himself to eat the bread and other food brought by the villagers, fearing that the food was not kosher. Israel only ate potatoes that he baked in the fire, and he eventually died of starvation. I see much heroism in his deed: he never lost his spiritual essence and his deep beliefs. When I compare his final journey to the journey of the many thousands of Russian POW's who, while passing through our town, fought each other to get to food that was thrown to them by the Nazis, I can particularly respect him.

Another resistance was by Arka Alperovitch, who attacked a policeman who was taking him to be killed. Arka managed to strike the policeman in the head and take his rifle away; he escaped to the fields, but other policemen killed him. Yankeleh Alperovitch, the son of Orchik and Maryl showed another example of bravery. I will tell about his act of bravery later.

First, I must tell you about my mother in a few sentences. Her resistance to the enemy was heroic and lasted throughout all the days of the Nazi occupation, until the German killers took her from her hiding place to her death. Even there, she never stopped cursing them and despising them. She spit in the face of one of them and hit him with her skinny, tired hand. For that, they killed her right on the spot. Days later, the villagers who saw the incident were still talking about it. They were amazed at how brave my mother was.

Most of these heroic occurrences were spontaneous, but the story that I am going to tell you is about organized, thoroughly thought-out resistance that was done by a small number of teenagers. We were members of the youth movement Hashomer Hatzair in Kurenets, even in the days of the Soviets; we worked in secret on our commitment to the youth movement. The group numbered only about ten to twelve people; it was small only because it had to be underground. During the Nazi occupation, when people realized the existence of our band of resistance, many who were years older than we were implored us to let them join our troop.

The active members of the troop in 1941, when the Germans invaded our area, were: Yitzhak (Yetzkaleh) Einbinder age sixteen, Benjamin (Nyomka) Shulman age fifteen, Shimon Zirolnik, Zalman Gurevitch, the brothers Elik and Motik Alperovich, Chaim Yitzhak Zimmerman, and me. Later we were joined by Berta Dimenstien, Noach Dinnerstien, Josef Norman and others. I was seventeen at that time. The only survivors of this group were Zalman Gurevitch, Yosef Norman, and me. Yetzkaleh Einbender and Nyomka Shulman were renowned for their heroic deeds and their complete commitment to fighting the enemy. Yetzkaleh received many important medals after his death. Our strong commitment to fighting the enemy came from our involvement with HaShomer Hatzair; the movement's slogan was "Brave and Strong." For us it was much more than a slogan. It was our way of life and our motto. Another important rule of the movement was absolute commitment to looking out for each other.

HaShomer Hatzair precepts were: to help each other, to live a life of purity both in the physical and spiritual sense, to cherish nature, to love Eretz Israel, and to train to be farmers in our homeland. This way of life was encouraged and achieved by means of journeys through the forest and participation in summer and winter camps alongside youth from other towns. Those youthful experiences helped us, especially during the hard times of the German occupation.

I was drawn to HaShomer Hatzair from a very early age, following my older sisters' example. My oldest sister, Hannah, was one of the first youths in our town to join the movement. Later, my sisters Henia and Rachel joined the movement too. Hannah spent many seasons in training camps. She yearned to become a *chalutza* and was waiting for years for a permit to leave for Eretz Israel. Her dream was finally realized in 1938, still without a permit. Using fake papers, she reached Israel on a boat of illegal immigrants. I was the only son—we were one boy and five girls. Our mother was very brave and clever. In

1917, she was very committed to the Russian revolution. Although she was married at the time and had two young daughters, she deeply believed in and fought for communism. Eventually, she lost some of her zeal for communism.

At our house, my mother's brothers (Castroll) were often mentioned. Two of her brothers left for America before I was born; one of them had a candy store. His financial situation was not great and I remember that in one of his letters he wrote, "I have a sweet business with a sour income." My mother's other brother in America was Chanan Castroll. He was the secretary of the Communist Party in New York. In 1938, he was a member of a committee that went to Moscow, and people said that he even met Stalin! Hence it must have been a familial trait, this interest in political action.

Father, on the other hand, was very different—quiet and much more cautious. Perhaps his somber encounters in youth made him cautious. When he was very young, he immigrated to the United States, but was not satisfied with the way of life in the U.S. After a short time, he returned to the town.

Mother was very involved with the youth movement, and sometimes I felt that if she were younger, she would have chosen the path of the youth movement. From this, you can probably gather that I never needed to rebel against my parents, even though outwardly it seemed that their lifestyle was similar to that of the rest of the town's Jews. Half of our house, which stood in the market center, was for our personal use and the second half was a fabric store.

My education was the typical education in the shtetl. First I went to a cheder, and later to Tarbut school, where we spoke only Hebrew; there I finished four grades. There was no fifth grade, so the next year we had to continue our studies in a Polish public school. When the school year started I was tested, but I failed the test. Considering that I barely knew Polish, this was not a surprise. Instead of putting me in fifth grade, they wanted to put me in third grade. The teacher and headmaster in the school was a Polish man named Mataras. Mother, who was fluent in Polish, came to Mataras and told him that I knew the material; it was only the language that I was weak in. Then she started talking Yiddish to the principal and repeated everything she had said earlier, but in Yiddish. Mataras said, "How are you talking to me, Madam? What happened to you?" "Nothing happened," my mother said in Polish, "I was telling you the same things in Polish, a language you know well; in contrast, now I said it in a language you have no knowledge of. This is my son's state. He knows the material; he just doesn't know the language. If you accept him, you will immediately realize that he will be a good student and in time will overcome the language barrier."

Mataras was very impressed with my mother's cleverness and accepted me to fifth grade on the condition that I would work very hard the first half of the year, and he would then reevaluate the situation. When the first half-year came, I was still unable to overcome the language barrier, so my mother went again and asked to extend the period; he gave me another half year. By the time the end of the year arrived, I was one of the best students in the class.

It was well known in town that Polish people love gefilte fish—especially the way the Jews make it. Therefore, at the end of the school year mother made some gefilte fish delicacies. She brought the "Jewish gift" to our Polish headmaster, who was so kind to me. Our families became friendly from that day. We also had friendly relations with the Polish teacher of mathematics, Mr. Scrantani. He was very happy with my progress now that I could speak the language and he would always test me with math riddles—a subject that I was very able to perform. In 1936, I graduated from seventh grade in the Polish school.

I was very capable with technical skills. These were financially hard times in town; father was hardly able to support the family. Now he suggested that I should get a profession so I would be more independent and be able to help the family. Father started working as an accountant in the lending establishment, Gmilut Chesed. However, that still was not enough, so we decided that I would go to work as a blacksmith in the neighboring town of Vileyka.

I worked at an establishment that belonged to a Christian man. In that place, there was another young Christian man who was constantly drunk. One day, he came to work and started torturing me. He took a container full of gasoline, started pouring it on the ground around me, and threatened to set it on fire. I ran out of the establishment and returned to Kurenets. My parents decided that I should never go back there and that I should look for another profession.

We had a relative in Vileyka named Mandelis who was a merchant of bicycles and radio equipment; he even had one motorcycle, which was a new commodity in our area at the time.

Vileyka was a more modern town than Kurenets and it had a printing house that was owned by a Jewish man named Flexer. Flexer was very successful and decided to open a second store to sell bicycles. Mandelis was very upset, and decided to open a printing shop in retaliation. He bought printing material and stole Flexer's best worker, a man by the name of Abraham Berkovitz.

I had an aunt in Kurenets, my father's sister, Reshka Alperovitch. She was a very capable woman, well known in town and even outside of town. She was a widow, and besides taking care of her home, she ran a store that was renowned all over the region. Aunt Reshka said that in her opinion it was much more respectable to work in a printing house than to be a blacksmith. Since my aunt's opinion was much respected by the rest of the family, I joined the workers of the printing place as an assistant, along with a young man named Yosef Norman. After Yosef was trained and learned the profession well, Flexer offered him a large sum of money. He started working for him, so now I was the only worker in the Mondavi printing house that was under the management of Abraham Berkovitz.

We had a contract for three years. The first three years I was supposed to get five "units of currency" per month. In the third year, I was supposed to get ten. Thus I started working six days a week, and on Saturday I would return home to my family and to the youth movement that was so important to me. Among my friends in the youth movement I was much respected, since a person who was able to support himself as a laborer was looked up to. I, on the other hand, truly wanted to continue my studies, but there was just no opportunity to do that since my parents needed the little help I could give them.

During those days, my good friend from the youth movement, Motik, son of Reuven Zishka Alperovitch, was studying in the Vileyka high school. Motik would visit my place of work many times and would always say how jealous he was that I was able to accomplish the proletariat commandment of being productive, while he, on the other hand, must study. He said, "For you, everything is good. If I could only exchange situations with you." I wished to exchange situations with him. Our printing press was electric, but you could also manually move it either by hand or by foot. Motik came to help me many times and was very excited when I let him use the arm or foot piece, which made him feel like he was part of the labor force. Eventually, I was so experienced that Abraham Berkovitz would let me run the place all by myself.

Even a few years before World War II we could sense that the spirit of anti-Semitism was growing in Poland. Next to the meeting place of HaShomer Hatzair lived a Christian male nurse named Solkevis. Surrounding his home there was a fruit grove. Many times while we were playing in the yard, a ball dropped in the garden. Any time we tried to retrieve our ball, his son would start fighting with us. He hated Jews. There was a funny story about Solkevis. People said that he once came to visit a terminally ill person for whom he could not find a cure, and he decided that the man had a contagious disease. Solkevis started screaming that the house's inhabitant should not wait but should immediately take the sick man out of the house and bury him.

Kopel Specter was the leader of our troop, so whenever we got in trouble with Solkevis's son, he would stand halfway between the son and us, and he would somehow manage to stop the fights. One day, I went to get some water from the well near Smorgon Street. The Christian, Pietka Gintoff, saw me. He took my pail, which was full of water, and dumped it on the ground. I was furious. I took the pail and whacked Pietka on his head. He immediately fell to the ground. A gentile who saw the fight started screaming, "A Jew killed a Christian boy!" After a few minutes, Pietka got up and the Christians who gathered around saw that he was okay. All the Jews who came to see what was happening had to calm the gentiles so there wouldn't be a bigger fight.

Kopel would plan our activities and teach us about socialism and Eretz Israel. He would teach us to sing Hebrew songs and Chasidic songs, and we danced many folk dances, the most popular of which was the hora. Our meetings were not only held in the school, but also in the fields and in the forests. We especially liked to walk to the big boulder, two huge rocks in the middle of a field; we always wondered how they got there. Sometimes, Elik and Motik Einbinder would invite us to the barn that belonged to Reuven Zishka, their father, and there we would hold the meetings. During our vacation, we would walk to the village of Mikolina, near Dolhinov, a distance of about 20 km. There we would spend many days in what we called either our summer camp or our winter camp. We would meet members of HaShomer Hatzair from the Dolhinov *ken* (unit), from the Dockshitz *ken*, and from the Krivich *ken*.

During the winter, we would go to Ratzke to sled. Ratzke was a tiny town. It was probably named after the river that was on its border and it was most famous for its hills; to us, they looked like mountains and we called them the Ratzkelberg. In the evening, we walked in groups through the town. Many times the young Christian kids liked to trick us by putting barbed wire on the road, and sometimes we would get hurt. One time, Pesach, the son of Pinke Alperovich the town's butcher, caught one of those Christian boys getting ready to put the barbed wire down. He punched him very hard. Pesach was a very good-looking boy, very strong and brave, and we were all very proud of him. This scared the Christian kids, and after that, they stopped bothering us. We were especially proud of Pesach, since his brother Tevel was a member of our troop.

In our meetings, we would discuss events that happened very far away from Kurenets. In 1936, we had major arguments among members concerning the situation in Eretz Israel. This was during the bloody fights with the Arabs. We argued about whether the Jews should compromise with the Arabs to keep the peace or whether they should fight. We were all about thirteen or fourteen at the time, and for some of us it was difficult to obey the rules of HaShomer Hatzair. One of the most dedicated members was Shimon Zirolnik. He was a very serious and kind person, and he would always follow the rules and keep a pure lifestyle.

When I was thirteen, for my bar mitzvah my mother gave me her father's tefillin. I was named after my mother's father, Nachum Castroll. Nachum was a *shochet* in Kurenets for many years. He went blind when he was old. Just before he died, he told my mother that if he were to be lucky enough to have a grandson in Kurenets (he had other grandsons in the U.S. and the Soviet Union), she should name him Nachum and he would inherit his tefillin. I was very disappointed when my mother gave me the tefillin. When my friends had their bar mitzvahs they got new tefillin that looked beautiful, while mine were old and shabby-looking. Mother kept explaining how important it was to keep the tefillin, that it was a tradition that passed for many generations in our family. Finally, I was convinced, and by the time I read the Torah and Haftorah, I could already appreciate the importance of the old tefillin. I argued with my friends and won the argument that mine were superior. Just about then, the youth movement Beitar was becoming very popular in town and we fought with them for the recruiting of new members.

A New Spirit in Town

World War II started and the Soviets came to our area (in what is now Belarus) after the partition of Poland. Many members of our youth movement believed that the Soviets would understand our nationalistic desires, particularly our youth movement's desires, since these were based on Marxist ideology.

Particularly excited among us were Shimon Zirolnik and Nyomka Shulman. Nyomka was fourteen at the time, already a deep thinker, brimming with energy and a leader type. Both of them had hoped that the Soviets would help us accomplish our nationalistic desires as Jews. Nyomka and Shimon started studying Marxism very tenaciously. Nyomka even read Marx in German to be sure that he did not miss any of the intent. When the Soviets had just arrived, there was a feeling of comfort for some of us. The Christian boys who used to bother us were very quiet now. No one was allowed to say the word "*Jeed*." The judge who came to our area from Russia was a Jew, and I must say that the political committee was working hard to try to educate the public. We, the members of HaShomer Hatzair, would gather in Nyomka's house no longer in secret. We would talk and argue. Some of us even had girlfriends who were Russian (not Jewish). In general, there was much more communication among the Jews and Russians.

I had new opportunities for education, particularly since prior to the Russian arrival I was a proletariat, a laborer in a printing place; consequently, my situation was very favorable now. As I told you earlier, I finished seven grades in the Polish school. I could be accepted to the fifth grade in the public high school. The elementary school in town now became a high school. Many of my friends were accepted to fifth grade, but some of us who had previously stopped our studies were about sixteen and seventeen, much older than the rest of the students, who were about fourteen. Some of the teachers were Polish but a few came from Russia. Now, many students came from Russia, from territories that prior to the war had belonged to Russia. Some people among us thought that there was no sense in studying, since we soon would be eighteen and would have to serve in the army. There was a huge difference in capabilities between the Jews and the non-Jews. The Jews were all very good students and, in no time, there was a big gap. Other than studies, the school also had many social activities now. There was singing and dancing and we had many lessons on communism. My biggest desire in those days was to continue to study medicine, but that was a long-term dream.

During the summer vacation of 1940, I went to work for the train station. My job was to check the tracks; the train tracks were made of wood and there was iron on top of them. I had to check that the wood was not rotten. The tracks would get affected by heat and cold so I had to be very diligent in my job and report the situation to a Christian, named Bogdonyuk, who was the head of the train station. At that time, they started widening the train tracks that had previously belonged to the Polish territories, since they were slightly narrower than the ones that the Russians used. Therefore, I was traveling on a little bicycle from Kurenets to Molodechno, and I would check things and report to Bogdonyuk.

I did my job so well that they suggested I should go to Leningrad to study in the Techniyon. I came home and told my mother that I had gotten an offer. My mother asked me, "Why the Techniyon? You always talked about being a doctor." At that time, we had a renter who was responsible for the communist propaganda in the region. He was a Jew named Israel Guzman, and he suggested that if I could finish the ninth grade in high school before my time in the army, he would arrange for me to go to medical school. At that time, people from the Polish area were allowed to finish high school by graduating from ninth grade, rather than tenth grade, which was more common in Russia. I listened to Guzman, but I thought it would be impossible to finish four grades in the time that I had left before I would have to serve in the army. Mother did not agree with me. She said that I could study very hard during the summer and learn everything needed for sixth grade, so the next year I could go to seventh grade, and then we would get a postponement to finish ninth grade. Guzman agreed with mother, so I immediately discontinued working on the tracks and started preparing for seventh grade. Most of my friends also did the same, and by the time the year started we were even able to help some of the Russian students who were not so good in their studies.

The "Days of Honey" Do Not Last Long

The first weeks of Soviet rule seemed like days of honey. However, this period was done with in no time, and many troubles subsequently came to the town's population, particularly to "richer Jews," such as the merchants. Many Jews were imprisoned and some were sent to Siberia. Our hope that the Soviets would recognize our nationalistic desire disappeared. In town there were many Jewish soldiers from the Red Army, and they would tell us that in Russia they lacked nothing and that they had everything they needed. One soldier who fell in love with a Jewish girl from the town would say in Russian, "*Me yee vosof emiem*," meaning, "We have everything." The clowns in town would say that what he meant was that the word *mayeem* is "water" in Hebrew, so they do not lack water in Russia. We would learn about the true situation of the Russian people from the way the soldiers behaved. They would buy anything from any merchant in sight. They would even agree to buy two left shoes in two different colors! Soon the stores were empty of all merchandise and even local residents were waiting for merchants to arrive from Russia.

Now merchandise would come to the cooperative store and it would be divided among the residents, who would stand in lines to get the rations. The payment for the supplies was originally made with both Soviet and Polish money, Soviet rubles and Polish zloty. The cooperative stores opened in a few places in town. The Soviets made a few stores into one big store. The part of our house that was a store was taken. It became a component of a cooperative of leather goods. The smell of the leather spread all over our house and it was very hard to breathe. All day long, people would come to these stores to shop. No one knew what products would be found on a particular day. The main seller was a Jew from town, Moolah (Shmuel, the son of Yehoshua Alperovich). He was a true comedian and would have all kinds of stories to tell. We would come to him and ask in Yiddish, "Moolah, *mas vin hind kind*?" Moolah would answer, "Today only balalaikas." One day, Moolah said that they sold many locks, but there was only one key to all the locks; still, everyone was ready to buy the locks.

The authorities fired teachers in the school. This was the situation of the headmaster, Mataras. To replace the fired teachers, they brought teachers from the Vostok and some local residents became teachers. One was Yitzchak Zimmerman who was called in town Ytza Ckatzies', meaning Yitzhak son of Yechezkel. Ytza was known as a very learned man. He became our teacher for Russian studies. He was renowned among the students and the teachers alike. He was a very educated man, knew the Hebrew language very well, and would win any argument. He had a good voice and was very involved in the synagogue. The teacher, Josef Scrantani, continued teaching. He taught mathematics. His wife also became a Russian teacher, but their situation was very difficult. Scrantani became sick with tuberculosis but continued smoking. I, myself, did not smoke. I was not allowed to, according to the rules of HaShomer Hatzair. However, I had an easy time getting cigarettes, so I would buy cigarettes and come to school to give them to Scrantani, pretending that I was trying to stop smoking. The fact that I never saw anyone from the Scrantani family stand in line for cigarettes or anything else made me think that I should do something for them. We really believed that sugar had a healing effect. During the Polish days, there were posters saying, "*Sukiari keshpeh*," meaning, "Sugar makes you strong." Therefore, I decided to get a large amount of sugar for Scrantani to compensate for the fact that I was giving him cigarettes that I knew were bad for him. My sister Henia worked as a checker in the restaurant in Vileyka. I approached her, told her about Scrantani, and asked her to sell me two bags of 1kg each. Although it was much more expensive to buy it there, my financial situation was good, so I did not mind paying a higher price if I did not have to wait in line. Henia gave me the sugar. The next day, I approached Scrantani's wife. She was very excited when she received the sugar and said, "You don't know, my dear, how we appreciate your deeds. At the same time, I think how things have changed. In the old days, I would have been extremely insulted if someone had tried to help me like this, but these days things are different. I cannot express how wonderful it is that you care for Scrantani so." I paid for the sugar with 32 rubles. She assumed that I had stood in line and paid me 20 rubles. I said that I only paid 10 rubles, so that is what she gave me. Scrantani, who was a Polish

Christian, told Mataras (who was also Christian) about what I had done for him. The reason I am telling this story is that they were very helpful to us in the days to come.

In the Christian villages, there was hatred toward the Soviet rulers. Many of the villagers who had horses were forced to work for the Soviets. There were also rumors that soon they would establish *kolchozes* and confiscate the farms, including the cows and horses, and bring them there. So now, many villagers tried to get rid of their horses. They would bring them to the meat market and sell them very cheap. They would pretend that the horses were sick, slaughter them, and take the skins to sell to the government. The rule was that in order to establish that a horse was sick, a veterinarian had to assess the health of the horse. Sometimes, the veterinarian was paid under the table, so many healthy horses were killed. Many of the Jews and the local authorities were involved in this practice and were eventually caught and sent to Siberia. The situation with cows and other livestock was similar to that with horses. Those days, many cows were sick with tuberculosis, but many people pretended that healthy cows were sick with tuberculosis so that they could sell the cows for meat and leather.

I remember that, about that time, my parents bought another cow to add to the one cow we already had. We bought it from a Christian farmer named Kostya. Truly, the cow was healthy, yet when they checked her, they said that she was sick with tuberculosis. Moreover, she must be slaughtered immediately. Kostya and his wife were very honest people and came to us saying that when they brought the cow to us she was very healthy; therefore, she had turned sick more recently. They told us that as a consolation they would give us a one-year-old calf. In the end, we did not agree but we became very friendly with them.

Father, the Enemy of the Proletariat

At just about the same time, someone informed on my father, saying that he used to be a "major merchant." So on his identification card it was put that he was an enemy of the proletariat. This was not enough reason to send him to Siberia, but he was limited in his ability to get a job and was only allowed to do menial work. Father, who was only a middle-class merchant who had worked in accounting for Gmilut Chesed, now had to start doing manual work. He would go to work with one of the gentiles from town, Meetzkovsky, and would be his assistant in building furnaces. Father would hand him the bricks and other materials. Meetzkovsky was a very friendly person. He could speak Yiddish fluently, and when he spoke it sometimes, his language would be much nicer than that of the town's Jews.

The Russians not only confiscated apartments and stores; they also confiscated the synagogue that was called Beit Hamidrash, where the Mitnagdim prayed. There were other prayer houses. Two belonged to the Chasidim and there was a minyan of the rabbi where only the most religious of the Chasidim would pray. The synagogue they confiscated became a community center. There were meetings and speeches, and movies would even be shown there. The Jews took out all the bibles and the head of the community center took out the beautiful *bima* so that the place would be larger inside. Now most of the townspeople, Christians and Jews, would come there to watch movies. The older people of the town would tell how the *bima* was originally made. In 1924, Max Shulman, a former town resident who had immigrated to the United States and become very rich, arrived in town. He gave a vast sum of money for, among other things, improving the synagogue and putting in the *bima*. He even brought a painter from Vilna to paint unique scenes for the *bima*.

In those days, father was dreaming of becoming a farmer. If he had to do manual work, he decided to get a parcel to farm. At that time, anyone who lived near a land parcel was told that he could get the land next to the house if he wanted to be a farmer. Therefore, father decided to register to get such land. Among the persons who were granting the land was a Jew from Russia. He abruptly whispered to my father in Yiddish, "*Da oom vah ava rhysm. Af laka tif din art*," meaning, "Here you must know that a person who owns some land ends up being buried in the land." Father immediately understood the meaning and decided to return to his job with Meetzkovsky.

Aunt Reskah's house was also confiscated and now it became the home for the Russian authorities and my aunt and her children had to leave. The same was the fate of the house that belonged to the Einbinder family, the parents of my friend Yetzkaleh.

Test Time

The meetings of our youth movement became increasingly covert. In many ways, this was the beginning of our underground activities. The core of the youth movement for us was our leader Kopel Spektor, although he didn't spend much time in town.

Kopel finished his Techniyon studies in Vilna with very high grades. When the Soviets realized his skills, they sent him to work in Molodechno, where he had a lab. He was working on an invention. He made something to do with trains.

He was beloved by all of us teenagers and we waited impatiently for the times he would come to Kurenets. At some point Josef Kaplan came to town. He was one of the principal leaders of HaShomer Hatzair in Eastern Europe and now he came to communicate with us and tell us how we could still immigrate to Palestine. He told us that we should go to Vilna. From there, people would go to Japan and from there somehow to Palestine. Our friend Chaim Yitzhak Zimmerman went to Vilna to inquire about it. It was very difficult to reach Vilna, which now was on the other side of the border; therefore, he had to pay a large sum of money to bribe someone to let him proceed. When he returned to Kurenets with the needed information, some of us prepared to leave for Vilna. However, Vilna soon thereafter became part of the Soviet Union and this plan was not viable anymore.

One time the chemistry teacher was trying to do an experiment with dangerous chemicals and since I was experienced at such things, I told him this was dangerous. He told me "If you are so scared, go to the back benches." I immediately did as he told me. I was right, and the teacher got a burn on his face while doing the experiment. The next day I showed the class how to do it in a safer way. Therefore I got a good grade, but I was sent home for bad behavior—being disrespectful to the teacher. Mother came to the high school to talk to the headmaster the next day. He was from Soviet Russia and he was a Jew by the name of Fishkin. She said "There was something wrong with my son's behavior but the punishment was too strong. Everyone admitted that there was something wrong with the way the teacher did the experiment, not only wrong but also dangerous. Nevertheless, despite the mistake, the teacher is staying in school. My son, who is sorry for his behavior, is taken out. Is that justice?" The principal was convinced and I was let back into school.

Meanwhile, since I planned to skip some grades, I had to bring a note from the doctor saying that I could withstand such a difficult task. A Jewish doctor named Cyrynsky came to our area in 1937. He was highly respected by all. He was very helpful to the poor people. I went to see him and asked for a note. He tried to convince me not to undertake such a difficult task and asked me why I was in such a hurry to skip grades. I explained the fact that I was older, and eventually he gave me the permission. So I took the difficult tests and managed to get into the eighth grade in high school in Vileyka. In the evening I would go to classes for ninth grade. One time, the head of the education department in Vileyka came to see me; he sat in the classroom during a test. When I finished the test, he came to me. He said, "What grade were you in last year?" I told him, "I was in fifth grade." "Can you explain, if you were in fifth grade, how you are in ninth grade? In Russia, there was one person named Lomonosov who was able to do it. You must try to be like him."

Now, I was emotionally prepared to study medicine one day. Some years earlier I had another great desire. I was studying Spanish because of the civil war in Spain. The war of the Republicans against Franco appealed to workers all over the world. Many volunteers came to fight, and I dreamed of volunteering; that's why I studied Spanish. Finally we reached June 15, 1941. I graduated from the ninth grade, as I needed to do. My sister Henia would say that she was ready to clean floors so we would have enough money to send me to medical school.

The Way It Began: To Run or Not to Run?

I was able to enjoy my vacation only for a few days. I felt that now my dreams could be realized and a bright future was waiting for me. Then the fateful moment of June 22, 1941 came, the day of the attack by the Nazis, their invasion of the USSR. That day, at four in the morning, German planes bombed the train tracks in Molodechno. People said that many were wounded and killed there. Even though there was obvious pandemonium all around us, the authorities in Kurenets tried to calm us down and promised that very soon the Germans would be annihilated, so we shouldn't panic. Still, many of us thought we shouldn't stay, that we must escape to the east.

People started arguing about what we should do. Should we run or stay? There was a library on Vileyka Street with many books in Polish, Russian, Hebrew, and Yiddish. For unknown reasons, someone from the Soviet authority ordered that the library be destroyed, and all the books were thrown into the street. I looked at the books and—how ironic—among them I found a Spanish-Yiddish dictionary that I had searched for a few years earlier. I took the book. I was hopeful at that point, sure that the Red Army would overcome the Germans very soon. Someone who saw me with the book laughed at me and said, "This is an unreasonable time to learn Spanish. Now that the Germans are coming you should be learning German." On the other hand, our renter Guzman was very sure that the Red Army would win soon. He said to me "We'll push them out. The Red Army will show the awful Nazis that they are not dealing with the Polish army anymore."

A few days passed and the Germans were going from one victory to next and the Soviets were retreating from our area. Now pandemonium was everywhere. Mother told me that it would be better if I would run away to the east. She prepared supplies for me. I didn't know what she put in the bag; she just gave it to me and said, "Run away my son, run east. The situation is very bad." Many started leaving town in the neighboring community of Ratzke, which had about fifteen Jewish families; I met with Meir Mekler, Abba Narutzki, and the son of David the shoemaker. I also remember a few of the policemen and members of the Soviet authority there. We rested near Ratzke, about 8 km from our town. A Soviet officer came to us, told us that the situation at the front was improving so there was no reason for us to run east, and that we should return to Kurenets. We didn't trust him and decided to wait there a little longer. It was around noon and we got hungry. I opened the bag for food, but I found out that instead of food my mother had packed many boxes of cigarettes. Again I realized that my mother was very clever. Although she knew I was not smoking—my youth movement had rules against it—nevertheless she knew that cigarettes were worth more than money. She was thinking about my future. Therefore, I gave some cigarettes to one of villagers who gave me food in return. I shared my food with a girl from Kurenets who was with me.

Most of the people who were with us didn't accept what the officer said and continued going east. The girl and I decided to return to town. We reached the village of Bogdanova, which was 4 km from Kurenets, and since it was already dark we decided to sleep there and go back in the morning. We slept under a tree. It was a nice summer night and there were many fruit trees in the area. In days of peace, the Jews would lease those fruit orchards. Early in the morning, we were awakened by the young villagers who took their cows to pasture. They must have thought that we were lovers. We got up and returned to town. When we returned we were told that those few policemen we had met in Ratzke had also returned but didn't stay long. They immediately left to go east. Therefore, on the evening of June 25, 1941 there was no one left from the Russian authority. Everyone had gone east.

That morning when I passed by my aunt Reshka's house, which had been confiscated by the Soviet authorities two years earlier, I decided to enter; there was no one there. The house was a total mess. I found many papers, documents, and IDs with pictures, so I took many of those documents saying to myself, "Who knows what the days will bring? Maybe they can help me somehow." I also went to Chaim Sotzkover's house, which was also confiscated by the Soviets prior to the German invasion, and there I found a lot of papers and I took them too. I returned home, hid everything, and went to rest. I was very tired and fell asleep immediately.

The town was now without rulers. Villagers from the surrounding villages started coming to town, planning to rob the Soviet stores and the Jews. An amazing phenomenon occurred, and this gave us Jews a little encouragement. The Christian inhabitants of our town organized a committee to prevent the villagers from robbing our town. We soon found out that they were doing it because they didn't want our possessions to be taken by others. Dr. Shostakovitch, who later was a German sympathizer, now was with the Jews, organizing a patrol of Christians and Jews, and we started a watch all around the town. This patrol lasted about two days and then the Christian residents started robbing the Soviet supplies and a few of them took supplies from the Jewish stores. In addition, some of the villagers managed to come and rob our homes too. I remember something funny that occurred, which—if it were not such hard time, would be a good comedy. One Jew, Zalman Neta Wexler, was very sneaky and clever; when the gentiles came to rob his house, he mixed in with them and pretended to be one of the robbers and managed to "steal" some of his own possessions.

On June 28, six days after the war began, a few Germans soldiers entered the town. They came from Vileyka Street riding motorcycles and cars. They stopped for a while at the corner of Vileyka Street and Smorgon and continued passed Dolhinov Street. The gentiles gave them flowers and milk. Among them were Kasick Sokolovsky, who was holding a rifle in his hand, Pietka Gintoff, and Pelvic. The three were later collaborators and killers of many Jews. Some Jews observed the arrival of the German soldiers, and I was among them. The fact that they crossed town and didn't strike anyone encouraged us. Someone said, "They passed and didn't cause us any harm; maybe the monster is not so bad."

At eleven in the morning, tanks came into town. Now there was an ominous foreboding. The soldiers' first question when they met us was "How many Jews are in town?" One of the people standing there answered. A Germans said, "Too bad, too bad. They'll all have to be moved out of here." Still some Jews said, "Don't take it seriously, he's just talking." Others said that during World War I, the German invasion was good for the Jews.

The picture of the Germans approaching Kurenets and the gentiles giving them flowers and milk was printed in one of the German newspapers. The tanks went through Myadel Street to the market center and went east to Dolhinov. At 1:00 P.M., there was an order by the Germans that everyone who had a weapon had to return it to the authorities. Two young boys, cousins with the same last and first name, Shimon Zimmerman, returned the weapons. When they returned them, they were murdered.

Fear spread all over when we found out about it. Even the ones who thought the Germans would be okay, based on memories of World War I were asking, "What should we do?" They tried to find a reason for the murder of the two boys. Since the two murdered boys were members of our youth movement and our good friends, we were all shocked. Nyomka came to me very upset and said we should do something. Therefore, we decided that we should all meet with Kopel Spektor and decide what to do, and this is how our underground activity started.

Kopel said that we must meet in a secret place, so we met by the swamps behind the bathhouse, a place crowded with bushes that could not be seen from the main road. So here we met: Kopel Spektor, Nyomka Shulman, Yitzkale Einbender, Zalman Gurevitch, the brothers Motik and Elik Alperovich, Yechiel Kremer, Shimon Zirolnik, and me. It was clear to us that in the coming days death could come from any corner. We vowed to fight. The question was how to fight, how to get weapons. Our ideas were still unclear. Someone suggested that in our situation there was only one option: jump on a policeman, kill him, and take his weapon. That was the way of the Underground. Shimon said that besides physical fighting we must also have political fighting, i.e., posters and propaganda. We must make flyers to distribute among the villagers and tell them to fight the Nazis invader. He told me that I should organize it. I used to work in a printing house.

As we came out of the bushes we met Josef Zuckerman, who was much older than we were. He told us that a few days earlier, when the Russians left, he saw that one of them who passed through the swamps threw a gun somewhere. He showed us where it was. We looked for it and found it; it had three bullets.

Although the two Shimon cousins were killed cruelly, people still tried to not judge the Germans. They wanted to see if it was an unusual case, not one that foretold the future. People whose homes were taken by the Soviets now returned; that looked to some to be a good thing. It was July 1st when the Germans actually entered the town and put officers there. The first order that day was that all male Jews had to go to the town market to register. Anyone who would not come there would be killed immediately.

When we came to the market, we were told that we must choose a Jewish committee, a Judenrat that would be our communication with the authorities. A refugee from Austria by the name of Shuts was elected a head of committee. He came to town in 1939. He was expelled from Austria and was badly hurt. When he came to our town he had a head wound, but he found a place here and became a German teacher in the Polish school and a physical education teacher. He was respected in town and his German was excellent, so he was suitable for the job. The SS let it be known that from this time forward, the Jews had no rights. From now on, we were ordered to do whatever told. We had to wear a yellow tag, could not cross the street, and could not go on the sidewalk; rather, we had to walk in the middle of the street, like horses. No more were we allowed on trains or in cars. There were curfews at night from 6:00 P.M. to 6:00 A.M. We were not allowed to be in groups of more than three Jews. We were forbidden to have communication with gentiles. When the SS man ended his speech, he ordered us to disperse, and everyone left.

A few days later, the German army started coming to town. There was a never-ending parade of troops driving or walking through Vileyka to Dolhinov at night. It was impossible to cross the street, which was filled with German soldiers. It was very difficult to take cows to the pasture during the daytime, so we got up early, at 6:00 A.M., when there were few soldiers. We would somehow manage to cross the street to take the cows to the pasture. We used to take the cows to an area of abundant grass. I would usually take the cows and stay all day, until 6:00 P.M., and then I would make the cows run quickly to get back to our yard. On the way back home, I had to go by the house of Motka Alperovich. Now the Germans had taken his house, so this part of the walk was very dangerous. At that point, we were told not only what not to do, but also what we should do from then on. There was an order that every time we saw a German, we had to take our hats off and greet him with respect, in recognition of his superiority.

One time when I passed by a German, I deliberately didn't take my hat off, so they beat me mercilessly. Next time I decided to be smarter and walked without a hat. When they caught me this time, not only did they beat me up: they also shaved my head in the shape of a cross, one ear to the other and forehead to neck. My mother cut off all my hair. The third time, I was wearing a hat and took it off when they came by. When they saw that I was baldheaded, they figured I was a Russian soldier who had escaped from being a POW, so for that they would kill me. One German was holding a gun and another German passed by and said to the other guy, "Look this is a perfect example of what Jews look like. You shouldn't kill him. Now when the time comes for no Jews, he can be an example of what Jews look like, with long noses." They laughed and let me go. Even when I think about it today, I cannot believe how sure they were about their victory, thinking that one day there would be no more Jews left. Sometimes my father would go with the cow, and he experienced horrible treatment. This was on Kosita Street, not far from the train tracks. Some German soldiers came off the train and when they saw him, they called for him. When he went to them, they beat him severely. He returned home but didn't tell anyone what had happened. Later that day, my sister Rachel told him that she met some German who treated her well, like a human being; Father got upset and took his shirt off and showed us the injuries on his back. We were shocked and immediately gave him first aid. He told us of his memories of Germans from World War I. Even then, he was almost killed one day and it took a miracle to get out alive. From then on, we avoided taking the cow to pasture and most of the time we would take grass from the field and bring it home for the cow, which stayed in the barn.

Not far from our home, between the house of the Wexler family and the house of Yitzhak Moshe Meltzer, the hatter, there was a row of stores that were used during Soviet times as supply rooms. The Germans continued to use the supply rooms and they put flour and other supplies there. Now they made the Jews carry the sacks full of flour. One time, when I was carrying a sack on my back, I unintentionally touched a German who stood guarding us, and the flour from my clothes came onto his uniform. He was very mad and started screaming and said to the other German standing there, "When will I get a new uniform? I was in other battles for the homeland in Czechoslovakia, Austria, and Poland and they would always give me a new clean uniform. So when will I get one in this war with the communists?" His friend said that the day of victory would come and he'd get a new uniform, "but until that day, this Jew will clean it for you." I had no choice: I took a brush and cleaned his uniform and knelt to clean his pants.

We Decide To Fight

A few weeks passed following the announcement of the new rules. Many people suffered, and we only knew a little of their suffering. One day at 9:00 A.M. we gathered at the house of Nyomka Shulman. Yitzhak Zimmerman, who was much older than we were and a member of HaShomer Hatzair since 1928, was also told of our plans. Nyomka Shulman had a very old and blind grandmother and she had her own room. Her room was always dark and she seemed as if she was not aware of the present. All day she would repeat a sentence. She said this sentence in Soviet times as in the German days. "God in heaven, please help every Jew and keep everyone healthy and safe." Despite the fact that she seemed unaware of what was around her, in her sentence you could hear something of the horrors outside the room. Occasionally the old woman would leave the room, but even when she sat in the corner we could discuss everything; she was ignoring the outside world. So now we met, five people—Nyomka, Itzka, Zalman, Shimon, and I—to discuss what to do. We all realized that the situation was getting worse and that we must not sit and do nothing. Getting weapons was an intricate assignment and we didn't even fathom what to do with a weapon once we got it. However, at this time we were more concerned with how to obtain it. Someone said that near the river between Poken village and Myadel, not far from Chaim Zokofsky's carpentry, there was a rifle. At that time, the Germans took Zokofsky's carpentry and it was dangerous to walk around it at night or in the morning. Nevertheless, we decided to check the spot.

Mother was told about it and she suggested she would help. Zalman and I went with mother. We pretended to be collecting grass for the cow. Mother thought that if she joined us we would appear less suspicious. We paced on all sides as if collecting grass and after a while we found the rifle; we took the sack that we had and put the rifle into the sack, laden with grass. The sack was too short and the rifle stuck out, so part of the way I put it under my jacket. Finally we reached home. When my father saw the rifle, he became worried. He said that we were taking a tremendous responsibility on ourselves. We were playing with fire. Dad was a traditional Jew even prior to the war, but now he became intensely Orthodox. He said, "Whatever God has decided for us will happen, and we will not change his will." He would continuously repeat this sentence. Father was now taking part in every funeral in town, and at this time there were many funerals. One day two young guys—one was Mendel the grandson of Leib Motosov, the other, Mendel, the grandson of Chaim Velvel, the owner of a store for metal work—were sent to work in Vileyka. The order for their new job came from the Gvitz Commissar. On the way to work, they met Shernagovitz, a local policeman who worked for the Germans. He killed them both on the spot. One gentile from a nearby village found the bodies and brought them in his buggy to Kurenets. Leib Motosov, the grandfather of one of the youths, who was a very intelligent man, was mourning and extremely distressed. "What is the reason here?" he said. "There must be some logic in things. They were ordered to go to work by the Gvitz Commissar. Each one was holding a saw and ax, ready to work as they were ordered. Nevertheless here comes a policeman and kills them. This is a crime that the Gvitz Commissar cannot ignore. We must complain." Father believed that everything was decided in heaven. He told us, "We can never understand the reason why things are. Moreover, there's no reason to complain to the Gvitz Commissar. It will just open the mouth of Satan." This was in the first month of German rule. People didn't believe that things that were more awful were going to happen. Moreover, that they would happen almost daily.

The rifle that we found near the river was hidden in our attic. The rifle had no bullets. Nevertheless, the ingenious Nyomka Shulman said, "Even if we have no bullets, it's worth something. If you meet a policeman, you point the rifle at him; he won't know that you don't have bullets. The policeman will hesitate and you might be able to overcome him and take his own weapon." That day we managed to get a gun from a villager from Volkovishtzina by exchanging some salt, and this gun was also hidden in our attic. In a meeting in Nyomka's grandmother's room, Shimon suggested again that we should start propaganda and showed us that he had already done something about it. He brought a specially made frame that could be used to make flyers. That same day I almost was killed when I walked through the market, which was usually empty. I heard the voice of a German watchman far from me. He told me to stop, yelling, "Why didn't you greet me?" He started readying his weapon to shoot. I knew that if I tried to run, he'd kill me. Therefore, I started to tell him something. Luckily for me, an officer came and the soldier changed his tune. He screamed, "Bloody Jew, get away. Don't come near me." I was still afraid that if I did as he said and ran, he'd shoot me. For some reason, the officer allowed me to go home. I didn't know why the first one was upset and I didn't know why the second one let me go. Therefore, in a hurry, I left the spot.

In the Meat Market

The victory of the Germans at the front brought many prisoners of war to town. The meat market became a station for transferring the thousands of POWs who continually passed through town. There was barbed wire around the meat market and there were watchtowers with lights at the corners. POWs would stay one night and would be transferred west. Many of them would die there in the meat market; they would be buried right there, and the next day there was a new group of POWs. Many were wounded and starving, and they were kept under extremely inadequate sanitary conditions. The gentiles, the residents of the surroundings towns, would stand at the side of the road and throw food to them, potatoes and fruits. They had a lot of compassion for them. The POWs would run to the food and start fighting each other to get something. The Germans, who hated any disorder, would hit them and threaten the people who gave them food. "If you want to give them food, it has to be in an orderly manner," they said. The officer would constantly yell, "There must be order. You must collect the food in one place and we will divide it among the POWs." Many of the Jews brought water from the well and the river by Dolhinov Street. The POWs who were wounded badly would be killed prior to arriving at the market. However, some badly wounded POWs would be brought to the other market in buggies. The gentiles did as they were ordered and put food in one place. The Jews and non-Jews would take the wounded off the buggies and lay them on the ground, as told. We were ordered by the Germans to put the heads in one straight line. At first, we didn't understand why they cared if they were in straight lines, but soon enough we learned the reason. The officer stood across from the row of heads with an automatic rifle, opened fire, and killed all of them.

One day a German officer caught me and Yechiel Kremer, the son of Yekutiel Meir, who was much older than I, and we were ordered to wash the car of one of the officers. He told us, "If I find out that you didn't clean it well or sabotaged it, I'll kill you like dogs." This was on Dolhinov Street, not far from the meat market. He ordered me to take the wheels off and clean them. At first it was hard to take them off, but eventually we did it. Then the officer demanded that we remove the seat covers from the car and clean the inside. He was teasing us, saying, "We are going to Moscow and I must come there with a clean shiny car." When I was done with the job, I asked the German officer if I could go to eat. While we were standing there, I saw what was happening in the meat market. When I was done with the job, the officer decided to send us to work with the POWs. As we walked there, we passed a garden in front of a Polish house. I saw that in the bushes close to the sidewalk there was a weapon. Carefully, I moved the weapon to a more hidden place in the bushes. When we reached the meat market, we were told to help with the distribution of food to the POWs; the gentiles had collected it in one area. Among the POWs who were brought to the market, I saw a young Jewish man from Ratzke, named Hoinsihof. I saw that he threw a note on the ground when he saw me. With his eyes, he signaled me to pick up the note. I did it and saw the first two lines. He was begging me to let his family know he was there. I threw the note to the side immediately. One of the Germans saw this and thought I was the one writing the note. I explained to him that I had seen it on the ground and was curious. He didn't believe me, put me next to a wall, called a guard, and said to him, "Aim at the head." Nevertheless, a second later he changed his mind, thinking maybe he was wrong, and instead of "Fire," he yelled, "Halt," meaning stop. The soldiers put their weapons down. He asked me, "Are you going to continue to spy?" I couldn't say a word; my tongue was paralyzed. With the stick he had, he hit my hands and that brought me back to reality. I explained that I didn't write the note. I wasn't guilty. He listened to my defense but still ordered me to lie on ground, and he hit me. Eventually I fainted. They poured water on my head and I woke up. Then he let me go home but reminded me that I must return to work the next day. It was already dark, and I managed to crawl from the market to my home. My whole back was full of wounds and I was bleeding everywhere. My mother put dressings on the wounds, and although the situation was bad she was happy I was alive.

The POWs continued to pass through town. The situation was heartbreaking, and one day we met at Nyomka's and talked about how we could help the POWs. We decided to do something. We went to the Judenrat and demanded that Shuts send us to work in the meat market. While we were working there, some of us managed to give the POWs clothes. When we left, a few escaped with us. Among the escapees was a man who later was code-named Vlodia and who became one of the leaders of the Underground in our area. The sight we saw in the meat market was horrible. It was so crowded that some POWs couldn't find a place to lie down and rest. During the day, flies enveloped the place and the heat was unbearable; at night, it got cold. The POWs who still had some capabilities managed to cut pieces of wood for small fires, to keep warm. I can never forget one of the POWs: from what was left of his uniform I could tell he was an officer. He managed to get water and he washed and changed clothes. He arranged a fire pit to warm himself. One German was watching him the entire time and didn't like what he saw. He approached him from behind and with great force hit him on the back with a rifle. The officer collapsed lifeless.

Even at that point, some believed that the Soviets would overthrow the Germans. Our group would discuss the subject, but we didn't know how to help the Russians. Shimon Zirolnik would particularly talk about it; he believed that the day of revenge would come soon. Moreover, the Nazis would be annihilated in a short time. The Germans put electric lights in the meat market so they could watch the POWs at night. The villagers brought food and clothes, since they felt pity for the POWs who many times walked around almost naked. The clothes would be put in one pile. There were rumors that among the POWs many managed to get clothes and then mix with people who came to work, and escape. I was prototypically Jewish-looking and the POWs knew that they needn't fear me. I was approached by one of the POWs and was asked how he could escape. I pointed to the clothes and he understood my sign and managed to escape. One night the electric power was cut off and there was darkness. People were whispering in secret that it was done by Dania Alperovich, the son of Chaim Abraham, who worked in the carpentry of Chaim Zokofsky. The carpentry was right next to the meat market and the electric lines ran through the carpentry. Among the escapees that day were two POWs who managed to reach the Ungerman pool. When they realized that someone was following them they hid under a bridge, and there they were found and murdered.

The Flyers

It was the end of August and the nights became colder. We still met at Nyomka's house and still didn't know what to do. Shimon was very excited about the POWs who escaped. He said that some were experienced soldiers and they could help us with the Resistance unit. He suggested that we make flyers and that perhaps they would reach some POWs who had escaped and were now in hiding. Meanwhile, he improved the printing press, but there was still a problem. We didn't have letters to use for the printing. Josef Norman, the man with whom I learned to print, was working on the printing press that was now in the hands of the Germans. Therefore, we decided that I would meet with him and tell him our plan. Perhaps we could get the letters from him.

In the first days after the Germans entered the Vileyka district they ordered all the Jewish males from Vileyka to come to a certain place. From there, they took them to a bridge next to the river and murdered them. The few who didn't show up as the Germans had ordered managed to survive. Now many Jews of Kurenets were taken under police watch to Vileyka to do different jobs: cutting wood, cleaning streets, doing park work, and other work. I was also taken. One day when I was near the printing place, I found the courage, entered the building, and met Josef. I told him promptly what I wanted, whispering for him to collect a few letters for me. When I came back three days later, he gave me a little package with letters, papers, and black ink. We managed to meet a few times and eventually I had a lot of letters and printing materials to accomplish the mission.

The Germans at that point were not watching us strictly. If they were suspicious of anything, they would just kill us on the spot. That's why it was doable. My mother helped me. She took pieces of cloth and made pockets and that's where I kept the letters. In each pocket, I had a different letter. We thought that if there was a moment of danger, we could immediately use the cloths as aprons and we wouldn't look so suspicious. One day when we returned from Vileyka to Kurenets, I had a little package from Josef. The Germans started taking us to a different location. I was very worried, but soon we realized that they wanted to show us something—two gentiles they had hung for robbing someone. They wanted us to see what happened to all who disobeyed. After that, they let us go home. When I went home, I saw that they had also hung someone in the town center for robbing.

We dug a hideout in the ground and there I hid the letters and printing materials. Except for my cousin Zalman, no one knew where we were making the printed materials. Even our own troop members did not know. We decided that if anyone got caught, it was better if they didn't know where it was. At that time, the house of Nathan, my uncle, also became a meeting place for us. Nathan sensed that we were doing something dangerous and was very fearful. Nathan's wife, Batia nee Ayeshiski was sick; she was in a nursing home when the war started. She tried to go back home, but she died from starvation on the road.

Nathan felt very responsible for his orphaned children and was fearful that what Zalman was doing would cause danger to his other children.

At that time the Germans printed flyers for the villagers saying, "Farmer, keep your bread. Don't give it to the criminals. They will eat it and then they will hurt you and burn your farm. Keep your bread for the German army that released you from communism." As an answer, Shimon Zirolnik wrote our first flyer. It said, "Farmer keep your bread for yourself and your heroic brothers who fight the horrible conqueror. Don't give one seed to Germans. Death to Hitler." We printed about 100 and distributed them in various places. Our Shimon was able to see the first flyer, but a few days later Shimon didn't come to the meeting. We found out he was imprisoned; with him a non-Jewish farmer was taken and another town resident was also imprisoned, our town barber Leibe with the beautiful voice. When he would cut hair, he would sing beautiful songs. After a time, we found out that the Germans murdered them and it was a horrible blow to us. We so loved Shimon. If I mention the barber Leibe, I must say a few words about him. As I told you, while he cut hair he would sing songs. I still remember one of his songs, which he sang in Russian. He would sing it with deep expression, and it would go like this. "I will die, I will die. They will bury me and no one will know where my grave is and no one will know to come to my grave. But one morning in spring a nightingale will see it and sing." How ironic the song was. Could Leibe ever imagine that this song would accurately foretell what was going to occur?

During that time, there was little Underground activity in our area. There were rumors that the Russians had parachuted some troops in and they managed to burn many German supply rooms; that's what the Germans were referring to in the flyers regarding criminals. Our own flyers were found by Jews from the town, and this gave them hope that there was an Underground. Someone even showed me a flyer. Zalman Gurevitch, who had many friends among the villagers, helped a lot with the flyers. He knew who should be informed. Moreover, he knew who could distribute them among the population.

No Secrets

The desire to do something, to fight, existed in many Jews, but the possibilities were close to nil. As for us, our small group, we were particularly united since we had a similar past with strong ties to the youth movement. Besides, we were so young and still believed in the impossible. At times we received emotional pleas from older people, as well as from very young ones, to join our company. I remember how Shimon Alperovich, the son of Zishka (son of Shimon), once came to the house of Nyomka Schulman when we gathered there. Shimon was much older than we were and he was a much-respected person. And now he approached us sounding very worried and not knowing where to get help. He asked us to let him join our group. In Yiddish he said, "*Fragst nit anmir*" (Don't forget me). He was almost begging. [Later on he joined the Partisans and died fighting.] Also very emotional was the plea of Araleh Gordon, son of Shaptai, brother of Riva and Mikhla, who was much younger than we were, still a child. He asked to join us. We said to him, "Araleh, do you have a weapon?" And Araleh naively and with a hint of embarrassment said he didn't have a weapon at the time but he knew how to play the mandolin. He tried to explain to us that there was a need in the Resistance for a social life, and that until the day he received a weapon he could be an entertainer. Until today I feel excitement when I remember his plea. We were sure that our Resistance unit was secret and soon it was clear to us that there were no secrets in our world and that many knew about our unit. We still had a very unclear idea as to how we would resist, and many would come to us urging us to take them into our ranks. [Araleh Gordon was killed while hiding from the Germans (in a tree?)]

Chaim Zukovsky owned a sawmill and carpentry mill that had been taken away by the Nazis, and now an army officer managed it. Someone told us in secret that the officer was actually a decent man, a unique person who disliked the Germans' behavior towards the Jews. To us it was an unbelievable phenomenon, particularly remembering our neighbor Shernagovitz, the murderer who killed Jews daily; thus, to find a person among the Germans who was such a righteous person was a true miracle. We were told that once, when the drunken Shernagovitz approached the area aiming to torture the Jews who worked there, the German hid them inside a cold boiler and saved them from being murdered. We somehow found out that this German was willing to sell weapons to the Jews. I don't remember now who gave us this information, but we found out that he was willing to sell a Nagan with seven bullets for ten gold rubles. We gave the money to Yankeleh, the son of Chaim Zalman, so he could give the money to the son of Lazar Shlomo, who had contacts with the German man, and he bought the weapon. When we sent someone to Lazar Shlomo to transfer the Nagan to us, he refused to give us the weapon, so we decided to trick him into returning the weapon. Some of us approached his house at a night hour when there was a curfew. We pretended to be Germans and yelled, "*Juden heraus*!" We gave them enough time to run, and when we found out that they had hidden and the house was empty, we left a note in which we said that if they would not give us the weapon, the consequences would be severe. We sent Yankeleh, the son of Chaim Zalman Gurevich, and he also wanted to keep the weapon for himself after receiving it, but after some threats he gave it to us. I point this out to you to show how many wanted weapons so they could fight the Germans.

The Germans kept demanding money from the Judenrat. Some of the members of the Judenrat were dishonest and took some of the money for themselves. In our home were a new couch and carpet that we bought before the war for my sister Henia, who was about to be married. When the war started, Henia's groom was taken to the Polish army and died during a battle between the Polish and the Germans. One of the Judenrat people, the very worst among them, knew about the sofa and the carpet, so now he demanded that we give those things to the Germans, who asked for furniture and carpets. My sister Henia was very much against it. These things were very dear to her as a reminder of her dead groom, and she asked that they be left with her. The Judenrat man slapped her and took her things by force. When I found out about it, I came to the Judenrat and I said to the man, "You must know that we will never let you, a Jew, slap another Jew. It's enough the way we are treated by the Germans." He answered, yelling, "What do you think? Do you think I am afraid of your gun? Do you think I don't know you own a gun?" "It is not a secret that I have a gun," I replied, and I pulled out my weapon. He must not have thought I'd react so fast and he went pale and never came to our home again.

The head of the Judenrat and some of its members were new arrivals from other towns. They were not always decent or honest, and it wasn't the rescue of the community that was foremost in their minds. The people who were the public servants before, whose names were famous for dedication and good deeds, like Zalman Gvint and others like him, clearly knew that being a member of the Judenrat meant having to fulfill the wishes of the Germans, and they could never accept such a job. Zalman Gvint, who was experienced with pharmaceuticals, established an enterprise at this time with Nathan Gurevich to make chemicals for soap, shoe polish, and ink. They suffered much at the hands of the Judenrat, which demanded their products. Leib Motosov had a place in the deep forest before the war that made turpentine and tar. He knew all the little paths in the forest. He also clearly understood that the Nazis would soon annihilate us. So he came to Zalman Gvint, who agreed with him, and suggested that they should escape to the forest, where he knew many of the villagers in the area and thought that since they were friends they would help him. They started planning their escape. I also remember that my mother in those days talked a lot about leaving the town and escaping to the forest. While everyone was planning such an escape, a tragic event took place. Some families escaped to the forest secretly from everyone, among them Zishka Alperovich's family, but someone informed on them and the mutilated bodies were brought to town. It was a huge disappointment for all who dreamed of going to the forest, and it momentarily shocked everyone and caused them to postpone their plans. Nyomka Shulman, who was very energetic and a go-getter, was still full of excitement and plans. He was the leader of our group, and he came with an idea to lift the spirits of the people. We did something that was dishonest, that we should not have done. We made a pamphlet of encouragement, filled with imaginary events that had no basis in reality. In this pamphlet we wrote that the wonderful Red Army pushed the Germans out of the Polaczek area and soon would free our entire area. We ended it with the words, "Death to Hitler."

There was a rumor that something might happen in Polaczek, but to say that the Germans lost there was a greatly exaggerated statement. Anyway, the Jews were greatly encouraged by this pamphlet and talked about it, especially Motl Leib Kuperstock, who used to have a flourmill. He would stand in the synagogue among the Jews, spreading the rumor that the pamphlet had come from the Soviets. They beat the Germans, he would tell everyone, and were going through Polaczek. This had to have been done by planes, he added, and since we were only 120 km from there, it would not take long until they reached our area. Motl Leib was very interested in politics and strategies. There was a time when he lived in the United States, and he knew how to add certain sentences in English that greatly impressed the people, the residents of the town. Among the people who spoke with him, there was someone who took his samples and said he really knew that the retreat of the Soviets was only a trick and that they would quickly show the Nazis their might. For some days they were talking like this, but there was great disappointment when nothing happened. We felt bad about what we had done and from then on we decided to write only real news.

Time passed and Noach Dinestein from Vileyka joined our group.

He was older than we were but was once a soldier in the Polish army. In 1939, when the Germans and the Polish fought, he was drafted. After a battle with the Germans, his unit suffered greatly. He was somehow able to escape, and he came back to our area. When the Germans killed the man in Vileyka near the bridge on the Vilia during the first month of the war in our area, Noach somehow escaped from the place and arrived at Kurenets. Here he taught us how to use weapons and trained us in other military operations.

The Code Name is Volodia

One day I was told that a Christian person had come to our house and asked for me. She later returned and met with me. It was a young village girl who looked much like a Christian, but she was really a Jewish girl by the name of Bertha Dimmenstein from the village of Khalafi, a little village near Vileyka. I didn't know her earlier and had no idea she was Jewish. She showed me our first pamphlet and said that she knew there was a secret printing press in Kurenets. I was very worried and I pretended to know nothing about it. I continued being worried when she told me she belonged to a group of young villagers who organized themselves to fight the Nazis. She said that these young villagers wanted to meet us, since they knew we were also an Underground unit. She also told me that she had a text that was ready to be printed by our unit. She said to me that if I could print the text it would be proof that they could rely on us, and they would get in touch for later missions. She said she would come back the next day and take the pamphlets and they would distribute them on their own.

The text she gave me was very similar to what we had written. It asked the locals to organize against the Nazi invaders and unite with the Resistance. I was very confused and didn't know if I should trust her. I asked my friends to come to a meeting. Among them were Eliyau Alperovich, Itzkaleh Einbender, Zalman Gurevich, Noach Dinestein, and Nyomka Shulman, at whose house the meeting took place. We met in a dark room in his home. Once again, the question arose as to whether someone was tricking us. Some thought yes, some thought no. I thought that we should wait a while, but Nyomka Shulman finally won. He said that there was no reason to wait, that we had to print the pamphlet. So, that night I already sat in our hideout and joined letter to letter, and after a short time the pamphlet was ready. I only printed twenty copies. I thought that to prove our loyalty and reliability this would be sufficient. All the time I was very fearful that Bertha would arrive with someone from the authorities, and a great weight was lifted from my heart when I realized she had come alone. I explained to her that I could only print twenty pamphlets. Bertha took them and promised to return shortly. Many years later, when I met Josef Norman in Israel, he told me how Bertha had found out about me. Bertha, who knew Josef from Vileyka and knew that he was working in the printing house, thought that Josef might know something about those secret pamphlets. So when she met him, he told her about me. He knew that she was very reliable and didn't hesitate to give her all the information. And this was how she found me.

Shortly thereafter, Bertha returned and told me that their unit was ready to join with us for missions. She also told me that eventually they were planning on going to the forest and starting to fight the Nazis. She also asked me if we had any weapons. I told her that we had only two rifles. I didn't tell her about the guns. She suggested that one of our people should come to them. The meeting would take place in the village of Volkoviczina. At the entrance to the village, she said, there was a small building, a Christian prayer house. She said that one of our people should be there during a certain night, and there he would call out a certain code word that would let him into the house. The code word was Volodia.

Once again, we met. The energetic Nyomka insisted that he should be the first messenger. Nyomka went during a late night hour and met with one of their people. The fellow suggested that at this point we should keep our group small and not add any members. Most of our energy should be put into collecting weapons and food to be ready to go to the forest. During that meeting the man told Nyomka that he must never come to Volkoviczina without first being contacted by them. We would receive instructions from them, and Bertha would be the main contact. Most important, from now on the code word would be Volodia. Nyomka slept there, and the next day, early in the morning, he returned to town and told us all the details. At about that time I was told by Josef Norman that he could not give me any more letters, since they realized that something was not right at the printing press and they thought that something dangerous was going on.

At this point, the Germans only killed single Jews in Kurenets, here and there in small numbers, and life continued like that until Simchat Torah in 1941, when they killed 54 Jews of Kurenets.

The Fifty-Four

Now, in years of peace and quiet, we refer back to those days as the Day's of Torment. The synagogues were filled with people praying. Most people seemed a bit numb. They didn't scream or cry. To people on the outside, it appeared as if people had put up some kind of barrier, but in the synagogue it seems that this barrier was broken. The tears and the cries were heartbreaking, and the line of people who said Kaddish for the dead was very long. The people in our group who were secular in nature also went to the synagogue.

The management of Zukovsky's old carpentry mill called for Kopel Spektor because there was something wrong with the main machine there. Maybe now it is time to talk about Kopel.

Something was kept very secret. During the Soviet days Kopel, who was an engineer and an inventor, worked on a machine to automatically load coal to keep the fires going in train engines. It was almost ready to be patented when the war started. In the train station in Molodechno, Kopel had a laboratory where he had all the papers that had to do with his invention. During the war between the Germans and the Soviets, he went to his laboratory and burned his papers and inventions so they would not fall into the hands of the Nazis.

Back to that Simhat Torah.... As usual we went that day to Vileyka. The women walked in front and I walked at the back along with the men. We passed by the village of Zimordra, and all of a sudden, two policemen from Kurenets and the Nazi collaborators, Pietka Dovsky and Pietka Gintov, who studied with me at the Polish school, appeared and ordered me to return to Kurenets. I felt that there was some danger facing me, so I asked, "Pietka, why do you stop me? We used to be friends."

"Satan is your friend," Pietka answered, "Not me. Come with us." So I was brought to town and put in the store of Itzka Leah, the place the police now used to keep prisoners. When I got there I met other Jews from the town, among them Kazdan, Chaim Zukovsky, Zev Rabunski, and others, more than twenty people. Once in a while they would bring new prisoners. We looked outside the windows and saw that they had assembled the families of the prisoners. One person who was with us said he was arrested for the red flag found in his home. During Soviet days, everyone had a red flag, and he forgot about it. Now he was taken to the prison along with his flag. Some of the prisoners started screaming that for this flag, everyone would be killed. They wanted to take the flag, rip it up, throw it on the ground, and cover it with their shoes. While the prisoners were talking about it, the police came in and took out ten people. We watched through the shutters as these people were given the hose and marched away. Once again people wondered what was going on. Some said they were being taken out for a job. Chaim Zukovsky, who was badly beaten and depressed, said they were not being taken to work, but were being taken to dig their own graves. All of a sudden the door opened and into the room came a German Oberlieutenant who called me by name. He took me outside and told me that I should point to my relatives who were standing outside. "This is my mother and those are my sisters." I pointed to my mother, Rohaleh, Rashkaleh, and Doba. "Take them and go home," the officer told me, and I was ready to do it but all of a sudden he hesitated, as if he had changed his mind. "Jew, you still need to receive some beatings."

I lay on the ground in the presence of my mother and sisters, and he beat me many times. Finally he stopped and ordered me to leave. I could hardly get up, and left with my mother Rohaleh. I had no idea why I was taken out of the prison room and separated from the fifty-four Jews, residents of our town, who were murdered that day. After they got the hose, they were made to dig their own graves, as Chaim Zukovsky foretold while we were in there. When we got home, my sister Doba said she had seen me being taken from the people who went to Vileyka and she realized my life was in danger, so she left the group of girls and ran to Kurenets. As soon as she got home she told my mother what had happened. They knew it was a very dangerous situation and they had to do something immediately.

Without hesitation they immediately went to Mataroz, the Polish teacher, to ask for his help. In town, people already knew that the Germans were planning to do something against the communists. They decided that my father and my sister Henia, who were known as communists, should flee and take the cows to the meadow, so when they came for them they wouldn't find them at home. Rohaleh and Doba spoke to Mataroz, who liked me very much from when I was a student and who was now the mayor of the town appointed by the Germans, and they told him about my imprisonment. As soon as they left Mataroz, they were taken by the police, as were my mother and Rashkaleh, and it was Mataroz who decided to save us all from our deaths. Two days later I went to Mataroz to thank him for what he had done. At that point we were all heartbroken over what had happened in town. He asked me to sit down and I told him I could not sit down because my back had awful wounds from the beatings I had received. When I thanked him, he said I shouldn't thank him and that I should pray to God and stay a human being as I had been in the past, and stay decent despite the tortures that occurred every day.

I felt strongly that to show our thanks we should give him some material from the old store we used to own. Material could be used for suits for him and his son. He was very much against it and got mad at me. I was very embarrassed and didn't know what to do, so I suggested something else. I asked him to take our cow, since our lives seemed to be pretty much over, with or without a cow. He answered that he agreed to take the cow, since we had so much trouble even trying to take it to the meadow, but he had one condition. He would accept it if we would take half of the milk from the cow each time he milked it. I said to him that this could cause him great troubles as the mayor of a town, sending milk to a Jewish family. At the end we reached an agreement and gave him the cow. Secretly, in all sorts of ways, he was able to transfer milk to us. Now I know how he saved me from certain death: after Doba and Rohaleh visited him, he went to the German officer who was conducting the murder of the fifty-four people for being communists. He told the officer about how I helped him during the Soviet days by giving sugar and food to the teacher Skarntani, who was anti-communist, and that I had helped him when he was very sick and put myself in danger. This proved I was anti-communist, so I could not be blamed for communism. The officer accepted his opinion, and this was how I was rescued.

The Jews were shocked at the killing of the fifty-four who were supposedly communists. Everyone was talking about how the fifty-four men, women, and children were taken to the forest of Lovitz, and there they were ordered to dig their graves before they were killed. The Christians, especially the villagers who were present, told many stories about the killing, especially the brave stand of Yankeleh Orchik's (son) Alperovich. When Yankeleh stood at his open grave, he said to the officer who was ordering the killings, "If you kill me because I am a Jew, there is nothing I can do since I am a Jew and this is my faith. But if you kill me because I am a communist, you should know that since the Soviets sent my father to Siberia, I am an anti-communist. Can you really believe that my father who is being tortured in Siberia is a communist?" The officer decided to release him as well as his younger brother. The Christians who were watching admitted that Orchik Alperovich was sent to Siberia.

They also told about Tevel Alperovich, the son of Pinhas the butcher. Tevel, who was a very strong and good-looking man, was able to escape from the killers but he encountered Volodka, the son of Mishka from the alley. With a hoe in his hand, he hit him on the head and wounded him. Then he called the Germans to kill him. The reason why the Christians would gather in such places to watch the killings was so they could collect belongings such as clothes, shoes, etc. Some of the Christians would sing while the Jews were being taken to their deaths. They made a sang, "*Zhydi, zhydi, tzerti. Kali vas femerti,*" which means "Jews, the son of Satan, die already! When? When?" During their singing they would sometimes throw rocks at the Jews and curse them. Many of the Jews in town wanted to believe the Germans: that this murder was meant only for communists. They were hoping that now all the murders would be done with, but our group, as well as many others in Kurenets, knew that this would not be the end, that it was only the first in systematic killings, and our desire to fight increased tenfold.

For My Benefactor, Mataroz

Once again, I visited Mataroz. Mataroz, in his true nature, was liberal. As far as the Jews, he tried to help; this was not unknown by the Belarussian population, and they greatly disliked him. One of his opponents was the son of the surgical practitioner, Surikvas. There was a certain rumor that the son secretly put a picture of Pilsudski in Mataroz's office and told the German police that Mataroz was secretly organizing Polish Resistance. The Germans imprisoned him, but he somehow immediately returned to become mayor. [Reminder: the Germans killed him with his family.]

I came to Mataroz after he asked me to come to him. He immediately told me that murder was facing me everywhere I went and that he would try to help me. Further, he said, "You must know that between wishes and ability there is a big distance. I truly wish that all my students will survive, but what can I really do? As far as you are concerned, I suggest you come to the school as a laborer doing cleaning and cutting wood for the fire, as well as operating the furnaces." At that point he was no longer head of the school, but since he was mayor he was able to do it. He was also in cahoots with one of the teachers. He still said to me that I must be very careful to be there only when the school was empty of students. I later found out that the person he was in touch with was the wife of Skrentani, who was a teacher in the school. Skretntani himself worked for Mataroz in the municipal building, as head of the food distribution department.

I was told to be in school during afternoon hours until the time of curfew, when I was supposed to be home. Mataroz said that since danger faced me in every direction, it would be easier to escape from the school in times of extreme danger than from places where Jews were plentiful. Further, he said he would try to get me a special permit as a worker of the municipality, so I could work outdoors even during curfew hours. Once again he emphasized that in case of an action where they would kill the Jews, I would have to hide in the school. There would be a greater chance of survival there, since it was unlikely that they would look for Jews in the school. There was a huge basement with many secret corners that I could hide in. He also gave me a letter to take to the police which asked for permission to work at night, since I needed to clean the school after the students left. When I entered I only found Baliznuk, who was known as the most evil torturer. "How do you think this will help you? With such a Jewish face, to get a permission from the police!" He started laughing. "Before I would ever get a look at the permission you might receive, I would shoot you with a bullet and the permission would not bring you back to life." Still, he gave me the permission.

In the school worked a Polish woman who explained my duties to me. She was generally kind to me but she was very fearful that my presence in the school would hurt her. She begged me to be very careful and to make sure that no one would suspect that she was hiding a Jew at the school. Every time she had a hint of danger, she would quickly tell me to go hide in the basement.

The first day after finishing my work I didn't stay at school. I went home with my permit. It was a late night hour; I quietly passed the market and saw not one living soul: no Germans, no policemen. When I told my friends about it, someone said that even the Germans were afraid to walk around at night, and we felt some pleasure in knowing that. I don't know if it was smart, but I always carried my gun with the three bullets, though I didn't know if they were viable. I was thinking that if someone bothered me at night, I would draw the gun and this would hopefully be enough. One night I remembered that I had hidden a knife in the gardens near the school. I went there and found it and took it to our cowshed, and there I wrapped it in a rag and hid it.

Nights passed and no one bothered me. The only person who seemed to follow me with her eyes was my mother, who stood by the window and looked out from behind the shutters to see if I was coming. Only when I arrived could she sleep. She begged me to stay in the school and not come at night. One night, when I returned home, all of a sudden I heard a shout of, "*Stoi! stoi!*" which means "Stand! Stand!" I was very afraid that someone was shooting my direction. I went through the gardens behind the houses until I reached the middle synagogue. I went to the central floor, where the women sat, and slept. In the morning I came home and found my mother very fearful. As it turned out, she didn't sleep a wink that night. She also heard the shouts and thought that maybe I was killed. The next day we found out that it was a drunken policeman who had yelled at a pig to quiet down. When the pig didn't listen, he shot it. From that night on, I stayed in the school's basement and only when morning came did I return home. In the basement I found a small tool that could be used for counterfeiting money. I thought that I might be able to use it to counterfeit ID cards, but in the meantime I left it there. Zalman Gurevich was able to connect with Kostya from the village of Litvinki. He was the son of Januk. Anyway, he sold Zalman a gun with a few bullets.

The winter of 1941-42 was a very difficult winter. The hope that the so-called communist Jews would be the last to be killed proved wrong. One day the Germans came from Vileyka and kidnapped some Jews and demanded that they take their clothes off. Half naked, they were put in cars and driven through town. The Jews in town were told that they must pay large sums of money in order to avoid their killing. The large sums were paid. On another day, the killers Egov and Shernagovitz played a bloody game. They killed thirteen Jews, among them the rabbi of the town, Rav Moshe Aharon Feldman. He was a gentle soul, pure and honest. His death was very torturous. They broke his arms and legs and his entire body until he passed away. His body was put out in the main market for days, until finally the killers allowed the Jews to take him for burial. Our group continued to meet, fully knowing that our fate was written and our situation would become worse and worse. As I said earlier, many tried to join us. Among them was Shimon Alperovich, who eventually was added to our ranks. When I speak of that, I remember the image of Arczik Shulman [the translator's great-grandfather], the father of Nyomka, who was a tanner by profession. He knew very well what we were talking about in the dark room in his home, but he never, ever tried to say anything against it. We felt very much that in his quietness there was full agreement with what we were doing. One day, Lazar Shlomo said to him, "Arczik, don't think for a minute that I don't know that your son came behind my home one night to scare me. You must know that those children, and among them your son Nyomka, are playing with fire." In those days it was enough for one tiny ember to spark a great fire that could engulf the entire community of Jewish Kurenets. He was referring to the time we demanded that he return the gun that we had bought. Although Nyomka's father, Arczik, told us about the meeting, he was not complaining. He told it to us only for informational purposes.

Mataroz also arranged for Nyomka to work for the municipality. Nyomka became responsible for the warehouses where the food was stored. During the wartime, the town had no money and payments were done with an exchange of food.

A Tale of a Mouse and a Tartar

As soon as Bertha found out that Nyomka was responsible for the food warehouses, she decided that this could be used for our missions, so once in a while someone would come from Bertha's group to Nyomka and would take food supplies secretly to Volkoviczina. This took place shortly after Mataroz was imprisoned one day and later released. Bertha told me there were rumors he would be imprisoned again. They found out that someone was spreading rumors against him. Anyhow, sometime around January of 1942, or maybe February, on a Sunday that was very cold, I collected papers and put them in a container near the furnace. I didn't pay attention, but while I was transferring the papers to the furnace a big mouse somehow went in, and when I threw the papers in, he started burning and the smell became horrible. Although I opened the furnace, it didn't help, so when the students came back on Monday the smell was horrible. Mataroz called me to his office immediately.

"What happened?" he asked me when we were alone. I told him about the mouse, and while we were conversing he told me he had heard a rumor that Nyomka was taking certain provisions from the warehouses and transferring them to underground elements. He was worried about the idea of Nyomka putting himself in such danger and not maintaining our secrecy well enough. While speaking, he suddenly asked me, "And what about you? It is clear that in such situations you will not be able to continue working in the school. Are you also thinking of joining some underground group?" I was not worried about Mataroz and I was very honest with him. I said I belonged to such a group and I urged him to join us. He immediately answered, "My dear, our ways are very different, and what is appropriate for you is not appropriate for me. Our ways are very different." I answered, "Our ways may be different, but our enemy is the same enemy!" He looked at me with a sad expression and said, "Go, child, and may God take you on the right route. But remember to be careful and not to burn any mice. To Nyomka Shulman, tell him to be very careful too." [About six months later, in the summer of 1942, the Germans killed Mataroz and his family.]

At that point I would stay in the school at night and during the day I would write pamphlets for Bertha. As soon as my mother would see me putting my boots on, she knew I was going to a place other than the school and ask me, "Where are you going, Nachum? You must tell me." I tried very hard not to tell her and explained to her why it was important that she not know. "As I told you before, about the time I found the old Soviet IDs in the apartment of Aunt Rashka [which was used as the headquarters of the Soviets from 1939 to 1941], I used one of the IDs with one of my pictures and used the name Hantieb (a Tartar name), and I kept working on saying my name and information with a Tartar accent." My mother, who knew of my doings and very much agreed with me that I should help the Resistance asked, "What do you need with these fake IDs? They will not help you; they will only cause you trouble." "Look, Mother, there is much value in these fake names. If I am killed and they find this ID, they will think I am a Tartar in the service of the Soviets and they will not come to Kurenets to ask questions. But in case I am only wounded and they torture me, they might come to you, and it's better if you don't have any information." My mother accepted my explanation and didn't ask anymore.

The other people with Bertha were Ivan Sirotzin, Basilik, Yorka Balashov, Matyo Kevitz, Nikolai Sirotzin, Sovatz, and Zina Bitzon, all non-Jews. At this point, all we did was print pamphlets and talk about going to the forest. By then, we had already printed twenty different pamphlets. We waited impatiently for the winter to pass, and the dream to go to the forest was postponed.

As time passed, the number of Partisans in Volkoviczina grew. At the head of the group was Volodia [codename], who escaped from the POW camp in Kurenets, and who now worked for one of the villagers.   In the month of February 1942, we were invited to meet the Partisan troop. One night Itzkaleh Einbender, Nyomka Shulman, Zalman Gurevich, and I were invited to come to Volkoviczina. We arrived at a small forest at the edge of the village, and there we met with Volodia, the head of the troop, after saying the code word "Volodia." He urged us to collect weapons and to ready ourselves to go to the forest at the end of the winter. He also told us to prepare clothes and food, but to keep everything very secret. When he found out that I was the one responsible for the pamphlets, he said that they were planning to write a periodic newsletter; for that, the supplies I had would not be enough, so he urged me to go to work at a printing press in Vileyka, where I might be able to confiscate some more letters. He also urged us to give them all the rifles and weapons we had so they could keep them for us until we moved to the forest. We sat with him for half an hour and then returned to Kurenets. We went in a roundabout way so they couldn't find us, through the fields that took us to the forest of Tzavina, and then we separated and each one went to his home, back to the daily tortures of our lives.

Nyomka continued to transfer products to the Volkoviczina group, and Bertha would visit us and tell us news she had heard on the radio about the situation at the front. One Sunday, we once again went to Volkoviczina and returned at a very late hour. We used the fields near Smorgon Street and not Vileyka Street. Vileyka Street used to be the street that people took long walks on. It had old cedar trees, and it would take you to Jewish Vileyka. But now there was no more Jewish Vileyka, and Vileyka Street was also out of our reach as Jews, since now the German police were situated there, so we returned home in a roundabout way, and arrived in the village of Tzavina: Itzkaleh, Nyomka, Zalman, Yorka Balshov (a non-Jewish Partisan from the Volkoviczina troop) and me. Yorka came from the Vostok (the east, Soviet territory). He was a serious young man and very dedicated to his job. When we neared the village of Tzavina, we heard sounds of singing and dancing. A party was taking place in one of the homes. Itzkaleh looked through a window and realized that that among the celebrators was Pietka Gintov, a policeman who was one of the evil and ugly killers. Itzkaleh came back and said that this was a good time to pay Pietka what he deserved. He was ready to go in and do the deed. Yorka was very much against it, since Itzkaleh would be easily recognized and this would endanger all the Jewish residents of the town. He volunteered to do it, since no one knew him and the town would not pay for it. So he went into the house with a drawn gun, and since he didn't know what Pietka Gintov looked like, he asked, "Who here is a policeman?" Someone was able to darken the place immediately. Itzkaleh immediately ran, trying to identify Pietka in the darkness, but Pietka was able to escape, as did the celebrating people who thought that a big Partisan troop had come there. Itzkaleh was at first very mad that he was not allowed to do it the way he wished, but Yorka said he shouldn't take it so deeply, because even if we didn't succeed now, we would succeed later, and even if we didn't succeed, we had learned something from it. We could see that the policemen were scared to death of the Partisans, and this was something we should not forget.

Letters and an Author

It seems as if the Nazis would choose Jewish holidays on purpose for their evil deeds. The holy day of Purim was approaching, and the cold was horrible that year, but despite the fact that we had no more wood to burn in our furnaces, the idea that the German army was suffering this cold on the Russian front pleased us greatly, especially since we found out that there were certain battles where they were defeated. But then came Purim, and our pleasure in knowing about the German defeats was eclipsed by our huge tragedy. During that day, the Germans killed the last of the surviving Jews of Vileyka, and many of the Jews were brought in for forced labor, among them Jews from Kurenets. The information was brought to us by Zina Bitzon, a woman who belonged to the Partisan group in Volkoviczina. She said they would bring workers from Kurenets to Vileyka, and she suggested that this would be a good time for me to be accepted into the printing house in Vileyka. Soon everyone found out about Vileyka, and the Judenrat told us that the German authorities demanded certain professional people, among them carpenters, shoemakers, tailors, furriers, metalworkers, and others.

Our family was very worried about the fate of my sisters Henia and Rochaleh, who worked and lived in Vileyka. We knew that Rochaleh worked for the Germans in the post office, and Henia worked for the group of painters by cleaning their rooms and cooking for them. We hoped they had escaped the killing, but soon we found out that they were both murdered. My sister Henia, who was so close to me, who said she was ready to wash floors and do everything so I would be able to study and improve my life, was dead. How my heart cried for my sisters Henia and Rochaleh, my beloved sisters, who in their lives and in their deaths did not separate.

My mother, who was heartbroken, begged Doba and me to go to Vileyka and find a job. I didn't tell my mother or my sister of my plans to work at the printing press. Many of the Jews of Kurenets came to Vileyka to be taken to work. Some of them had no profession but hoped they would be lucky and get accepted there, thinking that might save their lives.

We arrived in Vileyka in the afternoon and we were put in front of the Gvitz Commissar Schmidt. With him was his assistant Handl, who said to us, via the interpreter from Kurenets, Schatz (an Austrian Jew who came to Kurenets and who was now the head of the Judenrat in Vileyka), "Shoemakers, go to this site, carpenters to this site, tailors to this site…" Handl never once mentioned anything about printers. I was very confused and didn't know what to do. My sister Doba kept nudging me quietly and said, "Why are you standing here and waiting? Go and mingle with the professionals." Finally Handl called me and asked what my profession was. I was very confused and said, "*Schriftsteller*" which in German meant, "Author." At that moment I thought that this was the right name for someone who puts letters together in a printing house. The word "*Schriftsteller*" made Handl very mad. He started screaming at me with disgust, mocking me. "*Du bist ein Schriftsteller? Ah. Ein Schriftsteller bist du?*" I was sure that my fate was sealed, but I immediately started correcting myself, explaining that I fixed letters in a printing place. Handl quieted for a minute and was pensive, then all of a sudden said, "Tomorrow to the printing press." That's how it was. The next day I was accepted as a worker at the printing press.

The grief that came over my family when we found out that Henia and Rochaleh were killed was unbearable. My father took it as a sign from heaven, and he cried bitterly before God when he recited the Kaddish for them. I remember that one day our Christian friend Kostya from Diaditz came to us to take part in our mourning. He once again clarified that he would always help us, and his house would be open to us; even if it would endanger him, we would be able to hide there. We gave him some of our belongings, clothes, and supplies to keep. We knew that he was an honest man who was telling us the truth and that we could always rely on him. I found out about Kostya's visit when I came one Sunday for a vacation. We would work for six days, and on Sundays we would get time off to go to Kurenets. We were taken both ways by policemen. The reason why they wanted us to go to Kurenets was so we could clean ourselves and change clothes. The Germans wanted to maintain certain hygienic conditions.

My first day of work at the printing press was a difficult day. When I entered and said that Handl had sent me there, I was greeted by the manager of the printing house, a Christian by the name of Byelosov. Other than my friend Josef Norman, there were two other non-Jews who worked there. One was Nikolai Lazar, and the second was Matvei Matvievich, who was once a Soviet POW who somehow was able to get a job there. There were also two Christian girls, Manya and Sonia, who helped with the printing but who mainly kept the place clean. So as soon as I came there, Byelosov looked at my boots and said, "You have nice boots. It would be a good idea if you gave me your boots since the Germans will murder you and take your boots anyway." I answered, "I don't care who will take my boots after I die, but in my lifetime I will not give them to anyone."

Matvei was a very gentle and spiritual person. You could see it from his expression. He thought I was a remnant of the Jews of Vileyka, who at that point had all been killed, and he whispered to me, "After what happened here, why are you sitting here and working for them? Why aren't you escaping to the forest?" When I heard what he said I became worried. Despite his face, which appeared very gentle, those were difficult days and it was hard to know where trouble might come from. Who knows? Maybe he would spy on me and trick me, I thought. So I looked at him quietly, like a person who didn't understand the hint when he said "the forest." Secretly, I told Josef Norman about the plans and why I was sent there. Josef once again emphasized that it was very dangerous, that they might notice that letters were missing. As I continued working there, I discovered that Byelosov was not a bad person; he was just a chatterbox and didn't mean ill. When he asked me for my boots it was just chatter, and it contained no evil.

Most of the work involved printing announcements, letters, and accounts of office supplies for the Germans. Most times the letters were in both Russian and German. The German letters were smaller than the Russian ones, but since we wanted the printing to be pleasant and not uneven, we added something to the letters and I became the specialist in this. I also became more fluent in German during this time. Truthfully, the other workers in the printing shop did not know any German. Often I was sent to the Gvitz Commissar to see him and his assistant Handl, or to Kiborik, who was the education officer, and I became the go-between. They gave me materials to print and they received the finished materials from me.

Each day when I was done with my work, I would go to the ghetto in Vileyka and stay there until the next morning. It wasn't the usual ghetto, but this was the place where they kept the Jewish workers. It was located behind the public park and the municipal hospital, close to the Jewish slaughterhouse from years before. The place was not really guarded. There was no fence, and Schatz was responsible for the guarding. Schatz used to be the head of the Judenrat in Kurenets and now was situated here in Vileyka. Also there was my sister Doba, and also Kopel Spektor with his brother Eliyau and his two sisters, Esther and Dinka. Kopel was very, very close to his family, and now never separated from them, and this is how we explained to ourselves his not being so close to us at this point. Once in a while Handl, the assistant to the Gvitz Commissar, would come around and torture whomever he encountered. Every once in a while I, too, suffered a beating with the stick that he always held in his hand. One time he hit my hand so hard that I thought it had become paralyzed. I feared I would never be able to move it. The people in the ghetto were tortured not only by German head officers like Handl, but also by every German. They were all permitted to treat us as they wished. Zalminka Alperovich, the son of Masseh Alperovich, brother of Rivka Gilat who is now in Israel, used to work for a German who would torture him and beat him mercilessly, so much so that we were worried about his survival. One time he returned to the ghetto all beaten up and wounded, in horrible shape. But the next morning the German came to the ghetto and demanded that Zalminka, and no one else, be sent to him. Many tried to explain the horrible situation of the young boy, but the German just became enraged and said, "I will make him well," and he drew out his weapon. So with no choice, Zalminka got out of bed and went to work. Who could ever dream during those days that this Zalminka, who was so tortured, would one day escape from the ghetto and arrive at the forest, and from there go to the Red Army, where he would get his revenge on the German killers, something I will tell you about later. Most people in the ghetto of Vileyka suffered greatly. Other than the people from Kurenets, there were remnants from other neighboring towns. Many of them were very depressed. I remember our Motik Alperovich, who was with us. Even when his heart was very bitter, Motik used three words to describe the situation, "*Seiz nit gut*" (The situation is not good). He was a member of our Partisan group and there was hope at least that we might leave for the forest.

When I worked next to Matvei, I saw that among the many letters he kept in his drawer were many Red Army buttons with Soviet emblems of the hammer and sickle. I am sure that he meant for me to see them, but still I pretended that I was not paying attention. One day, Josef Norman found in the printing house the original announcement that ordered all the Jewish men in Vileyka to come for a roll call, which ended with all of them being taken to the bridge and killed. When we looked at the paper we saw it was signed with the Polish name Sapieska. During the Polish times, Sapieska was the head of the Vileyka archives, and as soon as the Germans entered he became the mayor. Josef showed me the paper and I thought that it might be historically important, so I took it and hid it somewhere. I think that this paper, among others, helped at the time when the Soviets came after the war, during Sapieska's trial, which got him sentenced to ten years in prison.

One time the Gvitz Commissar came and said that we should take some printing materials off the trucks. When I came to take them down, he said to me, "These are my materials, and I am telling you that if there is anything missing or imperfect, you will pay with your head." I don't know why Schmidt made me responsible for these materials, which were brought from Oshmany, where they had a printing house that was now closed. We did as we were told and took all the printing materials down from the trucks and into the printing house. Among other things, we found a box filled with letters and I immediately realized I could take from this box without making them suspicious. One day, Itzkaleh Einbender came to the printing house unwatched, and told me that the Partisans from the Volkoviczina group were asking about the letters, since it would soon be time to go to the forest. I said that I would probably be able to bring something soon.

Under the Nose of the Germans

We found out that in the yard of the Gvitz Commissar there were many letters for Russian print from an old printing house that had been used by the local daily paper in Vileyka, *Salinskiya Gazetta*, during the Soviet times. Since I would often go to the Gvitz Commissar to transfer materials, I decided to make good use of my visits there. The guard knew me well and didn't bother me. Bertha met me near the yard of the Gvitz Commissar and we both entered as if we didn't know one another. Bertha, who appeared non-Jewish and acted in a way that was filled with self-confidence, exuded trust and the guard didn't even check her. Bertha put a note in my hand and continued walking. When I had a chance to look at the note, I realized it was the text for a flyer, with an instruction that it should be printed very quickly. I couldn't figure out what Bertha was planning. Did she mean that I had to leave for Kurenets now and make this with the letters that I had kept there? Or did she want me to print this pamphlet right here in Vileyka? I considered the possibility of printing it in Vileyka, but I couldn't find a way at first. Slowly, I came up with a plan. I discussed this with Josef Norman and we realized that going to Kurenets was impossible, so I decided to go to the manager, Byelosov, and I said to him that I was very worried since I found out that soon there was going to be an action where they would kill the Jews in Vileyka. I begged him to let me sleep in the printing house. Byelosov, who was a devout Christian, had a job as the choirmaster and a deacon (?) and many times he used the printing press for the church. The Germans had no knowledge of what he was doing. Byelosov thought about it for a second and then said, "Well, if you want to sleep here maybe you can print some things for me. I immediately agreed and I decided to use this opportunity. I would do the Byelosov job and our pamphlet on the same form. When I was finished, I would separate them.

Josef Norman also asked to stay in the printing house; since he was also a Jew, it would seem natural he would want to join me. The young girls, Manya and Sonia, used the printing house as a permanent place to sleep, and as soon as they fell asleep on some tables, we started working, right under the Germans' noses. First we prepared the form for Byelosov, and then our pamphlet, which was very short. Byelosov told me before he left that once I finished printing I must separate all the letters so that no one would catch him. So as soon as I was done with the printing, I immediately separated the letters and started cutting the papers, separating the ones that belonged to us from the ones that belonged to the church. I hid our pamphlets in the print house and waited impatiently for someone to come and get the materials. It wasn't a large amount of material. I somehow was able to inform Bertha that she must not meet me at the Gvitz Commissar but must come to the yard behind the print house and wait there. So that is what happened. She came when it got dark and I gave her the package.

The relationship among the workers in the printing house was good. There was a sort of good socializing among them. Lazar and the two young women often joined Byelosov in singing. A very special person was the POW whom I talked about. Once in a while he would still ask me why I didn't join the Partisans and say, "What are you doing here? I am a Russian and it's not as dangerous for me to be here. But you are a Jew. You have no future here." I could see that he was truly worried about me. Obviously he had no idea about my connection with the Resistance, so he was pleading with me, thinking he would save me if he taught me certain things about the forest. He also taught me how to make fake stamps for IDs and how to put letters in a round shape. He was a very gentle person. He had some kind of infection on his hands and he was very careful not to use the public soap. He would very carefully cut a little piece of the public soap for himself. Soap was a very precious commodity, and one day Byelosov realized that pieces of the soap were cut, and he started yelling, "Who is stealing our soap?" Matvei didn't hide the truth. He admitted that he took some of the soap and showed Byelosov his infected hands. He explained that he did it because he feared that his infection could spread to others. Byelosov would not accept his explanation. He was very mad and went to the German who was responsible for us and told him about Matvei stealing the soap. The German hit Matvei very cruelly. Eventually he was kicked out of the printing house and sent to Germany.

Now we continued working with Lazar, whom I still couldn't figure out. I wondered if he had anything to do with Matvei getting sent to Germany. I decided to check out his character. Since he told me that his brother-in-law was a watchmaker, I asked him to give my watch to his brother-in-law to get it fixed. Bertha suggested that if he was not to be trusted and might cause us trouble, we should get rid of him. By getting rid of him she meant killing him. During those days, if someone was killed all of a sudden, no one would check the reasons. So when Lazar didn't bring back the watch and days passed, we didn't know what to do. Lazar promised me that on Sunday when he would be in the village, he would ask his brother-in-law to hurry up, but his brother-in-law was very busy.

When he returned on Monday, the watch was still not with him. I told him to just give me back the watch, whether it was ready or not. But he said the watch had been taken apart. When I told Bertha about it, I realized it could all end very badly, but luckily enough, just then, Lazar brought back the watch and proved he was not a bad man. So I notified Bertha and I was happy that he was not hurt, since someone worse could have been sent there.

On Sunday, I decided to make a short pamphlet while I did a general pamphlet for the Germans. I was sure that on Sunday no German would come to the printing house. I was just about ready to print the pamphlet, when to my great shock, the Gvitz Commissar, Schmidt, and another high-ranking officer, entered the printing house. I was shaking and I felt like I was standing over a huge chasm. So all I could do was to drop it all of a sudden, as if I was careless, and that is what I did. The entire form fell with a loud noise, and the letters spread all over. Schmidt immediately came to me and hit me for being so careless and said to me, "You must work carefully. Do not do any *stakhanov* here." ["Don't rush or try to overproduce."] I started gathering the letters and scrambling them, especially the letters from my pamphlet. All of a sudden there was an order to stop working. Now I was no longer worried that they would recognize the letters. Once again I was hit by the Germans before they left, and they said, "Be more careful. Don't do such a lousy job." Then they left the printing house.

Those were the days between Purim and Passover, and I spent almost all my time in the printing house in Vileyka. I found out that once again they had killed thirty-two Jews in Kurenets. This took place on the 6th day of the Hebrew month of Nisan, 1942. The killers were not Germans, but collaborators from the local area. One was from Kurenets and the second was from the village of Kastzinevitz. This is the information I got from Yehezkel Zimmerman, the son of Yitzhak Haitze's. Yehezkel Zimmerman is now known as Charles Gelman, and he wrote a book in English about his experiences during the war.

The two Christian hoodlums were policemen for the Germans. They were Shernagovitz and Balzinyuk. They went, as they said, to create a *polevanya*, meaning a hunt. One of these killers was a student of Yitzhak Zimmerman in the public school in 1941, but these so-called privileges did not help Yitzhak. He was the first to be killed by them. The daughter Ethel tried to escape but didn't go far. They caught her and killed her. The second daughter, Minya, was shot while holding her baby in her hands, a baby just a few months old. She fell in the snow, in a pool of her blood, and died immediately. The baby, Shimshon, fell on the snow but was not hurt. Feyga Zimmerman, the mother, saw the whole thing from the window of their home. She was in shock and practically fainted, but still she was able, after a short time, to go outside and take the baby from the snow. But Feyga Zimmerman was not able to stay in the house. She took the baby to Zalman Mendel Tsipilevich, who was distantly related to her, and there she stayed with the baby until the day of the annihilation of Kurenets, September 9, 1942.

I would like to say more about Yitzhak Zimmerman. He was a very learned Jew with an excellent memory. He was a deep thinker who understood the depths of ideas, and he was very articulate and able to explain everything to his students in a very clear and simple way. People who knew him said he was an amazing mathematician and was also very proficient in Hebrew grammar. All his knowledge was self-taught. He didn't have any formal education. In addition to that, he had the most beautiful and clear voice, and he served as prayer leader for the congregation in front of the Ark in the synagogue.

Yehezkel [Charles Gelman], his son, was at that time in the Vileyka ghetto with the other Kurenetsers and knew nothing of what had happened to his family. But people looked at him strangely and he understood that something had happened, so he left Vileyka for Kurenets and learned about the awful tragedy. He met with his mother and his nephew, and together they went back home to mourn his father and his two sisters. Yehezkel wrote that the piercing cries of his mother could have made the blocks of his house melt. During that time he also met with Artzik Dinestein, who was also known as Artzik Gatze's, and he told him that he, together with other Jews, went out and collected the bodies of the thirty-two martyrs and buried them in the Jewish cemetery. Artzik told him that when they checked the pockets of the people who were killed, they found in Yitzhak Zimmerman's pocket a detailed list of all the fifty-four martyrs who were killed during Simhat Torah that year. The list included the names of the people, their parents' names, their ages, etc. Surely, Yitzhak Zimmerman hoped that there would come a day when the fifty-four martyrs would be brought to a Jewish burial and their headstones would be put on their graves.

Leaving for the Forest

From the beginning of April 1942, the Underground unit from Volkoviczina urged us to come to the forest and establish a permanent newspaper from there. Since we had a lot of work in the printing house, and I knew I was about to leave, I suggested that Byelosov bring a young woman from Kurenets who was in the labor camp to help in the printing house. I gave her a great recommendation and said that since Matvei left, someone needed to replace him. The reason I wanted a Jewish girl to come there was to help Norman and me take letters and also to keep an eye on the Christian girls while we were printing the pamphlets. The girl I recommended was Riva, the daughter of Shaptai Gordon. She was full of energy and self-confidence, and

I knew that she would be very good at the job. But it wasn't enough for her to want to do it and for Byelosov to ask for her. We needed permission from the Gvitz Commissar. So Riva went to Schatz and asked him to recommend her. Schatz knew her well because when he came to the area of Kurenets, he lived in Riva's parents' home and liked them a lot. So he went to do as she wished, and after Schatz pleaded her case to the Gvitz Commissar, she got her position. Schatz had no idea we would use her for the Resistance.

Riva was very good at her job. She was able to transfer letters to the yard near the printing house, and Bertha would meet her. Riva would always sit by the printing press while we were doing pamphlets. She would clean the area, volunteering so that the Christian girls would not have to do anything, leaving us to print without worrying about them seeing anything. Riva stayed at the printing house after I left the area, and many years later when I met her, she told me that when they asked why I left, she told them that it was hard to know and that it must be that I was murdered when I went to visit Kurenets. She stayed there until October 1942. Eventually they organized an escape from the Vileyka ghetto, and the first to escape was Riva , with a group of ten young men. She was the only woman. The rest of this group were Shimon Zimmerman, later the husband of Riva, and Yehezkel Zimmerman (Charles Gelman) the son of Yitzhak Haitze's. With them were Tevel, the son of G'daliyahu the blacksmith, Lazar Shlomo, and others.

At this point I was still printing pamphlets as well as some materials for the church. Since the nights were still long in April, I could do much work, but still I was always tense, despite the fact that the Germans didn't usually come there at night. One night, after I printed some things for Byelosov and also short pamphlets for us, one of the Christian women for some reason started cleaning the printing house. Once in a while she would come near me, so I had no choice but to drop the form and mix the letters. I had to wait for her to finish and it took a long time, and then once again I joined the letters and finished the job. In our area it was mainly favorable news from the front. The next morning, Bertha came and took all the pamphlets.

Among the pamphlets I did in Vileyka, there was one that called for the residents who worked for the German police to join the fight against the Nazis. It said that the Germans had lost many battles on the Russian front. We announced that if they wanted to find the Partisans, all they had to do was go to the forest with the announcement and a weapon, and the Resistance would accept them. We signed this pamphlet with the words "Death to Hitler!"

Beautiful spring days came and the snow melted. We could see the days but since we were indoors we really did not experience them. The non-Jews in the Partisans kept asking us if we had sufficient weapons, papers, and letters so we could join them in the forest. They were not ready for all the Jewish members to join them, but they wanted me to come so I could start printing the newspaper. Since I needed more letters, I remembered the letters I had seen from the old Soviet printing house. I told Byelosov about it and said we should ask Handl for the letters, since many of our letters were not functional anymore. Byelosov sent me to Handl to ask for them. I explained to Handl that Byelosov sent me to collect those letters for our job, and he told me to choose the letters that were in good shape so I could take them to the printing house. Handl ordered me to weigh what I was going to take so that everything would be exact, so I sat there for a whole day so I could examine the letters, and I took a bag of about 30 kg of letters. When I showed the bag to Handl he forgot about weighing it. I hid them near the printing house and I gave Byelosov only a small package of letters, saying that most of the others were non-functional.

The people from Volkoviczina came the next day. Yorka Balshov took the letters back with him to Volkoviczina. The Germans had their eagle symbol on a stamp and we thought that we could make a stamp from it if we added the appropriate words in a circle around the eagle. So I brought the raw material to Kopel who was among the skilled Jews that the Nazis needed. There was also a dentist there. Kopel took some plaster from him and he was able to somehow make a print with the eagle and the appropriate letters. Now we had an official German stamp that we hoped to use for the Resistance. Since the labor camp was crowded with many Jews, it was impossible to hide such an operation from them, and someone started yelling that because of this stamp, everyone would be murdered. But someone else yelled to him, "Tell me, do you really believe that if we didn't have the stamp they would keep us alive and not kill us?"

Kopel Spektor was well respected, even by the Nazis. One time, when they were repairing a toilet in the German headquarters, the different technicians were arguing about which way a toilet should be designed. Should it be the French way, where you pull a string, or the English way, where you press a button or lever for it to flush? Since they all respected his technical skills, they called Kopel and asked his opinion. Kopel, who didn't lose his sense of humor, said that there was also a Russian system, in which there was no need to flush at all, since the toilet was not in the house but at the edge of the yard. The Germans loved this answer and they all laughed, thinking of how backward the Soviets were. Kopel made them so happy that they gave him cigarettes.

In reality, Kopel Spektor did everything he could to help people who were going to fight the Germans. He was the head of the committee that had planned the escape from the camp to the forest. They were an Underground group. One of the other heads of the committee was Jonah Riar, from the town of Ilia. He was able to steal a gun from one of the German gendarmes, but when he tried the gun it had some kind of defect and Kopel Spektor was able to fix it in no time at all.

When I think of those days I remember how we all wished to get revenge, and every little bit of revenge would please us. In Vileyka, there was the daughter of Doctor Shostakovich from Kurenets. He was born in one of the villages nearby, and now, since the Germans came, he became their assistant, and maybe because of his collaborating with the Germans, his daughter now received an important job as an editor for them. Lazar, who worked with us, fell in love with that girl, and would often go from the printing house to deliver the prints we made. Despite the fact that it could endanger us, we were so angry and revengeful that we would change the letters and make, as if by mistake, errors that would say something nasty. That would make us feel a little bit better, that we were able to embarrass her in some way.

At the end of April, I was told that I should go to Volkoviczina to meet with Ivan. The letters were in his attic, and he asked me to check what we could do with them. While I was checking the letters and separating them, the Germans came to the village to get some chickens. I immediately hid, but I could see the Germans looking. From where I was hiding, I also saw one of the soldiers making love to a local girl from the village. At the end, he gave her a loaf of bread as payment, and a big smile lit up her face. Finally, the soldiers left and I was able to get out of my hideout and continue with my job. During that meeting, Ivan informed me that the next morning I had to go to the forest with two other people. We decided that Zalman Gurevich and Elik (Eliyahu), the son of Ruven Zishka Alperovich, would join me. Meanwhile, Itzkaleh Einbender went to Vileyka and spread a rumor that I had been murdered. A decision was made that if Schatz, the head of the Judenrat, would start investigating, Itzkaleh would kill him. My sister Doba worked in Vileyka for the German officer Riddle, putting together clothing for the soldiers, and she also helped them make packages to send home that basically consisted of pillage from the Jews.

Monday morning, while I walked to Vileyka with Itzkaleh, I transferred my rifle with three bullets to Itzkaleh Einbender so he could threaten Schatz if needed. Near the village of Zimadora, I decided to leave. I fell off the little bridge, and a policeman who saw me asked what had happened to me, and I said that something was wrong with my shoe and that I must fix it. They continued walking and I stayed there as if fixing my shoes. As soon as I saw them passing, I ran to the forest nearby, and there I stayed the entire day. When night came I went to Volkoviczina, where I met Yorka Balshov, who told me that Zalman Uri and Elik were ready and that we would leave that night.

Weeks later, Itzkaleh told me that Schatz was very helpful and spread the word that I had been killed, in spite of the fact that he knew I had really left for the forest. More than that, Schatz said that if he could only do it, he would join the Partisans in the forest. Doba also told me years later that Itzkaleh and Kopel Spektor came to her and told her not to worry about my escape and that no one would hurt her for revenge.

The Dream of the Forest

I met with Elik and Zalman Uri as well as the other Partisans. They had the printing press deep in the forest area. This was the end of winter, the beginning of spring. The ground was wet from the melting snow and the rain that came often. I was very tired, and naively I asked one of the Partisans who seemed knowledgeable in the ways of the forest where I could lie down to sleep for a bit. "A good question," answered the Partisan, mockingly. "In the place where you stand, that's the place where you sleep, either lying down or standing." So that's how it was. We would close our eyes in the place where we stood, and since we were so tired, we were able to sleep while standing.

The head of our unit was a person by the name of Andrey Ivanovich Volinitz. He was a very pleasant man from a village near Vileyka. Zalman Uri Gurevich knew him well. His sister worked for Zalman's family as a housekeeper before the war. The reason they used a housekeeper was because Batia Gurevich, Zalman's mother, was sick and needed help with the house chores.

The place where we rested was in the forest near the village of Tsentzevitz, not far from the ranch of Luban. We had a lot of food supplies: eggs, potatoes, flour, butter... The area was one of marshes. At this point they didn't use us Jews for any missions. We were only used in guard positions, because they were afraid that since we were Jews, if we were caught as Partisans, the entire Jewish community would pay for it.

The first Sunday we spent in the forest, many of the Partisans went to a dairy near Tsintzevitz to get some food. The guard at the dairy asked them to beat him up so the Germans would not suspect that he collaborated with them. They also took a horse and carriage and brought some alcohol with them. When they returned, most of them were drunk and fell asleep while we were guarding them. This was in the early morning hours, and all of a sudden I saw a shepherd not far from us. I did not know that he was the Partisans' contact. In his hand he held a horn made of an animal's horn. All of a sudden he started making loud sounds with the horn, and he announced that the Germans were approaching. There was a big commotion. Everyone ran from the place and the whole camp dispersed. We could hear many shouts of the Germans, and then there was quiet. We, the three Jews, also ran some distance from the camp, but when it turned quiet, we returned to the camp in the marsh area. We didn't know what to do next, since there were a lot of supplies. Elik decided that he should watch the supplies while the two of us went looking for the Partisans. Elik had a hunting rifle in case people came. So Zalman and I went to look for the Partisans. All of a sudden we heard an announcement. "Comrades, where are our people?" It was Volodia, one of the heads of the Partisan unit. While we were talking we heard heavy fire. People were running all over the forest. In one place we saw a large group of Germans approaching the area. We saw that there was a large fir tree that was very thick, so we hid in the branches and very fearfully we waited to see what would happen. The Germans came very near us and we could hear them talking, saying, "There must be some near here. We must be careful lest they surprise us and attack us."

"Maybe we should bring some dogs with us," said another soldier. And that was all we heard as they walked farther way.

We sat there in the branches of the fir tree for a long time. It was mostly quiet, but once in a while we could still hear shots. When evening came, we came out of the tree and looked at where we left Elik that morning, but we didn't see anyone there. We continued towards the road between Karlietza and Kurenets. All of a sudden we heard dogs barking and Volodia said that I should go check the place. I went to check but found nothing. I was very tired and sat for a minute, and somehow I fell asleep. All of a sudden I woke up and didn't know where I was. I stood and started looking around, and I saw a shepherd with cows. When he saw me he became very scared and tried to run. I approached him and told him not to worry. I asked him where the village of Karlietza was. He pointed to a few homes and said that was it. I sat with him to talk and he told me that in a village named Uzla, the Partisans had burned the big mill and that there were police forces on that bridge, and the guards kept changing. I was very hungry, and the shepherd took some meat from his bag and shared it with me. I wanted to give him something in return, but all I had was a cigarette lighter, so I gave that to him as a present and then we parted.

The Unit is Spreading

I didn't know what to do. I didn't know where to look for Zalman and Volodia, so I decided to try to get to Kurenets, and from there I tried to contact them. Carefully I passed the ranch of Luban where there were still some Jewish workers, but I didn't enter. I kept walking and got to the village of Diyadich around eight in the morning. There had already been daylight for hours, and all of a sudden I heard the sound of bicycles coming behind me. To my great shock it was the two evil policemen from Kurenets whom I knew very well. One was the son of Polevick and the second was Belziniyuk. At first I wanted to run to the forest and hide, but it was too late, so I decided to just act naïve.

"Why are you walking around so early in the morning?" one of them asked. Since I had papers showing I worked at the printing press, I showed them my permit. They immediately said, "If you work in Vileyka, what are you doing here in Luban?" I told them I visited my sister who worked here and decided to sleep here, and that I was on my way to Vileyka. They asked me if I had seen any Partisans in Luban. They seemed to be very busy with their own problems, and they didn't really pay any attention to me. They were talking about the Partisans who had burned some buildings and taken cows and other livestock, and they gave me back my permit and continued on their bicycles to Kurenets, and I walked behind them. Since I was near the village of Diyadich, I decided to visit my family's friends, the family of Kostya where we once bought a cow. Now a lot of our belongings were hidden, so as soon as the policemen disappeared, I went there. Anyway, as soon as I arrived in Diyadich, I saw that there were Germans with weapons shooting towards the forest, so I couldn't continue. I went to the home of Kostya and Agassia. They were scared to see me and I told them a lie, that I was in Luban and had come back and I was just here to visit them. They told me about Partisan activities in the area, and how the Germans were searching for them. They worried that the Germans might find me, but they still gave me food. "In any case, I had already prepared a hiding place in my barn, in the hay," Kostya told me, adding, "From that barn there is a secret way to the forest. So go there and rest. If you see that the Germans are coming, run to the other side, to the forest, to live."

I entered the barn and lay down in the hideout. Shortly thereafter, I heard people speaking in German. They were soldiers, who had come to get water for their horses from the well in the yard but were not looking for anyone, and they left. I was so tired that I fell asleep and woke up in the afternoon. It was quiet.

When it turned dark, Kostya's wife came in and brought me bread, honey, butter, and milk. She said this would be a good time for me to leave, since it was dark. Further, she said that the Germans might come again that night to look for me. Although I promised her I would leave when it got a little darker, as soon as she left I fell asleep again and I stayed there until morning. I was very embarrassed that I hadn't done what they wished, so I didn't go to say goodbye. I came out via the secret way and continued towards Kurenets. I passed by the village of Litwinki, and came to the end of Myadel Street, a place that we used to call Der Shvashtzapola. The first person I encountered was Zinia, a member of the Judenrat. From him I found out that our Elik Alperovich was killed in the forest, that in Kurenets it was not a secret, and that everyone knew we had left for the forest. He further said, "You only bring troubles for us." He told me that the Jews paid a huge sum of money to Silak, a Christian villager, so he would not tell the Germans that the person they had killed was a Jew from Kurenets, something that would mean the destruction of the entire Jewish community. Silak was a forester who was very familiar with the area. He was a collaborator with the Germans, and he would guide them in the forests when they would chase the Partisans. He was the person who brought the Germans who chased us, and he witnessed the killing of Elik. We found out from Silek that Elik fought fearlessly, but the Germans caught him while he was standing guard. They caught him and interrogated him. It must be that during the interrogation he decided to scare them, saying that the Partisan camp had hundreds of people with heavy weapons and grenades and machine guns. We understood that he did it so the Germans would not continue looking, but would organize themselves, giving the Partisans enough time to escape. After the interrogation they killed Elik. Silek, who witnessed this, was the father of two of our friends from school. He would often visit the home of Ruven Zishka Alperovich, the father of Elik, so Silek knew Elik very well. When he found Elik, he didn't tell the Germans who Elik was, and for his silence, he received money. He was the very first person to reach the parents of Elik and tell them of the death of their son.

I left Zinia and arrived home. Soon thereafter, the mother of Elik came to our house to ask me more details about the tragedy. Meanwhile, Zalman returned and for now our activities ceased.

What's Ahead?

From that point on, I had to be very careful since there was a rumor that I had been killed. I tried not to be seen, but I still had to meet with people and decide what would come next. We met again at Nyomka Shulman's house. Motik Alperovich, the brother of Elik, came to this meeting. Although we were mourning deeply, on the outside we acted as if we were frozen. All we talked about during the meeting was what we should do next, and how we should continue, since the brief journey in the forest had ended with a question mark. We all came to the conclusion that there was only one choice for us, and that was to escape the town and go to the forest. We decided to go to the forest to wait for information from Volkoviczina at this time.

As for my family, we realized that the central market where our house was located was a very dangerous place, so we moved to an empty apartment in the alley. My father particularly liked the apartment because it was next to the "rabbi minyan," where he often went to pray and to open his bitter heart to express his distress with passages from Psalms. Father, at that point, became deeply religious. He said he believed that God decided everything and that our fate was sealed and there was nothing we could do about it. I knew that Bertha had already left and was in the forest, and now she didn't come to contact us anymore. So I decided to go on my own during the night to Volkoviczina and try to meet with Ivan to find out what we should do. I came to the edge of the village but I was too afraid to enter. I was hoping to meet with someone but no one came around, so I returned with empty hands.

During those days, I met with a girl from Dolhinov. Her name was Bushka nee Katzovitz. She used to visit often in Kurenets because she was a member of Hashomer Hatzair, and we knew her well. This was the first time I saw her since the war had started. "What are you doing here?" I asked her, very surprised. Bushka told me of her ordeal, a story that was very common to most of us. At that point, most of the Jews of Dolhinov had been killed, but Bushka and her sister Chaia had escaped to the forest. However, the situation was difficult there so she decided to come to Kurenets. I brought her to my house, and my mother was happy to take her and she stayed with us for a while. Eventually she went to the Kenanina Camp, a place where survivors of slaughtered towns were taken for forced labor. Eventually she escaped and went to Russia. Now she lives in Israel with her two sisters.

Once again, I went to Volkoviczina, and on the way I met with some members of our Partisan unit who stopped in the village of Ivanovitz to meet with Matyokevitz to get instructions. Matyokevitz volunteered to serve in the German police as an agent for the Resistance. He wanted to find traitors and to get information about the plans of the Germans. Under his command they attacked a police patrol of the Germans that guarded one of the bridges on the Vilia River. This took place when Matyokevitz was guarding the river. When the Partisans arrived at the bridge, they killed the other guards and burned the bridge and took two machine guns. After this attack, Matyokevitz had to hide from the Germans, who realized his loyalties and started looking for him. We didn't know about his involvement in this mission, and we went directly to the village of Ivanovitz to get information. This was during a late night hour, and when we entered the village we encountered the wife of Haikovitz, who used to own the ranch there. It seemed that she stood there on purpose near the home of Matyokevitz to warn us, since the Germans were watching the home of the Matyokevitz family, looking for the son they were very suspicious of. We found out that she had been standing there for many nights, on guard, to warn anyone who came to the village about the dangerous situation. I am sure she saved us from certain death. Not only that: she immediately took us to her home and gave us food and drinks and also gave cigarettes to the people who smoked. Years later, when the war ended and I came to the area, I looked for Mrs. Haikovitz, wanting to thank her, but I was told she went to Poland. When I was in Poland I also looked for her but could never find her.

When the Germans realized that Matyokevitz was not to be found, they imprisoned his father and interrogated him. In the end they hanged him. Once again we didn't know what we should do. We received no instructions, and then we received a note. We learned that the Germans hadn't found the letters that were located near the place where Elik was killed, and that these were now in the possession of the Partisans. Once again I went in the direction of Volkoviczina and met with Bertha. A Partisan whom I had never met before, Lonka Verebayov, was with her. He asked me if I was ready right then to go to the Vostok, meaning to the east, to the area that was still in the hands of the Soviets. I didn't know what to say. My friends had sent me there so I could tell them the situation. How could I just leave them? Anyway, I didn't like Lonka. Before I even had time to answer him, he asked, "Do you have a weapon?" I was naïve and showed him my gun. He took it from me and refused to return it. Instead he gave me an old Colt with no bullets. "Why aren't you returning my gun?" I asked him. He said, "Now it's my gun."

I felt that Bertha was uneasy with him and a bit scared. Once again he asked me if I was ready to go to the Vostok. I answered, "From here I cannot go anywhere. I am connected to some comrades and I have to return and give them a report about our situation. We will all go together when we are ordered to go." The place where we met was located near one of the bridges where there was a train track running between Kurenets and Vileyka. All of a sudden Lonka said to me, "You know, I would like to know if you are at all suitable to be a Partisan. Are you able, for example, to put explosives under the bridge of this train track and blow up the bridge? You must understand that only if I watch you can I test whether you are suitable to be a Partisan." I explained to him that up until then I had not blown up any bridges, but I was sure it would not be too complicated if he told to me how to do it. Lonka gave me the explosives he had, and also a fuse that was only about 30 cm in length. He further explained that 30 cm was sufficient for only 30 seconds, so I would have a very short time to run from the place after lighting the fuse. "After you blow up the bridge, you can return to your friends in Kurenets and wait for our instructions."

There was no continuous patrol on the bridge. Only once in a while would there be a patrol that checked the place, so I took the explosives and quickly went under the bridge. I did what he told me to do, and as soon as I realized that the fuse was burning, I started running away from the bridge with all my might. Those seconds seemed like an eternity to me. I was so nervous. Only when I heard the explosion could I relax. There were other bridges that the Partisan unit blew up at the same time, among them the bridge of the train tracks in the direction of the town of Kriviczi.

Don't Be Together

I returned to Kurenets feeling both excitement and some disappointment. I didn't meet with my friends because I was sure that the Germans would hurt the Jews. I sent my mother to talk to my friends. I discussed the situation with her and said that I must part. My mother thought that the fate of the Jews was already sealed and that most likely only a very few would be able to save themselves. In her opinion, the only way that we could survive was if we were far from one another, because together we would all be worried about one another and it would hurt our chances. She kept repeating the words, "We shouldn't be together. Maybe if we are separate, someone might be saved."

I must say here that every time a rumor started that the young people were escaping to the forest, someone in town would say how this would cause the killing of the entire Jewish community, since the Germans would use it as a reason to take revenge on the Jews. So now when my mother begged me to run away, I reminded her of what her peers said. She said, "Son, you are as experienced as all of us. Do you really think that the Germans need excuses to murder Jews? Run away, son, don't listen to all this nonsense." She told me that even the first time, when we went to the forest, one of the Judenrat people came to her and said, "Don't think for a minute I don't know about the preparations of your son to go to the forest. This can cause the entire community's destruction." My mother told him that her son was already an adult who could stand in his own right, and that he didn't need any permission from her to do whatever he wanted to do. "Further," she said to him, "if you want to hear my opinion on what he is doing, I must tell you very openly that it is very good that he is doing that, and I so wish that I could do the same thing."

Despite the fact that she urged me to go, now that it was finally a reality for her, she was very emotional. Her eyes filled with tears, but she was very strong in her commitment to walk with me part of the way. Her mother love was very strong, stronger than any rational thoughts. So when I left, she walked with me. We walked through Kosita Street. I was barefoot, holding my boots. It was very warm and pleasant weather, but when we came near the train tracks, we saw that there was some kind of commotion by the German army, and soon we heard shooting. The shooting was not in our direction, but still we decided to return home. When we entered our home I realized that one of my boots was lost. I decided to go to my friends and give them the information, since the Germans seemed to be busy in another area. I was only able to find Nyomka Shulman. I told him how we needed to leave town immediately. I also told him about Bertha and the bridge; I said that we needed to go to the forest and I asked him to relay my message to other people, and I immediately went home.

When I entered the house, I saw my mother talking to a young Christian girl. It turned out to be Zina Bitzon, whom I hadn't met before, but I knew her name. As soon as I entered, she said the code "Hantiev," which was my fake name. Zina was also a contact with the Partisans. She told me that she had come to take us to the forest and we must leave immediately. She said that Ivan was also in town and he would take the weapons that were now located in our second apartment in the alley. Zina said we must get some food supplies, clothes, and personal weapons, and we must leave immediately. Whoever was not notified now would be sent for at another time. Mother went immediately to Nyomka and she found out that he had only been able to contact Itzaleh Einbender so far. Zina was very nervous and impatient. She kept repeating that time was running out and that we could not wait. She told us that when we walked we should walk some distance away from her but watch her all the time. She said that the three of us should not walk together, but each one separately until we were some distance from town. We should not take off our yellow stars. When we started walking I saw, at the corner of Kosita Street and Dolhinov, Perla Einbender, the mother of Itzkaleh. She knew that her son was leaving for the forest, and she stood looking at him from afar with a quiet but sad expression. Who knows what she was thinking during those moments? Every time I remember the occasion of our leaving the town, I remember Perla and her sad expression. [Perla, her husband, and their other children all perished.]

That was the afternoon hour. We had no time to find our other friends, so it was only the three of us. I didn't even have time to really say an appropriate goodbye to my parents since Zina was in such a hurry. We walked as we were told, watching for Zina. When past the train tracks, all of a sudden Zina disappeared, but we continued towards the village of Kosita. All of a sudden we met with the Partisan Lonka Berbayov, the leader of the unit, and there were fifteen people with him. "It's very good that you came," he said, and we joined his unit. Now he was a little more personal, and continued going along the edge of the forest. Then Lonka ordered us to enter the forest for a short rest. Here he showed us a bag filled with the letters and other printing materials, like paper and ink. Here I would like to say that the Christians had great respect, which in my opinion was a bit overblown, regarding the subject of pamphlets. Lonka divided the materials among the different people, and said that as soon as we got to an appropriate spot for printing, we would print some pamphlets for the local population so they would feel that the Partisans in the area were alive and active.

We Are the Masters Here

We continued walking and met with a Partisan by the name of Hubjanksi. I was excited to find out that Hubjanski had found one of the pamphlets that I had written; that was how he came to be with the Partisans. He used to be a policeman in the German service before joining the Partisans. There was another Partisan by the name of Kolbosin, who had a Czechoslovakian rifle. A short time later we met with Matyokevitz. He had a rifle and binoculars. They all walked around with their weapons unconcealed. We were not used to that and we saw it as very dangerous. I think that Matyokvetiz sensed our fears and tried to calm us down. He said, "You must understand that here we are the masters and the Germans are the ones who are scared of us here."

When we arrived at a bathhouse near a village, Lonka said that this would be an appropriate place to prepare a pamphlet, so we wrote something in the standard wording: "Don't Give the Horrible Ones Anything! Help the Partisans and Join the Ranks. Death to the Nazis." We also wrote some news from the front, some of it true, some made up. We also announced that we were the Partisans who had blown up the bridges. Shortly, the pamphlet was ready. The sun set and night came, and then we entered the village. This was an out-of-the-way village far from any road, and the Partisans had a party where they had *evetzerinka* and handed out pamphlets. Everyone was singing and dancing, and Lonka made a speech where he called on all the young people to join the ranks of the fighters. We, the Jews, did not enter the houses, worrying that someone would recognize us and inform the Germans, leading them to take revenge on our families and the Jews of Kurenets. The party continued until eleven in the evening, and then we continued on our way. The village was near the river Vilia. Before we left, we took a lamb from one of the yards. Some of the people were already across the river, and others were still on the other side, when all of a sudden, shots were fired. Kolbosin, who walked next to me, was wounded. His rifle was also shattered and became dysfunctional, so he threw it. He was wounded both in his hand and stomach, and he started running to the river. I entered with him, helping him. His condition became more grave. Nyomka and Itzkaleh were already on the other side of the river, where together with the other Partisans they started shooting back to cover us, which helped us get across. Kolbosin's situation was grim and he begged us to kill him. "Kill me. Why do I need such torture? Just kill me and end it all," he kept begging. I tore my shirt and a piece from someone else's shirt and made bandages. I covered his wounds and took care of him. He kept begging us to end his life, saying that if the Germans caught him alive they would torture him so badly and he didn't want to experience it. Lonka decided that two would stay with Kolbosin and the rest would go east, and that's what we did.

Once in a while new fighters would join us. It went on like this for days. We'd enter new villages and take food. Hudjanski was originally a native of Tservitz, a little village near Katzinovitz. Tservitz was really just a ranch that belonged to his uncle. Lonka decided to reach Katzinovitz first, since Hudjanski said he had some weapons hidden in Tservitz, enough weapons for all of us. We didn't go the usual way from Kurenets to Katzinovitz, meaning west to east, but we went in a roundabout way that took much longer. Hudjanski, who knew the area, served as our guide, and he told us that right after the First World War, when the area was near the Russian-Polish border, his uncle was a smuggler who knew the area very well. When we arrived at Tservitz, the uncle became our guide, and when we got to a certain bridge, someone opened fire on us. It turned out to be Polish residents of the area. One of them got up and yelled, "Why are you shooting and whom are you shooting?" But he was killed as he was saying it. Once again they returned fire and Hudjanski's uncle was mortally wounded, so now we were without a guide. We walked around the town of Dolhinov, which at that point was without any of its Jews. All had been annihilated.

We rested nearby and then left in the direction of Pleshensitz. Once again we made some pamphlets, and once again new fighters joined us and eventually we were joined by Bertha. At that point, one of the officers decided that Nyomka, Itzaleh, and some other fighters and I should go to the area of Borisov near the marshes, where the Partisan brigade Dyadia Vasya was situated. Dyadia Vasya was named for the head of that brigade, Vasya Narinaski. This brigade contained two battalions, one named "Revenge" and the other "The Battle." We walked for three days, until we came to the brigade that was in the middle of the marsh areas. Vasya himself was the first to welcome us. His first question was whether the printing press was functional and whether we could start with the job. Once again I saw how important it seemed to them to print. I said that I could start right away.

They sent us to rest and to get acquainted with the new place. There were thousands of Partisans in this area, and they were of different leadership ranks. They also had a hospital with many doctors. Here we met with a native of our town, Ita Gilberstein, who was renowned as a brave fighter. [She was later killed. Her sister survived and she is in Israel.] The Partisans lived in huts made from tree branches. They also had tents and many *zimlankas* built in the ground. It was a big settlement in the middle of the forest.

I showed the commander samples of my pamphlets and he was very complimentary. He asked us for information about how long it would take and what sort of productivity we could maintain. I told him that we could make thousands of pamphlets a day, even in such primitive conditions. That made him very curious.

On the Way to the Vostok

We found out that in this camp there was a unit of eighteen people who were also making pamphlets, but they had very low productivity. With their supplies it took a long time. I met with one of those people, who turned out to be an old Jew. It seems that our coming to the place made them upset. They saw us as competitors and decided to give us trouble. We didn't suspect anything. We were very encouraged by the warm welcome from the head of the brigade. My letters were all in the pockets of the special pieces of cloth that my mother had made for me, and I hung them nearby in the place we slept. When I woke up in the morning and looked for the letters, my eyes darkened. The pocket was torn and many of the letters had disappeared. We only had a few letters left and we didn't have the entire alphabet, so now when the commander asked me to start with the pamphlets I was in a very embarrassing situation. I didn't tell him the whole truth, but I said that I had lost many of the letters and I was not able to do anything at the moment. He didn't conduct any investigation. He said that we could join the group of fighters that did the usual type of job: guarding, blockading, and others. I received a rifle in which you had to load each bullet individually. Itzkaleh and Nyomka also received such weapons. I remember a conversation I had at that point, while I was sitting next to a small bonfire that I started. An officer approached me. He was friendly to the Jews. He sat next to me and asked, "Why are the Jews going like lambs to the slaughter?"

It didn't seem that he wanted to mock us; he just wanted to understand. He said that he had seen a hundred Jews taken to be killed by ten Germans, and not even one of the Jews tried to hurt the killers. Not only that: not even one of them was crying or begging. Like lambs to the slaughter. I told the officer that I could answer him if I could also ask him a few questions. "Look at those hundred Jews who are taken by ten Germans. More than half are women and children, and many of the others are old and sick. It may be that some men could have fought, but they did not because they didn't have weapons and also because of concern for the community. They think that every such act would cause the killing of thousands of Jews as revenge by the Germans; there is no weakness in the fact that they are not crying or begging. I see strength in it."

I told him about the resistance of Arke Alperovich, who hit the policeman who took him and who was able to take a rifle from one of them. I described this in the first chapter of this book. Now I wanted to ask him questions. How could he explain that a few Germans were able to take thousands of POWs down a very long road? These POWs were soldiers in the Red Army. They watched as the Germans killed anyone who was not able to walk. All of these people were men who knew how to use weapons, yet no one seemed to be fighting, and very few were trying to escape. And they were in a friendly area, where most of the population was Belarussian. He didn't really have an answer to what I said, and he accepted my explanation.

Shortly thereafter, we were called to the head of the brigade and he told us that we were going to join a group going east, past the front lines, near Witbesk. There we would go to the other side, to the east, where we would receive real weapons and also printing materials. On the way there, he said that we would encounter many wounded people and refugees and we should help them as much as we could. So we left, along with other Jews, like the Meyerson brothers from Dolhinov, the Schuster brothers, one whose last name was Kremer, a man named Bakshatz, and some non-Jewish Partisans. On the way east I met with the mother of Bushka Katzovitz from Dolhinov, whom I encountered in Kurenets. Her name was Chana nee Gitlitz Katzovitz Forman. She was there with her youngest daughter, Sarah nee Forman, who was about ten years old. She was wounded during their escape. There was a bullet in her right cheek. Earlier I had dreamed of being a doctor, and now I tried to take care of her as much as I could.

The leader who guided us was Captain Latishov. We kept transferring from one unit to the next. Itzkaleh befriended a Russian Partisan and they became like brothers, and his connection with Nyomka and me suffered. Itzkaleh was blond and didn't look Jewish. His personality was not typically Jewish either, but he was a very decent and honest person and was extremely courageous. Nyomka and I kept our friendship. Nyomka was in very bad shape and needed assistance; though spiritually he was very strong, physically he had many problems. He had eczema that had spread through his entire body. Also, his boots were too tight and since we walked so much, his feet were filled with blisters and cuts. We traveled about a thousand kilometers, most of it by foot. Once in a while I changed boots with him, since mine were a little bit bigger. This was the month of October 1942. We knew nothing of what had occurred in Kurenets. It took many months to find out that on September 9, three days before Rosh Hashanah, our dear family members were killed and most of the community in Kurenets was annihilated. It started getting cold and it was raining, but there was no snow. We kept walking towards the front. Itzkaleh seemed to me to lose all respect for the paperwork, as he called our pamphlets. Ever since the other Jewish unit sabotaged us, he only wanted to fight with weapons. Although I loved Itzkaleh, who was my childhood friend, I didn't think like him.

The front was near a town by the name of Vilich, which was located close to a big lake in the area of Smolensk-Witbesk. We hardly had food, and many could not endure the walk. All the areas where we walked were under German occupation, but

Partisan groups informally controlled the forest and the marshes. Once in a while we would hear shots, but we never knew where they came from. Among us was a group of refugees, women and children who walked with the fighters.

Despite the fact that I kept busy with combat operations, I saw a very important part of the war effort in propaganda. I aimed to go past the front to where I could find an appropriate printing press, and then return to the Partisan area—not just to any Partisan area, but back to Vileyka and Kurenets. We arrived at a place where there had been a German blockade the night before, where the entire group that tried to pass had been killed. We met with a few people from the Ditzkova brigade, and they suggested that whoever wanted to join them could receive real weapons and wouldn't have to pass the front. They didn't want to take any women, children, or wounded, but they wanted to take us. I didn't want to join this new brigade. I felt I could have stayed with Dydia Vasya; I was determined to go back to Kurenets and felt I didn't need a new brigade. Nyomka and Itzkaleh shared this opinion that we should return to Kurenets and Vileyka, but other fighters joined the new brigade. They let us rest for a few days while deciding what to do. All of a sudden, during night hours, they ordered us to go to the front. We went with women and children in the dark. Then there was gunfire, not directed exactly at us. For a few minutes there was panic, but shortly the situation improved. One Jewish child whose family escaped Myadel started crying, and a Partisan was ready to kill him to quiet him down, but somehow the child quieted down and we started running. Each one held a child and we ran quickly through an area that was filled with bunkers of the German army. We succeeded in crossing the dangerous area peacefully. I think the success was due to the dark night, which had no moon. Our group consisted of fifty people; among us there were Jews from Dolhinov and Myadel, and also some non-Jews from other places. There was even a non-Jew from Crimea, which was very far from this area. Even when we succeeded in getting to the eastern part of the front, controlled by the Soviets, we still carried the wounded, the sick, and the children. But as we went farther from the front, we encountered Soviet citizens, and they were really concerned about the state of the wounded and helped us. As soon as we encountered Soviet officials, they stopped us and decided where each one of us should go. They divided us into those who could help in the fighting and those who would be sent farther into the country. Since we were sent to the headquarters to fight, we didn't know the fate of the other people, the women, children, and wounded who came with us. Upon arriving at the deployment base, they decided who would go back to the front and who would go for more training.

The Demolition School

Nyomka and Itzkaleh were sent to demolition school and I was ordered to wait. All of a sudden they started investigating me as well as the others who had not yet been sent, and they asked us if we knew the Partisan Walter Hans, who had been with us during our wanderings. I knew him, and he was known among us as a dedicated and brave fighter who was always volunteering for dangerous missions. I looked up to him and I even admired him. Walter told us that he was a Jew and a native of Germany, that he had suffered greatly at the Nazis' hands, and that it was time to repay them. He spoke perfect German and he also spoke Russian very well, but he didn't speak any Yiddish. Still, it seemed natural to us and it didn't surprise us. Walter joined the Ditzkova Brigade and as a member of that group he came with us to the front, to help bring the women and children across. When Walter returned to the Ditzkova Brigade from the mission, a Russian Partisan saw him. This Russian had been a prisoner in Kovno and recognized him as a member of the Gestapo in Kovno. The Partisan immediately informed the headquarters. Further, he said that he and a friend had been taken to be killed by this Walter, who was a Gestapo member; the friend was executed, but he was able to escape. Upon hearing this testimony, they arrested him and began investigating. They learned that Walter was a fifth column planted in the brigade. He was supposed to pass the front and arrive in Moscow, where he was to spy and make contact with other German spies. I don't know all the details, but I know that Walter was executed.

As I said before, like many others I admired Walter for his dedication and bravery, and I truly believed he was a Jew. Since I could prove myself with all the flyers that I had kept from the different missions, they accepted the fact that I really was not involved with him and they told me the details of Walter's crimes.

Meanwhile, Nyomka and Itzkaleh were sent to Haburtshuka in the region of Smolensk for demolition school. Once I was cleared of any connection with Walter, I was sent to the school too. I was told that I should learn more about demolition and as soon as they could organize a printing house, they would send me there to run it. When I left the area they gave me food sufficient for one week: bread, a little bit of butter, flour, sugar, tea, and a few eggs. When I arrived at the school I didn't let them know I had food, so there I received food for another week.

When I arrived there, I joined Nyomka and Itzkaleh and seven other guys from Dolhinov; the food was used by all of us. This was in December 1942. The weather was pretty cold and windy. We would train in the snow with all sorts of weapons that the Soviets supplied. Some were German weapons that had fallen into Soviet hands. We were taught how to use explosives, how to lay mines, and how to disarm them; it was very serious training and every day we would train for more than ten hours. Itzkaleh and I were excellent target shooters. Nyomka did everything in a very dedicated way and with deep devotion, but his physical condition was very bad. He had eczema on his entire body, and it bothered him greatly.

We were not only busy with training. Among the ten of us, the ten Jewish guys, there were especially strong ties, since our circumstances were pretty difficult. Each one of us carried a wooden spoon inside our boots, and during meals we would take our spoon out of the boot and put it into the common pot of soup that was given to us. The soup contained mainly water and a very small amount of meat and potatoes. Since I was very depressed because of the incident with Walter, I hardly tried to get any food. I would just get some liquid and the guys would make fun of me, saying, "Tomorrow we will make *zatzirka*, so you will have no choice but to have something to eat." (*Zatzirka* is a soup made out of flour.) Many times we would talk about our friends from Kurenets and Vileyka. To make us feel better, we would mention how Motik would say, during the hard days in the ghetto in Vileyka, "*Hever, seiz nit gut*" (Friend, things are not good). So whenever someone would complain about the bad conditions, we would say, "What is new? Our Motik said the same thing a year ago."

We found out that the main headquarters was planning on organizing a new Partisan brigade to be sent near Molodechno, which was close to where we came from. They planned on taking about 100 people trained here, and they were hoping to use local people from the villages in the area for the rest. We decided to ask the headquarters to let us join that brigade. At first, Itzkaleh said that there was something un-kosher about a true fighter asking to be sent to the area he came from, thinking that a true fighter should go wherever he was told, without emotion. But eventually he joined us and asked to be sent to the area that he had originally come from. We came to the headquarters and explained that we knew a lot about the area and that we could be helpful. Despite that, it seems that we made very little impression on the guy who was assigning troops. He said we must finish our training in demolition, and then they would send us out somewhere. So we returned to our training.

Nyomka, whose condition became worse, could no longer tie his ammunition to his waist, since the eczema was now very bad. He was told to go to the hospital, but he refused and stayed. Itzkaleh was filled with a desire for revenge, and he felt he could only truly get his revenge with weapons. It seemed he was ashamed that much of the resistance he had participated in so far was a paper resistance, as he called the type of missions we had (printing pamphlets). The entire group of ten Jewish fighters that I belonged to was excellent in its abilities, but shortly after we asked to be sent to Molodechno, I was called to the headquarters and was told that I must go to another assignment. They didn't tell me where I was going. I was given new weapons and said goodbye to Nyomka and Itzkaleh. I climbed on a big truck that was ready to go, and I went far, far away.

From Place to Place

Together with two other guys, I traveled for many hours in a truck filled with papers. We went through marsh areas, and the roads were very difficult. When we couldn't cross the wetlands, we would cut wood from the forest and we would lay it on top of the water, and that's how we passed. Though it was winter, the land was wet and not frozen, so the truck got stuck many times. Finally we arrived at a village, and there I found out they were making a mobile printing house at the front. It was the kind of printing house that was always ready to be transferred. Everything was put in trunks; some were closed and some were open. There was a printing press, and there were letters and everything else that was needed. There was also a permanent house that stored different supplies. Before the war, this was where the army printed the newspaper of Witbesk, which was named *Witbesky Rabutzi*. There was also, on the other side of the front, a German paper by the same name, giving the Nazi version of the news.

The town of Witbesk itself was occupied by the German army; many times they would shell the area where we were located, so once in a while we would change our location There was a member of the staff of the newspaper by the name of Shikarda, with his driver, Schmidt; both of them were of German descent and they were Volga people. They were very loyal to the Soviet authorities and were treated with respect and trust. One night, when the shots came very near our area, we were ordered to leave immediately and the trucks were ready to go. When we arrived at a bridge over a river, it seemed as if the bridge would not tolerate the weight of the trucks; there was an order to burn the trucks so they would not fall into enemy hands, and the order was sent out to continue on foot. But Schmidt was stubborn and said we should attempt to get the trucks to the other side. A miracle occurred and the trucks drove across, and the bridge did not collapse. This brave act by Schmidt became known and he received a lot of praise. In the end we found out that the people who shot at us were only drunken German police.

It was January 1943. After driving from one place to another we were now at the front. One day I was working on the newspaper and I was told that someone was waiting for me outside and had asked to see me. When I went out my eyes filled with tears. Itzkaleh was standing outside. With excitement he told me that he was sent to SpetzGrupa, which was an elite demolition unit. We met for a short time. We talked about Kurenets, whose fate we still did not know. We so wanted to go back there and fight for the area. We parted with hugs and kisses and promised each other that whoever arrived in the area of Kurenets first would help the members of the family of the other as much as he could. We felt, at that moment, that Witbesk was foreign to us, and our ties to Kurenets were very strong. We had deep feelings for every piece of land, every road and forest that were known to us in our hometown, the places that made us want to fight. This was our last meeting. We never saw each other again. This meeting made me feel very lonely, and once again I went to the officer above me and asked to go back to the area I had come from, where I could be used in a better way. But once again I was told that we couldn't choose where to fight - we had to fight wherever we were ordered to.

After the First Mistake

A short time after I parted from Itzkaleh, I encountered three very young guys from Kurenets. One of them was Nyomka, son of Berlman the barber, the second was Yakov, son of Chaim Zalman Gurevich, and the third was Shmuel Alperovich, the son of Orchik and the brother of Nyomkaleh, whom I described earlier in the chapter about the fifty-four. They told me of the annihilation of our holy community, three days before Rosh Hashanah, on September 9, 1942. From them I also found out that of all my family members, only my sister Dova survived and that she was now in the forest. The news hit me very hard. I was extremely depressed and lonely and couldn't find any rest. One night I took my weapon and left, not really knowing where I would be going. I kept walking, but at one place I encountered the police and they forced me to return. In spite of my desertion, the head of the newspaper understood the reasons for it. He recognized my bad emotional state and gave me a few days of rest. Slowly I returned to work, and eventually things became better. Because a girl by the name of Yadviga, who was very professional, decided to quit her job, she taught me how to organize a page on the printing press, and soon I became responsible for designing the layout of the paper.

We kept moving around the areas of the front, near the towns of Witbesk and Smolensk. I remember that one time we were told they were showing the movie, *A Ray in the Clouds,* by Vanda Vasilavska, half an hour from where we were located. I walked many miles by myself until I got there. Not many people came to see the movie, and the audience also had to run the movie, changing the reels every few minutes. Despite the fact that I was very tired, the movie greatly affected me. It wasn't the plot itself – I was too sleepy to really follow it – but the fact that there were still movies in the world and they were being watched; this gave me hope of better days to come.

At that time I met a young man named Marek Shapira. He was from the town of Hormel. Even before the war his life was very difficult. He was practically on the verge of joining the criminal underworld. Now he worked for us. He was a good-looking man filled with energy. He could sing and dance and was very generous. I liked him very much. At one time, he was responsible for putting letters onto the printing press. He once typeset a speech by Stalin and he omitted some words. The head of the newspaper accused him of doing this on purpose, but Marek said that these words didn't appear in the handwritten version. Marek was fired and I tried very hard to help him. I shared my food with him. For a while he was accepted for work again, but ultimately he was fired.

Letters

Once in a while, the newspaper received permission to use an airplane to send materials and supplies to Partisans beyond the front. There was even some postal service. The person who ordered the use of a plane for postal purposes was Stulov, a high-ranking officer in the Red Army who was secretary of the party in Witbesk and who was also responsible for the printed materials. On those planes they would also fly doctors, so they could take care of the wounded and sick people at the front. I decided to use this service, since as a worker for the newspaper I had easier access to it. One time I found out that Dr. Shirinsky from Kurenets, the one who some years before had given me the special permit to take the test so I could skip some grades, was now a member of the Otkina Atriad Nikolayeva Partisan brigade. [Translator's note: I talked to this Dr. Shirinsky's grandson in Germany, the grandson of Dr. Shirinsky and Rachel nee Dinestein; we will look for the grandson's name.] I decided to send a letter to Dr. Shirinsky. Together with the letter I sent him blank paper, which was very precious in those days. This paper could be used for many purposes. It could be used to roll cigarettes and it could be exchanged for other things. To explain to you the value of paper in those times of the war, in the schools in Russia at the time, students would use newspapers to do their homework.

Sadly, I didn't receive any answer from Shirinsky, despite sending many letters. But one day I received a letter from my childhood friend Motik, the son of Ruven Zishka and the brother of Elik. As it turned out, Motik was in the same brigade as Shirinsky. The letter made me so excited and was so dear to me that I constantly read it until I knew it by heart. And here I am reciting the translated letter:

"Hello to you, my comrade in the fight, Nachum. In spite of the fact that you never, ever in any of your letters wrote to me, your friend, Motik Alperovich, I can't resist writing a few words to you. I assume you don't know that I exist here. I have some sad news. I found out that our friend Noah Dinestein fell in the battle. It was about two months after my brother Eliyau was killed. Also, our contact with the Partisans, Bertha Dinestein from Kalafi, was killed, and Nyomka was killed after he put explosives on a German train. That is about it, as far as our friends. Here with me is Shimon Alperovich, son of Zishka, as is Shirinsky. I am in good condition and I am now a soldier, but I still miss very much the old days that will never return.

"Do you remember our old friendship? In life you encounter situations and conditions you never anticipated. We used to be so naïve. Nachum, it could be that I will not be lucky enough to return to Kurenets, but maybe you will be lucky and return there. Do not forget to get revenge for all that was done to us. One day you will meet my cousins, Eshka and Bushka nee Kremer; please help them as much as you can.

"Your friend,
Motik"

I spilled more than one tear reading that letter and kept it as a very dear possession. In 1960, in Warsaw on the way to Israel, I visited the Israeli consulate there and showed the letter to the secretary of the consul. He said that he wanted to show it to a relative of his who was a writer. He promised to return the letter to me, but to this day the letter has not been returned to me.

Anyway, back to 1944. I responded to Motik's letter and I even sent more letters to him, but I never received an answer. Many years later, when I came to Israel and met with Avraham Aharon Alperovich, who was with Motik in the forest, I found out why Motik didn't answer any of my other letters. Avraham Aharon Alperovich's story was recorded in *Megilat Kurenets*. He told me of the condition of the Partisans around Polacheck during the retreat of the Germans. At that point the Germans' objective was to clear the forest. That was the only mission they were able to do well at that point. They tightened up the area in three rings. The first ring contained Belarussian and Ukrainian soldiers fighting for the Germans, the second ring was Polish and Latvian, and the third was German. Thousands of Partisans were killed during that blockade, among them several from Kurenets who fell in battle. Avraham Aharon Alperovich said he encountered Motik during battle and he was gravely wounded in both his legs. He told me that Motik was beloved by everyone, and they refused to leave him there. They wanted to do everything to save him, but he begged them and demanded to be left. "I am already lost," he told them. After throwing all his grenades at the Germans, he used his last grenade to kill himself.

I cried when I heard the story of my childhood friend and member of our Resistance unit, Motik. Avraham Aharon also told me about Zalminka Alperovich, the son of Moshe the brother of Rivka, whose torture in the Vileyka Ghetto I told you about. He was able to get out of the ghetto and escape to the forest. He was beloved by the Partisans. In the brigade where he was a member he became the contact person. When he met with Avraham Aharon, he suggested that he be transferred to his brigade with the other Jews from Kurenets, so they could all be together. But when the head of Zalminka's brigade heard this suggestion, he said he could not let Zalminka go. He said, "You will see him after the war." Nevertheless there were some battles where they fought together, side by side. In one of those battles, the Partisans were surrounded by German tanks and Zalminka would constantly run in front of the German tanks to throw grenades at them; you couldn't stop him. At the end of the war, when Avraham Aharon lived in Kriviczi, he received a letter from the Soviets, who thought that he was a relative of Zalminka. In the letter they wrote glorious words about the bravery of the boy Zalman Alperovich, who couldn't be drafted into the Red Army but who volunteered because he so wished to get revenge against the enemy of his people. He fell in battle in Prussia as a hero of the Soviet Union, and after his death he received two of the highest awards of the Red Army; the bravery of this young man should be considered an example of greatness in serving the Red Army.

With regard to the death of Bertha, I heard a rumor that Lonka Verbayov had murdered her. During a battle between the Partisans and the German army, Lonka was the number one, and Bertha the number two, shooter. At one time during that battle, all of Lonka's bullets were gone and he decided to leave the place during the battle, despite the fact that Bertha could supply him with more bullets. But Bertha pointed her gun at him and forced him to stay in the battle. People said he never forgave her for that, and at the first opportunity, he killed her. Further, people said that Volinitiz, who greatly respected Bertha, later killed Lonka. I don't know, however, if these are just rumors or are true facts.

As the war ended, there were a few places in the Soviet Union where they formed committees to look for friends and relatives. Also the Red Cross took part in such actions. I sent many letters to such committees to ask what had happened to the remnants from Kurenets, Vileyka, and Dolhinov. From one of the committees I received an answer concerning Meir Meckler from Kurenets, who left Kurenets with me on the day the Germans started the war with Russia. I met him in Ratzke after escaping. I quickly sent a letter to him, and he told me he was in the area of Gorky, where he worked at a tractor factory. He also sent me addresses of others from our town who had survived. He also asked for information on every other surviving Jew from the area.

Although at this point the Germans were retreating, I was wounded during a shelling. I was hospitalized, and near me was a Russian soldier who was badly wounded but who still had a clear memory. We started talking and he asked if I had relatives in Gorky. He said that he had had communication with a woman who worked with him and he said her name was Alperovich. My parents had told me that we had relatives in Gorky [The relatives in Gorky were a brother of his father by the name Itzhak Salomon Alperovich, who had two daughters.] Anyway, this man said that the name of the girl he knew was Mira Alperovich and he gave me her address. After a short time I received a letter from her saying, "Dear Partisan, I tried to find the roots of my family. At this time I could not find links to your family, though I may be your relative even if there is no obvious connection." She added a small package to the letter with some candy. I was very surprised to receive the package unopened, because supplies were so limited at the time that I expected someone would have stolen the food. Anyway, I kept in touch with Mira, and after the war I visited Gorky, where I found the brother of my mother from the Castroll family. He was by then an old Jew, 70 years old. I also met with Mira during that visit.

In June of 1944, the Soviets started an attack on the front in Witbesk. The area fell into Soviet hands, and the Red Army kept pushing west. During those days, the Katyushas became very famous. They were new Soviet weapons, and they may be the reason that the Germans lost so rapidly. Everyone would talk about the miracle Katyushas that were mounted on top of the trucks, facing the front; they would shoot twelve rockets from twelve different tubes at one time. So these Katyushas hit the Nazis hard, and one town after another was freed. Among them was Kurenets.

At that point we were already in the city of Witbesk, with the printing press. There are two rivers that meet in Witbesk: the Dvina, for which the town of Dvinsk is named, and the Vesiba. The town was empty of people when we arrived, and it was burning. The Germans blew up all the bridges when they retreated. Many of the residents of the town who hadn't escape east and who had stayed in town were German collaborators, so they now retreated with the German army. As soon as we arrived, I was sent to check the printing presses that the Germans had used. I found that the Germans had destroyed most of them before leaving, but I found lots of supplies, which I transferred. I was also told to look for workers, and at that point they didn't care if the workers were collaborators: I was told that right now we needed to use them and we could worry about punishment later on.

I was able to find a very experienced man named Sazunov. He was very excited to meet a Jew. He kept telling me about how thousands of Jews were annihilated in Dvinsk and Witbesk. He said he would see the Germans take them in boats to the deepest place in the river, and there they would either blow up the boat or capsize it. Anyone who tried to save himself was shot. There was another worker taken there who would get very angry upon hearing these stories, saying, "Why are you only talking about Jews who were killed? There are plenty of Russians who were killed." It greatly irritated me to listen to this worker, and I said, "There is a big difference between me, a Jew, and you, a Russian. I am sure that when you saw a Jew being killed you helped the killers. But when I saw Russians being hurt I aided them as much as I could." Although the man was corrupt, he was very good technically and for a while we used him, but finally he was sent away and we got someone else. The Germans left many supplies in different places, but they put mines all around the supplies. However, since I was trained to disarm mines, I was able to get the supplies.

To Kurenets

The authorities suggested that I should be the head of the police in the area, since the situation in the area was anarchic. But I didn't agree, and I asked to be released from my job so I could go to Kurenets. I knew that when I arrived in Kurenets I would not find any Jews, but each person from my town who survived became very dear to me. Not far from where I was, I found a girl from Kurenets, Merka Zimmerman, who had written me a letter asking for help, and since I was in a financially good situation, I helped her. Near the printing press was a hospital, and there I met a Jewish doctor who was the head of the hospital. He was married to a female doctor. They had no children and we all became very close.

There was no electricity at the time. During the night hours we used a generator to provide power for the printing press. I let the doctor use the generator during the daytime to provide electricity for the hospital, and that is how we became close. Since the doctor and his wife had no children, and they knew that my parents had been killed, they asked to adopt me. But despite the fact that I really liked them, I couldn't do it. I told them that the war was not over yet; besides, our friendship was more important than such a formal act.

At that time, I found out that Josef Norman, my friend from the printing house in Vileyka, had survived. I received a letter from him and we started a regular exchange of letters and we tried to arrange a meeting in Vileyka. I worked for the *Witbeski Rabutzi*, but there was another newspaper that was printed in Witbesk by the army, and we kept in close contact with the other press and we helped each other. This was in September 1944, and I found out that a truck from their newspaper was going to the town of Polaczek. I asked for permission to go with them, and I received a few days' vacation. I left Witbesk with a heart full of fear for what I would encounter. The truck that took me was filled with paper; the roads were badly damaged by the war, and in one place we had an accident. I remember telling the people who were in the truck with me, "We went through this whole war and survived, and now we'll get killed in a truck carrying paper?"

But we survived and arrived in Polaczek; there I found out, at the main station in the town, that there was a train going to Molodechno but that it would not stop at this side station. I entered the station anyway and told the head of this station my story, and I said I would give him some paper, which was still a very hot commodity, if he could do something to stop the train right there, or even make it go slower so I could jump onto it. It was late at night and he went towards the train with a red lantern, a signal for it to stop. The train stopped for a minute and I quickly went onto the platform. It was an open train car, and it took five hours for it to reach Kurenets. When the train arrived near Kosita Street in Kurenets, I jumped off and ran away, fearing someone would chase me to ask questions.

It was a dark day in autumn and it suited my dark heart. Externally I looked like an army man, with my green uniform, but this shiny green did not express my mood upon seeing the dark vistas where once my hometown stood. Everywhere I saw empty fields where only chimneys stood, and also some damaged buildings that had been made of cinder blocks. All of the homes that had been made of wood had been burned to the ground. I crossed land that once had been gardens for homes and arrived at the area where synagogues used to be. This place was also empty of buildings. Across from me stood the central market, which was now empty and desolate. Only on the western part of the market did I see one home still standing. It was our home, which had been made of blocks. I couldn't understand why it was still standing. I wanted to go there, but my legs felt paralyzed; finally, though, I was able to walk and slowly I approached the house and entered. I cannot describe the meeting with my sister Doba, my only sibling to survive out of the whole family, other than my sister Hanna, who left for Eretz Israel before the war. For a long time we sat there crying.

During that day I met with other remnants of our Jewish town who had returned from the forest. Some of them had escaped from the ghetto in Vileyka, among them Dinka Spektor, the sister of Kopel. They told me about the last days of the Vileyka ghetto, which was known by the Germans as "the Ghetto of the Useful Jews." They gave me information about what had happened in the ghetto after I left. I learned that the Vileyka ghetto existed for seven months after the annihilation of Kurenets. I found out information about Kopel Spektor and his activities in the ghetto. Kopel was very helpful to young people in escaping the ghetto; he refused to join them at first, fearing that if he escaped he would endanger the people who remained in the ghetto, since he was very important to the Germans, who knew him well and used his technical skills. He decided to wait for the day when all would escape, and he became one of the organizers. Then he worked tirelessly to collect and fix weapons for the day of the escape. One time he was asked to fix some locks on a door in the supply depot of the Germans. While he was fixing the lock, he saw that in this depot there were many weapons and ammunition, so he immediately made copies of the keys so he could secretly get some weapons out of there for the use of the Partisans. Kopel was able to repair many dysfunctional guns and to replace missing parts so that they would work.

Kopel was one of the organizers of the escape. They contacted the Partisans in the forest, and there was a Christian man who would arrive in the ghetto with his horse and buggy and would bring wood for furnaces, and they would hide weapons on his buggy as he was unloading the wood. Then he would take the weapons out to the forest to hide them. They would do this by making holes in the wood and hiding the weapons and bullets inside. They called them their "Revenge Tablets." Originally, some young people escaped. Among them was Riva, the daughter of Shaptai Gordon, and later her husband Shimon Zimmerman. After they escaped they joined the Partisan brigade that was headed by Shaptzenko, and they asked him to get the

Jews out of the ghetto. But Shaptzenko said that first they must prepare weapons for them, so Shimon got in touch with this person who would transfer the weapons. His name was Januk and he was from the village Vilovitz, but his nickname among them was "the One with the Yellow Beard." The person who arranged permission for him to get into the ghetto was Schatz, who was responsible for the workers in the ghetto.

Anyway, this Januk arrived in the ghetto a few times and was successful in transferring the weapons. Shortly before the day of the escape, March 18, 1943, he came with a letter telling them that on Saturday the Partisans would send horses and buggies to the forest behind the train station. Everyone was very excited, but then a woman saw a policeman coming towards Januk, and they took him to the police station. This woman thought Januk was arrested, and she started screaming that soon the Germans would come and kill everyone. This was in the afternoon, and the Germans were resting. All the Jews of the ghetto were very frightened, and they decided to use this time to escape. Many, many people were killed during that escape; among them were Kopel, his brother Eliyau, and two of his sisters.

My sister Doba escaped from the ghetto that day. At that time, she worked in the warehouses in Vileyka for a German by the name of Rydel. She worked separately from the other Jews, and her job was to fix the clothes brought over from annihilated Jewish communities. Once in a while, Doba took some of those clothes and shoes and gave them to Jews in the camp who were ready to escape, and also to people who were already in the forest. Doba herself had some clothes ready for the time when she would escape. Anyway, she had everything for herself ready to go, but during that day, March 18, she didn't know anything. It turned out that she was going to the train station with some clothes that she was getting ready to give to Gershon Eiyshiski, who worked in Vileyka near the train station. Gershon was somehow able to transfer the clothes to his relatives who were already in the forest. At that point she found out about the escape and she took her clothes and started running with the rest of them. She quickly put on the long coat that she had prepared ahead of time so people would not recognize her. After some hours of running, the long and warm coat made her running very difficult. Also, carrying a bag of clothes was very difficult, so she threw it away. The escapees who passed on their way and recognized the clothes as Doba's were sure that she had been killed. So when they arrived in the forest, they told the rest of the people that Doba was dead. When she came there eventually, everyone was greatly shocked to see her alive.

Later on, Doba told me about the fate of my parents. During the day of the annihilation, my father was with other Jewish men in the prayer house that we called "the rabbi minyan," and from there he was taken to his last walk. My mother and my youngest sister, Rashkaleh, who was sixteen at the time, together with six other women, were able to escape during the day of the annihilation. They arrived at the village of Poken, and hid in the barn of Tkachuk, a resident of the village. They hid for three days. When Tkachuk realized there were people hiding there, he notified the Germans. They came there and caught all the women. The Christians who saw it said that my mother fought the Germans. She cursed them and spit in their faces and slapped one of them. So she was the first to be killed; then they murdered the rest of the women. I had two grenades with me. The story was very painful to hear, and I decided that night to go to the village Poken and to get revenge on Tkachuk for the blood of my mother and sister. I arrived at the house where a person told me Tkachuk was living. I left a grenade at the door, thinking that if someone would open it, it would explode. But when I left the area, I all of a sudden asked myself, "But what if not Tkachuk but someone else opens the door? And is it really the right place? Is it Tkachuk's place?" So I returned and removed the grenade and left the area. I realized that the memory of my mother and Rashkaleh left such a deep hurt in my heart that no revenge would make it heal. My heart filled with emotion, and I threw away the two grenades. I returned home, to the only home that survived out of all the homes in the market. Our house. From that point on, we stopped talking about the tragedies and we became frozen. I still needed to go to the village of Dyaditz to visit my Christian friends Kostya and Agassia, who were true friends. My sister told me that Kostya brought back the possessions that our family had left with them. Kostya and Agassia received me with much warmth. They kept bringing glasses filled with vodka and we drank it as a sign of our friendship. They said that they would do whatever they could for us. I told them that there was nothing that I needed and I only wanted to thank them for all that they had done and all that they had wished to do for our family.

As the years passed, we slowly learned the fates of different people during the annihilation of September 9, 1942. Years later I found out from Yehezkel (Charles Gelman), the son of Yitzhak Zimmerman Z"L, about Zalman Mendel the tailor who was his relative. His mother, Feyga, and her grandson Shimshon, who had survived an earlier killing, were hiding in his house. On the day of the killing, Zalman Mendel, who was a sick man, as well as the mother of Yehezkel, with a baby less than a year old, knew they could not escape to the forest. Before the annihilation, Zalman Mendel was known as a very able person, and the Germans used him for tailoring and shoemaking; the house was filled with shoes and clothes and Zalman would work day and night as a laborer for the Germans. Fearing that someone would steal the Germans' belongings, police surrounded his house at all times. Still, there was a hideout in the house, where the daughter of Zalman Mendel, Dishka, and her husband, Hirshel, the son of Elhanan Alperovich the butcher, lived. They were still very young and they planned to go to the forest. But since the place was surrounded by police, they decided to hide there, and when the opportunity came, they would escape to the forest.

Anyway, they were able to hide there, but when they finally decided to escape to the forest, they had to move a big bureau that was covering the hideout, and the policemen who watched the door heard it and caught them and killed them.

There was also another person from the Dinestein family who was able to hide with his family that day. He begged his family to come to the forest with him, but they refused. He warned them that in the hideout they would surely die, but to no avail. Although he showed them he was able to leave and come back, he left them there to die. He was able to reach the forest, where he stayed for some years, walking around as if there was a curse put on him. There, in the forest, he found his death.

After a few days I went to visit Joseph Norman. This was October 1. We also encountered Lazar, who used to work in the printing house. At least externally he looked happy to see us. He said to us, "You must think that I didn't know about all the secret pamphlets you printed. I already knew then that you belonged to some Partisan unit that was working underground, but I am not one to talk idly. I saw everything but I knew how to keep quiet." We suspected that he was lying, but we didn't confront him. In Vileyka we also met with Volinitz, one of the Partisans I met during my walk to the front, to the Vostok. During those years he became a high-ranking officer. He became the commander of a full brigade of Partisans. He became known as the Partisan who freed Vileyka from the Nazis when the Red Army started to come near Vileyka. The rumors were that when the town of Vileyka was given to the Red Army by the Partisans it was free of Germans. From Volinitz we heard much about Itzkaleh Einbender and Nyomka Shulman. "Brave fighters, they were," Volinitz said, "and this Einbender was a true hero. Can you imagine? Eighteen trains this guy derailed! From this you can imagine how many Nazis he killed."

I also heard about the bravery of Itzkaleh from other people. Of all the Jewish members of our Partisan unit, only Zalman Gurevich and I survived, but we were not together. After some time I moved to Molodechno, and Zalman was in Smorgon and later in Poland. As I later found out from Zalman, he met Itzkaleh when he returned to the area, where he stayed for more than a month. The story can be found in *Megilat Kurenets*. From that story we learn that he also came to the town of Kurenets and, together with Zalman, did many missions against the collaborators. Itzkaleh was known as Dvitka, and his bravery was renowned, and many collaborators feared him. During the summer of 1943, after derailing a train, Itzkaleh went home with other members of his unit to Dolhinov, to celebrate the success of their mission. One of the villagers who saw them went to the Germans and told them about the party. German soldiers surrounded the house. Itzkaleh was able to escape from the house, but while he was fleeing he was shot and killed. After his death he received the highest awards from the Soviets.

A Fateful Meeting

Years passed, and in September 1947 I was invited to a cousin's wedding in Minsk. The house was filled with guests. During the party I met a girl by the name of Tzila. She was younger than I. Like me, she went through the hellish years of the war, she lost relatives and friends, and she escaped from her hometown and hid in the forest through periods of cold and starvation and other troubles. Now she was in Minsk, in accounting. We started dating each other. Although it was hard to admit in Soviet Russia that I wanted to go to Israel, I told it to Tzila. I told her that I had a sister there who left before the war, and that my second sister had left Russia, on her way to Israel. I found out that Tzila was actually born in Eretz Israel. During the First World War, before she was born, her family lived in Pleshensitz. At the end of that war, during the battles between the Polish and the Bolsheviks, the family was in Dolhinov, and they stayed there during the time when the Polish took charge of the town. Since Pleshensitz was now part of the Soviet Union, they could not return there. The only way they could think of getting to the Soviet Union was from another country, not from Poland. So they decided to go to Eretz Israel and, one day, to go from there to the Soviet Union to be with the rest of the family. But they lived in Haifa for ten years, and Tzila's father, who was very able, found different jobs. So Tzila was born in Israel, but when she was about six years old, the family left the country and went to the Soviet Union. The reason they left was because her mother became sick and could not handle the warm climate. But despite some of the difficulties they had encountered in Israel, they still had a deep love for the country, and Tzila was fluent in Hebrew and even knew some Arabic.

Some months later we decided to marry. In October of that year, we arrived in Pleshensitz for our wedding. Our party took place in a private home, and we served bread and salted fish, and of course some vodka. We sang in Russian and Yiddish, but still my heart was saddened knowing that not one of my family members was there. After drinking some vodka, I started singing in Hebrew, songs from distant days, days of school in Kurenets – the songs of Bialik. Tzila's father joined me, and his eyes filled with tears. From that day on we became very close to each other. I moved with Tzila to Molodechno, where our children were born. Here we found out about the establishment of Israel. We were excited when Golda Meir came to the Soviet Union as an ambassador for Israel. On the other hand, we suffered anti-Semitism and the trials of Jewish doctors (who were accused of some conspiracies). As Jews, we knew that the Soviets were spying on us. We always had to be very careful. I would like to tell a story that happened to me.

In 1948 I received a letter from my cousin Moshe Alperovich, from Israel. Moshe was the son of my Aunt Rashke, the sister of my father. Moshe, together with his mother and his sister Sarah, was able to escape to the forest during the day of the annihilation. But Rashke died there from starvation. After the war, my cousin Moshe went to Israel, and the letter supposedly came from Tel Aviv and was written in Yiddish. The return address was Shderot Rothschild Street, Tel Aviv. Tzila and I were very excited. The letter said that he was married and had a daughter, and it even had a drawing by a baby. Although we so wanted to have a contact, when we thought about it, we became very suspicious. First, how was Moshe able to find our address? And the fact that he was so soon a father to a girl who could draw with a pencil seemed unbelievable. I knew that he had left Russia only two years earlier, and he was not married then. So we never answered the letter, knowing that it must be a trick. As we later found out, Moshe Alperovich married only in 1952. This letter must have been sent by the secret police, who waited for my answer.

Quiet Hatred

Among the people who worked with me in the Molodechno printing house was Marek. Once in a while, he would announce loudly, "Whatever our Alperovich here says is not really important. I wish I could read his thoughts, because his thoughts are what are really important," implying that what I said and what I thought were two different things. I was greatly upset by his constant teasing. I remember what happened one day in particular, during our break. It was an ordinary day. Although it wasn't a holiday, people would still drink. Then they wouldn't know how to keep their mouths shut. There were very few Jews left in Molodechno, but even this small number didn't please the other residents. A young Jewish guy passed by, and he was naturally overweight. Immediately one of the writers of the newspaper started saying to me, "Tell me, what is the name of this man? I'm already writing a satire about a Jew who is a parasite living on the account of others, who never knew what starvation was, even at times when the entire Russian population was starving. This man is very suitable for the satire that I am writing and I want to use his name, since it would be appropriate."

This was in the 50s, during the time of the doctors' trials, when there was great hatred toward Jews in Soviet Russia. You would often encounter conversations in which people said how they were afraid to go to doctors, since most of the doctors in Russia were Jews and they betrayed the nation. In the winter of 1953, my wife Tzila and I went to a health resort. They would have cultural activities at the resort, and a Soviet colonel came to speak about the technical advancement of Soviet Russia. At the end of the speech, it was usual to ask questions, and people felt that they showed their loyalty to the Soviet Union by being interested in the subject and asking lots of questions. Since many of the people who were present for this speech knew nothing about technology but still wanted to show loyalty, they asked questions that had nothing to do with technology. Because the Soviet system was that you had to answer the questions whether or not they were on the topic, and not dismiss anything, he answered them. Most of the questions had to do with the so-called Jewish betrayal. At the end of the speech, someone came to me with a worried sound in his voice and said to me quietly, "I would like you to know that I have a very important political position in this area, and I am not supposed to tell you this, but I would like to ask your forgiveness for the questions in regard to the Jews that these people asked here. I am sure that times will change and the Soviet people will show a nicer side of their personality. This ugly wave of hatred will subside." Although I believed that the man was really honest with me, as a person who looked very Jewish I still had to be very careful, and it was very hard for me to really rest in this place, where the atmosphere was so hateful.

There were also Jew-haters in the printing house. There was one mechanic, named Katzan, who was very talented at his job. In 1946, I was the head of the printing department in this printing house, and here as well as in Vileyka, Riva nee Gordon Zimmerman from Kurenets worked with me and lived in one of the rooms in the printing house. Since the nights were very cold, she collected some discarded papers to burn in the furnace in her room. When Katzan saw her holding papers, he started looking at the ones she took and decided that some of them were of value, and he went to call the police to inform them of her disloyalty to the USSR. Riva came to me to tell me what had happened. I told her to immediately go and burn the papers in the furnace, and I went to the telephone room to talk to Katzan. I informed him that his job was to take care of the technical side of the printing, and that as far as the papers were concerned, I was the one who was responsible and he should not get involved in it. I also informed him that I told Riva to take the papers, and since the papers were already burned as I had informed him, Katzan knew there was nothing he could do and he didn't contact the police.

In 1948, my wife went to visit her parents in Pleshensitz, and I had my lunches in the cafeteria-style restaurant in Molodechno. I took my soup and sat at the table, and a drunken Christian man kept saying loudly, "*Bey zidov say Rasia*", meaning, "Beat the Jews and save Russia." Another person in the restaurant said to him, "Why are you yelling like this? Here is a real Jew sitting here. Beat him up and save Russia." Immediately, the drunk approached my table and tried to take my soup away from me. I took a flowerpot that was on the table and hit him on his head. The drunken man shook and fell to the floor. Immediately, people in the restaurant started cursing me, and some wanted to beat me up in revenge for the comrade who had fallen. I felt I was in real danger, and I was very lucky that Andrey Volinitz entered the restaurant. He was well known as a hero of the Soviet Union and beloved by many. As soon as he found out what had happened, he pushed the crowd aside and came to me. He shook my hand and hugged me and told the people, "You must know that this Jew fought with me as one of the most loyal and dedicated Partisans." The spirit in the restaurant immediately changed. The drunken man was taken out and now everyone wanted to be our friend. They tried to give us vodka, and they wanted to appear open minded.

Obviously there were other people who were honest and open minded among the Russian population, people like Kostya and Agassia, and Bakatz, the citizen of Kurenets who proved his good will toward the Jews and endangered himself by staying with them through the toughest days. One of the most sensitive deeds done by this righteous Bakatz was when he invited some of the remnants of the Kurenets community, as soon as they returned to town from their forest hideouts, and he gave them the big Torah book from the synagogue, which he had saved in his house through all the days of the destruction of the community.

It was very hard for me to visit my hometown, where my family was killed, but still I had a desire to see Bakatz and talk to him. I felt as if I was going on a pilgrimage to a holy man, but I delayed this desire for pilgrimage for a long time. The son of Bakatz worked in the Molodechno post office. I met him often and always tried to show our feelings of deep love for his father, which existed in the hearts of all the remnants of the Jews of Kurenets. Bakatz belonged to a Baptist sect that believed in a life of piety and purity. He was very old by the time I came to him. He lived in a little village near the water mill that once belonged to the Jew Mota Leib Kuperstock, who perished with his sons Zeev and Josef and their families. When I expressed my admiration for all that he had done, he said to me that considering the horrors and the travails he witnessed, what he did was so little that there was no need to thank him. He further expressed thanks for the heaven that kept him from being engulfed by the evil waves of hatred for Jews that swept through the rest of the population. I sat with him for a while and then said goodbye.

In 1950, I visited Kostya in the village of Diyadich, and Agassia told me about something that had happened eight years earlier, in 1942, that was affecting Kostya's life now. What happened was that after our first Partisan mission, when Elik died, I was in a very depressed state. I went to Luban to look for Noah Dinestein from Vileyka, who trained us in military action. I couldn't find him there, but when I returned to Kurenets with my gun, I passed by Kostya's house and I saw that two armed men were trying to take the cow from him. I pretended to be part of a Partisan unit and scared them, and they left the area. Now Agassia told me that a relative came to visit them from a faraway place, and Kostya went to the Kehanina train station but didn't return; a long time passed and she was worried about their situation. I asked for permission to check the situation, and I had to take a day off from work. I went to Kehanina station and approached the police there, but could not get any information. It was as if he had vanished without a trace. So I had no choice but to return to Molodechno, and Agassia went to Diyadich. She said that Kostya had returned home in a very bad state: he was beaten up and his toes were blue from being frozen. What had happened was that in Kehanina, two men who pretended to be policemen came up to him. One of them, he thought, was one of the people who had attacked him eight years before. During this encounter they took everything he had, beat him, and pulled him into the snow. They took off his boots and he was left alone, barefoot in an open field. It took a long time and help from people he encountered for him to finally arrive home. He was in very bad condition and was taken to a hospital in Vileyka. They had no solution but to cut his toes, and he was in the hospital for many months. When he finally recovered, I was able to get him a job in the printing house, where he became the carpenter. So now I would see him daily in Molodechno, and I was very happy to help take care of him.

The Secret Ring

Every day I dreamed of the time when I would leave Molodechno for Poland and from there go to see my sisters Hana and Duba in Israel. Many times it seemed to me a dream I would never achieve, so I continued to work dedicatedly in the printing house. Generally, I treated the people with whom I worked with camaraderie and good will, except for those who showed open anti-Semitism. If truth be told, after the war ended I acquired very few true friends. In my heart I was saying goodbye to the place and didn't allow myself deep friendships. But the one person I felt very close to was Vlodia, a member of our Partisan unit from the days of Volkokviczina. Vlodia was only his codename when he was with our unit; his real name was Danilotsky. Vlodia lived in Molodechno. He was a friendly man who was very honest and truly loved the Jewish people. It was a constant love that was unusual in those days in the Soviet Union. Vlodia, as I said before, became a POW of the Germans during the first few days of the war and was taken with thousands of other POWs to the market in Kurenets. When he arrived there, some Jewish members of our Partisan unit (which would be formed later) helped him escape. Later I met him when we were in the area of Luban and Uzla where Elik Alperovich was killed, but since that time, when the three of us hid in a tree from the Germans, I hadn't encountered him again.

Vlodia belonged to the brigade of Volinitz and he was the commissar. He continued in a similar job after the war, serving in the department of propaganda and education in the region of Molodechno. Vlodia lived very much in the past, and all that happened during the war was still alive inside him. He loved talking about those old days and recalling the missions of the Partisan units. He would tell of the dedication of the Jewish fighters and tell of their large part in all the missions. One day he asked all the surviving members who were still in the area to go to Volkoviczina, the base of many Partisan missions. For me this was a very bitter reminder of the time of the annihilation of the residents of Kurenets and the surrounding area, and in spite of his excitement about this, I could not take part in it. Although I didn't take part in this nostalgic mission, our friendship still remained strong and he still saw me as his confidant.

In the year 1948, there was much talk in the USSR of new treatment by the authorities for different nationals, and it was decided to give the various nationalities some independence. This was manifested by taking away the political jobs of those who came from other areas and giving them to people who were born locally. So Vlodia's job as *politruk* for education and propaganda was taken from him and given to a Belarussian. Vlodia was very bitter, and I think in many ways he wanted me to express how he felt to Volinitz, the hero of the Soviet Union who was from here and very popular and loved by the public and the authorities. He figured he could help him keep his job. Eventually, though, the plan to take his job away was canceled and he returned to work there.

Since Vlodia often mentioned the names of Jewish people who took part in the fight, others would say to him, "I'm getting tired of your talking about Itzkaleh Einbender and Nyomka Shulman, Bertha Dimmenstein, etc. as if they were the only heroes of the Soviet Union." But these complaints didn't stop Vlodia. He never changed his mind about the role Jews played in the Resistance, and he constantly mentioned in conversation a need to write stories about it in the paper. He wanted to collect all the names of, and detailed information about, the members of the Resistance, Jews and non-Jews. So Vlodia wrote detailed stories about all the missions of the unit and gave them to the secretary of the Communist Party in Molodechno. The secretary was not very excited about the article and said, "This is very strange. The Soviet people fought heroically and sacrificed themselves, and now people come around and try to stick this heroic Russian bravery onto the Jews." Until 1953, Vlodia was not able to publish this information, and they didn't even return his original material.

In 1953 they started investigating me, and I am sure it had something to do with Vlodia's story, since in his essay he mentioned my name as one of the members who was still alive in Russia. During the investigation they kept asking me about my missions during my days as a Partisan and why I had decided to work in the German printing house in Vileyka and to serve the enemies of the Soviet Union. During the investigation I kept repeating the story and the explanation as I wrote them here. I emphasized that it was not my idea that I wasn't a member of the Partisans, but I could not convince the investigators until finally Vlodia sent a letter to the investigators explaining how I helped the Partisans by printing pamphlets and by going to the forest, and how I was instructed to go to Vileyka by the Partisans. After the letter they me go, but Vlodia continued to try to get the story published.

In 1956, my wife and children and I went with Vlodia's family to vacation near an amusement park. They had a shooting range in this place where you had to shoot five bottles that stood next to each other. As people watched me shooting, someone yelled, "Let's see what this Jew can do," in a mocking voice. Five times I aimed, and each time I made a bottle fall. Vlodia became very excited and said, "Yes, yes, we knew how to fight. But who wants to hear about it?" He ended the conversation with a hint of disappointment.

During that year, my wife went to the market with Mikhla the daughter of Shaptai Gordon (nee Alperovich?), the sister of Riva. She had heard from her something very exciting that filled us with hope, something about the dream that we couldn't talk about, the dream to immigrate to Israel. Mikhla told her that she had received a letter from my cousin Leah nee Gurevich Shogol saying that she was able to go to Poland, and there she found out that the Polish authorities allowed everyone who lived in Poland before the war to return there so that families could stay together. In the letter she hinted that there was a possibility of emigrating from Poland to Israel. One night we met at the house of Mikhla and Leibl, the son of Alte Zimmerman from Kurenets, and we found out that many of the Jewish families of Kurenets who had survived were also trying to leave Russia through Poland. They decided that I should go to Moscow to the Polish consulate and ask for permission for four families to go to Poland: Moshe Alperovich's, Mikhla and Leibl Zimmerman's, Riva and Shimon Zimmerman's, and mine.

Here I must tell you that my cousin Leah Shogol (the daughter of my first cousin Nathan) did much to help. Since there were family ties, she asked to unite the families. In the Polish consulate in Moscow, I didn't encounter any difficulties. They seemed to want the citizens of the former Polish state to return, but then I had to go to the Department of the Interior. It took a long time for the four families to receive permission.

Here I would like to talk about David Katz. In 1945, the head of the printing house, Leiblin, asked me to find a job for a Jew by the name of David Katz, who had no profession. He was a native of the town of Kerve near Molodechno, and during the war he lived in the forest. On the day he returned to his town after the victory, the residents of Kerve attacked him and tied him to a tree and started beating him. They treated him with brutality and accused him of being an American spy. When the police came by, instead of imprisoning the thugs, they imprisoned David Katz for being an American spy. When Leiblin, who was involved in the Communist Party, found out about it, he talked to the authorities on behalf of David and explained that he was a very simple man who could speak only Yiddish and that it was totally irrational to think he could be an American spy. So now I gave him a job mixing the chemicals. Katzan, whom I mentioned before, was a true anti-Semite; he tortured David on a regular basis and was ready to kill him. One day I found that the pail used to mix the burning lead was filled with water, and if it had been put in the boiler it would have exploded and killed the person in charge of it, who was David Katz. After a short investigation I found it was Katzan who had filled it with water. I immediately called him and said that it was totally unacceptable. "I can tell you this because during the days of the war when I was fighting the German tanks, you collaborated with them and you fixed their tanks."

A few times David was able to escape the beatings, but one time at the Molodechno train station a few men jumped him and beat him up. He went to the hospital for several days, and when he left he was blind in one eye. He could no longer work at mixing the lead, and we found him a job cutting paper. But soon David and the rest of us realized we had no life in the Soviet Union. He immigrated to Poland and then to Israel long before I was able to reach the area.

Parting

The year was 1957, forty years after the Bolshevik Revolution. The Soviet newspaper policy was to write about the anonymous heroes of the nation, and Vlodia felt he could accomplish his old dream of publishing the stories of our old Partisan unit. He asked for the exact names of the Jews in our unit. I told him to use the names they were known by among Jews, such as Itzhak Einbender, Binyamin Shulman, Eli Alperovich, and so on. If we used those names, we didn't need to mention that they were Jewish; people would just know.

Vlodia contacted the central archive in Minsk, where you could find information on the different Partisan units, and then he expressed his wish to write the story. To my surprise, they were very receptive to this idea and gave their full assistance. So a few days later, a few workers from the Minsk archives arrived in Molodechno and met with Vlodia. They said that they should visit all the places tied to those events. We left Molodechno in two cars, together with the three people from the Minsk archives. First we went to Kurenets, to the house that once belonged to Nathan Gurevich, who was already in Israel at that point. The house was situated on Smorgon Street, which was renamed Partisan Street. This house was one of the only ones left in the market, and now it was Partisan Street. Two Russian teachers lived there. At first when we went there, the two teachers were worried that we had been sent by the authorities to confiscate the apartment that now belonged to them. When we explained our true mission to them, they relaxed. We told them that during the war a Resistance unit that fought the Nazis had come there. They said they had encountered things in the apartment that surprised them. They found the double walls in the attic, and in certain areas the floor was collapsing. I explained to them that this was the house of my uncle, that the area that was collapsing was the cowshed, and that under the ground there was a hiding place where I printed pamphlets against the Nazis, first for the unit in Kurenets, and later for the unit that started in Volkoviczina. As I was telling the story, I remembered that many years earlier I had hidden a knife that I found in our cowshed, wrapped in cloth. Although sixteen years had passed, I wanted to find it. So we started digging in the cowshed and I found it. The knife was all rusted. After telling them some more details, we continued on our way.

We visited the mother of Motyokevich, a member of the Volkoviczina fighters, in the village of Ivonzovitz. As I told you before, the Nazis executed her husband because they weren't able to find her son, who had been sent by the Underground to work for the Nazis as a police officer, and at that post he had managed to kill some Nazi policemen. We also visited the place where Elik Alperovich was killed, and there I told them about Mrs. Haikovitz who waited for us and notified us that the Germans were in town, thus saving our lives. Once again, Vlodia wrote the story and gave it to the publisher of the newspaper in Molodechno, and once again he was told that there was too much about Jews in the story. He then gave the story to another newspaper, *Znanaya Nyunisti* (Flag of the Youth) and they ran a full-page story; in its center was a picture of the wooden home of Nathan Gurevich and also pictures of a few members of the Partisan group, among them my picture. The material was edited by Irena Magzis and by Alexander Harkevich, who was a Russian.

They edited it as they wished. They mentioned the names of all the Jews who took part in the fighting except for Zalman Gurevich and Josef Norman, who had left the Soviet Union. They made it clear that Jews were a major part of this unit. After the piece was published, Irena Magzis was investigated and fired. Shortly thereafter, they printed the same article in the daily of Molodechno, *Salinskaya Gazetta*, but in this article they didn't include my picture. At that point I had already asked to leave the Soviet Union for Poland, so it made me unworthy, although the head of the newspaper said it wouldn't be right to include a picture of someone who worked for the paper. This was in 1959. As soon as people found out I was going to leave the USSR, Vlodia came to me and said, "You shouldn't do it. Now that you have become known in these articles in the paper, it could affect your future greatly."

Volinitz also came to convince me to stay. I couldn't tell them that my true aim was to go to Israel; rather, I explained that I was born a Polish citizen and that I wished to return to my nation. However, they were both disappointed and parted from me greatly upset. This was November of 1959. During the last evening of my work with the printing press, they had a celebration where they showed much love and respect for me. That evening I also said my good-byes to Kostya and Agassia. They cried quietly while we separated, remembering the strong connection to my family. Kostya told me that he was ready to follow me to the ends of the earth. While we were sitting in our apartment, a big group of young people who worked in the printing house suddenly came in to say their good-byes. They brought a *garushka* and vodka bottles and started celebrating. They said that they had left in the middle of work to send me off. I begged them to go back to work, and I promised to stay and let them in when they were done. At around midnight they began to come, singing and dancing and drinking as only Russians can, and they stayed until the morning hours. And this is how we left the Soviet Union.

We stayed more than a year in Poland, and in 1960 we arrived in Israel.

Afterword

Many years passed and I was an active citizen of Israel, but Kurenets still kept coming back to me in my dreams. I kept meeting natives of Kurenets, among them natives who settled the village of Kfa-harif. In one of my many visits to this village, I came to the house of Abba Nerutsky, and during conversations about the old days of the Second World War, Nerutsky told me of his experiences. His stories were so amazing that no imagination of a writer could even come close.

I would like to mention something here about the killing of the fifty-four. I wrote about our meeting when he was about fifteen years old when we escaped from Kurenets, in June of 1941. He told me how his family wanted to make sure that he would survive and urged him to go to Russia across the old border. After he separated from his father and the rest of his family he went, alone with a small bag on his back, away from the town, and when he reached the edge of Dolhinov Street, the street that would take you east, a Jewish resident of the town saw him from his window and came out. He called to him in a mocking voice, "You are also escaping from town? If I, an adult, will live, we will find a way to work it out with the Germans. I don't panic and escape, so what reason do you have, a young and healthy person, to spread fear and rumors of disasters? Go, you wild guy, go home. Don't unnecessarily plant seeds of fear among the population." Abba ignored this respected elderly Jew's advice and left the town. And for that he could now sit with me and tell of all that he experienced during those years of the Holocaust. But so many years earlier, who knew what would be the right thing to do? So I must point out here that confusion was natural in those horrible days.

After four years of escape, service in the Red Army, disease, and other troubles, Abba Nerutsky returned to Kurenets as a young man of nineteen. As soon as he heard that Kurenets was free, all he wished was to return there. Although he was told that there was no reason to return to Kurenets, that he wouldn't find anyone alive, he still knew he must go there. As long as he didn't fulfill this wish, he would not be able to rest. So for twenty days he traveled in different freight trains until he arrived in Molodechno. During those days and nights he rode through desolate towns where everything was destroyed. From Molodechno he took another freight train to Vileyka and jumped off the train when it stopped for a minute. Then he took the old, familiar road between the two towns, the one with the cedar trees. "When I arrived at the place where the town was once located, I saw a desolate and destroyed field filled with broken homes, and I could only see the famous cloister that belonged to them, coming up from the ground. When I arrived at the place that was once the central market, I found that it was empty of homes and people. This was the early morning hour and I was all alone. I sat on a mound of destruction and started crying, not knowing what I should do with myself. While I was sitting there crying quietly, a Christian man came to me and in a voice that had much empathy he started talking. I found out that this was our Bakatz. At this point I didn't know of his generous deeds for the Jewish community of our town. He told me about what occurred here during the war years. He tried to console me by saying that there were other remnants who had survived and gathered here after returning from the forest."

Abba Nerutsky told me that he later encountered members of his distant family. He met Itzhak Zimmerman and his wife Rachel and their two children. He became like their son, and they moved to the house where he was able to recover and find a job. Now Abba told me a story about the killing of the fifty-four. I always felt I belonged to those fifty-four. It was only through the intervention of Mataroz that I was able to survive. Despite the fact that I was able to survive close encounters with death many times, this incident of the fifty-four was the most prominent in my memory. Abba Nerutsky told me that he and other survivors, among them Meir Mackler, took the bones of the fifty-four from the killing field fifteen years later and brought them for Jewish burial. This took place after he became a resident of Vileyka, where he married and worked in the warehouse. He told me about the first year after they returned from the forest, how they met for Yom Kippur in the house of Ruven Dimmenstein and prayed deeply and cried desperately. When he moved to Molodechno and later Vileyka, he kept coming to Kurenets to visit the graveyard. One day when he came to visit, a villager who knew that he was a Jew originally from Kurenets told him that she came from the village of Kalinn and that when she went to the forest near Mikolinova to gather mushrooms, she arrived at the area where they had originally killed the fifty-four. The woman said, "I went to gather mushrooms, but then I arrived at the place where the graves of your brothers were located. A huge fear came over me. I saw in the ground, near the graves, many bones of people." When Abba Nerutsky investigated the story, he found out that the residents of the area kept coming to search the graves, thinking that there might be some valuables that had been buried with the people. Immediately, together with Meir Meckler, he searched the graves and found out that the woman was telling the truth. So they gathered the bones and returned them to their graves without saying anything to the authorities.

Every year on the ninth of the Jewish month of Av, they would gather with the survivors and go to the cemetery in Kurenets, where they would mourn the dead. One year on the ninth of Av, they found that the graves were open again and the bones were strewn about, so once again they gathered the bones and returned them to the graves. In the year 1957, during the ninth of Av, many came to Kurenets. The Fiddler family came from Vilna, and one Jew came all the way from Arkhangelsk. During that day they had a meeting to discuss what to do. They decided to take the remnants of the fifty-four from the killing field and bring them for Jewish burial in the old Jewish cemetery of Kurenets. Since many of the Jews were planning to leave the Soviet Union and go to Poland, they knew that this was the last chance to fulfill this commandment and that it should not be left undone. They decided to do it secretly and not notify the authorities, who would not allow such an undertaking.

During the day they hired a horse and buggy, and Abba who was responsible for the warehouses of Vileyka, brought some new sacks made of burlap and some digging tools, and they quietly went about doing their holy mission. They divided themselves into two groups. One group dug open the original graves and gathered the remnants into the sacks. The second group went to the old cemetery and dug two graves, one for men, the other for women. "We did it," said Abba, "with broken hearts and our bare hands. We did it deliberately that day, so we could touch our dear ones without any filter. Many tears were spilled during those hours, and as much as we could, we separated the bodies of men from women according to the clothes that they wore and other signs, such as long hair and braids. We did it very carefully. Among us there were some women: Chanka Minkov, or Chanka Nehamasheina's (as she was better known) and her daughter Masha, Tzirka Shklir, Zelda (nee Botwinnik) Alperovich (the second wife of Orchik) from Rakov, and Nachamka Zimmerman. They were among the people who gathered the bones. Among the people was Yankeleh Orchik's (Alperovich), who was one who was taken with the fifty-four; I told you the story of how he was able to escape and in the forest help many to survive. Nachamka Zimmerman was able to identify, among the bodies, Pesia Yente Zukovzky, the mother of Chaim Zukovzky and Dvoshel Zukovzky, the gentle soul, the talented Kurenets teacher who founded the youth movement Hashomer Ha'zair in Kurenets. Nachamka was able to recognize the clothes of Pesia Yente, who was hiding at her house together with her son Chaim when the Nazis came to take them, and recognized the clothes she was wearing when she was taken away. People said the clothes survived all those years because of something special in the land in the area that kept them in good shape."

After they gathered all the bones, they took them to the Jewish cemetery and covered the new graves with earth. They recited prayers of mourning and left the area, hoping that the authorities would never find out about what they had done. But the authorities did find out and started investigating them, emphasizing that this could cause disease since they had used their bare hands to transfer the bones. Abba said that if they were so worried about the public health situation, why were they not concerned about the many times the graves were opened by the villagers, who didn't use any special care when they exposed the dead bodies during their treasure hunts. "On the other hand, we, who did it out of special commitment to our dear ones, you now find a reason to complain and to punish us?" Abba said it to them in a very bitter way. He said that among the investigators there were some sensitive people who understood him and this whole affair ended with no complications. Since most of the people left the area to go to Poland on their way to Israel, they had no time to put gravestones in the cemetery.

Since I didn't take part in these events, and I feel much guilt and see it as a failure on my part, I would like to end my story with this chronicle. I would like to add that in my chronicles I want to bring up not only brave deeds, but also our failures and our inability to fight during those horrible days. We shouldn't be ashamed to express it, because without reporting it, something of the dark atmosphere of those days would be denied, and we would not get a true image of the time.

Top: In the little town of Kurenets in Belarus, the town that is located on the road between Molodechno and Lake Narutz, at Partisan Street #1 there stands a home not different from other homes. Now the family of the teacher Moskvitzeva lives here. They arrived here a short time ago. When they first came, they found strange things in the cowshed that was adjacent to the home. They found a deep area that had been dug out under the floor, and they also found a double wall in the attic. They were very surprised and wondered what the reason for it was. Now this is what happened here some years before:

In the dug-out area under the cowshed, a small oil lamp burned. There, Nachum Alperovich was situated. He had stains of printing dyes and he was sweating. His hands moved quickly, nervously looking for letters. Slowly the letters became words, and here is the first pamphlet: "Farmer! Keep your bread. Don't give one seed to the fascists. Help the Partisans."

The first victim of the unit was Ilia (Eliyau) Alperovich from Kurenets, and this is what happened: The Partisan *atriad* rested after a mission. Ilia Alperovich was the guard. When he realized the Germans had surrounded the unit, he fired a warning shot. There was a bitter battle and the *atriad* retreated. The shots stopped for no clear reason. Afterward we found out that Eliyau was caught and wounded, and he purposely told the Germans that there was a very large force of Partisans, about 250 people, with the most modern weapons. That was why the Germans stopped shooting and retreated, leaving about forty of their people killed.

When we returned to the base we buried young Ilia with military honors. Only a few of the unit's members were lucky and survived to see the day of liberation. Heroic deaths among the members of this unit were Zina Bitzyon, Vladimir and Nadzadeh Sobol, Bertha Dimmenstein, Victor Sokholov, Yitzhak Einbender, Yora Bilshov, Binyamin Shulman, Nikolai and Alexander Sherutzin, Noach Dinnestein, and other heroes, sons and daughters of the Soviet nation. Among the survivors were Piotr Mikhailovich Donilotskin, the secretary of propaganda of the party in the town of Molodechno; Nikolai Motyokevich, an engineer and an architect; Nachum Alperovich, a chief typesetter of the district; Ivan Sherutzin, a member in the Kollhoz named for Yakov Kolles in the Vileyka district; and Mikhail Basilik, the leader of the firefighters in Molodechno.

Memoir of infancy in the Vileyka camp

by Jay (Yosef) Rabunski

*"Dedicated to my parents, Rose nee Chosid and Wolf (Zev) Rabunski,
for my children and grandchildren to become aware of our family history"*

Chapter 1

I was born in 1938 in a shtetl named Kurenitz. At the time of my birth, the region belonged to Poland. Kurenitz was part of the Vilnius district and set about 80 kilometers distant from Vilna. During the term of the Polish rule in the Vilnius district, (1922-1939) the profession of the head of the household greatly influenced his family social standing and reputation in the community. If you were a minor tailor, a shoemaker or a handyman your family would be considered a lower class family. If you were working in an office, you were middle class family. If you owned a reputable business, you were considered as part of the upper class. Grandfather Mendel Chosid, my mother's father, was a businessman. His line of business was selling herbal pharmaceuticals made from natural vegetation such as weed, grass, mushrooms, wheat and tree roots. He would collect the specimens in the fields and forests that surrounded the town and later he would export it all over the world to be sold as natural medicine. Mothers' mother was a descendent of the Shulken family, who was well known in the area on their own rights. Due to the numerous properties, they owned in many areas of Poland, they owned forests land, farming land and other real estate the land that they had owned near-by would be leased out to the local population for farming.

My very beautiful mother had one brother who was in business with my grandfather, he was a chemist. His name was Paul Chosid. He would travel all over Europe, selling the raw materials grandfather collected to be made to medicine. My most vivid memory of him prior to the war is the oranges and fancy chocolates he would bring me, from abroad. Such delicacies were considered luxury items, which were rarely found in Poland. He was a very caring uncle. He was a tall and very handsome man with sparkly blue eyes and full of charm. The family's original last name was Frankfurt. My great-grandfather came from Frankfurt Germany. At the time he left, the region had a large Jewish population. He was forced to move east. He was a very religious and righteous man therefore the Rabbi of Vilna had changed his name to Chosid, which means, "a very religious man". Grandfather Mendel was known by everyone as a very kind and generous person and people would take advantage of his very large heart. (I seem to take after my grandfather). Grandmother was about four to five inches taller than grandfather was and she was the boss of the family.

Mother was an outstandingly beautiful woman. She was a member of a Jewish youth organization, "HaShomer Hatzair", (the young gatekeepers) which was a Zionist socialist movement that emphasized the necessity for all Jewish youth to immigrate to Eretz Israel (Palestine) to work the land. Their principal belief was that we must create a State for Jews. The State of Israel should be on our ancient land. Mother was also very active in sports. She loved to sing and dance. Most of all, she loved people and was very kind to them. I think she was very much like her father.

The great inflation of the early 30's affected the economy of Europe. In addition, the Nazi movement gained power in Germany, anti-Semitism was spreading rapidly in Poland. My grandfather's business began to dwindle down and the family was compelled to move to a different town, the town in which I was later born, Kurenitz.

When mother was a teenager, she met my father. Father was an extremely handsome man. Blonde and with deep green eyes. Certainly, he did not appear Jewish. Father was born in Kurenitz. His father Yitzhak Rabunski was at one time the Mayor of the town, my grandfather Yitzhak was a devout Communist. He believed very strongly in Communism as the solution to the Jewish problem. He might have changed his mind regarding communism had he lived longer. He died in the early 1920's, at the young age of 50 after a bout of tuberculosis. At that time, there were no antibiotics and tuberculosis was usually a fatal disease. When my grandfather died, he left five children, without a man to provide for them.

My grandfather's sister, Hada and brother in law Eliyahu Alperovich died a few years prior to my grandfather's death. Their children were sent to America to live with their older sister all except for the youngest girl Noima who was less then two years old at the time. She was left behind to be raised by my grandmother who was at this time also running a large factory that previously belonged to her husbands' sister and brother in law. The factory would produce root beer out of black bread and sugar, called Kvas. She had soon joined in partnership with her brother, who was the father of Shimon Peres, the ex-prime minister of Israel. The maiden name of my grandmother was Perski. She had several brothers and sisters that were scattered all over the world. One of them was the father of Loren Becall. (Who used to be called Perski).

During the thirties, my grandmothers' brother, Shimon's father, Getzel Perski, joined a special commando unit in the British army, it was purely Jewish unit. The unit was sent to Palestine to fight the German Army that was trying to gain control of North Africa. He took with him a large sum of money that was part of the cash flow of the factory to be used for the war against Germany. That left my grandmother back in Poland with meager means of support. My father started running the factory, which by now produced just enough income to put meat, occasionally, on the family's table.

Times had changed and after the partition of Poland in 1939, the Soviets entered our area. The Soviet ideology was greatly different then the Polish. Very rapidly everything turned upside down, the handyman, the tailors and proletariats became the "ideal people of the Soviet society". They were now rewarded with good political positions and owners of businesses were now castigated. We at this time were very poor. At night, our dining room tablecloth would double as our bed cover. On cold nights we would sleep on our self-made stove for warmth and would cover ourselves with the tablecloth.

My parents were young and very much in love. There were many anecdotes of which I was told by their friends, some of whom had been with us during the horrors of the holocaust and survived. Others had fled to England, Russia and other parts of the world prior to the Holocaust. The anecdotes indicate that father was very much in love with my mother even during their high-school years. He would turn very jealous if mother would just talk to someone else. Some times, he would turn violent. My mother was very attractive. She was recognized as the most beautiful girl in school. Her real name was Rachael. However, her name was altered to Rose because she wore very bright and colorful clothes, she had a unique style and people nicknamed her Rose.

At the dawn of World War 2, father attended school to become a professional man. He was studying to be a CPA. My Uncle, Alan (Eliyahu), who was known as very bright man, was drafted into the Army. My Uncle Leo ever since early youth had more of a carefree attitude about life and my grandmother did not approve at all of his lifestyle. As my father had told it he was the kid who would constantly be blamed for anything wrong that happened in the household. He would often be punished for no reason at all. It seemed like he could not find his place amongst the hard working, ambitious Rabunski family members. He unceasingly liked expensive clothes and the best of fruits, such as oranges, which, in Poland, were almost impossible to get. As he was growing up, he often got himself into trouble. From what people had said father would usually get him out of those troubles.

My Aunt Hannah was a young teenager. She was actively involved with the Zionist movement and was considering marriage. At that time, girls used to marry at the age of 16 or 17. Naturally, we were not observing any religion, only tradition, since as I told you my grandfather was an active Communist and that affected the entire family out look on life. As I mentioned before there was a cousin living with us, her name was Noima (Naomi). She ended up living with my grandparents in my father's home due to both of her parents passing away shortly after she was born from an unspecified disease that was not curable at that time. She grew up in the house as another child, she was truly part of the family.

During the Soviet rule, my father had to find other jobs due to the fact that the factory was seized by the authorities.

My parents were married on January 13, 1937. From what I am told, it was a beautiful, outdoors wedding and all the young people from the surrounding areas came to celebrate with them. Father took on jobs such as carrying heavy loads of rolls of fabric, loading them onto a horse and buggy and riding throughout the night to distribute the goods to the town of Vilna. On the way, he would stop and converse with numerous merchants in other villages and would attempt to sell them the Kvas that he used to manufacture. He would also pick up every empty bottle that was left, by virtue of that back then, bottles were refillable with a pressure cork.

All I can remember, as a small child is that the place I lived in was a rustic little house on Hazza Gestle. (The Pig Street.) It was a distressed section in the Hamlet of Kurenitz. As well as remembering my parents being in love. Father was the kind of man that could never raise his voice at me. He was a very gentle. Very emotional. In time of great stress, mother would have to take over. She was the stronger one. She was constantly positive about all things. My father tended to get depressed quickly. As years went by, I discovered that it was not just my imagination, these were the real facts of life in our household.

Shortly prior to the war, the common conversation in the shtetl was concerning the Germans plans to invade Poland. My grandparents from both sides were mature and looking forward in their thinking and realized adverse times were coming and wanted to make certain kind of move. They tried to immigrate to Palestine or to America. However, due to both families having financial difficulties at that point and visas that were very hard to obtain, even for well to do people, we had no means to go anywhere.

I remember my very early childhood. One vivid recollection from happy times is of Russian soldiers who would come to our village occasionally. They would eat outdoors at wooden tables and bring with them their accordions and vodka. They certainly had lavish parties. I was, for some reason, always selected out of the crowd and placed on the table around which they would dance. I guess dancing was a component of my upbringing even as a little boy of two-years-old. I would constantly be dressed with the finest of clothes by my adoring grandparents. As it turned out, I would be the only grandchild they would get to know, they all perished when I was four. I was blond with curly hair and I, as my parents, did not appear Jewish. I was called Ishia, which is a Russian name for Isaac. They would clap their hands and drink their vodka and go on and on with the singing and playing and would have me dancing on the table. This is something that is very hard to forget since I would always be rewarded by my parents and grandparents with new clothes after such occasions and I specially remember getting a pair of white boots. Therefore, life went on peacefully in the Community of Kurenitz under the kerosene lamps and with the handmade stoves and firewood that we had to fetch for heating and cooking.

I can remember the fresh fruits and vegetables that my grandmother would buy in the local market. I guess, as a child prior to the war, I thought life could not be any better. In Kurenitz, people were not wealthy in finance, but people seemed very happy. I did not know what a funeral was. I heard only of weddings and celebrations before the war.

On June 22, 1941, Germany attacked Russia.

My Uncle Paul was able to escape to Russia with his girlfriend (later wife) Brunia, shortly before the war he was living in another shtetl. The day the Germans invaded Russia he hired a horse and buggy. He asked his girlfriend and her family to join him in his attempt to cross the old border, only his girlfriend took the offer. My Uncle Leo and my Aunt Naomi had also escaped to Russia on the day of the invasion, each to a different place. The entire family tried to escape though unlucky for the rest of us, we were turned back by the Russians when we reached the border. The Russians had different policies toward refugees depending on what point of time you reached the borders.

My Uncle Alan, a tall, handsome man, who was a very quiet and very peaceful man, was drafted earlier into the Russian Army. As we now know, he was killed in one of the major battles in St. Petersburg, Russia and buried in a massive grave.

The Germans eventually entered our village. It was very peculiar and scary for me to see different uniforms as well as an army with heavy machinery, tanks, and men dressed with helmets, pushing, shoving, and screaming at us in foreign language. The inhabitants of the village were divided into groups. Families were separated. Kinsmen were sent to different locations.

A couple of months past, one night, father with other Jewish men from our town was taken from our house by the police. The Germans sentenced them to be shot the next morning for being communists, only they were sentenced in absence, and were told lies about what the Germans were planning to take them. Now I know that the other men were killed in a massive grave that they dug with their own hands. They were killed together with their wives and children. This "actzia" was later known as the "killing of the 54".

My mother, who was very clever and radiant woman realized the danger that my father was facing when he was taken out of the house, and immediately decided to do something to try to save him. She snuck out of the house during curfew time, which was from 7:30 at night to 5:30 in the morning. She went directly to the SS headquarters. I tried not to ask. As I said before, you do not ask or question anything that happens. I remember my mother coming back hours later, with her clothes totally ripped, beaten up, and full of blood. She could barely walk. She walked like a hunchback. You could see in her eyes the pain and the fear. I could read her feelings. I saw Hell in my mother's eyes. Her eyes reflected an internal burning flame. Every time she took a step forward, it was as if kerosene was added to the flame. I tried to comfort her by hugging her, but my mother, who loved me very much, pushed me away harshly. I guess she did not feel clean. I never spoke to my mother about those incidents. Even when my mother was ill in her later years, it had never been brought up. Whatever my mother had to do that night, father was released the next day. He was the only one of the men who got the death sentence that day who survived.

Some time later Professional people were put in a labor camp in a town nearby called Vilejka. At a later point, their wives and children joined them. Anybody that the Germans decided was capable of performing hard labor was also put in other camps in Vilejka. . The camp we were sent to was located in barracks that were put up by Polish laborers who were also imprisoned by the Nazi's. You could see in between the spaces between the boards when you would lie down on the wooden beds without mattresses. Some days I would be alone so I would lie on the bed looking to that space to see if my parents were coming back.

Life in the Vilejka ghetto was horrible. The men would be taken out every morning to small factories that were set up by the Germans. There, they would make uniforms, shoes, medicine, and war products. The day would start at 5:30 in the morning when everyone would be taken outside for a head-count. It was very cold and we had very little covering for our bodies. Horse and buggy's would come and load us up to take us to our destinations. Breakfast would be given out before work, which would start at about 6:00am. Breakfast consisted of bread and pig fat and a mixture of hot water that had the color of tea. There was no sugar or salt. Salt was a very expensive commodity during the war. The women would also be taken out, with the children, and a head-count would be taken. Some of the women would be taken to work in a hospital for wounded German soldiers. Some would be reserved to care for the SS soldier's families.

The children would be crowded in one massive room we were forced to grade buttons for uniforms. Some would be ordered to put medicine into bottles according to color, which would then be sent to the German front for the soldiers. Some of the women that were pretty were taken for experiments in a hospital and some for personal use for the SS soldiers and their collaborators.

I can remember on several occasions seeing my mother coming back to the barracks with her clothing ripped and with a terrible gaze of horror in her eyes. As a young child, I could not understand precisely what was going on. Being curious and concerned, I would ask some of the older boys in the camp why my mother looked that way. However, they would never answer me. The rapes and the experiments were so horrible that they did not fathom how to explain to a three-year old child what was going on. At times, I would see her cry until there would be no more tears in her eyes. Her face would be red and there would be scratches on her arms and her legs. She would sometimes sink into my father's arms when he returned from work shaking with horror, crying and saying, "why!?" There was constant dread and terror in her eyes. They would quietly comfort each other, trying not to let me see their reactions. However, since we were all living in one very small room, about 6 by 10 feet, one could not help but see everything. I would sometimes see my mother's personal clothing full of blood. Buttons missing from her clothes. You learn, very quickly, not to ask questions anymore, you just try to survive another day. You learn to keep quiet, to stay in your corner, since you fear that tomorrow might not come, that there might not be another day for you. You learn fast what pain, horror and death is. You learn not to say anything, but to wait solely for the little bit of food, the little bit of bread and water. You learn to watch your meager personal belongings, especially your shoes. You become aware that people you know disappear with no trace. They just vanish and no one talks about them any more. I still don't know to where my grandparents were sent. I knew not to ask. The constant fear for your life makes you sort of numb to any emotions and blind to the brutality of your surrounding.

So life continues and you don't think of tomorrow. You just hope of surviving today.

One day in November, I remember my father taking me by the hand, and going to a group with another 40 to 50 men with their children. We were driven by horse and buggy outside of the ghetto quarters near a field. I remember many German soldiers with heavy machine guns and automatic weapons surrounding us. We were told to remove all of our clothes. I think at that time that people were more like animals than humans. I don't think anyone thought of decency, modesty or shame. The German soldiers were brutally hitting all of the men with their weapons to hurry them up. It was cold. In the distance, about 10 to 20 feet from us, there was a massive crowd of young women undressed, nude as the day they were born. I guess as a child in the ghetto, nudity meant nothing. A little time passed by and I can remember the sound of the machine guns. I could see pieces of human flesh scattered all over. There was a big hole, which had been dug by Polish laborers. All of the men with the children were forced to identify their beloved ones. They were pushed by the German soldiers with clubs and weapons, shouting "Filthy Jews, you'll be next." I remember my father identifying parts of his sister, Channa, he started vomiting. I did not ask anything. I grabbed onto him, holding him so tight.

My father was shaking, trembling. He was all…green. His eyes bulged out of his head. His mouth went crooked. He held me as tight as he could. I guess tears could not come out of either one of us, because we had no more tears. He mumbled with his crooked mouth and his shattering teeth. His body was bent, his hands were numb and I think his legs were just about to give out. The Germans forced us to get dressed again. The men were taken back to work. The children were taken back to the massive room. That day, I could not tell the difference between any color. I can still remember and will never forget a woman with a soldier's belt was hitting me very hard because I was not putting the right colored buttons into the right place. I felt no pain. I could hear her screaming at me, yet she sounded to me like an echo coming from 100 kilometers away. I looked forward to the punishment, I rather liked it. There was a lot of blood coming out of my little body. I was just skin and bones. Yet, I felt no pain. Moreover, if I did feel it, I looked forward to the pain, I wanted to torture myself.

I guess the woman was of Jewish decent, could understand what was going on in my little head. After a little while, she stopped hitting me. I did not bother cleaning my wounds and sores. I wanted it to stay their forever. I can remember my father coming to our tiny place that night, I could not recognize him. His eyes were almost closed. With his fists and feet, he was kicking and banging against the wall, without letting out a sound. I could see his agony and his bitterness. My mother was aware of what was happening. She tried to calm him down. She herself was trembling. This is something that one can never forget. It will always stay with me. Many nights, that vision comes up. And when it does, I think of death. I think of Hell. And I know what Hell is like.

Days had gone by and fresh vegetables would be brought in to the camp on a daily basis by horse and buggy for the SS soldiers. A Christian man would deliver the vegetable. The buggy had two layers. On the top layer would be vegetables, on the lower layer, the partisans smuggled weapons for us to be used when we break out of camp. We clearly knew that one day we would be killed and it would be done in a horrible way. We had been paying for the weapons with personal possessions we had hidden in the ground. Gold fillings, gold teeth, etc. also we were smuggling out bullets we stole from the Germans and gave to the partisans.

I understood, somehow, from all of the boys whispering among themselves, that something big was about to take place. Being it was a labor camp, it was not watched quite so closely. There was not so much security as compared to the death camps. I understood, after a while, that we would try to break out one day. You get to be smart and knowledgeable at a very young age if circumstance call for it. Moreover, you say nothing; you keep all the secrets. You do only what your parents tell you to do. There is never a "no". There is never a "why".

One day in February of 1943, the vegetable wagon came as usual, to supply the SS men with fresh vegetables. We saw an SS man stop the wagon, and we thought that he had found the layer where the weapons were concealed. Panic spread in the camp among the women who were running and screaming that the SS had detected the weapons.

Unfortunately, we did not have time to find out the real reason the Christian man, who was so helpful to us, was stopped. A German SS Officer had stopped the wagon to be used for his pregnant wife to be taken to the local hospital. However, the panic that spread could not be stopped. German soldiers started to run into the Jewish crowds that were running away, shooting everyone in sight. Mothers and children, husbands and wives, separated. Children were left all alone. My father, who had a pistol, left my mother and me alone. I understood what it was. I started begging my mother, "do not leave me, I want to live".

My mother's chances to survive with a four-year-old on her arm were almost non-existent. Yet my mother ripped off the Jewish star from her clothes, which we all wore and put on an old Russian scarf and covered me in her arms. I could feel her trembling heart. She started to run towards the hospital. A German SS man stopped us and said to us "Zine Ze Ad Uten?" (Are you Jewish?) He was screaming, shouting, and pointing his automatic machine gun at us. Mother replied in Russian, "No, my baby is sick, I live in the Village, and I am in need of a doctor." She opened her scarf and showed him that she had a baby in her arms. She showed him only my face. I guess that due to all the panic and commotion, the SS soldier let us be. It was truly amazing luck.

My mother hid in a section of the hospital that she knew very well. Mother had worked in the hospital. She was a very learned woman, she was a chemist in this hospital at one point. She knew every corner as well as each shelter in that old hospital. At one point that day, she met with two Jewish women. One was wounded in her leg, and the other had two children with her. We all hid in the old hospital until nighttime came. The children had learned not to cry, and not to ask for anything. We knew not to question a thing. The other children were two boys. One was named Al in later years, the other was named Stanley. They were the sons of Isaac and Besheva Halperin. The other woman was from a well-known family in Vilna. Her name was Rachel.

As nightfall came, my mother made a proposal to the others, we should hideout in the Old Russian school in town that had a double-layered floor. There was snow on the ground, and we had to find a way to cover our tracks so that the SS would not discover where our hiding place was. To go across to the area that was controlled by Russian-partisan was infeasible at that point. There were railroad tracks, which divided the constantly patrolled German side of Poland to the area in the forest, were the Russian-partisan had a base.

The German's had placed, every 16 meters, machine guns, and anyone who would try to cross the railroad to the other side would be shot down immediately. Therefore, for five days and four nights, almost all we ate was snow. My mother would sneak out at night to a couple of local farmers which my grandfather used to do business with, and she would bring back some bread and sometimes some boiled potatoes. The women did not ask anything about their husbands, nor did the children ask anything about their fathers. We knew not to ask. Mother was neurotic about dreams and she constantly spoke to her dead mother, in her imagination, in her mind. My mother imagined a dream or a vision. She had heard her mother tell her that we needed to leave this place at once since one of the farmers was going to inform the Nazi's of our hiding place. He would do this because he would get a kilo of salt for every Jewish head that he would bring in.

Therefore, we quietly made our escape by crawling out that night and we hid in the bushes next to the railroad. This was the first time in my life that I truly feared that my mother did not want me. "She is not going to make it with me", I thought to myself. I remember her putting me down in one of the bushes and somehow, I knew that she would not return. As young as I was, I looked at my mother and I said to her, "Mom, I want to live, don't leave me". I knew what life was all about. I did not cry. I did not know how to cry any more. Mother did walk away a good couple of steps, turned around, then took me back into her arms, covered me up with that scarf, and hugged me tightly. She said nothing. I could only feel through her hugging, that it could be the last time that we would be together, or even to be alive. I have seen so much death, and so many bodies scattered all over, I knew what death was all about although I was only four years old.

We hid in the bushes for several hours. It was a full moon night. If someone walks in the snow under to moon, you can see a shadow. However, we knew we could not stay until morning because the Germans were searching the entire area with dogs looking for escapees. We were three women, three children. One of the women wounded in the leg, bleeding lightly. We tried to go towards to railroad. As we proceeded, we saw two shadows from afar coming towards us. Mother and the others turned around with their backs towards the shadows and someone said, "if we are going to be shot, we might as well be shot in the back". We thought the shadows were of German soldiers. The three women all cried out, "Shoot! We are ready to die!"

Several moments passed by, and the shadows behind us had turned their backs to us. They obviously did not see or hear us. As nothing had happened, we turned toward them and proceeded walking in their direction. They had done the same thing. As we came closer, we realized that one of them was my father. He was with another man from camp. It was the miracle of life. If one wants to believe that the Messiah came for us, he came at that moment.

There were no emotions shown between anybody. My mother, as usual, possessing the nature of a leader, made a decision for all of us that we were to cross the railroad at a certain place where she knew it would be easier. It was a wooded area. Everywhere else the Germans cut the woods to make the watch easier. So, on that February 1943 night, father, the stranger, who I later met, the three women and the three children, successfully crossed over to the area that was controlled by Russian partisans.

NAME INDEX

A

Adamovich, 141, 142, 225
Adamovitz, 249
Agov, 196
Aidelman 312
Alberts, 36, 45
Alparovich, 215, 216
Alparovitch, 121
Alperovich, 4, 5, 6, 7, 8, 9, 10, 11, 14, 20, 24, 25, 26, 27, 28, 29, 30, 32, 35, 36, 46, 57, 62, 69, 71, 79, 82, 86, 88, 91, 95, 97, 98, 102, 104, 119, 120, 122, 123, 126, 140, 150, 151, 152, 154, 157, 158, 161, 162, 163, 164, 165, 166, 167, 169, 177, 178, 179, 180, 182, 184, 185, 186, 188, 189, 191, 193, 195, 196, 197, 198, 199, 200, 201, 203, 208, 213, 215, 222, 227, 229, 232, 233, 234, 235, 236, 237, 249, 250, 256, 257, 258, 261, 262, 264, 266, 274, 276, 277, 278, 279, 280, 281, 282, 283, 284, 286, 287, 290, 292, 293, 294, 296, 297, 299, 303, 304, 305, 306, 307, 310, 311, 312, 316, 323, 337, 338, 339, 340, 342, 343, 344, 345, 346, 347, 348, 349, 350, 352, 354, 358, 361, 362, 363, 364, 366, 367, 370, 374, 376, 380, 383, 384, 385, 387, 389, 391, 392, 394, 395, 396
Alperovit, 108, 320
Alperovitch, 25, 36, 37, 53, 74, 88, 136, 217, 220, 229, 326, 336, 350, 352
Alperovitz, 4, 9, 10, 26, 30, 36, 45, 51, 53, 54, 75, 76, 77, 78, 81, 84, 88, 89, 91, 105, 108, 125, 136, 138, 139, 171, 172, 203, 207, 208, 217, 232, 236, 240, 241, 243, 244, 245, 247, 250, 253, 254, 255, 268, 320, 323, 327, 334, 339
Alpert, 14, 51, 53, 65, 67, 265
Alpervich, 8
Alporevitch, 249, 250, 251, 252, 254
Alprorvitz, 326
Altman, 88, 91, 121
Anzelevich, 11
Ash, 69
Ashkenazi, 164, 2874, 302
Ashknazi, 8
Auigenfeld, 220
Axelrod, 103
Ayeshevsky, 163
Ayeshiski, 361

B

Babiniyar, 167
Babniyar, 167
Baker, 21, 24, 116
Bakshatz, 380
Balashov, 368
Baliznuk, 366
Balshov, 30, 368, 373, 374
Balzinyouk, 265
Bankover, 99
Baranovitch, 141
Bardan, 31, 88, 91, 238, 239
Bartz, 181
Basilic, 250
Basilik, 368, 395
Baslik, 250
Bat Noach, 284
Becker, 289
Belizniyuk, 137, 138, 375
ben Chanan, 202
Ben David, 86, 99, 101
ben Rav Eliyau, 62
Bender, 4, 31, 32, 82, 108, 109
Benes, 7, 83, 91, 128, 207, 223, 264, 349
Bengin, 251
Bengis, 45
Benis, 282, 290
Berbayov, 378
Berger, 8, 285
Bergstein, 224, 310
Berkovitz, 352
Berman, 177, 189
Berzinjuk, 214
Betinov, 249, 250
Bevinar, 216
Beviner, 304, 306
Biager, 122
Bialsky, 324
Bilshov, 395
Birok, 217
Biruk, 254, 267, 268, 269
Bitzkovsky, 46, 47
Bitzon, 251, 368, 369, 378
Bitzyon, 395
Biyalik, 116
Blat, 199, 323, 324
Blinder, 6, 151, 189, 191, 279, 287, 308
Bogdanyook, 248
Bogdonyuk, 353
Bogin, 258
Bolshov, 250
Botianitz, 324
Botwinnik, 339, 394
Bratz, 285
Brazovbiski, 252
Bronstein, 295
Brunstein, 10
Bunimovitz, 34, 35
Burk, 146
Byelosov, 369, 370, 371, 372, 373

C

Canterovitch, 163
Carman, 298
Castrol, 23, 25
Castroll, 351, 353, 385
Catznelson, 341
Catzovitz, 7

Chadash, 5, 137, 157, 182
Chait, 4, 45
Charas, 4
Charivitz, 217
Charnas, 9, 81, 125, 150, 151, 172, 212, 218
Charnes, 291, 292
Charney, 290
Charnez, 216
Chasid, 57, 149, 152, 153, 267
Chayit, 297, 301
Chazkeles, 75
Cheres, 173, 198, 199, 200, 274
Cherney, 9
Chesed, 56, 124, 351, 355
Chesler, 306, 307
Chetzkales, 75
Chosid, 88, 395, 396
Cohen, 41, 50, 104, 105, 109, 132, 223, 297, 298
Cooper, 313
Cooperstock, 294
Cyrynsky, 356

D

Danilotsky, 390
Danishevsky, 161
Dardak, 81, 84, 85, 86, 108, 109, 117
Dardek, 109, 110, 111, 112
Darduk, 116
de bakerke, 91
de Lyubiker, 8
de Shamach, 58
den Schmidt, 35
Denis, 37
der Biager, 122
der Einbender, 27
der Eiser, 24
der Kalasnik, 115
der Klashnik, 97
der Koymen Karer, 26
der Kutler, 35
der Malach, 24
der Maliskai, 67, 68
der Malisker, 67, 68
der Moller, 35
der Muler, 24
der Ragatchaver, 72
der Schneider, 20
der Shaffer, 78
der Stoller, 35
der Tantzer, 93
der Vaser Trager, 24
der Viner, 20, 24
Deteloh, 56
Dickstein, 47
Dimenstein, 45, 88, 91, 117, 247, 250
Dimenstien, 350
Dimmenstein, 118, 123, 261, 364, 391, 394, 395
Dimnestein, 288
Din, 20, 23, 64, 72, 73
Dinerstein, 45, 55, 88, 91, 131, 141, 142, 143, 145, 180, 249, 250, 262, 279, 285, 287, 298, 339, 350
Dinerstien, 140, 152, 229, 231, 232, 256, 350
Dinestein, 25, 363, 364, 372, 383, 384, 388, 390
Dinnerstein, 6, 8, 249, 250
Dinnerstien, 234, 350
Dinnestein, 120, 197, 264, 395
Dizengoff, 101
Dobkin, 99
Dodge, 46
Dodger, 47
Donilotskin, 395
Dovsky, 365
Drashtzki, 34
Dubin, 8, 283
Dudik, 89

E

Eesak, 8
Eetzah, 149
Einbender, 57, 215, 240, 242, 243, 247, 250, 350, 358, 364, 368, 370, 374, 378, 388, 391, 392, 395
Einbinder, 11, 14, 192, 240, 250, 254, 255, 256, 296, 303, 309, 312, 350, 352, 355
Eisak, 88, 91
Eisar, 45
Eiser, 24
Eisheski, 81, 174
Eishiski, 28, 238
Eishisky, 289, 290, 300, 312
Eiyishiski, 81, 82
Eizen, 88
Elishkavitz, 308
Ephron, 26, 39
Eyeshski, 32

F

Feigenson, 276, 277
Feldman, 71, 137, 178, 180, 196, 215, 223, 300, 367
Feldsher, 296
Feygelson, 325
Feyglson, 5
Fiddler, 93, 189, 193, 394
Fidler, 4, 92, 262
Fiedler, 274, 301, 302, 310
Fingerhut, 41
Finkelshteyn, 341
Fishbein, 199
Fishkin, 356
Fistonovitz, 9
Fladsher, 11
Fleisher, 200
Forman, 7, 282, 380
Foster, 321
Frankfurt, 396
Fredkin, 305
Fridman, 6, 7
Friedman, 195, 198, 279, 281, 287, 288

G

Garfinkel, 63
Gedaliah, 301
Gelberstein, 275
Gelman, 71, 78, 95, 122, 137, 150, 151, 154, 160, 180, 195, 196, 203, 216, 229, 232, 236, 264, 306, 308, 309, 320, 372, 373, 387
Gelmans, 55
Gelemson, 306
Gevelman, 285, 286, 291, 311
Gevint, 290
Gilberstein, 5, 379
Gintoff, 352, 357
Gintov, 365, 368
Ginzburg, 84
Glasser, 325
Glazer, 3, 326
Golov, 47
Gordin, 1, 12, 20, 31, 36, 38, 46, 50, 53, 67, 69, 71, 72, 78, 83, 91, 98, 104, 106, 115, 118, 121, 122, 126, 136, 141, 146, 171, 175, 195, 217, 221, 224, 227, 260, 349
Gordon, 7, 9, 10, 45, 85, 88, 160, 188, 223, 224, 225, 226, 243, 262, 268, 282, 291, 294, 295, 299, 317, 319, 320, 362, 372, 386, 389, 391
Gorev, 32, 211, 238
Gorfenkel, 230
Gorfinkel, 25, 46, 308
Gotzes, 177
Grava, 226
Green, 313
Grossbein, 313
Gurevich, 10, 14, 20, 23, 24, 25, 32, 65, 79, 82, 88, 91, 211, 213, 214, 215, 217, 218, 219, 362, 363, 364, 367, 368, 374, 383, 388, 391, 392, 393
Gurevitch, 174, 250, 256, 316, 350, 358, 362
Gurevitz, 2, 4, 7, 8, 11, 30, 31, 32, 36, 76, 77, 81, 97, 102, 103, 108, 109, 190, 199, 200, 207, 238, 239, 241, 243, 252, 255, 258, 349
Gurfenkail, 229
Gurfinkel, 88, 89, 91
Gurvitz, 283, 296, 312
Gutkovich, 102, 103
Guzman, 354, 356
Gvalman, 25
Gvellman, 8, 9
Gvint, 3, 81, 86, 88, 89, 106, 114, 116, 117, 121, 173, 175, 211, 241, 243, 256, 261, 264, 265, 363
Gwint, 106

H

Ha-Cohen, 23
Hadash, 276, 288, 298, 299
Haikovitz, 377, 392
Halevi, 35, 39
Halperin, 400
Harav, 22, 300, 310
Harkevich, 393
Harnas, 261
Hashochet, 58
Hasid, 287
Hayet, 345
Herbert, 31, 239
Hetskales, 37
Himmelfarb, 25
Hirshbein, 69
Hubjanksi, 378
Hudjanski, 379
Hurwitz-Gurevich, 25

I

Isak, 284, 285
Isaras, 48
Itzha, 30

J

Jokovski, 5
Jokovsky, 5

K

Kagan, 313
Kalashnikov, 201, 202, 203, 210
Kalasnik, 115
Kalkovitz, 251
Kanterovich, 174, 183
Kanterovitz, 206, 265
Kantor, 301
Kantrowitz, 302, 303
Kapelovitch, 157, 165
Kapilovitz, 150
Kaplan, 240, 356
Kasdan, 149, 150, 151
Kashdan, 297
Kastrel, 51, 151, 245
Kastrol, 4
Katsavitz, 242
Katz, 196, 313, 392
Katzenbogen, 325
Katzovitz, 16, 281, 376, 380
Kaygan, 145
Kempin, 344
Kepelevich, 117
Kevitz, 368
Klashnik, 97
Kloyzner, 118
Kolbosin, 378, 379
Koobah, 159
Kooperstock, 78
Kooperstooch, 97
Koor, 20, 33
Kopel, 154, 161, 171, 239, 240, 244, 323, 352, 355, 358, 364, 365
Kopelovich, 8, 160
Kopelovitz, 204, 248
Kopershtook, 183, 184
Kopershtuch, 10
Kopilevitz, 88
Kopilovich, 82, 83, 85
Kopilovitch, 88

Kopilovitz, 11, 45, 158, 283, 284, 289, 296, 297, 303, 308
Kostya, 355, 367, 369
Kotavitzky, 324
Koymen Karer, 26
Kozak, 199
Kozch'akov, 110
Koznietz, 281
Kramer, 5, 6, 14, 38, 39, 40, 41, 42, 44, 55, 56, 60, 61, 66, 91, 99, 100, 101, 108, 119, 123, 124, 191, 240, 257, 277, 279, 289, 304, 307, 308
Kramnik, 81, 85, 91, 109, 124
Kravitz, 307
Kremer, 23, 25, 28, 54, 81, 86, 94, 153, 196, 215, 358, 360, 380, 384
Kremnick, 150
Kremnik, 84, 298, 310
Kribitzky, 46
Krivitsky, 52
Krivitzki, 43
Kronik, 313
Kupelovitz, 91
Kupershtooch, 125, 182
Kuperstock, 65, 139, 363, 390
Kur, 33, 34, 35
Kurenitser, 39
Kushnir, 306
Kutler, 35
Kuzniatz, 7

L

Labadower, 32
Landa, 309, 313
Landau, 13, 15, 20, 22, 25, 129, 136, 140, 269
Lapkin, 311
Laptzlter, 34
Latishov, 380
Lehrman, 31
Lemon, 10
Levin, 35, 82, 196, 262, 288, 289, 294, 341, 346
Levine, 10
Levinson, 300
Levitan, 1, 2, 12, 16, 20, 38, 50, 53, 67, 72, 78, 83, 91, 98, 104, 106, 115, 118, 121, 122, 126, 136, 141, 171, 175, 195, 221, 224, 227, 238, 260, 267, 293, 316, 349
Liberman, 262, 314
Lifshitz, 313
Limanadniks, 79
Limon, 10, 88, 141, 196, 294
Loria, 23
Lubka, 21
Luria, 45, 111
Lyubiker, 8

M

Mackler, 394
Magzis, 393
Mahar'sha, 23
Maizel, 152
Makler, 6

Malach, 24
Malahshekvitz, 162
Maliskai, 67, 68
Malisker, 26, 28, 35, 68
Maneh, 318
Markman, 88, 91, 150, 161, 289, 302
Markon, 28, 223, 311
Markov, 325, 332
Matarosz, 216
Mataroz, 365, 366, 367, 368, 394
Matorose, 247
Matosov, 215, 277, 289, 296
Matvievich, 369
Matyokevitz, 377, 378
Meckler, 338, 385, 394
Meetzkovsky, 355
Meirovich, 62, 67, 78, 89, 90, 127, 129, 136, 269
Meirovitch, 1, 2, 88, 91, 114, 117
Meirovitz, 3, 4, 14, 88, 89, 108, 349
Meirowitz, 288
Meizel, 291, 292
Mekler, 262, 277, 278, 301, 357
Meltzer, 11, 88, 91, 106, 124, 211, 296, 297, 359
Melzer, 173
Mendel, 21, 53
Meshulam, 22
Meyerson, 380
Meyrovich, 110
Mindel, 88, 114, 299, 300
Minkovitz, 137
Mironovich, 341, 346
Mizel, 9
Moller, 35
Monies, 37
Motisov, 14
Motiyokevitch, 251
Motosov, 4, 5, 11, 24, 25, 32, 71, 78, 81, 141, 150, 180, 185, 226, 243, 260, 261, 350, 359, 363
Motyokavitz, 247, 250, 251
Motyokevich, 392, 395
Muler, 24
Munis, 11
Muniz, 20

N

Narinaski, 379
Narotzki, 287
Narutzer, 36
Narutzki, 357
Naruzki, 262
Nashesh, 56
Nasis., 341
Nehemsik, 20
Nerutsky, 393, 394
Nigal, 69
Noach, 92, 93, 98, 103, 132
Norman, 115, 163, 246, 247, 304, 350, 352, 361, 364, 369, 370, 371, 372, 386, 388, 393
Norvitz, 252
Novogin, 252

O

Orlov, 323
Oshpal, 71, 72
Oshpol 310, 311
Oshtashkover, 36
Ostrovsky, 82
Oyeshisky, 243
Ozer, 43

P

Paikon, 223
Paritcher, 35
Patrapas, 148
Peikon, 276, 297
Peres, 59, 109, 110, 117, 146, 269, 396
Peretz, 151, 152, 286, 287
Perlman, 233
Perski, 59, 109, 146, 396
Persky, 269
Peykin, 3, 45
Peykon, 5
Piastonovitz, 292
Pieshka, 267
Pintov, 4, 112, 113, 116
Plavius, 84
Plevski, 220
Polevick, 375
Potropos, 79
Potzotsky, 83
Putrpas, 146, 147
Pyeshka, 80

R

Rabbi Zishka, 13, 23, 39, 264
Rabinovich, 109
Rabinovitz, 34, 35
Rabonski, 4
Rabonsky, 274, 290, 312
Rabunski, 59, 88, 89, 109, 112, 146, 149, 159, 170, 365, 395, 396, 397
Rabunsky, 267
Racha-Rasha, 82, 281
Ragatchaver, 72
Raginholtz, 206
Raider, 307
Raiz, 276, 277, 300
Ramanovsky, 197
Rashish, 31
Razin, 72
Reitstein, 314
Reyder, 91
Riar, 161, 162, 323, 374
Rice, 52
Riddle, 374
Rider, 248
Robonsky, 324
Rod, 196, 197
Rodanski, 339
Rodantzki, 137
Rodinidky, 9
Rodinisky, 9
Rodinski, 7, 88, 111
Rodinsky, 143, 305
Rodinitsky, 280, 290
Rodnizki, 258
Rogovin, 229, 231
Rogovin, 313
Roitstein, 275, 278, 299
Romankov, 267, 268
Roshka, 20, 22, 183
Roytstein, 4, 6
Rozenshtein, 106
Rubin, 10, 45, 108, 292, 293, 309
Rudnitsky, 141
Rugbin, 183, 185, 186, 187, 265
Rydel, 387

S

Salovitz, 324
Samuilovna, 339
Sandler, 10, 216, 293
Sapieska, 370
Sapir, 45
Sazunov, 385
Schatz, 196, 369, 370, 373, 374, 387
Schkalia, 82
Schmidt, 35, 159, 369, 370, 372, 382
Schneiorson, 225
Schneorson, 295
Schneur, 116
Schnitzer, 313
Schostekowitz, 213
Schraga, 25
Schulman, 113, 240, 336, 362
Schuster, 380
Scrantani, 351, 354
Sekliar, 301, 310
Sepelevitz, 268
Serls, 11
Sernack, 266
Sesensky, 313
Sesonsky, 14
Shaefer, 190, 191
Shafer, 4, 45
Shaffer, 78, 288
Shafran, 258, 324
Shamach, 58
Shapira, 5, 311, 383
Shapiro, 51, 327
Shaptzenko, 386
Shastakovitz, 269
Shavetz, 171, 227
Shebetznko, 323
Sheffer, 297
Sherangovich, 178, 181, 182, 183
Sherganovitz, 137
Shernagovich, 196
Shernagovitz, 137, 359, 362, 367, 372
Shernegowicz, 214, 215

Shernogovitch, 162
Sherutzin, 395
Shestokovitz, 177
Shetonov, 251
Shevetz, 298
Shevitz, 197
Shiff, 29
Shihanover, 26
Shikarda, 382
Shilak, 201, 204, 210
Shimsheleventch, 163
Shimshelevetz, 162
Shirinsky, 383, 384
Shirotzin, 253
Shirutzin, 247, 250
Shkolnik, 6, 278
Shlah, 23
Shletzer, 254
Shmookler, 162
Shmukler, 5, 88, 91, 183, 276, 304
Shnayorson, 216, 217
Shneirson, 226
Shneirsons, 226
Shnerson, 223
Shnitzer, 249, 254, 257
Shogol, 32, 218, 219, 238, 239, 391, 392
Shohel, 24
Shorekvas,, 269
Shoshan, 104, 105
Shostakovich, 266, 374
Shostakovitch, 357
Shostakovitz, 243
Shostokoviz, 180
Shotan, 258
Shots, 160, 251
Shotz, 153, 243, 321, 323
Shotzs, 245, 246
Shuberty, 346
Shugol, 313
Shulken, 395
Shulman, 2, 4, 6, 10, 11, 14, 28, 31, 45, 46, 71, 79, 81, 82, 116, 117, 122, 125, 180, 182, 215, 219, 221, 222, 224, 233, 238, 240, 242, 247, 248, 250, 251, 253, 254, 256, 261, 262, 275, 279, 293, 295, 308, 316, 340, 350, 353, 355, 358, 359, 360, 363, 364, 367, 368, 376, 378, 388, 391, 392, 395
Shuts, 154, 155, 156, 157, 159, 160, 161, 162, 164, 358, 360
Simhas, 28
Sirotzin, 368
Skarntani, 365
Skrentani, 366
Smallshaness, 145
Smetinko, 213, 216, 217
Smitenko, 213
Sobol, 395
Soborov, 248, 325
Sokholov, 395
Sokolinsky, 309, 310
Sokolov, 250
Sokolovsky, 137, 149, 150, 152, 357
Soliminsky, 9

Solominsky, 291
Sorinski, 249
Sosanski, 7
Sosensky, 151, 169, 201, 202, 203, 206, 207, 209, 210, 221, 222, 223, 224, 293, 339, 350
Sosnasky, 303
Sosneski, 281
Sosnesky, 281, 309
Sosonoski, 256
Sotzkover, 6, 11, 357
Sovitch, 250
Sovitz, 250
Sozkover, 180, 207, 245
Specter, 154, 158, 161, 192, 352
Spector, 71, 109, 110, 112, 137, 171, 288, 308
Spektor, 3, 121, 122, 165, 195, 239, 240, 243, 244, 323, 355, 358, 364, 370, 373, 374, 386
Sperber, 299, 300
Statoayudviga, 266
Stenkivitch, 216
Stolar, 139
Stoler, 78, 204, 205, 313
Stolier, 286
Stoller, 35, 209
Stulov, 383
Surikvas, 366
Sutzkever, 296
Sutzkevor, 280
Svirsky, 290

T

Takchonik, 183
Takontzik, 137
Takotznik, 119
Tantzer, 93, 94
Taubes, 6, 115, 279, 309
Tewel, 341
Tillis, 287
Tkachuk, 387
Tkatchuk, 216
Tkatzonik, 177
Torov, 4, 6, 112, 123, 160, 182, 195, 198, 200, 223, 274, 279, 280, 300
Tsinstung, 9
Tsipa, 69
Tsipilevich, 25, 96, 372
Tsipilovich, 196
Tunik, 311
Turov, 195, 198, 274, 279
Tzedek, 22, 23, 26, 27, 29, 32, 55
Tzeplevitz, 295, 300
Tzernechovski, 112
Tzinstang, 291
Tzipilevitz, 10
Tziras, 27
Tzirinsky, 312
Tzirolnik, 216
Tzirolnik, 280, 286, 305
Tzirtoka, 74
Tzivoni, 104, 264

Tzodikov, 312

V

Varfman, 288
Vaser Trager, 24
Vasilavska, 383
Verbayov, 384
Verebayov, 377
Vexler, 190
Vilkovsky, 117
Viner, 20, 24
Vinik, 307
Vlodia, 245, 247, 248, 249, 250, 252, 255, 361, 390, 391, 392, 393
Vlodka, 250
Volinitz, 247, 249, 250, 251, 252, 374, 388, 390, 391, 393
Volkavsky, 110
Volkovsky, 110
Volodia, 364, 368, 375
Volozhinski, 34, 35
Vorbviov, 254
Voroshilov, 232, 316, 332, 337

W

Weiner, 303
Weinstein, 305
Weisenholtz, 287, 305, 311
Weiss, 45, 49
Wexler, 258, 298, 357, 359
Wolf, 146, 223, 224

Y

Yashteshev, 162
Yentes, 28
Yoran, 103, 217
Yoshekevitz, 256

Z

Zaev, 21
Zaif, 5
Zal, 22, 23
Zalman, 11, 23, 29, 200, 296
Zamoshchik, 277
Zavodnick, 51
Zavodnik, 50
Zeif, 277
Zemushzik, 5
Zendel, 302
Zikovsky, 113
Zimerman, 4, 5, 6, 7, 8, 30, 44, 45, 88, 91, 117, 121, 137, 149, 151, 175, 202, 203, 212, 225, 241, 255, 262, 317, 319, 320
Zimmerman, 1, 3, 8, 20, 23, 25, 47, 67, 80, 95, 118, 123, 127, 137, 154, 160, 177, 181, 196, 199, 216, 222, 229, 232, 236, 240, 243, 249, 254, 258, 261, 264, 275, 276, 278, 280, 282, 285, 286, 288, 298, 302, 310, 313, 314, 316, 350, 354, 356, 357, 359, 372, 373, 385, 386, 387, 389, 391, 394
Zipelevitch, 254
Zipelevitz, 11
Zipelovitz, 11
Zipilavitz, 81
Zipilevich, 110
Zipilevitz, 137
Zipilovitz, 108
Zirinsky, 236
Zirolnik, 7, 240, 242, 244, 246, 350, 353, 358, 361, 362
Zirtzis, 312
Ziskand, 6, 278
Ziskind, 7, 195, 283, 290
Zivoni, 4, 105, 108, 320
Zokofsky, 148, 169, 359, 361
Zokovski, 88, 89
Zokovsky, 46, 104, 223
Zokovsy, 197
Zoshas, 18
Zrinski, 228
Zuckerman, 138, 154, 155, 158, 161, 162, 164, 296, 310, 323, 358
Zukerman, 3, 4, 11, 12, 45, 47, 51, 171, 244
Zukofski, 143
Zukofsky, 265
Zukovski, 143, 150, 151, 200, 321
Zukovsky, 126, 275, 362, 364, 365
Zukovzky, 394
Zushas, 18, 19
Zushibebes, 145
Zusman, 39

Supplements

Do Not Go Gentle

The Kurenets Chapters From a book by Charles Gelman (Known in Kurenets as Yechezkel, son of Yitskhok Iche Hatsyes Zimmerman)

https://www.amazon.com/Do-Not-Gentle-Resistance-1941-1945/dp/1511736852

July 1941. We were huddling in the backyard of our neighbor, Mote-Leyb Kopershtooch, sitting on the ground, our backs against the wall, and talking in whispers. The German army had arrived in town barely one week earlier. No specific orders or edicts against Jews had been proclaimed at this point. Yet the air was more and more permeated with fear each passing day. Even on bright days it felt as if a heavy cloud had descended on us.

Mote-Leyb's house stood next to my father's. I reached his yard by going through a hole in the back fence, as did a couple of neighbors from the other side of Mote-Leyb's house. We met there daily just to stay out of the way of the police and the Germans, to exchange the latest rumors, and to kill time. Our former routine of living had been broken, most likely forever.

That day, Leybke the barber was there and so was my friend, Nyomke Shulman. Leybke regretted not having escaped with the retreating Russians while there was still time. Not that he hadn't tried. In fact, he told us, he had made a half-hearted effort to go east. He acquired a horse and buggy, a real fancy one, a brichke they used to call it, and he put his wife and two children in it and drove off. They got as far as Kostenevich, a small town about seventeen kilometers from our town of Kurenits (sometimes pronounced, but never written, Kœrnits; in Polish KurzŽniec, in Russian KurenŽts). Leybke's wife kept begging him to return home, where things were familiar and safe. She couldn't take the hardship and uncertainty of what lay ahead along the way--air raids, hunger, trouble with bandits, just to mention a few. So they turned back. Leybke concluded his story by saying he could see he'd made a mistake in giving up so easily; he should have pressed on.

I couldn't help but agree with him--in though only, of course. Leybke was more vulnerable than most of us because of the high standing he had had with the Soviet authorities. Being a barber and a real proletarian, his background was, from the Soviet political view, impeccable. We lived in the eastern part of Poland. When the Soviets occupied it on September 17, 1939, they promptly divided the population into politically "acceptable" and "unacceptable" segments. Anyone who didn't have his passport stamped with the designation "worker" or "peasant" could eventually expect trouble from the authorities. Because a large segment of the shtetl (small town) Jews made their living before 1939 buying and selling, they had been designated "businessmen." Many were just peddlers and small merchants; they earned barely enough to keep body and soul together. Nevertheless, they received the negative designation. It didn't bode well for the future.

The Soviet authorities were helped along in these and other matters by local activists who cooperated with them, often to the detriment of others--Jews as well as non-Jews--and informed on them as to their wealth, political reliability, and so forth. Some people were taxed into poverty, deprived of their houses, furniture, and all material goods. Some were even sent to Siberia as a result of the activities of these informers.

Leybke was considered an activist, although of a different kind. So far as I know, he was not an informer, but he had high-placed friends in the local hierarchy. I know for a fact that he had saved the life of my brother-in-law, Sam Spektor. Sam had been inducted into a work brigade about three months before the Germans invaded Russia on June 22, 1941. Leybke convinced the authorities that Sam was the only person capable of organizing and training a city orchestra, which the Soviets very much desired. So Sam was left behind. The Soviets mobilized quite a few men from our town of Kurenits and sent them to the German border to build fortifications. None of them ever returned and they were never heard from again.

Most of these activists had retreated along with the Soviets, well ahead of the approaching Germans, because they feared retribution from the non-Jewish population who were anti-Soviet. Some fled with their families. Others left wives and children behind, mistakenly believing that only they themselves were in danger. Many of those who fled survived the war. Of the families that activists left behind, none survived. During the first few weeks of the German occupation, such an outcome could not be foreseen. Had anybody described such a scenario as eventually coming to pass, we would have considered them deranged.

Rumors abounded: "The Russians are counterattacking." "They've taken back this or that city." "The Germans have taken Smolensk (a Russian city on the way to Moscow)." "The war can't last more than a month longer." Few of them were true. Confusion was the order of the day; for real news we were utterly in the dark. Listening to radio broadcasts was forbidden under penalty of death. News from the front was unavailable. What we did hear was mostly sketchy and unreliable.

The, only a few days later, Leybke told us he had been summoned to the police station; he had been informed he must appear there the following day, ready to be shipped out to an unknown destination. He would be allowed to take with him only five pounds of food and clothing.

We were sitting in our usual place and discussing this latest development. Leybke said he though the Germans would send him to a labor camp. He wasn't worried about himself, because he thought he could always survive if they allowed him to take his barbering tools with him. "Even in a labor camp, hair must be cut," he said. He was confident that he would make out all right.

Thoughts like that seemed quite plausible at that time. We had not heard of any German atrocities yet, except for two instances, which the Jewish population interpreted as unfortunate accidents.

Between the time the Russians fled Kurenits and the time the German army arrived, the town was without any real authority. It was decided to organize a sort of civil guard; gentiles and a few young Jewish men participated in order to guard against looting. The men were armed with rifles left by the Russian police and even used the local police station. Unwisely, this action continued several days after the Germans entered. Early one morning two young Jewish men, coming off duty and walking back to the police station, were confronted by German soldiers, who discovered they were Jews and arrested them. No explanation was acceptable and the young men were promptly shot. They were cousins and both had the same name--Shimon Zimmerman. One was also known as Shimon dem fishers.

The other incident involved two prominent men from Kurenits, both of them merchants and quite rich by our standards. They suffered greatly under the Soviets, who confiscated their businesses and all their merchandise and taxed them so severely--hundred of thousands of rubles--that they lost their houses and savings and fled to another town about thirty-five kilometers away. A good thing they did, too. If they hadn't, they might well have been sent to Siberia. A couple of weeks into the German occupation these merchants started to walk back to Kurenits to try to reclaim the houses that had been theirs. They were intercepted on the road by Germans, recognized as Jews, and promptly shot.

These incidents, unfortunate as they were, were in no way recognized as a harbinger of things to come.

Leybke reported to the police station as directed and was never seen or heard from again. He was probably shot somewhere out of town. Yet such a fate, at that time, was incomprehensible because it was unbelievable. After all, the Germans are civilized people, we though. They might weed out the communists, but surely they would investigate with at least some semblance of orderly procedure.

Were we all na•ve? With the benefit of hindsight, I can say we certainly were. The truth is that up to that time we had not yet heard of any real atrocities.

Throughout the period of Russian administration there were Jews living in our town, as well as in surrounding towns, who had come from the western part of Poland, occupied by the Germans in September 1939. These Jews had managed to come to eastern Poland, even after living several months under the Germans. The stories they told were not pleasant. Jews in German-occupied territory had to wear a yellow star of David on their clothes. At times they were mistreated and demeaned, for example, by being made to wash public latrines and streets. Jews had no right to use the sidewalks; they had to walk in the middle of the street. Religious Jews in the street often had their beards cut by force, or grabbed and a handful of hair pulled out. Sometimes a German officer would order an individual Jew, or a group, to dance for him and then proceed to mercilessly beat up those who hadn't jumped high enough or who had otherwise failed to perform to his liking. There were other stories like these of Jews being humiliated and brutalized. Nonetheless, we heard nothing, not even rumors, of outright shootings.

When the Russians offered these displaced persons a chance to return to their former homes in western Poland, a large number of them said yes and signed up to be transported back to the German part of Poland, something they would not have done, we believed, had they thought conditions there to be unacceptable. Of course the Russians never intended to keep their offer; instead, they shipped these transportees east to Siberia. In so doing the Russians unintentionally saved the lives of thousands of Jews. Some died on the way from the primitive conditions of transport, which could last for several months on each leg of the journey. Others perished from the harsh conditions in remote parts of Russia. A majority, though, survived and surfaced in the West after the war.

Even much later--after fifty-four of our Kurenits Jews had been shot outside of town on the Simchas Torah holiday of 1941, after thirty-two more had been shot by two policemen in March of 1942, after news reached us of Jews being massacred in surrounding towns--people would still come up with explanations, no matter how feeble, to give the events some justification. For instance, in one town they said the Germans supposedly found a gun. In another they said the Jews hadn't filled their assigned quotas of money, furs, or other goods. In the case of fifty-four, as these martyrs became known, the excuse was that they had been Russian activists, or families of activists, left behind. People excused the massacre of thirty-two by saying the Germans had no direct role in it: the hapless Jews were shot by two drunken Polish policemen.

People desperately looked for excuses in order to continue believing that somehow they would survive. Married people with young children were especially prone to this syndrome, as were older people. A case of drowning men grasping for straws. The real truth of things did not crystallize and hit home for some time. In 1941, especially during the summer, we were still innocents.

After Leybke disappeared, I continued to get together with a few friends in Mote-Leyb's backyard. The news and rumors that filtered through to us were getting more and more grim every day. It was becoming clearer that the Russians were being defeated on every front and that the Germans were capturing major cities deep inside Russia--all in a matter of only a few weeks. It was discouraging.

In this connection, I especially remember the feldsher of our town, a man by the name of Szostakowicz. (Feldsher is a Russian medical title, roughly equivalent to "physician's assistant", given to a person with medical experience and the authority to treat patients, but without a regular medical degree.) One morning I met him as he was walking in the town square, holding in his hand a German grenade, the type with a long wooden handle. It had obviously been given to him by one of his high-ranking German officer friends. He was just toying with it and intended no harm. (Later on, when I was a member of the partisan underground, I had occasion to use grenades like these on the Germans, with their intended purpose.) As we met, he stopped and talked to me for a moment or two before continuing on his way. What I remember most is what he said just before he went on. "You mark my words. This German Reich will last for a thousand years." He was, of course, parroting words from a recent speech of Hitler's, but to me he conveyed the message that he completely believed what he was repeating. Having said his piece, he strutted away like a peacock, proud of the achievements of his newfound German friends. You can imagine what this chance meeting did to my already sagging spirits. The future looked bright to him, but to usÉWe were on the opposite ends of a seesaw; the higher he rose, the lower we sank.

How different things had been only a month earlier. There was no war here then and, with the tight control which the Soviets exercised over news sources, we had absolutely no inkling that war between the Russians and the Germans was in the offing. (The outbreak of war came as a surprise to the Soviets, too.) Under the Russians, we Jews felt for the first time--aside form the lack of freedom and the shortages of food and material things that affected everybody--that we were full-fledged citizens, with anti-Semitism prohibited under severe penalty of the law.

I was not quite eighteen then and lived at home with my parents, Yitskhok Zimerman (Iche Khatsyes), my father, and Feyge, my mother. I was the youngest of the five children. My oldest sister, Sarah, was married and lived in the town of Volozin. My youngest sister, Dina, about four years older than I, was also married and lived deep inside Russia, out of reach of the Germans. Also living at home were my two middle sisters, Ethel and Minya. Minya was in the last stages of pregnancy. Her husband, Sam Spektor, had received permission to visit his brother in the city of Kharkov in Russia two weeks before the war started. When war broke out, he couldn't get back. He remained deep inside Russia throughout the war and survived.

Our future looked bleak now. What would become of us? Minya was ready to give birth almost any day. How would she cope with a baby in times like these, and without a husband? There were many questions and no good answers.

2

One day an official order of the German commandant was posted in the public square. In both German and Polish it ordered all Jewish males between the ages of fourteen and sixty-five to assemble in the public square at two in the afternoon the next day. Failure to comply, it stated, was punishable by death.

No one knew the reason for this order, though many tried to guess. "Maybe they'll make us wash the cobble-stones in the marketplace," some said. "Maybe they'll amuse themselves by making us dance for them," others suggested. Many other explanations like these were offered, which is to say, no one expected the worst. Yet failure to appear at the ordered time and place would probably be unwise because the Germans might check the people present against a list of town residents.

As it happened nothing much really did occur. About eight hundred men showed up at the appointed hour and were made to stand in the hot summer sun, facing the German Kommandantur (commandant's office and garrison headquarters). After about an hour had passed, German soldiers with machine guns came out of the building and took up positions facing us. They remained in that attitude for about another hour. This was the low point of the day. The Germans, with their machine guns, certainly looked menacing enough and I had second thoughts about the wisdom of having showed up. Then, after we had been standing there for more than two hours, the German commandant finally came out. He was a man about fifty years old and held the rank of major. He told us not to worry. He wished to have a Judenrat (council of Jews) appointed. Then and there he selected an Austria Jew, a man by the name of Schatz, to be the Judenrat leader. And then he dismissed the entire group and told us to return to our homes. Except for a few cases of sunburn and of one person fainting from the heat, nothing bad had happened to anyone.

We didn't appreciate how lucky we were until a month or so later when we found out that in the town of Vileyka, only seven kilometers away, all the Jewish male population from fourteen to sixty-five years of age had also been ordered to assemble before their local commandant, at approximately the same time we were before ours. But all of them--about two thousand men--were taken away and vanished without a trace. This was followed by all kinds of rumors as to their whereabouts. Some peasant had seen them in a labor camp thirty kilometers away. Or they might be in another labor camp eighty kilometers away. Needless to say, all these reports were false. The men had in fact been shot the same day they were taken away. Their place of execution was not discovered until after the war.

Obviously, then, local commandants had discretionary power to determine the fate of the Jews within their jurisdiction. We were lucky to have gotten a commandant with a human heart. He would prove this again a little later in an incident involving my family.

The Judenrat was organized the day after the assembly in the Kurenits public square and consisted of eight to ten Jews, with Schatz as leader. It served as the instrument through which the Germans conveyed all their orders and wishes to the Jewish population. For example, a certain number of Jews were required to go and work at Lubanye, a state-run farm not far away. Other Jews were detailed to clean the offices of the German administration, the police, the civil administration, and so on. Money, furs, jewels, Persian rugs, and paintings were expropriated from the Jewish population. All these orders were given to the Judenrat, which then apportioned them among the Jewish population. This was not always done fairly.

Towards the end of July, I was among the 150 Jewish young people between the ages of seventeen and thirty sent up to the state farm of Lubanye for three days of work in the fields. After the three days were up, we were relieved by another group of the same size. Each of us had to go work there about once every two weeks. The rest of the time we worked in or around town. Lubanye was about six kilometers away, but no transportation was provided; we had to walk there and back. Each of us brought our own food for three days with us. I remember bringing along only a loaf of bread and a bottle of milk. Food was getting scarce and little could be spared. So we supplemented the food we brought from home with cabbage and carrots from the gardens we tended. Of course we weren't entitled to do this, so we took the vegetables on the sly. Carrots posed no problem; nothing obvious was left after you pulled one or two out of the ground. All you had to do was dispose of the inedible green leafy part. Cabbages were a problem, though, because if you removed the whole head, it left an empty space that could easily be spotted. Getting caught could conceivably mean punishment by beatings or maybe worse, so I used to eat only the inside of a cabbage head, carefully leaving the outside leaves in place. Unless the plant was scrupulously examined, no one could tell that it had been tampered with. At any rate, I was never caught, and I don't recall anyone else was either.

I particularly remember one out of many jobs I had to perform in or around our town of Kurenits. During the months of August, September, and part of October 1941, the Germans operated a Durchgangslager (transit camp) in Kurenits--a temporary way station for Russian prisoners of war. Thousands of them were marched in on foot from the eastern front and kept in Kurenits for two or three days of rest before being driven further west. They were kept out in the open at the horse market, where, prior to the war, horse trading had taken place.

Day and night, fair weather and foul, the prisoners remained exposed to the elements. When it rained, they got soaked. As time passed and it started getting chillier, their situation quickly became desperate. Every morning a number of dead bodies had to be disposed of, a task assigned to the Jews. Fortunately, I never had to do this. In the transit camp a few of us were given the job of bringing in water in a huge barrel mounted on wheels, from a water source located outside the camp perimeter. The camp was surrounded by barbed wire and electrified wires, with armed guards in watchtowers. The prisoners were usually in bad shape, suffering from malnutrition, fatigue, and exposure. Once a day they got a water soup and about 250 grams of moldy bread. The soup was cooked from moldy cabbage into which had been dropped a few pieces of rotting fish or meat.

The camp operated for about three months. It finally closed down at the end of October or maybe the beginning of November 1941. While it operated, at least 100,000 POWs passed through on their way to more permanent sites. We very much pitied them and, when we could, tried to help with a piece of bread, a drink of water, or a found cigarette butt. But their miser was so great that our best efforts amounted to no more than a drop in the ocean. Of course, at the time neither they nor we had any inkling of the scope of the calamity that awaited us all. Of the estimated six to eight million prisoners the Germans captured in Russia, only twenty-five percent survived. The rest were executed or died from systematic hard labor and starvation. The Jews of Europe fared even worse. They had only about a ten percent rate of survival; most of the other ninety percent died by direct execution.

During the last days of July 1941, an order came from the German authorities for all Jews to surrender any and all Persian rugs they might have in their possession. My sister Minya, who was in the last days of her pregnancy, owned one of decent quality and about two by three meters in size. She had me help her drop it off at the Kommandantur. The commandant saw us bring it in and, I am sure, noticed Minn's condition.

That afternoon a German soldier drove up to our house with a horse and wagon loaded with several sacks of flour and potatoes and proceeded to unload the wagon. "Courtesy of the commandant," he said. Needless to say, these food supplies were a godsend and we made them last quite a while. That major was obviously a decent man and, in the limited framework of his position, apparently tried to do as little harm as he could get away with and even to help when possible. It was always my sincerest hope that he would survive the war in good shape.

In early August 1941 my sister gave birth to a beautiful baby boy, without medical assistance. By pure chance we were fortunate enough to have stayed with us for a couple of days a Jewish woman from the town of Ilya, about forty-five kilometers away, and she was of considerable help in the delivery.

This lady--whose name, I regret, I cannot recall--had an Aryan "appearance" and easily passed for gentile. Because of this she could move from town to town without too much difficulty. People with this particular endowment were considered lucky and were much envied by others considered to have the more traditional Jewish look. No doubt many owed their survival to this lucky chance. The woman was looking for her husband and her only son. They had all been in the town of Vileyka at the time all Jewish males fourteen to sixty-five were ordered to assemble in the town square, and her husband and her son vanished with the local Jews. It was through this woman that we first heard of what had occurred in Vileyka. She was on her way to some other town or village to investigate a rumor that Vileyka Jews had been seen there. She had already checked several other leads, all false. She stayed with us only a few days. Who knows how many more rumors she would subsequently investigate. Quite a few, I would venture to guess.

Two days before Simchas Torah of 1941, I was sent to the state farm at Lubanye for three days of work as part of the contingent of young people sent there periodically. It was the time of the year for potato harvesting. One of the regular non-Jewish workers, working with a team of horses, plowed a furrow about half a kilometer long to expose the potatoes. Our job was to follow and pick these potatoes and bag them. Before we finished one furrow, the next usually lay exposed, ready and waiting for us. Thus we were under constant pressure to work faster. The overseer berated and harassed us with shouts of "Keep moving, you lazy sons of bitches. You're delaying the horses." By the end of a day like that we were naturally pretty exhausted and our backs hurt from all that bending.

On our third and last day of work, the day of Simchas Torah, we were out in the fields as usual, spread four to five meters apart from each other, facing a furrow with freshly exposed potatoes. Off in the distance we noticed two people with guns approaching. As they got closer I recognized them both as two young men from our town of Kurenits and barely a year older than me. One was called Blizniuk and the other, Polevik. They were now members of the town police force and both were well known to us. I was not on unfriendly terms with either of them.

As all of us workers stood facing the approaching policemen, I had an uneasy feeling in the pit of my stomach, like everyone else, I suppose. Never before had Kurenits police come up to Lubanye. The sight of them now did not bode well, especially as they were carrying guns. One was holding some sort of paper in his hand and he glanced down at it from time to time. The pair marched up the line of Jewish young people facing them and, as they went by, from time to time they called out one of our names and plucked that person out of the line. In all they pulled fourteen of us out and I was one of the fourteen.

We got only vague answers to our questions about what was happening. My mind started running at high speed, looking for some explanation of why I had been selected to be arrested. I had certainly been no activist for the Russians; in fact, during the almost two years of their administration, I had come to dislike their system. It must be, I thought, that my name had somehow got mixed up with the name of a distant relative of mine, with the same family name, who was an activist. Yes, that must be it, I thought. I'd be able to straighten this out once we got to the police station. A feeling of hope and belief in some order--a feeling that the world wasn't totally upside down--still prevailed then.

It was about six kilometers from Lubanye to Kurenits. The first five kilometers were through woods and the last, just before Kurenits, was through open fields. In the woods we walked together with the policemen, mingling and talking like old friends. One of our group of fourteen was a young man by the name of Arke Ruvke's, Aaron the son of Ruvke Alperovich. He was about three years older than I and quite strong physically. Halfway through the woods something happened that shook me to the core. Arke walked alongside me for a while and whispered, "They're going to kill us. Let's overwhelm them now before we get out of the woods." Properly organized, this could probably have been accomplished easily. But the idea seemed preposterous. Why should these people kill us? I considered myself innocent of any wrongdoing and so did everyone else in the group. And what would happen after the pair was overwhelmed? Where would we go then? We would be fugitives and unable to move freely. And what bout our families? They might all be punished, even shot. Much later, by the way, after we had become less naïve and the true nature of what the Germans intended became clearer, that uncertainty about what could happen to their families kept most people in check and restrained them from running away to the woods or giving more open expression of revolt. Needless to say, I disregarded Arke's suggestion and so did others he also tried to persuade.

What really impressed me at the time, though, was the look in his eyes. It took me back to my schooling under the Soviets, where I had to read quite a few of the Russian classics. In one story, by Lermontov, a young nobleman in the military is assigned, because of some infraction of discipline, to an out-of-the-way garrison where there are no young women. The boredom is great. When the commander's daughter comes to visit, the young nobleman promptly falls in love with her, as do several other officers, and one of them challenges the young nobleman to a duel over the young woman. A friend of the nobleman's, in the course of preparations for the duel, foretells that the nobleman will die in the coming encounter. When asked how he can know an outcome before it happens, he answers that the eyes of a man who is about to die reflect death for an hour or two before the event and that this can be seen by anyone who looks into them. The nobleman fights the duel and, of course, is killed.

The story made quite an impression on me. I remember wondering whether that was really possible. Now, looking into Arke's eyes as he talked to me about overwhelming the policemen, I was sure I saw death. I remember thinking clearly, "Oh my God, if he is just about to die, then the fate of the rest of us is also sealed. Can this really be?" The mind will not accept such a verdict willingly or easily--not on such short notice and especially not if known to be based on a work of romantic fiction.

We all continued walking together toward Kurenits, still in a more or less friendly atmosphere. I began feeling more nervous from the moment I saw Arke's eyes and I now considered the chances of a satisfactory ending to this episode greatly reduced. Where were they taking us? And what actually lay in wait for us when we got there? The answers to these questions were not long in coming.

As soon as we came out of the woods into the open country, the policemen's demeanor changed abruptly. They fell back about three meters behind us and pointed their rifles at us. Gone was their former amiable and comradely behavior. We now had behind us two snarling policemen ready to shoot at the slightest provocation. They began and kept up a diatribe accusing us Jews of helping the Soviets, and spat out a story about how a man called Peter--one of their unofficial leaders, who had been arrested by the Soviets shortly before the war started--had been executed in the jail in Vileyka.

This last was probably true. We had heard rumors that the Russian security forces executed all their prisoners in that jail, and most likely in all the other jails under their control, because there was not enough time to evacuate them. After the Russians left and before the Germans arrived, relatives and friends of prisoners rushed to the jail and discovered the remains of their loved ones, all executed. It was easy to imagine the anger and rage of the two policemen at such atrocities, but why pick on us? Peter was young and well like in the Jewish community. He mixed with Jewish men his age in friendly fashion and was definitely no Jew-hater. His arrest had nothing to do with Jews, his execution even less. Both were the result of a brutal political system that victimized Jew and non-Jew alike.

But all of this was of no interest to the two policemen. It became more and more clear that what motivated them was a need for revenge--not for something we had done, but for something the Soviets had done. Throughout history Jews have been scapegoats for people who wanted to vent their anger at a higher authority beyond their reach, an authority at whom they could only grit their teeth. What a convenient punching bag the Jews made under the Germans. No one was punished for injuring or even killing a Jew. Little did I suspect at this time that one of these two policemen, together with yet another, would a few months later in March 1942, go on a rampage and kill thirty-two Jews in Kurenits, my father and two of my sisters among them. And for this the pair was not punished at all, but actually praised by the Germans. I was told that an article appeared in a White Russian newspaper printed in the German-occupied city of Minsk, the capital of White Russia, describing the pair as great patriots of White Russia.

We were well out of the woods now with only open space between us and the first houses of the town. As we got closer, we came upon some armed German soldiers, which was very odd because there weren't supposed to be any Germans in town. There were none when we left for Lubanye two days earlier. The German major and his company of troops had been in charge for just the first five or six weeks of the German occupation. When they left, the town came under civilian administration and there had been no Germans in town since then.

The German soldiers let us pass. At close range their uniforms and insignia looked different. They were, as we found out later, SS Einsatzkommandos (SS Emergency Strike Force), who specialized in exterminating supposed enemies of the German Reich within conquered territories--communists, Jews, gypsies, and others. (SS stood for Schutzstaffel, or "Protection Detachment," an elite guard also known as the "Black Shirts.") We were going by houses now. A little farther on was the house of a schoolmate of mine, a young woman whose name was Khayke Rabunski. As we walked by, I saw her standing at a window, looking out. When she saw us being led by policemen, she threw her hands together in an exclamation of horror and I distinctly heard her cry out, "Oh, dear God, they're taking Khaskl away." (Khaskl is my Jewish name.)

It soon became apparent something horrible was happening in Kurenits. The street we were being marched down led to the public square in the center of town. We were coming to a small bridge over a stream, and right next to this bridge stood Arke's house. As we marched past, Arke suddenly bolted into his yard and sprinted on through into the open fields, with one of the policemen in hot pursuit. The other policeman ordered the rest of us to start running and hit me in the back with his rifle butt by way of encouragement. We were driven at a fast trot over the remaining half kilometer to the police station in the town square.

Before we were herded into the police station, we saw a group of about twenty-five Jews, mostly women and children, standing under guard in front. Once inside, we were locked up in a small room. Two Kurenits Jews who had been put there before us were sitting on the floor in a corner. One was a childhood friend of mine and a classmate, Nokhum Alperovits, and the other was Velvl Rabunski. "What's going on here?" The question seemed to come from everybody at once. "They're going to kill us. That's what's going on," they answered and proceeded to tell us how they had been arrested the night before. One group, they said, had already been taken outside of town, made to dig their own graves, and had then been shot. "They'll be coming for the rest of us soon."

Velvl Rabunski's wife, Rosa, worked as a maid at the police station. Thanks to her intervention and pleading, Velvl had been allowed to stay behind temporarily. Nokhum had been picked up too late to be sent out with the first party. They said they had no hope of getting out of this alive. I remember proposing that when we were taken out we should all run in different directions so that one or two might survive. The response I got was, "What's the use? They'll get us anyway." I had to admit the chances of success were really slim. And so we too sank to the floor ready for the worst. We too lost all hope.

We arrived at the police station about noon. We would stay there until five or so in the afternoon. All that time we expected that the door would open at any moment and that we would be led away by the Germans and shot. When the door finally did open, the person who came in was Matros, the former principal for the public high school Nokhum and I had both been students. He was a major in the Polish army reserves and a recognized leader in the local Polish community. Matros later paid for this honor with his life, along with his wife and one of their two grown sons, late in the spring of 1942, when the Germans liquidated the Polish leadership and intelligentsia. There were rumors that the other son, who at the time lived with a relative in another town, later became a German collaborator. The principal spoke to us encouragingly and when he left we felt at least a glimmer of hope returning.

About an hour later, we were all released. To this day I'm not sure why we were let go. The principal, I realized later, wasn't influential enough to accomplish our release on his own. There were rumors that the Germans, after taking the second group (the one we saw standing in front of the police station when we came in) and disposing of them in the same manner as the first, were too lazy to take out another group, especially so late in the afternoon. Maybe they had another job scheduled somewhere else the next day. In any case, by then they had disappeared from Kurenits.

For a period of several hours we had been without any hope at all. I remember Velvl Rabunski saying at one point, "What a beautiful world this will be after the war. Hitler is definitely going to be defeated"--in this we all concurred--"but we aren't going to be around to see him defeated or to enjoy life afterwards. Because we're all going to be dead in a few hours." No one contradicted him. It certainly looked true enough at the moment. I was barely eighteen; at such a tender age it is quite terrible to expect life to end in a short hour or two. But miracles do happen and here I was, back with my family, free of the nightmare.

By the next morning it was possible to take stock of the terrible events of the previous thirty-six hours: in all, the SS had killed fifty-three Jews, over half of them women and children. Some of those picked up were the families of the activists who had fled eastward. Some were young men who never cooperated with the Soviets except by holding a regular job. They went to their deaths with their families--parents, sisters, and brothers. They were forced to dig their own mass grave and were then shot.

Two young men--one, about twenty years old, the younger son of Pinye Alperovits the kosher butcher and the other, Osher from Dolhinov Street, about thirty years old--managed to break away from the pit and run back toward town with Germans and police in pursuit. They made it to a barn on Dolhinov Street and tried to hide there, but were discovered, beaten severely, and then dragged back to the pit and shot.

I was very anxious to find out what had happened to Arke, one of the fourteen in our group brought back from Lubanye, who had run away. The news was not long in coming. According to witnesses who saw and heard everything, the policeman giving chase to Arke caught up with him, whereupon Arke turned around and grabbed the policeman's rifle. Being of superior strength he was able to wrestle it away from the policeman. This was more the result of inspiration of the moment than calculation because as soon as Arke found himself in possession of the gun, he realized that he didn't know what to do with it. As I explained previously, we weren't yet psychologically ready to oppose the authorities actively, much less grab a gun and shoot a German or a policeman and then escape into the woods. The policeman senses Arke's state of mind and took advantage of it. In a honeyed voice he said, "Oh, come on, Arke. Stop fooling around. Give me the gun and we'll walk back." Arke hesitated, his fate hanging in the balance as seconds slid by. Then, spurred by his desperate will to survive, Arke made a final attempt to escape. After heroically wrestling the gun away from the policeman, he had some measure of hope and encouragement.

With the gun in his hands he took off at high speed heading towards the village of Pukien and the woods beyond it. But his act of desperation was like jumping from the fire into the frying pan. The chances of making his escape were practically nil. The town was surrounded by police and SS troops. Arke was running in an open field and made quite a visible target. Shots were fired at him from several directions and before Arke covered the first thirty meters he was brought down by a bullet. He crumpled to the ground unable to move. Several policemen surrounded him. Then Blizniuk, the first policeman who chased Arke from the moment he broke away from our group closed in, retrieved his gun and shot Arke death at close range as he lay wounded on the ground. He became the fifty-fourth victim.

My father compiled a detailed list of all fifty-four of the victims, including their first and last names, their ages, their addresses, and the names of their parents. The list was found in his suit pocket after he himself was killed, about six months later, by this same Blizniuk.

It was a miracle I had not succumbed along with the fifty-four. What we needed in those times was something on the order of a new miracle every day. The great majority of the Jews didn't get the benefit of even one; a few were saved miraculously not once but several times over, only to run out of miracles after successfully dodging death these three or four more times. However, there were no miracles for Arke that day. I believe he somehow sensed that his end was at hand, and even though he tried desperately to avoid it, his growing agitation brought the inevitable to pass.

3

Before the war, Vileyka was an unpretentious, middle-sized town of about 15,000 inhabitants, 4,000 of whom were Jews. Late in October 1941 it became the seat of the provincial government. Actually the Soviets had earlier raised Vileyka to this high status by making it the capital of what was once called Vilner gubernie (Vilno province). The city of Vilno (Polish Wilna Lithuanian Vilnius) had always been the capital of Lithuania, except for the period between the two world wars, when it was annexed to Poland. In October 1939 the Russians generously returned Vilno to Lithuania, along with a few neighboring towns, and Vilno once more became the capital--only to be annexed by the same Russians a few months later, along with the rest of the country, and made one of the Soviet republics as it still is today.

The Germans cut Vileyka province in two. Gluboke was made the capital of the northern half, while the city of Vileyka was retained as the capital of the southern half. The provincial governor--called Gebiet Kommissar--along with scores of officials, both military and civilian, took up residence in Vileyka. Dozens of German businessmen also settled there in order to appropriate as much grain, cattle, and clothing as possible from our province for the

German population back home. The military did their own separate requisitioning. All these people, with their staffs and secretariats, constituted quite a sizable number of Germans in need of living quarters and office space.

All that was left of the Jewish population of Vileyka at this time were women, children, and a few old men. All the men between the ages of fourteen and sixty-five had been executed at the beginning of the German occupation. Many of the houses and offices of Jews were empty and abandoned; some had been partially destroyed by looters. The Germans needed these living quarters and office space restored quickly for their own use. They ordered a number of carpenters, cabinetmakers, and painters to be sent from Kurenits to work in Vileyka. I joined the ranks of the painters.

Painting came naturally to me even though most of what I knew about it came only from watching painters working. As a child I loved to watch people at work, any kind of work. I could stand for hours watching, with equal fascination, blacksmiths, shoemakers, tailors, carpenters, painters, and all the other artisans as they practiced their trades. My brother-in-law, Sam Spektor, was a trained artist-painter and produced beautiful canvases, undoubtedly the kind of work he loved best. However, to make a living in those days, he had to devote some of his time to other, less artistic work, like painting houses. I had the opportunity to watch him at work more than anyone else and I picked up enough about painting houses to be able to pass as an experienced house painter.

It was becoming clearer that working people who could make themselves useful to the Germans stood a better chance of survival. If work was required, then so were workers. And the more important the job, the better this chance was. Suddenly everybody wanted to work, especially if they could get an official certificate indicating their new job status. A work certificate was very desirable and became a much sought-after talisman, as if this alone could make the difference between life and death. Many paid a high price, even gold, to obtain one. A few unscrupulous people, helped by some officials and even some Germans, made a thriving business out of selling work certificates. But in the end most of these certificates proved of little value. Only a few of the most highly skilled workers--those the Germans really needed and could not do without--were spared, but only for a while.

I became one of the painters working for the Gebiet Kommissar in Vileyka. Because his was the highest provincial authority, working for him gave us a greater sense of protection. This proved valuable when the Germans decided later on to finish off what remained of the Vileyka Jews. I was one of the five painters from Kurenits: two adults, Yosef Zuckerman (Yosef Saras) and Irma Meir-Aarons Alperovits, and three young male apprentices, Hershl Zimmerman (Hershl der Krivitser), his brother Judl, and I. We worked six days a week. Saturday afternoons we were allowed to go home to Kurenits, stay there overnight and part of Sunday, and then return to Vileyka Sunday afternoon. We were not paid, nor were we supplied with any food. We had to bring with us food enough to last the week.

There wasn't much I could take with me, since food reserves at home were meager and dwindling. But there was bread enough to eat. Sometimes in the evening, after work, we used to cook a soup of barley, beans, or such. Once in a while we obtained milk. And that was pretty much our constant daily fare. Such delicacies as meat, butter, and eggs were seen only in dreams. Breakfast consisted of bread and hot water. I called it "tea with buttered bread (broyt mit puter mit tey)" because that was what I used to have for breakfast at home before the war. So what if there was no butter to put on the bread and no tea or sugar to go with the hot water. I made believe it was the same old "tea with buttered bread." Once I got used to it, it wasn't so bad really, especially since I knew that some people had it much worse.

The first few weeks we painters were in Vileyka we slept on the floor of whatever house we were working in. These houses were unoccupied at the time and the Germans would not move in until all the work was completed and the houses thoroughly cleaned. After four or five weeks of this sleeping about, we were placed in a house where an old Jewish woman lived by herself. She had lost her husband and two sons in August when the Germans took all the men away. It was arranged for a young woman from Kurenits to be our cook and prepare some dishes for us from the few supplies available. She was Nokhum Alperovits's middle sister, Henia. The house was small and had only a kitchen, a bedroom, and a living room. Henia slept in the bedroom with the old woman, while the five of us painters slept in the living room, the older men on the two couches, one person on the table, and the other two on the floor. It was crowded and not easy to get a good night's sleep.

One day I met a young man a few years older than I who was a native of Vileyka and one of only a handful of younger Jewish men still alive in Vileyka. This young man invited me to sleep in his house, where there was a sofa I could use. I accepted gladly. For about two months I spent my evenings and stayed overnight with his family, which included his father, about seventy-five years old, and his older sister, about forty. Her husband had been taken away with the other men in July. They were nice people and I felt quite at home with them. Food was scarce, so I never ate with the family at their house. I had my supper, or what passed for supper, at the house where the other painters stayed.

One of our first jobs was to paint the inside of a house that was to be used by the Gebietskommissar. The Germans supplied the paint and other materials. How important the job was and how quickly it had to be done was underlined when the civil administration of Vileyka sent over some non-Jewish painters to lend us a hand. These men were paid a full wage in money and got extra food rations and cigarettes. This was the only time we ever worked on any job with non-Jews. As it turned out we had to repeat this particular job several times over before receiving the Gebietskommissari's nod of approval. Only after the third or fourth painting was he finally satisfied and then he gave us each a pack of cigarettes. Cigarettes were the unofficial currency of the time and could be traded for food or other essentials. I used to bring mine home to my father, who craved cigarettes. Smoking was more important than food for him.

After the governor's house was finished, we had to pain the houses and offices of lesser officials. We also worked on repainting their theater. What I remember most, however, was working on the house of the chief of the local SD, which stands for Sicherheitsdiensti (Security Service). The SD were part of the SS and their sole mission was exterminating Jews and gypsies and all others they considered undesirable. The number of Germans in these local SD units was not great--perhaps about thirty in all--but in less than two years they were responsible for exterminating about eight-five percent of all the Jews in the province under their jurisdiction. Only a few Jews managed to survive through 1943 and into 1944. Other provinces had similar SD units who also proved themselves equal to their assigned mission.

The Germans couldn't accomplish this all by themselves. It wouldn't have been physically possible. They were assisted by special volunteers recruited in Latvia, Lithuania, and the Ukraine--countries known for their widespread anti-Semitism. These volunteers were part of the SD units and wore the same uniforms as the Germans did, with the same skull insignia on their hats. They were zealous and efficient and did most of the actual killing, while the Germans took on more of a supervisory role. It was a labor of love for these volunteers, who all seemed to be selected for size: they stood at least two meters tall or more and weighed at least 100 kilos. Their imposing presence and the wild look in their eyes instilled fear in our hearts and mesmerized us as effectively as a cobra mesmerizes its prey.

The house of the SD chief formerly belonged to the warden of the big jailhouse in Vileyka under the Polish administration. Later the warden's house was taken over by the Russians and then by the chief of the SD. It stood next to the courthouse, in the same compound, on a hill overlooking the jail. Both buildings were of impressive size. The former courthouse was used by the SD for offices, interrogation, and torture.

It took us about three weeks to complete the paint job to the SD chief's satisfaction. During the time we were working on the house, he came by a couple of times to check on how the work was progressing. You could not imagine a more soft-spoken, amiable man. We were, nonetheless, under no illusions about what cruelty the man was capable of. The distinctive smell of burning human flesh assaulted our nostrils most of the time we were working on the chief's house. Relief came only when the prevailing winds shifted for a while. Dozens of human beings were being shot in Vileyka every day, then thrown into a huge pit near the old courthouse and burned. The fire in the pit was fed by a constant flow of gasoline or kerosene and it burned day and night for as long as the SD was there, that is, approximately three years. People were continually brought into the old courthouse to be interrogated, tortured, and incarcerated. Sooner or later most of them wound up in the pit, where they were converted into reeking particles that permeated the air for blocks around. Anyone approaching the SD compound within a wide area was assaulted by the stench of carbonized human bodies.

During the time we worked there, around Christmas of 1941, the victims were mostly non-Jews: gypsies, communists or people suspected of being in sympathy with the Soviets, and intellectuals were considered unreliable, especially if they were Polish and in the Polish leadership. Several months later, the former head of the Kurenits public school, Matros, was brought in along with his wife and grown son. They ended up in the pit. There were undoubtedly some Jewish victims too, but I knew of only one such family.

Late one afternoon, after work, when I came into the house where I was staying temporarily, I found a frightened little girl of about ten sitting at the table. There was caked blood behind her left ear, her eyes were glazed and showed signs of shock and stress, and her speech was semi-coherent. She'd already told the family with whom I was staying the story of what had happened to her and her family.

Her parents and the three children, of which she was the youngest, lived in the village of Neyka, about nine kilometers east of Kurenits. Their family was one of only three still living there; most Jews had abandoned village life and moved into the larger towns after the first world war. But there were still a few holdouts. The girl's family decided to move into Kurenits to be near other Jews during these difficult times. They may also have had relatives there. They were on the road, coming in by horse and wagon, when they were arrested. Jews had no right to move from one place to another without specific authorization. Jews also had no right to use a horse and wagon. Actually they had no right to anything. If caught on a road traveling, they were especially fair game. It was not clear whether the girl's family was intercepted by chance or whether they were denounced by their former neighbors. They wound up in the SD compound in Vileyka.

A visit to the SD compound was a one-way trip. There should have been a sign on the gates of the compound with these words, to reflect its true function: "Through these gates people enter but never leave." The girl's whole family was shot. Sometimes bodies weren't thrown into the burning pit right away, and that's what happened in this case. Fortunately, the bullet did no more than graze the girl's skull behind the left ear and leave her stunned. We could only guess how long she had remained in that state. It may have been minutes, or it may have been an hour or two. When she did come to, she crawled to a hole in the fence around the compound and escaped. She wandered around in shock for a while and then knocked on the door of a house, of non-Jews as it turned out. By chance, good people lived there and they brought her over to our house. We calmed her down as best we could and she stayed the night with us. The next day she was somehow smuggled into Kurenits, where she must have shared the eventual fate of most Kurenits Jews; I don't believe she survived.

After two months we decided that because of the strict night curfew it would be best for me to come back and stay overnight with the other painters. So I gave up the more comfortable lodging I had enjoyed with the family and moved back with my co-workers.

Later we heard that the old man of the family had been arrested one evening and was being held in the jail. A strict curfew was in force from sundown to sunup. At night all windows had to be covered so that no light could show through. The old man's chouse had wooden shutters that effectively blocked the light their kerosene lamp gave off. It so happened, however, that a knot in the shutter wood shrank just enough to become loose and fall out. This left a hole the size of a quarter which nobody in the family noticed. Unfortunately, one evening the police or the SD passed by and saw the tiny ray of light coming through the shutter. They arrested the old man. His young son who had befriended me recognized what the nighttime knock at the door might be and managed to hide successfully.

I saw the old man once more, and I wish I had not, because whenever I think of him and his family, this last scene comes back before my eyes. One afternoon, while I was coming back from the jail, under guard, digging and pushing a stalled German car out of a snowbank. The old man's face was marked with welts and cuts; one eye was swollen shut. He was obviously being beaten and tortured. Maybe this was the last time he was outside of that jail. Just when he actually perished I do not know, but neither he nor his son nor his daughter survived the final liquidation of the Vileyka Jews in March of 1942.

One night I awoke to the sound of church bells ringing loudly in my ears. It was as if the bells of all the churches in town were tolling at once. I lay where I was for a long time trying to comprehend why church bells would be ringing in the middle of the night. Soon my head ached and my temples throbbed. This, coupled with the difficulty I had raising my head off the pillow, finally made me realize I was experiencing carbon monoxide poisoning. I was familiar with the symptoms because, when growing up, I had heard many stories of people found unconscious or even dead as the result of a poorly ventilated stove that allowed the poisonous gas to build up. I forced myself to get on my feet and wake up the others. The girl, Henia, and the old woman were only half conscious, but they revived quickly when we took them out into the fresh air outside. It was a narrow escape for all of us.

The month of March 1942 arrived. It wasn't spring yet. There was still plenty of snow on the ground and the nights were still cold. But the relentless grip of the winter cold had eased and the days were getting slightly, but noticeable, warmer. A definite promise of spring was in the air. The festival of Purim was only a few days away.

News began filtering in that Jews were being massacred in several towns. Some massacres were partial and lasted only a day or two. Whoever got caught during the roundup was eliminated, but those who survived by escaping or hiding were allowed to return and resume their lives in town. After such an "action" (aktion, the Germans called it), the authorities usually put the few surviving Jews into a ghetto. Some towns went through several such purges before the Germans pronounced them Judenrein, that is, "clear of Jews." The final massacre ran for as long as necessary. With many non-Jewish neighbors assisting, Jews were discovered hiding in attics, under floorboards, behind double walls, and in many other ingenious places. Some Jews managed to avoid discovery for days, even weeks. But in the end, unless they were able to slip away without being seen and reach the safety of the woods, they were discovered. One could not stay in hiding in the middle of a town forever. And the chances of getting out of a hiding place and away were best the first night. As the searches got more thorough, the chances of getting away diminished steadily each successive night.

The Germans explained away the partial massacres with some excuse or other and assured the survivors they were now safe. It didn't necessarily follow that the Germans were believed, but what else could Jews do? Where else could they go? People always hoped that the next time they'd again manage to hide or escape. At this time the woods afforded at best only temporary safety because there were few partisans there. The measure of protection the partisans would eventually provide didn't materialize until the end of the summer of 1942. During the first half of 1942, few Jews chose to stay in the woods permanently. Survivors of partial "actions" usually returned to the towns they lived in. The few survivors of complete and final "actions" sought refuge in towns that had not yet been touched by the full German fury.

Then came the news that the Jews of the town of Volozin, where my oldest married sister, Sarah, had been living for ten years, had also been executed. A faint ray of hope still remained in my heart at the time; maybe by some miracle she had survived. But of course the bitter truth was that she perished in the massacre of the great majority of the Volozin Jews. After the war a survivor told me about it.

We still hoped, no matter how weakly, that somehow we would live to see the Germans defeated, a defeat we all believed would eventually occur. Slowly but surely, however, the ultimate German plan for the Jews was becoming clear to us. They intended to empty all captured lands of all Jews. It took time for this realization to crystallize, but it was a conclusion everybody came to sooner or later--except those who consciously chose to close their eyes and ears to logic and reality. Unfortunately, there were many people in this category. Their way of coping with the situation was to say that Jews should carefully avoid provoking the Germans and conscientiously perform the tasks the Germans assigned to them. Then the Germans would leave them alone. These people refused to believe the word reaching us about all the massacres or, rather, they found ways to explain away what was happening--as if there could be a rational explanation for the murder of a whole town of Jews. But this was the road to survival these distressed people chose.

I remember one case clearly. This particular Jew was about forty years old and came from a town about fifty kilometers away. The Germans had just murdered all the Jews they could get their hands on there, including the man's wife and children. He was lucky enough to escape with his life and somehow or other made it to Vileyka. I happened to meet him one day while he was telling his story and giving his opinion that the Germans would eventually do the same to every Jew in every town.

I saw no reason to disbelieve the man, and I did not entirely disagree with his assessment of what was awaiting us. Yes, it did sound extreme, but it also sounded plausible. Some of the younger people who were there and heard the man speak felt more or less the same way I did. Others, however, said the man was crazy and suggested that the terrible loss of his family had made him deranged. Young single people still had a sense of freedom of action and tended to see things differently than men who were weighed down with the responsibilities of caring of r a wife and children and felt there was no way they could run off to the woods, where the hardships of existence would be multiplied many times over. They put all their hopes into doing good work for the Germans and in making themselves as useful as possible. They actually tried to block out any information that might contradict their false assessment of the situation. Then came the festival of Purim.

We couldn't celebrate Purim in any really traditional way, of course. In the evening I read the Megilla (Book of Esther), which is read in all synagogues in normal times. The best we could do was to gather a few of the neighbors, who made the trip to our house through backyards. They were mostly women and a couple of young girls. After the reading we all exchanged wishes that the latter-day Haman should meet the fate of the original one. Then everybody went back home and we bedded down for the night. Except for its being Purim, this was an evening like any other.

Later we recognized the pattern, but by the time we did, most of the Jews had already perished. The pattern was that most German "actions" against the Jews were carried out on Jewish holy days or, in order to confuse us, a few days before or after a holy day. Soviet Russian holidays could also trigger these "actions."

Thus, around three in the morning of Purim, 1942, I was suddenly awakened by a loud banging on the front door. This door was never used in the winter and the snow on the steps normally lay fresh and untrampled. So I knew from the first what the knocking meant. "This is it," I remember thinking. "The SD have come for us."

The animal instinct for self-preservation takes over automatically in time of danger. My first thought was to run. "Maybe out the back door," I thought. I started to put on my pants in the dark. I always used to leave my clothes on a stool next to where I slept so they would be handy in case of an emergency. I grabbed what I thought were my pants, which I usually left on top, and tried to get into them. In the excitement and terror of the moment, I couldn't get my foot through the leg. Then there was knocking at the back door. Somebody opened it and Germans came in. The kerosene lamp was lit and there I was standing half-naked with my shirt in my hands. No wonder I hadn't been able to get my foot into the sleeve.

The Germans told us to finish dressing. We were facing three huge men in SD uniforms, with the dreaded skull on their caps. All carried submachine guns. They led us out the back door and into the yard. There we were confronted by three more SD men, making six of them all told. There were seven of us--the two women and the five of us painters. The SD men marched us out of the yard and into the street towards a truck visible about a block away. A full moon glowed in the sky and the light it gave was intensified by reflections off the snow that lay on the ground. It was bright enough to read a newspaper. "Once we get to that truck we're doomed," I remember thinking. "I must keep my eyes open for a good time and spot, and then I'll make a run for it."

At one point I was all set to make the fateful sprint, and had even taken the first step, but something held me back. I suddenly realized there was no way I could have gotten away. And lucky for me I didn't try. I would have been cut down before taking a few steps.

We got to the truck and were ordered to climb in. A few people were there already and more were arriving all the time. In only five minutes the truck was filled to capacity. Canvas flaps at the back and on the sides were lowered. We stood in total darkness with guards on the truck all around us. Then the truck started moving. We couldn't tell what direction it was going in, but it did not really matter. There was no question in our minds that we were being taken to our deaths. We were more seasoned now; eight months under the Germans had dispelled much of our earlier naivetŽ. Now we knew just what we could expect. We said goodbye to each other. I stopped thinking about trying to flee because I knew by this time it would be impossible.

About ten minutes later the trucked stopped. The canvas flaps were raised and we were ordered out. The place was well lit with artificial light. As we got off the truck, one by one, we were yelled at to run a gauntlet of SD men holding wooden clubs about the size of baseball bats. Two rows of facing SD men stretched from the truck to a building about thirty meters away. The building turned out to be a large garage, and I now recognized we were inside the SD compound that included the jail, the courthouse, and this garage. This was the dreaded place with the one-way ticket reputation.

To keep us moving, the SD men swung the clubs at and around our heads and shoulders. I made it through without getting hit. Others weren't so lucky. Several had received wounds that were bleeding profusely. Others, who had taken blows to the head, were in a semi-stunned condition. There was a purpose in all that yelling and swinging of clubs and making us run the gauntlet. It was not primarily to inflict pain or injury but to confuse us psychologically so that we could not orient ourselves or take stock of the situation. In this way no one would think of bolting. Cowboys use the same tactic herding cattle. All the noise and shooting in the air are for the purpose of driving the startled animals in the desired direction.

Once inside the garage, we were put in a corner and told to wait. Diagonally across from us, in the opposite corner of the garage, I saw a large group of about 300 people, mostly women and children. The "action" was in full swing now. Trucks arrived bringing more and more people, who were then driven into the garage. This continued all through the nigh and most of the following day.

We heard later that some people had not been picked up by the SD that first night. Jewish houses were obviously on a list prepared well in advance. But by faulty intelligence or simple oversight some houses had been missed. The next morning they started to walk to work, unaware of what had taken place during the night. They were then picked up on their way to work, or where they worked if they got that far, and trucked off to the garage.

Many of the Jews rounded up were originally from Kurenits, and a large number were young women working at menial jobs in Vileyka. One way or another they were all swept up by the "action." In the garage, smaller groups of Jews stood around and apart from the large group. I recognized the chief of the SD as he walked up to one of these smaller groups. He talked to the people there and one by one motioned with his hand for them to join the large group. Within a few minutes he had disposed of all the small groups in this way--by making them a part of the large group--all except ours. We were still standing apart. The chief of the SD now approached us. My knees felt weak. With a flick of his finger this man had sent who knows how many people to their deaths with no more emotion than it takes to swat a fly. Over 300 people in just the last hour or two. And in his whole career, maybe as many as 100,000! Yet to hear the man talk you would think him the gentlest and most civilized person in the world who could not possibly wish you any harm.

"Wo arbeiten Sie? (What is your place of work?)," he politely asked the first person he reached in our group, using the formal and polite Sie instead of the informal and intimidating du. To address somebody as Sie in German indicates a modicum of deference, especially when coupled with the honeyed tones the chief now used.

"Wo arbeiten Sie?" each person in our group was asked in turn and all answered. The older ones who didn't work said so. The chief's finger flicked in the direction of the large group. People who had work said where it was: the post office, the German police station, other offices. In all, about ten different places of work were mentioned. The chief's response was the same to all--a flick of his finger towards the main group.

When the chief finally got to one of us painters, the answer to his question was, "I'm a painter and I work for the Gebietskommisar (provincial governor)." This time the finger didn't move. "Have you the certificate to prove it?" the chief asked. We each took out the certificates that stated we were working for the Gebietskommissar as painters, each certificate bearing the signature of a high-ranking official and the stamp of the Gebietskommisar. They had been given to us just two weeks earlier. The SD chief glanced at the certificates and told the five of us to stand apart by ourselves.

A tiny glimmer of hope kindled within us. We hadn't been put in with the main group that was obviously marked for death. I nourished that small flame of hope. Maybe, just maybe, he would let us live. It was far from a sure thing, of course; we were still in the hands of the SD, in the center of the infamous SD facility from which, so far as we knew, no Jew had ever come out alive. And what was to prevent the chief from changing his mind? Or to prevent one of his men from throwing us in with the others by oversight or malice?

Presently we were led into a small side room; there we joined eleven other people who had been picked out of previous truckloads. Later, we were joined by one more couple. Besides the five of us, two others, carpenters, were from Kurenits. The rest were from Vileyka: two saddlers with their wives and one twelve-year-old son, one candle-maker and his wife, one soapmaker and his wife, and, I believe, one printer and his wife. All told there were eighteen of us in the room.

We began to hear shooting outside and saw a yellow-reddish light coming through the small barred window high up near the ceiling, as it usually is in jails. We wanted to get up to the window to see what was happening outside. There was nothing in the room to stand on, so I hopped onto somebody's shoulders. We realized this was dangerous. If caught, we would probably have to join those outside. But the desire to know, if we could, what was going on was strong. I watched for no more than a minute.

What I saw were two SD men, each one leading a group of three people towards the fire. One group was close to the fire. The other group was just leaving the building. The fire came from the infamous pit about which we already knew.

And then I jumped down, glad we hadn't been caught watching. We heard shooting again and knew what it meant. The shooting continued throughout the rest of the night and through most of the next day.

Once, around midday, the door to our little room swung open and two Lithuanian SD burst in. They were drunk and their glassy eyes looked full of murder. In their foreign-sounding German one of them said," Was machen die Scheisse hier? (What are you shit doing here?)" For a moment or two we thought we'd had it. Luckily a superior officer happened by and ordered the men out of there and to leave us alone.

The day dragged on. No food or water was brought to us, but worry and tension depressed our appetites anyway and nobody felt hungry. Early in the evening the door finally opened and an officer came in. He announced that we were going to be released and told us to step back into the main garage.

How different the place looked now from when we had been brought in. The whole main group of Jews was gone. They had all been shot and burned not more than 150 meters from where we had spent the last fifteen hours. They had been taken out in small groups to the burning pit, shot with small-caliber weapons, and then shoved into the flaming hole in the ground. All of those brought in after us, even during the day, met the same fate. I'm not certain of the exact number of those that perished in this "action," but judging by the size of the Jewish population of Vileyka before the war, it could have been as many as 2,000, including the fifty Jews from Kurenits who were also killed. Eighteen people out of 2,000 were spared by the SD; eleven of the eighteen were natives of Vileyka.

But the garage was not entirely empty. Two women, both strikingly good-looking, were no where the main group had once stood. One was from Kurenits, Khayke Rabunski, who had gone to school with me and who, as I have recounted earlier, was looking out of the window as I was led by, coming from the Lubanye farm on Simchas Torah on October 1941. The other woman was a native of Vileyka, intelligent and cultured, and perhaps in her late twenties, with a teaching degree. To what purpose these two had been kept back, we could only speculate.

When we were marched back out into the big garage, the two women stood there facing us about seven or eight meters away. Khayke called out my name a couple of times in a hoarse whisper and asked me to let people know at the police station, where she worked, what had happened, in the hope they would come to her rescue. She repeated this plea several times, not being sure whether or not we had heard it. Poor soul, we couldn't even acknowledge with a nod that we had. We were afraid of antagonizing the Germans and imperiling our own chances for release. But the possibility that someone at the police station would come to Khayke's rescue was nonexistent. The power of the SD was so great and their latitude of activity so broad that even high-ranking German officials were afraid to take them on. SD authority went unquestioned.

In the almost empty garage, a German officer sat behind a long table covered from end to end with all sorts of valuables--gold, diamonds and other jewels, stacked in places a foot high and made up of rings, bracelets, brooches, pins, chains, earrings, and watches, perhaps weighing a good twenty-five kilos. Obviously it had all been taken from the victims before they were killed. The German officer asked us if any of our valuables had been taken away and if so, we were to look through the pile and retrieve them. But none had been taken because we didn't have any. I remember thinking at the time that if anything had been taken, I certainly would not call attention to myself by asking for it. Let them keep it. We just wanted to be released.

So I was astounded to hear one man, the candlemaker, I believe, answer, "Yes." A golden pocketwatch had been taken from him and he could see it there in the pile. I was even more astounded to hear the officer tell him to go ahead and take it. The man did so.

Then the officer took our names and addresses in order to provide an escort for us back to where we lived. When he asked Irma for his address, instead of giving the street and number of the house we stayed in, Irma blurted out that we were from Kurenits. The officer responded by saying he couldn't send us back to Kurenits at night. He put the five of us painters back in the little side room to spend another night and promised to see what could be done the next day.

Back in the room, behind the locked door, we once more felt dejected and forlorn. We had been so close to freedom only to be denied it at the last minute by an unfortunate remark from one of our own. It was really more than we could bear. Who could predict how the SD would feel the next morning? Understandably, Irma felt terrible. After somebody tried to reproach him for saying what he did, he picked up a brick lying on the floor and began to hit himself on the head with it to punish himself, as if that could help us in any way. The man was really on the verge of suicide. We had our hands full just trying to quiet him down and console him.

That night was the longest I can remember. Sleep was out of the question. Again we had no food or drink and again we felt neither hunger nor thirst. We heard sporadic shooting, but on a much smaller scale.

Morning came, but there was still no sign of our being released. Several hours went by. Fresh doubts arose about the outcome of this drama; if they intended to release us, then why were they still holding us? That was the nagging question at the back of our minds and it had no satisfactory explanation.

Then about eleven in the morning the door finally opened. An officer called us out into the garage. This time it was really empty. The long table was still there but now it lay bare. The valuables that 2,000 Jews consigned to oblivion, their lives extinguished by the flick of one man's finger to satisfy the bloodlust of the leader of the Herrnvolk (master race) and his henchmen. The two women--one a schoolmate and lifelong friend--had disappeared to who knows what fate before they, too, would be killed.

A mere thirty hours before, these people had been live human beings, each with their own aspirations and, above all, a desire to survive. I had known many of them personally and some had been close friends. Gone now was the family at whose house I had slept for two months recently. Gone were the neighbors who had come to hear me chant the Megilla: the older women and the two young daughters of one of the women, sixteen and seventeen years old, both of them redheads, beautiful, and intelligent. Gone too were our landlady and the young woman from Kurenits who had prepared our meals. All of them gone. Despite all this and despite the ordeal we had just been through, we simply felt happy we were still alive and elated that we were being released.

At the place we were taken to on the outskirts of Vileyka the Germans created a ghetto. Sixty families had been brought in from Kurenits, all headed by artisans, or, as they were called at the time, Spezialisten (skilled workers): tailors, shoemakers, carpenters, blacksmiths, sheet-metal workers, glaziers, and others the Germans had need for. All were allowed to bring along their wives and their children up to the age of fifteen.

The ghetto consisted of two long buildings the Russians had originally built as army barracks. The buildings were in a sorry state, without doors or windows, but we were moved in anyway. We were given permission to take what we needed from Jewish houses in Vileyka, now all unoccupied since the Purim "action." Within a few days, doors and windows were found and fitted and the barracks were made more livable. Officially, we were known as the Gebietskommissarsgetto (provincial governor's ghetto) because we worked for the Gebietskommissar.

Only real, experienced mechanics were brought to Vileyka and they came eagerly, even though it meant exchanging homes with many rooms and familiar surroundings for the cramped corner of a dormitory that had to be shared with several other families and that was without privacy or conveniences. It would also have been easier to cope with the food situation in Kurenits, where people knew some non-Jews and where bartering of clothing and articles for food would have been easier than in Vileyka, where all the people and surroundings were unfamiliar. Officially, Jews were prohibited from any social or business contacts with non-Jews; in Kurenits this would have been easier to circumvent because many Jewish houses were located in among the others.

Nonetheless, all these workers and their families were quite happy to move to Vileyka. By this time it was understood that working for the Gebietskommissar in Vileyka afforded some measure of protection. Not absolute protection--few were na•ve to believe that--but a measure of protection for the immediate future. News of the Vileyka Purim massacre, together with rumors and reports of Jews being wiped out in other neighboring towns, made Kurenits's Jews realize that Kurenits afforded no protection at all, even for workers. Sooner or later Kurenits would follow the same fate as the other towns.

Our two master painters, Yosef and Irma, brought their wives and children to Vileyka to be with them. About twelve of us, mostly young and unmarried, shared one room, sleeping on army cots. After some breakfast in the morning, we all--except the married women and the children--went to work and did not return until dark.

After a few days I managed to take off from work and go visit my family in Kurenits. This time, however, unlike all previous times, I had no official permission to go to Kurenits, much less to be absent from the new ghetto.

The route to Kurenits from the ghetto required crossing the entire town of Vileyka from one end to the other, a distance of about one and a half kilometers. There was, however, little danger in walking the streets of Vileyka because both the police and the Germans were used to seeing Jewish workers walking from one job to another. Once outside of town, though, you had to negotiate seven kilometers of public highway between the two towns. Here the danger was greater but still acceptable. Vehicles with Germans passed by and you could never be too sure whether they might take into their heads to "stop that wandering Jew." To forestall identification by taking off the yellow star of David we displayed on our clothes, front and back, could have proved even more dangerous. I actually worried about meeting up with the non-German policemen who sometimes traveled the road to Kurenits on bicycles. I kept a sharp lookout for them and whenever I spotted any in the distance, I hid in the bushes by the side of the road until they had passed.

In this way I arrived back home safely and was enthusiastically greeted by my parents and sisters. They had learned, as had everybody else in Kurenits, about the events in Vileyka on Purim from one Kurenits carpenter working in Vileyka just like us. He happened to wake up in the middle of the night of the "action" and, hearing all the commotion in the street, he got out as fast as he could. Using backyards and side streets he crossed the town of Vileyka and reached Kurenits before dawn, unchallenged. Within an hour the whole town of Kurenits buzzed with the news. At first, for a period of thirty-six to forty-eight hours, my family assumed I was among the dead. Then they heard I had been released. Naturally they were quite relieved to receive the news and anxious to see me. I stayed overnight in Kurenits and returned to Vileyka the next day.

Back in Vileyka I found the people in a somewhat more optimistic frame of mind. The living quarters in the ghetto barracks had been made more livable with the addition of a table and a couple of extra chairs. There were even curtains at the windows of our room, courtesy of the young women. This better mood came mostly as a result of feeling that we had just been handed a new lease on life--not permanent, or even long-term, but what we hoped would last for a while at least. The Germans wouldn't go to all the trouble of bringing in master craftsmen and allowing us to fix up the ghetto buildings unless they needed us. So went the thinking and there was some logic in it.

Spring had just begun and the weather was getting warmer. The often sunny days that followed also played a part in helping to lift our spirits. With the full encouragement of the Germans we built a small bathhouse between the two barracks. Germans were sticklers for cleanliness. They were afraid of epidemics that uncleanliness might bring on.

For me the euphoric feeling didn't last very long. One day, when I came home from work and walked into our room, I noticed that all conversation among the ten people present came to an abrupt halt. I didn't pay much attention to it at first, though it did seem odd. The next day I also noticed some whispering going on among the people around me. When I tried to join a group that was engrossed in conversation, they quickly separated. My questions were answered in a vague and offhand manner. I got the feeling that information was deliberately being kept from me and it all pointed in the direction of my family in Kurenits. Something must have happened, perhaps something terrible.

I decided then and there to leave for Kurenits in the morning and find out for myself what was up. It had been three weeks since my last visit back home and it was no longer possible to move between Vileyka and Kurenits as easily as before. Ghetto residents had been forbidden to be absent from the ghetto for any reason at all except work.

So the next morning I left the place I was working, with the other painters covering for me. Getting across Vileyka still presented no problem. Once outside of town I turned to the right off the main road, wen through some fields and reached a small village (the name of which I have since forgotten). There I picked up a small farm road leading almost the rest of the way to Kurenits. This detour added about two or three extra kilometers but was safer since I met no one at all the whole way.

My apprehension grew with each step as I approached my hometown. I could sense that something disastrous must have happened there, but I could not imagine the extent of it. As I entered the town square, I noticed Jews in the distance walking and going about their business in a quite normal manner. This confused me, but gave me a slight measure of hope that maybe this had all been a false alarm after all.

I soon ran into my friend Nyomke Shulman and asked, "Tell me what's happened. Has anyone been killed?" "Well," he answered evasively, "there are no exact figures yet. Many people ran away. And some of them haven't come back. It's not known how many are missing."

"What about my family? Are they all right?"

"Yes," he said. "Your mother is at the house o Zalman Mendl the shoemaker."

I didn't have to inquire any further. Without telling me outright, Nyomke had indirectly indicated the extent of the disaster.

I ran all the way to Zalman Mendl's house. There I found my mother holding little Shimshon, Minya's son, on her lap. Mother's eyes were puffy and red. She burst out crying again when she saw me and we cried in each other's arms for a long time. Shimshon, even when he was not crying, looked hopelessly sad and forlorn. This was not the happy baby who used to greet me with a big smile. His face showed how much he missed his mother. It was as if he understood. And I too knew what the tragedy was. All that was left was for Mother to tell me how it had happened.

The disaster had struck two days earlier, at about ten in the morning. Without warning, two Polish policemen, both of them drunk, barged into the house. They ordered everybody, except Mother, out into the backyard--my father, my sister Ethel, and my sister Minn with the baby in her arms. Then they shot Father and Minn dead. The baby fell from Minn's lifeless arms into the snow. Ethel tried to run away. She made it through an opening in the fence and across the street into another yard. There one of the policemen caught up with her and shot her dead, too. Mother was standing by the kitchen window and saw everything. There had to be an added measure of deliberate cruelty in murdering a woman's husband and children before her very eyes.

These policemen were not only accustomed to cruelty, they positively reveled in it. One, Blizniuk, was a native of Kurenits; he was the same policeman who had hauled me out of the Lubanye farm in the fall of 1941 and who, the same day, had shot Arke Ruvkes as he lay wounded on the ground. The man got a taste of blood then and apparently he liked it. The other policeman, from Kostenevich, a small town about seventeen kilometers away, was named Szarenkiewicz. He had participated in the killing of the fifty-four on Simchas Torah of 1941 and had also taken part in the liquidation of the Vileyka Jews on Purim. Besides my sisters and father, the pair of them had murdered twenty-nine other Jews in Kurenits, a total of thirty-two.

After the two policemen left, Mother went outside and lifted the terrified baby up out of the snow. She was helped to move into Zalman Mendl's so she would not have to live by herself with the baby in the house where the murders had occurred. Father and Minn were buried the next day in the Jewish cemetery outside of town. By the time I got to Kurenits only Ethel remained unburied, and with the help of a couple of men, we laid her to rest next to my father and Minya.

Artsik Gotyes, a friend of the family, was one of those who helped in the burial of all three members of my family. He handed me a piece of paper he had taken from my father's pocket. On the paper were listed all the names, and other detailed information, of the fifty-four victims who perished in the fall of 1941. To this list we now added the names of the thirty-two who had just been killed. I kept the paper on me for a long time, until it disintegrated over the next couple of years.

Yitskhok (Iche Hatsyes), my father, was about sixty-three years old when he was murdered. He was highly respected by both the Jewish community and the gentiles. He was a recognized scholar in all the holy scriptures, including the Talmud. He knew Hebrew and Russian and had a good knowledge of mathematics. He was a teacher most of his life and even taught Russian and mathematics in our public school and in night school. The policeman who shot him, Blizniuk, had once been a student of his in night school. To me he was more than a father; he was also my teacher, from the age of five through the age of fourteen, in all nonsecular subjects. He had a unique talent in explaining difficult passages in the scriptures in such a way as to make them easy to understand. His lectures on Mishna and Gemara were very much appreciated and well attended. He was considered a special authority on these subjects and he was even consulted on some difficult and tricky passages of law by the local rabbi. He had a sharp, analytical mind and all who knew him acknowledged him to be a brilliant scholar.

As a young teenager I never ceased to be amazed at my father's ability to demolish every argument an opponent in a discussion could come up with. He answered with such ease and logic that everyone present was soon won over, including the opponent. He also possessed a beautiful voice and was a cantor. His rendition and interpretation of the prayers, especially on the High Holidays, were deeply moving and soul-inspiring. He was also an excellent bal kriah--reader of the Torah. People who had the privilege of hearing him read the Torah and chant while leading the congregation in prayer still speak of it with a praise reserved for masters of these crafts.

It is told that an important Talmudic discussion once took place in Kurenits between a visiting rabbi from the city of Lublin and our local rabbi and several local scholars, my father among them. The topic was one aspect of a certain work by Rambam Maimonides. It was not unusual for this kind of discussion to last for several hours, as the learned men brought out and carefully analyzed all the fine points of law and brought to bear the many commentaries, all in the presence of a large congregation that would gather for such an event. At the end of this discussion the visiting rabbi turned to the congregation and, pointing to my father, said: "Here in Kurenits you have a priceless pearl. You should consider yourselves blessed by his presence among you." This took place when I was still a little boy and too young to know of it at firsthand, but it is related in a chapter by Abraham Dimenstein (Avrohom Merkes) in the book Megilat Kurenits (edited by Aaron Meirovitch 1956).

And now my father was gone. No longer would I be able to listen to his wise counsel or, with the numerous other students of his, children as well as adults, be able to drink at the deep well of knowledge he possessed.

Gone, too, were my two sisters Ethel and Minn, at the ages of thirty-one and twenty-eight. Ethel was a pretty brunette, the brainiest one among my sisters. Minya, my favorite, was not only ver pretty but also gentle, warm, very loyal to the family, and well-liked and well-thought of by all who came in contact with her. My sisters were cut down by two drunken policemen, eager for Jewish blood.

If there is any consolation, it is in the knowledge that some measure of justice came down on the pair of killers. They soon received their just due. One, the native of Kurenits, was killed four months later by partisan**Don't Go Gentle**

Chapters From Charles Gelman's Book (Yechezkel Zimmerman)

July 1941. We were huddling in the backyard of our neighbor, Mote-Leyb Kopershtooch, sitting on the ground, our backs against the wall, and talking in whispers. The German army had arrived in town barely one week earlier. No specific orders or edicts against Jews had been proclaimed at this point. Yet the air was more and more permeated with fear each passing day. Even on bright days it felt as if a heavy cloud had descended on us.

Mote-Leyb's house stood next to my father's. I reached his yard by going through a hole in the back fence, as did a couple of neighbors from the other side of Mote-Leyb's house. We met there daily just to stay out of the way of the police and the Germans, to exchange the latest rumors, and to kill time. Our former routine of living had been broken, most likely forever.

That day, Leybke the barber was there and so was my friend, Nyomke Shulman. Leybke regretted not having escaped with the retreating Russians while there was still time. Not that he hadn't tried. In fact, he told us, he had made a half-hearted effort to go east. He acquired a horse and buggy, a real fancy one, a brichke they used to call it, and he put his wife and two children in it and drove off. They got as far as Kostenevich, a small town about seventeen kilometers from our town of Kurenits (sometimes pronounced, but never written, Kœrnits; in Polish KurzŽniec, in Russian KurenŽts). Leybke's wife kept begging him to return home, where things were familiar and safe. She couldn't take the hardship and uncertainty of what lay ahead along the way--air raids, hunger, trouble with bandits, just to mention a few. So they turned back. Leybke concluded his story by saying he could see he'd made a mistake in giving up so easily; he should have pressed on.

I couldn't help but agree with him--in though only, of course. Leybke was more vulnerable than most of us because of the high standing he had had with the Soviet authorities. Being a barber and a real proletarian, his background was, from the Soviet political view, impeccable. We lived in the eastern part of Poland. When the Soviets occupied it on September 17, 1939, they promptly divided the population into politically "acceptable" and "unacceptable" segments. Anyone who didn't have his passport stamped with the designation "worker" or "peasant" could eventually expect trouble from the authorities. Because a large segment of the shtetl (small town) Jews made their living before 1939 buying and selling, they had been designated "businessmen." Many were just peddlers and small merchants; they earned barely enough to keep body and soul together. Nevertheless, they received the negative designation. It didn't bode well for the future.

The Soviet authorities were helped along in these and other matters by local activists who cooperated with them, often to the detriment of others--Jews as well as non-Jews--and informed on them as to their wealth, political reliability, and so forth. Some people were taxed into poverty, deprived of their houses, furniture, and all material goods. Some were even sent to Siberia as a result of the activities of these informers.

Leybke was considered an activist, although of a different kind. So far as I know, he was not an informer, but he had high-placed friends in the local hierarchy. I know for a fact that he had saved the life of my brother-in-law, Sam Spektor. Sam had been inducted into a work brigade about three months before the Germans invaded Russia on June 22, 1941. Leybke convinced the authorities that Sam was the only person capable of organizing and training a city orchestra, which the Soviets very much desired. So Sam was left behind. The Soviets mobilized quite a few men from our town of Kurenits and sent them to the German border to build fortifications. None of them ever returned and they were never heard form again.

Most of these activists had retreated along with the Soviets, well ahead of the approaching Germans, because they feared retribution from the non-Jewish population who were anti-Soviet. Some fled with their families. Others left wives and children behind, mistakenly believing that only they themselves were in danger. Many of those who fled survived the war. Of the families that activists left behind, none survived. During the first few weeks of the German occupation, such an outcome could not be foreseen. Had anybody described such a scenario as eventually coming to pass, we would have considered them deranged.

Rumors abounded: "The Russians are counterattacking." "They've taken back this or that city." "The Germans have taken Smolensk (a Russian city on the way to Moscow)." "The war can't last more than a month longer." Few of them were true. Confusion was the order of the day; for real news we were utterly in the dark. Listening to radio broadcasts was forbidden under penalty of death. News from the front was unavailable. What we did hear was mostly sketchy and unreliable.

The, only a few days later, Leybke told us he had been summoned to the police station; he had been informed he must appear there the following day, ready to be shipped out to an unknown destination. He would be allowed to take with him only five pounds of food and clothing.

We were sitting in our usual place and discussing this latest development. Leybke said he though the Germans would send him to a labor camp. He wasn't worried about himself, because he thought he could always survive if they allowed him to take his barbering tools with him. "Even in a labor camp, hair must be cut," he said. He was confident that he would make out all right.

Thoughts like that seemed quite plausible at that time. We had not heard of any German atrocities yet, except for two instances, which the Jewish population interpreted as unfortunate accidents.

Between the time the Russians fled Kurenits and the time the German army arrived, the town was without any real authority. It was decided to organize a sort of civil guard; gentiles and a few young Jewish men participated in order to guard against looting. The men were armed with rifles left by the Russian police and even used the local police station. Unwisely, this action continued several days after the Germans entered. Early one morning two young Jewish men, coming off duty and walking back to the police station, were confronted by German soldiers, who discovered they were Jews and arrested them. No explanation was acceptable and the young men were promptly shot. They were cousins and both had the same name--Shimon Zimmerman. One was also known as Shimon dem fishers.

The other incident involved two prominent men from Kurenits, both of them merchants and quite rich by our standards. They suffered greatly under the Soviets, who confiscated their businesses and all their merchandise and taxed them so severely--hundred of thousands of rubles--that they lost their houses and savings and fled to another town about thirty-five kilometers away. A good thing they did, too. If they hadn't, they might well have been sent to Siberia. A couple of weeks into the German occupation these merchants started to walk back to Kurenits to try to reclaim the houses that had been theirs. They were intercepted on the road by Germans, recognized as Jews, and promptly shot.

These incidents, unfortunate as they were, were in no way recognized as a harbinger of things to come.

Leybke reported to the police station as directed and was never seen or heard from again. He was probably shot somewhere out of town. Yet such a fate, at that time, was incomprehensible because it was unbelievable. After all, the Germans are civilized people, we though. They might weed out the communists, but surely they would investigate with at least some semblance of orderly procedure.

Were we all na•ve? With the benefit of hindsight, I can say we certainly were. The truth is that up to that time we had not yet heard of any real atrocities.

Throughout the period of Russian administration there were Jews living in our town, as well as in surrounding towns, who had come from the western part of Poland, occupied by the Germans in September 1939. These Jews had managed to come to eastern Poland, even after living several months under the Germans. The stories they told were not pleasant. Jews in German-occupied territory had to wear a yellow star of David on their clothes. At times they were mistreated and demeaned, for example, by being made to wash public latrines and streets. Jews had no right to use the sidewalks; they had to walk in the middle of the street. Religious Jews in the street often had their beards cut by force, or grabbed and a handful of hair pulled out. Sometimes a German officer would order an individual Jew, or a group, to dance for him and then proceed to mercilessly beat up those who hadn't jumped high enough or who had otherwise failed to perform to his liking. There were other stories like these of Jews being humiliated and brutalized. Nonetheless, we heard nothing, not even rumors, of outright shootings.

When the Russians offered these displaced persons a chance to return to their former homes in western Poland, a large number of them said yes and signed up to be transported back to the German part of Poland, something they would not have done, we believed, had they thought conditions there to be unacceptable. Of course the Russians never intended to keep their offer; instead, they shipped these transportees east to Siberia. In so doing the Russians unintentionally saved the lives of thousands of Jews. Some died on the way from the primitive conditions of transport, which could last for several months on each leg of the journey. Others perished from the harsh conditions in remote parts of Russia. A majority, though, survived and surfaced in the West after the war.

Even much later--after fifty-four of our Kurenits Jews had been shot outside of town on the Simchas Torah holiday of 1941, after thirty-two more had been shot by two policemen in March of 1942, after news reached us of Jews being massacred in surrounding towns--people would still come up with explanations, no matter how feeble, to give the events some justification. For instance, in one town they said the Germans supposedly found a gun. In another they said the Jews hadn't filled their assigned quotas of money, furs, or other goods. In the case of fifty-four, as these martyrs became known, the excuse was that they had been Russian activists, or families of activists, left behind. People excused the massacre of thirty-two by saying the Germans had no direct role in it: the hapless Jews were shot by two drunken Polish policemen.

People desperately looked for excuses in order to continue believing that somehow they would survive. Married people with young children were especially prone to this syndrome, as were older people. A case of drowning men grasping for straws. The real truth of things did not crystallize and hit home for some time. In 1941, especially during the summer, we were still innocents.

After Leybke disappeared, I continued to get together with a few friends in Mote-Leyb's backyard. The news and rumors that filtered through to us were getting more and more grim every day. It was becoming clearer that the Russians were being defeated on every front and that the Germans were capturing major cities deep inside Russia--all in a matter of only a few weeks. It was discouraging.

In this connection, I especially remember the feldsher of our town, a man by the name of Szostakowicz. (Feldsher is a Russian medical title, roughly equivalent to "physician's assistant", given to a person with medical experience and the authority to treat patients, but without a regular medical degree.) One morning I met him as he was walking in the town square, holding in his hand a German grenade, the type with a long wooden handle. It had obviously been given to him by one of his high-ranking German officer friends. He was just toying with it and intended no harm. (Later on, when I was a member of the partisan underground, I had occasion to use grenades like these on the Germans, with their intended purpose.) As we met, he stopped and talked to me for a moment or two before continuing on his way. What I remember most is what he said just before he went on. "You mark my words. This German Reich will last for a thousand years." He was, of course, parroting words from a recent speech of Hitler's, but to me he conveyed the message that he completely believed what he was repeating. The, having said his piece, he strutted away like a peacock, proud of the achievements of his newfound German friends. You can imagine what this chance meeting did to my already sagging spirits. The future looked bright to him, but to usÉWe were on the opposite ends of a seesaw; the higher he rose, the lower we sank.

How different things had been only a month earlier. There was no war here then and, with the tight control which the Soviets exercised over news sources, we had absolutely no inkling that war between the Russians and the Germans was in the offing. (The outbreak of war came as a surprise to the Soviets, too.) Under the Russians, we Jews felt for the first time--aside form the lack of freedom and the shortages of food and material things that affected everybody--that we were full-fledged citizens, with anti-Semitism prohibited under severe penalty of the law.

I was not quite eighteen then and lived at home with my parents, Yitskhok Zimerman (Iche Khatsyes), my father, and Feyge, my mother. I was the youngest of the five children. My oldest sister, Sarah, was married and lived in the town of Volozin. My youngest sister, Dina, about four years older than I, was also married and lived deep inside Russia, out of reach of the Germans. Also living at home were my two middle sisters, Ethel and Minya. Minya was in the last stages of pregnancy. Her husband, Sam Spektor, had received permission to visit his brother in the city of Kharkov in Russia two weeks before the war started. When war broke out, he couldn't get back. He remained deep inside Russia throughout the war and survived.

Our future looked bleak now. What would become of us? Minya was ready to give birth almost any day. How would she cope with a baby in times like these, and without a husband? There were many questions and no good answers.

2

One day an official order of the German commandant was posted in the public square. In both German and Polish it ordered all Jewish males between the ages of fourteen and sixty-five to assemble in the public square at two in the afternoon the next day. Failure to comply, it stated, was punishable by death.

No one knew the reason for this order, though many tried to guess. "Maybe they'll make us wash the cobble-stones in the marketplace," some said. "Maybe they'll amuse themselves by making us dance for them," others suggested. Many other explanations like these were offered, which is to say, no one expected the worst. Yet failure to appear at the ordered time and place would probably be unwise because the Germans might check the people present against a list of town residents.

As it happened nothing much really did occur. About eight hundred men showed up at the appointed hour and were made to stand in the hot summer sun, facing the German Kommandantur (commandant's office and garrison headquarters). After about an hour had passed, German soldiers with machine guns came out of the building and took up positions facing us. They remained in that attitude for about another hour. This was the low point of the day. The Germans, with their machine guns, certainly looked menacing enough and I had second thoughts about the wisdom of having shown up. Then, after we had been standing there for more than two hours, the German commandant finally came out. He was a man about fifty years old and held the rank of major. He told us not to worry. He wished to have a Judenrat (council of Jews) appointed. Then and there he selected an Austrian Jew, a man by the name of Schatz, to be the Judenrat leader. And then he dismissed the entire group and told us to return to our homes. Except for a few cases of sunburn and of one person fainting from the heat, nothing bad had happened to anyone.

We didn't appreciate how lucky we were until a month or so later when we found out that in the town of Vileyka, only seven kilometers away, all the Jewish male population from fourteen to sixty-five years of age had also been ordered to assemble before their local commandant, at approximately the same time we were before ours. But all of them--about two thousand men--were taken away and vanished without a trace. This was followed by all kinds of rumors as to their whereabouts. Some peasants had seen them in a labor camp thirty kilometers away. Or they might be in another labor camp eighty kilometers away. Needless to say, all these reports were false. The men had in fact been shot the same day they were taken away. Their place of execution was not discovered until after the war.

Obviously, then, local commandants had discretionary power to determine the fate of the Jews within their jurisdiction. We were lucky to have gotten a commandant with a human heart. He would prove this again a little later in an incident involving my family.

The Judenrat was organized the day after the assembly in the Kurenits public square and consisted of eight to ten Jews, with Schatz as leader. It served as the instrument through which the Germans conveyed all their orders and wishes to the Jewish population. For example, a certain number of Jews were required to go and work at Lubanye, a state-run farm not far away. Other Jews were detailed to clean the offices of the German administration, the police, the civil administration, and so on. Money, furs, jewels, Persian rugs, and paintings were to expropriated from the Jewish population. All these orders were given to the Judenrat, which then apportioned them among the Jewish population. This was not always done fairly.

Towards the end of July, I was among the 150 Jewish young people between the ages of seventeen and thirty sent up to the state farm of Lubanye for three days of work in the fields. After the three days were up, we were relieved by another group of the same size. Each of us had to go work there about once every two weeks. The rest of the time we worked in or around town. Lubanye was about six kilometers away, but no transportation was provided; we had to walk there and back. Each of us brought our own food for three days with us. I remember bringing along only a loaf of bread and a bottle of milk. Food was getting scarce and little could be spared. So we supplemented the food we brought from home with cabbage and carrots from the gardens we tended. Of course we weren't entitled to do this, so we took the vegetables on the sly. Carrots posed no problem; nothing obvious was left after you pulled one or two out of the ground. All you had to do was dispose of the inedible green leafy part. Cabbage were a problem, though, because if you removed the whole head, it left an empty space that could easily be spotted. Getting caught could conceivably mean punishment by beatings or maybe worse, so I used to eat only the inside of a cabbage head, carefully leaving the outside leaves in place. Unless the plant was scrupulously examined, no one could tell that it had been tampered with. At any rate, I was never caught, and I don't recall anyone else was either.

I particularly remember one out of many jobs I had to perform in or around our town of Kurenits. During the months of August, September, and part of October 1941, the Germans operated a Durchgangslager (transit camp) in Kurenits--a temporary way station for Russian prisoners of war. Thousands of them were marched in on foot from the eastern front and kept in Kurenits for two or three days of rest before being driven further west. They were kept out in the open at the horse market, where, prior to the war, horse trading had taken place.

Day and night, fair weather and foul, the prisoners remained exposed to the elements. When it rained, they got soaked. As time passed and it started getting chillier, their situation quickly became desperate. Every morning a number of dead bodies had to be disposed of, a task assigned to the Jews. Fortunately, I never had to do this. In the transit camp a few of us were given the job of bringing in water in a huge barrel mounted on wheels, from a water source located outside the camp perimeter. The camp was surrounded by barbed wire and electrified wires, with armed guards in watchtowers. The prisoners were usually in bad shape, suffering from malnutrition, fatigue, and exposure. Once a day they got a water soup and about 250 grams of moldy bread. The soup was cooked from moldy cabbage into which had been dropped a few pieces of rotting fish or meat.

The camp operated for about three months. It finally closed down at the end of October or maybe the beginning of November 1941. While it operated, at least 100,000 POWs passed through on their way to more permanent sites. We very much pitied them and, when we could, tried to help with a piece of bread, a drink of water, or a found cigarette butt. But their miser was so great that our best efforts amounted to no more than a drop in the ocean. Of course, at the time neither they nor we had any inkling of the scope of the calamity that awaited us all. Of the estimated six to eight million prisoners the Germans captured in Russia, only twenty-five percent survived. The rest were executed or died from systematic hard labor and starvation. The Jews of Europe fared even worse. They had only about a ten percent rate of survival; most of the other ninety percent died by direct execution.

During the last days of July 1941, an order came from the German authorities for all Jews to surrender any and all Persian rugs they might have in their possession. My sister Minya, who was in the last days of her pregnancy, owned one of decent quality and about two by three meters in size. She had me help her drop it off at the Kommandantur. The commandant saw us bring it in and, I am sure, noticed Minn's condition.

That afternoon a German soldier drove up to our house with a horse and wagon loaded with several sacks of flour and potatoes and proceeded to unload the wagon. "Courtesy of the commandant," he said. Needless to say, these food supplies were a godsend and we made them last quite a while. That major was obviously a decent man and, in the limited framework of his position, apparently tried to do as little harm as he could get away with and even to help when possible. It was always my sincerest hope that he would survive the war in good shape.

In early August 1941 my sister gave birth to a beautiful baby boy, without medial assistance. By pure chance we were fortunate enough to have staying with us for a couple of days a Jewish woman from the town of Ilya, about forty-five kilometers away, and she was of considerable help in the delivery.

This lady--whose name, I regret, I cannot recall--had an Aryan "appearance" and easily passed for gentile. Because of this she could move from town to town without too much difficulty. People with this particular endowment were considered lucky and were much envied by others considered to have the more traditional Jewish look. No doubt many owed their survival to this lucky chance. The woman was looking for her husband and her only son. They had all been in the town of Vileyka at the time all Jewish males fourteen to sixty-five were ordered to assemble in the town square, and her husband and her son vanished with the local Jews. It was through this woman that we first heard of what had occurred in Vileyka. She was on her way to some other town or village to investigate a rumor that Vileyka Jews had been seen there. She had already checked several other leads, all false. She stayed with us only a few days. Who knows how many more rumors she would subsequently investigate. Quite a few, I would venture to guess.

Two days before Simchas Torah of 1941, I was sent to the state farm at Lubanye for three days of work as part of the contingent of young people sent there periodically. It was the time of the year for potato harvesting. One of the regular non-Jewish workers, working with a team of horses, plowed a furrow about half a kilometer long to expose the potatoes. Our job was to follow and pick these potatoes and bag them. Before we finished one furrow, the next usually lay exposed, ready and waiting for us. Thus we were under constant pressure to work faster. The overseer berated and harassed us with shouts of "Keep moving, you lazy sons of bitches. You're delaying the horses." By the end of a day like that we were naturally pretty exhausted and our backs hurt from all that bending.

On our third and last day of work, the day of Simchas Torah, we were out in the fields as usual, spread four to five meters apart from each other, facing a furrow with freshly exposed potatoes. Off in the distance we noticed two people with guns approaching. As they got closer I recognized them both as two young men from our town of Kurenits and barely a year older than me. One was called Blizniuk and the other, Polevik. They were now members of the town police force and both were well known to us. I was not on unfriendly terms with either of them.

As all of us workers stood facing the approaching policemen, I had an uneasy feeling in the pit of my stomach, like everyone else, I suppose. Never before had Kurenits police come up to Lubanye. The sight of them now did not bode well, especially as they were carrying guns. One was holding some sort of paper in his hand and he glanced down at it from time to time. The pair marched up the line of Jewish young people facing them and, as they went by, from time to time they called out one of our names and plucked that person out of the line. In all they pulled fourteen of us out and I was one of the fourteen.

We got only vague answers to our questions about what was happening. My mind started running at high speed, looking for some explanation of why I had been selected to be arrested. I had certainly been no activist for the Russians; in fact, during the almost two years of their administration, I had come to dislike their system. It must be, I though, that my name had somehow got mixed up with the name of a distant relative of mine, with the same family name, who was an activist. Yes, that must be it, I though. I'd be able to straighten this out once we got to the police station. A feeling of hope and belief in some order--a feeling that the world wasn't totally upside down--still prevailed then.

It was about six kilometers from Lubanye to Kurenits. The first five kilometers were through woods and the last, just before Kurenits, wa through open fields. In the woods we walked together with the policemen, mingling and talking like old friends. One of our grouop of fourteen was a young man by the name of Arke Ruvke's, Aaron the son of Ruvke Alperovich. He was about three years older than I and quite strong physically. Halfway through the woods something happened that shook me to the core. Arke walked alongside of me for a while and whispered, "They're going to kill us. Let's overwhelm them now before we get out of the woods." Properly organized, this could probably have been accomplished easily. But the idea seemed preposterous. Why should these people kill us? I considered myself innocent of any wrongdoing and so did everyone else in the group. And what would happen after the pair was overwhelmed? Where would we go then? We would be fugitives and unable to move freely. And what bout our families? They might all be punished, even shot. Much later, by the way, after we had become less na•ve and the true nature of what the Germans intended became clearer, that uncertainty about what could happen to their families kept most people in check and restrained them from running away to the woods or giving more open expression of revolt. Needless to say, I disregarded Arke's suggestion and so did others he also tried to persuade.

What really impressed me at the time, though, was the look in his eyes. It took me back to my schooling under the Soviets, where I had to read quite a few of the Russian classics. In one story, by Lermontov, a young nobleman in the military is assigned, because of some infraction of discipline, to an out-of-the-way garrison where there are no young women. The boredom is great. When the commander's daughter comes to visit, the young nobleman promptly falls in love with her, as do several other officers, and one of them challenges the young nobleman to a duel over the young woman. A friend of the nobleman's, in the course of preparations for the duel, foretells that the nobleman will die in the coming encounter. When asked how he can know an outcome before it happens, he answers that the eyes of a man who is about to die reflect death for an hour or two before the event and that this can be seen by anyone who looks into them. The nobleman fights the duel and, of course, is killed.

The story made quite an impression on me. I remember wondering whether that was really possible. Now, looking into Arke's eyes as he talked to me about overwhelming the policemen, I was sure I saw death. I remember thinking clearly, "Oh my God, if he is just about to die, then the fate of the rest of us is also sealed. Can this really be?" The mind will not accept such a verdict willingly or easily--not on such short notice and especially not if known to be based on a work of romantic fiction.

We all continued walking together toward Kurenits, still in a more or less friendly atmosphere. I began feeling more nervous from the moment I saw Arke's eyes and I now considered the chances of a satisfactory ending to this episode greatly reduced. Where were they taking us? And what actually lay in wait for us when we got there? The answers to these questions were not long in coming.

As soon as we came out of the woods into the open country, the policemen's demeanor changed abruptly. The fell back about three meters behind us and pointed their rifles at us. Gone was their former amiable and comradely behavior. We now had behind us two snarling policemen ready to shoot at the slightest provocation. They began and kept up a diatribe accusing us Jews of helping the Soviets, and spat out a story about how a man called Peter--one of their unofficial leaders, who had been arrested by the Soviets shortly before the war started--had been executed in the jail in Vileyka.

This last was probably true. We had heard rumors that the Russian security forces executed all their prisoners in that jail, and most likely in all the other jails under their control, because there was not enough time to evacuate them. After the Russians left and before the Germans arrived, relatives and friends of prisoners rushed to the jail and discovered the remains of their loved ones, all executed. It was easy to imagine the anger and rage of the two policemen at such atrocities, but why pick on us? Peter was young and well liked in the Jewish community. He mixed with Jewish men his age in friendly fashion and was definitely no Jew-hater. His arrest had nothing to do with Jews, his execution even less. Both were the result of a brutal political system that victimized Jew and non-Jew alike.

But all of this was of no interest to the two policemen. It became more and more clear that what motivated them was a need for revenge--not for something we had done, but for something the Soviets had done. Throughout history Jews have been scapegoats for people who wanted to vent their anger at a higher authority beyond their reach, an authority at whom they could only grit their teeth. What a convenient punching bag the Jews made under the Germans. No one was punished for injuring or even killing a Jew. Little did I suspect at this time that one of these two policemen, together with yet another, would a few months later in March 1942, go on a rampage and kill thirty-two Jews in Kurenits, my father and two of my sisters among them. And for this the pair was not punished at all, but actually praised by the Germans. I was told that an article appeared in a White Russian newspaper printed in the German-occupied city of Minsk, the capital of White Russia, describing the pair as great patriots of White Russia.

We were well out of the woods now with only open space between us and the first houses of the town. As we got closer, we came upon some armed German soldiers, which was very odd because there weren't supposed to be any Germans in town. There were none when we left for Lubanye two days earlier. The German major and his company of troops had been in charge for just the first five or six weeks of the German occupation. When they left, the town came under civilian administration and there had been no Germans in town since then.

The German soldiers let us pass. At close range their uniforms and insignia looked different. They were, as we found out later, SS Einsatzkommandos (SS Emeregency Strike Force), who specialized in exterminating supposed enemies of the German Reich within conquered territories--communists, Jews, gypsies, and others. (SS stood for Schutzstaffel, or "Protection Detachment," an elite guard also known as the "Black Shirts.") We were going by houses now. A little farther on was the house of a schoolmate of mine, a young woman whose name was Khayke Rabunski. As we walked by, I saw her standing at a window, looking out. When she saw us being led by policemen, she threw her hands together in an exclamation of horror and I distinctly heard her cry out, "Oh, dear God, they're taking Khaskl away." (Khaskl is my Jewish name.)

It soon became apparent something horrible was happening in Kurenits. The street we were being marched down led to the public square in the center of town. We were coming to a small bridge over a stream, and right next to this bridge stood Arke's house. As we marched past, Arke suddenly bolted into his yard and sprinted on through into the open fields, with one of the policemen in hot pursuit. The other policeman ordered the rest of us to start running and hit me in the back with his rifle butt by way of encouragement. We were driven at a fast trot over the remaining half kilometer to the police station in the town square.

Before we were herded into the police station, we saw a group of about twenty-five Jews, mostly women and children, standing under guard in front. Once inside, we were locked up in a small room. Two Kurenits Jews who had been put there before us were sitting on the floor in a corner. One was a childhood friend of mine and a classmate, Nokhum Alperovits, and the other was Velvl Rabunski. "What's going on here?" The question seemed to come from everybody at once. "They're going to kill us. That's what's going on," they answered and proceeded to tell us how they had been arrested the night before. One group, they said, had already been taken outside of town, made to dig their own graves, and had then been shot. "They'll be coming for the rest of us soon."

Velvl Rabunski's wife, Rosa, worked as a maid at the police station. Thanks to her intervention and pleading, Velvl had been allowed to stay behind temporarily. Nokhum had been picked up too late to be sent out with the first party. They said they had no hope whatever of getting out of this alive. I remember proposing that when we were taken out we should all run in different direction so that one or two might survive. The response I got was, "What's the use? They'll get us anyway." I had to admit the chances of success were really slim. And so we too sank to the floor ready for the worst. We too lost all hope.

We arrived at the police station about noon. We would stay there until five or so in the afternoon. All that time we expected that the door would open at any moment and that we would be led away by the Germans and shot. When the door finally did open, the person who came in was Matros, the former principal for the public high school were Nokhum and I had both been students. He was a major in the Polish army reserves and a recognized leader in the local Polish community. Matros later paid for this honor with his life, along with his wife and on of their two grown sons, late in the spring of 1942, when the Germans liquidated the Polish leadership and intelligentsia. There were rumors that the other son, who at the time lived with a relative in another town, later became a German collaborator. The principal spoke to us encouragingly and when he left we felt at least a glimmer of hope returning.

About an hour later, we were all released. To this day I'm not sure why we were let go. The principal, I realized later, wasn't influential enough to accomplish our release on his own. There were rumors that the Germans, after taking the second group (the one we saw standing in front of the police station when we came in) and disposing of them in the same manner as the first, were too lazy to take out still another group, especially so late in the afternoon. Maybe they had another job scheduled somewhere else the next day. In any case, by then they had disappeared from Kurenits.

For a period of several hours we had been without any hope at all. I remember Velvl Rabunski saying at one point, "What a beautiful world this will be after the war. Hitler is definitely going to be defeated"--in this we all concurred--"but we aren't going to be around to see him defeated or to enjoy life afterwards. Because we're all going to be dead in a few hours." No one contradicted him. It certainly looked true enough at the moment. I was barely eighteen; at such a tender age it is quite terrible to expect life to end in a short hour or two. But miracles do happen and here I was, back with my family, free of the nightmare.

By the next morning it was possible to take stock of the terrible events of the previous thirty-six hours: in all, the SS had killed fifty-three Jews, over half of them women and children. Some of those picked up were the families of the activists who had fled eastward. Some were young men who never cooperated with the Soviets except by holding a regular job. They went to their deaths with their families--parents, sisters, and brothers. They were forced to dig their own mass grave and were then shot.

Two young men--one, about twenty years old, the younger son of Pinye Alperovits the kosher butcher and the other, Osher from Dolhinov Street, about thirty years old--managed to break away from the pit and run back toward town with Germans and police in pursuit. They made it to a barn on Dolhinov Street and tried to hide there, but were discovered, beaten severely, and then dragged back to the pit and shot.

I was very anxious to find out what had happened to Arke, one of the fourteen in our group brought back from Lubanye, who had run away. The news was not long in coming. According to witnesses who saw and heard everything, the policeman giving chase to Arke caught up with him, whereupon Arke turned around and grabbed the policeman's rifle. Being of superior strength he was able to wrestle it away from the policeman. This was more the result of inspiration of the moment than calculation because as soon as Arke found himself in possession of the gun, he realized that he didn't know what to do with it. As I explained previously, we weren't yet psychologically ready to oppose the authorities actively, much less grab a gun and shoot a German or a policeman and then escape into the woods. The policeman senses Arke's state of mind and took advantage of it. In a honeyed voice he said, "Oh, come on, Arke. Stop fooling around. Give me the gun and we'll walk back." Arke hesitated, his fate hanging in the balance as seconds slid by. Then, spurred by his desperate will to survive, Arke made a final attempt to escape. After heroically wrestling the gun away from the policeman, he had some measure of hope and encouragement.

With the gun in his hands he took off at high speed heading towards the village of Pukien and the woods beyond it. But his act of desperation was like jumping from the fire into the frying pan. The chances of making his escape were practically nil. The town was surrounded by police and SS troops. Arke was running in an open field and made quite a visible target. Shots were fired at him from several directions and before Arke covered the first thirty meters he was brought down by a bullet. He crumpled to the ground unable to move. Several policemen surrounded him. Then Blizniuk, the first policeman who chased Arke from the moment he broke away from our group closed in, retrieved his gun and shot Arke death at close range as he lay wounded on the ground. He became the fifty-fourth victim.

My father compiled a detailed list of all fifty-four of the victims, including their first and last names, their ages, their addresses, and the names of their parents. The list was found in his suit pocket after he himself was killed, about six months later, by this same Blizniuk.

It was a miracle I had not succumbed along with the fifty-four. What we needed in those times was something on the order of a new miracle every day. The great majority of the Jews didn't get the benefit of even one; a few were saved miraculously not once but several times over, only to run out of miracles after successfully dodging death three or four more times. However, there were no miracles for Arke that day. I believe he somehow sensed that his end was at hand, and even though he tried desperately to avoid it, his growing agitation brought the inevitable to pass.

3

Before the war, Vileyka was an unpretentious, middle-sized town of about 15,000 inhabitants, 4,000 of whom were Jews. Late in October 1941 it became the seat of the provincial government. Actually the Soviets had earlier raised Vileyka to this high status by making it the capital of what was once called Vilner gubernie (Vilno province). The city of Vilno (Polish Wilna Lithuanian Vilnius) had always been the capital of Lithuania, except for the period between the two world wars, when it was annexed to Poland. In October 1939 the Russians generously returned Vilno to Lithuania, along with a few neighboring towns, and Vilno once more became the capital--only to be annexed by the same Russians a few months later, along with the rest of the country, and made one of the Soviet republics as it still is today.

The Germans cut Vileyka province in two. Gluboke was made the capital of the northern half, while the city of Vileyka was retained as the capital of the southern half. The provincial governor--called Gebietskommissar--along with scores of officials, both military and civilian, took up residence in Vileyka. Dozens of German businessmen also settled there in order to appropriate as much grain, cattle, and clothing as possible from our province for the German population back home. The military did their own separate requisitioning. All these people, with their staffs and secretariats, constituted quite a sizable number of Germans in need of living quarters and office space.

All that was left of the Jewish population of Vileyka at this time were women, children, and a few old men. All the men between the ages of fourteen and sixty-five had been executed at the beginning of the German occupation. Many of the houses and offices of Jews were empty and abandoned; some had been partially destroyed by looters. The Germans needed these living quarters and office space restored quickly for their own use. They ordered a number of carpenters, cabinetmakers, and painters to be sent from Kurenits to work in Vileyka. I joined the ranks of the painters.

Painting came naturally to me even though most of what I knew about it came only from watching painters working. As a child I loved to watch people at work, any kind of work. I could stand for hours watching, with equal fascination, blacksmiths, shoemakers, tailors, carpenters, painters, and all the other artisans as they practiced their trades. My brother-in-law, Sam Spektor, was a trained artist-painter and produced beautiful canvases, undoubtedly the kind of work he loved best. However, to make a living in those days, he had to devote some of his time to other, less artistic work, like painting houses. I had the opportunity to watch him at work more than anyone else and I picked up enough about painting houses to be able to pass as an experienced housepainter.

It was becoming clearer that working people who could make themselves useful to the Germans stood a better chance of survival. If work was required, then so were workers. And the more important the job, the better was this chance. Suddenly everybody wanted to work, especially if they could get an official certificate indicating their new job status. A work certificate was very desirable and became a much sought-after talisman, as if this alone could make the difference between life and death. Many paid a high price, even gold, to obtain one. A few unscrupulous people, helped by some officials and even some Germans, made a thriving business out of selling work certificates. But in the end most of these certificates proved of little value. Only a few of the most highly skilled workers--those the Germans really needed and could not do without--were spared, but only for a while.

I became one of the painters working for the Gebietskommissar in Vileyka. Because his was the highest provincial authority, working for him gave us a greater sense of protection. This proved valuable when the Germans decided later on to finish off what remained of the Vileyka Jews. I was one of the five painters from Kurenits: two adults, Yosef Zuckerman (Yosef Saras) and Irma Meir-Aarons Alperovits, and three young male apprentices, Hershl Zimmerman (Hershl der Krivitser), his brother Judl, and I. We worked six days a week. Saturday afternoons we were allowed to go home to Kurenits, stay there overnight and part of Sunday, and then return to Vileyka Sunday afternoon. We were not paid, nor were we supplied with any food. We had to bring with us food enough to last the week.

There wasn't much I could take with me, since food reserves at home were meager and dwindling. But there was enough bread to eat. Sometimes in the evening, after work, we used to cook a soup of barley, beans, or such. Once in a while we obtained milk. And that was pretty much our constant daily fare. Such delicacies as meat, butter, and eggs were seen only in dreams. Breakfast consisted of bread and hot water. I called it "tea with buttered bread (broyt mit puter mit tey)" because that was what I used to have for breakfast at home before the war. So what if there was no butter to put on the bread and no tea or sugar to go with the hot water. I made believe it was the same old "tea with buttered bread." Once I got used to it, it wasn't so bad really, especially since I knew that some people had it much worse.

The first few weeks we painters were in Vileyka we slept on the floor of whatever house we were working in. These houses were unoccupied at the time and the Germans would not move in until all the work was completed and the houses thoroughly cleaned. After four or five weeks of this sleeping about, we were placed in a house where an old Jewish woman lived by herself. She had lost her husband and two sons in August when the Germans took all the men away. It was arranged for a young woman from Kurenits to be our cook and prepare some dishes for us from the few supplies available. She was Nokhum Alperovits's middle sister, Henia. The house was small and had only a kitchen, a bedroom, and a living room. Henia slept in the bedroom with the old woman, while the five of us painters slept in the living room, the older men on the two couches, one person on the table, and the other two on the floor. It was crowded and not easy to get a good night's sleep.

One day I met a young man a few years older than I who was a native of Vileyka and one of only a handful of younger Jewish men still alive in Vileyka. This young man invited me to sleep in his house, where there was a sofa I could use. I accepted gladly. For about two months I spent my evenings and stayed overnight with his family, which included his father, about seventy-five years old, and his older sister, about forty. Her husband had been taken away with the other men in July. They were nice people and I felt quite at home with them. Food was scarce, so I never ate with the family at their house. I had my supper, or what passed for supper, at the house where the other painters stayed.

One of our first jobs was to paint the inside of a house that was to be used by the Gebietskommissar. The Germans supplied the paint and other materials. How important the job was and how quickly it had to be done was underlined when the civil administration of Vileyka sent over some non-Jewish painters to lend us a hand. These men were paid a full wage in money and got extra food rations and cigarettes. This was the only time we ever worked on any job with non-Jews. As it turned out we had to repeat this particular job several times over before receiving the Gebietskommissari's nod of approval. Only after the third or fourth painting was he finally satisfied and then he gave us each a pack of cigarettes. Cigarettes were the unofficial currency of the time and could be traded for food or other essentials. I used to bring mine home to my father, who craved cigarettes. Smoking was more important than food for him.

After the governor's house was finished, we had to pain the houses and offices of lesser officials. We also worked on repainting their theater. What I remember most, however, was working on the house of the chief of the local SD, which stands for Sicherheitsdiensti (Security Service). The SD were part of the SS and their sole mission was exterminating Jews and gypsies and all others they considered undesirable. The number of Germans in these local SD units was not great--perhaps about thirty in all--but in less than two years they were responsible for exterminating about eight-five percent of all the Jews in the province under their jurisdiction. Only a few Jews managed to survive through 1943 and into 1944. Other provinces had similar SD units who also proved themselves equal to their assigned mission.

The Germans couldn't accomplish this all by themselves. It wouldn't have been physically possible. They were assisted by special volunteers recruited in Latvia, Lithuania, and the Ukraine--countries known for their widespread anti-Semitism. These volunteers were part of the SD units and wore the same uniforms as the Germans did, with the same skull insignia on their hats. They were zealous and efficient and did most of the actual killing, while the Germans took on more of a supervisory role. It was a labor of love for these volunteers, who all seemed to be selected for size: they stood at least two meters tall or more and weighed at least 100 kilos. Their imposing presence and the wild look in their eyes instilled fear in our hearts and mesmerized us as effectively as a cobra mesmerizes its prey.

The house of the SD chief formerly belonged to the warden of the big jailhouse in Vileyka under the Polish administration. Later the warden's house was taken over by the Russians and then by the chief of the SD. It stood next to the courthouse, in the same compound, on a hill overlooking the jail. Both buildings were of impressive size. The former courthouse was used by the SD for offices, interrogation, and torture.

It took us about three weeks to complete the paint job to the SD chief's satisfaction. During the time we were working on the house, he came by a couple of times to check on how the work was progressing. You could not imagine a more soft-spoken, amiable man. We were, nonetheless, under no illusions about what cruelty the man was capable of. The distinctive smell of burning human flesh assaulted our nostrils most of the time we were working on the chief's house. Relief came only when the prevailing winds shifted for a while. Dozens of human beings were being shot in Vileyka every day, then thrown into a huge pit near the old courthouse and burned. The fire in the pit was fed by a constant flow of gasoline or kerosene and it burned day and night for as long as the SD was there, that is, approximately three years. People were continually brought into the old courthouse to be interrogated, tortured, and incarcerated. Sooner or later most of them wound up in the pit, where they were converted into reeking particles that permeated the air for blocks around. Anyone approaching the SD compound within a wide area was assaulted by the stench of carbonized human bodies.

During the time we worked there, around Christmas of 1941, the victims were mostly non-Jews: gypsies, communists or people suspected of being in sympathy with the Soviets, and intellectuals were considered unreliable, especially if they were Polish and in the Polish leadership. Several months later, the former of the Kurenits public school, Matros, was brought in along with his wife and grown son. They ended up in the pit. There were undoubtedly some Jewish victims too, but I knew of only one such family.

Late one afternoon, after work, when I came into the house where I was staying temporarily, I found a frightened little girl of about ten sitting at the table. There was caked blood behind her left ear, her eyes were glazed and showed signs of shock and stress, and her speech was semi-coherent. She'd already told the family with whom I was staying the story of what had happened to her and her family.

Her parents and the three children, of which she was the youngest, lived in the village of Neyka, about nine kilometers east of Kurenits. Their family was one of only three still living there; most Jews had abandoned village life and moved into the larger towns after the first world war. But there were still a few holdouts. The girl's family decided to move into Kurenits to be near other Jews during these difficult times. They may also have had relatives there. They were on the road, coming in by horse and wagon, when they were arrested. Jews had no right to move from one place to another without specific authorization. Jews also had no right to use a horse and wagon. Actually they had no right to anything. If caught on a road traveling, they were especially fair game. It was not clear whether the girl's family was intercepted by chance or whether they were denounced by their former neighbors. They wound up in the SD compound in Vileyka.

A visit to the SD compound was a one-way trip. There should have been a sign on the gates of the compound with these words, to reflect its true function: "Through these gates people enter but never leave." The girl's whole family was shot. Sometimes bodies weren't thrown into the burning pit right away, and that's what happened in this case. Fortunately, the bullet did no more than graze the girl's skull behind the left ear and leave her stunned. We could only guess how long she had remained in that state. It may have been minutes, or it may have been an hour or two. When she did come to, she crawled to a hole in the fence around the compound and escaped. She wandered around in shock for a while and then knocked on the door of a house, of non-Jews as it turned out. By chance, good people lived there and they brought her over to our house. We calmed her down as best we could and she stayed the night with us. The next day she was somehow smuggled into Kurenits, where she must have shared the eventual fate of most Kurenits Jews; I don't believe she survived.

After two months we decided that because of the strict night curfew it would be best for me to come back and stay overnight with the other painters. So I gave up the more comfortable lodging I had enjoyed with the family and moved back with my co-workers.

Later we heard that the old man of the family had been arrested one evening and was being held in jail. A strict curfew was in force from sundown to sunup. At night all windows had to be covered so that no light could show through. The old man's house had wooden shutters that effectively blocked the light their kerosene lamp gave off. It so happened, however, that a knot in the shutter wood shrank just enough to become loose and fall out. This left a hole the size of a quarter which nobody in the family noticed. Unfortunately, one evening the police or the SD passed by and saw the tiny ray of light coming through the shutter. They arrested the old man. His young son who had befriended me recognized what the nighttime knock at the door might be and managed to hide successfully.

I saw the old man once more, and I wish I had not, because whenever I think of him and his family, this last scene comes back before my eyes. One afternoon, while I was coming back from the jail, under guard, digging and pushing a stalled German car out of a snowbank. The old man's face was marked with welts and cuts; one eye was swollen shut. He was obviously being beaten and tortured. Maybe this was the last time he was outside of that jail. Just when he actually perished I do not know, but neither he nor his son nor his daughter survived the final liquidation of the Vileyka Jews in March of 1942.

One night I awoke to the sound of church bells ringing loudly in my ears. It was as if the bells of all the churches in town were tolling at once. I lay where I was for a long time trying to comprehend why church bells would be ringing in the middle of the night. Soon my head ached and my temples throbbed. This, coupled with the difficulty I had raising my head off the pillow, finally made me realize I was experiencing carbon monoxide poisoning. I was familiar with the symptoms because, when growing up, I had heard many stories of people found unconscious or even dead as the result of a poorly ventilated stove that allowed the poisonous gas to build up. I forced myself to get on my feet and wake up the others. The girl, Henia, and the old woman were only half conscious, but they revived quickly when we took them out into the fresh air outside. It was a narrow escape for all of us.

The month of March 1942 arrived. It wasn't spring yet. There was still plenty of snow on the ground and the nights were still cold. But the relentless grip of the winter cold had eased and the days were getting slightly, but noticeable, warmer. A definite promise of spring was in the air. The festival of Purim was only a few days away.

News began filtering in that Jews were being massacred in several towns. Some massacres were partial and lasted only a day or two. Whoever got caught during the roundup was eliminated, but those who survived by escaping or hiding were allowed to return and resume their lives in town. After such an "action" (aktion, the Germans called it), the authorities usually put the few surviving Jews into a ghetto. Some towns went through several such purges before the Germans pronounced them Judenrein, that is, "clear of Jews." The final massacre ran for as long as necessary. With many non-Jewish neighbors assisting, Jews were discovered hiding in attics, under floorboards, behind double walls, and in many other ingenious places. Some Jews managed to avoid discovery for days, even weeks. But in the end, unless they were able to slip away without being seen and reach the safety of the woods, they were discovered. One could not stay in hiding in the middle of a town forever. And the chances of getting out of a hiding place and away were best the first night. As the searches got more thorough, the chances of getting away diminished steadily each successive night.

The Germans explained away the partial massacres with some excuse or other and assured the survivors they were now safe. It didn't necessarily follow that the Germans were believed, but what else could Jews do? Where else could they go? People always hoped that the next time they'd again manage to hide or escape. At this time the woods afforded at best only temporary safety because there were few partisans there. The measure of protection the partisans would eventually provide didn't materialize until the end of the summer of 1942. During the first half of 1942, few Jews chose to stay in the woods permanently. Survivors of partial "actions" usually returned to the towns they lived in. The few survivors of complete and final "actions" sought refuge in towns that had not yet been touched by the full German fury.

Then came the news that the Jews of the town of Volozin, where my oldest married sister, Sarah, had been living for ten years, had also been executed. A faint ray of hope still remained in my heart at the time; maybe by some miracle she had survived. But of course the bitter truth was that she perished in the massacre of the great majority of the Volozin Jews. After the war a survivor told me about it.

We still hoped, no matter how weakly, that somehow we would live to see the Germans defeated, a defeat we all believed would eventually occur. Slowly but surely, however, the ultimate German plan for the Jews was becoming clear to us. They intended to empty all captured lands of all Jews. It took time for this realization to crystallize, but it was a conclusion everybody came to sooner or later--except those who consciously chose to close their eyes and ears to logic and reality. Unfortunately, there were many people in this category. Their way of coping with the situation was to say that Jews should carefully avoid provoking the Germans and conscientiously perform the tasks the Germans assigned to them. Then the Germans would leave them alone. These people refused to believe the word reaching us about all the massacres or, rather, they found ways to explain away what was happening--as if there could be a rational explanation for the murder of a whole town of Jews. But this was the road to survival these distressed people chose.

I remember one case clearly. This particular Jew was about forty years old and came from a town about fifty kilometers away. The Germans had just murdered all the Jews they could get their hands on there, including the man's wife and children. He was lucky enough to escape with his life and somehow or other made it to Vileyka. I happened to meet him one day while he was telling his story and giving his opinion that the Germans would eventually do the same to every Jew in every town.

I saw no reason to disbelieve the man, and I did not entirely disagree with his assessment of what was awaiting us. Yes, it did sound extreme, but it also sounded plausible. Some of the younger people who were there and heard the man speak felt more or less the same way I did. Others, however, said the man was crazy and suggested that the terrible loss of his family had made him deranged. Young single people still had a sense of freedom of action and tended to see things differently than men who were weighed down with the responsibilities of caring of r a wife and children and felt there was no way they could run off to the woods, where the hardships of existence would be multiplied many times over. They put all their hopes into doing good work for the Germans and in making themselves as useful as possible. They actually tried to block out any information that might contradict their false assessment of the situation. Then came the festival of Purim.

We couldn't celebrate Purim in any really traditional way, of course. In the evening I read the Megilla (Book of Esther), which is read in all synagogues in normal times. The best we could do was to gather a few of the neighbors, who made the trip to our house through backyards. They were mostly women and a couple of young girls. After the reading we all exchanged wishes that the latter-day Haman should meet the fate of the original one. Then everybody went back home and we bedded down for the night. Except for its being Purim, this was an evening like any other.

Later we recognized the pattern, but by the time we did, most of the Jews had already perished. The pattern was that most German "actions" against the Jews were carried out on Jewish holy days or, in order to confuse us, a few days before or after a holy day. Soviet Russian holidays could also trigger these "actions."

Thus, around three in the morning of Purim, 1942, I was suddenly awakened by a loud banging on the front door. This door was never used in the winter and the snow on the steps normally lay fresh and untrampled. So I knew from the first what the knocking meant. "This is it," I remember thinking. "The SD have come for us."

The animal instinct for self-preservation takes over automatically in time of danger. My first thought was to run. "Maybe out the back door," I thought. I started to put on my pants in the dark. I always used to leave my clothes on a stool next to where I slept so they would be handy in case of an emergency. I grabbed what I thought were my pants, which I usually left on top, and tried to get into them. In the excitement and terror of the moment, I couldn't get my foot through the leg. Then there was knocking at the back door. Somebody opened it and Germans came in. The kerosene lamp was lit and there I was standing half-naked with my shirt in my hands. No wonder I hadn't been able to get my foot into the sleeve.

The Germans told us to finish dressing. We were facing three huge men in SD uniforms, with the dreaded skull on their caps. All carried submachine guns. They led us out the back door and into the yard. There we were confronted by three more SD men, making six of them all told. There were seven of us--the two women and the five of us painters. The SD men marched us out of the yard and into the street towards a truck visible about a block away. A full moon glowed in the sky and the light it gave was intensified by reflections off the snow that lay on the ground. It was bright enough to read a newspaper. "Once we get to that truck we're doomed," I remember thinking. "I must keep my eyes open for a good time and spot, and then I'll make a run for it."

At one point I was all set to make the fateful sprint, and had even taken the first step, but something held me back. I suddenly realized there was no way I could have gotten away. And lucky for me I didn't try. I would have been cut down before taking a few steps.

We got to the truck and were ordered to climb in. A few people were there already and more were arriving all the time. In only five minutes the truck was filled to capacity. Canvas flaps at the back and on the sides were lowered. We stood in total darkness with guards on the truck all around us. Then the truck started moving. We couldn't tell what direction it was going in, but it did not really matter. There was no question in our minds that we were being taken to our deaths. We were more seasoned now; eight months under the Germans had dispelled much of our earlier naivetŽ. Now we knew just what we could expect. We said goodbye to each other. I stopped thinking about trying to flee because I knew by this time it would be impossible.

About ten minutes later the trucked stopped. The canvas flaps were raised and we were ordered out. The place was well lit with artificial light. As we got off the truck, one by one, we were yelled at to run a gauntlet of SD men holding wooden clubs about the size of baseball bats. Two rows of facing SD men stretched from the truck to a building about thirty meters away. The building turned out to be a large garage, and I now recognized we were inside the SD compound that included the jail, the courthouse, and this garage. This was the dreaded place with the one-way ticket reputation.

To keep us moving, the SD men swung the clubs at and around our heads and shoulders. I made it through without getting hit. Others weren't so lucky. Several had received wounds that were bleeding profusely. Others, who had taken blows to the head, were in a semi-stunned condition. There was a purpose in all that yelling and swinging of clubs and making us run the gauntlet. It was not primarily to inflict pain or injury but to confuse us psychologically so that we could not orient ourselves or take stock of the situation. In this way no one would think of bolting. Cowboys use the same tactic herding cattle. All the noise and shooting in the air are for the purpose of driving the startled animals in the desired direction.

Once inside the garage, we were put in a corner and told to wait. Diagonally across from us, in the opposite corner of the garage, I saw a large group of about 300 people, mostly women and children. The "action" was in full swing now. Trucks arrived bringing more and more people, who were then driven into the garage. This continued all through the nigh and most of the following day.

We heard later that some people had not been picked up by the SD that first night. Jewish houses were obviously on a list prepared well in advance. But by faulty intelligence or simple oversight some houses had been missed. The next morning they started to walk to work, unaware of what had taken place during the night. They were then picked up on their way to work, or where they worked if they got that far, and trucked off to the garage.

Many of the Jews rounded up were originally from Kurenits, and a large number were young women working at menial jobs in Vileyka. One way or another they were all swept up by the "action." In the garage, smaller groups of Jews stood around and apart from the large group. I recognized the chief of the SD as he walked up to one of these smaller groups. He talked to the people there and one by one motioned with his hand for them to join the large group. Within a few minutes he had disposed of all the small groups in this way--by making them a part of the large group--all except ours. We were still standing apart. The chief of the SD now approached us. My knees felt weak. With a flick of his finger this man had sent who knows how many people to their deaths with no more emotion than it takes to swat a fly. Over 300 people in just the last hour or two. And in his whole career, maybe as many as 100,000! Yet to hear the man talk you would think him the gentlest and most civilized person in the world who could not possibly wish you any harm.

"Wo arbeiten Sie? (What is your place of work?)," he politely asked the first person he reached in our group, using the formal and polite Sie instead of the informal and intimidating du. To address somebody as Sie in German indicates a modicum of deference, especially when coupled with the honeyed tones the chief now used.

"Wo arbeiten Sie?" each person in our group was asked in turn and all answered. The older ones who didn't work said so. The chief's finger flicked in the direction of the large group. People who had work said where it was: the post office, the German police station, other offices. In all, about ten different places of work were mentioned. The chief's response was the same to all--a flick of his finger towards the main group.

When the chief finally got to one of us painters, the answer to his question was, "I'm a painter and I work for the Gebietskommisar (provincial governor)." This time the finger didn't move. "Have you the certificate to prove it?" the chief asked. We each took out the certificates that stated we were working for the Gebietskommissar as painters, each certificate bearing the signature of a high-ranking official and the stamp of the Gebietskommissar. They had been given to us just two weeks earlier. The SD chief glanced at the certificates and told the five of us to stand apart by ourselves.

A tiny glimmer of hope kindled within us. We hadn't been put in with the main group that was obviously marked for death. I nourished that small flame of hope. Maybe, just maybe, he would let us live. It was far from a sure thing, of course; we were still in the hands of the SD, in the center of the infamous SD facility from which, so far as we knew, no Jew had ever come out alive. And what was to prevent the chief from changing his mind? Or to prevent one of his men from throwing us in with the others by oversight or malice?

Presently we were led into a small side room; there we joined eleven other people who had been picked out of previous truckloads. Later, we were joined by one more couple. Besides the five of us, two others, carpenters, were from Kurenits. The rest were from Vileyka: two saddlers with their wives and one twelve-year-old son, one candle-maker and his wife, one soapmaker and his wife, and, I believe, one printer and his wife. All told there were eighteen of us in the room.

We began to hear shooting outside and saw a yellow-reddish light coming through the small barred window high up near the ceiling, as it usually is in jails. We wanted to get up to the window to see what was happening outside. There was nothing in the room to stand on, so I hopped onto somebody's shoulders. We realized this was dangerous. If caught, we would probably have to join those outside. But the desire to know, if we could, what was going on was strong. I watched for no more than a minute.

What I saw were two SD men, each one leading a group of three people towards the fire. One group was close to the fire. The other group was just leaving the building. The fire came from the infamous pit about which we already knew.

And then I jumped down, glad we hadn't been caught watching. We heard shooting again and knew what it meant. The shooting continued throughout the rest of the night and through most of the next day.

Once, around midday, the door to our little room swung open and two Lithuanian SD burst in. They were drunk and their glassy eyes looked full of murder. In their foreign-sounding German one of them said," Was machen die Scheisse hier? (What are you shit doing here?)" For a moment or two we thought we'd had it. Luckily a superior officer happened by and ordered the men out of there and to leave us alone.

The day dragged on. No food or water was brought to us, but worry and tension depressed our appetites anyway and nobody felt hungry. Early in the evening the door finally opened and an officer came in. He announced that we were going to be released and told us to step back into the main garage.

How different the place looked now from when we had been brought in. The whole main group of Jews was gone. They had all been shot and burned not more than 150 meters from where we had spent the last fifteen hours. They had been taken out in small groups to the burning pit, shot with small-caliber weapons, and then shoved into the flaming hole in the ground. All of those brought in after us, even during the day, met the same fate. I'm not certain of the exact number of those that perished in this "action," but judging by the size of the Jewish population of Vileyka before the war, it could have been as many as 2,000, including the fifty Jews from Kurenits who were also killed. Eighteen people out of 2,000 were spared by the SD; eleven of the eighteen were natives of Vileyka.

But the garage was not entirely empty. Two women, both strikingly good-looking, were no where the main group had once stood. One was from Kurenits, Khayke Rabunski, who had gone to school with me and who, as I have recounted earlier, was looking out of the window as I was led by, coming from the Lubanye farm on Simchas Torah on October 1941. The other woman was a native of Vileyka, intelligent and cultured, and perhaps in her late twenties, with a teaching degree. To what purpose these two had been kept back, we could only speculate.

When we were marched back out into the big garage, the two women stood there facing us about seven or eight meters away. Khayke called out my name a couple of times in a hoarse whisper and asked me to let people know at the police station, where she worked, what had happened, in the hope they would come to her rescue. She repeated this plea several times, not being sure whether or not we had heard it. Poor soul, we couldn't even acknowledge with a nod that we had. We were afraid of antagonizing the Germans and imperiling our own chances for release. But the possibility that someone at the police station would come to Khayke's rescue was nonexistent. The power of the SD was so great and their latitude of activity so broad that even high-ranking German officials were afraid to take them on. SD authority went unquestioned.

In the almost empty garage, a German officer sat behind a long table covered from end to end with all sorts of valuables--gold, diamonds and other jewels, stacked in places a foot high and made up of rings, bracelets, brooches, pins, chains, earrings, and watches, perhaps weighing a good twenty-five kilos. Obviously it had all been taken from the victims before they were killed. The German officer asked us if any of our valuables had been taken away and if so, we were to look through the pile and retrieve them. But none had been taken because we didn't have any. I remember thinking at the time that if anything had been taken, I certainly would not call attention to myself by asking for it. Let them keep it. We just wanted to be released.

So I was astounded to hear one man, the candlemaker, I believe, answer, "Yes." A golden pocketwatch had been taken from him and he could see it there in the pile. I was even more astounded to hear the officer tell him to go ahead and take it. The man did so.

Then the officer took our names and addresses in order to provide an escort for us back to where we lived. When he asked Irma for his address, instead of giving the street and number of the house we stayed in, Irma blurted out that we were from Kurenits. The officer responded by saying he couldn't send us back to Kurenits at night. He put the five of us painters back in the little side room to spend another night and promised to see what could be done the next day.

Back in the room, behind the locked door, we once more felt dejected and forlorn. We had been so close to freedom only to be denied it at the last minute by an unfortunate remark from one of our own. It was really more than we could bear. Who could predict how the SD would feel the next morning? Understandably, Irma felt terrible. After somebody tried to reproach him for saying what he did, he picked up a brick lying on the floor and began to hit himself on the head with it to punish himself, as if that could help us in any way. The man was really on the verge of suicide. We had our hands full just trying to quiet him down and console him.

That night was the longest I can remember. Sleep was out of the question. Again we had no food or drink and again we felt neither hunger nor thirst. We heard sporadic shooting, but on a much smaller scale.

Morning came, but there was still no sign of our being released. Several hours went by. Fresh doubts arose about the outcome of this drama; if they intended to release us, then why were they still holding us? That was the nagging question at the back of our minds and it had no satisfactory explanation.

Then about eleven in the morning the door finally opened. An officer called us out into the garage. This time it was really empty. The long table was still there but now it lay bare. The valuables that 2,000 Jews consigned to oblivion, their lives extinguished by the flick of one man's finger to satisfy the bloodlust of the leader of the Herrnvolk (master race) and his henchmen. The two women--one a schoolmate and lifelong friend--had disappeared to who knows what fate before they, too, would be killed.

A mere thirty hours before, these people had been live human beings, each with their own aspirations and, above all, a desire to survive. I had known many of them personally and some had been close friends. Gone now was the family at whose house I had slept for two months recently. Gone were the neighbors who had come to hear me chant the Megilla: the older women and the two young daughters of one of the women, sixteen and seventeen years old, both of them redheads, beautiful, and intelligent. Gone too were our landlady and the young woman from Kurenits who had prepared our meals. All of them gone. Despite all this and despite the ordeal we had just been through, we simply felt happy we were still alive and elated that we were being released.

At the place we were taken to on the outskirts of Vileyka the Germans created a ghetto. Sixty families had been brought in from Kurenits, all headed by artisans, or, as they were called at the time, Spezialisten (skilled workers): tailors, shoemakers, carpenters, blacksmiths, sheet-metal workers, glaziers, and others the Germans had need for. All were allowed to bring along their wives and their children up to the age of fifteen.

The ghetto consisted of two long buildings the Russians had originally built as army barracks. The buildings were in a sorry state, without doors or windows, but we were moved in anyway. We were given permission to take what we needed from Jewish houses in Vileyka, now all unoccupied since the Purim "action." Within a few days, doors and windows were found and fitted and the barracks were made more livable. Officially, we were known as the Gebietskommissarsgetto (provincial governor's ghetto) because we worked for the Gebietskommissar.

Only real, experienced mechanics were brought to Vileyka and they came eagerly, even though it meant exchanging homes with many rooms and familiar surroundings for the cramped corner of a dormitory that had to be shared with several other families and that was without privacy or conveniences. It would also have been easier to cope with the food situation in Kurenits, where people knew some non-Jews and where bartering of clothing and articles for food would have been easier than in Vileyka, where all the people and surroundings were unfamiliar. Officially, Jews were prohibited from any social or business contacts with non-Jews; in Kurenits this would have been easier to circumvent because many Jewish houses were located in among the others.

Nonetheless, all these workers and their families were quite happy to move to Vileyka. By this time it was understood that working for the Gebietskommissar in Vileyka afforded some measure of protection. Not absolute protection--few were naïve to believe that--but a measure of protection for the immediate future. News of the Vileyka Purim massacre, together with rumors and reports of Jews being wiped out in other neighboring towns, made Kurenits's Jews realize that Kurenits afforded no protection at all, even for workers. Sooner or later Kurenits would follow the same fate as the other towns.

Our two master painters, Yosef and Irma, brought their wives and children to Vileyka to be with them. About twelve of us, mostly young and unmarried, shared one room, sleeping on army cots. After some breakfast in the morning, we all--except the married women and the children--went to work and did not return until dark.

After a few days I managed to take off from work and go visit my family in Kurenits. This time, however, unlike all previous times, I had no official permission to go to Kurenits, much less to be absent from the new ghetto.

The route to Kurenits from the ghetto required crossing the entire town of Vileyka from one end to the other, a distance of about one and a half kilometers. There was, however, little danger in walking the streets of Vileyka because both the police and the Germans were used to seeing Jewish workers walking from one job to another. Once outside of town, though, you had to negotiate seven kilometers of public highway between the two towns. Here the danger was greater but still acceptable. Vehicles with Germans passed by and you could never be too sure whether they might take into their heads to "stop that wandering Jew." To forestall identification by taking off the yellow star of David we displayed on our clothes, front and back, could have proved even more dangerous. I actually worried about meeting up with the non-German policemen who sometimes traveled the road to Kurenits on bicycles. I kept a sharp lookout for them and whenever I spotted any in the distance, I hid in the bushes by the side of the road until they had passed.

In this way I arrived back home safely and was enthusiastically greeted by my parents and sisters. They had learned, as had everybody else in Kurenits, about the events in Vileyka on Purim from one Kurenits carpenter working in Vileyka just like us. He happened to wake up in the middle of the night of the "action" and, hearing all the commotion in the street, he got out as fast as he could. Using backyards and side streets he crossed the town of Vileyka and reached Kurenits before dawn, unchallenged. Within an hour the whole town of Kurenits buzzed with the news. At first, for a period of thirty-six to forty-eight hours, my family assumed I was among the dead. Then they heard I had been released. Naturally they were quite relieved to receive the news and anxious to see me. I stayed overnight in Kurenits and returned to Vileyka the next day.

Back in Vileyka I found the people in a somewhat more optimistic frame of mind. The living quarters in the ghetto barracks had been made more livable with the addition of a table and a couple of extra chairs. There were even curtains at the windows of our room, courtesy of the young women. This better mood came mostly as a result of feeling that we had just been handed a new lease on life--not permanent, or even long-term, but what we hoped would last for a while at least. The Germans wouldn't go to all the trouble of bringing in master craftsmen and allowing us to fix up the ghetto buildings unless they needed us. So went the thinking and there was some logic in it.

Spring had just begun and the weather was getting warmer. The often sunny days that followed also played a part in helping to lift our spirits. With the full encouragement of the Germans we built a small bathhouse between the two barracks. Germans were sticklers for cleanliness. They were afraid of epidemics that uncleanliness might bring on.

For me the euphoric feeling didn't last very long. One day, when I came home from work and walked into our room, I noticed that all conversation among the ten people present came to an abrupt halt. I didn't pay much attention to it at first, though it did seem odd. The next day I also noticed some whispering going on among the people around me. When I tried to join a group that was engrossed in conversation, they quickly separated. My questions were answered in a vague and offhand manner. I got the feeling that information was deliberately being kept from me and it all pointed in the direction of my family in Kurenits. Something must have happened, perhaps something terrible.

I decided then and there to leave for Kurenits in the morning and find out for myself what was up. It had been three weeks since my last visit back home and it was no longer possible to move between Vileyka and Kurenits as easily as before. Ghetto residents had been forbidden to be absent from the ghetto for any reason at all except work.

So the next morning I left the place I was working, with the other painters covering for me. Getting across Vileyka still presented no problem. Once outside of town I turned to the right off the main road, wen through some fields and reached a small village (the name of which I have since forgotten). There I picked up a small farm road leading almost the rest of the way to Kurenits. This detour added about two or three extra kilometers but was safer since I met no one at all the whole way.

My apprehension grew with each step as I approached my hometown. I could sense that something disastrous must have happened there, but I could not imagine the extent of it. As I entered the town square, I noticed Jews in the distance walking and going about their business in a quite normal manner. This confused me, but gave me a slight measure of hope that maybe this had all been a false alarm after all.

I soon ran into my friend Nyomke Shulman and asked, "Tell me what's happened. Has anyone been killed?" "Well," he answered evasively, "there are no exact figures yet. Many people ran away. And some of them haven't come back. It's not known how many are missing."

"What about my family? Are they all right?"

"Yes," he said. "Your mother is at the house o Zalman Mendl the shoemaker."

I didn't have to inquire any further. Without telling me outright, Nyomke had indirectly indicated the extent of the disaster.

I ran all the way to Zalman Mendl's house. There I found my mother holding little Shimshon, Minya's son, on her lap. Mother's eyes were puffy and red. She burst out crying again when she saw me and we cried in each other's arms for a long time. Shimshon, even when he was not crying, looked hopelessly sad and forlorn. This was not the happy baby who used to greet me with a big smile. His face showed how much he missed his mother. It was as if he understood. And I too knew what the tragedy was. All that was left was for Mother to tell me how it had happened.

The disaster had struck two days earlier, at about ten in the morning. Without warning, two Polish policemen, both of them drunk, barged into the house. They ordered everybody, except Mother, out into the backyard--my father, my sister Ethel, and my sister Minn with the baby in her arms. Then they shot Father and Minn dead. The baby fell from Minn's lifeless arms into the snow. Ethel tried to run away. She made it through an opening in the fence and across the street into another yard. There one of the policemen caught up with her and shot her dead, too. Mother was standing by the kitchen window and saw everything. There had to be an added measure of deliberate cruelty in murdering a woman's husband and children before her very eyes.

These policemen were not only accustomed to cruelty, they positively reveled in it. One, Blizniuk, was a native of Kurenits; he was the same policeman who had hauled me out of the Lubanye farm in the fall of 1941 and who, the same day, had shot Arke Ruvkes as he lay wounded on the ground. The man got a taste of blood then and apparently he liked it. The other policeman, from Kostenevich, a small town about seventeen kilometers away, was named Szarenkiewicz. He had participated in the killing of the fifty-four on Simchas Torah of 1941 and had also taken part in the liquidation of the Vileyka Jews on Purim. Besides my sisters and father, the pair of them had murdered twenty-nine other Jews in Kurenits, a total of thirty-two.

After the two policemen left, Mother went outside and lifted the terrified baby up out of the snow. She was helped to move into Zalman Mendl's so she would not have to live by herself with the baby in the house where the murders had occurred. Father and Minn were buried the next day in the Jewish cemetery outside of town. By the time I got to Kurenits only Ethel remained unburied, and with the help of a couple of men, we laid her to rest next to my father and Minya.

Artsik Gotyes, a friend of the family, was one of those who helped in the burial of all three members of my family. He handed me a piece of paper he had taken from my father's pocket. On the paper were listed all the names, and other detailed information, of the fifty-four victims who perished in the fall of 1941. To this list we now added the names of the thirty-two who had just been killed. I kept the paper on me for a long time, until it disintegrated over the next couple of years.

Yitskhok (Iche Hatsyes), my father, was about sixty-three years old when he was murdered. He was highly respected by both the Jewish community and the gentiles. He was a recognized scholar in all the holy scriptures, including the Talmud. He knew Hebrew and Russian and had a good knowledge of mathematics. He was a teacher most of his life and even taught Russian and mathematics in our public school and in night school. The policeman who shot him, Blizniuk, had once been a student of his in night school. To me he was more than a father; he was also my teacher, from the age of five through the age of fourteen, in all nonsecular subjects. He had a unique talent in explaining difficult passages in the scriptures in such a way as to make them easy to understand. His lectures on Mishna and Gemara were very much appreciated and well attended. He was considered a special authority on these subjects and he was even consulted on some difficult and tricky passages of law by the local rabbi. He had a sharp, analytical mind and all who knew him acknowledged him to be a brilliant scholar.

As a young teenager I never ceased to be amazed at my father's ability to demolish every argument an opponent in a discussion could come up with. He answered with such ease and logic that everyone present was soon won over, including the opponent. He also possessed a beautiful voice and was a cantor. His rendition and interpretation of the prayers, especially on the High Holidays, were deeply moving and soul-inspiring. He was also an excellent bal kriah--reader of the Torah. People who had the privilege of hearing him read the Torah and chant while leading the congregation in prayer still speak of it with a praise reserved for masters of these crafts.

It is told that an important Talmudic discussion once took place in Kurenits between a visiting rabbi from the city of Lublin and our local rabbi and several local scholars, my father among them. The topic was one aspect of a certain work by Rambam Maimonides. It was not unusual for this kind of discussion to last for several hours, as the learned men brought out and carefully analyzed all the fine points of law and brought to bear the many commentaries, all in the presence of a large congregation that would gather for such an event. At the end of this discussion the visiting rabbi turned to the congregation and, pointing to my father, said: "Here in Kurenits you have a priceless pearl. You should consider yourselves blessed by his presence among you." This took place when I was still a little boy and too young to know of it at firsthand, but it is related in a chapter by Abraham Dimenstein (Avrohom Merkes) in the book Megilat Kurenits (edited by Aaron Meirovitch 1956).

And now my father was gone. No longer would I be able to listen to his wise counsel or, with the numerous other students of his, children as well as adults, be able to drink at the deep well of knowledge he possessed.

Gone, too, were my two sisters Ethel and Minn, at the ages of thirty-one and twenty-eight. Ethel was a pretty brunette, the brainiest one among my sisters. Minya, my favorite, was not only ver pretty but also gentle, warm, very loyal to the family, and well-liked and well-thought of by all who came in contact with her. My sisters were cut down by two drunken policemen, eager for Jewish blood.

If there is any consolation, it is in the knowledge that some measure of justice came down on the pair of killers. They soon received their just due. One, the native of Kurenits, was killed four months later by partisan. The other was dispatched by the SD, for whom he often worked so diligently, into the same flaming pit into which he himself sent so many.

--For the rest of the book which is a story of escape and resistance .https://www.amazon.com/Do-Not-Gentle-Resistance-1941-1945/dp/1511736852

Charles Gelman (Yechezkel Zimerman) was twenty (born in 19200 when eternal night fell on his town Kurenets. It was June 1941 and the Holocaust had tragically reached the region. Gelman lost his family , and felt the cold, dead hand of the "Final Solution" even as its victims continued to hope. But he had one chance many did not have, and he took it. Charles Gelman fought back. Gelman was part of the Russian resistance; very few partisans survived to talk about their experiences. It was a difficult task for Gelman to find the desperate warriors hiding in the forests. Food had to be begged for; shelter was scarce; weapons were nearly impossible to come by and were a condition for joining the partisans. Courage, ingenuity , and self-sacrifice were both shared and assumed in the underground.

Gelman became part of an organized force and attacked German outposts, derailed trains, blew up bridges, ambushed tanks, and neutralized the occupation infrastructure. Neither side expected or gave a quarter. Gelman explains the scourge of anti-Semitism. He shows how and why so many outwardly decent Poles and Byelorussians became indifferent to the fate of their Jewish neighbors. He understands the psychology of the German plan and why so many Jews struggled silently or went in comparative quiet to their own destruction. But most of all, Gelman gives us a participant's story of the armed resistance to Nazi genocide- and the story of those who did not go gentle. https://www.amazon.com/Do-Not-Gentle-Resistance-1941-1945/dp/1511736852

The Spektor Family of Kurenets

Told by Dina Dreillich nee Spektor

My father Natan Spektor was born in Dolhinov in 1890 to Ita and Kopel Spektor. As far as I know he was an only child. At some point he moved to Kurenets to become a teacher there. He married my mother Rivka born c1890. She was the daughter of Henia and David who was from the Frankfort family of Soli, (a small shtetle near Smorgon) now in Belarus. I also had some relatives in Oshmiany and some immigrated to the U.S. long before the war. My father was very involved in the community life in Kurenets. For some years he was the head of "Gmilut Chesed"- a charity organization. Hs was an accountant and also a teacher for bible studies in "Tarbut" school.

I was born in Kurenets in the Vileyka-Vilna area in 1923. At the time I was born it was part of Poland. Kurenetes was a small town and many residents were pretty poor. The majority were Jews that supported themselves with stores they owned. There were a few that worked in offices, in education, and social services. The town was surrounded by villages where most of the population was of Belarussian origin. The high officers and the authorities at the time when I was growing up were Polish people who were sent from the south western part of Poland to run the region that became part of Poland in 1921 after a hundred and twenty five years of Russian rule.

My father (Nathan Spektor, Z"L) was a teacher of Torah in the school, as well as my oldest sister Esther Spektor (born in 1914), who later on joined the staff at the Tarbut school. Hundreds of children of the town were educated by them, but tragically, most of them perished in the Holocaust, and my siblings and our parents who were amongst them.

There was a strong attachment to the Land of Israel in Kurenets. Most of the children studied in the Hebrew school, Tarbut, and were deeply ingrained in the Hebrew language and culture. Zionist ideology flourished and many of my peers were members of Hashomer Hazair were my brother Kopel (born in 1919) was a beloved leader of the Youth Movement Hashomer Hazair. Since the town was small, almost everyone knew the entire population as we were growing up.

The sleepy, relaxed sort of life continued until the year 1939, when the war started, and even then, after the Russians came, things didn't change much. But then, when the Germans attacked Russia in June of 1941, our world was turned upside down. Shortly after they entered the town, they announced new rules against Jews, and from then on, they started systematically killing the population, and many of the local, non-Jews became their collaborators. The main actzia (killing) took place on 9/9/1942, three days before Rosh Hashanah. On that day, about one thousand forty people were killed, which was most of the population of Jewish Kurenets. My parents Rivka and Natan perished that day. My sister Ester was transferred to the Vileika ghetto camp to work there (but she was later killed). More than a hundred people succeeded in escaping and hiding in basements, attics. Some of them were later caught by local farmers who brought them to the Nazis, who killed them on the spot.

Many who hid were able to escape since it was a foggy day. They survived hiding outdoors in the forests. They survived there for almost two years of deprivation, living in a constant state of starvation and through two very cold winters, hiding outdoors until the area was freed in the summer of 1944.

I was amongst the few who survived. On the day of the killing of the Jewish community of Kurenets when my loving parents perished, I was in the camp in Vileyka with my sister Sarah born in 1914, my brother Koppel born in 1919, and my youngest brother Eliyau born in 1924. Both of my brothers were strong like lions, and since we were all in very good condition and able to work any kind of job, the Germans used us for hard labor.

In 1943 we escaped from the ghetto with a few dozen Jews.

Tragically, although my brother Koppel was amongst the leaders of the escape, and everything was prepared for an orderly escape, things didn't turn out so, and we had to escape all of a sudden. The Nazis and the locals who helped them ran after us, using dogs, and they shot at us, killing many, including my brothers Kopel and Eliyahu and my sister Sara. I was wounded but survived as the only remnant of my entire family, the last of the Spektor family that does not exist anymore. With the little bit of might left in me, I was able to run to the forest with other survivors and together we survived the hard years in the forest until the war ended.

After the war, many of us were able to go to Israel, and to build a new life there, and rehabilitate ourselves.

I kept in touch with every survivor, amongst them the Cheres family. Since Shalom's wife was caught in the forest and killed, the father Shalom, with his four children, went to Germany after the war and met another woman who he married and had a daughter with.

After I married, Shalom would visit our family often in Herzelia. He would often talk about his son, Yehudah, who later immigrated to Israel. He particularly loved his daughter-in-law Wanda. In Israel we are still in great contact with all the Kurenets natives and survivors. Here in Herzlea where I live, I have a good friend, Chaiat Tzirolnik Sheingood. She is also a Kurenets native and a survivor who is left as the only remnant of her family. She's also in touch with the Cheres family. We all greatly appreciate Yehudah Cheres for all his activities for the sake of our own Kurenets, and now his involvement, great involvement in the issue of making a street named after Kurenets in Israel.

From a phone call with Eilat Gordin Levitan:

When the war started I was sixteen years old, I had two brothers and two sisters. My oldest sister, Ester had graduated form a seminar for teachers in Vilna. She was a teacher in the Kurenets "Tarbut" school and engaged to be married to a young man from Soly.

Sometime after the Germans invaded our area we had an opportunity to work in the German camp in Vileyka. We saw it as the only chance to survive. My sister Ester refused to leave my parents and perished with them and about 1040 of their neighbors, on 9-9- 1942.

My brothers Kopel and Eliyahu, my sister Sara and I were in the Vileyka camp for about a year. Many wrote in their memoirs about my brothers — here is some...

We were students of the daily Hebrew school, Tarbut and members of the socialist Zionist youth movement, HaShomer Hatzair. We spoke Yiddish and Hebrew fluently and dreamed of Aliyah to Eretz Yisrael. We were affected by Hitler's rise to power and information about the sad situation of the Jews. Poland also saw a rise in anti-Semitism in the thirties and we were closely watching the Spanish Revolution. All of these factors affected us. We believed in the justice of socialism and desired to accomplish it by living in an Israeli kibbutz. But we were young boys, still a long way from being able to make this a reality. Most of us were born between 1922 and 1924 and our troop leader, Kopel Spektor, was our strongest influence...

Our original troop leader, Kopel Spektor, was a man of all seasons- an athlete, a bookworm, a mathematician, and a generous and dedicated person. He was like a father to us. During the days of the Soviets, he was a technician and a cartographer in the central train station in Molodechno, 30 kilometers from Kurenets. He was a graduate of a technical institution in Vilna and an extremely capable man.

His job compelled him to travel throughout the USSR. When he came back from his trips he was very disappointed. He asked Benjamin Shulman to congregate in his house. It was the winter of 1940. We sat in the dark and listened to his sad statements. He told us about Minsk, the capital of Belarus,It had a large Jewish population. He only found one Jewish school there, and when he went to the one Jewish Theater to see "Fiddler on the Roof", they had changed the essence of Tuvia and made him a fighter against Czarism. He found a lot of mixed marriages there and people pulling away from Judaism. Our dream that the Jewish problem would be somehow resolved in the Soviet Union and that the Jewish entity would be recognized as a separate minority was abolished. In conclusion Kopel said, "The Jewish population in the Soviet Union will mix with the general population and in no time there will be no independent Jewish entities."

At the end of the evening Kopel passed the flag to Nyomka Shulman and suggested that we should find a way to get in touch with the movement headquarters in Vilna.

June 1941-....They called us to take part in the congregation, and we all decided to arrange watch groups. Mendel, the son of Henia Motosov, marched us to the house of Reshka Alperovitz, the former headquarters of the Soviet police. We found rifles and ammunition there. The rifles were divided among the young people who knew how to use them. Shostakovitz, the Belarussian doctor who was later a German sympathizer, was at that moment on the side of the Jews. He organized patrols of gentiles and Jews to patrol the town. I was stationed at a watch point near the railroad, together with Eliyahu Spektor.

The farmers started coming with horses and buggies. We told them that they couldn't enter town and that if they did, we would shoot them. They all left, and for two days, there was silence in the area. But then the town's gentiles started robbing the Soviets' storage areas and a few of them also robbed some Jewish homes…

…Kopel Spektor had just returned to Kurenets, so we asked him to secretly meet us in a hideaway on June 30 1941. This was our first meeting since the German occupation. The main question on our mind was "What are we going to do?". We all came to the same conclusion: we must fight the Nazis. Most of us were only 17 and 18, and we were still naive enough to believe that there was something we could do. We believed in the slogans of the Youth Movement about our collective and personal responsibilities. Kopel knew that the situation was grave, but didn't try to stop us. All he said was "I hope that you will succeed". We devised a practical plan. Firstly, we were to collect weapons and organize a Partisan group. Secondly, Shimon Zirolnik suggested that we print flyers urging people to fight the Nazis. Nachoom Alperovitz, who prior to the 'Soviet time', had worked in a printing office, decided to organize this. Lastly, and most importantly we would try to find other people that could join us. We hoped, in particular, to contact the Russian resistance….

- **Zalman Uri Gurevitz**

Kopel would plan our activities and teach us about socialism and Eretz Israel. He would teach us to sing Hebrew songs and Chasidic songs, and we danced many folk dances, the most popular of which was the Horah. Our meetings were not only held in the school, but also in the fields and in the forests. Particularly, we liked to walk to the big boulder, which were two huge rocks in the middle of a field that we always wondered how they got there.

Sometimes, Elik and Motik Alperovitz would invite us to the barn that belonged to Reuven Zishka, their father, and there we would hold the meetings. During our vacation, we would walk to the village, Mikolina, near Dolhinov, a distance of about 20km. There we would spend many days in what we called either our summer camp or our winter camp. We would meet members of the HaShomer Hatzair from the Dolhinov Ken (unit), from the Dockshitz ken, and the Krivich ken.

By 1940 the meetings of our Youth Movement became increasingly covert. Therefore, in many ways this began our underground activities. The core of the Youth movement for us was our leader, Kopel Spektor, although he didn't spend much time in town. Kopel finished his Techniyon studies in Vilna with very high grades. When the Soviets realized his skills, they sent him to work in Molodechno where he had a lab. He was working on an invention. He made something to do with trains.

He was beloved by all of us teenagers and we waited impatiently for the times he would come to Kurenitz

- Nachum Alperovitz …

How shocked I was when Hertzel told me that you could not even try the gun because it did not have the barrel with bullets.

My heart broke. My spirit was lifted again thanks to Kopeleh Specter who was an absolute genius, and in his hands, the gun became lethal. He fixed the gun according to the exact rules. Now all I needed were bullets. Therefore, again I started running around looking for the correct bullets amongst my Christian acquaintances. Finally, I got three bullets….

...After horrible arguments, we managed to elect a committee for the escape. The members of this committee were Mordechai, son of Havas Alperovich, who now lives in Israel; Hertzel Alperovich, may he rest in peace; Yosef Zuckerman, who now lives in Israel; Kopel Spector, may he rest in peace; our manager Shuts; Yonah Riar, from Ilya, both live in Israel; and I. The mission seemed very difficult. How would we be able to get the women and children out? .....The gun worked. From near the train tracks, I heard sounds someone walking and saying, "God, what did you do to us? Mommy and daddy, your situation is better. You already live in a better world." I tried to see who it was. At first, I saw a shadow on the snow and slowly I saw a short person wearing boots with a dark coat and messy hair. It was a woman who was limping. All of a sudden, I recognized Dinkah Spektor. She stopped, confused, and scared. She fell on the ground saying, "Where am I?" The snow around her was red from the blood coming from her leg. The blood kept coming, so I took my shirt and tore the sleeve and put it on the wound. I started covering her bloody footsteps and transferred her to another location. She told me that together with many of the camp workers, she already passed the train tracks and on the other side, they met German soldiers who shot all the escapees. She told me who ran with her and who she knew was killed. How she survived, she did not know. Instead of running to the Kurenets area, she somehow returned to the other side of the tracks back to Vileyka. She did not see my wife and son. I put some snow on her wound. Quietly, she twitched from pain. I thought that I should take the other sleeve and put it on her wound. Unexpected, I heard more steps, quick steps. I peeked from the hiding place, it was Doba Alperovich. Her jacket was open and her hair was messy. I yelled to her and she stopped but couldn't see me. I yelled to her again and she saw me and started crying from excitement. She also thought that she was on the other side on the way to Kurenets. Lacking any energy and depressed, we decided that when night came we would cross the tracks. From the bushes, we could see the road. I saw some people riding bicycles. I crawled closer to the road and saw that it was a farmer that I knew from the Soviet days. He greeted me, "Hello," and told me that I must quickly go to the other side of the forest since the Germans were coming to this side. He blessed me and quickly departed. I returned to the girls and told them. We decided to somehow go near the road to Molodetchna. Dinka had horrible pain. Doba and I supported her and walked toward the road....

Zev Rabunski

.....Our escape started at exactly four o'clock in the afternoon. We went together with Kopel Spektor, his brother Eliyau, and his sister, Sarka, may they rest in peace. I want to tell you about them for all the good they had done for us. The escape was very difficult for me and my wife. We had to carry our baby and I asked Kopel, "Don't desert us at this time. Please help us. It is very difficult for us with the baby."

He immediately answered, "Yosef, we will never desert you. We remember all you have done for us." He was talking about the time I helped him buy a gun. Since our escape from the Vileyka camp was unplanned, he didn't have time to take his gun. Until Kopel, Eliyau, and Sarka were killed, they ran with us, and every few minutes, we switched who would carry the baby in their arms. The snow was very deep, and we were running and falling, running and falling. The road was full of bushes and thorns that stuck out of the snow, so the journey was a truly thorny one...

Yosef Zukerman

Dina told me that when she arrived at the forest she met with Yitzhak Einbender who was a leader of a partisan unit and he helped her with her wound and other things. He was later killed near Dolhinov.

Another story that mentions Dina/Dinkah Spektor:

Excerpt from Zev Rabunski's The Struggle to Survive:

(The complete story can be found here: http://www.eilatgordinlevitan.com/kurenets/k_pages/stories_struggle.html)

I warned him not to go to the train tracks. All of a sudden, we heard the sounds of a German voice, "Rashkas Slinchas." We started running and I lost Yitzhak and his child. I did not hear any more German voices but I could hear many shots that were getting closer and closer. I lied there all by myself and a thought came to me. I never shot my gun. What if the gun does not work? I must try. Among all the shots, no one would hear my shot. From all the ammunition that I had collected through time, I was only able to take seven bullets. I pulled the trigger and shot. The gun worked. From near the train tracks, I heard sounds someone walking and someone saying, "God, what did you do to us? Mommy and daddy, your situation is better. You already live in a better world." I tried to see who it was. At first, I saw a shadow on the snow and slowly I saw a short person wearing boots with a dark coat and messy hair. It was a woman who was limping. All of a sudden, I recognized Dinkah Spektor. She stopped, confused, and scared. She fell on the ground saying, "Where am I?" The snow around her was red from the blood coming from her leg. The blood kept coming, so I took my shirt and tore the sleeve and put it on the wound. I started covering her bloody footsteps and transferred her to another location. She told me that together with many of the camp workers, she already passed the train tracks and on the other side, they met German soldiers who shot all the escapees. She told me who ran with her and who she knew was killed. How she survived, she did not know.

Instead of running to the Kurenets area, she somehow returned to the other side of the tracks back to Vileyka. She did not see my wife and son. I put some snow on her wound. Quietly, she twitched from pain. I thought that I should take the other sleeve and put it on her wound.

Unexpected, I heard more steps, quick steps. I peeked from the hiding place and saw it was Doba Alperovich. Her jacket was open and her hair was messy. I yelled to her and she stopped but couldn't see me. I yelled to her again and she saw me and started crying from excitement. She also thought that she was on the other side on the way to Kurenets. Lacking any energy and depressed, we decided that when night came we would cross the tracks. From the bushes, we could see the road. I saw some people riding bicycles. I crawled closer to the road and saw that it was a farmer that I knew from the Soviet days. He greeted me, "Hello," and told me that I must quickly go to the other side of the forest since the Germans were coming to this side. He blessed me and quickly departed. I returned to the girls and told them. We decided to somehow go near the road to Molodetchna. **Dinka** had horrible pain. Doba and I supported her and walked toward the road. All of a sudden, we heard horses running, and the sounds of Belarussian and Latvian voices. We fell on the ground in the bushes. I held my gun ready. We could see them. They were policemen. We all decided that we would commit suicide if they caught us. Dinka was begging that she should be shot first since she was wounded anyway and would not survive. Doba was begging that she should be shot first. Dinka was shaking so much while talking that she sounded as if she was stuttering. We were all watching the killers' every step hence we would not fall in their hands alive. I was almost ready to use the gun, but **Dinka** stopped me, "Maybe you should wait a minute." Doba said, "They are coming right by us. What are you waiting for?" unanticipated, I saw the police going in our direction turn to the right. They continued looking for people in a further direction from us, so now we had some hope of escape. Finally, we could not hear their talking. It was getting much darker and the air was getting colder.

A meeting at midnight.

We waited for the late night to come so we could pass the train tracks, but we were not lucky. The night was very clear, the moon was shining, and the snow was very bright. We stayed lying on the ground and our clothes froze and became hard. I looked at my watch, it was 10pm. I decided that we must leave. I was also starving. I helped **Dinkah** get up. She was lying on the ground and it was impossible for her to move. I tried to encourage her to get some strength telling her that we must go to the other side of the tracks, because if we stayed here until daytime, we would be dead. From among the trees, we could see the lights of the houses where other people sat safely in their homes. We walked and the snow was making a swish sound beneath our feet. This made us very upset. We were very fearful. We thought that someone was waiting behind every tree. We reached the edge of the forest. We hid under a bush, looking at the train tracks that were about 50 meters away from us. All of a sudden, we saw red flares then green flares then other colors. The Germans were busy watching. They were not going to sleep. We went to another area and we saw shadows of people on the train tracks. We heard sounds of talking but could not understand. It was already midnight and the watchmen were busy patrolling. Without warning, we heard the sound of breaking snow as if someone was running.

We were lying on the ground quiet and scared. Could the Germans be searching so late at night or could it be Jews? We were very fearful. From afar, we could see the barracks with the red flag and swastika. We could see two shadows going toward the barracks. It must have been the watchmen returning from the patrol. Then we saw the running people returning to where they came from, stopping in certain spot and searching for something. For some reason, in my heart I was very sure they were Jews who were lost like us. I started running and the girls tried to catch me being fearful that they would lose me in the dark. The two shadows must have heard our sounds. They stopped, as if they hesitated, I stopped and waited too. A woman's voice started calling, "Don't shoot!" It was like an electric shock going through my body. I recognized the voice, I could not talk for a second. I then yelled, "Rosa!" My son immediately recognized me and yelled, "Abbah!" He ran to me and we all started hugging and crying from excitement. The second shadow was of Batshevah, the wife of Yitzchak Alperovich, with her children. Doba and **Dinkah** started hugging Batshevah and her children. I told Batshevah that around 5pm, I saw in the forest her husband with her son but I had lost them. I carried my little son. He hugged me very tight and said, "Now we won't leave you daddy. Now we will be with you." Somehow, he felt much safer now, believing that I could protect him. Life seemed much dearer now, I had a reason to live and fight and try to get out of here.

Dina at age 89 on the right

The Kremer and the Eishishki, families of Kurenets

by Moshe Kremer

I was born in Kurenets in 1926. I was the youngest child of Chana, born in 1890 in the hamlet Kusta (a small farming community near Kurenets) My mother was the daughter of Bluma and Pinchas Eishishki. My father was Mendel, born in Kurenets in 1880 to Eshka Ester nee Alperovich and Yehushua Leib Kremer. My father Mendel had 4 children with his first wife Miriam, daughter of Cherna and Cheikel Velvel Alperovich. Baruch was born in 1905. Baruch was a merchant. He was married to Batia and lived in Molodechno with their children Yehoshua born in 1928 and daughter Miriam born in 1939 (just before the war started). My very smart sister Busia Bushka was born in 1906. She was married to Meir Shkolnik who was born in 1903. They lived in Kurenets. Bushka was a confidential unofficial advisor and therapist to the women of Kurenets. In extreme cases of rape or jilted young women she even arranged for abortions. Jacob was born in 1907 and lived in Svir with his wife Ester Henya ,he was a merchant. Chaim was born in 1911. He lived in Kurenets with his wife Zlata nee Dokshtzy from Dolhinovo. They had a baby girl during the war. He was also a merchant. His mother Miriam passed away while giving birth to him.

Some of the older siblings.

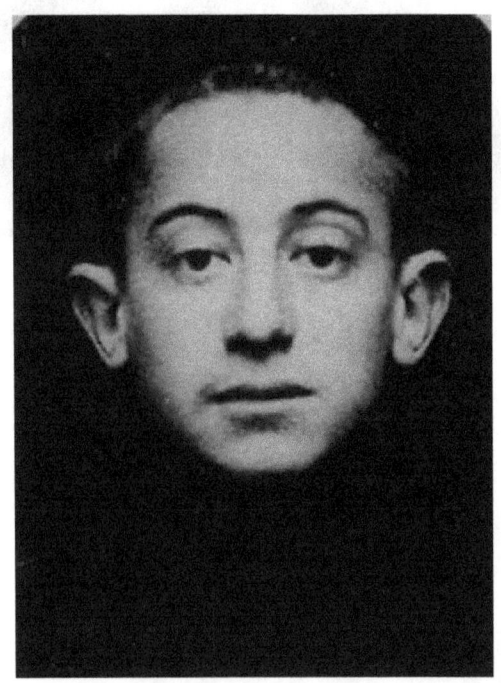

My brother Baruch who was murdered by the Nazis in 1942. His children survived the Holocaust.

Chaim Kremer (1911- 1959) survived the Holocaust.

My parents; Chana and Mendel Kremer

Since Miriam Kremer passed away when all of her four children were still very young, my father married my mother Chana and she helped him raise the kids from his first wife as if they were her biological children. In 1914 my parents had their fifth child, my brother. Gershon. He was a merchant and lived in Kurenets before the war. In 1918, they had their sixth child, my sister Henia. She was clever and beautiful. She was a book keeper and lived in Kurenets. The seventh, my sister Ashka was born in 1921 (she is my only full sibling who survived the Holocaust. She lived with her husband and 2 daughters in Chicago) The eighth, my brother Yehoshua was born in 1924. Then I was born in 1926 with a twin brother. He passed away when he was still a baby..

My sister Henia Kremer (1918- 1942). She perished in the Holocaust.

My Sisters Eshka and Bushka, shortly after the war ended.

Here is what the well-known Rabbi Landau wrote about my Kremer/ Kramer family of Kurenets: "At that time, a person who became important in our town was Yekutiel Meir Hakoen Kremer '(the brother of my father). He was very God fearing and honest in his ways, and he would teach Mishna to the community of the old shtiebel. His father was Reb Yehoshuah Leib Hakoen Kremer the Melamed. Reb Y. Leib was very knowledgeable in all the Mishna and many times would repeat the Mishna by heart. All his sons were honest and God-fearing people. Besides Yekutial Meir, there was Nachman Yosef Kremer, Mendel Kremer, and Chaim Zalman Kremer. All of them were businessmen, and Yekutiel Meir was also a merchant. He had a flour store but he was still busy learning Torah. Whenever you passed by his store you could see that there was a book in his hand. He was the son-in-law of Reb Yehiel Yentes and lived in his house. His brothers-in-law were the son of Yakov Mendel Markon, the owner of the flour mill in the village Ivontsevich, near Kurenets. Another brother-in-law was Zishka, son of Shimon Alperovich. Everyone in Kurenets respected the family."

Another sister of my father was Dobe Isaacson who immigrated to Eres Israel. She was the great grandmother of Gilad Jafet (owner of Geni and My Heritage). Both wives of my father came from very respected families. My mother was the oldest daughter of Pinchas and Bluma. Her siblings lived in Kurenets with their families Her brothers were

Gershon, Mordechai and Zeev Ayeshisky. Her sisters were Batia Gurevich, Sara Alperovich and Bela. Sadly not one of them survived the Holocaust, but the children of Batia Gurevich and Sara Alperovich survived and came to Israel after the war.

Our family was considered well-to-do. My father and my older brothers were merchants. They would buy grass from farmers who collected it in the many forests that were found in the area. My father had a special process that made the grass into feed for livestock. The feed was sent to Germany and Belgium and sold to Jewish merchants who lived there and they sold it to the farmers in their countries. We had a good income. My father had a phone (only two other households had phones in Kurenets of the 1930s).

My father was very generous. He hosted minyans at our house twice a week. 90% of the residents of Kurenets were Jewish. Zionist organizations and Youth movements were very popular (especially the socialist Hashomer Hazair). Like most young kids in Kurenets, I attended the Tarbut school which had six grades. We spoke Hebrew in class in almost all subjects (other than the mandatory Polish class where the teacher was a non-Jew named Matarass who during the Holocaust was appointed a mayor of Kurenets by the Nazis. He tried to save his students and at the end paid for it with his life.

The teachers for other subjects were trained in Jewish-Zionist teaching schools in Vilna. Such was the nursery/kindergarten school teacher Rashka Shulman and Rivka nee Spector/Gurevich whose father was born in Kurenets. (Rivka survived the Holocaust.)

I had many cousins in Kurenets. Most of them were slightly older than I. I was also very close with the children of the sister in law of my sister Bushka Skolnik. Motik and Elik Alperovich. They lived next door to us. Life was very good for me in my childhood.

After Hitler came to power in 1933 my father's business had some challenges. Jewish businesses were closed by the Nazis in Germany. It was the main country in which my father sold his products. Eventually he was able to find buyers in Poland and other countries in Europe and did ok until September of 1939.

Poland was attacked by Nazi Germany and with the agreement between the Nazis and Soviet Russia, our area became part of the Soviet Union.

Most Jews in Kurenets welcomed the Soviets. At least Jews who were simple workers were equal to any other Soviet citizens and their children were entitled to free schooling (including colleges) For families like ours, it was not so good. On my father's and older brothers ID it said that they were former business owners and as such not allowed to live in big cities like Minsk or Moscow.

Our school become a public school in Yiddish. Hebrew was considered a Zionist language and was not to be spoken in school. Zionist organizations were dissolved. Yiddish culture was fine since the Soviets consisted of many different cultures.

Our business was closed and my father retired. My older siblings found other jobs working for the Soviets. The Soviets were ready to send some of our family to Siberia for capital activities in the spring of 1941 but did not have time to do it since the Nazis attacked Russia in June of 1941. It would have been better if we would have been deported since almost all the Jews who were deported survived.

Much of the story of Kurenets during the Holocaust was already recorded by other survivors. Regarding my family my brother Baruch with wife Batia and children Yehoshua and Miriam moved from Molodechno to Kurenets right away. Baruch perished in Kurenets in 1942. His wife and the two children escaped to the forest with my parents and my brother Chaim. My brother Yaakov and his wife Henia stayed in Svir. Eventually they were taken by the Nazis to a hard labor camp in Estonia and were murdered there in 1943.

Meir Shkolnik, the husband of my sister Bushka perished in Kurenets in 1942. Bushka escaped to the forest and survived. My brothers Gershon and Yehoshua perished in Kurenets in 1942. My sister Henia perished in Vileika. My sister Eshka survived in the forest. On the early morning of the killing of the Jewish community of Kurenets, our family went into hiding together with the Alperovitz family (in-laws of my sister Bushka). Since it was a very foggy morning and the family could hear some Nazi collaborators looking for us they decided that it would be fine for Motik Alperovitz and I to try to escape to the forest and if it is possible to eventually return and take the rest of them. Motik and I ran to the forest. Just before we reached it a Ukrainian collaborator heard us and started shooting in our direction. He could not see us because of the fog and assumed that we were killed when there was no sound. We were able to reach deep in the forest but at one point I was lost alone in the forest not knowing the area (unlike me, Motik knew the area well) after some days I found Motik and our families' members who were able to escape late at night after the killings. We lived outdoors in the deep forest. We would beg the farmers from the area for a little food and we would get warm by sleeping next to bone fires. As winter was coming, we built zimlankas (covered bunkers) in the ground and covered them with plants to hide them. Tragically my parents and my sister-in-law Batia contracted typhus and passed away, I and my brother Chaim recovered. There were two blockades by the Nazis and we ran away to the marches to hide in the muddy waters. In one blockade, 4-year-old Miriam was left alone in the zimlanka. A miracle occurred and we found her alive when we returned many hours later. In 1943, I joined the Soviet partisans. Our job was to blow up trains.

Moshe Kremer- Partisan
son of mendel
son of Yehoshua Leib

As the war ended in our area I was conscripted to the red Army. I served for many years. By the time I was allowed to immigrate to Poland as an old Polish citizen (1958), I was married with two children and we lived in Oshmany.

From Poland we immigrated to Israel. There we met with my niece Miriam (now Gdor) who was adopted by Rivka Alper, a relative of her grandmother Miriam Kremer from the Alperovich family.

Tragically, her brother Yehoshua was killed as a soldier in the Israeli army during the war of independence in 1948. He was only two weeks in Israel when he was killed in a battle in Dgania. In Israel we also found my first cousin Israel Alperovich who also survived as a partisan and also our cousins Zalman, Leah and Gershon Gurevich (Gorev) who survived in the forest with their father Nathan. On my father's Kremer side, there was Moshe Kremer born in Kurenets in 1935 to Yechiel and Zisla. His brother Zalman Kremer was born in 1931. Their father Yechiel perished. They survived with their mother. Moshe was an important person in Kibbutz Ein HaShofet, A brother of their father

Yechiel was Shaya (Yishayahu) Kremer (1908- 1981). He also survived and came to Israel. He lived with his wife and daughter in Haifa.

My 3 surviving siblings went to Germany as soon as the war ended. My sister Emma Eshke married a Holocaust survivor Leo Greisdorf. They had two daughters; Chana and Ruth. My sister Bushka married Shmerl Lipski Leeb.

My brother Chaim married Zoya and had a son Michael in Germany in 1950. From there they immigrated to the US with their new spouses and newborn Michael in 1950.

Moshe Kremer with his sister Bushka and his wife at the wedding of his son Menachen and his bride Dori.

From left: my brother Chaim, my sisters Eshka and Bushka, Eshka's husband Leo, and the young girl Miriam Kremer Gdor

Shaya Kremer with wife and daughter.

My nephew, Holocaust survivor Yehoshua Kremer (1928-1948)

On the right, my cousin Shaya Kremer. On his left, his nephew Zalman Kremer, his sister-in-law, and his nephew Moshe Kremer.

Moshe Alperovitz, son of Rashka and Zalman

Moshe Alperovitz/Alperovich was a Holocaust survivor from Kurenets. I spoke with Moshe in 1995 at his home in the Tel Aviv area. Moshe's mother, Rashka, was the sister of my great grandmother, Frida. Here is some of what Moshe told me:

I was the youngest son of Zalman Alperovitz. My father was the son of Chaia Sara and Yechezchel and the paternal grandson of Binya Alperovitz. He had two brothers, Mendel Alperovitz and Moshe Alperovitz, and their families lived in Kurenets. My mother, Rashka, was the youngest daughter of Yehuda Alperovitz (the common ancestor of Eilat and mine). The last name Alperovitz/Alperovich, which both of my parents were born with, was very common in Kurenets. My parents might have been distantly related but I am not sure that they were.[1] Both of my parents came from similar well-off backgrounds. Their ancestors were very respected in Kurenets for their charity, their piety and their service for the community.

We were four siblings: My sister Fiya (Phaia) was born in 1905. She left home when I was still a young child. She married Shimshon Rubin and they lived with their children in Dolhinov before the war. The picture below is of my sister Fiya during the First World War, when the region was under German occupation.

My brother Meir lived at home with us and helped my mother with her thriving business. He was very charming and spoke a few languages fluently. In the following photo, my brother Meir is the young boy on the right. You can see our home, which was at the main market in Kurenets. The picture was taken during the First World War.

---

[1] DNA tests of the Y male line of sons of Moshe's paternal and maternal first cousins show that they were not related on the male Y Alperovich line but still somehow distantly related.

פינה בשוק, עם ביתה של לאה-אטקה בן הקומתיים

My sister Sarah was my only immediate family member who also survived the Holocaust. In the US she was married to Jacob Geller. Before the war she was married to someone else and had two young sons. As the war started, she had some problems with her husband. She returned and lived at our home with her two sons.

By the time I was born, my family was not as religiously observant as their ancestors. We celebrated all the Jewish holidays and on special occasions we would attend the synagogue. However, I did not attend a Yeshiva. This was like most of the families of Kurenets after the turn of the century, who also did not send their sons to Yeshivas. By the time I was ready to attend school, I attended the Hebrew Tarbut school, like almost every Jewish kid in town. Almost every subject was taught in Hebrew. The school had a secular Zionist socialist flavor.

Our father was a merchant. Sadly, he passed away when I was very young. At that time, life was very difficult for a widow who was raising her children alone. There was little respect for single or widowed women. My mother Rashka was very smart, forceful, confident and a great business woman. Despite running the business alone, she became very successful. She was very respected in the community and many people would come to her asking for advice.

Mother would often tell me about her childhood and her beloved siblings, who were now spread all over the world. She spoke of her brother, Wolf, who was smart and ambitious. Wolf was very unlucky. He served as a naval officer in the Czar's army in 1904. During that year, Japan offered to recognize Russian dominance in Manchuria in exchange for recognition of the Korean Empire as being within the Japanese sphere of influence. Russia refused and demanded the establishment of a neutral buffer zone between Russia and Japan in Korea, north of 39th parallel. The Imperial Japanese Government perceived this as obstructing their plans for expansion into mainland Asia and chose to go to war. After negotiations broke down in 1904, the Japanese navy launched a surprise attack on the Russian Eastern fleet at Port Arthur, China on 9 February 1904. Some time during that Russian-Japan war, which lasted a little longer than a year, Wolf was killed. The family never found the exact circumstances or date. Later, to keep his memory alive, some of his nephews were named after him.

My mother's brother Solomon Yitzi was involved with the 1905 failed revolution. It was primarily sparked by the international humiliation as a result of the Russian defeat in the Russo-Japanese War, which ended in the same year. Calls for revolution were intensified by the realization of the need for reform. Politicians such as Sergei Witte had succeeded in partially industrializing Russia but failed to reform and modernize Russia socially. The revolution failed, but its events foreshadowed the 1917 Russian Revolution just twelve years later. Mother's brother Solomon Yitzi moved to the Soviet Union and lived in Gorky.[2] In the 1930s my mother would send them Jewish inspired food during the holidays, as she knew that it was not available in the Soviet Union.

My mother had a sister who lived near Vilna when I was a young child. I can't recall her name but she had many sons and after her husband passed away, she and the teenage children, immigrated to Brazil.[3]

My mother's oldest sister was Frada (Frida, Frydel), born in 1870. She was married to Mordechai Gurevich, who was known as a religious scholar. He studied in his youth in a well-known Yeshiva and many times he would travel to meet with the Chabad Lubavitch Rebbe. The family owned a hardware store. Since Mordechai was always busy with religious studies, Frada ran the business and raised the children. They had 6 children. Nathan was born in 1898, Meir (Eilat's grandfather) was born in 1901, Batia (Bender) was born in 1905, Sima (Lerman-Herbert) was born in 1911, Luba (Bardan) was born in 1914. There was also a brother Yehuda who died as a young child. Unlike their father, all the children were secular, with strong Zionist and Socialists ideologies. By 1925 Meir and Batia made Aliyah to Eretz Israel (Palestina) Batia and her husband Yizhak Bender were among the founders of Kibbutz Givaat Hashlosha and in 1952, Kibbutz Einat. Meir and his wife Bela Shulman were among the founders of Moshav Bitzaron. Sima and Luba also followed and settled near Meir in Moshav Bitzaron. Soon after, the parents came and settled near Batia.

By mid-1930, only Nathan was still living in Kurenets. Nathan lived with his wife, Batia Ayeshisky, and their children, Leah Shogol (born in 1922), Zalman (born in 1924) and Gershon (born in 1928). Nathan was a merchant and owned a few stores. In the 1930s he owned a large textile store. He was well educated and led the parents' association of the Tarbut Hebrew school in Kurenets. The kids were very involved with the Hashomer Hatzair movement, a left-leaning socialist Zionist youth movement that was very popular with the youth in Kurenets. I was a

---

[2] The city of Gorky was renamed after writer Maxim Gorky, who was born in Nizhny Novgorod in 1868. In 1990 it went back to the original name, Nizhny Novgorod.

[3] I, Eilat, found the family via a strong DNA match that her grandson had with my mother. The name of the sister was Taiba Beila Gordon. She was married to Menachem Mendel Gordon in 1889. She lived in Adutiskis (Haydutzishok in Yiddish), a small town in present day eastern Lithuania, 15 miles west of the district capital, Svencionys. From 1920 to 1939 the district was in Poland. Taiba and Menachem had sons - Herzl, Simon, Volf, Meir- and a daughter, Hasse Karazin. They were all born between the 1890s and 1910. Menachem Mendel died in 1927. Shortly after, the entire family immigrated to Brazil. All but one brother lived in São Paulo.

member of the much less popular Bitar Youth Movement, which was more to the right. Both youth movements were Zionist and had the same emphasis on Aliyah to Eretz Israel.

Other than the mother Batia, the entire family survived the Holocaust by hiding in the forests and joining the partisans. Zalman and Leah wrote about it in the Yizkor book. After the war, they made Aliyah to Eretz Israel.

Next door to them in Kurenets lived my mother's brother, Michael, with his clever wife, Pesia Kastrol, and their children. They had five daughters, Chana, Henia, Rachel, Rashka and Doba. Their only son, Nachum, was born in 1923. He wrote a book about his survival with the partisans and later crossing the front and joining the Red Army. His sister Doba also survived, hiding in the forest after escaping from the Vileyka camp. Both he and Doba immigrated to Israel and joined their sister Chana, who came there in the early 1930s. The parents and the sisters Rachel, Rashka and Henia perished in 1942.

My mother had a brother named Yaakov Moshe who lived close by in the town of Radishkovich, near Minsk. My mother told me that he was a very well-off merchant. He sent his two sons to study in France. I do not know if any of the family members survived the Holocaust. Maybe the sons in France?[4]

It is difficult for me to talk about the Holocaust. Some things that I never shared with my sister can only be told after she passes away. Early in the morning of September 9th 1942 my mother, my sister and I realized that Kurenets was surrounded by Nazi forces. We talked to a neighbor and unanimously felt that it is the day that we feared for so long - the last day for Jewish Kurenets. They planned to annihilate all of us in a few hours.

We decided to try to escape and run to the forest. We made a huge, tragic mistake. Being in a hurry, we wanted to first try to get my mother and my sister into the forest and then if we would succeed, I would return and get the young boys who were still asleep. It took us a long time to run by foot deep into the forest. By the time I returned, I found our boy shot and killed in the doorway, which he must have opened to the killers. The baby was murdered in his bed. There was nothing I could do. I just ran back to the forest. My sister to this day never asked me about her children. My mother told me to never share the information with my sister.

Mother was murdered in March of 1943 during the first blockade, which was organized by the Nazis against the resistance and the Jews who were hiding in the forests. When we returned to the hiding area after escaping the Nazis deep in the forest, we found mother shot while sitting on a tree.

My brother Meir was working for the Nazis in the Vileyka camp. From a group of Jews who escaped to the forests and joined the resistance I heard that my brother was liked by the Nazi officers who ran the Vileyka camp. He made the mistake of thinking that he had a better chance of survival in the camp since the Nazis needed him and some other Jews from Kurenets and the area to do some essential work for them. He did not try to escape when he had a chance (many were killed during the escape). We know that he survived until the Red Army freed the area. We found

---

[4] Sadly I, Eilat, investigated it and not one survived, based on Yad Vashem reports. Vula Zeev Alperowicz was born in Radoszkowicze, Poland in 1905 to Yakov and Stirka. He was an engineer and married Yehudit, the daughter of Peretz Gitlin. They had two sons, Leibale (born c. 1935) and Yodele (born c. 1937). They lived in Radoszkowicze, Poland before and during the war. Vula, Yehudit and their two sons were murdered in the Shoah in March 1942. This information is based on a page of testimony that was submitted by their neighbor, Binyamin Zilburg. Here is the Radishkovichi Yizkor book information about those who perished: Alperovitz Ya'acov Moshe, Alperovitz Ze'ev, his wife Yehudit, and their children, Yodele and Leibele. Alperovitz Lazer, his wife, Zlata, and their children.

out that the Nazis took the Jews by force when they retreated back. I was told that some or all of the Jews from the camp were found dead, killed by the Nazis at the outskirts of Vileyka. The Nazis did not like to leave any Jews alive.

I was amongst the first to get a visa to immigrate to Eretz Israel/Palestina, where I had many first cousins. I built my life here. I married Sharlota and we have two wonderful sons. My sister came to California and married Jacob Geller. They have one son.

Survival stories of Kurenetzers
(Told to Eilat Gordin Levitan)

The Survival Story of Chaya Esther Reich (nee Gurevich):

I was born in Kurenets in 1923. My mother, Cheyena D'vorah, was born in Myadzyel in 1885 to Chaya Esther and David Wolf Gordon. Many Gordons from the Vilna region originated in the district of Myadzyel. The surname came to fruition when Jews were ordered to take last names by the leaders of the Russian Empire in 1815.

My mother's first husband was Yehoshua Leib Pliskin from Glubokie. They had two children: Shmuel was born in Glubokie in 1910 and Sonia Sara was born in Glubokie in 1912. Sometime in 1918 - just before the end of the First World War - Yehoshua Leib passed away of illness. My mother was left alone with two young children, ages eight and six, during very difficult years in the history of the region.

It was a very dangerous time for a woman to live alone. During those war years there was so much devastation, famine and illness. The region was at the front lines of the war for some years. It passed hands between the fighting forces nine times! First it passed from the Russians to the Germans and back until the First World War ended with the German defeat on November 11, 1918. Then after the Russian Revolution it was under the Bolsheviks' control. Finally, after wars between the Bolsheviks and Poland it passed to Poland in 1920. Most of the homes were broken and falling down. Most families hid in their broken homes, fearing the soldiers of the different invading armies during those years. My father, Chaim Yisroel, was born in Kurenets to Sara nee Zimerman and Zalman Uri Gurevich (My paternal brothers changed their last name from Gurevich to Horowitz when they came to the US).

Photo: Chaim Yisroel Gurevich

Before I was born, my father was a *Shochet* (a ritual slaughterer) in a village next to Kurenets named Zaneretz. His first wife was Toibe Raizsel. She was the daughter of the well-known Shmuel Alperovich, who was nicknamed in Kurenets "The Angel" for his charity and many good deeds. My father had five boys and two girls with his first wife. The boys immigrated, and settled in New Haven, Connecticut before my birth. Their names in the United States were Samuel (1887-1979), Joshua Heshe (1892-?), Maxwell (1893-1989), Abraham Elia (1895-1965) and Yizhak Elchanan (1896- 1982). There was a daughter named Leah, who was born in 1890 and lived in Kurenets with her husband, Zusia Benes. They had no kids. Leah's sister's name was Rivka.

In 1918 Toibe Raizel passed away. The Jewish tradition was that men should not live alone, even if they are sixty years old. My mother married my father, who helped her raise her two children from her previous husband at his home in Kurenets. I was born in 1923 to my mother, who was almost 40, and my father, who was about 65. Leah Benes, my half-sister on my father's side, was about 33 when I was born. She and her husband Zusia, who lived next door to us in Kurenets, were like second parents to me (since they had no children). I was still a young child when my half-brother on my mother's side left home. My brother Shmuel studied in a Yeshiva to become a Rabbi. He later migrated to the United States and was a rabbi in Baltimore. My maternal half-sister, Sonia Sara, married when she was still a teenager and lived with her husband and children in Dohinov.

Photo: Survivor Chaia Esther (age 93) with her son in 2016

My parents were strictly Orthodox. I grew up very sheltered. In September of 1939 the Soviets took control of our region. When I was sixteen, the Hebrew school changed to a Yiddish school. All Zionist activities had to stop. In June of 1941 the Nazis invaded our region. Soon after, we started hearing rumors that some Jewish communities in our area were being liquidated and all Jews, including women and children, were murdered. There were a few massacres of Jews in Kurenets and we were all very fearful. Just before Rosh Hashana of 1942, the Nazis surrounded Kurenets from all sides. We understood that they were going to murder us all. Most of the younger people decided to use the fog to try to avoid being detected by the Nazis and try to get to the forests and hide there. I hid in the forest for almost two years. Since much was already told by some of my cousins and others who hid and survived, I am not going to say much about it. I would rather talk about our extended family (mine and yours, Eilat).

My father had two brothers and three sisters:

1. My father's brother Mordechai (your great grandfather, Eilat, as you know) lived in Kurenets with his five children the year I was born. In the 1930s, Mordechai and his wife Frada followed four of their children: Meir Gurevich born in 1901, Batia Bender born in 1905, Sima Herbert born in 1911, Luba Bardan born in 1914. The children were all secular and devoted Zionists and socialists. During the 1920s (and some in the early 1930s) they settled in Kibbutzim and moshavim in Eretz Israel. My uncle's oldest son Nathan was also a secular Zionist. He lived in Kurenets with his 3 children: Leah born in 1922, Zalman born in 1924 and Gershon born in 1928. They all (other than their mother Batia) survived the Holocaust by hiding in the forest and joining the partisans. After the war they made Aliyah to Israel.

2. My father's brother Yankel, born in 1878, changed his last name to Spector and moved to Vilna to avoid service in the Russian army. He was the husband of Rachel Leah nee Brik. They were the parents of Yitzchok Spektor, who

passed away before the war. Their daughter Rivka was born in 1905. She was for a few years a teacher in the Hebrew Tarbut school in Kurenets. She was married to the well-known artist David Labkovski, a painter of Jewish images. They were revolutionary in their youth and chose to live in the Soviet Union, which was a lucky move during the war. After the war ended, they made Aliyah to Israel and settled in Zfat, where they passed away in the early 1990s. They had no children. Zlata/Zahuva was born in 1906. She was married to Reuven Reznik. As the war started, she and her twin babies were planning to join her husband, who had moved to South Africa. However, it turned out that it was too late. They were not able to obtain visas after the Soviets took control of the area. They perished in the Holocaust in Vilna with her parents. Arthur Abraham Spektor was born in 1908. He immigrated to South Africa and married Sally Mauarberger. They had four children: Patricia Kaimowitz, Robert, Barbara Barishman and Norman.

3. My father's sister Perla was born in Kurenets in 1880. She was married to Nathan Einbinder and had 3 children: Maryashka Rebecca Shapiro born in 1905, Jacob born in 1912 and Eli Tzvi born in 1913. In the early 1920s they moved to the United States and settled in New Haven, where many other Kurenetzers lived including some of Perla's nephews. Perla passed away in New Haven in 1964. Some of the grandchildren became well known rabbis of Chabad in the United States.

4. My father's sister Liba was born circa 1870. She was married to Yoel Shafer, a teacher of the Talmud High school in Vileika. They lived in Kurenets with their children: Rishka born in 1899, Israel born in 1900 and Alonzik born c 1905. Yoel Shafer passed away c 1930. Liba passed away of old age the week the Nazis entered Kurenets in June of 1941. Riszka married Ziska Sokolinski from Koblinik. They lived in Postavy and they were merchants. They had three children: Sara born in 1919, Avraham born in 1922 and daughter Michell born in 1928. The entire family perished in 1942 in Postavy, murdered by the Nazis. Israel married Etel and they had two sons. Yoel was born in 1931 and Michl was born in 1933. Israel Shafer was a watchmaker. Israel was known in Kurenets for his great sense of humor. Tragically, Israel was checking on his sister who was living in Postavy in 1942 and was murdered there by the Nazis. His wife was murdered in Kurenets on September 9, 1942. The two sons, Yoel age 11 and Michl age 9, escaped to the forest and were able to hide there for almost a year. Eventually they became sick and died of starvation. Alonzik Shafer left Kurenets for Argentina years before the war. For a while he kept in touch with his first cousin Aharon Meirovitz (the editor of the Kurenets Yizkor book). Yoel Shater was the brother of Aharon's mother Perla Meirovitz nee Shafer. Aharon told me that all connection with his cousin Alonzik Shaffer in Argentina was lost a few years after the war.[1]

5. My father's sister Chana was born circa 1879. She was married to Elchanan *HaKatzav* (the latter was a title referencing the fact that he owned a kosher butcher shop in Kurenets). Chana perished on the day of the Kurenets massacre. Her husband Elchanan died of natural causes before the Holocaust.[2] Note from Eilat: Chaya Esther Reich had a hard time speaking to me about Chana's family. All she said was that a young grandson of Chana who was about four or five years old survived a blockade in the forest but his parents, Chaim and Shoshka, and his sister were killed. Chana said that the child later hid with the Russian partisans and she knew nothing else about him.

---

[1] All the information about the Shafer family was given to me (Eilat) by Aharon Meirovitz, born in 1910. We spoke many times about 20 years ago. He also told me about his direct family. He, his three sisters and his brother Michael grew up next door to his uncle Yoel Shafer (the brother of his mother) and his wife Liba. He still remembered my great great grandfather Zalman Uri Gurevitz, who moved with his daughter Liba when he was very old. It was after his wife Sara passed away. Aharon recalled that he passed away c 1920. Aharon's younger brother Michael, who was a member of Hashomer Hatzair and wanted to make Aliyah to Israel, was not able to do it in time. Michael was murdered by the Nazis alongside his father, Ben Zion, the beloved teacher. His sister Fruma Varfman (born in 1903) perished with her husband and daughters, Bashinka and Perla, in 1942 in Kurenets. Another sister, Leika, died before the Holocaust and so did his mother, Perla. Aharon and his sister Sarah Eisen (born in 1918) made Aliyah to Israel before the war. Aharon was a poet. He helped other Kurenetzers who survived by recording, editing and publishing their memoirs. He implored me to include more stories, pictures and information from survivors and their family members.

[2] The information here is from a note by Eilat Gordin Levitan, based on a phone call with Israel Alperovich, the grandson of Elchanan.

I remembered Shimon Zimerman's story about the son of Chaim and Shoshka. Shimon wrote:

"After two months, this idyllic stage of hiding in relative safety ended. One morning our contact, Roman, with his son, came and told us that the Germans knew of our hiding places and that we must leave immediately. We had no choice, so we took our belongings and put them on our two sleds, one of which I had bought from a farmer. We went to more hidden away woods and fixed up a place to sleep. With the first morning lights we were awakened by shots. The Germans surrounded us. This was the first blockade. From the shots we understood that they were closing in on us. We had no time to think. We had to try to go through the ring of the Germans or go across an area that was clear of brush that was approximately 500 acres in size. We guessed that the Germans had come from Andreiky and surrounded the woods from three sides. The fourth side that was the part clear of trees was also clear of Germans. The Germans did not believe that anyone would try to go there. Despite the clear danger, I decided to cross that area, thinking that since the Germans were at least 600 meters away they would have a hard time catching us. Riva and I were the first to cross the clearing crawling. The snow was melting and in some areas its height was one meter. Above our heads the bullets whistled. But we had no choice, we had to continue. We were already in the middle of the clearing and could see a wooden area with no Germans, and then a bullet hit me in my left knee. My boot was filled with blood. I couldn't move and I begged Riva to go on without me. I lifted myself up praying that the Germans would kill me and not catch me alive. But Riva caught me and pulled me to the direction of the woods. Exhausted, we reached the woods. There we met some people that succeeded to cross the prairie. I tore my clothes to stop the blood. We had no medicine or first aid kit. The sun went west and the Germans stopped shooting. All of a sudden, I saw in the path made by me being dragged across the snow, a very tiny image slowly walking towards us. This was four years old Lazerke, son of Chaim Alperovich. From far away he saw us and followed behind. We waited for him to reach us. His father, mother and little sister were killed and he was the only one left from his entire family. We didn't have enough time to recover him and we heard a horse with a sled coming. Everyone ran away but Riva and I stayed because I couldn't move. The horse came right next to us. Riva caught the horse that the Germans must have lost. Inside the sled we found furs that must have belonged to a farmer. We called our friend Itzka Londers, and he took us back to our hiding place."

I (Eilat) could not let go of the information. My family left a young boy who survived in the Soviet Union and no one could tell me what happened to him after the war ended? After asking everyone I already spoke with before about him, I found out that they did not know anything else about him. I implored them to ask others who were there. I was directed to Israel Alperovitz, who shared first cousins with my mother (Leah, Zalman and Gershon Gorev/Gurevich). My mother was related to them on their father' side and Israel was related to them on their mother's side.

The survival story of Israel Alperovich:

Israel was born in Kurenets in 1923. His father, who he was named after, died in tragic circumstances before he was born. Yisrael the father was the son of Elchanan *HaKatzav* and his first wife. Chana, the sister of my great grandfather Mordechai, was Elchanan's second wife. Chaim, the father of Leizerke (the young boy who survived) was the half-brother of Israel's father.

Israel's mother Sarah, daughter of Pinchas Aishisk,i was the sister of Batia Gurevich nee Aishiski (my mother's first cousin's mother, Batia was the mother of Leah, Zalman and Gershon). Israel had two older siblings: Zeev born in 1919 and Ela born in 1921. In spite of the fact that Israel was orphaned from his father, he had a happy childhood. He had many uncles, aunts and cousins from both sides of his family and he also had grandparents and loving older siblings. Israel was a friendly child and had many friends his age in Kurenets.

Israel wanted to explain to me why the family let the Soviet partisans take care of young Leizerke, the son of his uncle Chaim. The best chance of survival for a young Jewish child homeless and hiding in the forest in very cold winters was with the Soviet partisans who had food and camps in the forest. Most of the young Jewish men who did not have families to take care of joined the Soviet partisans (if they were willing to accept them). Others who had young children had to build underground shelters and endangered their lives almost daily going to gentile farmers who lived in the outskirts of the forests asking for food. At that point a few Jewish children who were alone in the forest passed away of starvation and illness (including the second cousins of Leizerke, the orphaned grandsons of Liba Shafer, the sister of Chana, Leizerke's paternal grandmother). As the Nazis lost the war in that area, the Jewish survivors left the forests in the summer of 1944 trying to rebuild their lives and as soon as the Western areas were freed in 1945, they left the Soviet Union if they could. All men below a certain age were called to serve in the Red Army immediately after the area of Kurenets was freed by the Red Army in the summer of 1944. Some fought the Nazis, chasing them all the way to Berlin. Others fought Nazi collaborators and others in Belarus under Soviet rule. Israel was the sole survivor of his immediate family. His mother Sarah, his older brother Zeev and his sister Ela perished in Kurenets on September 9, 1942. All his uncles and aunts on his mother's side perished (see the story of his first cousin Moshe Kremer). His mother's brothers, Mordechi and Gershon Eishiski, perished with their wives and all their children. His mother's sisters, Batia Gurevitz and Chana Kremer, perished. Batia's husband Natan survived with children Leah, Zalman and Gershon (they all made Aliyah to Eretz Israel). From the children of Chana and her husband Mendel Kremer, Moshe Kremer and his sister Eshka survived and her step daughter Bushka survived as well as her step grandchildren Yehoshua and Miri (they were the children of Baruch Kremer who perished). Yehoshua Kremer was killed while fighting during the War of Independence.

On his father's side, those who perished included his uncle Chaim with his wife Shoshka and daughter Chiena, his uncle Yosef Alperovich with wife Feiga and son Moshe age 5, and his aunt Rivka. His uncle Hirshel perished along with his wife Dishka (a teacher). His aunt Tzirka survived with son Zalman. They made Aliyah to Israel and lived in Nazareth Ilit. Zalman had two sons.

Israel did not know where the young child Leizerke was when he looked for him after returning from army service. By then, all the relatives left the Soviet Union. He was unable to leave the Soviet Union until there was permission for former Polish citizens to move to Poland. In 1958, just before he left the Soviet Union for Poland, he was able to find Leizerke. He wanted to tell him that he could move to Poland and from there immigrate to Israel. It turned out that Leizerke grew up in a Soviet orphanage. Leizerke showed little interest in his Jewish relatives who he did not remember. That was the last attempt of connection of the family to Leizerke as far as the survivors knew. I am still hoping to find some information about Leizerke.

Israel married and had children They came to Israel in 1958. Israel had a happy life in Israel. He never forgot Kurenets and gave hundreds of Yad Vashem reports for the residents of Kurenets.

The Survival Story of Mendel (Marvin) Fidler and his parents, Yitzahak and Chana

In September of 2021 I received an email from Mina Nemirov. She wrote:

Dear Eilat Gordin Levitan,

My father, Marvin (Mendeil) Fidler and I were very happy to discover your website commemorating the people of Kurenets. My father is almost 91 years old (born 1931) and survived in the woods about 20 km outside of Kurenents with his parents Chanah Fidler (nee Piastonovich, born 1898, died 1972) and Yitzkhak Fidler (born 1898, died 1975). He is the only one of their 4 children that survived. Sara Fidler died by lightning in their home in 1940 at the age of 14/15 and his sister Mina was murdered by the Nazis in a roundup in Vilayka in 1942. His brother, Isser was caught by the Nazis while he was with the resistance and perished in 1943.

We are sharing photos my father has. The first 2 pictures of the men standing in the grave with the group of people and the one with the horse, I think are additions to other pictures you have of the town people properly burying those that perished. The two pictures of the groups of men were taken in Germany in 1947. These are all Kurenets survivors who relocated to Germany and were in displacement camps and later made their way to the US and Israel. In the picture with the wall, my grandfather, Yitzhak Fidler is in the rear, 5th from the right. And Charles Gelman (wrote a book about his survival. Was known in Kurenets as Chezkel Zimerman) stands in the front left and directly behind him is Velvel Rabunski.

My answer:

I would love to add the survival story of your father and his parents, as well as pictures and information about your relatives from Kurenets. Many years ago, I created a tree on Geni.com for both sides of your family. The tree of the Fidler's side is based on the story about the Fidler family of musicians which includes information about the grandfather of your father, Isar Fidler, his siblings and their parents. The information on your grandmother's side is based on Yad Vashem reports by Levik Alperovitz. His sister Nacha married Yaakov Leib Pistanovicz, the brother of your grandmother Chana. According to the Yad Vashem reports they were the children of Pesach and Mina. Mina passed away long before the Holocaust since at least two of her granddaughters (oldest of Yaakov Leib, and oldest sister of your father) who were born in the 1920s were named after her[3] (both perished as teenagers). Maybe Pesia, the youngest Daughter of Yakov Leib Pistonovicz who also perished in the Holocaust was named for her grandfather Pesach. The two sons of Yaakov Leib and Necha were Yechezkel and Zalman who were named after members of Nechas family. Thanks.

---

[3] It is an Ashkenazi Jewish custom to name babies after deceased ancestors, not living ancestors.

Photos: From the email from Mina Nemoriv, Marvin Fidler's daughter

I also spoke with Marvin Fidler directly. Since Marvin already had his very detailed story recorded by the Steven Spielberg Foundation (which is available online), we mostly spoke about two of his young cousins who also survived in the forests near Kurenets. On his father's side we spoke about his first cousin Chaim Dimenshtein, the son of Maszha nee Fidler (the sister of his father). Chaim was born in 1933 in Cholopy, a small farming village next to Kurenets. Chaim survived as a child hiding in the forest near his home for two years. After the war he stayed in the Soviet Union and had a family. Many years later he immigrated to Israel, where he passed away in 2017.

Photo: Chaim Dimenshtein

On Marvin's mother's side we spoke about his cousin Mendel Rabunsky, who was born in Kurenets in 1927. Mendel's mother was Leike (Leah Liza) nee Pistonovicz and was the sister of Chana, Marvin''s mother. Mendel's father was Yizhak Rabunski. His brother Shmuel was born in 1921 and his sister Chaia was born in 1924. I heard about her from my mother's first cousin Zalman Uri Gurevich. He was her classmate and her good friend. He said that she was very nice looking and smart. Sadly, only Mendel survived. His parents and siblings perished in the Holocaust. His brother Shmuel (Mula) joined the partisans and took Mendel with him to fight for the resistance. Tragically, Mula was killed while fighting.

Photo: Mendel Rabunsky

We also spoke about Marvin's aunts and uncles who came to the United States before the Holocaust.

After the liberation of the area by the Red Army in the summer of 1944, Marvin and his parents came out of their hiding place in the Naarutz forests. They returned to Kurenets, where they united with other Jews who survived. They reburied the Jewish victims and felt that it was too painful to try to rebuild their life in Kurenets. As soon as Germany was freed from the Nazis, they and other families from Kurenets left the Soviet controlled area for a refugee camp in the American controlled area in Germany. They waited there for a few years to get visas for either Palestine or the United States. After a few years of being refugees, with the help of their parents and siblings in the US, they received the desired visas and settled in the New York area. Today Marvin lives in New Jersey next to his good friend Natan, also a survivor.

I spoke to Natan many years ago. He is related to me via his mother Mina nee Sosensky, who was a second cousin of my grandmother, Bela nee Shulman.

Natan Kasdan was born in Glubokie to Mina (daughter of Chana and Nachum Sosensky) and Yosef (son of Fruma and Avraham Kasdan of Kurenets). Natan had a younger sister named Chanale. Shortly before the war, Natan's beloved mother Mina passed away after a short illness. Chanalel was still a toddler and it was difficult for Yosef to take care of her on his own. He went to the Kurenets/Ilya area (where he had some cousins and also brothers and sisters in law) and there he found a wife. He married Fruma Zira Alperovitz, the daughter of Chana Pesia nee Ginsburg and Avraham Chaim Alperovich.[4]

Yosef Kasdan brought his new wife back to Glubokie. His son Natan did not like his stepmother. He was very upset and asked to live with the family of his mother. The father took him to Kurenets to live with Natan's aunt Riva Tzirulnik (Cirulnik) nee Sosensky, born in 1902. Riva was the sister of Natan's mother. Her husband was Yitzhak and they had two sons: Shimon born in 1922 and Avraham born in 1926. Natan's cousin Shimon was a very bright guy and an active member of the socialist Zionist movement, *Hashomer Hatzair*. As soon as the Nazis arrived in the area, Shimon organized a Jewish resistance cell in Kurenets with his younger friends from *Hashomer Hatzair*. They printed flyers calling for resistance, which they secretly spread in the region and made contact with non-Jewish former communist (read Zalman Uri's story for details). Sadly, Shimon was reported to the Nazis as a communist and was taken to a camp, where he was killed shortly after.

On the day of the Kurenets Massacre, Natan's aunt had just a minute to tell Natan to be silent and to cover him with blankets when the police knocked on their door. She knew that they would not look for him since he was not registered as their child in Kurenets. Natan was able to escape and hide in the forest. At one point he united with his father, who had also escaped.
In the Yizkor book of Glubokie, Tzvi Rier wrote about Natan's father Yosef Kasdan during the time they hid in the forest:

"We found some other Jews after wandering around in the forest for a few hours: Eli Gordon and his family, Alia Padnos, Yosel Kasdan, who had been with me in the pit, Chaim–Meir Bipkin (a young boy). Later, Motke Genshteyn, Meir Bliachman, Motke Markman, and others arrived. Gordon's wife, Vichne, gave me a shirt. The Jews had built a primitive bath and heated it in honor of the 'guests.' I washed up and put on my 'new' shirt. I felt human again! They were well entrenched in Zemliankes and in Beidelech (primitive huts)."

After the liberation, Yosef and his son Natan came to the United States. Yosef married another Holocaust survivor from Kurenets. Her name was Chaya Ida, the daughter of Freidke Belka and Arie Leib Ziskind. She was married first to Chaim Lewin who perished in Kurenets. She survived with their son Zelig Lewin, her parents Arie Leib and Freidka Belka and her 3 sisters: Zina Zelda Kuperberg (born in October of 1926), Rivke Siegman and Dverke Dora (born in 1925 married another Kurenets survivor David Motosov - see his story in the Yizkor book) Dora had 2 daughters and a son Moti Inbar, who wrote me. They lived in Haifa. I spoke with Dora Matosov and her daughters many years ago. She as well as her sisters told their survival story to the Steven Spielberg foundation. The only son of Arie Leib and Freidke Belka, was Mordechai Ziskind, who was born in 1916. Mordechai joined the resistance and was killed in May of 1944 about a month before the liberation.

The Survival Story of Dvora nee Rubinstein:

From a phone conversion with Dvora of Ness Ziona, Israel in 2000:

Dvora nee Rubinstein was born in Rezke in the early 1920s. Technically she was born in Kurenets, at my (Eilat) great-grandparents house (Mordechai Gurevitz and Freydel nee Alperovitz). Her grandmother Rachel, the wife of Chaim

---

[4] I helped Ann Chana Sharoni, the daughter of Fruma Zira's sister Fanny to find information about her father Yosef Schmukler. Her mother Fanny (Feiga) is the only survivor from the siblings of Fruma Zira. Fanny lost her first husband Peretz Zeidenkop and their toddler daughter Batsheva age 3 in the Shoah. Batsheva was named after her grandmother Batsheva nee Kremer, who was the sister of Moshe Eliezer Kramer who brought Chabad to America (read his story in the Yizkor book). After the liberation Fanny met a survivor from Vileyka by the name of Yosef Shmukler who also lost his family. They were married and had a daughter Ann in Germany, where they were living in a refugee camp waiting for visas. Shortly after In 1947, Yosef Shmukle was killed.

Baruch Gordon, was a relative of Mordechai's from his father's side (Zalman Uri Gurevitz). Since there was no midwife in Rezke, her mother was taken to Kurenets to deliver her babies. When Dvora was growing up, there were about twenty Jewish families in Rezke. Some names included:

- The Gordon Family: Dvora's mother had a brother, Berl Gordon, who married Gitel nee Rubin from Dolhinov. Her mother had a sister, Asna Kaplan, who had a daughter Rachel. They all perished with her father and the three children he had with his second wife from the Fiddler family of Kurenets. The Fiddler family was known in the entire area as Musicians. Only one brother, Yizhak Fiddler, his wife Chana and their son Mendel Marvin survived. See his story in this chapter.

- Chodesh Family: Rabbi Chaim Meir and Liba nee Alperovitz Chodesh (died recently), their daughter Judy of Philadelphia. A relative of his, Batia Chodesh lives in Chedera, Israel and speaks only Yiddish or Russian. The sister and mother of Shabtai Gordon, who lived in Kurenets also lived in Rezke. Shimon Zimerman, the head of the Kurenets society in Israel was the husband of Shabtai's daughter Riva. He lives in Kfar Charif in Israel. Rivka Feygelman was the married name of Shabtai's sister. Rivka and Shabtai perished together with their family in Kurenets. Shabtai's older daughters Riva Zimerman and Michla who married Arye) son of Alter Zimerman from Kurenets) were the only survivors from the entire family. Their husbands and children live in Israel.

- The Salzman Family: they were well off and the mother was from the United States. Before the war they moved to Vileyka. Their son Yaakov lives in the United States. He went many times to Rezke and has pictures. Shimon Zimerman and him went for a visit there together and can provide his phone number.

- Mendel Levin Family and the Zichok family, whose daughter just came from Russia to Israel. There are still some other family members in Russia. The family of Yehuda Alperovitz (Liba Chodeshfrom Philadelphia was his daughter).

Dvora said that there was not a Dinerstein family there when she lived in Rezke. (Steve Rosen has a list of fifty Dinersteins who lived there in 1838)

Rezke was known for the mountains, where people would sled and ski in the winter. It also had rivers. Most of the people in the area were not Jewish. They had a heder where Dvora went to school. Her grandfather Chaim Baruch Gordon was very educated in Jewish studies and he would teach her. She told me that her grandmother would tell her that her father used to live and work for the wealthy Pariz (the nobleman and big land owner in the area). Dvora's great grandfather found out that Chaim Baruch, who was studying in the Yeshiva in another town, was a very learned man and chose him for his daughter (her grandmother) even though he was a hunchback.

One of the teachers in Rezke was Ben Zion Meirovitz from Kurenets. His son Aharon is a writer in Israel. Dvora did not study with Ben Zion Meirovitz because her family said that he was not religious enough. He was a great teacher who made his students speak in Hebrew and many became Zionists with his support. The Rabbis also came from other places, mostly from Kurenets. They buried the Jews mostly in the cemetery in Kurenets.

Dvora's mother died when she was eight years old. She was buried in Vileyka because she was taken there to the hospital. Eight years old Dvora organized a minyan to say Kaddish for her mother every day for the first year.

The school in Rezke was only up to four grades and then many children went to school in Kurenets or Vileyka. Dvora did not have the opportunity to attend high school because the family could not afford to pay for it. That was during the Polish time. However, after the Soviets entered the area, she had new opportunities of going to school since she was from a working-class family. The Soviets gave preferred admission to children from working class families and school and lodging was free for them. In 1941 Dvora worked and studied in Vileyka.

Her father was a "glass man." When the Germans invaded the area, she was sent with other workers to the Vileyka train station to put some important Soviet papers on the train to Russia. She and others were pushed to the train by a Soviet officer who said to her, "You are a Jew and a Communist. You must leave." The non-Jewish people jumped off the train. Dvora stayed with nothing but the summer dress she was wearing. She never saw her family or Rezke again. She told me much more about her very interesting life as a refugee. Later, when the war ended, she received a letter in Russia from the Chodesh family that her entire family had perished. She decided to leave Russia and go to the west. She became an illegal immigrant crossing many borders without papers. Eventually she met her later-to-be husband in Poland in 1945, right when the war ended. They were right near the Kielce incident, where a mob of Polish soldiers, police officers, and civilians murdered at least 42 Jews and injured over 40 in the worst outburst of anti-Jewish violence in postwar Poland. On the day of the Polish Pogrom, amongst those who were killed there were about twenty Jews that came back from the Holocaust and were with Dvora on the same train the day before. Two years and many refugee camps later, on an illegal boat to Israel she saw the lights of Haifa, but was taken to the camp in Cyprus by the British
and somewhere there she had a daughter.

The Survival Story of Yente Rudnitsky-Baranovitch nee Dinerstein and her sister, Rachel:

I called the sisters Rachel and Yente nee Dinerstein in Cholon, Israel. Here is some information that I received from the sisters:

Their father was Leib, son of Gotza Dinerstein. He had two brothers. One was Artzik Aharon Dinerstein from Kurenitz. On 9-9-1942 he was hiding with his wife and children in the ground by his house. He asked them to run to the forest and they refused. He left for the forest, telling them he will return to take them after they realize that it is safer there. They refused to go and were found and killed by the Germans. Arzik was killed in 1944, days before the liberation.

The other brother lived and perished in Volozhin with his family. His name was Natan Dinerstein. Yente's father had a first cousin in Vileyka named Moshe Natan Dinerstein. His son Fibel came to Israel and lived in Zur Shalom. They still have a family there. Yente told me that she lived with them for a few weeks when she took a class on how to use the Zinger sewing machines that her father sold in Vileyka. There was also the family of Noach Dinerstein, who was a partisan from Vileyka and had relatives in Kurenets.

Yente's father also had three sisters: One was Nechama, who married Aharon Arka Alperovitz. They perished with their daughter in Kurenets. Many wrote about Arka's fighting and overcoming one of the policemen that took him to be killed. Another sister was Chaya Rocha Rogozin, who lived and perished in Smorgon. The third sister was from Molodechna and her name was Chana Ashinovski. She has a daughter named Zvia Mishkin, who lives in Rehovot, my hometown in Israel.

From the mother's side: the mother was from the Gurfinkel family. Their first cousins were Michael and Batia Rivka Gurfinkel, who perished, and their brother Yitzhak, who lives in a Kibbutz in Israel. Yente wrote a chapter in the Yizkor book about her survival. You can read more about the Dinerstein family in the Yizkor chapter about the Vostok territory, written by Abraham Aharon, son of Naftali Alperovich. Here is a section about their uncle Artzik:

"I also remember Artzik (son of Gutzes) Dinerstien. He had a huge fur coat that he never separated from. When we were walking through the forest, we felt very sorry for him. He kept tripping over his coat. But we were very jealous

during the cold nights. After many, many troubles and wandering, we passed the old Russian-Polish border, the border prior to 1939. We passed near Pleshentznitz, about 10 km from Poloshnitz. A few days later, the first snow fell. We didn't dare go to the local homes. We slept in the forest. The weather was very cold and only one person had the appropriate clothes: Artzik, the owner of the fur coat."

Yente and Rachel had a brother named Gershon who made Aliyah to Eretz Israel and settled in Rehovot long before the Shoah. His son Prof. Ariel Dinar (nee Dinerstein) told me about his aunt Rachel. She had a child with Dr. Tzrinski, who lost his wife and children during the Nazi massacre in Kurenets on 9/9/1942. The boy was born while they were in the forest fighting the Nazis as members of the Soviet resistance. After the war ended Dr. Tzerinski took the child to Germany. Ariel was in touch with the child's son, who lives in Germany.

The Survival Story of Rachel Frydman (née Alperowicz):

Rachel was born in Kurenets on May 8, 1926, to Chaya Leah (born in Volozhin in 1900 to Rachel and Moshe Bunimovitz) and Avraham Alperovich. Rachel discussed her life in Kurenets before World War II in a video for the Steven Spielberg Foundation.

Some highlights from her story: After the Nazis invasion in June of 1941, there was not a Jewish ghetto in Kurenets because it was so small and almost the entire population was Jewish. The Germans arrived abruptly in June 1941. Her sister Chana (later Galinsky) immediately left with a neighbor to cross the old border deep into Russia. She survived and came to Israel after the war. There was no full government established yet, only the army (she did not say that already on the first day the Germans arrived, they took 3 Jewish young men, cousins name Zimerman, and murdered them right outside the town). She shared that once the Gestapo came, gold and silver was demanded from everyone via the Jewish Committee. Rachel discussed the selection process, during which individuals age 16 and up were taken away. She discussed being made to work (they were not taken away. They were taken in the morning and returned in the evening. Only months later they were taken to Vileyka and Luban a few kilometers away. There they stayed in camps). Rachel stated that just before the High Holidays approximately 50 men and a few women, including her neighbors across the street and two cousins, were slaughtered in the streets and how one man escaped.[5]

Yenta Dinerstein, who I spoke with, watched her husband being killed and they were going to kill her and their baby. The Polish mayor of the town came running and asked the Nazi head officer to let Yente and her baby go. The Nazi did it, saying to Yente "Next time don't marry a communist." The man Rachel said was not killed was Yankale, son of Artzik Alperovich. He arrived after they had already murdered most of the men. When he heard that they were killed for being communist, he said, " Ask all the locals here. My father was sent to Siberia. Why would I be a communist?" I (Eilat) spoke to his brothers, who were among the last family who lived in Kurenets after the war.

Rachel also spoke in her interview about the specific men who committed atrocitie. She spoke about working as a cleaning lady. She also spoke about the liquidation three days before the High Holidays, hiding with her family in a false attic her brother had built, a non-Jewish neighbor reporting on them to the Germans and a Jewish family down

---

[5] There were 54 people. They were not killed in the street, They were taken to the forest. It was during Simchat Torah of 1941. They were people who had a good job when the Soviets were there and their wives, mothers and kids.

the street committing suicide by starting a fire on the day of the killing, 9-9-1942.[6] Rachel also spoke about sneaking out of the attic and hiding in the woods and losing track of her brother. She spoke about living in a hole in the ground with 18 people, her mother being caught one winter night. Sheina Liba Cheres and her mother Chaya Lea Alperovitz went back to Kurenets to get clothes and food for the children. They were caught by German collaborators and tortured but refused to tell where the Jews were hiding. They were killed on the spot. Rachel was now alone in the forest. A family with 3 kids from Kurenets let her join them. The forest was divided by numbers and each village had a part of the forest. The Germans surrounded their area of the forest on April 29, 1943. She spoke about escaping the Germans, not joining partisan groups but making them food, the rainy summer of 1943 and hearing that her brother Moshe was alive in the Vilna ghetto. Rachel also spoke about going to several villages before returning to the woods, hearing that her brother was sent to Estonia, and later hearing that he was not. He escaped and joined the resistance. Rachel started searching for her brother Moshe Alperovich in villages and partisan groups. She spoke of the happiness of finding him in the forest. She also shared that she was shot at by German soldiers but avoided being hit by running in a zig-zag.

List of Kurenetzers' Testimonies that were recorded by Spielberg's Shoah Foundation

These video testimonials can be ordered online at https://sfi.usc.edu

1. **Marvin Fidler** (Mendel Fidler name at birth)
Date of Birth: 2/10/1931
Went into hiding in bunkers in the forests
Liberated by Soviet armed forces
Was in displaced persons camps in Germany waiting for visas
Language(s) of Interview: English.
Length of Interview: 3 hours and 30 minutes.
Interview Code 39943

2. **Rachel Frydman** (Rachela Alperowicz name at birth)
Date of Birth: 5/8/1926
Went into hiding
Was a member of Underground Partisan Group Hiding or living under false identity in Niewiary and the Narocz Forest (before the war; Poland today Belarus) Also in the Rudnicka Puszcza Forest.
Liberated by the Soviet armed forces, Location of liberation Narocz Forest.
Was in displaced person camps
State of Interview Florida.
Language of Interview: English
Length of Interview: 3:00 hours
Interview Code: 41491

3. **Gurewitz, Uli** (Also known as Zalman Uri or Salman)
Date of Birth: 8/10/1924
Went into Hiding
Member of Underground, Resistance or Partisan Group. (Location) Narocz Forest. Resistance Group; Orlianski-Borba Battalion.
Liberated by armed forces, Soviet. Location of liberation Smorgonie.

---

[6] It was my grandfather's first cousin Ethel nee Gurevitz and her husband Zusia Benes, well off Jews with no children. They decided to kill themselves and burn their home so the Nazis would get nothing. Etel's youngest sister Esther Reich, survived and lived in New Haven.

State of Interview Baden-Württemberg, Germany
Language(s) of Interview: German
Length of Interview: 3:30
Interview Code: 34600

4. Dorothy Kleinkopf (Devorah nee Cheres maiden name)
Date of Birth: 6/10/1925
Ghetto/ camp: Wilejka
Went into Hiding
Was a Member of Underground, Resistance or Partisan Group.
Type of hiding place: forests and bunkers.
Liberated by armed forces, Soviet. Location of liberation Vilna.
Other Experiences: displaced persons camps.
State of Interview: Florida
Language(s) of Interview: English.
Length of Interview: 1:41
Interview Code: 5565

5. Ita Klenicki (Itka Cheres maiden name)
Date of Birth: 1/9/1927
Camp: Liuban
Went into hiding in the forest
Liberated by armed forces, Soviets
State of Interview: Florida.
Language of Interview: English
Length of Interview: 1:30
Interview Code: 9717

6. Zina Kuperberg (Name at Birth: Zelda Ziskind. False Name: Sonia Alprowitz)
Date of Birth: 10/20/1925
Ghetto(s) Wilejka (Poland: Ghetto)
Camp(s)
Went into Hiding
Member of Underground, Resistance or Partisan Group
Hiding or living under false identity (Location) Vilna
Type of hiding place forests and barns.
Liberated by armed forces, Soviet. Location of liberation: Vilna
Displaced persons camps in Germany.
State of Interview: Florida
Language(s) of Interview: English
Length of Interview: 2:30
Interview Code: 24269

7. Esther Lewitan. (Maiden name: Charnas. Other name: Kalé)
Date of Birth 6/3/1913
Went into Hiding
Was a Member of Underground, Resistance or Partisan Group
Type of hiding place: forests.
Resistance Group(s) resistance groups, Soviet. Other resistance groups, Jewish.

Liberated by armed forces, Soviet.
Location of liberation: Wilejka.
Other Experiences: displaced persons camps.
State of Interview: Florida
Language(s) of Interview Yiddish: Length of Interview 1:00
Interview Code: 7569

8. **Mikhail Liberman** (Release name: Mikhail Abramovich Liberman. Hebrew name: Moishe. Other Name: Michael Liberman)
Date of Birth: 1/1/1931
Went into Hiding
Member of Underground, Resistance or Partisan Group
Hiding or living under false identity (Location) Vilna region. Type of hiding place forests.
Liberated by armed forces, Soviet. Location of liberation Vilna
Other Experiences: orphanages and children's homes. concealment of identity. concealment of Jewish identity. Escaped from mass shootings. evasion of roundups.
Country of Interview: Israel
Language of Interview: Russian.
Length of Interview: 2:00
Interview Code: 16661

9. **Le´ah Shugol** (Name at Birth: Elizabieta Gurewicz)
Date of Birth: 1/24/1922
Went into Hiding
Member of Underground, Resistance or Partisan Group.
Hiding or living under false identity (Location) Vilna region. Type of hiding place: forests. Resistance Group(s) resistance groups, Soviet.
Liberated by armed forces, Soviet
Location of liberation: Vilna region.
Other Experiences: evasion of roundups
Country of Interview: Israel
Language(s) of Interview: Hebrew
Length of Interview: 2:30 hours
Interview Code: 26596

10. **Shim`on Tsimerman** (Name at Birth: Shim'on Hilel Tsimerman. Other Name: Shimon Zimmerman)
Date of Birth: 2/2/1923
Camp(s) Wilejka
Went into Hiding
Member of Underground, Resistance or Partisan Group.
Hiding or living under false identity (Location) Vilna. Type of hiding place: forests
Resistance Group(s) Voroshilov brigade
Liberated by armed forces, Soviet. Location of liberation: Vilna region
Other Experiences: escapes from the camps
Country of Interview: Israel
Language(s) of Interview: Russian
Length of Interview: 3:00
Interview Code: 37289

www.ingramcontent.com/pod-product-compliance
Lightning Source LLC
Chambersburg PA
CBHW082007150426
42814CB00005BA/248